The Random House Guide to Business Writing

THE RANDOM HOUSE GUIDE TO BUSINESS WRITING

JANIS FORMAN
Director of Management Communication
University of California, Los Angeles

with

Kathleen A. Kelly
Babson College

McGraw-Hill Publishing Company
New York St. Louis San Francisco Auckland Bogotá Caracas Hamburg Lisbon London
Madrid Mexico Milan Montreal New Delhi Oklahoma City Paris San Juan São Paulo
Singapore Sydney Tokyo Toronto

THE RANDOM HOUSE GUIDE TO BUSINESS WRITING
INTERNATIONAL EDITION

Copyright © 1990 by Janis Forman.
Exclusive rights by McGraw-Hill Book Co—Singapore for manufacture and export. This book cannot be re-exported from the country to which it is consigned by McGraw-Hill.

All rights reserved. Except as permitted under the United States Copyright Act of 1976, no part of this publication may be reproduced or distributed in any form or by any means, or stored in a data base or retrieval system, without the prior written permission of the publisher.

1 2 3 4 5 6 7 8 9 0   JJP SW   9 4 3 2 1 0

This book was set in Times Roman by The Clarinda Company.
The editors were Steve Pensinger and Mary M. Shuford;
the production supervisor was Stacey Alexander.
Design was done by Scott Chelius.
The cover was designed by Katherine Urban,
and the cover photograph is by Tom Grill/Comstock.

PHOTO CREDITS: 4, Courtesy of Janis Forman; 5, Joel Gordon; 8 *(top left)*, Courtesy of Allied-Signal; 8 *(top right)*, Courtesy of Johnson & Johnson; 8 *(bottom)*, Charles Grupton/Southern Light; 10, Courtesy of Janis Forman; 11, Bill Bachman/Photo Researchers; 12, Courtesy of the Los Angeles Times; 13 *(top)*, Brian Coyne/Southern Light; 13 *(bottom)*, Allan Carey/The Image Works; 24, Courtesy of Hewlett Packard; 53, Howard Dratch/The Image Works; 128 *(top)*, Lanier Business Products, a sector of Harris Corp.; 128 *(bottom)*, Van Bucher/Photo Researchers; 186, Peter Vandermark/Stock, Boston; 207, The Photo Works; 227, Teri Leigh Stratford/Photo Researchers; 265, The Photo Works; 320, Ulrike Welsch; 320, The Photo Works; 382, Frank Siteman/Taurus Photos; 414, Gabe Palmer/The Stock Market; 421, Ellis Herwig/The Picture Cube; 459 *(top)*, Hazel Hankin, 459 *(bottom)*, David Schaefer; 464, David Schaefer; 480 *(top)*, Courtesy Irene Cohen Personnel Services/The Photo Works; 480 *(center)*, James Schaefer, 480 *(bottom)*, Teri Leigh Stratford/Photo Researchers; 496, Ellis Herwig/Stock, Boston; 508, The Photo Works; 563, Dave Schaefer/The Picture Cube; 586, Ellis Herwig/Stock, Boston; 587, Susan Lapides/Design Conceptions; 588, Courtesy of the Long Island Lighting Company, photo by Brian M. Ballweg; 591 *(top)*, J.D.S. Loan/The Picture Cube; 591 *(bottom)*, Joel Gordon; 619, Rae Russel; 620, David Schaefer; 621, Ulrike Welsch; 623, Joel Gordon; 664, Joseph Nettis/Photo Researchers; 665 *(top)*, Michal Heron/Woodfin Camp & Associates; 665 *(middle)*, Ken Robert Buck/The Picture Cube; 665 *(bottom)*, Joel Gordon; 666, Courtesy Apple Computer; 691, Courtesy of Irene Cohen Personnel Services/The Photo Works; 708, Steve Payne; 738, John Coletti/Stock, Boston; 765, Courtesy of Hewlett Packard; 778 *(top)*, Richard Pasley/Stock, Boston; 788 *(bottom)*, Sarah Putnam/The Picture Cube.

Library of Congress Cataloging-in-Publication Data

Forman, Janis.
  The Random House guide to business writing/Janis Forman, with Kathleen A. Kelly.
    p.   cm.
  Bibliography: p.
  Includes index.
  ISBN 0-07-557221-4
    1. English language—Rhetoric.   2. English language—Business English.   3. Business report writing.   I. Kelly, Katheleen A.
II. Title.
PE1475.F67 1990
808'.066651—dc18

When ordering this title use ISBN 0-07-100723-7

Printed in Singapore

For Don and Michele

CONTENTS

Checklists   xvii
Preface   xix

CHAPTER 1   INTRODUCTION   1

What Is Business Writing?   1
How Important Is Business Writing to Success in Business?   2
    Writing Is Built into Your Job   3
    An Effective Job Search and Job Promotion May Depend on Your Ability to Communicate   5
    Writing Is a Way of Thinking   6
How Will the Business You Go into Affect the Writing You Do?   7
    Organizational Expectations about Writing   7
    Office Environment   10
What Skills and Experience Can You Draw on to Become a Successful Business Writer?   14
    Problem Solving   14
    Project Management and Team Work   14
    Speaking   15
    Reading   15
    Essay and Exam Writing   15
Summary   16
Preview of Chapters to Come   16

CHAPTER 2   WRITING AS A PROCESS   17

Setting the Goal   19
Assessing the Reader   21

Gathering Information and Generating Ideas   23
    Gathering Information   23
    Generating Ideas   25
Organizing   27
    The RTA Formula: Rapport, Thinking, Action and Attitude   35
    Analysis Trees and Outlines   35
Writing a Draft   39
Revising   40
    Role-Playing Your Reader   40
    Asking an Associate to Review Your Writing   41
Editing and Proofreading   41
Summary   42
Exercises   42

CHAPTER 3 REVISING AND EDITING   49

Revising Holistically   50
Revising Locally: Paragraphs   59
    Revising Paragraphs for Organization and Completeness   59
    Revising Paragraphs for Coherence   62
Revising Locally: Sentences   69
    Using Strong Verbs and the Active Voice   69
    Using Emphatic Word Order   76
    Avoiding Noun Clusters   76
    Avoiding Needless Words   77
    Using Language Appropriate to Your Reader   80
Proofreading   86
Summary   87
Exercises   87

CHAPTER 4 THE BASICS OF BUSINESS LETTERS: WRITING TO READERS OUTSIDE THE ORGANIZATION   105

Setting the Goal for the Business Letter: Action and Attitude   107
Assessing the Reader   108
Gathering Information, Generating Ideas, and Organizing: The RTA Formula   108
    Using the RTA Formula   109
Writing a Draft   120
    Using Dictation   121
Revising the Business Letter: Holistic and Local Revision   124
    Revising Holistically: The RTA Formula   124
    Local Revision: A Friendly Tone and a Conversational Style   125

The Format of the Business Letter   134
    Four Styles for Letter Format   134
    The Letter Parts   141
    Envelopes   146
Summary   148
Exercises   149

CHAPTER 5 WRITING AND RESPONDING TO REQUESTS   159

The Good-News Direct Letter Pattern   160
    Using RTA for the Good-News Letter   162
The Bad-News Indirect Letter Pattern   167
    Using RTA for the Bad-News Letter   169
A Direct Approach to the Bad-News Letter   172
Writing About Products and Services   173
    Orders for and Inquiries about Products and Services   173
    Replies to Orders and Inquiries   176
Writing about People: Requesting and Writing Recommendations   185
    Requesting a Recommendation   185
    Writing a Recommendation   188
Writing about Claims and Adjustments   191
    Making Claims or Requesting Adjustments   191
    Responding to Claims   194
Writing about Credit   201
    Checking Credit References   201
    Replying to Credit Checks   201
    Approving Credit   201
    Refusing Credit   203
Writing to Refuse Requests for Favors   206
Summary   208
Exercises   208

CHAPTER 6 LETTERS THAT PERSUADE   223

Selling   224
    Setting the Goal: Your Proposition   228
    Assessing the Reader: The Mailing List   228
    Gathering Information and Generating Ideas: Determining the Sales Appeal   229
    Organizing the Sales Letter: Using RTA   233
    Testing the Sales Letter   241
    Envelopes for the Sales Letter   243

Requesting Favors   247
    Setting the Goal: Know What You Are Asking   251
    Assessing the Reader: Understanding Reader Benefits   251
    Gathering Information and Generating Ideas   251
    Organizing: Using RTA to Request Favors   252
Collecting   263
    Setting the Goal of the Collection Series   263
    Assessing the Reader of the Collection Series   265
    Generating Ideas for and Organizing the Collection Letter: Using RTA   267
    The Collection Series   268
Communicating in Controversy   280
    Public Misperception   281
    Changing Social Values   287
Summary   292
Exercises   292

CHAPTER 7 GOODWILL LETTERS   307

Setting the Goal   308
Assessing the Reader   309
Generating Ideas and Organizing for Goodwill   309
    Generating Ideas and Organizing: Using the RTA Formula for Goodwill   310
Letters of Congratulation   312
Letters of Appreciation   319
Letters of Sympathy   328
Season's Greetings   328
Letters of Welcome   334
Summary   334
Exercises   340

CHAPTER 8 MEMOS   347

Setting the Goal   348
Assessing the Reader   348
Gathering Information and Generating Ideas   351
Organizing Memos That Give or Request Information   351
    Checking for Completeness   356
Organizing Memos That Give Bad News or Persuade   359
    Bad-News or Persuasive Memos to Subordinates   359
    Bad-News or Persuasive Memos to Peers or Superiors   361
Writing a Draft   363
Revising: Checking for Tone   363

Memo Format   366
    Memos Have a Similar Heading Format   366
    Memos Are Short   368
    Memos Use Page Layout to Reinforce Their Message   369
    Memos Often Have a Conversational Tone and Style   370
The Functions of Memos   371
    Memos That Announce   371
    Memos That Give Instructions or Explain a Procedure   371
    Memos That Make a Routine Request   374
    Memos That Confirm an Agreement   377
    Memos That Clarify   379
    Memos That Remind   379
    Memos That Promote Goodwill   382
Summary   384
Exercises   385

CHAPTER 9   THE BASICS OF REPORT WRITING   391

Problem Solving and Report Writing   392
    Determining the Question the Reader Wants Answered   392
    Analyzing the Problem   393
    Establishing Criteria   395
Writing the Problem-Solving Report   397
    Setting the Goal   397
    Assessing the Reader   397
    Gathering Information and Generating Ideas   399
    Organizing   399
    Writing a Draft   400
    Choosing a Format   405
    Revising   407
Other Types of Short Reports   413
    Meeting and Trip Reports   413
    Progress or Status Reports   421
    Reports on Procedures   425
    Proposals   430
Summary   436
Exercises   436

CHAPTER 10   THE FORMAL REPORT: GOAL, READER, IDEAS, AND INFORMATION   451

Setting the Goal and Assessing the Reader   453
Making a Schedule   454

Gathering Information and Generating Ideas: Secondary and Primary Sources 456
    Ten Types of References to Consult 457
    Suggestions for Using the Library 463
Using Secondary Sources 466
    Taking Notes 466
    Quoting 468
    Paraphrasing 470
    Summarizing 473
Using Primary Sources 477
    Making Observations 478
    Conducting Experiments 479
    Conducting Surveys 481
    Designing and Administering Questionnaires 483
    Conducting Interviews 494
Summary 497
Exercises 498

CHAPTER 11 THE FORMAL REPORT: ORGANIZATION, DRAFT, FORMAT, REVISION, AND GROUP WRITING 507

Organizing 508
Writing a Draft 509
Parts and Format of Formal Reports 542
    Introductory Material 542
    Body 547
    Supplementary Material 550
    Format 556
Revising the Formal Report 556
    Poorly Developed Conclusions and Recommendations 556
    Excessive Use of Quotations, Paraphrases, or Summaries 557
    Lack of Transitional Paragraphs and Sentences 559
    Secondary Material Put in the Body of the Report 560
    Organization According to Sources or Research Design Rather Than by Argument 560
    Irrelevant Information 560
    Poor Headings and Subheadings 560
    Long Executive Summaries That Rehash the Whole Report 561
Group Writing 562
    Coordination of the Group's Efforts 562
    Group Writing Within the Framework of the Writing Process 564
    Pitfalls in Group Writing 565
Summary 567
Exercises 567

CHAPTER 12   SPEAKING   585

Links Between Writing and Speaking   585
Oral Presentations   588
    Setting the Goal   590
    Assessing the Audience   592
    Gathering Information and Generating Ideas   593
    Organizing   593
    Outlining or Writing Out the Copy for the Presentation   603
    Rehearsing to Revise and to Polish Your Delivery   615
Other Common Speaking Tasks   621
    Conducting Interviews   621
    Holding Meetings   626
Summary   630
Exercises   630

CHAPTER 13   VISUAL AIDS   635

Tables   635
    Design of Tables   636
Graphic Aids: Bar Charts, Line Graphs, and Pie Charts   645
    Bar Charts   645
    Line Graphs   646
    Pie Charts   651
Graphic Aids: Organization Charts, Flow Charts, and Maps   652
    Organization Charts   653
    Flow Charts   654
    Maps   654
Visual Aids for Oral Presentations   657
    Text Visuals   658
    Displaying Visual Aids   663
Computer Graphics   663
Summary   671
Exercises   671

CHAPTER 14   THE JOB SEARCH   677

Making a Schedule   678
Exploring Career Options: Self-Assessment and Research   678
    Self-Assessment   680
    Research   685
Writing Your Resume   689
    Setting the Goal   690

       Assessing the Reader   691
       Gathering Information and Generating Ideas   692
       Organizing the Resume   692
       Writing the Draft   706
       The Appearance and Format of Resumes   711
       Revising   711
The Search   714
       Want Ads   715
       Research on Specific Companies   717
       Business Contacts   720
Letters of Application   722
       The Solicited Letter   722
       The Unsolicited Letter   727
       Revising Letters of Application   730
The Job Interview   732
       Planning for the Job Interview   732
       Rehearsing   737
       At the Interview   737
Thank-You Letters   739
       Setting the Goal and Assessing the Reader   740
       Gathering Information and Generating Ideas   740
       Organizing   740
The Letter of Acceptance   741
Letters of Refusal   741
Summary   744
Exercises   744

CHAPTER 15   THE BUSINESS WRITER AND THE COMPUTER   763

The Benefits of Computer Technology   767
The Computer and the Writing Process   769
       Setting the Goal and Assessing the Reader   769
       Gathering Information and Generating Ideas   769
       Organizing   770
       Writing a Draft   770
       Revising   770
       Editing, Proofreading, and Formating   771
Common Errors in Using the Computer for Business Writing   773
       Focusing on the Mechanics Rather Than on Writing   773
       Inappropriate Use of Electronic Mail   773
       Revising Only What Appears on the Display Monitor   773
       Computer-Generated Errors   774

The Computer and Group Writing   774
Summary   775
Exercises   775

APPENDIX A   WRITING RESPONSES TO CASES   777

Problem Solving and Case Assignments   778
    Determine the Question the Reader Wants Answered   779
    Analyze the Problem   784
    Establish Criteria   786
The Process of Writing a Response to a Case   787
    Setting the Goal   787
    Assessing the Reader   787
    Gathering Information and Generating Ideas   788
    Organizing   789
    Writing a Draft   790
    Revising a Case Write-Up   792
Summary   797
Exercises   797

APPENDIX B   A BRIEF GUIDE TO GRAMMAR AND PUNCTUATION   807

Abbreviations   807
Apostrophe   808
Capitalization   809
Colon   811
Comma   812
Comma Splice   813
Dangling and Misplaced Modifiers   815
Dash   816
Fragments   817
Hyphen   817
Italics (or Underlining for Italics)   818
Numbers   819
Parallelism   821
Possessive Pronouns   823
Pronouns   823
Pronoun Agreement in Number   824
Pronoun Case   825
Quotation Marks   827

Run-on Sentences   828
Semicolon   828
Subject-Verb Agreement   829

Notes   833
Index   839

Checklists

Formulating a Goal Statement   21
Assessing the Reader   23
Gathering Information and Generating Ideas   27
Organizing Business Communications   39
Revising Holistically   58
Revising Paragraphs   69
Editing Sentences   86
Writing the Good-News Letter   167
Writing the Indirect Bad-News Letter   171
Writing the Sales Letter   247
Requesting Favors   257
Writing the Collection Letter   276
Communicating in Controversy   291
Writing the Goodwill Letter   312
Writing Memos That Give or Request Information   355
Assessing Completeness   356
Writing Memos That Give Bad News or Persuade   363
Revising Memos for Tone   366
Reviewing Format   371
Solving a Business Problem   397
Assessing Readers of Reports   398
Writing a Problem-Solving Report   405
Reviewing Report Format   406
Revising a Problem-Solving Report   412
Making a Schedule   456
Using the Library   466
Quoting, Paraphrasing, and Summarizing   473
Making Observations   479
Developing a Sample   482
Reviewing a Cover Letter   493
Reviewing a Questionnaire   494
Preparing for an Interview   497
Writing Executive Summaries   547
Revising the Formal Report   561
Doing Group Writing   566
Assessing the Audience   593
Organizing Presentations   603
Rehearsing Presentations   619
Conducting Interviews   626
Holding Meetings   630
Using Tables   645
Using Bar Charts, Line Graphs, and Pie Charts   652
Using Organization Charts, Flow Charts, and Maps   657
Using Text Visuals   663
Evaluating Career Exploration   689
Writing Your Resume   705
Reviewing Job Search Efforts   722
Writing Letters of Application   732
Preparing for and Performing at a Job Interview   739
Solving a Business Problem Presented in a Case   786
Responding to a Case   792
Revising a Case Response   797

PREFACE

TO THE STUDENT

In preparing *The Random House Guide to Business Writing*, we talked to a number of successful business writers. Many indicated to us that they have found their business careers to be limited only by the number of people they can influence. Mastering writing and speaking skills will enable you to present yourself persuasively to those people who are important to your career. Our goal for *The Random House Guide to Business Writing* is to teach you the skills to handle all of your business writing assignments successfully, both in the classroom and on the job.

We take a process approach to writing in this text because such an approach demonstrates not only what good writing is, but also how it is produced. In the introductory chapters as well as in the chapters on memos, letters, and reports, you will see how business people engage in seven activities as they write their business communications: (1) setting the goal of the business communication, (2) assessing the reader, (3) gathering information and generating ideas, (4) organizing, (5) writing a draft, (6) revising, and (7) editing and proofreading. Later chapters also use the process approach to teach you the related communication skills of making oral presentations, using visual aids, conducting the job search, and using computers.

In an effort to be completely up-to-date on how business writing is being done in the 1980s and 1990s, we have consulted numerous business people who work in diverse industries, functional areas, and parts of the country. From these discussions and from reviews of portfolios, we found that business people are confronted with challenging communication problems that draw on sophisticated communication skills. We have used their experiences to demonstrate the dynamic process of writing. For example, you will see how the manager of a travel agency uses a report to persuade her boss, who is afraid of computers, to invest several thousand dollars in computer equipment. You will also find a personnel manager using a memo to finally settle a long-simmering office feud between smokers and nonsmokers. And you will see how a director of corporate communications writes a public letter intended to reassure an entire town that is concerned about a chemical leak that the corporation has in fact safely contained.

The business writers whose work appears in this book are either the people we have observed and interviewed or they are composite portraits of several of these people. All demonstrate how essential communication skills are to success in business.

The experiences of these business writers will give you an idea of the business situations you may encounter during your career, the purposes for which you may have to write, and the roles you may have to play as you deal competently—and even imaginatively—with communication problems. The exercises at the end of each chapter put you in the shoes of similar business people as they help you to apply to specific writing tasks the principles you have studied in the chapter. Checklists provided throughout the chapters provide clear summaries of these principles as you progress.

THE RANDOM HOUSE GUIDE TO BUSINESS WRITING

TO THE INSTRUCTOR

As scholars and as teachers of business communication both in universities and industry, we discovered the need for a more effective business communications textbook that would take advantage of new insights into the composing process and its relation to discourse communities. *The Random House Guide to Business Writing* is the result of a collaboration that began when we met as postdoctoral fellows at a National Endowment for the Humanities seminar on composition.

We believe that we have provided a combination of features not available in any other textbook:

- A theoretically consistent process approach to business writing and speaking
- Chapters built around extended, realistic cases that situate the writing process in the business context
- A wealth of authentic samples of both good and poor writing and speaking, demonstrating that the written product is as important as the writing process
- Coverage of important subjects neglected by most texts: a problem-solving approach to report writing, written responses to cases, crisis communications, group writing, the effect of the computer on process and product, and holistic revision
- Effective coverage of traditional topics: letters, memos, reports, oral presentations, interviews, meetings, visual aids, and the job search
- Traditional textbook apparatus: checklists, chapter previews, chapter summaries, and a grammar appendix
- Exercises based on challenging business cases that require students to apply the principles discussed in the chapter

HOW TO USE THIS BOOK

Some instructors may want to use only a few of the chapters in the text; others may have time for a wide range of topics covered by all the chapters taken together. Because of its consistent process approach, this text can be adapted for use in a variety of ways. We do suggest, however, that you read the first three chapters before going on to the specific writing or speaking task that you wish to cover. These first chapters introduce the seven activities of the writing process that, in turn, provide the framework for the chapters on specific writing and speaking tasks.

One feature of our text that may be especially welcome to new instructors of business communications is its quantity of scenarios, examples, and exercises derived from our extensive research in business. Our work with business people from a number of industries and across functional areas revealed to us at once the variety of communication tasks and contexts that business people must confront, but at the same time the common process underlying these activities. We have designed our book to enable an instructor to provide richness of example usually available only to one who has been working years in the field, while at the same time we focus on the fundamental processes common to all communication tasks.

PREFACE   xxi

SUPPLEMENTARY MATERIAL AVAILABLE TO INSTRUCTORS

Instructor's Manual: An *Instructor's Manual*, written by Janette Lewis of UCLA's Writing Programs, suggests ways to effectively use the book to complement various teaching approaches. It also provides sample syllabi, chapter-by-chapter discussions of how to use the book in class, discussion questions, responses to sample exercises, additional exercises and answers, and a bibliography for instructors.

Acetate Transparencies: Acetate *Transparencies* include outlines of each chapter, illustrations of the main points of each chapter, and sample business communications. To request samples or order any of these supplements, please contact your local McGraw-Hill representative or write to:

McGraw-Hill Publishing Company
College Division
P. O. Box 448
Hightstown, New Jersey 08520

Requests received at the above address will be sent to your representative for processing.

ACKNOWLEDGMENTS

Business writers—both students and people in the workplace—gave generously of their time and knowledge. We especially want to thank the following writers: John T. Adams, Rachel Baker, Terry Beaton, Adrienne Bernstein, Diane Bolger, Phillip Boucher, Don Brabston, Camille M. Caiozzo, Dan Cane, M. A. Cartwright, Gloria Cline, Anita Davis, Karen Davis, Tom Digioia, Becky S. Drury, Tom Dunn, Sue Cohen, Robert Feren, Robert F. Foster, Sarah Frank, Gary Futterman, Gail Gaumer, Steve Geyer, Jonathan Goldstein, Simone Gross, Richard M. Grubb, Lisa S. Hamilton, Rowland Hill, James Hilvert, Laura Horowitz, Dick Howell, Martha Foley Jackson, Jean Jarvis, Susan Jelonek, Judy A. Kilduff, Patrick J. Kirwin, H. C. Kung, Randy Kunin, Rick Lipton, Susan Longhito, John D. Lyon, Barbara Maas, Dale H. Marco, Virginia Maynard, Beth Milwid, John W. Moore III, Agnes Moy, Florence M. Murphy, Steven C. Pippin, Carl H. Renezeder, Betsy Samuelson, Robert Saxe, Bruce Schecter, Dirk A. Smith, D. R. Stephenson, Nathaniel Sutton, Dilys Tosteson, Robert L. Young, and Craigie Zildjian.

Various organizations cooperated by permitting us to use communications written by their employees. Some organizations also invited us to visit their offices to see how business writing and speaking are done on the job and to interview their employees. We thank the following organizations: the Alexander Group, the American Judicature Society, American Friends Service Committee, the Atlantic, Augat, the Babson College Internship Program, the Bank of America, Baybank, Boise Cascade, Boston College Library, Cambridge Trust, Cedar-Sinai Hospital, Citicorp, Cosgrove Landscape, Credit Check, Dow Chemical of Canada, Dydee Diapers, First Woman's Bank, General Mills, The Graduate Management Admissions Council, Interactive Systems, Johnson & Johnson, Munroe Regional Medical Center, Masonite Corporation, Needham Oil, the New England Anti-Vivisection Society, Patton Electric, the Red Onion Restaurants, Software Publishing Corporation, Stockton Wire, Teddygrams, Texas Commerce Bancshares, Texas Instruments, Time Incorporated, Tosco, University of New Hampshire Admissions, UNOCAL, and Xerox.

Individuals also supported our research efforts. Our appreciation goes to Avril Archibold, Charlene Bourgue, William Broesamle, Arline Chambers, Michael A. Cinelli, Robert R. Delaney, Jr., Claire Donohue, Sherry G. Dyer, Lawrence G. Foster, Peer Ghent, JoAnna Henderson, Henrietta Holsman, William L. Hunt III, Marc Jacob, Sally Jacobs, Ted Jernigen, Susan Littlewood, Bill MacDonald, John Mcartle, Barbara Mentel, Christina Nicolson, Ellen Ruben, Robert T. Scherer, Jack Shurman, Henry Spira, Dana Stetson, Michael Thacher, Terry J. Thompson, Kathleen Vadnais, George H. Williams, John O. Wilson, Warren A. Witte, William Woodcock, and Mary K. Young.

Faculty and staff at UCLA and Babson helped us in a variety of ways. Janette Lewis wrote the *Instructor's Manual;* Mike Moore, Lynne Markus, and Neal Thornberry contributed business reports; Pat Katsky and Gretchen Thompson put us in touch with managers known for their speaking and writing abilities; Barbara Lawrence reviewed our use of statistics; Jason Frand provided advice about computer graphics; the staff at the Babson College Library assisted with the research on business topics; and Sonja Maasik used several chapters of the book in class. We owe special thanks to Joan Mitchell for testing the book in her business communication classes at the University of California at Santa Barbara. We also want to acknowledge Mike Granfield, Mike Hanssens, Al Osborne, Ernie Scalberg, and Carol Scott of the Anderson Graduate School of Management at the University of California at Los Angeles for establishing an academic environment in which management communication is valued.

Many people at Random House and McGraw-Hill contributed to the publication of this text. We are grateful to C. Steven Pensinger, our editor, for his wisdom and persistence, and to his assistant editor, David Morris; and to Cynthia Ward, Elaine Romano, and Mary Shuford, for their editorial expertise. Recognition and thanks go to our reviewers: Santi Buscemi, Middlesex Community College; Mabel Stone Cipher, University of Kentucky; Helen Ewald, Iowa State University; Paula Feldman, University of South Carolina; Melinda Knight, New York University; Stanley Kozikowski, Bryant College; Tim Lulofs, University of California at Davis; Hank Sparapani, University of Wisconsin at Stevens Point; and Ron Sudol, Oakland University.

Finally, we owe our boundless appreciation to our husbands Don Brabston (Janis's husband) and Peter Kirwin (Kathleen's husband). Their encouragement and wise counsel helped us through many months of research and writing. Don also gave generously of his time and computer expertise, allowing us to take over his house and his computers during two long summers.

ABOUT THE AUTHORS

Janis Forman designed and now directs the Management Communication Program for the Anderson Graduate School of Management at UCLA. As director of management communication, she coordinates instruction in business writing and speaking, teaches an elective course in management communication, supervises a large staff of teaching assistants, and conducts IBM-sponsored research on collaborative business writing and computing. She also consults for Fortune 500 and smaller companies. After receiving her Ph.D. from Rutgers University, she did postdoctoral work in composition theory as a National Endowment for the Humanities (NEH) fellow at the University of Southern California. She was also awarded an NEH grant to direct a writing-across-the-disciplines program, an NEH fellowship to study women's nontraditional literature, and a Fulbright Lectureship to teach business writing, literature, and translation at the Centre Universitaire de Savoie à Chambéry. Dr. Forman has published articles on business communications, composition theory, literature, and translation theory, including publications in *Computers and Composition*, *The Journal of Basic Writing*, *The Journal of Business Communication*, *Semiotexte*, and *Translation Review*. Currently she is studying the relationship between translation and composition, designing an assessment of group written business reports, and planning a collection of critical essays on collaborative writing for Boynton/Cook Publications.

Kathleen A. Kelly is associate professor of English at Babson College in Wellesley, Massachusetts, where she coordinates the writing program at both the undergraduate and MBA levels. She received her Ph.D. from The Ohio State University and did postdoctoral work in composition theory as a National Endowment for the Humanities fellow at the University of Southern California. Besides teaching business writing at Babson, she has taught at The Ohio State University Business School, in the Radcliffe Seminars in Management Programs, for programs at the Babson Center for Executive Education, and for Fortune 500 firms. She has published literary critical articles and has written numerous papers on writing theory and pedagogy, including publications in *ABC Bulletin*, *ABC Proceedings*, *CEA Forum*, and *College Composition and Communication*. Currently she is working on applying a cognitive process model of writing to the speech composition process.

1
INTRODUCTION

PREVIEW

This chapter should help you to

1. Understand what business writing is
2. See the importance of strong business writing skills to success in business
3. Consider how the particular business you go into affects the writing you do
4. Identify the skills and experiences you can draw on to become a successful business writer
5. Understand what each chapter in this textbook covers

Several questions may be on your mind as you begin reading this text:

- What is business writing?
- How important are strong business writing skills to success in business?
- Will the particular business I go into have anything to do with the kinds of writing expected of me?
- Do I already have any skills or experiences I can draw on to become a successful business writer?

WHAT IS BUSINESS WRITING?

Business writing is writing to accomplish the work of an organization. Through writing, business people can request and give information, make recommendations, persuade, promote goodwill, gain approval, consult, plan and coordinate, and give orders.

Letters, memos, and reports are the most common forms of business writing, and they constitute the major subject matter of this text. Business people write **letters** when dealing with outside organizations and individuals. They write **memos**—short communications written for a single purpose—to others within the organization. Memos go *up* the chain of command to superiors to gain approval and to recommend change; *across* to associates to inform, persuade, and consult; and *down* to subordinates to give directions and orders. For bigger tasks, business people write **reports** to convey information and to argue for their recommendations. No matter where you, as a business person, are located on the organization chart, you will be a writer and a reader of business communications (see Figure 1.1).

1

Figure 1.1

KINDS OF BUSINESS WRITING

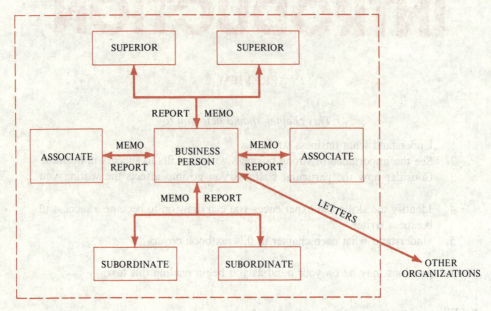

HOW IMPORTANT IS BUSINESS WRITING TO SUCCESS IN BUSINESS?

Surveys of business people reveal the importance of writing to success in business. In two separate studies reported in the *Journal of Business Communication*,[1] the vast majority of respondents stated that business communication was important in their current jobs. A 1984 *Harvard Business Review* survey of corporate presidents and personnel directors revealed that over half of them saw the need for stronger communication skills in MBAs. (Only about 15 percent of the same group indicated dissatisfaction with the graduates' analytical skills and knowledge of their content area.)[2] Preliminary findings from a survey by the Graduate Management Admissions Council of 2,200 business students at ninety-three business schools further support the importance of communication skills. Eighty-nine percent of the first 910 students—those respondents whose questionnaires had been analyzed at the time of this writing—identified communication skills as "very important" in becoming a successful manager. Communication skills ranked highest among the eleven attributes surveyed (see Figure 1.2).[3]

Despite the evidence, some people falsely believe that successful business people need only good ideas, because a subordinate, a secretary, or an assistant will be on hand to translate those ideas into clear prose. Not only does the testimony of successful business people prove that this notion is wrong, but changing office technology in-

INTRODUCTION 3

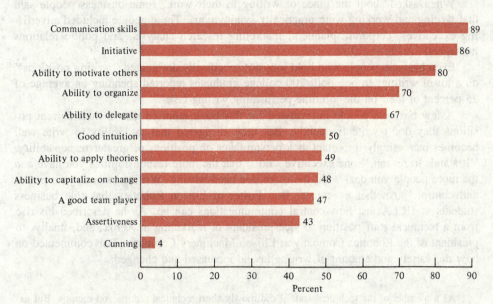

Figure 1.2

PERCENTAGE WHO NAME VARIOUS PERSONAL TRAITS AS "VERY IMPORTANT" IN MANAGEMENT

creases the likelihood that managers will do more and more of their own writing, from inputting their ideas at a terminal to making corrections on the final draft.

From business people we interviewed, we found that strong writing ability helped them for at least three reasons:

1. Some amount of writing is built into almost every job.
2. An effective job search and job promotion depend on the ability to communicate.
3. Writing is a way of thinking; it helps business people to analyze problems, understand others, and make decisions.

We think that your experience on the job will confirm the opinion of those we interviewed.

Writing Is Built into Your Job

Whether or not you plan to seek a business position in which writing is at the heart of your work, you will need to write in order to perform most business jobs with even minimal competence. Writing is one way you will explain procedures to subordinates, confirm decisions with associates, recommend policy changes to superiors, promote products with consumers, and perform many other tasks necessary to carry on business. Whether your company produces goods or performs services, you will be turning out written messages as part of your role as a business person.

When asked about the place of writing in their work, some business people said that writing and working were practically synonymous. These people included advertising executives, corporate planners, marketing research analysts, and public relations managers.

Even business people who hold jobs not specifically designated "writing positions" do a lot of writing. In one poll, 200 college graduates reported spending an average of 25 percent of their on-the-job time performing writing tasks.[4]

A few business people interviewed for this book reported that in their current positions they don't write frequently. But they all agreed that the ability to write well becomes increasingly important as a person takes on positions of greater responsibility. "It stands to reason," one executive said, "that the more responsibilities you have and the more people you deal with, the more you need writing. Writing extends your power and control." Another executive, Bob Foster of Ellison Robotics, has told business students at UCLA just how central communications can be. As he described his rise from a technical staff position to vice president of marketing at Xerox, and, finally, to president of the Robotics Company at Ellison Machinery Company, Bob commented on how the variety and amount of writing he did increased and changed:

> As a member of the technical staff, I did mostly short technical reports and memos. But as I rose through the Marketing Division and then moved on to becoming a president, I was called on to produce a greater number of memos and reports, written to both nontechnical and technical people. When I started out with a B.S. in engineering, I had no idea how important communications would be.

Bob Foster, president of robotics at Ellison Machinery Company.

INTRODUCTION   5

As your responsibilities increase, you will have less time for face-to-face communication and will need to depend on writing to communicate—to make your ideas clear and persuasive to a variety of audiences who are more or less knowledgeable and receptive to your views.

An Effective Job Search and Job Promotion May Depend on Your Ability to Communicate

A second reason for acquiring good writing skills is that an effective job search and job promotion usually depend on your ability to communicate. A person who can write well is a valued member in any organization. Thousands of students with good-to-excellent grade-point averages graduate every year from colleges and business schools. But few of them can write effective resumes or letters of application. Even fewer interview effectively. And once on the job, only a small number are singled out as excellent communicators. Recruiters place a high value on the ability to communicate. A recruiter at a brokerage firm in Connecticut "makes the first cut" by interviewing. But before proceeding further, he subjects the applicant to a writing test: he presents him or her with a case (a problem requiring a solution) and wants to see a decent piece of writing at the end of an hour. "Of course we want great credentials in finance. But if a broker can't communicate, what good is he to us?"

Having strong writing skills should give you a competive edge in job applications. And once you have landed a job, these skills will be essential for promotion. Rick Lipton, a young marketing representative, pointed out that although some entry-level jobs require more legwork than writing skills, "If you want to move up to an executive

Recruiters often look for skilled communicators in interviews.

position, you have to build writing skills. You can't make it without that. A lot of people at my level will not go higher because they are not polished enough to be able to write a good letter." After years of experience in corporate banking, Nat Sutton knows that some people can get in the door without much writing ability, but if they don't learn quickly, they are soon stuck:

> There's no way to become a successful executive without being able to communicate on paper. I'm convinced of that. Most of the executives I've worked with put their words on paper in a very interesting way. I'm talking about imagination and freedom and conversing without a lot of constrictions. Successful executives have integrated writing successfully into their work as managers.

A single well-timed and well-written communication can, in fact, make a big difference in your career. One personnel manager we know wrote an eight-page report addressed to her superiors arguing for the creation of a training program in communication. The document was the major reason that the program was instituted, two new staff members were hired, and her own responsibilities and salary were increased. A second manager, a marketing representative for a major paper products company, came up with a new advertising concept. He outlined his idea in a memo to his boss who agreed with the idea, used it, and helped the manager get a major promotion.

Think of writing, then, as an expression of your competence and of your eligibility for promotion. If effective, every sample of your writing will both accomplish a specific task and create a good impression on the people to whom you are writing. Over a period of time, your letters, memos, and reports will give your superiors tangible evidence of your abilities and motivate them to promote you.

Writing Is a Way of Thinking

Besides writing to carry on daily business and to gain job promotions, some business people write as a way to solve problems and make decisions. In other words, they use writing as a way of thinking. From the business people we interviewed we have heard these comments:

> I don't know what my main point is until I begin writing down things.

> When I'm stuck, I take pen to paper and write a note to myself to clarify my question or problem or the decision I have to make.

> Writing clears my head. Usually I find talking or thinking aloud easier. Strangely, the fact that writing slows down my thoughts forces me to look at my ideas more closely. And then I have a record that I can look back on and revise. The decision I am to make may appear on the page.

> I keep a record of my library research and conversations in my computer and go back to the file frequently to hunt among the details for significant patterns.

In Chapter 9, "The Basics of Report Writing," we review a three-step approach to solving a business problem: identifying the problem, analyzing it and doing research, and selecting the best solution. Writing can help a business person clarify and explore a problem *at any point in this process*.

In some companies, writing helps new managers build the business skills they need to perform well in the professional group they have joined. According to researchers Lisa Ede and Andrea Lunsford, a new manager's writing and the constructive review of that writing by a senior person who serves as a mentor help the new manager develop analytical skills and the ability to work on problems with other members of the group.[5] In a study of writing at Exxon Corporation, researchers James Paradis, David Dobrin, and Richard Miller reached similar conclusions: Writing acted as "a social process to help individuals to fit themselves into the work community."[6]

HOW WILL THE BUSINESS YOU GO INTO AFFECT THE WRITING YOU DO?

As an employee, you can assume that writing will be built into your job. But what will your organization expect in the way of communication, and how will the office environment affect how you get your writing assignments done?

Organizational Expectations about Writing

The writing you do depends, in part, on your company's policies and informal attitudes about writing and speaking. Companies popularly known as "writing cultures" place a priority on writing. In one such company, a young accountant had to write a long memo to his boss requesting that he be permitted to join a professional accounting association and serve several days a year on its board. At another firm, with less emphasis on writing, the same request would have required just a brief phone call or an informal conversation.

Companies in particular industries—for example, insurance, banking, and accounting—tend to be writing cultures. These companies are forced by the nature of their work to use formal written communications, such as insurance policies, financial analyses, and auditing reports. Companies with many levels of authority also tend to be writing cultures because the size of the company makes doing business face-to-face or over the phone inefficient, if not impossible (see Figure 1.3).

In contrast some companies can be characterized as "oral cultures." In these companies writing is avoided when possible. Small entrepreneurial and family-run companies often fall into this category. So do new companies and those run by a powerful individual. Organizations that are less stratified and that like to do business informally also tend to belong to this group.

THE RANDOM HOUSE GUIDE TO BUSINESS WRITING

The Allied-Signal Code of Conduct

The Corporation's basic objective is to conduct its business to benefit our customers, shareholders, employees, suppliers and society in general. We seek to achieve our goals of profitability and growth while fulfilling the responsibilities of a corporate citizen.

COMMITMENT TO CUSTOMERS
■ We provide to our customers high quality products and services on schedule and at fair prices.

COMMITMENT TO EMPLOYEES
■ We believe employee relations must be based on mutual trust, respect and a clear recognition of the dignity of all employees. We are committed to providing competitive pay and benefits.

We also recognize our obligation to provide a safe and efficient workplace, and an environment conducive to open and frank communications. We are committed to equal employment practices.

COMMITMENT TO SHAREHOLDERS
■ We strive to provide a reasonable return to our shareholders and to protect and increase the value of their investment.

COMMITMENT TO SUPPLIERS
■ We deal honestly and fairly with our suppliers. We give all suppliers fair consideration, basing purchasing decisions on value offered, price, reliability and integrity.

COMMITMENT TO SOCIETY AS A WHOLE
■ As a Corporate citizen we have certain responsibilities. For example, we obey laws and regulations; we pay our taxes; we produce safe goods and services that consumers want; and we protect the environment. We also assume wider social responsibilities. We support community organizations, encourage employee involvement in civic causes, help the disadvantaged and conserve energy and other valuable resources.

Our Credo

We believe our first responsibility is to the doctors, nurses and patients, to mothers and all others who use our products and services. In meeting their needs everything we do must be of high quality. We must constantly strive to reduce our costs in order to maintain reasonable prices. Customers' orders must be serviced promptly and accurately. Our suppliers and distributors must have an opportunity to make a fair profit.

We are responsible to our employees, the men and women who work with us throughout the world. Everyone must be considered as an individual. We must respect their dignity and recognize their merit. They must have a sense of security in their jobs. Compensation must be fair and adequate, and working conditions clean, orderly and safe. Employees must feel free to make suggestions and complaints. There must be equal opportunity for employment, development and advancement for those qualified. We must provide competent management, and their actions must be just and ethical.

We are responsible to the communities in which we live and work and to the world community as well. We must be good citizens — support good works and charities and bear our fair share of taxes. We must encourage civic improvements and better health and education. We must maintain in good order the property we are privileged to use, protecting the environment and natural resources.

Our final responsibility is to our stockholders. Business must make a sound profit. We must experiment with new ideas. Research must be carried on, innovative programs developed and mistakes paid for. New equipment must be purchased, new facilities provided and new products launched. Reserves must be created to provide for adverse times. When we operate according to these principles, the stockholders should realize a fair return.

Johnson & Johnson

A "writing culture"

An "oral culture"

Different organizations have different expectations for handling communications.

Figure 1.3

LEVELS OF AUTHORITY IN TWO DIFFERENT ORGANIZATIONS

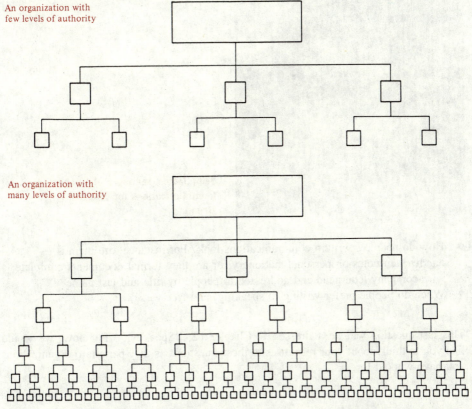

An organization with few levels of authority

An organization with many levels of authority

The more complex the organization, the more likely it is to communicate in writing.

How do you, as a new employee in a company, determine your organization's expectations about writing? Jean Jarvis, manager of Corporate Communications for Kaufman-Broad, a Los Angeles financial company, recommends that you learn to "read" your organization. That is, you should observe and ask associates about what gets done orally and what gets done in writing. In particular, look carefully at the communications that cross your desk, and if possible look in the company's files of past communications sent out by your office. Notice, too, how your superior and associates handle communication tasks, and if possible review your superior's written communications for style and presentation. To build your understanding of how writing functions in your organization, answer these questions:

- When do employees use the phone, when do they write, and when, if ever, do they send messages electronically?

Jean Jarvis, manager of Corporate Communications for Kaufman-Broad.

- How do people's written communications look? For instance, are memos handwritten notes on personal stationery, or are they formal documents complete with company letterhead and addressed to people by title and last name?
- When do people prefer writing to speaking, and *vice versa?*

This last question will be addressed in Chapter 12, "Speaking." For now, we would like you to think about your responses to these questions as they pertain to organizations you have worked for.

Office Environment

Your organization will affect how you do your writing. Sometimes your organization can frustrate your efforts to get your writing done. For instance, you will most likely have to do your writing in a busy office amid phone calls, meetings, and conversations. Such an environment will require you to find some way to manage your writing workload. At other times, your organization can make writing easier for you. For example, if computer technology is available, you will be able to write more quickly and effectively.

MANAGING YOUR WRITING WORKLOAD

Because efficient business writers know that they must meet deadlines on their writing assignments despite distractions and other demands on their time, they have developed strategies for managing their writing workload. These include:

INTRODUCTION 11

Writing must sometimes be done amid the buzz of other office activities.

- Establishing priorities
- Setting aside time for important writing, while handling routine writing tasks during busy or less productive hours

We think that you may be able to benefit from the experience of these efficient business writers.

Establishing Priorities. To establish priorities for the tasks you face on the job, you will want to develop a system for identifying which tasks deserve your greatest and most immediate attention. One manager has developed a personal system for managing the tasks involved in running his company's computer center. He uses a "hot seat"—an office chair on which his secretary leaves messages that he needs to handle immediately. When he gets to work at 8 A.M., he first takes care of the requests he finds on the chair. Then he goes through his "in" box, which contains a random collection of messages. He puts everything requiring immediate attention in an orange folder and low-priority items in a green folder. You may not want to work with a "hot seat" and colored folders, but you will want to develop a method for setting priorities.

Setting Aside Time for Important Writing Tasks. You know from your college experience that you have to set aside blocks of time to complete a complex writing assignment such as a research report, and you have to find an empty classroom or a corner of the library in which to work undisturbed. In business, you may have to write important communications that take as much concentration as the papers you write in college, but you will find yourself working in a busy office where you can't control noise or interruptions. Given this environment, how can you manage to get your writing done?

Some business people we interviewed do their important writing early or late in the day, when they can work undisturbed by co-workers, clients, or customers. Others work in offices that have instituted "quiet hours," times when phone calls are taken by the switchboard operator or by a secretary and when co-workers have agreed not to disturb one another. Still others identify the time of day that they write best and try to arrange their schedules so that they can work steadily during those periods. You will want to determine when is the best time to write, given the circumstances in which you work.

USING COMPUTER TECHNOLOGY

Computer technology is increasingly a part of most business environments and can assist businesses with everything from inventory control to form letters. Writing in the work place—and in the university for that matter—is done more and more with the aid of computers. A recent study revealed that over half of the country's largest companies plan to automate their offices.[7] Another study, a survey of eighty-nine business people representing all levels of management, revealed that many of them already use computers for their writing tasks instead of having secretaries do their typing.[8]

As a business person you can expect to have computers in your office and to find their communication capabilities helpful in your writing. Besides **word processing,** you may have access to **computer graphics** for displaying information visually and to **electronic mail** for composing and sending messages from one terminal to others. Chapter 15, "The Business Writer and the Computer," and to some extent Chapter 12, "Speak-

Today business people use computers for handling their writing tasks.

INTRODUCTION 13

ing," and Chapter 13, "Visual Aids," treat this subject in greater detail. For now, if you are already proficient, we encourage you to use the computer for your writing assignments. If you are still in college and have not learned to use the computer, we urge you to find out about your school's computer facilities and training programs.

Many writers now use computer graphics to display their data.

WHAT SKILLS AND EXPERIENCE CAN YOU DRAW ON TO BECOME A SUCCESSFUL BUSINESS WRITER?

Even if you have done little writing, you can draw on experiences and habits you have acquired in other areas of your life to develop business writing skills. If you have solved problems, planned projects, worked in an organization, argued for your point of view, read widely, or written essays and exams for courses, you will be able to apply your background to business writing.

Problem Solving

If you have solved problems in math or science courses, you can apply your problem-solving skills to your business writing tasks. Problem-solving skills have helped at least one executive organize ideas for the memos and reports she turns out regularly. As this banker told us, "My background in chemistry—in getting to a particular point in an experiment, in proving something—has been most valuable in banking. If you have scientific training, you start by defining an unknown and move to a known through steps." Similarly, a marketing representative who works for a pharmaceuticals company and flies a private plane in her spare time draws on her training in problem solving as a pilot to write effective reports:

> I look at writing as a kind of problem solving and that's why I like doing it. What helped me most with problem solving was learning how to fly a plane. When you fly an airplane, you have maybe thirty seconds to make a decision. When I started flying, I used to keep a notebook of questions—"What if's"—that I'd study as I walked my dog. I'd present myself with a problem and mentally go through all the information that would be relevant and decide what I would do. In the many hours I flew and the different planes I flew, there were actually a couple of situations, landing gear collapsing and circumnavigating in a thunderstorm, which demanded that I make emergency decisions. Because I was so darn systems-oriented, I didn't sit there and fall apart. My mind was mentally trained to identify the problem, collect the data, and react. I write this way too.

Project Management and Team Work

Have you been successful in planning a project? If so, you have probably gathered and analyzed information and coordinated your team's activities to launch the project on schedule. You can now apply your research, organizational, and time management skills to much of the business writing you will do. If you haven't run a project but have belonged to a team, social club, or other college organization, you have worked in groups and have some understanding of group dynamics and of how you come across in social situations. As a result of your experiences, you will be able to handle group writing projects.

Speaking

If you enjoy arguing a point in conversation, you can learn to do so in writing as well. Your ability as a speaker to persuade others to adopt your point of view or to take an action prepares you for developing matching skills as a persuasive writer.

Reading

Anyone fascinated by language can apply this love of words to developing business writing skills. One executive who is an excellent business writer noted:

> When I was younger, I was very impressed by how writers put together words to make a sentence. I was very interested in words and how they were related to each other. My orientation was not so much the long paragraph as it was each word. I would think, Why? Why did the writer do that? I am constantly asking myself that in my writing. I want to put words together to do something.

Your sensitivity as a reader to a writer's use of language can help you become aware of the words that will make your business communications accomplish what you want them to.

Essay and Exam Writing

You have no doubt written essays and exams for class. If you have been successful, you can figure out your instructor's expectations about the assignment, you can organize information, and you can revise and edit your work for style and clarity. Adept essay and exam writers who also know the principles behind writing find the transition to business writing easy because some of the same principles apply to both academic and business writing.

Of course there are differences between the writing you do for class and the writing you do on the job. In general, the essays and exams you write for class travel a one-way street from you to your instructors. Their job in reading your work is to check to see whether you have mastered the subject matter of the course. Your writing, then, is a vehicle for showing what you have learned. By contrast, business communications have as their primary purpose to get work done. They may travel several streets—your writing may go out to several readers. Finally, business writing calls for conventions of style, layout, and graphics that differ from the essay forms you are familiar with. In this text, you will learn about the unique features of business writing. Knowing them will help you bridge the gap between academic and business writing.

Right now, you may want to take stock of your skills and experiences as they apply to your goal of learning to write effectively for business. You may also want to track your growth as a business writer during the school term. To do so, think about keeping a portfolio of your writing and reviewing it periodically to see how you have progressed.

SUMMARY

As you begin learning to write business letters, memos, and reports, keep in mind the variety of tasks your business writing allows you to do. Remember, too, how important business writing can be to your current job, to your job search and job promotion, and to your ability to solve business problems. As you enter a specific organization, notice how the company affects the writing and speaking you do. Consider whether the organization is primarily a "writing culture" or an "oral culture," and figure out how you can best manage your writing workload and how you can make use of computer technology to accomplish your writing tasks. Before reading further in this text, think about the skills and experiences you may be able to draw on to become a successful business writer.

PREVIEW OF CHAPTERS TO COME

In this textbook, you will learn about the process of writing letters, memos, and reports. You will look at writing as a process (Chapters 2 and 3) and at letter writing (Chapters 4 to 7) and memo writing (Chapter 8). Then you will consider report writing—problem solving and report writing (Chapter 9) and formal reports (Chapters 10 and 11). In the final chapters, you will learn about a variety of related communication tasks: speaking (Chapter 12), visual aids (Chapter 13), the job search (Chapter 14), and business writing and the computer (Chapter 15). Two appendixes cover supplemental material: responding to business cases (Appendix A) and a selective summary of grammar and punctuation (Appendix B).

2 WRITING AS A PROCESS

PREVIEW

This chapter should help you to

1. See writing as a process that consists of
   - Setting the goal for the communication
   - Assessing your reader
   - Gathering information and generating ideas
   - Organizing
   - Writing a draft
   - Revising
   - Editing and proofreading
2. Recognize and apply techniques that good writers use
   - For gathering information: note-taking
   - For generating ideas: talking to an associate, using a tape recorder, writing nonstop, and making a list
   - For organizing: using the RTA formula, analysis trees, and outlines
   - For revising: role-playing your reader and asking an associate to review your writing

A casual observer watching administrative assistant Diane Bolger would see her writing the final draft of a three-page report in less than thirty minutes. Although the observer may think he or she has seen Diane take only thirty minutes, in fact she has been "writing" the report for three days, ever since her boss asked her to explain some procedures.

Writing is much more than putting final words on a page. It is a process that begins the moment you decide you need to write and includes everything from your initial decision to write to your final proofreading. Writing can be thought of as a process that consists of the following seven activities:

1. Setting the goal for the written communication
2. Assessing the reader
3. Gathering information and generating ideas
4. Organizing

5. Writing a draft
6. Revising
7. Editing and proofreading

In this chapter we discuss each activity and suggest techniques that effective writers use to accomplish their writing goals. Right now, we would like you to consider the activities in sequence. But you should keep in mind that good writers often shift quickly and effectively among the activities, even dealing with more than one at a time. Once you become familiar with the activities in the writing process, you can observe your own writing process and decide what works best for you.

Before we look at the activities, let's see how Diane put together her report. (The report appears in Chapter 9, pp. 426–427.) When asked to reconstruct how she got to the last thirty-minute draft, Diane looked over her earlier drafts and flipped back through her calendar of the last three days to refresh her memory. Then she tried to remember everything she did to write the report. Her remarks can be classified according to the seven activities of the writing process.

1. Set the Goal:

My boss told me Accounting would be using new computer-assisted procedures. He asked me to write a report explaining the new procedures so that everyone requisitioning funds would have a step-by-step description.

2. Assess the Reader:

There are two groups, new managers and old-timers. Neither group knows the procedures. The old-timers would probably resent getting the report because they like the old company style of casualness and camaraderie. Since the company has recently been acquired by a much larger organization, the report would be just one more sign to the Old Guard that "bigness is bad." So I can't send out the report cold to them. I have to take them aside individually—there are only seven of them—and let them know how they'd benefit from the change. The new people, who are from the larger organization, would be receptive to the report since they are used to following formal computerized procedures.

3. Gather Information and Generate Ideas:

That first day, I attended a meeting of the Accounting Department on the new procedures. Since Accounting provided me with a worksheet, my note-taking on the meeting itself was sparse—just vital bits of information, especially examples that I thought I would not be able to remember. I asked questions and took notes on the answers, since I knew I'd be writing the report.

Later that day, I talked to a few key people—people who are sensitive to how others react and who would be affected by the procedure. I wanted to find out what, if anything, they knew and felt about using forms that the computer would have to process.

4. Organize:

I reviewed my notes from the Accounting meeting and from my discussions with key people, and I came up with three categories for grouping all the information people needed. The categories reflect the big questions I figured people would have: the "what" ("What is the new procedure?"), the "how" ("How do you fill out requisitions?"), and "special cases" ("How can you handle special requisitions?").

5. Write a Draft:

After organizing my notes from the Accounting meeting and from my talks with people, I began, immediately and with complete confidence, to write a full draft in pencil and completed it in an hour. I had a clear sense of all the details, so I thought I could pour the report straight out onto the page. I wrote for about fifteen or twenty minutes and then was interrupted. My writing got bigger and less controlled on the draft when I realized that there's a difference between understanding something in my own head and explaining it to someone else. You can see on the draft a beautiful beginning and toward the end all the crossing out—the first hour's thinking and writing. By the end of the hour, my cockiness had diminished—see all the cross-outs. "They'll never know what I'm talking about," I thought. I finished the draft and had my secretary type it so that people could look at it.

6. Revise:

I made some changes in the draft and showed the new version [draft 2] to a few key people. The questions they raised made me decide to add a new section on additional information. I also read the draft aloud and tried to imagine how the reader would take it. I wanted to find the gaps. Gaps are the "dues you have to pay" if the report is not clear. This kind of reading helped me realize that the managers were concerned primarily with how to fill out requisitions and not with the fact that this is a new procedure. So I changed the subject heading from "New Accounting Procedures" to "Filling Out Requisitions." It's a simple thing, but it's a sign of what I have to do when I reexamine the whole piece.

7. Edit and Proofread:

I let the report [draft 3] sit overnight so I'd be able to give it a fresh reading. In reading it again, I underlined key phrases so that the reader wouldn't overlook their importance, and I added sentences to clarify my point. I was particularly sensitive to my weakness—I'm in love with long, complicated sentences. I broke long sentences into two. Then I had it typed and proofread it.

When we did a graph of Diane's writing process (see Figure 2.1), it became clear that she shifted often and easily among the activities of the writing process. Although the basic movement of her activities was from setting the goal to proofreading, she moved back and forth as new information and insights caused her to revise. For instance, once she received responses on her second draft from key people, she knew she had to add a new section that anticipated questions her readers might ask.

Let's look now in greater detail at the activities in the writing process that experienced business writers use to get their writing tasks done.

SETTING THE GOAL

Setting the goal of a business communication, and using that goal to guide you through the subsequent activities of the writing process, is the kind of planning that distinguishes effective business writers from poor ones. Whenever you decide to write, you should ask yourself what you want your readers to think and what you want them to do.

One technique effective writers use to clarify their goal is to express it in a single sentence that answers the question, "What is this letter, memo, or report supposed to

Figure 2.1

DIANE'S WRITING PROCESS

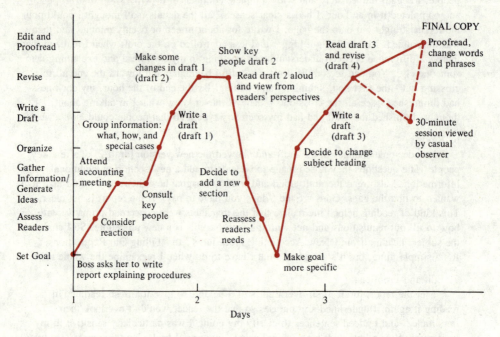

accomplish?" John D. Lyon, a vice president at an energy corporation, advises, "Don't lose sight of why you set out to write the document. Think about what you want readers to have at the end that they didn't have at the beginning." After you have formulated a goal statement, you can use it as an objective against which to measure everything you think of putting into your business communication. But not all statements are equally effective. Poor goal statements typically announce a general subject area:

Poor Goal Statement: I'm going to discuss the reward system for entry-level managers at our company.

The resulting communication could be anything from a description of salary and benefits to a comparison of the current reward system with that at comparable organizations. Effective goal statements make clear what the reader is to be informed of and how the reader is to use this information:

Effective Goal Statement: I'm going to compare the reward system for entry-level managers at our company to that at two of our competitors in order to recommend to our decision makers any adjustments they need to make in our system.

Sometimes a manager who asks you for a communication is vague in expressing what he or she wants to know. It can then be difficult to write a goal statement. Your boss may say, "Find out what you can about the new tax code" or "Tell me about your trip to the branch offices." When you can, you should ask your boss what specifically he or she is going to do with the information. You may learn, for example, that the request is for information about the tax code's impact on oil shelters or about how to handle absenteeism at the branch offices. When you can't ask for clarification, you may have to rely on your own judgment and previous experience working with your boss to determine why he or she might need the information.

The accompanying checklist will help you review the goal statements of your communications.

CHECKLIST FOR FORMULATING A GOAL STATEMENT

1. Does the goal statement express what you want your readers to think?

2. Does the goal statement express what you want your readers to do?

ASSESSING THE READER

Knowing the purpose of your communication is not enough. Diane Bolger knew her goal. She had to explain the new accounting procedures. But she also had to think about how the old-timers as well as the new managers would react to her report.

Like Diane, you will need to determine who your readers are and to assess what they are like in order to write a letter, memo, or report that is understandable and convincing. Usually the question, "Who are my readers?" has an obvious answer. When Diane planned her report on new accounting procedures, she knew she would be addressing it to all managers who use the accounting procedures. These people are her **primary readers,** people who can take action on the basis of the communication. Sometimes your communication will have **secondary readers,** readers who are less obvious. In fact, all written communications can have secondary as well as primary readers. For instance, a letter that goes outside an organization will have the addressee as primary reader. But anyone to whom the addressee shows the letter becomes a secondary reader.

Once you have identified your readers, you will want to consider them carefully so as to make your communications understandable and convincing. You will want to think about four things:

1. *Your reader's business relationship with you:* When you are writing to someone outside your company, your relationship to your reader should be cordial and busi-

nesslike. When you are writing to someone within your company, your formal relationship to your reader helps to define your role. If your reader is your superior, you will want to explain and support the rationale for your recommendations. If your reader is your peer, you can use an engaging tone to encourage your associate to participate in your thinking and decision making. If your reader is your subordinate, you will want to avoid sounding dictatorial, but you can focus on presenting your order or information to show how it benefits your subordinates.

2. *Your reader's knowledge of the subject:* You will want to consider how familiar your reader is with the subject of the communication. If your message belongs to a long line of discussions and written exchanges between you and your reader, you don't want to waste your reader's time spelling out what is obvious. On the other hand, if your reader is uninformed about the subject, you will want to give essential background information and explanations.

If you are writing as a specialist, you will also need to consider whether your reader has sufficient expertise to understand the concepts and vocabulary you use to convey your message. A computer specialist writing to someone familiar with data processing can write, "Main memory's larger in this CPU than in the old one." But to a generalist, these terms would need to be explained, perhaps at length.

3. *Your reader's expectations about how the communication should be presented:* You will need to know what your reader expects in the way of the content, style, and format of your business communications. One management consultant told us that most corporations she works for expect her reports to be in the form of charts and graphs, with a minimal amount of prose. Most executives want recommendations presented on the first page, but some want to see the arguments first. As for letters, most people expect them to be cordial and informal and to contain mostly short paragraphs and short sentences.

4. *Your reader's attitudes toward you and toward the subject of your communication:* You will want to know how your reader feels about you and about your message. Will he or she be inclined to think and feel the way you do about the subject of the communication, perhaps because of common beliefs, experiences, or objectives? If so, you will probably decide to be straightforward in the way you express yourself. If not, you will want to build a case for your views before presenting them.

When sending her report to the new managers, Diane Bolger could begin by explaining the accounting procedures, since her readers were accustomed to formal, computerized procedures. But before she could send the same report to the old-timers, who were against the system, she had to prepare them for the unpleasant news. Since she knew all seven of them, she spoke to each one individually, arguing personally for the long-term benefits of the changeover to the automated system. If people find you and your ideas threatening or unpleasant, you too will have to give reasons for your point of view and acknowledge and respond to their objections—in person, in writing, or both. In fact, if Diane had not had a working relationship with the old-timers or if they had been a large group, she might have chosen to write *two separate reports,* one to the new managers consisting of a straightforward description of the procedures, and the

WRITING AS A PROCESS

other to the old-timers arguing for the benefits of the procedures as well as describing them.

The accompanying checklist will help you assess the readers of your communications.

CHECKLIST FOR ASSESSING THE READER

1. Who are your primary and secondary readers?
2. What is your reader's business relationship to you?
3. What does your reader know about the subject of your communication?
4. What does your reader expect in the way of content, style, and format?
5. What is your reader's attitude toward you and toward the subject of your communication?

GATHERING INFORMATION AND GENERATING IDEAS

If you know what you want to tell your readers and how to say it best, writing the communication can be a simple matter of getting started and following through to the end. For example, if you are responding to a letter, all the "research" you may need to do is to have the letter beside you as you write. Sometimes, as in the case of Diane Bolger, your notes will contain much of the data you need for the communication. But for most writing assignments, you will need to gather information and generate ideas before you can write the communication.

Gathering Information

If you have ever written a research report, you know that gathering information for it can be the biggest part of your job. Doing research includes everything from reading books, newspapers, and periodicals to conducting surveys, attending lectures, talking to experts, making observations, and retrieving information from computerized data bases. But in business you will find that doing research is not limited to preparing a formal report. Some business writers need to gather information constantly—for memos, letters, and presentations—on such issues as competitors, technology, and legislation. And they have to seek that information from experts, trade journals, newspapers, magazines, computer data bases, and other sources. As a business person, you will find that your research will take you not only into your company's offices but out into the field and to the library as well.

In Chapter 10, "The Formal Report," you will learn about techniques for gathering information for a research report. For the present, just note that there are two sources of information, primary and secondary. **Primary sources** refer to sources of information that you yourself gather firsthand; they include what you learn from doing a survey, conducting an interview, attending a meeting, or observing a situation. **Secondary sources** refer to information that has been gathered by another researcher. They include books, articles, company reports, newspapers, and brochures. Regardless of the source you use, however, doing research involves *selecting* information that is relevant to your writing goal.

To assist you in answering questions that arise as you do your research, we recommend that you take notes. Effective note-taking will serve you well whether you are making an inquiry over the phone, reading several books and articles, or like Diane Bolger, attending an important meeting on procedures you have been asked to write about.

NOTE-TAKING

Whether you take notes on scraps of paper or on index cards, in a notebook or in a computer's filing system, the important thing to remember is to comment in writing on what you read, see, hear, and observe, relating it to the communication you are planning to write. Careful note-taking will help you establish connections between your research and the communication you want to write.

Some avid note-takers like to "house" their research under one cover—a notebook that holds material likely to be useful in their business writing. As more material is added to the notebook, it becomes a rich storehouse of information. In addition, keeping a notebook helps business people develop the habit of thinking about the potential use-

Business people who keep a notebook always have a store of data to call on.

fulness of what they read, hear, and observe. As one executive remarked, "I jot down observations and facts about a situation as soon as I realize I'll have to write about it."

Barry Jamison, a marketing analyst for a pharmaceuticals company, takes a notebook everywhere he goes on the job, because he never knows when a member of his staff will raise an important question, when a timely research study will come his way, or when a superior will ask him to look at a new angle for the company's marketing campaign. Barry gets information and inquiries from so many sources that the only way he can keep track of everything is to keep a notebook. By dividing it into sections, he can compartmentalize all this material. He keeps a section on his staff's questions and ideas, one on studies of consumer behavior and related literature, another on government regulations, and yet another on his own research and analysis of marketing trends. If your writing tasks require you to gather and pull together detailed information from numerous, varied sources, you too may want to keep a notebook.

Generating Ideas

Taking notes about what you read and observe allows you both to gather information and to generate ideas. But at times you may need to find other ways to generate ideas. You may have **writer's block**—that is, you may be unable to decide what to say and how to say it. In every chapter we give suggestions for generating ideas relevant to specific communications, but here are some techniques you can use in any situation.

TALKING TO AN ASSOCIATE

Too many students and business people suffer from "resource myopia": They hold the false belief that all writing must be solitary. When they have trouble writing, they don't see that someone whom they work with every day may be able to help them come up with ideas or indicate what has worked for him or her in the past, whom to talk to, or what source is worth reading.

Talking to an associate can also help you better imagine who your readers are, what you need to tell them, and how you need to express your ideas. As Diane Bolger told us, "Sometimes someone else's vantage point will be 'right on.' I might be floundering around, trying to plan what to say. Interchange with people can give me the right perspective." For routine business communications, you should work on your own; for important and complex assignments, you should think about asking associates to set aside some time to assist you.

USING A TAPE RECORDER

If you are more comfortable talking than writing, you can use a tape recorder to "talk out" your thoughts about your letter, memo, or report. Some business people—especially those who are better talkers than writers and who get bogged down thinking about all the different directions they could take in handling a writing task—find that using a tape recorder is an effective way to stop worrying and start writing. There are two potential advantages to using a tape recorder:

1. You can imagine you are talking to the person you have to write to.
2. Since your natural way of speaking will come through on the tape, you will be better able to incorporate this conversational style in your communication.

Using a tape recorder will allow you to generate ideas and test them out on yourself—without risk—before subjecting them to your reader's scrutiny. In playing back the tape, you can begin to formulate your message, for within the material may be found the complete or partial message you want to put in writing.

WRITING NONSTOP

Like using a tape recorder, writing nonstop helps you by-pass worries and get words down on a page. With this technique you begin to write even when you are uncertain about what to say and where or how to start. If you find yourself blocked, you can try the following technique:

- Write for ten minutes about any aspect of your communication.
- Put down everything that comes into your mind—even write about why you can't write.
- Begin with what you know. Articulate as clearly as you can questions about what you don't know.
- Don't stop writing. Don't worry about finding the exact word, the right phrase, the best sentence. Your problem was how to begin; now you are getting words down on paper.
- Stop at the end of ten minutes.
- Read over what you have written. Ask yourself: Are there any ideas here that I can work with for my communication?

In the process of writing quickly and freely, you may discover some of the content of your communication—even appropriate words and phrases.

Ted Gaynor, president of Manufacturers' Representatives Association (MRA), used this technique to get started on a difficult letter he felt it necessary to write in order to keep a new customer. MRA is a wholesaler of high-technology equipment in the New England area. The new customer, Paulsen, Inc., manufactures such equipment and had contracted with MRA to sell for it.

Ted had just heard formally by letter from Paulsen's vice president and general manager, Joe Stipanski, that Paulsen wanted to terminate its contract with MRA as of March 1 of the coming year. As Ted reread Joe's letter, he began thinking about several

WRITING AS A PROCESS

strategies for persuading Joe not to terminate the contract. Ted also felt frustrated that all the work he had put into this account had not as yet panned out. Since Ted didn't know how to begin his letter to Joe or what to cover, he decided to do some nonstop writing to get his mind working in more concrete terms about the problem. Figure 2.2 shows Ted's first ten minutes of nonstop writing.

After rereading his nonstop writing and thinking about it from his reader's point of view, Ted extrapolated two major points that might convince Paulsen to continue with MRA. First, it would be more costly for Paulsen to switch manufacturers' representatives, given MRA's knowledge of the New England market. Second, despite the small size of the market for Paulsen's products, MRA is eager to continue making efforts to sell them and these efforts would cost Paulsen nothing. Clearly Ted's final letter would look a lot different from the nonstop writing, but this exercise allowed him to discover the key ideas he had to convey in his message.

MAKING A LIST

Some people who may feel uncomfortable using a tape recorder or doing nonstop writing like to make lists of their ideas to keep track of them. These people like to sit down with a sheet of notes and begin drawing lines and circles to group and order items into a list.

When gathering information and generating ideas, you will find the accompanying checklist helpful in reviewing your efforts.

CHECKLIST FOR GATHERING INFORMATION AND GENERATING IDEAS

1. Have you taken notes to assist you in gathering information? Have your notes helped you answer questions relevant to the communication you must write?

2. Have you used any of the following techniques to help you generate ideas: talking to colleagues, using a tape recorder, writing nonstop, making lists?

ORGANIZING

Taking notes, talking to associates, using a tape recorder, writing nonstop, and making lists are all techniques to help you get your ideas out on paper. These ideas will most likely be in the form of brief notes, phrases, or key words. Or they might be long drafts of prose that are rich in ideas but without any shape or focus. Grouping and ordering your ideas will help you develop and sharpen your thinking, so that your main points can become clear to yourself and understandable and persuasive to your reader. In organizing your ideas, you may also be rethinking your goal and reassessing your reader.

Figure 2.2

NONSTOP WRITING

I've worked hard trying to position this account but it's very frustrating. Paulsen is tough to sell in this territory. They're used to selling their stuff in high volume, but very few firms in this area use mil spec hybrids in volume and three of these firms have their own in-house facilities for manufacturing them. Then why shouldn't Paulsen just get out of the market? Why should I even try to convince Joe to stay put. Because we've made a time and money investment in selling Paulsen. While the Northeast is not fertile field for Paulsen's type of product, we've planted seeds and generated interest and contacts. We expect results in the future. We can continue to make these efforts. We're in the field everyday. It won't cost Paulsen anything to let us keep trying. We've learned more and more about this market and hiring another manufacturer's rep will cost Paulsen money just to give them the time to get up to speed about this market. There's a learning curve associated with new representation. They shouldn't switch now. We need their business and giving it to

> someone else will cost them more. We see the market in New England for the types of hybrids they produce is limited to a few programs that generally don't buy in volume the $100,000 per year per part requirements Paulsen sets. Paulsen's customers have historically been manufacturers of missiles and high-volume radar. These are rare in our area. But we don't miss whatever limited opportunities do exist for their kind of product.

Imagine yourself in Barry Jamison's shoes. In his notebook he has collected comments from several members of his staff on the cough syrup that they market. He now recognizes it is time to call a meeting to provide some answers.

Figure 2.3 shows Barry's notes on the comments made by Janet, a sales rep; Dan, another sales rep; Ed, the assistant market researcher; and Phil, the advertising account executive.

To prepare for his meeting, Barry could just go down the list in his notes, answering the questions one by one. But by grouping questions on the same or similar topics, he can see that he needs information primarily in three areas. Figure 2.4 shows how he ordered his notes. By grouping and ordering his notes, Barry has the agenda for the meeting and a list of "need to know" items that he will have to investigate before the meeting.

Grouping items into categories has made Barry's task in preparing for the meeting much clearer to himself. It will also make the meeting much more useful to his staff. Now, rather than enduring a meeting in which Barry gives out twenty bits of information, staff members will be able to see how each member's concerns fit into the larger picture, and they will be encouraged to offer their own points of view and ask further questions. Thus Barry not only anticipates their questions, but he also helps his staff work as a team.

Barry has an easy job of grouping and ordering his ideas because his notes readily fall into three categories easily understood by his readers. Other writing tasks can be more challenging to group and order. In more complex writing tasks, for example, grouping and ordering can reveal some ideas that need expanding and others that need cutting.

Figure 2.3
BARRY'S NOTES

Janet
- Are we going after children's market?
- Have no packaging just for children. Syrup's never displayed in the juvenile section.

Dan
- Our labeling's too "sedate," no "eye appeal," drab next to competitors' designs.
- R and R has come out with new bottle shape, looks great on the shelf. Our response?

Ed
- wants to conduct survey to find out:
  - which packaging for safety lids best
  - if we need to know anything else about safety lids
  - consumer preferences on
    - flavor
    - "back to nature" appeal
    - lozenges versus syrup

Phil
- Needs decisions on changes by mid-Nov. for advertising budget.

Ned Andersen, a vice president at Carlsberg and Kest (C&K), had a somewhat complicated assignment. The worst hot spell and drought in ten years had resulted in shortages of water and electricity. This crisis was threatening two million workers. Newspaper headlines warned that shortages of water and electricity in parts of the Far West could shut down many plants. Workers had already been laid off, and utilities were rationing power. In Arizona, one of the hardest-hit states, industries had been requested to reduce the amount of water and electricity they used. C&K, a large manufacturer of tractors, was one of the companies affected. Top management met to determine plans for handling this emergency. On the basis of advice from energy consultants, management decided on two measures: keeping the air conditioning turned off

Figure 2.4

HOW BARRY ORDERED HIS NOTES

1. Packaging
   - R and R's new bottle shape
   - Is our packaging too sedate?

2. Juvenile
   - Are we going after children's market?
   - Do we stay with separate child's dosage but no separate packaging for children?
   - R and R is convincing some doctors their dosage easier to use.

3. Consumer Survey
   - "back to nature" appeal
   - 3 good designs for safety lids
   - flavors
   - lozenges vs. syrups

until office and shop temperatures reached fairly high levels, and shutting down the water used to maintain the grounds at headquarters. At the same time, the company wanted to avoid the expense of overtime. Ned was responsible for writing the memo to inform workers of the new policy. Here are the notes he took away from the meeting:

>   Shortage of electricity and water
>   Other plants have already closed
>   Possible shutdown of C&K
>   Turn off sprinklers at headquarters
>   Absolutely no overtime
>   Allow office and shop temperatures to go up by Tues., July 16
>   > Shop 80 degrees
>   > Office 75 degrees

Ned could readily see that his notes fell into two groups, one describing the problem, the other the solution.

PROBLEM

>   Shortage of water and electricity
>   Possible shutdown of C&K

SOLUTION

>   Turn off sprinklers on grounds at headquarters
>   Absolutely no overtime
>   Allow office and shop temperatures to go up by Tues., July 16
>   > Shop 80 degrees
>   > Office 75 degrees

As Ned thought about his purpose in writing the memo, he could see that the list could be cut. For example, looking at his notes he knew that only a few employees would be concerned about the overtime. That information could be delivered by the appropriate department supervisor. He cut out that item. Then he imagined what his memo would look like:

> Extremely high temperatures and drought conditions have caused serious water and electricity shortages. Consequently, C&K will have to turn off the sprinklers on the grounds at headquarters and allow the temperatures in the shop and office to go up:
>
>   Shop: 80 degrees
>   Office: 75 degrees

WRITING AS A PROCESS 33

But reflecting on his purpose, Ned could see that his task involved more than simply informing employees they would have to endure high temperatures and parched grounds. He realized the news would make a lot of people unhappy so he also wanted to enlist the support of employees and help them recognize how they would benefit from their sacrifice. He looked again at the *groups* he had formed—"problem" and "solution"—and now realized he needed a third category, "benefits." Under this category, he added information that would be important to his employees.

PROBLEM

Electricity and water shortages, caused by drought and extremely high temperatures, have closed some plants and caused extensive layoffs in others. C&K wants to avoid shutdowns and layoffs but this requires drastic measures.

SOLUTION

One solution is to allow indoor temperatures to go up. Energy consultant says temperatures of 75 and 80 degrees are bearable.

Temperatures will be equalized to avoid hot spots and cold spots.
People can be comfortable if they dress appropriately.

Another solution is to turn off sprinklers on grounds at headquarters.

BENEFITS

Measures will save jobs and be fair to everyone.

After he had seen the problem and solution from the reader's point of view, Ned felt ready to write. After two drafts, he came up with the memo shown in Figure 2.5.

By grouping his ideas and recalling his purpose, Ned was able to generate the information that would help his employees see how their sacrifice would contribute to everyone's benefit. Although organizing is a later activity of the writing process, it can often lead you, as it did Ned, to circle back—to rethink your purpose and to generate more ideas.

Grouping related ideas helps you find the larger patterns in the information you have collected. How you order those ideas in your final draft will depend on what your letter, memo, or report is trying to achieve with your readers. Later chapters will offer detailed guidelines for organizing information. But for now, let's consider briefly three basic ways of organizing business communications: the RTA formula (for letters) and analysis trees and outlines (for all communications).

Figure 2.5

NED'S MEMO FOR DEALING
WITH THE HEAT WAVE

DATE: July 5, 199_
FROM: Ned Andersen, Vice President   NA
TO: All Staff
SUBJECT: Dealing with the Heat Wave

All of us know that due to the extremely hot weather and drought, electricity and water supplies are in jeopardy, and many people have lost work as a result of curtailments to industry in Arizona and other parts of the Far West.

I believe that all of us want to make some sacrifices so that as many people as possible can work. Therefore, beginning Tuesday, July 16, we will allow the temperature at the Tucson facility to go up a few degrees per day until we reach a level of about 75° in the office and 80° in the shop. Our energy consultants will help us equalize temperatures in the building. The consultants recommend that everyone wear light clothes to keep cool. We will also shut off sprinklers on the grounds at headquarters.

Over the past few weeks, we have heard about the willingness of people across the state to help out. We feel sure that people at our company will find our energy policy fair to everyone and will want to do their part in saving jobs.

The RTA Formula: Rapport, Thinking, Action and Attitude

Writing letters to get people to take action requires that you give special care to presenting yourself and your company courteously and persuasively. The **RTA formula** suggests that to be effective, business letters first establish *rapport* between writer and reader, then influence the reader's *thinking,* and finally motivate the reader to *act* and to have a positive *attitude*. Information to be included in the letter must be arranged to accomplish the three things in that order.

Notice that the RTA is called a "formula." It is not, however, a set of rules that you can follow to produce a letter in the same way you can use a chemical formula to produce a compound or an algebraic formula to solve a mathematical equation. Instead, RTA is a powerful organizing principle because it helps you keep in mind your goal and your reader as you organize the content of your message.

RTA can help you ask the right questions and look for the most useful information, but it is up to you to discover for a particular letter how best to establish rapport, influence thinking, and motivate action and attitude.

Analysis Trees and Outlines

So far we have watched business people group and order information for short memos. Longer memos, letters, and reports require the same grouping and ordering process, but organizing them will often be more challenging, because much more information is involved. In these cases it is especially important for you and your reader to understand how your writing is structured. Two helpful ways to see the structure of your ideas are to use analysis trees and outlines.

USING ANALYSIS TREES*

In complex writing, readers must be able to see quickly which are major ideas and which are supporting ideas. An analysis tree will help you clarify this relationship among your ideas. By showing the relationship between major and supporting ideas, an analysis tree reveals the hierarchical structure of your message. For example, let's imagine how Ned Andersen might have used an analysis tree to help him organize his memo on the water and electricity crisis. Instead of grouping and organizing ideas in outline form, he might have diagrammed them as in Figure 2.6. More extensive writing assignments, although more complex, have the same hierarchical structure—as the following situation illustrates.

---

* When analysis trees are used to organize business writing, they are sometimes called organization trees. Because business people are familiar with the term "analysis tree," we use it here instead of the term "organization tree."

Figure 2.6

NED'S ANALYSIS TREE

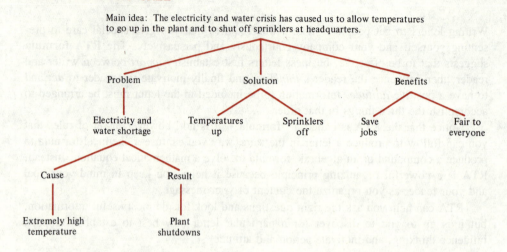

Donna Roemer, staff member in a training and development department of a major corporation, was handed an especially sensitive assignment. Recently the corporation had found itself involved in several cases of sexual harassment. Management needed to raise the employees' awareness—of the problem, of ways to avoid it when possible, and of ways to deal with it should it come up. They asked Donna to design a series of training seminars on the issue and to submit a proposal justifying her design.

Donna could see she would have to study the legal issues and find out about similar training programs. She also recognized how important it was to find out more precisely what top management wanted this seminar to accomplish. She made arrangements to talk with as many vice presidents and field managers as possible. Figure 2.7 illustrates some of the notes she made.

Figure 2.7

DONNA'S NOTES

> 1. Most managers did not witness alleged incidents but do believe a problem exists and something should be done.
> 2. The degree of seriousness varies considerably: high in Manufacturing and Field Services, less in Technical Services.

3. It is critical that the program be derived from the top; its success depends on how important top management makes it.

4. The program should lead to an action plan that has no mixed expectations about desired behavior.

5. Old norms are being challenged by more women in the workplace. The result is confusion and discomfort. The defense is harassment.

6. The real issue is male/female awareness.

7. Harassment affects the productivity of more than just the victim.

8. To avoid reverse discrimination, fairness should be stressed.

9. The seminars should have a mixed (male/female) audience and mixed faculty.

10. Consciousness raising and alternatives to legal action should be emphasized before discussing Equal Employment Opportunity/legal action.

11. Unwanted behavior is defined differently by different age groups.

Donna knew her report would have to show that her program was in line with what management saw as the problem. She also recognized that management would have to agree with her proposed seminars, so she looked at her notes to see how she could use them for support. First she noticed that her ideas could be grouped into two major categories: problem (including causes and symptoms) and solution. Then she tried arranging these groups into a hierarchical structure and used a tree to diagram them (see Figure 2.8). She then used this tree to write a proposal to management on the design and rationale for her training seminars.

USING OUTLINES

Another way to see the hierarchical structure of a report is to use an outline. For example, the same structure shown in Donna's analysis tree can be expressed in more traditional outline form:

Proposal: We need the training seminars to help solve problems related to sexual harassment.

I. Problem: Sexual Harassment
   A. Symptoms
      1. Managers believe problem exists (1)
      2. Degree of seriousness varies (2)
      3. Affects productivity (7)
   B. Causes
      1. Old norms challenged (5)
      2. Unwanted behavior defined differently (11)
      3. Real issue is male/female awareness (6)

II. Solution: Training Seminars
   A. Content
      1. Stress fairness (8)
      2. Use mixed audience and faculty (9)
      3. Emphasize consciousness raising vs. legal action (10)
   B. Implementation
      1. Should be driven from top down (3)
      2. Should lead to action plan (4)

Many business writers are comfortable using the traditional outline. But more and more managers are using analysis trees and other visual diagrams to help them see the structure of their ideas. This is partly because they learn to use analysis trees in solving business problems. And for some people, analysis trees show more clearly than outlines the logical relationships among ideas.

The accompanying checklist will help you review the organization of your communications.

Figure 2.8

DONNA'S ANALYSIS TREE

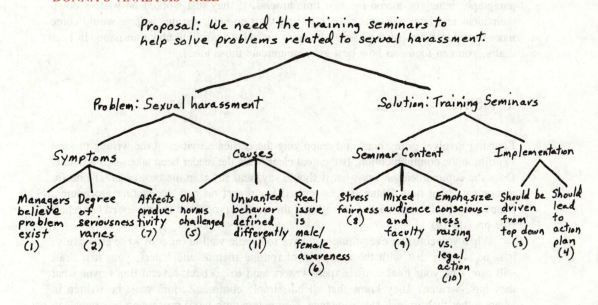

CHECKLIST FOR ORGANIZING BUSINESS COMMUNICATIONS

1. Are your ideas and information grouped into categories that are understandable and convincing?

2. Have you organized your communication hierarchically, with each point supported by subpoints?

WRITING A DRAFT

At some point you will want to write, type, or dictate a full draft of your business communication. It is only through turning that analysis tree, outline, list, or nonstop writing into full sentences and paragraphs that you will get a sense of the communication as a whole. Writing the draft will also enable you to discover gaps, irrelevant details and ideas, and new connections among ideas. You may also find that writing a draft will help you rethink your message and your relationship to your reader. All these discoveries about your communication can come to light only when you turn half-thoughts in the mind or notes on paper into the full, though not necessarily the final, words of the communication.

Most writers need to consider not only *what* to say but also *how* to present those thoughts clearly and persuasively. Writer's block is caused by trying to handle both these demands at once. Writers are so occupied with the shortcomings of what they are trying to say that they can't get a word down, or they try to write the perfect sentence, paragraph, letter, or memo the first time around. If they just worked on writing down their ideas and later went back to perfecting their communication, writing would come more easily to them. In the first draft, work out what you think about an issue. In later drafts, you can focus on how best to communicate those ideas.

REVISING

Revising involves going back and reapplying the earlier activities of the writing process to critique the communication: Is the goal clear? Has the reader been taken into account? Does the communication say what it should say, and say it in the best order? Think for a moment about how Diane Bolger revised her report on new accounting procedures. Diane went back to the earlier activities of the writing process as she reviewed her report (see pp. 18–19).

When you consider everything you have to handle well in order to write effectively, it is no wonder that with the exception of routine memos and letters, your first draft will rarely be your final draft. Expert writers tend to go back several times over what they have written. They know that all but simple communications must be written in layers rather than in lock-step sequence. Computers with word processing programs can considerably reduce the physical labor involved in rewriting and leave you more time for rethinking.

In Chapter 3, "Revising and Editing," we will look in detail at how whole communications, paragraphs, and sentences can be made easy to read. For now, let's look at two techniques for revising: role-playing your reader and asking an associate to review your writing.

Role-Playing Your Reader

Sometimes you may have trouble revising because you find it hard to be objective about what you have written. To get a fresh look at your communication, you can role-play your reader by getting out of your writer's chair and putting yourself in your reader's chair. As the reader, you might consider the following questions:

- Does the message produce the desired results?
- Is it clear and well organized?
- Does it adequately address the subject?
- As the reader, how do you react to the communication? Are you sympathetic? Detached? Annoyed? Angered? Do you believe what the communication says? Would it get you to act?
- How does the writer come across? As friendly? Bossy? Irritated? Helpful? Rushed? Encouraging? Reasonable? Well-informed?

One way to check your writing is to read your communication out loud. This may enable you to become more objective about how you sound and may help you discover gaps and redundancies in the communication.

Asking an Associate to Review Your Writing

You can verify whether your business communication will have its intended impact on readers, and whether it is well organized and complete, by asking an associate to role-play your intended reader and comment on the draft. An idea may be clear in your mind, yet others may have trouble understanding what you have written. Likewise, you may be unable to anticipate how the reader will respond. This is why an associate's review of a communication can lead you to rethink your message. When asking an associate to role-play your reader, you will find it useful to ask him or her to address the following specific questions:

- Can you easily identify the goal of the communication? Will the communication achieve the desired result?
- From what you know about the readers of the communication, will the message be understood and favorably received?
- Is the communication complete and well organized? What are the major and minor ideas? Should anything be eliminated or added?

Few people have an expert associate who is available to review all their writing. It is just too expensive and time consuming to have someone doing this work. But in many companies an important written document is typically reviewed by several people before it is sent out. As a new employee, you should find out if your organization has such a policy and if your boss expects to review your important communications. Even if no system of review exists, you should seek an associate's opinion when you are uncertain about the clarity and tone of an important business communication.

EDITING AND PROOFREADING

It is best to put off editing and proofreading your business communication for sentence-level changes—grammar, word choice, punctuation, and spelling—until you are fairly confident that you have expressed what you want to say. As one executive told us, "I worried too much about my grammatical mistakes. I found that I got so caught up in being correct that I forgot what I was trying to say. I now find I save a lot of time if I keep writing until I've gotten my entire letter on paper. Then I go back to see if it says what I want to say the way I want to say it." Being overly concerned with sentence-level changes as you put together your business communication can interfere with your efforts to improve your writing.

But even though grammar, word choice, punctuation, and spelling are the last things you should think about when you write, this does not mean that they are least important. Quite the contrary. People will judge you by your grammar, vocabulary, punctuation, and spelling. They will find that your errors will distract from your message. Editing and proofreading are discussed at length in Chapter 3; grammar and punctuation, are considered in detail in Appendix B.

SUMMARY

Once you understand that writing is a process that begins with understanding your goal and your reader, you will be well on your way to developing the ability to handle your business writing assignments effectively. Then you can use several techniques that good writers use to move through the activities of the writing process.

Good writers use note-taking to help them gather information, and they talk to an associate, use a tape recorder, write nonstop, and make lists to generate ideas. They use the RTA formula to organize letters, and analysis trees and outlines to organize letters, memos, or reports. When revising, they can call on two techniques: role-playing the intended reader of the communication and having an associate review their work.

EXERCISES

See "Setting the Goal," pp. 19–21, and "Assessing the Reader," pp. 21–23, for Exercises 1 and 2.

1. Staff research assistant Ned Beatty works in the energy division of a multinational corporation that has large investments in oil and gas exploration. His boss, Len Sapir, asked Ned to attend a workshop on the business climate in Mexico and to "tell me what you learn." The overall purpose of the workshop is to analyze recent political, economic and social trends in Mexico and to speculate about how those trends might affect government policy and the business climate over the next three to five years. Four Latin American specialists are to speak on the inner workings of the Mexican government and society.

As manager of the energy division and as an expert in the economics of oil and gas exploration, Len has the power and responsibility to influence the corporation's investments in oil and gas exploration in Latin America. He also knows that the recent political and economic upheavals in Mexico require that he take into account the current status of the country in making his recommendations to top management.

Write the goal statement for Ned Beatty's report. To do so, try to formulate the question that the report needs to answer. Consider what you know about Len Sapir that can help you identify this question.

2. Henrietta Saunders is a 35-year-old president of a wire products company that sells wire fencing for commercial buildings and low-cost private houses. As her summer

intern, you have been asked to "check on housing construction forecasts" for the next three months and hand in a short report on your findings within two weeks. Henrietta has recently acquired the firm from her parents and is new to the industry, which has been in a deep and prolonged recession. From your earlier experience writing reports for her, you know that she does not like long-drawn-out pieces that talk around the subject. One of her big concerns is whether to expand, maintain, or reduce her inventory of wire fencing in factory warehouses. Excessive inventory is costly, yet not having enough on hand will result in lost sales. She will base her decision on the trends in housing construction.

Write a goal statement for your report that specifies the purpose of your communication. Try to formulate the question you think Henrietta Saunders will want the report to answer. To do so, think about what you already know about her.

See "Gathering Information," pp. 23–25, for Exercises 3 and 4.

3. If you are required to do a formal report for this course, now is the time to think about the report. We suggest that you begin reading *Business Week, Forbes*, the *Wall Street Journal*, and comparable publications to stimulate your thinking about possible topics for the report. You may also want to set up regular meetings with a few people in the class to discuss interesting business issues.

4. Since you probably have more time now than you will have later in the term, go on a tour of the business section of your library and take notes on the reference books periodicals, and newspapers, and the procedures that will be useful to you when you write reports. Learning now about the library's computer services, about typical turnaround time for getting an interlibrary loan, and about the availability of major periodicals, books, and newspapers will help you budget your time properly when working on a report.

See "Analysis Trees and Outlines," pp. 35–39, for Exercise 5.

5. Marketing representative June Faldwell needs to send her boss a memo about the delay in her merit review. June's merit review was due several months ago. A positive review would entitle her to a raise of $400 a month. Her boss has been late in doing the review despite June's having asked him twice about it. He has also misplaced an important document that would have to be submitted to top management should he consider her eligible for promotion.

Figure 2.9 shows June's nonstop writing. Organize it into an analysis tree or outline that she can use to write the memo she will send to her boss. When doing the analysis tree or outline, be sure to consider the goal of her communication, her relationship to her reader, his probable awareness of the problem, and his likely attitude toward her message.

See "Writing a Draft," pp. 39–40, for Exercise 6.

6. Write a draft of June's memo using your analysis tree or outline (see exercise 5) to assist you.

Figure 2.9

JUNE'S NONSTOP WRITING

> I am furious with you for delaying my raise. I feel so angry I wish I could just go into your office and yell at you. You know I've made substantial inroads in new territory with our products and you said you'd get me a raise based on this performance. This writing's getting me more and more angry. The data's right in front of your face. Oh I better not show my anger in the memo. I might feel good for the moment but it's no way to get him to respond positively to any request.
>
> ... It's my understanding that merit raises for people at my level are due during the spring. You are several months late with mine. Can you please explain the delay to me? Why are you late? It's good I'm not saying this to him 'cause I can't get the anger out of my voice. I am submitting with this memo a copy of the table showing salaries of marketing reps at my level who work for comparable firms. This table is, as you've told me, important support for you when you go

before the committee on merit reviews that will say yes or no to your recommendation. As you may recall, we discussed the necessary steps I had to take before you could make your final evaluations. Why did he forget about this? $400 is a lot of money to me. Maybe it's not to him. These steps consist of providing you with sales figures over the past year, letters from any customers who commented on my work for them, and a list of seminars and extension courses I've taken in business. These are all in my folder. I hope he doesn't lose it too. If you need further information, I'd be glad to provide whatever you need. Let me take this opportunity to tell you too how much I enjoy working as a marketing rep. I better add something like this to keep things running smoothly between us. The quality of our products makes it a pleasure to sell for you. I also appreciate the track record of manufacturing and distribution in getting the product out the door on time. I see tremendous growth opportunities for me here and will continue to make every effort to do a quality

(continued)

(JUNE'S NONSTOP WRITING continued)

> job for you. I want him to see I'm not about to quit though I won't stand for being unfairly treated. Perhaps you can explain the delay in doing my merit review. I realize that you have extraordinary demands on your time but I've given you ample opportunity to consider my review.

See "Generating Ideas," pp. 25–27; "Organizing," pp. 27–39; and "Writing a Draft," p. 39 for Exercise 7.

7. Select two or three techniques you have read about in this chapter that you would like to encourage a friend to try. Write a letter to your friend explaining why you are recommending the use of these techniques. Take into account how much your friend already knows about this subject and his or her attitude toward writing so as to motivate him or her most effectively to try the technique. Use nonstop writing, work with a tape recorder, or make a list to generate ideas for the letter. Then group and order your ideas, and do an analysis tree before you write a draft.

See "Revising," pp. 40–41, for Exercises 8 and 9.

8. Reread the letter you wrote for exercise 7 and role-play your reader in order to revise it.
9. Eric Collins is a student trainee in a management development program sponsored by a national bank. The bank has had to discontinue offering the internship program and has asked Eric to write a letter to prospective student applicants explaining that the program cannot be run this year due to budgetary constraints. Here is a draft of Eric's letter:

Dear Prospective Applicant,

It is with great disappointment that I find it necessary to inform you that the bank's college management training program cannot be run this year due to budgetary constraints.

Currently the bank is experiencing hard times due to the recession. As a result, it had to cut back many programs that it normally runs.

On behalf of the bank I want to thank you for expressing interest in our program.

Think about how you would react if you received this letter. Suggest how Eric might revise it.

10. Reflect on the activities of the writing process in terms of your own writing. Answer the following questions, on a separate sheet, and prepare to discuss your responses in class. Use your review of the last two or three writing assignments you have completed as the basis for your answer. Be sure to note which activities you are stronger in and which ones you would like to develop or change. Ask yourself:

a. *Setting the goal:* Do I know what I want my writing to accomplish with readers?
b. *Assessing the reader:* Am I aware of my reader's relationship to me, knowledge of the subject, expectations about how the communication should be presented, and attitudes toward me and toward the subject? Am I clear about how these things relate to what I need to include in my message, how I organize it, and how I present myself in writing?
c. *Gathering information and generating ideas:* Do I know how to conduct research for a business letter, memo, or report? Can I take good notes at meetings or over the phone, conduct surveys, write and administer questionnaires, and locate and review books, periodicals, newspapers, and company brochures? Am I familiar with the business section of the library? Am I able to generate ideas of my own?
d. *Organizing:* Can I group and order information into an outline or analysis tree that helps me to write a communication that my reader will find both understandable and convincing?
e. *Writing a draft:* Can I write a full draft with little hesitation? Are beginnings easy for me to write? Middles? Endings?
f. *Revising:* Do I allow enough time for revising? Am I able to make changes so as to express more effectively what I want to say and how I want to say it?
g. *Editing and proofreading:* Can I make word- and sentence-level changes? Do I have any problems with grammar? Can I proofread?

Keep a portfolio of your writing throughout the term so that you will have a record of how you have developed. Go back to this list of questions, and answer them for a writing assignment you do in the middle of the term and at the end of the term.

3
REVISING AND EDITING

PREVIEW

This chapter should help you to

1. Revise whole drafts of your business writing by showing you
   - How to ask the "big" questions of your draft—to evaluate its overall effectiveness and to ensure that it demonstrates a clear purpose, answers the reader's questions, and is well organized
   - How to set up an agenda for revising
2. Revise and edit paragraphs and sentences of your writing by showing you
   - Techniques for making sure paragraphs are complete, organized, and coherent
   - Techniques for revising sentences—to create a forceful style with strong verbs and emphatic, concise phrasing
   - Techniques for revising sentences—to get rid of inappropriate jargon, sexist language, and clichés

---

A business person who has written a whole draft of a difficult letter, memo, or report might well feel a great sense of satisfaction and relief. Just getting a lot of ideas down on paper, in some kind of sensible order, is a substantial accomplishment. Yet although good writers might feel relieved at this point, they know they are not finished. They know they must revise and edit. In fact, studies have shown that what separates experienced from inexperienced writers most dramatically is that experienced writers know how to get beyond their first drafts to revise and edit their writing.

Of course not all business writing requires extensive revising. With repetition, some writing tasks become more or less routine. But others will demand your utmost care and attention. One marketing analyst we talked to represents the situation of many business writers. He always spends at least three weeks designing and writing his marketing proposals:

> I work with multiple groups, many of them my peers. Writing is the way I tell them what I'm going to do and how I'm going to do it. If I don't write up my proposal well, with clear reasons, if my proposal doesn't look good, it will never get to first base. So I'm constantly revising. How can I afford not to? I'm always seeing better ways to do things.

In a sense, the whole process of writing involves revising. Chapter 2 showed you that the activities involved in the writing process often lead you to rethink what you have already done. For example, thinking about how you want to organize a memo might lead you to reassess the reader of that memo, or to rethink your goal, or to come up with new ideas. Such rethinking naturally leads to reseeing—that is, revision.

But in addition to the revising that goes on as you write, there will usually be a point when you have finished a rough draft of your writing and can see your work as a whole. At this point, you can judge whether your writing comes across as having a clear purpose, whether it sounds persuasive, whether it is well organized, and whether it includes all essential parts. In other words you can check your writing as a whole, or **holistically.** Generally it is best to feel committed to the larger, or holistic, design of your writing before moving on to revising at the local level, the level of paragraphs and sentences. Let's look at some strategies for revising, first at the holistic and then at the local level.

REVISING HOLISTICALLY

As Glenn Lowenstein looked over the first print-out of his report on inventory problems at Fabco, he thought to himself, "This is typical of my first drafts. I've got everything down that needs to be covered, at least somehow, but it's a mess. The whole thing has to be totally reorganized. And there are always things I'm not sure about. This time I'm going to have to call Priscilla again to get this 'contract' vs. 'proprietary' straight. I don't think I really understand it after all."

A business major in his senior year, Glenn had been selected to participate in the business department's prestigious field experience program, in which teams of three to five students earn credit by doing consulting projects for area companies. Now, in the fifth week of the semester, Glenn's team is ready to draw up its preliminary report to the head of Accounting at Fabco, the area company that has asked for help in reorganizing its inventory control system. The report must state what problems the team found in the inventory system, and what solutions they recommend to overcome those problems. Glenn has volunteered to write up the description of the problems.

Studies show that when inexperienced writers approach revising, they merely check for spelling, or they change a word here or a sentence there. They talk about "fixing up" or "cleaning up" the draft. Experienced writers, however, approach revision as an opportunity to rethink what they have written. They know this can sometimes lead to recasting introductory and concluding paragraphs, to moving paragraphs around, to deleting sections, to adding new information, to rewriting whole sections, even to throwing out the entire draft and starting all over. But even if they end up starting over, experienced writers know they are still way ahead. They know that good writers often have to work through an ineffective approach in order to discover a better way to handle

REVISING AND EDITING

a writing task. The wastebaskets of professional writers are almost invariably filled with early drafts.

To get a sense of how one business student wrote a draft and revised his writing, let's look at Glenn Lowenstein's experience of drafting and then revising a report.

Glenn had to write a description of the problems his consulting team found with Fabco's inventory control system. Fabco is a small metal fabricating plant. Its inventory includes the raw materials necessary for production and the finished goods that are produced. Since storing inventory costs money, a good inventory control system should keep the amount stored to a minimum. Ideally, the company should have on hand only just enough raw materials for current production, and only just enough finished goods to fill orders promptly.

Before writing his draft, Glenn met with his team to find out what everyone had learned so far about the inventory system. He took notes, grouped and ordered his information, and then sat down at the computer to write the whole draft. Glenn told us that for short papers like this he usually can get a satisfactory product by the third draft. He types his first draft into the computer fairly quickly, to get down as much as he can. Then he prints it out and, working between the print-out and the computer screen, does extensive revisions for the second draft. For the third draft he also works from a print-out and concentrates on local revision, fixing up paragraphs and sentences. After working for an hour and a half, Glenn had the computer print the first draft, shown in Figure 3.1.

Figure 3.1

GLENN'S FIRST DRAFT

FABCO CONSULTING TEAM

SUMMARY OF PROBLEMS

Introduction

Fabco has an inadequate inventory control system. It is very difficult to find out exactly how much of a finished good item or raw material is on hand at a given point in time.

Records do exist, but in many cases the figures in one set of records do not agree with those in another set of records. This occurs for a variety of reasons:

1. Entries that should be made are omitted.
2. Erroneous figures are entered.
3. A number of different people make entries.

(continued)

(GLENN'S FIRST DRAFT continued)

Raw Materials

Examination of the purchase orders, invoices, and physical inventory sheets at Fabco for the 199_–199_ fiscal year shows that Fabco's primary raw materials are aluminum, stainless steel, moly sheet, Mu metal, and bearings. Copper, brass, lead, and aircraft alloys such as Inconel are of secondary importance.

It is not clear whether Fabco orders optimal quantities of raw materials. Company policies regarding size and timing of orders (EOQs, ROPs, etc.) need to be analyzed in detail.

Fabco officials question the advisability of buying precut circles vs. sheets, and buying directly from mill vs. warehouse. Should Fabco buy precut circles or rectangular sheets of aluminum for its spool cap and sheaves production? Is it more economical to purchase the circles, or to have Fabco workers do the cutting? What are the trade-offs involved in buying large quantities of aluminum or stainless steel directly from the mill vs. buying smaller quantities from a warehouse?

There is no raw materials control system. We plan to suggest one for implementation by Fabco.

Finished Goods

There is a dichotomy based on order size. If an order is large, it is handled as "contract"; if a small one, it is handled as "proprietary." We question whether this is the best way to define proprietary vs. contract work.

Fabco's products include both contract goods, which are made to order, and proprietary products, which are supplied from inventories of previously fabricated units. Although small orders of proprietary products are supplied from inventory, large orders are handled on a contract basis. The actual proportion of sales which are supplied directly from inventories of proprietary products is far from the stated corporate objective of 50-50. In fact, if large orders for proprietary products are reclassified as contract goods, the sales accounted for by proprietary products is well below 25 percent.

Multiple record keeping may not be a good idea.

REVISING AND EDITING

Computers are an aid in the drafting process.

Glenn's description of Fabco's inventory problems had to be ready for his team's meeting the following day, so he let this draft sit for just a few hours to let it "cool off." Then he read over what he had written so far, concentrating on what he calls the "big questions." We have classified Glenn's suggestions according to the stages of the writing process:

1. Set the Goal:
What am I trying to accomplish? We're a student team, but we want to prove we are professionals. I want this statement of the problem to show the company we have found out their main trouble spots. Also, the team has to agree that I've understood the problems and have gotten the reader to accept our definition of the problem and what we are going to do in the next ten weeks.

2. Assess the Reader:
What does the head of purchasing at Fabco expect? I'd say that by now he'd want to know we understand their operations and can talk their language. We certainly don't have to have everything worked out by now, but Fabco needs some evidence that we've got the basic issues well defined.

3. Gather Information and Generate Ideas:
Have I done my homework? It was clear from our last meeting that we have a lot of work to do before the final report. For now we need information on the main problem areas and ideas about how to organize the work ahead of us.

4. Organize:
Is it organized so it's convincing and readable? My write-up has to organize the problems in the way a company member would organize them, so they will see right off what I'm talking about.

THE RANDOM HOUSE GUIDE TO BUSINESS WRITING

With these questions in mind, Glenn read his draft to get an overview of what he had written. Then he read it again, this time making mental notes about what needed changing. Glenn described to us what he thought about before revising. In Figure 3.2, Glenn's comments appear right below the section of the draft they refer to.

Figure 3.2

DRAFT WITH GLENN'S COMMENTS

FABCO CONSULTING TEAM

SUMMARY OF PROBLEMS

Introduction

Fabco has an inadequate inventory control system. It is very difficult to find out exactly how much of a finished good item or raw material is on hand at a given point in time.

I'm concerned about my tone here. Can I come right out and say to the company, "you've got problems"? It sounds too accusatory. But the problems are what we're here for. The basic organization is good—"finished products" and "raw materials." But the order needs to be reversed. "Raw materials" logically comes first, and it comes first in the body of my report.

Records do exist, but in many cases the figures in one set of records do not agree with those in another set of records. This occurs for a variety of reasons:

1. Entries that should be made are omitted.
2. Erroneous figures are entered.
3. A number of different people make entries.

When I reread the report, I realized I'm talking about more than just the problem with record keeping, with knowing how much is on hand. We also have to figure out how to decide how much should be on hand: how much do they need in reserve and how low can inventory get before they must reorder? And we have to know this both for raw materials and for finished goods.

Raw Materials

Examination of the purchase orders, invoices, and physical inventory sheets at Fabco for the 199_–199_ fiscal year shows that Fabco's primary raw materials are aluminum, stainless steel, moly sheet, Mu metal, and bearings. Copper, brass, lead, and aircraft alloys such as Inconel are of secondary importance.

Do I need this paragraph? It shows that we learned what raw materials the company uses, but what does it have to do with inventory problems?

It is not clear whether Fabco orders optimal quantities of raw materials. Company policies regarding size and timing of orders (EOQs, ROPs, etc.) need to be analyzed in detail.

This is the big question not just for raw materials, but for finished goods too: How much of each kind should be ordered? When should they be reordered? Should I be using these abbreviations? The head of accounting will be familiar with them, but maybe he's going to pass this report on to other managers who don't know the terms.

Fabco officials question the advisability of buying precut circles vs. sheets, and buying directly from mill vs. warehouse. Should Fabco buy precut circles or rectangular sheets of aluminum for its spool cap and sheaves production? Is it more economical to purchase the circles, or to have Fabco workers do the cutting? What are the trade-offs involved in buying large quantities of aluminum or stainless steel directly from the mill vs. buying smaller quantities from a warehouse?

These were the major questions about raw materials we kept hearing about in our interviews. But how do they fit into the report?

There is no raw materials control system. We plan to suggest one for implementation by Fabco.

This repeats the problems with record keeping that are already talked about in the introduction. Save this for the statement of our objectives that Priscilla is writing.

<u>Finished Goods</u>

There is a dichotomy based on order size. If an order is large, it is handled as "contract"; if a small one, it is handled as "proprietary." We question whether this is the best way to define proprietary vs. contract work.

Fabco's products include both contract goods which are made to order, and proprietary products, which are supplied from inventories of previously fabricated units. Although small orders of proprietary products are supplied from inventory, large orders are handled on a contract basis. The actual proportion of sales which are supplied directly from inventories of proprietary products is far from the stated corporate objective of 50-50. In fact, if large orders for proprietary products are reclassified as contract goods, the sales accounted for by proprietary products is well below 25 percent.

(continued)

(DRAFT WITH GLENN'S COMMENTS continued)

> *This whole section is confusing because the company's definitions of the terms don't work. After talking with my teammate Priscilla about this, we realized that the company really has two definitions of these terms but they don't always jibe. At one point the company tells us a certain product is classified "proprietary" because they only get a small order for it and they can fill it from inventory. But then we'll find out that they'll get very big orders for the same goods and have to set up a special production for them. But that's what "contract" goods are supposed to be. I need to describe the company's confusion without getting confused myself!*
>
> Multiple record keeping may not be a good idea.
>
> *This repeats what is now in the introduction about poor record keeping. I'll have to figure out where it goes.*

After reviewing his draft, Glenn told us his **agenda for revising:**

- For this revision I see the biggest problem as organizing, so I'm going to concentrate on that. I want to keep the "raw materials" and "finished goods" division. But in *each* division, I should talk about the problem with figuring out what *is* on hand, and what *should be* on hand.
- I seem to talk about the problem with record keeping in several places. I should fit it into each major section.
- I have to explain the definition problem with "contract" and "proprietary" much better.
- I'm going to save the question about tone till I see the team tomorrow. And they'll have to tell me whether or not I've covered all the bases too.

With this agenda in mind, Glenn spent two and a half more hours at the computer and then printed out a new version, shown in Figure 3.3.

Figure 3.3

GLENN'S SECOND DRAFT

> SUMMARY OF INVENTORY PROBLEMS
>
> Fabco has an inadequate inventory control system. Currently it is very difficult to find out (1) how much of an item is on hand and (2) how much of an item is needed. This is true both for raw materials and for finished goods.

Raw Materials

1. <u>How much is on hand?</u> The current raw materials inventory record system requires record keeping by three different departments: purchasing, receiving, and the in-plant user. These multiple records should provide accurate records, but currently they do not because:

   - Entries that should be made are omitted.
   - Erroneous figures are entered.
   - A number of different people make entries.

2. <u>How much is needed?</u> Currently there is no systematic policy for deciding optimal quantities of raw materials. Company policies regarding size and timing of orders (EOQs, ROPs, etc.) need to be analyzed in detail. Fabco officials have questions in two areas in particular:

   - For aluminum in spool cap and sheave production, should Fabco buy precut circles or rectangular sheets that Fabco workers cut into circles?
   - What are the trade-offs involved in buying large quantities of aluminum or stainless steel directly from the mill versus buying smaller quantities from a warehouse?

Finished Goods

1. <u>How much is on hand?</u> Fabco's Sales Department needs an accurate account of finished goods stock in order to avoid stockouts. Right now, the inventory records in the Sales Department are so inaccurate that they are practically useless. Multiple record keeping may not be a good idea.

2. <u>How much is needed?</u> Currently Fabco inventories only those goods it classifies as proprietary. Fabco classifies its goods according to how large a quantity customers usually order. Small-order items are called "proprietary products"—these are fabricated in batches, and when a customer orders, the order is supplied from inventory. Large-order items are called "contract goods"—these are made to order at the customer's request.

But this classification system does not work as it is intended. Many so-called "proprietary," or small-order, items are often ordered in large quantities, so they are made on contract, as if they were contract goods.

Fabco's stated corporate objective is to have 50 percent of its sales supplied directly from inventories of proprietary products. But in fact, if large orders for proprietary products are reclassified as contract goods, the sales accounted for by proprietary products is well below 25 percent.

Fabco needs a new system for deciding which goods to inventory and which to manufacture only on contract. It also needs a system to monitor demand and determine stock quantities.

What did Glenn think were his strengths and weaknesses in this draft?

I'm sure the team will have some advice about things to add and change but I'm satisfied with what I've got so far. I think the hard part is done because I'm pretty sure about the framework.
    I think I finally did all right with that section on "contract" and "proprietary." I must have rewritten it four times, even after I was sure I knew what I was trying to say. I'd play around with it on the screen, then I'd try printing out a hard copy of that page, then go back to the screen. It was difficult. But I finally sorted everything out.

Glenn then told us about his agenda for his second revision:

This probably needs another rewrite, but I'm going to wait and see what the team says. When we start spelling out exactly what our objectives will be for the next ten weeks, we will probably see some changes we want to make. But for now, I think this gives us a pretty clear idea what the major problems are, and I think they're organized the way the company would see them. I still have questions about the tone and about exactly who we are supposed to be writing for. But I don't want to change anything till I get some feedback.

As it turned out, Glenn's team did have some additions and changes to make for his third draft, but they agreed that he had organized the problem very well.
    Glenn's writing process is only one approach to revising, but it suggests valuable strategies for holistic revision. These are summarized in the accompanying checklist.

CHECKLIST FOR REVISING HOLISTICALLY

1. Have you let your draft "cool off" for a few hours or days? Have you tried to see the draft the way the reader would see it?
2. Have you concentrated on the big picture?
   - What is your goal?
   - Do you answer the reader's main questions?
   - Do you have all the information you need to be convincing?
   - Is the organization logical and right for the reader?
3. Have you evaluated your draft's major strengths and weaknesses? Do you need to get an opinion from an associate about what needs to be changed?
4. What is your agenda for revision? What should you try to accomplish in your next draft?

REVISING AND EDITING   59

If you reach an impasse in your revising, you can ask these questions of your writing and your writing process. Checklists in subsequent chapters will help you revise by posing questions specifically related to the type of letter, memo, or report you are writing.

REVISING LOCALLY: PARAGRAPHS

Once you feel secure with the overall design of your memo, letter, or report, it is time to perfect your writing at the local level—the level of paragraphs and sentences. Your paragraphs may need revising for completeness, organization, and coherence.

Revising Paragraphs for Organization and Completeness

Organizing ideas within paragraphs is much like organizing for a whole letter, memo, or report. Paragraphs are small units within a larger piece of writing, and like the larger piece, they usually make one major point and develop that point with reasons, examples, or other details. (Exceptions to this pattern are paragraphs with special functions, such as introductory, concluding, and transitional paragraphs.) When we discussed organizing in Chapter 2, we suggested that an analysis tree could help you discover the hierarchical structure of your writing. An analysis tree can also help you at the paragraph level—to check whether the main ideas of your paragraphs are organized and completely developed. Let's consider a paragraph from the draft of a report that Carrie Aberdeen wrote to help improve communications in her condominium complex.

As you may know, in a condominium complex several people share ownership of a large building, each one owning a unit of that building. Often the complex is managed by a board of trustees, made up of volunteers from among the unit owners. As a retiring member of the board of trustees, Carrie is writing a report to provide her successors with the benefit of her three years' experience. In this paragraph she is analyzing the relations between the trustees and the regular unit owners:

DRAFT

>From the outset, the trustees agreed that unit owners must think of themselves as homeowners. The "tenant mentality" that most unit owners retained from apartment renting could potentially cause them to think of themselves as tenants, and the trustees as landlords. In order to eliminate this problem, the trustees attempted to involve unit owners in the care of their homes through activities such as spring and fall cleanups and gardening. Unit owners were encouraged to communicate comments and

suggestions via the newsletter, but only one unit owner commented in two years. The newsletter published minimal information regarding trustees' activities. Individual trustee votes were not recorded in the newsletter, so unit owners were unaware of how trustees voted. No unit owner sought additional information, and most appeared apathetic toward the management of their homes. The trustees assumed no news was good news.

Carrie felt uncomfortable about the paragraph. She could see that the first two sentences defined the problem confronted by the trustees, and that the third and fourth sentences showed how the trustees dealt with the problem. But after that she felt she had gotten carried away by the newsletter. She decided to make an analysis tree (see Figure 3.4).

Carrie's analysis tree revealed that although the ideas she had were well organized, she had not developed them completely. She saw that she wanted to do more than just announce what the trustees had tried. She wanted to explain how each attempt had worked out. That was why she had spent so much time discussing the newsletter. Her analysis tree revealed that she needed to discuss the results of the first approach too, that of encouraging yard work. And she needed to clarify why each attempt to solve the problem did not work. Figure 3.5 shows how she modified her analysis tree.

On the basis of this analysis tree, Carrie revised her paragraph as follows (the additions she made to the original are printed in bold type):

REVISION

From the outset, the trustees agreed that unit owners must think of themselves as homeowners. The "tenant mentality" that most unit owners retained from apartment renting could potentially cause them to think of themselves as tenants, and the trustees as landlords. In order to eliminate this problem, the trustees **tried two approaches. First, the trustees** attempted to involve unit owners in the care of their homes through activities such as spring and fall cleanups and gardening. **This was successful in getting a few unit owners involved in decisions about the appearance of the grounds, but only a few. Apparently not many unit owners take pleasure in yard work. The second approach was to encourage owners** to communicate comments and suggestions through the newsletter. **This did not succeed at all.** Only one unit owner commented in two years. **Perhaps this was because** the newsletter published only minimal information regarding trustees activities **and because** unit owners were not informed about how individual trustees voted. **Thus unit owners had no reason to seek** additional information, and most appeared apathetic toward the management of their homes. **Although the trustees saw their initial plans weren't succeeding, they nevertheless** assumed no news was good news.

REVISING AND EDITING 61

Figure 3.4

CARRIE'S ANALYSIS TREE

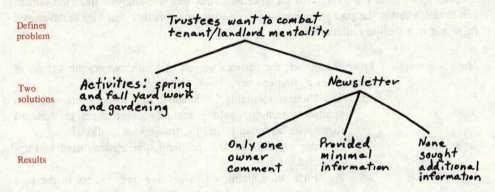

Figure 3.5

CARRIE'S MODIFIED ANALYSIS TREE

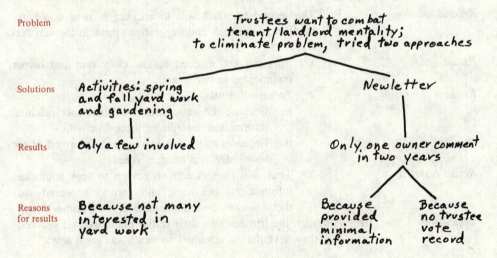

Notice that the additions Carrie made explain the trustees' solutions and help make the structure of the paragraph explicit to the reader. For example, "tried two approaches" signals the ways the trustees acted. Using a form of the word "succeed" after each approach shows that she is discussing results in both places. The words "apparently" and "because" show that she is giving reasons why the results turned out as they did.

Besides using analysis trees, another way to see the hierarchical structure of a paragraph is to use the traditional outlining method. Each indentation reveals a shift in the level of ideas from the general to the specific. Thus like the analysis tree, the outline can reveal whether the paragraph has one main idea, and whether that idea is developed fully and in a well-organized way.

Main sentence		From the outset, the trustees agreed that unit owners must think of themselves as homeowners.
Problem	I.	The "tenant mentality" that most unit owners retained from apartment renting could potentially cause them to think of themselves as tenants, and the trustees as landlords.
Solutions	II.	In order to eliminate this problem, the trustees tried two approaches.
First solution	A.	First, they attempted to involve unit owners in the care of their homes through activities such as spring and fall cleanups and gardening.
Result	1.	This was successful in getting a few unit owners involved in decisions about the appearance of the grounds, but only a few.
Reason for result	2.	Apparently, not many unit owners take pleasure in yard work.
Second solution	B.	The second approach was to encourage owners to communicate comments and suggestions through the newsletter.
Result	1.	This did not succeed at all. Only one unit owner commented in two years.
Reasons for result	2.	Perhaps this was
	a.	Because the newsletter published only minimal information regarding trustees' activities
	b.	Because unit owners were not informed about how individual trustees voted.
Result restated	3.	Thus unit owners had no reason to seek additional information, and most unit owners appeared apathetic toward the management of their homes.
Conclusion	III.	Although the trustees saw their initial plans weren't succeeding, they nevertheless assumed no news was good news.

Revising Paragraphs for Coherence

Analysis trees and outlines can help you catch the logical skips, irrelevant details, or faulty ordering of your paragraphs. But readers won't have access to your trees and outlines to help them move from one idea to another. To help readers see the coherence of your ideas, you need to provide verbal connections. Let's consider four kinds of connections that can help make your paragraphs cohere:

1. Providing transitions
2. Relating new information to given information
3. Retaining a single focus
4. Repeating key words

PROVIDING TRANSITIONS

As you have seen, analysis trees and outlines can show you when your paragraphs clearly have one main idea that is supported with reasons, examples, and other details. For example, if you review Carrie Aberdeen's modified analysis tree (p. 61), you notice the following pattern: She begins with one main idea at the top, then moves down to two attempted solutions, then on to results of those attempts, then down to reasons for those results. But how does Carrie translate this movement down the hierarchy of ideas into a paragraph? That is, how does she show the relationships among her ideas? If you examine her revised paragraph again, you will see that she uses transition words every time she moves from one level to another in the hierarchy of her ideas. Reprinted below, her revised paragraph has the transition words in bold type:

> From the outset, the trustees agreed that unit owners must think of themselves as homeowners. The "tenant mentality" that most unit owners retained from apartment renting could potentially cause them to think of themselves as tenants, and the trustees as landlords. **In order to** eliminate this problem, the trustees tried two approaches. **First,** they attempted to involve unit owners in the care of their homes through activities **such as** spring and fall cleanups and gardening. This was successful in getting a few unit owners involved in decisions about the appearance of the grounds, **but** only a few. **Apparently** not many unit owners take pleasure in yard work. The **second** approach was to encourage owners to communicate comments and suggestions through the newsletter. This did not succeed at all. Only one unit owner commented in two years. **Perhaps this was because** the newsletter published only minimal information regarding trustees' activities **and because** unit owners were not informed about how individual trustees voted. **Thus** unit owners had no reason to seek additional information, and most appeared apathetic toward the management of their homes. **Although** the trustees saw their initial plans weren't succeeding, they **nevertheless** assumed no news was good news.

As Carrie's paragraph demonstrates, transition words help the reader understand how ideas within a paragraph are related. Figure 3.6 provides examples of other such transition words.

Figure 3.6

TRANSITION WORDS

To Introduce Additional Items	To Introduce Reasons
again	because
also	in order to
and	so that
besides	
finally	**To Introduce Conclusions**
further	as a result
in addition	consequently
next	therefore
first, second, third, . . .	
what's more	**To Summarize**
	in brief
To Introduce Comparisons or Contrasts	in sum
	on the whole
although	to conclude
at the same time	
by comparison	**To Show Time**
but	after
conversely	at length
however	before
nevertheless	finally
on the contrary	first, second, third, . . .
on the other hand	later
in contrast	next
similarly	then
To Introduce Illustrations	**To Introduce Repeated Information**
as an example	
for example	in brief
for instance	as I said
that is	in other words

RELATING NEW INFORMATION TO GIVEN INFORMATION

Research has shown that for readers to understand what they are reading, they must be able to relate any new information they read to information they already have in their memories. For example, imagine you were to pick up an article entitled "Effective Throughput of a CSMA Network as a Function of the Number of Nodes." No matter how well written the article, chances are—unless you happen to be an expert in computer networks—you would not be able to understand the article. You simply have no previous information on the subject that could serve as a basis for understanding the article. Before you can absorb new information, you must already have information to which you can relate it.

The same principle holds true in paragraphs. For a paragraph to be coherent to a reader, any new information should be connected with information already given in previous sentences or paragraphs. To show how the principle of *given* and *new* information can help produce coherent writing, we will first analyze a sequence of two sentences and then look at a whole paragraph.

Research indicates that readers process most quickly those sentences that rely on information given in a directly preceding sentence.[1] For example, consider the following sentence pair:

1. *The executives* discussed our company's position.
2. *They* were misunderstood by a reporter.

The subject of sentence 2, "they," refers to information given in sentence 1, "the executives." The meaning of sentence 2 is first linked to that of sentence 1 before new information is added in sentence 2: that the executives "were misunderstood by the reporter." Since the new information of sentence 2 is directly linked to information given in sentence 1, the sentence pair is easy to read.

Here is another sentence pair:

1. *The executives* discussed our company's position.
2. A reporter misunderstood *them*.

Readers process this second sentence pair less quickly, because sentence 2 begins by introducing new information, "a reporter," information that is not related to sentence 1. At the beginning of sentence 2, then, readers may be slightly disoriented. By the end of sentence 2, however, its link to sentence 1 is clear: "them" refers to "the executives."

You will probably find the following sentence pair difficult to understand:

1. The executives discussed our company's position.
2. The story incensed stockholders.

Because nothing in the second sentence refers to information already given, the reader cannot make any connections between the second sentence and the first. Yet if a sentence linking the two is provided, they cohere:

1. *The executives* discussed our company's position.
2. *Their view* was distorted in a *reporter's story*.
3. *The story* incensed stockholders.

These sentence sequences illustrate the rule: the reader needs to be able to link new information with information given in previous sentences. Although this rule can be broken for surprise or emphasis, generally prose that is coherent obeys this rule. Now let's see how the rule works in a whole paragraph.

In their book *In Search of Excellence: Lessons from America's Best-Run Companies*,[2] Thomas Peters and Robert Waterman look at what makes excellent companies work. The following paragraph appears on page 57 of their book, preceded by a discussion of studies which show that people think very highly of themselves. For example, the authors explain that "in a recent psychological study when a random sample of male adults were asked to rank themselves on the ability to get along with others, *all* subjects put themselves in the top half of the population." In the following paragraph the authors draw some conclusions:

> The message that comes through so poignantly in the studies we reviewed is that we like to think of ourselves as winners. The lesson that the excellent companies have to teach is that there is no reason why we can't design systems that continually reinforce this notion; most of their people are made to feel that they are winners. Their populations are distributed around the normal curve, just like every other large population, but the difference is that their systems reinforce degrees of winning rather than degrees of losing. Their people by and large make their targets and quotas, because the targets and quotas are set (often by the people themselves) to allow that to happen.

Normally people read to learn something new, and most readers would agree that this paragraph probably taught them something they didn't know before, without boring them or being redundant. Yet if you analyze what is actually said, you will find that a good part of every sentence contains information you already knew before you read it:

The message that comes through so poignantly in the studies we reviewed is that we like to think of ourselves as winners.	*This whole sentence is given information, since it summarizes the main point previous paragraphs have been making. It does, however, express the main point succinctly, in a single clause: "we like to think of ourselves as winners." This is new.*
The lesson that the excellent companies have to teach is that there is no reason why we can't design systems that continually reinforce this notion;	*The idea that excellent companies have something to teach us is the main point the book has been making for fifty-seven pages, so this is given information. But the fact that we can design systems to make all company people believe they are winners is new.*

REVISING AND EDITING 67

Most of their people are made to feel that they are winners.	"Their people" is given information, referring to the excellent companies we already know; that most of these people feel like winners is new.
Their populations are distributed around the normal curves, just like every other large population, but the difference is that their systems reinforce the degrees of winning rather than the degrees of losing.	"Their populations" and "their systems" is given information, referring to "their people" in the previous sentence. That they are like normal populations is new and important information, since the reader might have assumed excellent companies had primarily exceptional people. Once we know what their people are like, we can understand what makes these companies different. The new information is that their systems reinforce degrees of winning.
Their people by and large make their targets and quotas, because the targets and quotas are set (often by the people themselves) to allow that to happen.	In the paragraph, the authors have been discussing the people in excellent companies, so the subject of the sentence, "their people," is given information. The fact that by and large they make their quotas is a more specific way of saying they are winners, so this is part given and part new information. The big news here is how they are enabled to make their quotas—they make them because they are given quotas that are reasonably easy to meet.

As this analysis demonstrates, when you read you can best follow the connections among ideas when the writer begins with something you already know and then adds new information gradually. The same must be true, then, of the sentences and paragraphs you write.

If you think your paragraphs are clogged with too much new information and are therefore hard to read, check each sentence to be sure it relates new information to given information, to something the reader already knows.

RETAINING A SINGLE FOCUS

Notice in the Peters and Waterman paragraph that the subjects of the sentences do not require the reader to shift focus radically, but, instead, to adjust the focus gradually to suit the gradual development of the topic:

> The message that comes through so poignantly in the studies we reviewed is that we like to think of ourselves as winners. The lesson that the excellent companies have to teach is that there is no reason why we can't design systems that continually reinforce this notion; most of their people are made to feel that they are winners. Their populations are distributed around the normal curve, just like every other large population, but the difference is that their systems reinforce degrees of winning rather than degrees of losing. Their people by and large make their targets and quotas, because the targets and quotas are set (often by the people themselves) to allow that to happen.

The subject of the first sentence, "the message," is closely related to the subject of the second sentence, "the lesson that excellent companies have." The subjects of the third, fourth, and fifth sentences—"most of their people," "their populations," and "their people"—refer to the excellent companies of the second sentence. Thus in no sentence does the subject ask the reader to shift the focus very far from the subject of previous sentences. Instead, the subject of the new sentence modifies the subject of previous sentences slightly as the topic is developed. In checking your own paragraphs for coherence, make sure they retain a single focus.

REPEATING KEY WORDS

Another device for achieving coherence is to repeat key words. Notice in the Peters and Waterman example that the writers introduce key words and ideas and then follow up on them sentence by sentence, repeating the key words to make connections explicit:

> The message that comes through so poignantly in the studies we reviewed is that we like to think of ourselves as winners. The lesson that the excellent companies have to teach is that there is no reason why we can't design systems that continually reinforce this notion; most of their people are made to feel that they are winners. Their populations are distributed around the normal curve, just like every other large population, but the difference is that their systems reinforce degrees of winning rather than degrees of losing. Their people by and large make their targets and quotas, because the targets and quotas are set (often by the people themselves) to allow that to happen.

Some writers mistakenly fear that repeating the same word in a paragraph will cause monotony, so they needlessly confuse readers by changing the key words. It is possible to overdo repetition, but as the above paragraph illustrates, good writing contains a great deal of repetition. Judge carefully. Repetition of key words is essential for the reader to make connections among your ideas.

You can use the accompanying checklist of questions to ensure that your paragraphs are organized, complete, and coherent.

REVISING AND EDITING 69

CHECKLIST FOR REVISING PARAGRAPHS

1. For organization and completeness, does your analysis tree or outline show that each paragraph is well organized and has one main idea that is developed with reasons, examples, or other details?
2. For coherence:
   - Does each paragraph provide sufficient transition words to move the reader from level to level of the hierarchy of ideas?
   - Does each sentence in the paragraph relate new information to given information?
   - Does the paragraph retain a single focus from sentence to sentence?
   - Does the paragraph repeat key words to show the relationship of ideas?

REVISING LOCALLY: SENTENCES

Frequently in putting together drafts, business people are concentrating so hard on getting out the whole idea that they build their sentences out of ready-made phrases without much thought, just to get the idea onto paper. But such ready-made phrases rarely express ideas forcefully and appropriately. Good business writers know that the final stage of writing—editing sentences and proofreading—can make all the difference in how effectively their writing delivers its message to the reader. Let's examine several techniques for editing sentences so that you can deliver your message forcefully and appropriately.

Using Strong Verbs and the Active Voice

Consider the following paragraph introducing a memo, and then look at the revision:

DRAFT

DATE: June 15, 199___
TO: All Departments
FROM: A. A. Mei, Director of Material Management
RE: Procedure for Requisitioning from General Stores

The purpose of this notification is to act as a reminder of the new policy regarding the utilization of the procedure for the requisitioning of stationery supplies and printed forms from General Stores. Immediate implementation of the new policy is mandated. There can be no acceptance of orders unless the correct procedure is used. An explanation is provided by this memo as to how the change will be beneficial to your department and to General Stores.

REVISION

Please remember to use the new procedure for requesting stationery supplies and printed forms from General Stores. After today, General Stores cannot accept your orders unless the new forms are used. By following this new procedure, you can benefit your department as well as General Stores. Let me explain.

The stilted and officious style of the first version often goes by the unflattering terms "gobbledygook" or "bureaucratese." Its wordy indirectness stands in sorry contrast to the straightforward style of the revised version. But can you say more precisely what is wrong with the original?

If you look at the subjects and verbs of the sentences in the original memo, it is hard to picture who is doing what:

SUBJECT	VERB
The purpose	is to act
implementation	is provided
no acceptance	can be
an explanation	is provided

But if you look at the subjects and verbs of the revised version, you get a very clear idea who is acting, and precisely what the action is:

SUBJECT	VERB
(you)	please remember
General Stores	cannot accept
you	can benefit
(you)	let me explain

Writers who use gobbledygook may be working under the false assumption that an inflated style will impress readers. But the reverse is true. Readers will be put off by not being able to see who is supposed to do what. Let's look at two ways to get rid of gobbledygook and make clear who is doing what—strong verbs and the active voice.

STRONG VERBS

Usually an action is more memorable than an object, a thing. Therefore, sentences with strong verbs—those that clearly express action—get your message across more force-

REVISING AND EDITING

fully than sentences that use weak verbs and load up on nouns. Let's consider two ways to find the strongest verb.

Change Nouns into Verbs. Compare the verbs in the draft and in the revised version of the memo you examined earlier. Here is the first sentence:

DRAFT

The purpose of this notification is to act as a reminder of the new policy regarding the utilization of the procedure for the requisitioning of stationery supplies and printed forms from General Stores.

REVISION

Please remember to use the new procedure for requesting stationery supplies and printed forms from General Stores.

In the second version, the writer has changed many nouns into action verbs and has used fewer syllables:

DRAFT	**REVISION**
notification is to act as a *reminder*	please *remember*
utilization of the new procedure	*use* the new procedure
for the *requisitioning* of	for *requesting*

Often prose creeps sluggishly along because the actions appear as polysyllabic nouns. Changing heavy nouns back into verbs makes sentences shorter and stronger:

DRAFT	**REVISION**
Department managers will be asked for *explanations* of their *implementation* procedures.	Department managers will be asked *to explain* how they *implement* procedures.
This step takes *the identification process* further and involves a *comparison* of each stamping method.	This step *identifies and compares* each stamping method.
The interview format provides a time *allowance* to both participants for *consideration* about what they consider *necessary information to be received* from the other person.	The interview format *allows* both participants the time *to consider* what they *need to find out* from the other person.
Prior *knowledge* of overseas work *contributes to the establishment* of easier working relations between the two liaison people.	*Knowing* overseas work *helps* the two liaison people *establish* easy working relations.

Avoid Overuse of the Verb "To Be." Another way to check writing for strong verbs is to look at all the occasions when you use some form of the verb "to be," and see whether you can change that verb into a strong verb. Often you can turn a nearby noun or adjective into the strong verb you need:

DRAFT	REVISION
The findings **were** helpful *in providing* . . .	The findings *helped provide* . . .
There **is** *a need for an investigation.* . . .	We *need to investigate* . . .
The result **was** *a discussion* of the procedures by top management.	As a result, top management *discussed* the procedures.
The analysis **was** *indicative* of . . .	The analysis *indicated* . . .
Therefore our *recommendation* **is** not to open a retail outlet at this time.	Therefore we *recommend* not opening a retail outlet at this time.

ACTIVE VOICE

Just as it is easier for the reader to create a mental picture if your action is expressed in strong verbs, so too is it easier if the doer or agent of that action is identified immediately as the subject of the sentence. To make sure the subject is the agent of the action, you should check to see that your sentences use the active rather than the passive voice.

ACTIVE

The research team finished the report on time.
    subject   verb

The above sentence is said to be in the **active voice** because the subject of the sentence, "research team," did the action that the verb, "finished," describes. When the subject does not act but instead is acted upon, then the verb is considered to be in the **passive voice.** With passive verbs, the agent may or may not be identified in the sentence.

PASSIVE (NO AGENT IDENTIFIED)

The report was finished on time.
  subject verb

PASSIVE (AGENT IDENTIFIED IN A PREPOSITIONAL PHRASE)

The report was finished by the research team on time.
  subject verb   agent

REVISING AND EDITING

Overuse of the passive voice creates two problems for readers: (1) wordiness and (2) confusion about the agent of the action. There are times when the use of the passive is acceptable, but, in general, you should avoid the passive voice. Let's look first at the problems the passive voice creates, then at acceptable uses of it, and finally at ways to avoid it.

The Problem of Wordiness. Passive voice makes sentences unnecessarily wordy and their meaning difficult to grasp. Consider the following sentences:

PASSIVE	ACTIVE
The concentration by the Training Division of its time, money, and other resources into a new program is not advisable from our point of view.	We do not advise the Training Division to concentrate its time, money, and other resources into a new program.
Our implementation of this new procedure is required by the board of directors.	The board of directors requires that we implement this new procedure.

In every case, changing the passive into the active has required fewer words to convey the same message. But more important, the meaning of an active sentence is easier for the reader to grasp. A passive sentence identifies the doer of the action only late in the sentence, after the action is described.

Concentration is not advised from *our* point of view.
Implementation is required by the *board of directors*.

These passive sentences force the reader first to picture an action, such as "concentration," and only later to identify who accomplished it. Yet it is much harder to picture "concentration" than to picture people concentrating.

The Problem of Confusion About the Agent. While some passive sentences identify the agent only late in the sentence, others never identify the agent at all. If you never identify the agent, your reader must work much harder to understand your meaning. Compare these examples:

PASSIVE	ACTIVE
In the design of the wheel assemblies, an attempt must be made to reduce the risk of lock-up. [Who must attempt to reduce the risk; who is responsible?]	In the design of wheel assemblies, engineering must reduce the risk of lock-up.

PASSIVE

In completing the following tasks, the planned $25,000 budget for June and July was exceeded. [Who exceeded the budget?]

ACTIVE

In completing the following tasks, we exceeded the planned $25,000 budget for June and July.

Changing these sentences from passive to active voice has forced the writers to identify who will do or has done the action. This makes the meaning much clearer for the reader. It also allocates responsibility. In the second sample set, for example, changing to the active voice has forced the writers to identify themselves as the ones who exceeded the budget: Not "the budget was exceeded," but "we exceeded the budget." Whereas the passive voice allows the writers to de-emphasize their role in exceeding the budget, the active voice makes their role clear. Using the passive voice, then, can help a writer de-emphasize the agent responsible for an action. But this strategy may backfire. If you do not identify the agent, your reader may become all the more concerned and intent on finding out who is responsible. Consider the following two versions of a sentence. Which do you think would be most effective? In what circumstances?

PASSIVE

By the first of the year, employees hired in the last six months will be laid off.

ACTIVE

By the first of the year, our new president will lay off employees hired in the last six months.

Acceptable Uses of the Passive Voice. As a rule of thumb you should avoid using the passive voice because it hides the agent of action. However, there may be times when de-emphasizing the actor is precisely what you want to do.

1. *Use the passive voice to avoid sounding accusatory.* Compare these examples:

ACTIVE

None of you has yet notified me.

You or your technicians did not properly install the instrument and therefore voided the warranty.

PASSIVE

I have not yet been notified.

Because the instrument was not properly installed, the warranty is voided.

2. *Use the passive voice when the action, and not the agent, is the focus of the paragraph.* Compare these examples:

ACTIVE

The newscasters received the company press release in time for the 5:00 P.M. broadcast.

PASSIVE

The company press release was received in time for the 5:00 P.M. broadcast.

REVISING AND EDITING

ACTIVE	PASSIVE
The installer anchored the computer to the desk top with a Secure-Lock.	The computer was anchored to the desk top with a Secure-Lock.

In these cases, the reader needs to know not who did the action but what happened to the object. Passive voice in these situations helps you retain paragraph focus. Yet even in these cases the sentences might fare better by being reworded in the active voice:

PASSIVE	ACTIVE
The company press release was received in time for the 5:00 P.M. broadcast.	The company press release arrived in time for the 5:00 P.M. broadcast.
The computer was anchored to the desk top with a Secure-Lock.	A Secure-Lock anchored the computer to the desk top.

Using Impersonal Agents to Avoid Passive Constructions. Many business writers use the passive voice because they or their superiors are reluctant to use the first person pronouns "I" and "we" in business reports. These people think, erroneously, that avoiding the first person makes what they say sound more scientific and more objective. Yet even experts in scientific style agree that using the first person makes scientific writing no less authoritative and often much more readable.[3] And the same can certainly be said of business writing.

It is, however, possible to overuse "I" and "we" so that it becomes distracting: "I investigated," "then I proceeded," "I recommend," "we found," "we uncovered." But instead of using the passive voice, you can avoid overusing personal pronouns by ascribing actions to **impersonal agents**—as was done in the last example: "A Secure-Lock anchored the computer to the desk top." Although a Secure-Lock certainly is not a person, nevertheless we ascribed an action to it: it "anchored" the computer. Look at the following revisions for examples of impersonal agents that can help you avoid the passive voice:

PASSIVE	ACTIVE
There are many positive aspects of check collection that are not brought out in this report.	*This report* does not bring out all the positive aspects of check collection.
From these findings it is indicated that . . .	*These findings* indicate that . . .
A weekly meeting is recommended as a way to reduce problems generated within the Training Division.	A *weekly meeting* would reduce problems within the Training Division.

Using Emphatic Word Order

In the English sentence, the most important positions are the beginning and the end, especially the end. Readers remember better what comes first and last than what comes in the middle. It makes sense, then, to put the most important information in the first and last positions in your sentences:

UNEMPHATIC ORDER	REVISED
Two of our members heard you speak in Dallas and praised you highly for your dynamic presentation when they returned.	Two of our members heard you speak in Dallas and, when they returned, praised you highly for your dynamic presentation.
The primary force behind most stress relief and exercise programs is that executives are more prone to stress and heart attacks, as shown by medical reports.	The primary force behind most stress relief and exercise programs is that, as medical reports show, executives are more prone to stress and heart attacks.
We feel we are missing some patients and therefore losing revenues by using this system.	We feel that by using this system we are missing some patients and therefore losing revenues.

By revising your sentences to end on an emphatic note, you reinforce the importance of your message.

Avoiding Noun Clusters

Normally in English sentences, nouns are modified by adjectives:

Inadequate space makes tax counseling difficult.

adjective   noun

But occasionally, a noun might be used to modify another noun:

Inadequate   desk   space makes tax counseling difficult.

        noun used as adjective   noun

Since using a noun as an adjective happens only occasionally in English, readers generally expect the first noun they read to hold the noun position in the sentence. But what happens when you read the following sentence?

Inadequate tax counselor interviewing desk space makes counseling difficult.

REVISING AND EDITING

With such **noun clusters** the reader becomes frustrated by continually having to postpone identifying the real noun. Long strings of nouns may make writing easier, because they contain so much information in a single phrase, but they are very hard for the reader to understand and they often sound ridiculous. You should break up such clusters into two or more phrases:

NOUN CLUSTER

Any *beverage industry market analyst* will tell you that Coke and 7-Up will sell even if medical research confirms that sugar is related to high blood pressure.

Our *Soviet truck plant contract price* does not include a margin for *foreign exchange rate transaction risks*.

Please revise the current *group member meeting dates scheduling package format* to allow us to record visits for each group member individually.

REVISION

Any market analyst for the beverage industry will tell you that Coke and 7-Up will sell even if medical research confirms that sugar is related to high blood pressure.

Our contract price for the Soviet truck plant does not take into account risks caused by fluctuations in the foreign exchange rate.

In the scheduling package for group members, please revise the current format of the meeting date to allow us to record visits for each group member individually.

Breaking up noun clusters in your writing will make your sentences more readable.

Avoiding Needless Words

Readers understand better and pay more attention to messages that are expressed in as few words as possible. So try to eliminate superfluous words from your writing. These include "all-purpose" nouns, excessively long or pretentious expressions, padding, and redundancy.

ALL-PURPOSE NOUNS

All-purpose nouns are words so abstract they can stand for a multitude of meanings. If you use any of the following words in your writing, you should try to find a word or phrase that conveys your meaning more precisely:

    aspect
    factor
    situation
    thing
    the fact (despite the fact that, regardless of the fact that)

ALL-PURPOSE NOUN

Another *factor* that has contributed to the need to raise the price of Great North campers is that we just signed a labor contract that increases wages and benefits 42 percent.

Despite the fact that I worked hard to service the Plummer account, they still switched to another agency.

REVISION

A 42 percent increase in labor costs has resulted in the need to raise the price of Great North campers.

Although I worked hard to service the Plummer account, they still switched to another agency.

LONG AND PRETENTIOUS EXPRESSIONS

You should avoid long or pretentious expressions that can be replaced by shorter ones. In Figure 3.7, compare the stilted expressions in the first column with their replacements.

PADDING

You will want to get rid of **padded expressions** too. These include

- there is
- there are
- it is
- it is interesting to note that
- one can observe that

PADDED

There is a program scheduled for Thursday.

There are several options we ought to consider.

It is management that controls hiring decisions.

REVISION

A program is scheduled for Thursday.

We ought to consider several options.

Management controls hiring decisions.

REDUNDANCIES

Yet another group of words you should try to eliminate from your writing are **redundant expressions.** A few of the most common redundancies are listed in Figure 3.8.

Figure 3.7

AVOIDING LONG AND PRETENTIOUS EXPRESSIONS

Instead of	Try
above mentioned	this, these
accordingly	so
at this point in time	now
to activate	to begin
advantageous	helpful, useful
after which time	then
aforementioned	this, these
ascertain	find out
at a later date	later
at your earliest convenience	as soon as you can
be good enough to	please
before you do anything else	first
to commence	to begin
due to the fact that	because, since
to endeavor	to try
to facilitate	to ease, to speed, to help
first of all	first
first and foremost	first
forthwith	now, at once, promptly
henceforth	after this
herein	here
in accordance with the request of Ron Miller	Ron Miller has asked me
inasmuch as	since, as
in the amount of	for
in the event that	if
I take the liberty to inform you	I am glad to tell you, you will be glad
optimum	best
per, as per	by, through
per your request	as you requested
take pleasure in	are pleased
to terminate	to end, to stop
therein	there
under separate cover	separately
utilization	use
We trust that this will meet with your approval	We hope you approve
what you need to do after you've done this	next

Figure 3.8

AVOIDING REDUNDANCIES

Instead Of	Try
reason why . . . is that	because, reason . . . is that
expectations in the future	expectations
memories of the past	memories
orange in color	orange
contemporary world of today	today, the world today
fifty years of age	fifty
true facts	facts
final result	result
at this point in time	at this point

Compare the sentences in these two columns:

REDUNDANT	REVISION
The reason why we are losing our share of the market *is that* foreign companies are flooding the U.S. with cheap steel.	We are losing our share of the market because foreign companies are flooding the U.S. market with steel.
The insurance agent used *personal examples from her own experience* to make her point.	The insurance agent used personal examples to make her point.
This job can be done in *an hour's time*.	This job can be done in an hour.

By omitting needless words you save your reader time and make your message clearer.

Using Language Appropriate to Your Reader

You should check your letters, memos, and reports to be sure that your language is appropriate to your reader. In particular, you should use jargon with care and try to avoid sexist language and clichés.

JARGON

Every group you belong to—whether family, friends, fellow sports lovers, or co-workers—shares a specialized language that is well understood only by members of that group. The specialized or technical vocabulary of a group is called its **jargon.** To be able to talk and write in the language of your group is a badge of membership, and people frequently take pleasure in knowing how to "talk the language" of their group. Academic fields and particular careers have their own jargon. As you take courses in your college major and enter the business world, you will learn the specialized language of your field and will begin to use the jargon readily and comfortably with others acquainted with it.

You may want to use jargon in your business writing when your readers will understand the meaning of the specialized vocabulary. Using it allows you to communicate quickly and effectively, because jargon is a shorthand for communicating complex ideas to fellow specialists. In fact, if you don't use the jargon in these situations, your readers may become impatient and irritated by your unwillingness to talk in the language that you share.

But if your readers are not specialists, using jargon will confuse, intimidate, or offend them. A tax expert can say to a colleague, "Take a look at the new rulings on *depreciation* and *rollovers* before you start *tax planning* for this company." But if she sends her client a letter using those terms, he might have only a vague sense of what she means.

Too often business people use the jargon of their specialization when they are not speaking or writing to a specialized group but to a lay audience. Jargon at such times alienates the listener or reader by making it obvious that he or she doesn't belong to the "in-group." For what readers would you consider the following excerpts from business communications to be appropriate?

> The purchasing department is still having some problems with invoices being paid on time. This is resulting in some accounts being closed and causing great inconvenience to the departments. One problem seems to be that the individuals charging items at the office are not aware that the yellow slip that the cashier hands them is not simply a receipt, but is in fact the invoice that must be vouched up and submitted to the accounting office for payment just as any invoice is paid. Please save these slips and vouch them up as soon as possible.

> Access to our new system requires that you install friendly terminals. Using it will allow you to take advantage of increased memory capacity, the electronic mail option, and word processing capabilities. Let me know if your department is interested in purchasing the necessary equipment.

Using jargon will enhance your business writing if used appropriately but will detract from it if used inappropriately. If you write with your readers in mind, you will know when to use jargon and when to translate it for the nonexpert.

SEXIST LANGUAGE

Is English a sexist language?[4] Some linguists would argue that it is for two reasons. First, English vocabulary contains nouns, adjectives, and verbs that more often favor men rather than women. Certainly governors, majors, and masters have more power and significance than governesses, majorettes, and mistresses. A virtuous man may have a number of admirable traits, but a virtuous woman is simply chaste. Although both men and women may make comments about people, laugh, and sometimes even yell, only rarely is a man accused of gossiping, giggling, or shrieking.

The second way English may be sexist is in the ambiguity of the supposedly generic term "man" and forms of the pronoun "he." Do these words refer to all people, as in "man and his environment," or do they refer only to male humans, as in "man and wife"?

While linguists are trying to agree on whether the language itself is sexist, no business person can afford to use sexist language unless he or she wants to risk offending everyone concerned about the fair treatment of both sexes. Let's take a look at two kinds of sexist language to avoid.

Stereotyping in Vocabulary and Usage. Figure 3.9 lists five types of belittling or stereotyping constructions that you should avoid when referring to women.

Supposedly Generic Terms. American English has yet to solve the problem created by not having a generic personal pronoun. Traditionally English has used "he," "him," "his," and some form of the word "man"—as in "mankind"—to refer to all people generically, that is, regardless of sex. For example, traditionally it was acceptable to say, "Everyone is requested to abide by the policies of his own department"; now such use of the word "his" is perceived to exclude women.

Old English (used from the fifth to the eleventh centuries) had a word to refer generically to all people. Whereas men were referred to as "wer," and women as "wif," all people were referred to as "man." But during the Middle Ages the word "man" gradually began to be used to refer not only to all people but also to adult males.

Recent studies have shown, however, that even though "he" and "man" are supposed to be generic pronouns, they carry with them a masculine connotation. In one study, for example, two groups of college students were given chapter titles for a sociology text and asked to submit photographs they thought appropriate to illustrate those chapters. One group received "man-linked" chapter titles—such as "Social Man," "Urban Man," "Political Man," and "Industrial Man." The other group received "non–man-linked" chapter titles—such as "Culture," "Population," "Race and Mi-

REVISING AND EDITING

Figure 3.9

FIVE TYPES OF SEXIST-STEREOTYPING
CONSTRUCTIONS TO AVOID

1. **Nonparallel terms**

INAPPROPRIATE	ALTERNATIVES
man and wife	husband and wife
men and ladies	men and women
department heads and their wives	department heads and their spouses
Mr. Brown and his family	the Brown family
Mr. Brown and his wife Julia	Julia and Eddie Brown
the men and girls in the office	the men and women in the office
the chairman, Mr. Coles, and the chairperson, Ms. Porter	the chairman, Mr. Coles, and the chairwoman, Ms. Porter
	OR
	the chairpersons Mr. Coles and Ms. Porter
prudent man, timid woman	prudent man or woman
man's shout, woman's scream	man's or woman's shout
man's talk, woman's chatter	man's or woman's talk
bitchy woman, outspoken man	outspoken woman or man

2. **Unnecessary reference to gender**

INAPPROPRIATE	APPROPRIATE
waitress	waiter, server
stewardess	flight attendant
male nurse	nurse
coed	student
woman doctor	doctor

3. **Belittling or stereotyping terms of address**
   honey, sweetie, dear, etc.

4. **Unnecessary descriptive expressions for one sex only**
   (references to hair color, clothes, marital status, or age)

INAPPROPRIATE	APPROPRIATE
The blond CEO, looking very businesslike in a dark brown pantsuit, strode into the boardroom and opened the meeting.	The CEO strode into the boardroom and opened the meeting.

(continued)

THE RANDOM HOUSE GUIDE TO BUSINESS WRITING

(SEXIST-STEREOTYPIING CONSTRUCTIONS TO AVOID continued)

---

5. Stereotyping Assumptions (that it is entirely a woman's responsibility to stay at home with the children; that homemakers don't work, because they don't get paid).

INAPPROPRIATE	**APPROPRIATE**
As part of our benefits package, we provide day-care facilities for the children of working mothers.	As part of our benefits package, we provide day-care facilities for the children of our employees.
Since more wives are working, we have had to extend our hours to evenings and Saturdays.	With the increase in two-wage-earner households, we have had to extend our delivery hours to evenings and Saturdays.

---

nority Groups,'' and ''Family.'' In the group receiving man-linked titles, 64 percent of the students submitted photographs depicting males only. In the group receiving non–man-linked titles, only 50 percent of the students submitted photographs depicting males only.[5]

This study and similar ones suggest that so-called ''generic'' pronouns do carry masculine connotations and, therefore, when used to refer to both men and women, actually exclude women. Fortunately, you can avoid sexist generic terms by using certain techniques. For ''man'' forms, you can substitute indefinite forms such as the ones shown in Figure 3.10.

Figure 3.10

SUBSTITUTING INDEFINITE FORMS FOR MAN FORMS

Man Form	**Indefinite Form**
salesman	salesperson, sales representative
chairman	chair, chairperson, department head
spokesman	spokesperson, representative
mankind	human beings, people, persons
man-hours	work-hours
manned	staffed
manmade	synthetic
workman	worker

REVISING AND EDITING

To avoid having to use "he," "him," and "his," you can use plural forms of nouns and pronouns whenever possible:

SEXIST

A manager knows that his success depends on the performance of his subordinates.

A good secretary knows how to make travel arrangements for her boss.

REVISION

Managers know that their success depends on the performance of their subordinates.

Good secretaries know how to make travel arrangements for their bosses.

Use "he or she," "him or her," and "his or hers" if you must, but be careful about overdoing it, as does this example:

No manager should enter his or her name on the expense account before he or she consults his or her supervisor.

In a document that cites several typical examples, you can avoid the "he or she" pattern by striking a balance between male and female examples. Here is an excerpt from a training division's brochure that succeeds in being nonsexist:

In a typical executive training session participants may be divided into teams to role-play a departmental crisis. One team member, designated team leader, may assume the role of outside adviser to the department. On the basis of the facts *she* gathers from the department members, *she* writes a report making policy recommendations subject to team approval.

When a team member receives the report, *he* must then assess the effect the recommended policy changes will have on *his* operations, determine feasibility, and report back to the team manager.

Although some publishers have recommended using novel constructions such as "s/he," and "his/her," readers who silently say words as they read them find these forms unpronounceable and obtrusive. You should avoid them.

CLICHÉS

Many people use clichés in casual speaking and writing when they don't have the time to rethink everything they want to say, but clichés are inappropriate for most speaking and writing. By using clichés, writers are telling the reader that they can't take the time to search for words that express exactly what they want to say.

Clichés not only reduce the impact of a sentence, but they also undermine the writer's authority with the reader. Compare the following examples:

CLICHÉ	REVISION
A new employee profit-sharing plan is a *tried and true way* to increase productivity.	A new employee profit-sharing plan will guarantee increased productivity.
The employees are *up in arms* about the lack of parking spaces within a block of the office.	The employees are furious about the lack of parking spaces within a block of the office.
The handwriting is on the wall: a tight monetary policy will have disastrous consequences.	Certainly a tight monetary policy will have disastrous consequences.
Your report made the need to purchase additional company aircraft *crystal clear*.	Your report proved that we need to purchase additional company aircraft.

The accompanying checklist will help you to review your business writing at the sentence level.

CHECKLIST FOR EDITING SENTENCES

1. In editing sentences for a forceful style
   - Do your sentences use strong verbs? Active voice?
   - Are your sentences ordered for emphasis?
   - Have you avoided noun clusters and wordiness?
2. In editing sentences for appropriate style, do you avoid inappropriate jargon, sexist language, and clichés?

PROOFREADING

Once you are satisfied that you have revised and edited sufficiently, you will want to proofread your work. Proofreading differs from reading in important ways. If you are a good reader, you do not see every letter and word when you read. Good readers can anticipate what some words and letters are going to be and skim across the lines looking for new information. That is why good readers have to change the way they read when they are looking for errors at the word and sentence level. Proofreaders have to slow down and make certain they see every word and letter. We recommend the following method for proofreading:

- Let the typed draft sit for several hours before proofreading it.
- Read it out loud.
- If you have access to a computer, use the spelling check to correct typographical errors and misspellings. (Some programs also help you correct errors in spacing, punctuation, wording, style, and basic grammar.)

SUMMARY

Once you have finished a draft of an important memo, letter, or report, you can feel a sense of accomplishment, but don't relax yet. You should use the techniques you have learned in this chapter to revise your draft. Revising involves reviewing your writing to be certain you have the content and organization to accomplish your goal with your reader. To revise the draft holistically, ask the "big" questions—about the communication's goal, its reader, its information and ideas, and its organization. Once you feel committed to the overall or holistic design of your draft, you can revise paragraphs and sentences. Use techniques you have learned in this chapter to ensure that your paragraphs are complete, organized, and coherent, and that your sentences have a forceful and appropriate style and are free of inappropriate jargon, sexist language, and clichés.

EXERCISES

See "Revising Holistically," pp. 50–59, for Exercise 1.

1. Various pieces of writing follow; imagine that associates have come to you to ask advice about revising them. To each of the pieces, apply the following questions: Does the draft accomplish a goal? Is the writer sensitive to the audience? Are the information and ideas complete and appropriate? Is the draft well organized?

a. Globe Airlines has received the following letter of complaint from Mrs. Stevens, a disgruntled passenger:

> On January 27th I was one of fifty passengers on your Los Angeles-Dallas/Fort Worth flight who was making connections in Dallas for Boston. But because of fog, our plane was unable to land in Dallas and was diverted to San Antonio. After waiting in San Antonio for one hour, the fifty of us were bussed to Dallas. But when we debussed at the Globe terminal, no one at Globe knew where we had come from, nor had anyone made any arrangements for our flight.
>
> After three hours of waiting, Globe personnel finally told us to go over to the Eastways Terminal, where we would find a flight to Boston. But when we fifty passengers arrived at Eastways, again no one had been expecting us or had any idea what to do with us. Meanwhile, it was getting past 6:00 P.M. and no arrangements for food or beverages had been made.
>
> Finally, after 7:00 P.M., bewildered and hungry, we were accommodated by an Eastways flight and the fifty of us boarded the plane.
>
> I am deeply disturbed by the neglect we experienced. I can understand airline delays and difficulties because of equipment or weather. But I can't understand such poor coordination and such callous unconcern for your customers' needs.

In response to this complaint, Mrs. Stevens is to receive the reply shown in Figure 3.11. How would you advise the agent who wrote this letter to revise it?

Figure 3.11

DRAFT OF LETTER TO MRS. STEVENS

18865 Ventura Blvd.,
Sherman Oaks, CA 91403
October 30, 199_

Mrs. Stevens
6231 Barcelona Ave.,
Yorba Linda, CA 92686

Dear Mrs. Stevens:

There is no doubt that you and all the other passengers scheduled to travel on flight 634 on January 27, to Boston, had a disappointing experience. Clearly, our performance did not meet our usual high standards and we apologize.

We know you were disappointed with the decisions made by operations personnel at Dallas/Fort Worth Airport. Because of the delayed arrival of the flight from San Antonio, we elected to operate the continuing segment of the flight on schedule. We are aware that this action to protect those passengers who otherwise would have been delayed at the Dallas/Fort Worth Airport caused you to be inconvenienced. Still, in view of the total number of passengers involved, we believed our decision was a sound one.

Since unforeseen difficulties can cause our flights to be delayed or canceled, neither we nor other carriers guarantee schedules. Our business is such that it is not possible to do so. While I apologize for any difficulties you experienced and can understand your reasons for requesting compensation for the expenses incurred, we must respectfully decline to make an adjustment. We do not assume responsibility for a passenger's expenses when a flight is delayed or canceled. Also, since there are numerous elements involved in our total service, we do not make adjustments in the fare, which is really charged for the transportation provided.

While your letter was unfavorable it is welcome, because we need to know when our passengers are dissatisfied. I have already alerted the right people so that corrective action can be taken.

> Please give us the opportunity to regain your confidence in our ability to meet your requirements. We want your business and we will work hard to earn it.
>
> Sincerely,
>
> Alice Wardson
> Staff Assistant
> Executive Office

b. An associate of yours, Ben Fraser, is planning to send a memo to Lou Burdick, his subordinate. Because of worker unrest in Lou's unit, Ben hired a consulting group to find out the causes of the unrest and to recommend solutions. The group pinpointed Lou's poor management of the unit as the major cause of the problem and recommended that Lou be relieved of his management position. Ben wants to send the memo shown in Figure 3.12 to Lou to tell him that his duties are going to be reduced. How would you suggest it be revised?

Figure 3.12

DRAFT OF BEN FRASER'S MEMO

> DATE: November 5, 199_
> TO: Lou Burdick, Manager
> FROM: Ben Fraser, Senior Manager
> RE: Your Dismissal as Manager of Unit B
>
> It is imperative that we resolve the labor dispute in your department quickly. Production schedules must be met now if we are to benefit from the Christmas shopping season. We will begin immediately to implement solutions developed at the executive level and with the assistance of outside consultants.

(continued)

(DRAFT OF BEN FRASER'S MEMO continued)

> The workers in your department voiced complaints about low rates of pay. But as you know, the compensation paid to our employees compares favorably with that for similar jobs in the surrounding area.
>
> I believe that the labor dispute stems from organizational problems and poorly assigned job responsibilities. With company growth, your position has become a difficult one. You are responsible for approximately 700 workers. This does not allow sufficient time to handle technical responsibilities as well as to maintain adequate communication with employees and top management.
>
> The changes that we will make involve some company reorganization and changes in your assigned responsibilities. We intend to utilize your technical abilities fully while giving you a more manageable position.
>
> These changes are necessary to alleviate labor problems in your department, prevent future problems, and ensure your continued success with this company. You have a strong track record with this company due to your technical expertise, and we want to see that continue.
>
> Please call my secretary to set up a meeting with me this afternoon. At that time, I will explain our plans and their effect on you in greater detail.

c. A consulting firm has received an assignment from Ms. Jean Copen. She is proposing to build a motel on her property in Clarks Ferry, South Carolina, and has requested that the consulting firm tell her whether it will be feasible to run a profitable motel business at this site. Although she has had no formal business training, Ms. Copen is a savvy business person and feels quite confident that a motel would succeed on her property. Figure 3.13 shows the report that the consulting firm intends to send her. Can you suggest ways the report ought to be revised?

Figure 3.13

DRAFT OF REPORT TO JEAN COPEN

COPEN SITE MOTEL FEASIBILITY STUDY

SITE

We evaluated the following factors regarding the proposed site:

- Traffic patterns
- Relationship to demand
- Relationship to amenities

Area Review

We gathered relevant economic data and interviewed officials of the cities and their chambers of commerce to determine the current and future economic environment. We found that the area economy is primarily dependent on tourism, with limited commercial development, and that this trend is not expected to change in the foreseeable future. The limited commercial development that will occur in the future is expected to be concentrated in Eagle Bay and East Aurora, as opposed to Clarks Ferry.

LODGING SUPPLY AND DEMAND

Existing Market Conditions

We interviewed managers of lodging facilities in Clarks Ferry, Eagle Bay, East Aurora, and Fair Haven (herein referred to collectively as the market area). The purpose of the interviews was to gather data regarding the current health of the lodging market, such as occupancy levels, average room rates, market mixes, patterns of demand, and quality levels.

We found that properties in the cities of Eagle Bay and Clarks Ferry were achieving occupancy levels of approximately 55 percent, whereas East Aurora and Fair Haven properties were achieving occupancy levels of approximately 76 percent. These higher occupancy levels are attributed to the more favorable locations of these cities. Moreover, we found that all properties operated at capacity during the summer months. As a result, many potential customers could not secure rooms in the market area during these peak periods, indicating unsatisfied demand.

(continued)

(DRAFT OF REPORT TO JEAN COPEN continued)

> Potential Additions to the Lodging Supply
>
> We interviewed developers of proposed lodging facilities to determine the probability of the proposed projects coming to fruition in the foreseeable future. We found that eight properties with 431 rooms were under construction in the market area.
>
> Demand
>
> Through our property interviews, we determined that demand within the market area comprised three segments: tourist, tour bus, and commercial. We found that both tourist and tour bus operators preferred East Aurora and Fair Haven to either Clarks Ferry or Eagle Bay, primarily because of available amenities and ease of access to the coastal highway. This explained the higher occupancy level of the properties in those cities.
> On the basis of the above findings, we are of the opinion that there would not be sufficient market demand to support the proposed motel.

See "Revising Paragraphs for Coherence," pp. 62–69 for Exercises 2a–d.

2. Revise the following paragraphs. Make whatever changes you think necessary, but pay special attention to the clues preceding each paragraph.

See "Providing Transitions," pp. 63–64, for Exercise a.

a.

> I highly recommend Anita Villalobos to any business organization. During her spring semester at The College of Business Arts, Anita prepared a description and analysis of marketing strategy at Communications Analysis Corporation (CAC). I was very impressed by the quality and depth of Anita's examination. Both I and the president of CAC found her report to be extremely valuable as we formulated our short- and long-term marketing strategy. A reexamination of corporate goals in regards to the potential dilution of our service capabilities with equipment sales and special projects was one recommendation. Her suggestion, as well as another cautioning us of the risks involved with depending on middlemen for sales distribution, has already proved to be extremely relevant to our business.

REVISING AND EDITING 93

See "Relating New Information to Given Information," pp. 65–67, for Exercise b.

b.

Inventory shortage is an important concern of management in our company. Shortage is a direct drain on profit. The store shortage was $10,000,000 in 199_. We must combat the growing shortage problem. We must identify which portion of the shortage is bookkeeping errors and which portion is actual theft.

See "Retaining a Single Focus," pp. 67–68, for Exercise c.

c.

Our proposal for tax-exempt money funds must take into account the competition. During the past two months several tax-exempt funds have been filed that invest exclusively in municipal securities from one state. Shareholders are offered an investment vehicle that is exempt from both state and federal taxes. Unit investment trusts do not compete directly with our fund because they have a fluctuating net asset value. The tax-exempt funds are unit investment trusts.

See "Repeating Key Words," pp. 68–69 for Exercise d.

d.

Production problems continually occur. In the highly technical coating operations area, Process Engineering groups have evolved to aid coating operators in solving these problems. Technical expertise and their ability to persuade are the only way Process Engineering groups have to influence coating operators. There is no financial responsibility for production losses on Process Engineering, nor rewards for improvements. Only coating operators have the responsibility of weighing Process Engineering advice and risking the financial consequences of technical errors.

See "Strong Verbs," pp. 70–72, for Exercise 3.

3. The following example consists of the draft and the revision of the opening paragraph to a report, written for a health maintenance organization, entitled "Streamlining Insurance Company Billing." The report recommends solutions for difficulties the health organization faces in collecting bills. The paragraph describes why collecting health care bills is more complicated than collecting for other businesses. Compare the original paragraph (draft) with the revision, and explain why the revision is more coherent than the original.

DRAFT

Since the 1940s, the use of private health insurance has become widely established in the United States. This third-party financier is the base of the present U.S. health care economy. In the exchange of service between the patient and provider, the fee has not been established by supply/demand forces, as in other services in our free market system. The service rendered is between the patient and the provider. The fee passes through many hands.

REVISION

Since the 1940s, the use of private health insurance has become widely established in the United States. Health insurance companies have become the financier of the U.S. health care economy. Whereas in other free market exchanges the fee is set by supply/demand forces, in the health care economy the fee is set by this financier, who acts as a third party to the health care provider (supplier) and the patient (the one who demands). The service rendered is between patient and provider. The fee passes through many hands.

See "Strong Verbs," pp. 70–72, and "Active Voice," pp. 72–75, for Exercise 4.

4. In the following sentences, change nouns into verbs and avoid overuse of the verb "to be":

a. At that time, suggestions from engineering are weighed, and a determination is made as to the appropriate approach to use.
b. The discontent of the hourly staff is an indication that the organization of the department is weak.
c. The definitions of objectives and goals must be systematically made in order to ensure a successful training program.
d. An insurance agent is a representative of the company in a sales and service capacity and receives pay on a commission basis.
e. Departments are given information at the vice president level.
f. The communication between top and middle management that occurred in the past is no longer occurring.
g. We have made a major investment of time, money, and resources in the development of the means to help companies solve this problem.
h. The "Key Data in the 90s" module is a half-day customer and prospect seminar for the identification of critical trends and issues facing all data-processing executives.
i. The designation of the new form is for the more accurate implementation of accounting for your time worked and time off.
j. The MBL Housing Office does not make provisions for assistance in searching for year-round rentals or house sales.

See "Active Voice," pp. 72–75, for Exercises 5 and 6.

5. Notice the use of the passive voice in each of the following sentences. Which sentences would you revise? Revise them by identifying the agent of the action and putting it in the subject position:

a. Timely delivery of merchandise to stores was stopped.
b. We were offered a low home mortgage rate for a house in western Pennsylvania by the Mellon Bank of Pittsburgh.
c. The decline in the number of people viewing prime-time network TV is caused by the growth of interest in cable TV.
d. The average American family will be forced to pay higher taxes by the new federal laws.
e. Concern about power shortages in January and February was expressed by the plant manager.
f. Power tools in the welding and machine shop were broken by inexperienced trainees.
g. Knowledge of the laws and regulations controlling foreign transactions was gained by Susan Bendix, the youngest member of the legal staff.
h. The manager of transportation was fired by the board of directors for losing 200 million barrels of diesel fuel.
i. The contract was breached by her.
j. We were recently addressed by the president of NBC.
k. His eligibility for an American Express card was made possible by his acquiring a full-time job.
l. Pocket calculators were bought by each of us once their prices fell.
m. The air conditioning is automatically adjusted to changes in the building's temperature.

6. Following is the draft of a letter written by one market researcher to another. Change passive into active voice so as to achieve a forceful, direct style.

Dear Mr. Shockel:

Three tasks were completed by me before the meeting in Bangkok began:
1. A thorough review of the protocol was made.
2. Comments were written on every section for consideration by the task force.
3. A list of all supplies that are needed by each center in order to carry out the studies was prepared.

I look forward to a productive meeting.

Best wishes,

Virginia Black

See "Using Emphatic Word Order," p. 76, for Exercise 7.

7. Revise the following sentences to achieve a more emphatic word order:

   a. This method has not been effective and many individuals have emerged more confused than when they arrived at the talk.
   b. The department managers had been working with these documents for a month or two before coming to the class.
   c. Please check with Sheila Larssen, the secretary responsible for ordering, giving her a description of your needs, if you need something more customized than those items on the shelves.
   d. You must know what is happening in your region in order to transmit information effectively and act as a good liaison.
   e. An analysis of the problems in this department and some recommendations that are straightforward, simple, and easily evaluated are presented in this report.
   f. Yet many companies simply cannot gain adequate access to the information they need to direct their market efforts efficiently, as our study shows.
   g. All of RAM's standard fixtures are provided with this unconditional guarantee, as seen in the enclosed General Products Catalog.
   h. Your company will be able to save a minimum of $1,500 per month, on the basis of the figures above and average usage costs of over $10,000.

See "Avoiding Noun Clusters," pp. 76–77, for Exercise 8.

8. The following sentences suffer from noun clusters. Try to figure out the meaning of each sentence, then revise it for clarity.

   a. The computerized gasoline pumping system analyst trainee chose an internship with the most experienced engineering group at headquarters.
   b. Due to the present Swiss franc dollar interest rate differential all time high, we ought to reconsider negotiations with our European suppliers.
   c. My investment consultant said he couldn't meet me this week because he is attending a seminar on tax advantaged copper investment development analysis.
   d. Here is our report on the strategic operations implementation design schedules that you will need to revise before we submit it to the board of directors.
   e. The recent thefts at the bank's automatic teller windows led the operations manager to devise a twenty-four-hour automatic teller machine safeguard program.
   f. Data Processing and Finance are meeting to discuss the data communications network cost analysis procedure.
   g. New state regulations have given rise to an infant smog inspection industry to check cars for illegal levels of pollution.

See "Avoiding Needless Words," pp. 77–80, for Exercises 9–13.

9. The following sentences are excessively wordy and pretentious. Turn them into clear, forceful prose.

REVISING AND EDITING 97

a. For the maximization of the achievement of our corporate goals, abate your personal altercations and make significant efforts to realize our mutual, cooperative ends.
b. Hereafter, the augmentation and proliferation of employees' demands will be received with silent indifference by management.
c. Social interaction among members of Levitson's staff is impaired by sexism.
d. We can streamline the organization by retrenchment of employees who can be identified as suboptimizers of our goals.
e. A resume should contain relevant data about the interrelationship of the job seeker's academic background and employment history.
f. Your taking an aggressive posture will exacerbate the disputatious aspects of our negotiation with headquarters.
g. To prioritize your long-range options for career development, retreat to an isolated setting and consider what you yourself want before approaching top management.

10. Here is part of a memo, written by the head of sales to his sales reps, explaining how they should handle customer relations. Make changes to give it a clear, forceful style.

    To facilitate efficacious interaction with customers and to obviate factors and elements that are in the nature of unpredictable phenomena, establish certitude in the following areas before contacting a customer:

    - History of company's interactions and transactions with customer
    - Analysis of potential utilization of products by customer
    - Prioritization of customers in terms of special customer privilege options.

11. Get rid of the "bureaucratese" in the following memo:

    Date: July 9, 199_
    To: All Product Managers
    From: Fred Jackson, President
    Re: Investment Bankers' Analysis and Recommendations

    After rumination and lengthy analysis, our investment bankers terminated their consideration of our portfolio of investments. Here are the results of the discussion:

    1. Divestiture of several investments that have been poor performers was strongly advised.
    2. Further discussion of several high-risk ventures that may result in optimization of our investments is postponed until next quarter.

12. Revise each of the following sentences to eliminate wordiness:

   a. As sales representative, Leslie is responsible for routine inspections of our retail outlets to ensure that products are displayed properly and according to guidelines.
   b. Any money we owe is the key essential in the collapse of the company.
   c. The fact that Harry's report fell into the wrong hands is one factor that contributed to his limited opportunity to advance.
   d. This is evidenced by the fact that the dollar discounts in points per month is higher for short periods than for long ones.
   e. It is because of overhearing the president speaking to his son that the manager learned of the company's recent acquisitions.
   f. There are three absolutely essential requirements that are not at all optional.
   g. It can be argued that any office desk bigger in size would be impossible to move into our cramped quarters.
   h. It seems that the computer that is light in weight can be carried on the plane rather than stored with the rest of the luggage.
   i. At the present time you are now eligible for one month's vacation.
   j. Although this option may be safer and less risky, there is an initial one-month period of time of great uncertainty at the start of negotiations.

13. Rewrite each of the following drafts so that they are concise:

   a.

   Dear Ms. Perniski:

   This is to thank you for your interest in our company and the fact that you sent us samples of brochures you have written and edited. We are returning them to you under separate cover in another mailing.
   The reason why I am writing to you at this time is that we are very sorry to say that we have had to choose another applicant whose work background and experience more closely match our needs and requirements at this time than do yours. Unfortunately there are many more qualified applicants than there were available positions. We wish you every success in your job search.

   Sincerely yours,

   Daryl Warner, Personnel

b.

    Date: August 13, 199_
    To: Harvey Barren, Director of Marketing
    From: Sarah Gorden, Marketing Analyst
    Re: Physicians' Interest in Management Consulting

The reader may be interested in learning the results of my research in several aspects of the use of management consultants by physicians in the business elements of their practices.

It seems that there is every reason to conclude that physicians who employed outside management consultants when their organizations were in need of assistance did benefit from our firm's assistance. These physicians are likely to hire us again when the need arises.

Results of the previously indicated study and analyses of the full range of physicians' responses point to the fact that there are few middle-of-the-roaders and that physicians either find beneficial or find useless the assistance of management consultants.

See "Jargon," pp. 81–82, for Exercises 14 and 15.

14. Identify readers who would understand each of the following sentences. Locate the jargon that would have to be explained so that a nonspecialist could understand the writer's message.

a. Fierce competition with companies dealing in currencies with less inherent exchange risk has forced us to narrow our profit margin.
b. The response time of this system is terribly slow because there are too few users.
c. Critics of quality control circles complain that they do not increase productivity.
d. Will the elasticity of demand for small cars change in the next ten years?
e. If we can target a wide enough market for our new product, we'll still have problems establishing efficient channels of distribution.
f. Disclosures made in the footnotes to the financial statement indicate that the company has suffered heavy losses due to its involvement in legal proceedings.
g. The risk associated with this proposal is that of a sharp increase in leverage that can hurt our future credit rating.

15. Read the following three memos. Underline the jargon that the writer must explain so that a nonspecialist will be able to understand the memos.

a.

Date: January 21, 199_
To: Paul Ryan, Personnel Manager
From: Vincent Parducci, Head of Planning
Re: Progress on long-range planning

Here is the current status of long-range planning:
- Unprofitable SBUs should be divested quickly
- Profitable ones should be acquired in only the oil and gas industries
- Cash cows should be used to finance a few question marks that have growth potential in the late 1980s.

Please let me know if you'd like the complete data supporting our recommendations.

b.

Date: February 13, 199_
To: Art Foster, Director of Public Relations
From: Phil Brown, Accounting Department Supervisor
Re: Class Action Suit 957

Here's the information you'll need to release to the public on our financial involvement in Class Action Suit 957:

1. Footnotes to the financial statements describe our losses due to the legal costs.
2. Use of inflation accounting methods has allowed us to show a smaller drop in revenues than was possible when we listed these losses in terms of historical costs.
3. Accelerated depreciation rulings will enable us to recover our losses more quickly than we had anticipated.

I'm sure that once you present these facts to the public, our image will improve.

REVISING AND EDITING   **101**

c.

    Date: October 11, 199_
    To: Dan Merrick, Management Trainee
    From: Byron Smith, Personnel Manager
    Re: Evaluation of Training Session I: Small Group Interaction

    I am pleased to give you my evaluation of your training session in small group interactions. Your strengths are as follows:

- You were able to scope problems and engage in authentic real life exchanges.
- Your leadership was nondoctrinaire, and you were nondriftive in your approach.

    For future sessions, I'd like to see you prioritize the tasks you set. This can be effected first by engaging in a procedure of self-assessment and then by introducing a new sequence and hierarchy of tasks to participants in your role as a pro-active individual.

    Let me know if I can be of assistance to you in helping you to actualize your goals.

See "Sexist Language," pp. 82–85, for Exercises 16–18.

16. Identify and remedy the sexist language in each of the following sentences:

a. An accountant should become acquainted with computer software designed to meet his needs.
b. Managers and their wives are invited to attend our Christmas party.
c. A marketing analyst needs both quantitative and verbal skills to write his reports.
d. We have adopted a flex-time program in order to be more adaptable to the schedules of working mothers.
e. Tell Maggie and Mr. Leighton that they've both been nominated for chairman.
f. Every typist should purchase her own ribbons.
g. No manager should enter his name on the expense account without consulting his supervisor.
h. Mrs. Jones and Sam joined our department at the same time last year.
i. After many complaints from accounting that they could hear chattering coming from Secretarial, we have decided to rearrange the office area according to the attached plan.
j. Let Diane know that she and the other girls did a great job processing the report.
k. A secretary needs to tell her future boss about her salary requirements, but an executive ought to be less direct with his boss.
l. A man who gets an MBA is more likely to become chairman of the board than a man without an advanced degree.
m. [headline] Divorcee is First Black Woman Elected Mayor

n. Mrs. Frank Reynolds and Mr. John Kelly were recently elected to key positions in their professional associations.
o. Salesmen need to spend twenty man-hours in training seminars to qualify for advancement.
p. All of mankind would benefit from an end to the economic recession.
q. Since you're the chairman, will you be spokesman for the committee at our annual meeting?

17. Revise the following memo so that it is no longer sexist:

Date: April 23, 199_
To: All New Students
From: Student Advisory Council
Subject: Registration Admission Cards

On Monday morning go to your mail boxes before your first scheduled class. Your registration envelope will be there with your class admission cards. You should give these cards to your professor on the first day of class. He will have a list of all students attending his class.
Your registration material will be held by your adviser. See him before you go to your first class.
Be sure to look for any changes made by the Registrar's Office. If there are any problems, see your adviser about them. He is prepared to make any adjustments that may be necessary.

18. The following paragraph is from a student's report on his internship at a restaurant chain's headquarters. Revise it so that it is no longer sexist.

The manager is, however, concerned about labor costs, which run 18–19 percent of each dollar sold. According to the manager, the girls who wait on tables at night want higher wages than the lunchtime waitresses. Any new manager the restaurant hires wants his contract to include full health benefits, which are costly to the chain.

See "Clichés," pp. 85–86, for Exercises 19 and 20.

19. Replace the clichés in the following sentences with fresh expressions that will gain and hold the reader's attention.

a. Believe it or not, microchip production at our Waltham plant increased 39 percent last month, an increase that exceeded our wildest expectations.
b. The awards ceremony for employees who've been at the firm for twenty-five years or more was an earth-shaking experience.
c. Let's face it, the current level of unemployment can result in the kind of internal strife that will lead to both civil and economic chaos.

d. Our marketing plan will let us strike while the iron is hot.
e. Congratulations on becoming the proud owner of a Northwoods camper.
f. Priscilla's ability to remain cool, calm, and collected in crisis situations will ensure her ability to move up the ladder of success.

20. Identify the clichés in the following examples, and revise them.

a.

    Date: January 12, 199_
    To: Brad Majors, Vice President of Production
    From: Bo McCallisters, Plant Manager
    Subject: Taking the Bull by the Horns

    Believe it or not, in the past two weeks we've processed three quarters of our backlog of orders. We have the bull by the horns and are now back on target. Within another week, we should be caught up.

b.

June 16, 199_

Mr. Steven Stubbs
Nippon Information Systems
Greenwich, CT 06830

Dear Steve:

    It goes without saying that we appreciated your talking to our staff about how your product can revolutionize our office procedures.

    Your talk was full of wit and wisdom. In one fell swoop you won us over to word processing as the wave of the future. Your coming down here was a valued service that every one of us truly appreciated.

                            Sincerely yours,

                            Wayne Sinclair

4
THE BASICS OF BUSINESS LETTERS: WRITING TO READERS OUTSIDE THE ORGANIZATION

PREVIEW

This chapter should help you to

1. Understand how to write business letters that aid in conducting business and encourage a positive attitude toward your company
2. Use the RTA formula to
   - Establish rapport with the reader
   - Influence the reader's thinking, both logically and psychologically
   - Motivate the reader to act and have a positive attitude
3. Dictate a letter
4. Develop a friendly tone and conversational style in your letters
5. Format letters to achieve a neat, businesslike appearance

With telephones, and lately even video conference calls, the business letter may seem to be a candidate for obsolescence, along with the slide rule and the manual typewriter. And yet far from decreasing, the volume of mail from businesses increases annually (see Figure 4.1).

Figure 4.1

TOTAL U.S. POSTAL SERVICE MAIL VOLUME, 1981–1987

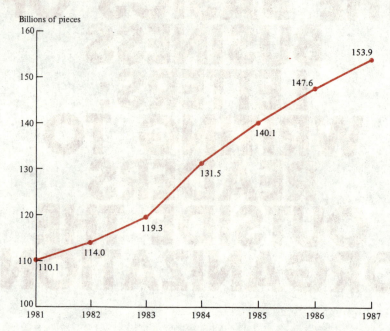

According to the U.S. Postal Service, over 90 percent of annual mail volume is generated by business.

    The reason is simple. Letters help you do business. Letters can put in an order, grant a claim, make a sale, or simply say congratulations—all at your convenience and the convenience of the person you address. Letters give you time to think your message through before you deliver it. And especially for routine transactions, letters can be much less expensive than phone calls.

    With these advantages of the business letter comes another feature that you can turn into either an asset or a liability: For many people, the image of your company will be determined entirely by the way you come across in your letters. Thus letters have two functions: to do business and to represent your company.

    Because letters represent your company, equally important as the business matters they cover are their business manners: the way letters show consideration for the reader. For this reason, business writers attend carefully not only to the facts and information their letters contain but also to their letters' tone, style, appearance, and appeal to the reader.

    In this chapter we take you through the process of writing the business letter. We will consider setting the goal, assessing the reader, gathering information, generating ideas, organizing, writing a draft, and revising. We also introduce an especially helpful strategy for generating ideas and organizing the business letter: the RTA formula. Finally, we offer suggestions for creating a friendly tone and conversational style, and for setting a format for such a letter.

THE BASICS OF BUSINESS LETTERS 107

Nan Foster puzzled over her notes from the Louisville Show. "How could Steve Gant complain about our company's service? Last summer we bent over backwards to get his two orders out. We knew he was a prize account." Nan looked up her records, and sure enough, they showed the orders were shipped within four weeks. "I've got to figure out how to let Steve know the facts. But I can't sound like 'I told you so' either. He's got to realize he has us mixed up with someone else."

SETTING THE GOAL FOR THE BUSINESS LETTER: ACTION AND ATTITUDE

Business letters make things happen. Your primary goal in writing them is to do business, either by requesting information and action from others, or by responding to others with information or action.

But besides inducing action, every business letter has another goal. Because business success relies on a good reputation, your letters must encourage the reader to have a positive attitude toward doing business with you. Your readers will form an attitude toward you and your company based on the manner in which you come across in your writing. They will respond not only to what you say but to how you say it.

Let's consider Nan Foster's goals in writing to Steve Gant. After Nan had talked to Steve at the trade show, she immediately decided a letter was in order. As marketing representative for a wood products manufacturer, Nan knew how important it was to reestablish the good image of her company in the eyes of Steve, buyer for Komfort, a bedroom furniture maker. At the show Nan asked Steve why he had stopped ordering from her. He explained that last year's orders were shipped late, so he took his business elsewhere.

But Nan was sure Steve had his facts confused. She explained her writing process to us in this way:

> I first looked up the shipping records to check my hunch. I was right. We hadn't shipped Steve's order late at all. I wanted to write the letter to show Steve he was wrong about late shipping. Not to say "you're wrong!" but to let him know our service *is* good.

Like most letter writers, Nan knew that her letter would have to convey information—in her case, the dates that Steve's orders were shipped. But the purpose of Nan's letter was not just to convey information. She wanted to encourage Steve to have a positive attitude toward her and her company. She wanted to demonstrate that she could serve his needs promptly and courteously. In other words, Nan wanted to convey the "service attitude" so essential to effective business.

ASSESSING THE READER

Since you write business letters to get readers to act or to encourage them to have a positive attitude, it stands to reason that you will have to have good rapport with them. To establish this rapport, you have to show careful consideration for your readers' needs and interests. After all, if you want people to do something or to think well of you, you can expect them to want some reason for doing so. The more you can relate your letter to the readers' concerns and interests, the more likely your letter will be received favorably.

Nan Foster, for example, told us that when she wrote, it was essential that she imagine her reader: "To figure out how to get my message across, I have a picture in my mind of who I am writing to." In explaining how she wrote to Steve, Nan told us that she kept Steve's concerns constantly in mind:

> I know I can serve Steve at least as well as our competitors, and probably better. Now, I know Steve's an easygoing guy, but he definitely likes to make up his mind for himself, and to take his time. So in my letter I did not want to come across with a big sales pitch. I felt I should be as no-nonsense as possible. Just give Steve the facts and let him decide for himself who he should be doing business with. I would just remind him I'm still around to help him get what he needs on time.

GATHERING INFORMATION, GENERATING IDEAS, AND ORGANIZING: THE RTA FORMULA

Most of your business correspondence will not demand elaborate information gathering for you to know what to say. Frequently, the information required for your questions or responses will be at your fingertips or will require only a quick look in the files. All Nan Foster had to do, for example, was to check her files to see when Steve's orders had been shipped.

But since the goal of business letters is not only to do business but also to create a positive attitude, writers need to generate ideas that will influence the reader's attitude. For example, when Nan thought about her letter, she knew she should not only tell Steve about the dates of his order. She should also show him that doing business with her would make his job easier. Nan wanted her letter not just to include information on his order but also to reinforce the idea that she could be very helpful to Steve in specific ways.

While you might have the information you want to include in your letter ready at your fingertips, frequently you will need to generate ideas that will help you show the connection between your goals and your reader's needs.

Because the writer's goals and the reader's needs are the major concern in almost any letter situation, training programs have traditionally encouraged business writers to use a "formula" to help bring together their goals and those of their readers. One such formula is **RTA**—**R**apport, **T**hinking, **A**ction and Attitude. Adapted from formulas long used by writers of sales letters, RTA can help you build a bridge between yourself and your reader. RTA not only helps generate ideas for your letters, but it also helps organize the letter.

Using the RTA Formula

RTA is based on the observation that good business letters have a three-part structure. The first paragraph *establishes rapport between the writer and the reader* by focusing on the reader's interests and concerns. The middle paragraphs build a bridge between writer and reader by providing information that will *influence the reader's thinking* about the connection between the reader's concerns and the writer's. And finally, the last paragraph *encourages the reader to take action and to have a positive attitude*.

If you already know what you want to say in your letter, the RTA formula can help you organize your ideas into a three-part structure. But much more than that, RTA can help you figure out what you want to say. RTA reminds you to generate ideas that will establish rapport with your reader, that will influence your reader's thinking, and that will encourage your reader to act and to have a positive attitude.

A seasoned letter writer, Nan Foster instinctively followed the RTA pattern when she wrote to Steve Gant. We asked her to comment on how she produced the letter that she sent off to Steve.

Establish Rapport: How did I get started? In this situation it was easy since I had just seen Steve. I just wrote what I might have said to him if I ran into him. I reminded him about the show and brought up the subject we talked about. Then I gave him the information I had found.

Dear Steve:

I enjoyed meeting with you at the Louisville Show. Although I am disappointed to find that you've changed sources on the Early American drawer pull, the attached documentation will recap our record of the service situation in 199__.

Influence Thinking: Of course before I sat down to write I had looked up the shipping records to verify my hunch. We hadn't shipped Steve's order late at all. I was hoping this information would make Steve change his mind and buy from us again, but obviously I wasn't going to push him.

We sold only two (2) orders to Komfort in 199_. We received orders #30529 and #30530 on June 16, 199_.

- #30529 was wanted on 9-17-9_, but we acknowledged to ship on 9-21-9_ and shipped on 9-18-9_. (Our lead time at that point was 12 weeks. We sent order acknowledgment copies to Komfort.)
- #30530 was wanted on 10-17-9_ and it was shipped on 9-28-9_.

Obviously, this is "water over the dam," but I did want to review the problem to satisfy your curiosity.

Motivate Action and Attitude: There was just one main message I was trying to get across to Steve: "We want your business and can give you excellent service." In the end, I put my sales rep in touch with him because I figured, well, just maybe Steve would feel like he was a little unfair to us; just maybe he would like to make up with an order. I wanted to make that just as easy as possible.

Steve, we would like to sell to you again. Whether it is a machine-highlighted part or a hand-buffed item, we can be competitive in price and service. Our sales representative in Los Angeles is Rick Henson. He will contact you in the next few days to discuss your future direction on drawer pulls.

Again, thanks for stopping at the show, and please contact me if I can ever be of help.

As a veteran business writer, Nan uses the RTA pattern instinctively to show her reader she is there to fill his needs. Now let's look at how RTA can help you generate and organize ideas for your letters.

ESTABLISHING RAPPORT WITH YOUR READER

Because readers are busy, they need immediately to be given some reason for reading on. If your first sentences establish rapport between yourself and the reader, the reader will be drawn to listen further to what you have to say. The exact way you establish rapport will depend on your relationship with the reader and your reason for writing, but in all cases the key is to focus on the reader's needs and interests. Showing concern from the start tells readers that you have not taken up their time thoughtlessly or merely for your own interests. Nan, for example, gained Steve's interest by telling him of the good feelings she had had in seeing him again: "I enjoyed meeting with you at the Louisville Show."

If you have trouble thinking of ways to establish rapport with your reader, here are some ideas you can consider.

Respond Immediately to the Issue of the Letter You Are Answering. People who have taken the time to write to you are interested in something you have to offer. Open your letter with a statement that responds to their reason for writing. Answer their questions, tell them how you have followed up on their request, acknowledge their problem or tell them that you need more information. Beware, however, of the humdrum opening, "Referring to your letter of August such-and-such regarding such-and-such." You are not a letter talking to another letter but a person talking to another person. Would you open a conversation by saying, "regarding our conversation of December such-and-such"? A letter must take the place of a direct conversation, so do not place artificial barriers between yourself and your reader.

Consider how each of these openings responds to the concerns of a person:

You can expect twelve twin gaslight fixtures (#M6986) that you ordered to arrive by April 18. They were shipped by UPS this morning.

Yes, children are permitted to use the pool areas in our adult apartment complex as long as they are accompanied by adults. Pool hours are 9 A.M. to 9 P.M. except for Saturday nights when the pool may be rented for private parties.

When you expressed concern that our sales reps have not been calling on your store, we immediately investigated the matter.

We will be happy to replace the gross of white marble tile we sent you. Just let us know whether you want ebony or moss green.

Raise an Issue of Mutual Concern. By raising an issue of concern to both yourself and the reader, you demonstrate that you have shared values.

As you know, last year's bumper crop was no blessing to the small farmer. Our local cooperatives have been able to do only so much. It is now time to lobby at the state level.

You and I both realize there is no magic or gimmick to collecting past due receivables. It's done through persistence, timing, and hard work, with a little luck thrown in.

State Your Appreciation. Thank your readers as a way of letting them know that you appreciate their taking the time to write to you. Such acknowledgment will put them in a frame of mind to read further.

> Thank you for your letter describing how much you have appreciated our services. Your generous praise makes us want to do even better.

> Thanks for sending us so promptly the color samples that we requested. We were able to order just what we needed in time for our opening.

> We appreciated your letting us know that delivery of the equipment we ordered from you would be late.

Use the Name of a Mutual Friend or Acquaintance. Referring to a mutual friend links you immediately to your readers. Sharing acquaintances also suggests that you and your readers may have common interests or values on which you can base a solid business association.

> Margaret Morrell told me about your interest in participating in money funds.

> Bow Lowery praised your talk on econometric modeling. He said that you have a unique talent for making abstract issues vivid and clear.

> While I was visiting your Toledo plant last week, I had a chance to meet with your purchasing agent, Charlene Gondolfo. She suggested that I write to you about how our line of drill-bits could solve a problem your Toledo plant is having with its presses.

Ask a Question. Asking a question prompts your readers to think about an answer and thus engages them in responding to your message.

> Have you forgotten our bill? Your account is past due.

> Can you tell us when you expect to ship the hair dryers we ordered (Invoice #7936)?

Try using **rhetorical questions.** These are questions to which you already know the reader's answer. Asking a rhetorical question can gain a reader's interest because the question establishes a common ground. As the reader silently answers your question, you can show that you and the reader agree on the answer.

> After years of being misused, does the word "quality" mean anything?

The writer of this sentence knows readers will answer "probably not," and then goes on to show why, for the writer's product, "quality" does mean something. Consider another example:

> How many times have you spent your entire lunch hour waiting to be served?

The answer, the writer knows, is "too many times." The writer can then offer a solution to this problem.

Suggest How Your Reader Will Benefit.   Just as you need a purpose for writing, readers need a purpose for reading. An opening sentence that tells readers how they might gain by what you have to say to them will encourage them to read on.

> The Securities and Exchange Commission has just issued a ruling that can save you thousands of dollars in broker's fees. That is why I am writing to you.

> We can reduce your heating and air-conditioning costs by 15 percent—if not, our service will cost you nothing.

> To ensure that copies of your company's annual report will be printed in time for your stockholders' meeting, please make sure the camera-ready copy you are preparing meets the following specifications.

> Please accept with our compliments the enclosed tickets to the 92nd Seattle Home and Garden Show.

INFLUENCING YOUR READER'S THINKING

Your first paragraph establishes rapport with the reader. It is usually short and makes a simple statement. But the goal of your letter is to get the reader to act and to have a positive attitude. To encourage the reader to go along with you, the body of your letter needs to provide information. Since readers will want to know how acting in response to your encouragement will satisfy their own goals and desires, your letter must provide readily understandable information that will influence them positively.

When Nan Foster wanted to show Steve Gant that her company did not ship his orders late, she provided evidence: "the attached document will recap our record of the service situation in 198—."

In your letters, the kind of information you provide to influence thinking will depend on the specific situation. The following three chapters offer many possibilities for gathering information and generating ideas important to common business letters, such as orders, requests, sales, and goodwill letters. Here we will discuss how to organize that information effectively.

THE RANDOM HOUSE GUIDE TO BUSINESS WRITING

Business letters are often so short that the information required to influence the reader's thinking may be quite easy to organize. Nan Foster's explanation, for example, required only seven sentences of information besides her opening and closing paragraphs. Longer letters, however, can be more challenging. In either case, however, you must be concerned not only with the logical order of the information you present but also with the psychological order.

Logical Order. Using the grouping and ordering techniques and the analysis tree introduced in Chapter 2 can help you logically organize letters that must contain a great deal of information. Consider the example of Pat Kirwin, president of Planned Music, Inc., a company that provides background music and installs speakers and other components of sound systems. News of two recent tragic fires in high-rise buildings made Pat decide that now was the time to point out to potential customers how valuable a good sound system would be in case of a fire in their buildings. He knew that by referring to these recent fires, he could gain interest in the opening of his letter. Then he wanted to make several points. Figure 4.2 shows what he jotted down.

Since Pat was going to gain interest by highlighting a problem—the recent fires in high-rise buildings—he could see that a problem/solution structure would work for his letter. He tried grouping all his points under problem/solution headings.

Figure 4.2

PAT'S NOTES

- Sound systems essential to good evacuation
- especially high rises
- Work with major building owners — Sheraton, Motorists Mutual
- Few buildings have speakers in stairwells, essential to good evacuation
- We are knowledgeable
- Been in business 30 years
- No charge for the initial consultation and survey

THE BASICS OF BUSINESS LETTERS

Major Idea: Use our sound systems to solve evacuation
I. *Problem:* Deaths from fires
II. *Solution:* Good sound system
   A. Are working with several building owners
   B. Are knowledgeable
   C. In business 30 years
   D. Need sound in stairwell
   E. No charge for initial consultation

From this initial grouping, Pat could see that his letter was focused much more on the solution than on the problem. This is what he wanted; but under the solution, his ideas needed to be better grouped and organized. He could see he wanted to emphasize that *his company* was the best solution. He further grouped his ideas this way:

I. *Problem:* Deaths from fires
II. *Solution:* Good sound evacuation systems
   A. My company can provide it because we
      1. Are working with several major high-rises
      2. Have been in business 30 years
      3. Discovered need for sound in stairwells
   B. It is not too difficult—we don't charge for initial consultation

Pat might also have used an analysis tree to help him organize his letter (see Figure 4.3).

Figure 4.3

PAT'S ANALYSIS TREE

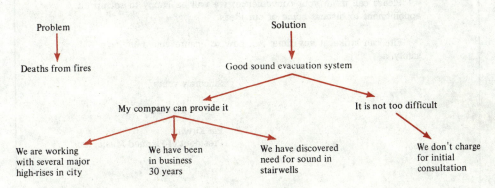

Satisfied that he had answered his questions about organization, Pat, after a couple of drafts, produced the letter shown in Figure 4.4.

Figure 4.4

PAT'S LETTER

Dear [name of potential customer]:

Fire strikes without warning! Are you prepared with a safe evacuation system?

The recent wave of fires and deaths in high rise buildings around the country has been a source of concern for owners and tenants alike. To ensure that you have a good fire and safety evacuation system, a reliable communication system is essential.

We have been in the communications business in Columbus for 30 years assisting many industrial and business firms in handling their communications problems. We can give you the sound system you need.

At present, we are working with several high-rise building owners in the downtown area, including the Sheraton Hotel and Motorists Mutual Insurance Company, in providing systems to evacuate tenants in case of fire or other disasters.

We have learned that, in evacuating people, the stairwell is one building area that especially needs sound coverage. Most buildings we have inspected appear to have little or no coverage in this area.

There is no charge or obligation on your part for consultation and survey activities. You may be surprised at how reasonable the investment is for a good fire and safety system.

Please call us at your convenience; we will be happy to set up an appointment to discuss some of our ideas.

Fire can strike at any time. Act now to ensure your building's safety.

Sincerely yours,

Pat Kirwin

Pat Kirwin
President of Planned Music, Inc.

Psychological Order. Readers respond to information not just with their logical minds but also with their psychological attitudes and emotions. Therefore, besides ordering your information logically, attend to your message's psychological order. Imagine how your reader will respond emotionally to each element of your message; then order those elements in the most psychologically appealing way. For example, since Pat Kirwin knew that his readers would first need to feel the threat of fire before they could become interested in his company, he began his letter by mentioning the recent fires and only later explained the service his company could provide.

Now consider the letter Sheila Levinson had to write. As consumer relations agent for Baby's World, a baby crib manufacturer, Sheila had to respond to a letter from Mrs. Johnson. Mrs. Johnson had recently learned that formaldehyde is used in making baby furniture and that it can cause serious allergic reactions. She wanted to know whether the crib she had purchased would be safe for her baby.

Sheila had just returned from a Juvenile Products Manufacturers conference, where she had obtained current information about formaldehyde from the Food and Drug Administration and the Consumer Product Safety Commission. Concerned to provide Mrs. Johnson with the factual information, Sheila first wrote this draft of the letter she wanted to send to Mrs. Johnson:

DRAFT 1

Dear Mrs. Johnson:

We use low-emitting urea formaldehyde (UH) particle board and plywood in the baby cribs we manufacture. Formaldehyde emission from particle board and plywood is currently a subject of concern at the Consumer Product Safety Commission. At present there is no consensus about the effects of inhalation nor about standard testing procedures. But any product emitting fewer than .03 parts/millions is considered within currently acceptable levels. Urea formaldehyde is well within the safety limits (.005/parts/million).

Because we use urea formaldehyde, which has been approved by the FDA, we can assure you that your baby's crib is safe.

In reviewing her draft, Sheila could see she had included all the information Mrs. Johnson would need to feel secure with her new crib. But Sheila could also see that Mrs. Johnson would have to read through the entire letter before she would be assured of her baby's safety. Sheila reorganized her letter so that she would reassure Mrs.

Johnson immediately and only then give her the technical information that explains why the crib is safe:

DRAFT 2

> Dear Mrs. Johnson:
>
> You can be assured that your child sleeps in a safe crib because we use only low-emitting urea formaldehyde (UH) in the cribs we manufacture.
>
> The Food and Drug Administration has approved urea formaldehyde because it falls well within the currently acceptable emission levels of .03 parts/million.
>
> Formaldehyde emission from particle board and plywood is currently a subject of concern at the Consumer Product Safety Commission. At present no agreement exists about the effects of inhalation or about standard testing procedures. But since urea formaldehyde emits only .005 parts/million, the FDA assures us that it's a safe substance.
>
> We are happy to reassure you that your crib is safe. Baby's World crib and all Baby's World products are designed for the comfort and safety of your child.

In her second draft Sheila not only provided her reader with information in a logical order but she also attended to the psychological order—by being aware of her reader's major concern and addressing that concern immediately.

MOTIVATING ACTION AND A POSITIVE ATTITUDE

The ending of a letter, like the beginning, is a position of emphasis. You can take advantage of that fact to reinforce your main message. Here you will want to motivate your readers to take the action you desire and promote their positive attitude toward you and your company.

Trying to reestablish Steve's good opinion of her company, Nan Foster closed her letter to him by making action easy, by expressing appreciation, and by offering to help in the future:

> Our sales representative . . . will contact you in the next few days to discuss your future direction on drawer pulls.
>
> Again, thanks for stopping at the show, and please contact me if I can ever be of help.

The following are two ways to motivate action and a positive attitude in your closing sentences.

THE BASICS OF BUSINESS LETTERS   119

State the Desired Action and Indicate How the Reader Will Benefit. These closing paragraphs encourage action by explaining the desired action and making clear how the reader will benefit by acting:

Fill in and return the enclosed card, Mr. English, and your reservation at the Regent will be assured.

If you'll just let me know what time would be most suitable for meeting next week, I'm sure we can settle your account to our mutual satisfaction. To set up an appointment, please call me at (501) 555-1895.

Tired tires are too dangerous to ignore. Why not stop in tomorrow and let us look at them?

To cancel your bill, we need the airline tickets we sent you. Please give me a call indicating whether we can pick up the tickets or whether you prefer to mail them to us.

Reinforce the Positive Relationship. These closing paragraphs encourage a positive attitude by expressing thanks for a past relationship and by looking toward a positive relationship in the future:

With you as our director, we know our drive will be a great success.

By honoring our original contract, you are assured of the best system available.

Thank you for your generous contribution to the success of our program. I hope we might have opportunities to work together again in our career awareness and development efforts.

Notice that none of these letters relies on the tired phrase, "If I can be of further help, do not hesitate to contact me." By telling your reader not to hesitate before contacting you, you imply you are so important that ordinarily the reader should hesitate. You should express your availability in writing as you would in speaking: "If I can be of further help, please give me a call."

The RTA formula—establish rapport, influence thinking, motivate action and attitude—helps business writers take into account the needs of the reader at the same time that they take care of business. But we want to emphasize that the formula is not a hard and fast rule. If you wrote letters by rules, all your letters would end up sounding exactly the same. In fact, what will make your letters most effective is letting a sense of yourself come through. As manager of a staff of writers in a consumer relations department, Anita Davis makes this clear:

> We have these seminars and we take a letter and say, how would you answer it? It's subject to interpretation. Five different people will answer the letter five different ways. Yet as long as the overall effect is correct, they can be very good responses.

By using RTA to help you generate and organize your ideas for letters, you will let a sense of yourself come through. The following sections, which discuss writing a draft, revising, and establishing a format, will also help you achieve an appropriate tone, style, and appearance for your business letters.

WRITING A DRAFT

Most business people who write a lot have their letter writing down to a routine. They are comfortable writing at certain times of the day and with certain props—be it the cup of coffee, the quiet office in the late evening, the dictating machine, or the word processor. Because business letters are frequently short, some business writers are eventually able to compose their routine correspondence with just one draft. But more challenging letters can take even the most experienced business writer several drafts.

Whether your letter is routine or challenging, have your goal clearly in mind before you write. Ask yourself what you are trying to accomplish with the letter and how it relates to the reader. Have the information you need at hand. If you are responding to a letter, have that letter in front of you. If you will need to refer to notes from conversations, to invoice numbers, or to other written materials, have those on hand. You will also want to arrange your materials and have some idea of what you will say and the order in which you will say it. The RTA formula can help you here.

Once you have your goal and reader in mind and the necessary information at your side, write, type, or dictate your draft. To help yourself with your draft, try to imagine what you would say if you were speaking face-to-face with that person. How would you want to sound? How would your listener respond?

If you feel stuck and don't quite know how to start, do some nonstop writing, talk out your ideas on a tape, or list your thoughts. At this stage, you should just get what is in your mind onto the page or into the word processor in any form you can. You can then rethink your goal, your reader, or your organization and begin rewriting the draft.

If you use a word processor for your correspondence, you will be able to make changes in your draft as you go along. But if you are dictating, your draft must make sense the first time through. This is why many business people feel uneasy with dictating until they have had considerable practice. Dictating routine correspondence—short letters on familiar subjects—is a good activity to begin building your skill. Then you can move on to routine short reports and to longer letters and memos. Some executives eventually become comfortable dictating whole sections of major reports, using the transcript as their first draft.

Using Dictation

It is especially important that you become proficient at using dictating equipment to generate drafts and even final copy of your business writing. Dictating over the telephone to machines connected to word-processing systems is beginning to dominate communications in government, business, industry, and the professions.[1] Although it is rare for business people to have a personal secretary who will take dictation, almost any business person can have access to electronic dictation equipment from which a secretary can transcribe letters, memos, and reports.

Recent research suggests that a majority of companies are increasing their use of dictation equipment, for the simple reason that dictation saves time—"up to 60% for short or routine messages, and somewhat less for long or complex messages."[2] And yet many business people who have access to dictation equipment don't use it. They feel it goes against the grain of their writing process. However, the writing process you use for writing or typing drafts can, with practice, be adapted to dictating.

As compared with writing or typing your own drafts, **three major differences characterize dictating:**

1. *You must provide special instructions at the beginning, and any special spellings or format as you go along*. The transcriber, perhaps a secretary in the word-processing pool, will not have the leisure to listen through your whole tape to find out your directions for how the message is to be typed. If you add changes at the end, attach written instructions about how these are to be included in the final copy.

2. *While dictating, you can review what you have written only by playing back the tape*. This makes reviewing and revising what you have written somewhat more difficult than when you work in longhand or with a computer print-out. If you are dictating a draft rather than a final copy, however, you can review the draft visually—but only after it comes back from the typist.

3. *Good dictating demands expert planning*. Because the transcriber must be provided with directions in advance, and because it is less easy to review and revise what you have written, people who dictate well always precede a dictating session with extensive planning. Before they begin to dictate, they know the purpose of their message, the order and detail of the content, and any special instructions the typist may need. They write detailed or key-word outlines, or at least make mental notes, to guide them through the dictation.

Even with detailed advance planning, however, people who dictate well do not start a tape and keep talking until the message is finished. On the contrary, many of them pause as they tape—as often as every six or seven words—to plan what they want to say next. They sometimes interrupt to make corrections, to clarify phrasing, or to give directions to the transcriber. Some make voice-over corrections on the tape, that is, they record changes over the original.

Initially, use dictation equipment to write rough drafts of letters and other simple messages. Later, you should feel comfortable enough to dictate final copy for routine letters and messages, and to dictate rough drafts of long, complex, or difficult messages. Figure 4.5 offers guidelines for effective dictation.

Figure 4.5

GUIDELINES FOR DICTATING

1. Plan the content of each letter before you begin. This includes determining your purpose, gathering information and generating ideas, selecting and organizing material, and choosing format and style. Write notes you can use during the dictating session.

2. Before you start the letter, give all special instructions: the format, approximate length, the number of copies, persons to whom copies must be sent, whether this is to be a rough draft or final copy, mailing instructions, and the like.

3. Speak clearly and at an even pace. Turn off the "Dictate" switch as often as necessary, for as long as necessary, to give yourself time to plan your sentences.

4. Spell proper names, unusual terms, and words that have more than one spelling. Dictate unusual punctuation. Indicate when a paragraph ends.

5. Play back your dictation occasionally. Are you coming across clearly and distinctly? Do your sentences need editing?

6. At the end of the dictating session, express appreciation to the transcriber.

7. When turning the tape over to the transcriber, include with it the letter you are answering or any other materials that may help in transcription. If you have dictated afterthoughts or changes at the end of the tape, provide written instructions about how these are to be included in the final copy.

8. Read and correct everything that comes back from the transcriber. Errors can be embarrassing and costly. You, not the transcriber, are responsible for any letters that are sent out over your signature.

THE BASICS OF BUSINESS LETTERS   123

SAMPLE DICTATION

Below is a transcription of how you might sound if you had prepared a dictation for an operator in your company's word-processing center. Your instructions to the person who will transcribe the letter are *in italics*. The letter itself is in regular typeface.

> *Operator, this is Elaine Sullivan in Sales, extension 4535. This is my standard telephone follow-up letter. Please make one file copy. Address the letter to* Mr. Partlow *P-a-r-t-l-o-w at* 49 Page Avenue, Kansas City, Missouri 64116. Dear Mr. Partlow *comma, use a comma and not a colon here. Paragraph.* At the Kansas City office of John Tucker, we offer a service that has helped many other successful professionals solve problems arising from today's tax and economic environment. *Paragraph.* The cost of this service is about thirty minutes *spell out thirty* of your time. *Paragraph.* I look forward to acquainting you with this service and will call in a few days to arrange a convenient time for a meeting. Sincerely, Elaine M. Sullivan. CLU, General Agent. *Enclosure:* Tucker Financial Services Brochure. *Operator, please include a brochure and return envelope. I'll be out of the office on Friday so please send this to my office for signature by Thursday. Thank you.*

In addition to the guidelines for dictating letters, you may also find it useful to take into account several myths about dictating (see Figure 4.6).

Figure 4.6

MYTHS AND FACTS ABOUT DICTATING

Myth no. 1	When using dictation equipment, one must talk continuously.
Fact:	Not true. When using desktop or portable units, one may turn off the "dictate" switch as often as necessary, for as long as necessary. The dictator may stop in mid-sentence and complete the sentence a week later and no one will be the wiser. Voice-activated telephone dictation systems allow varying periods of silence before the line is put on "hold." The length of these periods is determined by the purchasing firm and is part of the overall design which is tailored by the manufacturer to fit its needs.
Myth no. 2	Once dictated, words cannot be recalled and remain part of the text forever.
Fact:	Not true. Making changes or corrections is a simple procedure on most modern dictation equipment, once the proper techniques have been mastered. Training is essential in this area.

(continued)

THE RANDOM HOUSE GUIDE TO BUSINESS WRITING

(MYTHS AND FACTS ABOUT DICTATING continued)

Myth no. 3	It is not necessary to make corrections during dictation if transcription is done on word-processing equipment.
Fact:	Not true. Although correcting errors is easier on word-processing equipment than on standard typewriters, it is still time-consuming and thus costly to the company. Efficient transcription can only result from efficient dictation. The majority of "transcribing errors" are actually "dictating errors."
Myth no. 4	It is not feasible for those preparing lengthy or highly technical material to use dictation equipment.
Fact:	Not true. Countless writers in this category who have completed the necessary training dictate such material as a matter of course and report this method more effective than handwriting.
Myth no. 5	All dictated material must be rough drafted and retyped; it therefore makes better sense to correct the typed drafts than to make corrections during dictation.
Fact:	Not true. Once training has been completed and the dictator has acquired and practiced the proper techniques, only lengthy or technical material need be rough drafted. The goal of dictation training is final copy first time around. On occasion, of course, and particularly during the early weeks of the dictating experience, the writer may wish to change the final copy. This would be the exception, however, not the rule.

Source: Reprinted from the September 1979 issue of *Personnel Administrator*, copyright 1979, the American Society for Personnel Administration, 606 North Washington Street, Alexandria, Virginia 22314

REVISING THE BUSINESS LETTER: HOLISTIC AND LOCAL REVISION

When looking at the draft of your business letter, read to revise first holistically and then locally.

Revising Holistically: The RTA Formula

For holistic revision, the following summary of the RTA formula can serve as a checklist:

1. Do you know what you want this letter to accomplish? What action you want the reader to take? How you want to affect the reader's attitude?

2. *Establish Rapport:* Does your letter begin by making a connection to the reader? Do you show concern for the reader's needs and interests?

3. *Influence Thinking:*
   - Do you understand the reader's concerns and use information to build a bridge between the reader's concerns and your own?
   - If your letter covers a lot of information, is that information organized logically? Is it organized to take into account the psychological needs of the reader?

4. *Action and Attitude:*
   - Do your final sentences make clear the action you want your reader to take?
   - Do they indicate how the reader will benefit?
   - Do you reinforce positive relations with the reader and point to continued positive relations in the future?

Local Revision: A Friendly Tone and a Conversational Style

Once you have reviewed your letter holistically, read the letter for local revisions—revisions at the paragraph and sentence level. Remember that readers of business letters will be responding not only to what you say but also to how you say it. If your letters maintain a friendly tone and a conversational style, they can go far toward creating an image of your company as one with which people will want to do business. The **tone** of your letter is the attitude toward your reader and your subject that you convey in your writing. Although the style you use helps to create your tone, the term **style** here refers more specifically to the types of sentences and words you use.

Look at the letters in Figures 4.7 and 4.8, and try to analyze how their tone, and style differ from that of writing you might come across elsewhere—for example, in a term paper or a textbook. Compared with the impersonal tone and formal style of most term papers and textbooks, these letters come across as friendly and conversational. Textbooks store information for thousands of readers to refer to at any time and cover an extensive amount of material. In contrast, a letter is a short exchange between two people, so it should be less formal and more conversational. Even if you are writing to a large corporation or you are writing a form letter that will be read by hundreds of people, you want to create the impression that you are talking to each reader individually, one-to-one. Your reader wants to feel that he or she is being addressed personally.

When you write a letter, then, you want to come across well—just as when you meet a person face-to-face. You want to be friendly, courteous, and sympathetic. You want yourself to come through. In the words of Sarah Frank, director of Public Television Sales for Time Life "When I sit down to write, I want the gestures of my hands, the smile on my face, and my tone of voice to get translated onto the page."

126 THE RANDOM HOUSE GUIDE TO BUSINESS WRITING

Figure 4.7

SAMPLE BUSINESS LETTER 1

Midwest Lighting Co.
137 Highcrest Road
St. Paul, MN 55113
November 6, 199_

Mr. Henry Fleishmann
Rural Rt. 2
Iowa City, IA 52240

Dear Mr. Fleishmann:

You will be glad to know that your 5052 parts will be shipped to you on November 20.

Our shipment would have gone out earlier, but the chromium shortage has been forcing delays everywhere in the industry. We can report, however, that all our deliveries are now going out on schedule.

We look forward to supplying you with the materials you need when you need them.

Sincerely yours,

Ralph Wasden

Ralph Wasden, Manager

RW/gh

Figure 4.8

SAMPLE BUSINESS LETTER 2

                                                        Garfield & Hayworth, Inc.
                                                        532 16th Street
                                                        Phoenix, AZ 85016
                                                        October 5, 199_

Ms. Ellen G. Poulson,
Franconia Chemical Corporation
9 Burton Road
Dallas, TX 75227

Dear Ms. Poulson:

    To serve you better, our firm has appointed Dr. Elizabeth Genovese, a nationally recognized expert on energy and environmental issues, to our staff of consultants.

    Dr. Genovese's pioneering work in applying solar energy to the heating and air conditioning of large factories has been much publicized in the popular press as well as in the learned journals. We are enclosing a recent interview by Stanford Research Associates in which Dr. Genovese outlines her most recent work.

    Let us know whether we can extend our service to your company by offering to you Dr. Genovese's expertise. She would be happy to answer your questions, especially as to how solar energy can lower your overhead and increase profits. We think you will find her explanations exceptionally clear and relevant to your situation.

                                                          Yours truly,

                                                          Jake Garfield

                                                          Jake Garfield, Senior
                                                          Partner

JG/rs
enc.

When people sit down to write, many of them automatically become stiff and formal. To ensure a friendly tone and conversational style in your letters, keep in mind the person you are writing to. How would this person respond to what you have to say? While your exact tone and style will depend on you, your purpose, and your reader, we offer next some suggestions for ensuring that you have the tone and style you want in your correspondence.

There are many ways to dictate letters and reports.

A FRIENDLY TONE

When you talk, your tone of voice can tell your listener a great deal about your attitude—for example, whether you are bored or enthusiastic about the subject, and whether you feel distant or friendly toward the listener. Your writing also conveys a tone that allows readers to recognize how you feel about your exchange with them. Face-to-face, you can come across as a friendly person if you are courteous and sympathetic with your listeners, if you can put yourself in their shoes, and if you can make the best of a situation. Here are some ways you can achieve the same effect in letters.

Use a "You Attitude" In a friendly, person-to-person exchange there is a balance between your concerns and those of your friends. So too in a letter. A balance often shows up in a balance of pronouns. If your letter is full of "I-me-mine" or "we-us-ours" and is devoid of "you-your," chances are good you are focusing on your own concerns and neglecting those of your reader. This passage reveals a writer concerned primarily with his own situation, not with readers:

DRAFT

We are glad we can now ship our 5052 parts. We look forward to continuing to receive your orders and to getting them out on schedule.

By contrast, the following revision reveals a writer concerned with what the reader wants to know:

REVISION

You will be glad to know that your 5052 parts will be shipped to you on November 20th. We look forward to supplying you with the equipment you need when you need it.

As this example illustrates, the "you-attitude" does not mean you must avoid "I" and "we" altogether. On the contrary, too much "you" and "your" can make you sound insincere. Strike a considerate balance between your goals and your reader's.

Emphasize Reader Benefits. You demonstrate your concern for your readers by stressing what they will gain by taking in your information. This paragraph focuses primarily on the writer's situation:

DRAFT

>Let us know whether we can extend Dr. Genovese's services to your company. Her expertise considerably enhances the extent of our consulting services. We are now informed of the latest advances in solar energy research. We would be glad to answer any questions you might have.

The following revision focuses on how the reader would benefit:

REVISION

>Let us know whether we can extend Dr. Genovese's services to your company. She would be happy to answer your questions, especially as to how solar energy can lower your overhead and increase profits. We think you will find her explanations exceptionally clear and relevant to your situation.

Think Positively. When we reviewed the correspondence of a sales manager in a large retail firm, we were especially struck by the enthusiasm that came across in his letters. He explained it this way:

>I want to communicate that I want to do business with the person. If I'm aggressive and affirmative about where my company's going, I think most firms appreciate that. I want to communicate my energy, my desire to "grow the business."

Your letters should reflect your energy and your confidence in your abilities. To ensure a positive tone in your letters, check to see that you say things positively. For example, in Figure 4.9, phrases in the left-hand column create a negative image; those in the right-hand column put the information positively. Also, avoid asking a question if it invites the reader to think of a negative response:

>Why not return the enclosed card with your check today?
>[Possible response: because it's the end of the month and my bank account is empty.]

>Just return the enclosed card with your check today.

THE BASICS OF BUSINESS LETTERS

Avoid stating things tentatively. Instead, assume your offer or explanation has been clear, and be open for further questions. Among the tentative phrases to avoid are the following:

> If you'd like
> If we can help
> I trust you will have no further questions
> We hope you will understand

Figure 4.9
SAYING THINGS POSITIVELY

Instead of	Try
Our metal coating will not burn, scorch, or peel.	Our metal coatings are bonded permanently no matter how severe the climate.
Confirming your reservation will ensure against cancellations and delays.	Confirm your reservation before May 15 to ensure your place and on-time departure.
We cannot grant you credit.	By paying cash, you take advantage of our 10 percent discount.
Computer time is not available to individual accounts.	Have your department head fill out an authorization and we can schedule you for this Wednesday.
We don't offer 6-month leases.	We offer 1-year leases. Otherwise we rent on a monthly basis.

A CONVERSATIONAL STYLE

Although you are not face-to-face with the person you are writing to, you nevertheless want your letters to imitate the spirit of friendly conversation. One way, as you have seen, is to show concern for the reader. Another way is to imitate the rhythm and language of conversation.

The Rhythm of Conversation—Short Paragraphs and Sentences. In a conversation, if one person talked nonstop, sentence after sentence, never pausing to allow listeners to react, you would think that person a boor. In letters, too, paragraphs that go on and on without a break sound pompous and self-important.

Letter paragraphs are usually no longer than three or four sentences, to give the reader frequent pauses to react to what you have to say. And just as the exchanges in opening and closing a conversation are brief, so too the first and last paragraphs of letters are brief, usually only one or two sentences.

The sentences of business letters also tend to be shorter than those of other kinds of writing, to ensure that they are easy to read. The average length of your sentences should be around seventeen to twenty words. But beware! Short sentences are not necessarily the most readable. In fact, a series of short, staccato sentences can be more abrasive and difficult than a series of long but well-constructed ones.

The best stylists use a variety of sentence lengths. They occasionally use very short sentences, when they want to create emphasis. They occasionally use long, carefully constructed sentences, when length may be the clearest way to convey the relationship of ideas.

Compare the following three versions of an excerpt from a letter requesting a favor. Which version do you think is the most effective?

SHORT SENTENCES

We are developing an education booklet. It is specifically for teen-agers. It is called, "What Young Adults Should Know About Drinking and Driving." This booklet is meant for kids. It should inform them about the detrimental effects alcohol can have on driving ability. It is also meant to discourage kids from driving after drinking.

May we ask for your comments? You are knowledgeable and experienced in this area. Therefore, your comments would be valuable. They would help us ensure accurate and authoritative information. This is important. We need this information before we publish the final version.

LONG SENTENCES

We are developing an education booklet specifically for teen-agers—"What Young Adults Should Know About Drinking and Driving"—which is meant to inform kids about the detrimental effects alcohol can have on driving ability, and to discourage them from driving after drinking.

Before we publish the final version, we invite your comments because you are knowledgeable and experienced in this area and your criticisms would help to ensure the most accurate and authoritative information possible.

A VARIETY OF SENTENCE LENGTHS

We are developing an education booklet specifically for teen-agers called "What Young Adults Should Know About Drinking and Driving." This booklet is meant to inform kids about the detrimental effects alcohol can have on driving ability, and to discourage them from driving after drinking.

THE BASICS OF BUSINESS LETTERS

May we ask for your comments? Because of your knowledge and experience in this area, your comments before we publish the final version would help to ensure the most accurate and authoritative information possible.

As you can see from these three versions, the same information can be conveyed in long or short sentences, but only a variety of sentence lengths makes letter writing sound natural and conversational.

The Language of Conversation—Words and Phrases. If you want to sound friendly, you will use the natural language of conversation. What impression do you get of the writer when you read these words:

DRAFT

Pursuant to your request and as per the attached agreement regarding your account, we regret to inform you that the termination of said account cannot be forestalled.

Can you visualize anyone actually saying these words? And yet some writers feel so uncomfortable composing a letter that they retreat behind a barricade of stock phrases and pretentious words and cease to sound like human beings. As banker Betsy Samuelson told us, "I don't have to use polysyllabic words like 'facilitate' and 'utilize' when I can say 'help' and 'use.' Why talk like a machine?" To project a confident, friendly image, use language that is straightforward, courteous, and respectful:

REVISION

We are sorry that we cannot extend your account.

For advice on avoiding clichés and stilted phrases in your letters, refer to the section in Chapter 3 entitled "Avoiding Needless Words" (pp. 77–80).

Although there is a limit to how familiar a business letter can be, even the judicious use of contractions is often desirable (although they are not used in formal letters):

We're refunding your payment and canceling the order.

He doesn't think that beginning new construction now is advisable.

If you'll mail us your check now, we can ensure that your credit rating remains strong.

It's a safer, more effective system for controlling smokestack emission.

As you revise and edit your business letters, check for a friendly tone and a conversational style. Anita Davis suggests what the final test should be:

> Before you sign the letter, if you wouldn't say it, don't send it. If you don't say it on the phone, don't say it in a letter. If you wouldn't say "It gives me great pleasure to have the opportunity to rectify blah, blah, blah," then don't write it!

THE FORMAT OF THE BUSINESS LETTER

The appearance of your letters creates a powerful impression even before the reader gets to your message. No matter how well written your message, if your letter is full of erasures and typos, or is off-center and oddly arranged, you will come across as amateurish and careless of the reader's regard. On the other hand, if your letter is neat, correct, and in proper format on good quality stationery, you give the impression of being an established and successful business person.

To create a professional impression, choose your letter format from among the four conventional business styles.

Four Styles for Letter Format

Business letters usually follow one of four formats:

1. Full block
2. Modified block
3. Semiblock
4. AMS simplified

Choose the format that conveys the impression you want your company to give.

All four of these formats, which are explained in the sections that follow, require paragraphs that are single-spaced, with a double space between paragraphs. The most common punctuation is a colon after the salutation and a comma after the complimentary close. But some business writers prefer **"open" punctuation,** which omits these two marks.

THE FULL BLOCK FORMAT

Figure 4.10 shows that letters in the **full block format** begin every line at the left margin. Except for the AMS simplified format, it is the most efficient to type, since it saves the typist the keystrokes required for indenting. If you want to come across as efficient and time-saving, use this format. But since it may appear lopsided to the left, compensate by designing your letterhead so that your firm's name and address appear to the right of center.

Figure 4.10

THE FULL BLOCK FORMAT

Spry INC.
1279 ORANGE AVENUE COSTA MESA CA 92627

June 16, 199_

Mr. Al Spitvak
Municipal Recycling Center
56 Stroughton Road
Madison, WI 53714-2941

Dear Mr. Spitvak:

This letter illustrates the full block letter style, one of the most efficient letter formats to type.

As you can see, every line begins at the left margin, so that the typist never has to use a keystroke to center the date, to indent a paragraph, or to present the closing and signature.

While this letter style is very efficient, some people find its appearance almost too businesslike. They think the style presents a visual impression of being lopsided to the left. Also, because paragraphs are not indented, if a letter goes to two or more pages, it is sometimes hard to tell whether a sentence beginning on the second page is part of the paragraph of the last page or the beginning of a new paragraph.

Nevertheless, because of its neat, businesslike appearance, and because it is efficient to type, this letter style is acceptable to many businesses.

(continued)

(THE FULL BLOCK FORMAT continued)

> Mr. Al Spitvak
> page 2
> June 16, 199_
>
> Notice, too, that this letter does not use "open" punctuation. The open style of punctuation omits the colon after the salutation and the comma after the closing. But most businesses prefer to use the more conventional punctuation requiring the colon and the comma.
>
> Sincerely,
>
> *Georgia Tate*
>
> Georgia Tate
> Marketing Analyst
>
> GT/snu

THE MODIFIED BLOCK FORMAT

The **modified block format** (shown in Figure 4.11) is now the most popular. The date, complimentary close, and signature begin to the right of center. (The typist can set a tab stop at the center of the page for these items.) All other sections begin at the left margin. This format presents a more balanced appearance than the full block.

THE SEMIBLOCK FORMAT

As shown in Figure 4.12, the **semiblock format** is exactly like the modified block except that paragraphs are indented. Because the semiblock format gives the reader more white space, does not skimp on keystrokes, and is the convention for nonbusiness letters, many readers consider this a less businesslike and more friendly style.

Figure 4.11

THE MODIFIED BLOCK FORMAT (IN TWO PAGES)

CALVERTS AND SONS
CONSTRUCTION

1830 LINCOLN ST DENVER CO. 80295

October 28, 199_

Mrs. Diana Greene
Manager—CAD Analysis
Toro Company
3542 Forrest Dr W
Minneapolis, MN 55423

Dear Mrs. Greene:

Subject: The Modified Block Letter

This modified block letter represents the letter format most frequently used in business. It appears more balanced than the full block format and more businesslike than the semiblock format illustrated in Figure 4.12.

In this format, all lines begin at the left margin except the date, complimentary close, and signature sections. These three sections begin to the right of center.

The most efficient way for the typist to line up the date, complimentary close, and signature sections is to set a tab stop at the center of the page. Then by hitting just one key, the tab, each section can be properly placed.

Some typists, to ensure that the date and the longest line of the signature section end exactly at the right margin, go to the trouble of backspacing from the right margin. But this method takes much more time than simply setting a tab stop, and the results are not necessarily any more attractive.

(continued)

[THE MODIFIED BLOCK FORMAT
(IN TWO PAGES) continued]

Mrs. Diana Greene
page 2
October 28, 199_

Notice that this letter also uses the optional subject line. The subject line acts like a heading in a report and conveys the gist of the letter. The subject line appears below the salutation and may be centered (as it is here), or it may be indented, or it may begin at the left margin. You also have the option of typing it out in all capital letters or underlining it, as here. Finally, you have the option of including the introductory word "subject" or leaving the word out.

Since this letter is longer than about 300 words, it requires two pages. The second page needs its own heading, beginning six spaces down from the top and consisting of the name of the addressee, the page number, and the date. (Not all companies, however, bother to include headings for additional pages.) Continue the letter two or three spaces below the heading.

Best regards,

Alvin Applebee

Alvin Applebee
Assistant Vice
President

AA/dk
cc: Harold Binder

Figure 4.12

THE SEMIBLOCK FORMAT

NHD MANUFACTURING, INC.
135 CATOMA ST. MONTGOMERY, ALABAMA 36195

April 24, 199—

Ms. Sophia Hoffman
Sr. Development Engineer
Engineering Development Laboratory
E. I. Thornberry Co.
Wilmington, DE 19864

Dear Sophia,

    Do you like your paragraphs indented? If so, use the semiblock format.

    Strictly speaking, when a letter is single-spaced with a double space between paragraphs, then indentations aren't necessary to identify the beginning of a new paragraph. However, since all other kinds of print media indent paragraphs, many people are used to seeing paragraphs indented and find this letter format pleasing. It allows the reader more white space and can be easier on the eye.

                                          Sincerely,

                                          Paula Washington

                                          Paula Washington
                                          Manager—Product
                                          Marketing

PW/kak
enc.

cc: Paula Stiffey

THE AMS SIMPLIFIED FORMAT

Recommended by the Administrative Management Society, the **AMS simplified format** (Figure 4.13), is the most efficient letter style, saving the typist about nineteen key-

Figure 4.13

THE AMS SIMPLIFIED FORMAT

ENGINEERING RESEARCH ASSOCIATES
412 SOUTH CAMERON ST.
HARRISBURG, PA 17101

June 9, 199_

Russell Dietrich
Comptroller
Edlesberg Associates
1200 Broad Street
Shreveport, LA 71106

THE SIMPLIFIED LETTER

Do you like this letter format, Mr. Dietrich? It is recommended by the Administrative Management Society because it saves typing time—about nineteen keystrokes per letter. It appears attractive and businesslike, and to some people it comes across as sounding more friendly than the more conventional letter styles.

Notice the features of this format:

- Full block form and open punctuation
- Salutation omitted; instead, the reader is addressed by name in the first sentence or very early in the first paragraph
- Subject line in all capitals, omitting the word "subject"
- Complimentary close omitted
- Signer's name and business title typed in all capitals four blank lines below the last line of the body of the letter, and signature directly above typed name.

While this letter format is the most efficient style for typing, many people choose not to use it because it is too unconventional and may

> Russell Dietrich
> page 2
> June 9, 199_
>
> seem unfriendly. They think readers could be annoyed by the omission of the salutation, even though the reader is mentioned within the first few lines of the letter. Mr. Dietrich, you will have to decide for yourself whether you think your readers would prefer this style.
>
> *Ralph Leger*
> RALPH LEGER, CHAIR, TECH CONFERENCE COMMITTEE '86
>
> RL/or
> enclosure

strokes. This format omits the salutation and instead introduces the letter with a subject line, typed in capitals but omitting the word "subject." (A more streamlined version omits even the subject line.) The reader's name appears somewhere early in the first paragraph. This format also omits the complimentary close and uses open punctuation.

Besides being very efficient, the simplified form has other advantages. If you are not sure of the addressee's name or title, this form, by omitting the salutation, enables you to avoid offending people with an inaccurate or inappropriate salutation. Also, many people find the tone of the simplified form more friendly, since it omits the conventional salutation and closing, and instead addresses the reader directly in the first paragraph.

But the simplified form has a disadvantage. Because it does not use the conventional letter parts, it may appear as unfriendly, distracting, or faddish to readers who expect letters to follow the conventions.

The Letter Parts

Regardless of format, most business letters have seven parts, as illustrated in Figure 4.14. In addition, some letters may also have an attention line, subject line, enclosure notation, and carbon copy notation.

Figure 4.14

THE LETTER PARTS

Office Research Systems
ONE-HUNDRED BREWSTER PARKWAY, NASHVILLE, TENNESSEE

Heading

At least 2 blank lines

May 6, 199_

2–8 blank lines

Kent Jones
Retail Sales Manager
KRI Products, Inc.
778 Joseph Street
Pomona, CA 91768

Inside address

Dear Kent:

Salutation

This letter contains all seven parts of the business letter:

Body

1. Heading
2. Inside address
3. Salutation
4. Body
5. Complimentary close
6. Signature
7. Typist's reference initials

It also indicates how many blank lines separate the letterhead from the date, and the complimentary closing from the typed signature.

But how many spaces should you use between the date and the inside address? It all depends on how long your letter is.

> Kent Jones
> page 2
> May 6, 199_
>
> You want to create the appearance that the typing is more or less centered on the page. So if your letter is short, use between five and eight blank lines to separate the date from the inside address. If your letter is long, use just two blank lines.
>
> Observing these spacing suggestions should enable you to produce a letter that is nicely centered on the page.
>
> Cordially,   *Complimentary close*
>   *(3-5 blank lines)*
>
> *Marvin Scully* [signature]   *Signature*
>
> Marvin Scully
> Financial Consultant
>
> MS/tr   *Typist's reference*
>   *initials*

THE HEADING

The **heading** tells the reader where your letter comes from and when it was written. It usually consists of the company's letterhead with the date typed at least two lines below the last line of the letterhead.

If you do not use company stationery, the entire heading should appear at the upper right margin of the letter. It consists of the return address and the date:

> 15540 Briarwood Dr.
> Sherman Oaks, CA 91403
> August 5, 199-

THE INSIDE ADDRESS

The **inside address** appears at least two lines below the date of the letter and begins at the left margin. The inside address includes the name of the person to whom you are sending your letter, the name of the company for whom the person works, the street address, and the city, state, and zip code:

Mr. Charles M. Johnson
American Management Association
135 West 50th Street
New York, New York 10020

On an occasion when you do not know the addressee's name, use an **attention line** two lines below the inside address and two lines above the salutation:

American Management Association
135 West 50th Street
New York, New York 10020

Attention Membership Director

Dear Director:

THE SALUTATION

The **salutation** appears two lines below the inside address and begins at the left margin. Among the most common salutations are:

- Dear Mr. (Ms., Miss, Mrs.) Smith
- Dear Jim (June)—if you are on a first-name basis with the recipient of your letter

If you do not know the name of the recipient, you can use a title as a form of address: "Dear Purchasing Agent," "Dear Manager," "Dear Sales Representative." Avoid sexist salutations such as "Gentlemen" or "Dear Sirs," which imply that no business people are women.

Except when using the open punctuation style, follow the salutation in a business letter with a colon (:).

A **subject line** is optional and may appear two lines below the salutation. It acts like a heading, signaling the gist of the letter:

Dear Mr. Abrams:

Subject: Test Programs for Product Development

THE BASICS OF BUSINESS LETTERS

THE BODY

The body of the letter begins two lines below the salutation or subject line. It consists of paragraphs seldom longer than five sentences.

THE COMPLIMENTARY CLOSE

The **complimentary close** begins two spaces below the last paragraph of the body. In the following list, the most common complimentary closes are ordered from most formal to most familiar:

> Very truly yours,
> Yours truly,
> Sincerely yours,
> Sincerely,
> Cordially yours,
> Cordially,
> Best regards,
> Regards,

Except when using the open punctuation style, follow the complimentary close by a comma.

THE SIGNATURE

The **signature** consists of three or four items:

1. Sometimes your company's name above your signature
2. Your signature—in blue or black ink
3. Your typed name—three to five lines below the complimentary close
4. Your typed business title

Yours truly,

Ranger Boats

Charles P. Toland

Charles P. Toland, Jr.
Director of Marketing

In business-to-customer correspondence, it is best to omit the company name, since this format makes it appear that it is not a human being speaking but an impersonal company.

Some writers seem to feel uncomfortable with the convention of the complimentary close, and they run the last sentence of the body into the closing. It is far better to accept the closing as a convention than to reveal your discomfort by ending with an awkward nonsentence such as the following:

> . . . Until we hear from you further, we remain
>
> Yours truly,
>
> Paul Webster
> Production Manager

THE TYPIST'S REFERENCE SECTION

The **typist's reference section** contains your initials (in capital letters) and the initials of the typist (in lower-case letters). Usually, these initials appear at the left margin.

> JSF/sr

If the letter contains enclosures, it requires the **enclosure notation.** The word "Enclosure" appears one or two spaces below the typist's initials.

If you will be sending the letter to other readers, place the **carbon copy notation** one or two spaces below the enclosure notation or typist's initials.

> KAK/ch
> Enclosure
> cc: Jennifer Meldrum

Or

> KAK/ch
> Copy to: Jennifer Meldrum

Envelopes

Just as the appearance of your letter projects your company's image, so too does the appearance of your envelope. Most companies have good-quality envelopes printed with their return address in the upper left-hand corner in a format identical to the letterhead.

THE BASICS OF BUSINESS LETTERS 147

The sender's name and address, just as it appears in the inside address of the letter, is then typed in the lower center of the envelope. Figure 4.15 illustrates two properly addressed business envelopes.

Figure 4.15

PROPERLY ADDRESSED ENVELOPES

ENVELOPES FOR AUTOMATIC PROCESSING

You can quicken the processing of your mail, and also qualify for volume discounts, if you follow post office guidelines for preparing business envelopes for automatic processing. If you position and type or print addresses on your envelopes according to the specialized rules, the post office can use an optical character reader and bar code sorter to sort your letters automatically. If you also use the new **ZIP + 4 code**—the original zip code plus a hyphen and 4 additional numbers—the post office can sort your outgoing mail according to specific streets, specific buildings, or even specific floors within a building.

You can get the latest guidelines for preparing business mail from your local post office. Here we can briefly outline the current recommendations of the United States Postal Service.

Preparing Envelopes for Optical Character Readers. For machine processing, the postal service uses an optical character reader (OCR) to scan the lower center section of the envelope, called the "OCR read area," for the addressee's name and address (see Figure 4.16). To enable the OCR to read the address:

- Type or machine print the address. All capital letters are preferred.
- Single-space and block the address. Don't indent.
- Do not use punctuation in the address; it is not required.
- Use the last line for the city, state, and ZIP + 4 code.
- Use the second-last line for the delivery address: street address or box number first and then, if necessary, apartment, suite, or room number.
- Put all on-arrival instructions such as "Attn: Ms. Williams" or "Confidential" above the last two lines—for example immediately below the addressee's name.

Figure 4.16

WHERE TO POSITION THE ADDRESS FOR
MACHINE READING BY AN OCR ("OCR read area" is in white.)

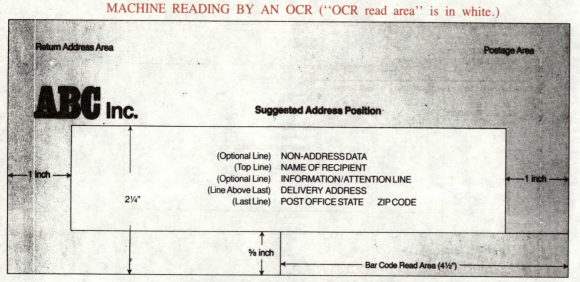

Last Line of Address *Must* be Completely Within White OCR Read Area

Figure 4.17 contains a sample address in a format suitable for machine processing, as recommended by the post office.

If, however, you do not wish to make use of the postal service's OCR, type your address the more traditional way, using upper and lower cases and punctuation, as illustrated earlier in Figure 4.15.

SUMMARY

Letters help you do business efficiently because they are convenient and provide an automatic record of your transactions. If they are well written, letters can also be your goodwill ambassadors. You can use the RTA formula to draft or dictate effective letters,

Figure 4.17

SAMPLE ADDRESS FORMATED FOR MACHINE READING

```
         MR AL SPITVAK
         CONFIDENTIAL
         MUNICIPAL RECYCLING CENTER
         56 STROUGHTON RD
         MADISON WI 53714-2941
```

ones that establish rapport with your reader; influence the reader's thinking, both logically and psychologically; and motivate the reader to act and to have a positive attitude toward you and your organization. To ensure that you get your messages across in a courteous and businesslike manner, develop a friendly tone and a conversational style using techniques you have learned in this chapter, and choose among the four business letter formats.

EXERCISES

See "Setting the Goal for the Business Letter: Action and Attitude," p. 107, for Exercises 1 and 2.

1. For the fourth time in a week, Lynn Cartwright, owner of a building supplies company, found herself on the phone long distance, asking customers to clarify the addresses her sales rep Red had scratched on the order forms. "Why can't Red get this straight? I've got to get these credit checks into the mail and I can't do it without addresses." Lynn decided to write Red and tell him what she thought. As she wrote, though, her irritation started to lift. She realized, "Red does great work for us and I can see why he can't stand the paperwork." Write a goal statement for the letter Lynn wants to send.

2. After completing management training courses in Atlanta, Georgia, Daniel Tyler has been assigned to his company's offices in Boise, Idaho. As a new resident in Idaho, Daniel needs to register his car and take the state's driving test. However, he has discovered that his company's credit union, located in Atlanta, will not release the title of his car (which shows that he is the owner) because they claim he has overdrawn his account by $50. On reviewing his records, Daniel finds that he has two accounts with

the credit union, one containing $25 and the other with $2,000. In the rush of moving from Atlanta to Boise, he had withdrawn the $50 from the smaller account. Write the goal statement for the letter he needs to send to the credit union.

See "Assessing the Reader," p. 108, for Exercise 3.

3. Jill Steinbrenner, a partner in a West Lafayette accounting firm, has been asked each year to speak at Purdue University's undergraduate accounting club. For the past five years she has been free to do so and has enjoyed exchanging ideas with the students and learning about their interests. Jill has been impressed by the level of their questions and the rigor of the program in accounting at Purdue.

This year Jill has been called away on a business trip that conflicts with the spring invitation from Purdue. She must now write a letter to the president of the club declining their invitation. What does she know about the students that might help her write the letter? Assess her readers.

See "Establishing Rapport with Your Reader," pp. 110–113, for Exercise 4.

4. Study the following opening sentences taken from business letters. Which ones do you think will immediately establish rapport with the reader? Why? Rewrite any opening that you find ineffective.

a. Here are the tickets you requested for the Home Builders Show.
b. July 27 is an important date for both of us, Ms. Godson.
c. In accordance with your written requests, we are herewith changing your address on our mailing list, and hereafter your future copies will be sent to your new address.
d. Here is the proposal you requested.
e. This letter is in response to your letter of April 9.
f. We would like you to participate in a demographics survey.
g. Ever since we heard you speak last year at the National Life Underwriters' Association, we have wanted to meet you in person. We believe someone with your wit and experience has much to teach us about sales.
h. Thank you for your letter of July 14 regarding your defective generator.
i. Would you please let us know when you can pick up your dry cleaning?
j. As chairperson of the Program Committee for the Oregon Jaycees, I am responsible for getting speakers. That is why I am writing you.
k. Your wedding dress is ready!
l. I am sorry that you have not answered my previous requests for payment of your long overdue account of $147.24.
m. Barbara Rogers, a former student of yours, has told us that you would be willing to write a recommendation for her.
n. Everyone knows about the plight of New York's neediest citizens.
o. How often have you felt as though you were being herded into a cattle car when you boarded an airplane.

p. I was sorry to learn that your husband's illness has prevented him from keeping up his car payments.
q. When I looked at your advertising circular I asked myself: "Does that company know about Smith ink?"
r. Thank you for your order. The shipping department is operating at a 3-day lead time, and so we expect to ship by Tuesday, March 8.
s. Thank you for your helpful comments on how we can improve our service to clients who do business in Europe and the Far East.
t. We are sorry but we have hired someone else for the position you applied for.
u. Our local police department has just released the latest crime figures for March: Burglaries have increased nearly 20 percent over last year. To combat crime, many communities have formed neighborhood watch programs.
v. Lester Hollins has spoken highly of your expertise in telecommunications.

See "Influencing Your Reader's Thinking," pp. 113–118, for Exercises 5 and 6.

5. You have hired a lawn care service but have been unhappy with the company's performance. You want to write a letter canceling your contract and giving the major reasons why. You want the company, Turftender, to give you a refund of exactly half of what you paid, and you would like the company to explain the reasons for its poor service. Read through the series of events explained below that led to your decision. Decide what information should be included in your letter to explain your reasons. Then write an analysis tree grouping and ordering the main ideas and information you would include.

- In early May you prepaid $165.30 for a series of four Turftender lawn applications. By prepaying, you saved $8.70, since paying for each application individually would have cost $52.20 for the first two applications, and $34.20 for the last two, for a total of $174.
- The Turftender program promises continuous, automatic treatments: properly timed fertilizer applications, crabgrass control, broadleaf weed control, and insect control. You were promised the "finest lawn service possible," and the opportunity to talk to your personal lawn specialist whenever you wanted information or advice.
- By mid-June you had not received your first, "early spring" application, so you called Turftender. A lawn specialist came out the next week to make the first application. You were at work at the time, but the lawn specialist left an invoice signed "Larry."
- By July you had not yet received your second application, the one designated "late spring/early summer," and you called. Since it didn't seem to you there would be enough time for the lawn to need three more applications of fertilizer before winter, you asked whether you could substitute a lime application for the fourth treatment. You were told that second treatments were still being applied until the end of July and that you could expect yours the following week. You asked to be called in advance of the application so that you could discuss weed control with your lawn specialist. (The weeds were clearly getting the better of the grass by this

- time.) You also wanted to explain to the specialist your unusual property lines. You suspected that a large area of the back yard had not been treated in the first application.

- By the third week of August you had not yet received your second application. You called to find out why. The person who answered said the application would be made the following week. You asked to be called the night before so that you could be sure to be home to talk with the lawn specialist.

- The following Monday morning (you were on vacation that week and so happened to be at home), on returning from a walk with your two-year-old daughter, you saw the Turftender truck pull into the driveway. You had not been called in advance. You asked to discuss lawn care with the lawn specialist, and he said he would be happy to as soon as he finished his paper work. But without coming to the door, he began to apply weed-killer to the yard. You ran out to explain the property lines. The lawn specialist applied fertilizer and then came to the door. You discussed the need for a lime application and asked that it be substituted for the fourth application, since it was too late in the season for two more applications of fertilizer. The specialist told you that there would be time for two more applications, and that a lime application would cost extra. You were told to keep your child and any pets off the lawn for the rest of the day, although the application should be safe as soon as it dries, in one hour. (You had been told earlier there were no potential hazards associated with the applications.)

- You looked at the invoice the lawn specialist had left with you. The application cost $34.80 and was acknowledged prepaid. Since the second application is supposed to cost $52.20, you assume the lawn specialist applied the third application (which does not contain insect or crabgrass controls, as treatments one and two do) rather than the second. The invoice was signed "Shawn."

- The next morning you took your daughter out and found a large, slick, oily spot on the driveway just where the Turftender truck had parked. You smelled the substance and realized it was weed-killer. This was precisely the place on the driveway where your daughter likes to play. You immediately spent half an hour hosing down the driveway to try to remove the chemicals. Meanwhile, you kept your daughter off the driveway until the next rain, two days later, when the oil slick finally washed away.

- Another lawn service company has offered you a $25 discount to begin a lawn program with them in the fall. You have decided to ask for a refund from Turftender and to change companies.

6. As a member of your community's chamber of commerce, you have been asked to write a letter requesting contributions from residents to a community council that

THE BASICS OF BUSINESS LETTERS 153

provides services to needy people in the community. Here is some of the information you might include in the letter:

- Goal of campaign to collect $35,000
- Council has good reputation
- Offers numerous services
- Has helped over 3,850 residents in past year
- Receives no financial assistance from government or United Way
- 130 people have been provided with food from our Pantry Shelf
- 200 people received holiday gifts while patients in community nursing homes
- 100 people took part in social activities with the Widowed-to-Widowed Program
- 250 people were transported to local hospitals and doctors
- 90 people were entertained at a Thanksgiving Day dinner
- 550 people were transported to medical appointments

Write an analysis tree grouping relevant information for your letter.

See "Motivating Action and a Positive Attitude," pp. 118–120, for Exercise 7.

7. Study the following concluding paragraphs taken from business letters. Which would get the reader to act as the writer desires? Why? Rewrite any paragraphs that fail to motivate action or a positive attitude.

a. We look forward to receiving your check within the next few days. Your prompt attention will protect your credit rating.
b. If you will tell us your recollection of the agreement, I am sure we can get the matter straightened out.
c. Thanking you in advance for your cooperation in this matter, and hoping to hear from you at your convenience, we are

                    Yours very truly,

d. We are glad to know of your interest in Gladding, McBrean and Company, and would like to retain your file in case anything unexpected develops.
e. Please give Mr. Epstein my best regards and sincere wishes for a speedy recovery.
f. If you follow these procedures, we'll see what we can do to help you out.
g. For these reasons, I'm enclosing a check for $196.18 to pay off the balance of my Sears account. If you cannot accept this settlement, please ask the branch manager to explain your store's policy *in writing*.
h. I look forward to meeting you at the NMA banquet. Should you have questions before then, please do not hesitate to give me a call.
i. I trust you now understand why we cannot let you charge additional items.

j. Until your back account is paid in full, I must ask that you pay cash for your purchases. Paying cash will allow you to avoid our monthly interest charges and to continue to enjoy shopping at Gimleco.
k. When you order your Bryant and Phillips 7154 drill, you can help us achieve our annual sales goal that much sooner.
l. Your failing to include your policy number means that we cannot make the change in beneficiaries that you requested.
m. Our Accounting Department will send you up-to-date figures which will show that the Mall Project is feasible.
n. I look forward to becoming your insurance agent.
o. Reviewing the Grimes account with Janet will allow her to take it over immediately.
p. Good luck with your new territory. Keep me posted on how sales are going.

See "Local Revision: A Friendly Tone and a Conversational Style," pp. 125–134, for Exercises 8–13.

8. Edit these paragraphs from letters to emphasize the "you attitude" and reader benefits:

a.

As a group of future entrepreneurs, my class was very interested in my paper, which was based on the personal interview I conducted with you on October 21. The class has a genuine interest in meeting successful entrepreneurs, and we would like you to come and share your experiences and success with us. It would be most convenient if you could visit our class on a Tuesday or Thursday at 1:30 in the afternoon.

b.

Order your Van der Vettering bulbs now! Van der Vettering's must order bulbs now to ensure its supplies for the fall rush. Help us meet our need by ordering early.

c.

I am looking forward to seeing your company's name among those offering internships to our students this summer. Our college believes that nothing can be more beneficial to a student than work experience. In this 8-week period, the student will become familiar with actual business practices, and if the experience is positive, it could lead to the student's eventual employment. If there is no job offer, the experience still will be a worthwhile venture for the student.

d.

In order for us to fulfill our responsibility to the tour group, we need to know how many group members will be taking the airport shuttle on Saturday, March 24th. Please fill out the form below to indicate your travel arrangements.

e.

As your local independent Cleaningworks specialist, I will be pleased to demonstrate our exclusive Cleaningworks process on your furnishings.

f.

I am writing to ask you for a favor. Last week, I received an assignment for a Presentation Skills class; we are to attend a business lecture outside the school or our jobs and then write a paper that analyzes the speaker as well as the speech. I was excited to notice that you are sponsoring Ken Berry, president of Dextra Equipment Corporation, at the dinner meeting next week. His speech would seem to meet several of my needs, and I would like to attend the lecture portion of the evening without having to pay for the banquet. I hope you will send me tickets.

g.

I have recently become associated with Hennessey Associates, Realtors. I am specializing in properties in the High Rock area. My firm, one of the most active in the town, has successfully handled a large number of sales in our area over the past 23 years. I will be contacting you shortly to become acquainted. Thank you.

9. Revise the following excerpts from letters so that they say things more positively:

a. Thank you for your trouble.
b. Because we deal only with wholesalers, we are unable to respond to your enquiry regarding our sheepskin products.
c. We are sorry, but we do not carry tiles in the 4" by 6" size you ordered.
d. Because the conference begins in four weeks, we cannot accept any program suggestions after June 28.
e. Smoking will be absolutely prohibited in the van.
f. I demand you refund my $25.92. Otherwise I will hold your hotel in very low regard and let others know what I think.
g. I am sorry, but right now I am simply too busy with my own responsibilities to accept the sacrifices expected of a volunteer assistant wrestling coach.
h. Our copying service guarantees that you will never receive your order late, never receive copies too dark, cloudy, faded, or irregular, and never hear a discourteous word from our staff.

THE RANDOM HOUSE GUIDE TO BUSINESS WRITING

10. Revise the following letter paragraphs so that they sound conversational.

a.

It seems funny to be thinking about vacation already, but Thanksgiving and Christmas are coming up fast and it is important that you plan your vacations early so as to ensure good values and convenient flying times for you and your whole family, especially since TransUS has a variety of special vacation packages, particularly to Florida, such as the new "See Your Way Clear to Florida" promotion that has been launched, offering perhaps the best package prices on the market to Florida, so if your vacation plans require air transportation, I would very much like it if you would please contact me, if you are interested, so that we can arrange a mutually agreeable time to meet and discuss what TransUS can offer.

b.

We are extremely happy! You have become a Westward Wagon customer! Westward Wagon will be your food shopping center. May we welcome you? May we extend you the enclosed Courtesy Card? You may need cash or a check while shopping. You can use the Courtesy Card in our market.

Bring this card with you on your next visit. We will validate it for you. Also please notify us of any change in address. This will help us keep our files up-to-date.

c.

On November 22, 199–, I wrote you to acknowledge Eddie has advised me that American Consolidated had lowered their prices to be competitive with ours so that your superiors chose to remain with them due to your fifteen-year association, although we found this very disappointing but were ready to understand your position.

d.

We wrote you a letter last week. It concerned the payroll deductions available. They were being offered by the Student Federal Credit Union. We thought you would like to have some more details. Let us tell you exactly what is being offered. Let us tell you who we are.

The Student Federal Credit Union is a savings institution. It was begun last year by undergraduate students. We opened in October 199–. Since then we have received shares of $41,000 and 147 accounts. We declared a first quarter dividend of 6.5 percent. We hope to do the same for our second quarter. The Credit Union is also a member of the National Credit Union Association. This Association insures each depositor for up to $100,000.

THE BASICS OF BUSINESS LETTERS

11. The new claims adjuster at your company handed you this draft for review. Can you make the style more conversational?

> In accordance with the request of Jim Schmeling, our service manager, I have reviewed your request that we issue you a refund in the amount of $36.10.
> We were sorry that you deemed the ½ hp motor (model 18023) unsatisfactory. In your letter you mentioned that it was used to drive a power-built chain saw (model #2916) and burnt out.
> In the instruction booklet that accompanied the motor, the manufacturer included a paragraph that expressly states that under no circumstances should power-built saws in the 2900 line be powered by engines of less than 5 hp. Inasmuch as we realize that there are occasions and times when customers overlook instructions when operating equipment and due to the fact we at Strong Brothers are always desirous of maintaining good customer-client relations, I took the liberty to ask our accounting staff to issue you a check for the above-mentioned sum. Please find it hereto attached.

12. As assistant director of a community outreach project, Barbara Fonseca was asked to hire ten more students as research assistants. Here is the draft of the letter she wants to send to Ed Williams, a student whom she had to turn down:

> Dear Ed Williams:
>
> Choosing students to participate as research assistants for the community outreach project was a very tough task due to the large pool of qualified applicants. The competition was strong.
> All applicants were thoroughly evaluated. Although your qualifications were impressive, your experience less directly fit what we had in mind than that of other students. You were, therefore, not chosen to be one of our research assistants.
> We appreciate your interest in applying for the position and wish you luck in pursuing an assistantship elsewhere.

Barbara's goal is to tell Ed no without making him feel bad about the rejection. Has she succeeded? How would you react if you received her letter? What suggestions can you give her for revising the letter?

13. For the past five years, Bob Farber has rented a cottage attached to his landlady's ranch-style house. Bob and his landlady share the backyard. Read the draft of the letter that Bob wants to send to his landlady to notify her that he will be leaving the apartment before his lease expires (Figure 4.18). Bob's goal is to break his lease without losing money and at the same time remain on friendly terms with his landlady. How would you change it to create a more conversational style?

THE RANDOM HOUSE GUIDE TO BUSINESS WRITING

Figure 4.18

DRAFT OF BOB'S LETTER

> Dear Janet,
>
> Personal and urgent matters force me to request that I be permitted to vacate the apartment at the expiration of two years on my three-year lease.
>
> I know that my lease contemplated a three-year commitment, but since I am aware that you will have no problems finding a renter to replace me (and probably at a higher rental), I hope that you will not object. I will be available to help you find a suitable new tenant.
>
> One other way around this problem is for me to find a sublessee but since in that case he would be paying the low rental that I am paying instead of a newly negotiated rental, I expect that you will prefer the new tenant route rather than the sublessee route.
>
> After inspecting my apartment to assure yourself that there are no damages (as there are none), I hope that you will send my deposit to me at the new address I will give you at the inspection. Please call me at work (555-2554) so that we can arrange for an inspection time. By the way, though I hesitate to mention this because of our amicable relations these past two years, prudence suggests that I remind you that the deposit was to stand for damages done to the apartment and not any pecuniary loss caused by my leaving the apartment earlier than I anticipated. That will be moot, probably, because you will find a suitable new tenant.
>
> Looking forward to hearing from you.

5
WRITING AND RESPONDING TO REQUESTS

PREVIEW

This chapter should help you to

1. Write effective business letters by showing you
   - How to convey good news and neutral messages directly and succinctly
   - How to convey bad news by showing consideration for the reader, providing sufficient explanations, and closing on a positive note
2. Adapt the RTA formula to
   - Writing about products and services
   - Writing about people
   - Writing about claims and adjustments
   - Writing about credit
   - Writing to refuse requests for favors

In business, you may often need to request information or action from people outside your organization. For example, you may need to order supplies, to ask customers what they think about your service, or to check references on a credit application. On the other hand, people outside your organization may often request information or action from you. They may ask you to confirm an agreement, to recommend a job candidate, or to make an adjustment. Although some of these transactions may be handled in face-to-face contacts or by phone, many of them will be handled through letters.

The most important consideration in writing and responding to requests is how your message will affect your reader. All the letters you write will be received by your reader as "good-news" or neutral messages, or as "bad-news" messages. In this chapter we show you how to use the RTA formula to write good-news and bad-news letters in the most typical letter situations for businesses: writing about products and services, writing about people, writing about claims and adjustments, writing about credit, and writing to refuse requests for favors.

THE GOOD-NEWS DIRECT LETTER PATTERN

As the new assistant of information services for the Fine Jewelers Association (FJA), Andrea Lindauer felt good about how quickly she had gathered together the reports and references that would help member Gerald Crafts. Mr. Crafts had written for information about ways to improve his jewelry business. But now Andrea sat perplexed before her keyboard, wondering about the cover letter. "I've looked at how they've written these letters in the past, but I'm not crazy about their standard reply." She looked at the copy of a letter sent out last week:

> Thank you for your inquiry dated 12/9/9_. In response to your request we have gathered the enclosed materials for your perusal.
>
> Thank you for your interest.
>
>   Yours truly,

Andrea thought, "I know I can be more helpful in my cover letter than this. But I don't want to end up rehashing all the information I'm enclosing. How do I write just enough to be helpful and to demonstrate my organization's goodwill?"

Letters that convey good news or neutral messages usually present few problems because your goal and your reader's needs are in harmony. You want to tell the good news, and your reader wants to hear it. So when you have good news for the reader, use the direct approach: Begin immediately with the news the reader wants to hear, then follow up with details and explanations. Above all, make clear how your information can be helpful to the reader. Before we discuss using RTA to write the good-news letter, let's look at how Andrea wrote her response to Mr. Crafts.

Andrea was right to feel she could write a more helpful letter than the standard response that her predecessor had written. She had gathered a great deal of information for Mr. Crafts. We asked her to explain how she decided to present it.

> When I read a letter from a retail jeweler asking a simple question, I want to figure out why he needs the information. Then, as I gather information that will answer the question, if I come across other material that might be helpful, I include that too. In Mr. Crafts' case, I found the information for most of the questions he asked, and then some. What my letter had to do was show him how to use all the information I'd found. I decided the best way to do that was to show how I'd answered the specific questions he'd asked.

To be sure he would understand her answers, Andrea looked at the letter Mr. Crafts had written (see Figure 5.1) to recall how he had phrased his questions.

Figure 5.1

MR. CRAFTS' LETTER REQUESTING INFORMATION

1107 Camino Del Mar
Del Mar, CA 92014
November 7, 199_

Fine Jewelers Association
101 East 50th Street,
New York, NY 10022

Dear FJA:

As a member of the FJA, I would like to avail myself of some of the statistical information you compile annually. I have operated an independent custom gold jewelry store in Del Mar (a resort in Southern California) for ten years. I am currently in the midst of difficult managerial decisions.

The most important decision is how to increase sales revenues another $50,000 (currently $100–150,000 annually). I am also considering changes in staff (currently 2 full-time and 1 part-time) and possible modification of inventory as ways to reduce operating expenses.

Any information on these subjects that you have available would be helpful. I would also like a representative profit and loss statement and a balance sheet for a similar size and type store, and a breakdown of sales by category. Also please send information on tumble polishing and equipment.

In short, almost any information you have to send me would be helpful. I will certainly appreciate any material you can get together for me.

Sincerely yours,

Gerald Crafts

Gerald Crafts
The Jewelry Box

GC/bn

Although Mr. Crafts had not listed and numbered his specific questions, his requests were quite clear. Before Andrea did her research, she circled what she saw as the major questions Mr. Crafts wanted answered (see Figure 5.2). Primarily he wanted to know how to increase revenues by $50,000, but to do this he wanted four things: (1) information on changing staff, (2) information on reducing operating expenses, (3) a profit and loss statement and balance sheet from a similar sized store, and (4) information on tumble polishing.

Andrea found the answers to his questions, and other information he would find useful, and decided to group the information under his own categories.

Finally, Andrea thought about how to begin her letter. She knew she did not want to go along with the stilted letter opening of her predecessor: "Thank you for your inquiry dated 12/9/9_." She thought again about what her letter was trying to do: "What I want to do is tell Mr. Crafts I've got answers to his questions. Why can't I begin immediately by saying just that?"

Once she had grouped her information and decided on a direct opening, Andrea wrote a response to Mr. Crafts' request for information, using her word processor to revise and edit as she went along. The final version of her letter is shown in Figure 5.3.

Andrea wrote an effective letter because she was sensitive to her reader's needs. Her reader, like all of us, wanted to hear the good news immediately. Andrea put her reader's concerns first by announcing the good news right away. She then followed up on the reader's concerns by explaining how the enclosed material would answer his specific questions. Finally, she ended on a positive, helpful note. To write effective good-news letters, use the RTA formula as Andrea did. It can help you keep your reader's needs in mind as you convey the good news.

Using RTA for the Good-News Letter

Establish Rapport: Put the good news or the main idea first. A short paragraph will emphasize the good news.

> Here is the information you requested.

> Your letter of recommendation should reach Mr. Holser at McGuinness within the week.

> Your $5,820 car loan has been approved and you may pick up your check anytime between 8:00 and 4:00 Monday through Friday at the Huron branch.

> Be assured that the 5052 Alloy Aluminum Scrap going to you by rail is straight 5052 with no 3003 mixed in.

WRITING AND RESPONDING TO REQUESTS 163

Figure 5.2

MR. CRAFTS' LETTER, WITH REQUESTS CIRCLED

1107 Camino Del Mar
Del Mar, CA 92014
November 7, 199_

Fine Jewelers Association
101 East 50th Street
New York, NY 10022

Dear FJA:

As a member of the FJA, I would like to avail myself of some of the statistical information you compile annually. I have operated an independent custom gold jewelry store in Del Mar (a resort in Southern California) for ten years. I am currently in the midst of difficult managerial decisions.

The most important decision is how to (increase sales revenues another $50,000) (currently $100–150,000 annually). I am also considering (changes in staff) (currently 2 full-time and 1 part-time) and possible (modification of inventory) as ways to (reduce operating expenses).

Any information on these subjects that you have available would be helpful. I would also like a (representative profit and loss statement and a balance sheet) for a similar size and type store, and a (breakdown of sales by category). Also please send (information on tumble polishing) and equipment.

In short, almost any information you have to send me would be helpful. I will certainly appreciate any material you can get together for me.

Sincerely yours,

Gerald Crafts

Gerald Crafts,
The Jewelry Box

GC/bn

Figure 5.3

ANDREA'S RESPONSE TO MR. CRAFTS

Fine Jewelers Association
101 East 50th Street   New York NY 10021

November 12, 199_

Mr. Gerald Crafts
1107 Camino Del Mar
Del Mar, CA 92014

Dear Mr. Crafts:

Here is the information to help you decide how to increase your sales revenues another $50,000. When appropriate, I have indicated how this information may be applied to reducing your operating expenses through modifying inventory or changing staff.

Enclosed you will find the following information:

1. A representative profit and loss statement and a balance sheet for two stores:
   - One store located in Aspen, Colorado, a resort comparable to Del Mar, attracting much the same population
   - A second store located in San Diego, nearly identical in size and history to yours

2. A study of the breakdown of sales by category for both stores

3. Information on changing staff:
   - Personnel guidelines for hiring and for determining efficiency of employees, wages, and benefits policies for Aspen and San Diego stores

4. Information on reducing operating expenses:
   - Advertising expenditures for different media and relative effectiveness of these ads
   - Three brochures on recent innovations in producing jewelry, concerned with ways in which to replace gold with substitute metals

Mr. Gerald Crafts
page 2
November 12, 199_

Information about and equipment for tumble polishing is available by writing to:

    Sorrento Fine China and Silver
    3869 El Camino Real
    Palo Alto, CA 94301

I have also included the latest predictions for our industry's growth in Sun Belt areas such as yours. These may suggest ways in which to plan ahead.

It has been a pleasure to assist you. If you have further questions, please write to me at FJA.

                        Sincerely yours,

                        Andrea Lindauer

                        Andrea Lindauer, Assistant
                        Information Services

AL/cd
Enclosure

Since your reader wants to hear the good news, don't delay with slow, stilted openers such as these:

    Acknowledging your request, we are enclosing herewith . . .

    Thank you for your letter of June 28.

    Referring to your recent request . . .

    We are in receipt of your letter dated September 8.

In the following examples, avoid the openings in the left-hand column. They emphasize your own pleasure when you should be concerned with giving pleasure to the reader.

INSTEAD OF	TRY
We are pleased to announce the results of our five-year product development project.	Our five-year product development project has paid off in dividends for you.
It gives us great pleasure to be sending this letter to notify you of our third annual Spinal Care Month.	To celebrate our third annual Spinal Care Month, we are offering you a free spinal examination during the month of November.

In her letter, Andrea immediately and succinctly showed that she had the answers for Mr. Crafts: "Here is the information to help you decide how to increase your sales revenues another $50,000."

Influence Thinking: Follow up on the good news with necessary details or explanations. Frequently, good-news messages are short and require very little explanation. But if necessary, once you have announced the main idea in your first paragraph, elaborate with details in the paragraphs that follow.

Notice in Andrea's letter that after she announced the good news—"Here is the information to help you decide how to increase your sales revenues another $50,000"—she then pointed out the features of the enclosed information that were most important to Mr. Crafts: "I have indicated how this information may be applied to reducing your operating expenses."

Sometimes you will write a letter with a **mixed message**—primarily good news, but not entirely. When doing so, de-emphasize the bad news. Embed it within more positive information, or instead of saying what you cannot do, say what you can do. Andrea could not provide Mr. Crafts with information about tumble polishing; but she did not say, "I am sorry I cannot provide you. . ." Instead, she emphasized what she could do: "Information about and equipment for tumble polishing is available by writing to . . ."

Motivate Action and Attitude: End on a positive note: recall the benefits of the good news, express appreciation, motivate action, or express willingness to help further. Andrea, for example, expressed her willingness to help further: "It has been a pleasure to assist you. If you have further questions, please write to me at FJA."

Whenever you have a good-news or neutral message for your reader, you can use the opportunity to create and reinforce company goodwill. You can emphasize the positive by putting the good news first and by ending on an appreciative or forward-looking note.

The accompanying checklist can help you review your good-news letters:

RTA CHECKLIST FOR WRITING THE GOOD-NEWS LETTER

R: Have you put the good news first and avoided slow openers such as "referring to your request"?

T: Have you explained the good news in adequate detail?

A: Have you ended on a positive note?

THE BAD-NEWS INDIRECT LETTER PATTERN

It had not taken Jeff Elliott long to establish his reputation in the Hardboard Division as a good writer, but he was not quite prepared for this. His boss had just asked him to ghostwrite a letter announcing to all wholesalers the company's latest price hike. "We don't like this any more than our wholesalers will, but it has to be done," his boss said. "I want to break it to them gently."

Letters give bad news when they go against the reader's wishes and expectations. If you must give the reader bad news, cushion that disappointment by taking an indirect approach.

The indirect pattern prepares the reader for the bad news because the letter uses the first one or two paragraphs as a "buffer"—providing information that may help the reader better accept the message.

To "break it to them gently," Jeff Elliott knew he would have to do more that just announce the new prices. He would have to explain to readers why prices had gone up. He also wanted to emphasize the positive whenever possible. But was there anything good about a price hike? Jeff talked to his boss and others in the firm to find out the reasons for his company's decision, and he also investigated the market situation of his wholesalers. With that information in mind, and after three drafts, Jeff produced for his boss's signature the letter shown in Figure 5.4. Notice how he buffers the bad news and emphasizes the positive.

Figure 5.4

JEFF'S BAD-NEWS LETTER

May 5, 199_

Dear Masonite Wholesaler:

Inflation has hit us all hard. To keep our costs down, and therefore yours, the Masonite Corporation has marshaled all its forces to control costs and improve productivity. We have been quite successful. In spite of high inflation, for sixteen months we have not raised our prices.

Unfortunately, there is no way we can completely offset rapidly escalating costs. In the 25 years I have been in business, I have not seen anything like the cost increases we have experienced over the last twelve months. Examples of some of these are:

Wood	20%	Natural Gas	35%
Resin	81%	Packaging Materials	28%
Fuel Oil	32%		

We hope the worst is over, but to remain a company producing quality products, we cannot continually absorb these inordinate cost increases. Therefore, we are forced to announce a price change effective September 17, 199_. Prices of all siding products will be increased 6 percent, with lesser amounts on other lines. Details of these changes and new price lists are being mailed to you by the Hardboard Division.

Although inflation has been difficult, economic factors influencing the building industry should make us optimistic. Housing starts for July were 1,799,000, a rate assuring good demand for building materials for the next several months. Home improvement remains strong.

We plan to meet the selling challenge ahead with an aggressive program and new products. We sincerely appreciate your continuing cooperation and support.

Sincerely yours,

Antony Jones

Antony Jones, President

AJ/bb

1 SOUTH WACKER DRIVE, CHICAGO, ILLINOIS 60606 • (312) 750-0900

Using RTA for the Bad-News Letter

When you are in the position of having to give unpleasant news—for example, announcing a price hike or refusing a favor, a claim, or a credit request—RTA can suggest guidelines for breaking the bad news gently.

Establish Rapport: Establish rapport by demonstrating that you have sincerely understood the issue from the reader's point of view. Begin with something relevant to the situation that both you and your reader can agree on. For example,

1. *Express understanding for the reader's need or problem.*

   We understand that it can be inconvenient to have to have repairs done on your brand new TV.

2. *Show you have taken the reader's situation seriously.* Explain that you have investigated promptly, have considered the situation carefully, or want to cooperate.

   We were very concerned to learn that the shipment you received contained only 25 electric coffee grinders rather than the 36 you ordered. We immediately checked our shipping records to verify the numbers.

3. *Express your appreciation—for the reader's interest or for information the reader may have provided.* But if you are denying a request, obviously do not say, "we were happy to receive your request."

   Thank you for your recent request for information about our Shakespeare reproductions.

   Jeff Elliott showed he understood his wholesalers situation by describing the inflationary situation they were all in and his company's efforts to hold prices steady: "Inflation has hit us all hard."

Influence Thinking: After establishing positive relations with the reader, first explain the reasons for the unfavorable news, then state the bad news.

Explain the Reasons. Although your letter brings bad news, it should convey a decision that is the result of a fair and honest analysis of the situation. You should be sincere and honest in explaining the reasons behind your decision. Be succinct in your explanations, and if appropriate, emphasize as much as possible that in the long run, fair dealing benefits the reader.

In explaining your reasons, avoid the following expressions, since they emphasize not what is good for the reader but what is good for the company:

It is our policy that . . .
We cannot afford to . . .
Much as we would like, we are unable to . . .

Also avoid sounding imperious or emphasizing the negative with phrases such as these:

We must reject . . .
We were surprised at your request . . .
Your failure to include the necessary . . .
You claim . . .
Surely you understand . . .

Notice in his letter how Jeff Elliott explained the reasons leading to his company's price hike, listing several examples of the price hikes his company had absorbed so far in its fight to keep costs down for the wholesaler.

State the Bad News.   Make your decision clear, but emphasize the positive. Keep the bad news out of the beginning and end of the paragraph. One way to accomplish this is to embed the bad news in positive information.

Rather than stating the bad news, you may be able to make your decision clear by implying it. For example, instead of saying "We do not sell individual cartons," try "We sell only by the gross." But never state your decision indirectly if there is any chance you may be misunderstood.

When you must state the bad news directly in order to be clear, try to de-emphasize it by subordinating the decision within a sentence containing positive information:

Although we can provide free delivery only to customers in our service area, we can arrange to have your order delivered for only a small handling charge.

As the last example suggests, one important way to emphasize the positive is to suggest an alternative or offer a compromise. For example, instead of refusing a favor outright, try to suggest someone to whom the reader may turn:

I will be out of town on February 24th, but my partner, who is an excellent speaker, may be available.

After explaining the reasons for the price hike, Jeff announces the bad news clearly: "Therefore we are forced to announce a price change." Notice, however, that Jeff then immediately discusses the positive side of his readers' situation: "Economic factors influencing the building industry should make us optimistic." In other words he suggests to his wholesalers that, despite inflation and the price hike, they should be able to sell his products without difficulty.

WRITING AND RESPONDING TO REQUESTS

Motivate Action and Attitudes: Since the end of the letter is a position of emphasis, close on a positive note. If you suggest an alternative to the reader, explain what action is required. Otherwise, reinforce a positive attitude by expressing one or more of the following:

1. Your appreciation for the reader as a customer
2. Your willingness to cooperate in the future
3. Your continued interest in servicing the customer

If you have been fair and reasonable, you can assume that the reader understands and approves. Avoid the following expressions, which convey doubts, suggest further trouble, or imply that you fear you have lost the customer:

We hope you will understand our decision . . .
We hope this meets with your approval . . .
If you have any further difficulties . . .
If we can be of further help, please call us . . .
We hope that this has not discouraged you from doing business with us . . .

Although Jeff Elliott knew his readers would not be pleased to hear about a price hike, he did not end his letter with a reference to the difficulties and inconveniences the hike might cause. Instead he relied on the body of the letter to persuade readers that the price hike was necessary. Then he used his conclusion to emphasize the positive things his company was doing for its wholesalers: "We plan to meet the selling challenge ahead with an aggressive program and new products." He also expressed his appreciation for his readers' willingness to cooperate: "We sincerely appreciate your continuing cooperation and support."

The accompanying checklist can help you revise your indirect bad-news letters.

RTA CHECKLIST FOR WRITING THE INDIRECT BAD-NEWS LETTER

R: Have you begun indirectly, with something relevant to the situation that your reader can agree with?

T: Have you given the reasons for the bad news *before* stating the bad news? Have you made the decision clear but at the same time emphasized the positive?

A: Have you closed on a positive note?

A DIRECT APPROACH TO THE BAD-NEWS LETTER

Although the indirect letter pattern is appropriate for most bad-news situations, bear in mind that some readers may not appreciate having to wait a paragraph or two before finding out your decision. These readers may prefer a direct approach, in which you announce your decision in the first sentence or paragraph. Even in these cases, however, buffer the bad news with a short phrase, expressing appreciation or giving a reason for your decision. Then announce the bad news and include whatever explanations for your decision you think appropriate. Consider these examples:

> Although your contract offer had attractive features, we have decided to do business with another firm. Thank you very much for the time you spent considering our needs and preparing the proposal.

> In order to repair the damage caused by this week's severe storm, we are closing the Children's Center this Thursday and Friday.
> We realize this may cause parents inconvenience, but these repairs are essential to maintain a safe environment for the children and the repairs cannot be done safely with children in the building.
> We will do everything we can to help you arrange alternative child care for these two days. Thank you for your cooperation.

> Because of the expense and staff time required, we are unable to exchange your tickets for the December 14th performance. In similar circumstances, many of our subscribers, however, do find it possible to sell their tickets to friends or at the theater on the night of the performance.
> We do still have good seats available for the January 7th performance and would be happy to take your phone order.

Whether your approach is direct or indirect, when you have bad news, remember to buffer the bad news, make the reasons for your decision clear, and end with the accent on the positive.

What you have learned about good-news and bad-news letter patterns can help with almost all your business correspondence. In the following sections of this chapter we look at some of the most common business letter situations, including:

WRITING AND RESPONDING TO REQUESTS

- Writing about products and services
- Writing about people
- Writing about claims and adjustments
- Writing about credit
- Writing to refuse requests for favors

For each situation we show you how to adapt the RTA formula, and we offer several letter examples.

WRITING ABOUT PRODUCTS AND SERVICES

As a business person, you may write about products and services both as a buyer and as a seller. As a buyer, you place orders and request information from suppliers about products and services necessary to the operation of your business. As a seller, you acknowledge orders and answer inquiries from your customers and distributors. Let's first look at writing your own orders and requests for information, and then at replying to orders and inquiries from others. (Persuasive letters about products and services, such as sales letters and special requests, are discussed in Chapter 6.)

Orders for and Inquiries about Products and Services

Ordering or requesting information from a business is usually a routine activity. Your reader will be happy to hear from you and often eager to respond. In these situations, you can be assured of an interested answer if you use the good-news direct approach.

Establish Rapport: Since your reader is prepared to respond to your request, establish rapport simply by stating your request. Be direct, polite, and to the point.

> Please ship us three PROOFWRITER: International/Scientific program disks. Please send UPS, to be received by January 24. You have already approved our credit application, so we assume the terms are 2/10 net 30.

> We would like your help in developing a new brochure in time for our July fabric show. I enclose samples of our most recent brochures to give you a sense of what we're looking for.

Figure 5.5

LETTER ORDERING SERVICES

Gordon's Delights
1670 Lincoln Ave.
Tacoma, WA 98421
May 9, 199_

Edward Marsden
Food Facilities Consultants
1414 15th Ave. W.
Seattle, WA 98119

Dear Ed:

This letter outlines the terms of agreement under which you will be retained by Gordon's to assist in evaluating food sanitation and handling procedures for Gordon's new sandwich program.

The scope of your work will be as follows:

1.	Read Gordon's New Direction Training Manual and evaluate	8
2.	Give verbal comments on manual	2
3.	Take field trip to familiarize yourself with Gordon's stores	4
4.	Review in-store procedure audits (2 Tacoma stores)	12
5.	Prepare written report (on manual and in-store procedures)	4
6.	Travel time (5 round trips from Seattle)	10
	TOTAL HOURS	40

We've agreed that for this work your fee will be $50 per hour, to a maximum of $2,000 for the total project. Expense reimbursement will be for mileage only, at a rate of $.20 per mile, with a maximum of 100 miles per round trip to either Gordon's headquarters or the sandwich stores in Tacoma.

In your verbal comments and written report, we would like you to address the following areas:

- Shelf life of meat: frozen, unopened in refrigerator, opened in refrigerator, portioned in sandwich setup. Are the shelf lives assigned correct, too stringent, or not stringent enough? Is the dating procedure adequate?
- Preparation procedures: any precautions necessary when portioning ingredients to ensure contamination is not introduced into the setups or opened bags of meat?
- Specific recommendations on equipment: procedures for cleaning and sanitation
- Acceptable emergency thaw procedures for meat
- Additional procedures for preparation that should be included

> Edward Marsden
> page 2
> May 9, 199_
>
> Ed, if you have any questions about these terms, please let me know prior to beginning work on the project. I look forward to working with you.
>
> Yours truly,
>
> *Mary Benson*
>
> Mark Benson, Manager
>
> MB/ef
> cc: L. Carson

Influence Thinking: While most orders and requests for information can be made over the phone or on standard forms provided by the supplier, you may have occasion to order or request by letter. If your request is more complex than a one-item order or a single question, help your reader think through your request. Make your questions clear and complete, and if you have several questions, group and number them for the reader's easy reference.

Motivate Action and Attitude: Since the reader is already motivated to act, close with a simple thank you and emphasize how the reader will benefit by fulfilling your request.

> By completing the enclosed resale certificate before July 30, you can satisfy our auditors that you qualify for exempt status.

Ordering Products. When ordering a product, include all the necessary information:

- Catalog numbers
- Product description
- Prices
- Method of shipping
- Desired delivery date
- Method of payment

Ordering Services. Ordering services may require a more elaborate letter than a simple order form, since the letter often represents a contract between you and the provider. In such a letter, you must take great care to specify precisely the terms of the agreement. Figure 5.5 represents a fast-food restaurant's letter of contract with a consultant for food handlers. Notice that the writer groups items into logical categories: times, fees, and expectations.

Inquiring About Products and Services. When inquiring about products or services, the more well thought out your questions, the more helpful your reader can be in supplying you with the information that will make it easy for you to decide.

In Figure 5.6 an office manager requests information about a copy machine. Why is this rather long letter more useful than a brief request such as, "Please send information about copy machines useful to a small office"?

Replies to Orders and Inquiries

Just as you may correspond with other businesses to place orders or request information about their products or services, so you may respond to similar inquiries from your own customers. Good business demands that you take this opportunity to retain and promote goodwill for your company. If you can say yes to a request, your letter is good news and by its very nature promotes goodwill. In these cases, use the direct letter pattern. If, on the other hand, you have to say no to a request, then retaining and promoting goodwill will be more of a challenge, requiring careful consideration of your reader's situation. For this, you should use the indirect pattern.

YES TO ORDERS AND INQUIRIES

Ordinarily, to respond to an order for your products, you simply fill the order and ship it as expeditiously as possible. To respond to an inquiry, you may have brochures or other promotional material available to send promptly (see Figure 5.7). But these transactions also offer you the opportunity to reinforce in your customers' minds your willingness to serve them. By writing a letter to acknowledge an order or to accompany brochures or promotional material, you can welcome new customers, encourage future sales, show your appreciation, and reinforce your desire to serve the customer. You should use the direct letter pattern to say yes and to promote further sales.

Establish Rapport: Begin directly with the good news:

NOT	BUT
We have received your order.	Your order is being shipped UPS today and should be at your door by Friday.
Concerning your inquiry . . .	The brass rail Cross T Connector you inquired about does come with a discount if ordered in quantities of 48 or more.

In acknowledging orders, confirm them by date, number, and name of item.

Figure 5.6

LETTER REQUESTING INFORMATION ABOUT A PRODUCT

Jackson Business Furniture
780 Old Dublin Road
Doylestown, PA 18901
September 5, 199_

Business Copy Associates
100 S. 10th Street
Philadelphia, PA 19107

Dear Sales Manager:

Subject: Purchase of Copy Machine

Our office is interested in buying a copy machine to serve the needs of our four sales reps. We are interested in what you have available for under $2,500 that meets the following criteria:

1. Must be able to reproduce the half-tones and the lines on our order forms (enclosed).
2. Must be capable of very high quality reproduction.
3. Must be able to handle 8½″ × 14″ as well as the standard 8½″ × 11″.

We would also be interested in discussing service contracts and the cost of options such as the ability to make transparencies and to collate.

If you have something that meets our criteria, would you ask a sales rep to make an appointment with us to discuss your machines.

We would like to make our purchase within the next four weeks, so the sooner you can contact us, the better.

Thank you.

Sincerely,

Clare Reinhart

Clare Reinhart
Office Manager

CR/mm
Enclosure

178 THE RANDOM HOUSE GUIDE TO BUSINESS WRITING

Figure 5.7

SALES BROCHURES

HEATING OIL/DIESEL FUEL
BOILER INSTALLATIONS
OIL BURNERS
FURNACE INSTALLATIONS
ENERGY SAVING PRODUCTS
HOT WATER HEATERS/ELECTRIC
& OIL—SALES AND SERVICE
HOT WATER AQUABOOSTERS
HOT WATER MAKERS
HEATING ADDITIONS
REMODELING SPECIALISTS
AIR CONDITIONING
INSTALLATION & SERVICE
MAINTENANCE & SERVICE
POLICIES
AUTOMATIC DELIVERY
DEPENDABLE 24 HR. SERVICE
RADIO DISPATCHED FLEET

OUR REGULAR BUDGET PLAN
IS AVAILABLE FOR SERVICE CONTRACTS

needham oil company
355 R Chestnut Street
Needham, Massachusetts 02192
444-3600

WRITING AND RESPONDING TO REQUESTS 179

**NOW, FOR THE FIRST TIME!
PROTECT YOUR TREES AND SHRUBS FROM WINTER-INJURY!**

Your trees and shrubs are a valuable asset to your property, an asset that deserves special care. But until now little could be done to protect trees and shrubs from winter-injury and winter-kill.

NOW THERE IS PRO-TEC® FOR COMMERCIAL AND RESIDENTIAL USE

When PRO-TEC is applied professionally to trees and shrubs it gives them positive protection from wind-burn, sun-scald and excessive water-loss.

PRO-TEC is non-toxic to animals and plants. It dries, quickly, to a clear, natural finish and protects pine, arborvitae, holly, yews, rhododendron, etc. all winter long.

LANDSCAPING IS A BIG INVESTMENT

Just as you protect your lawn with fertilizers and weed treatments, now give your trees and shrubs winter-injury protection.

LET US PROTECT YOUR VALUABLE TREES AND SHRUBS

Return this card. We will call you to answer any questions you have and arrange for an application of PRO-TEC.

_____

Please call me to answer questions and schedule an application of PRO-TEC.

Name _____

Address _____

City _____ State _____

Telephone No. _____

I have approximately _____ trees and shrubs to be protected.

Influence Thinking: Experienced business writers know that sales talk is important, even after a customer has placed an order. In a letter acknowledging an order they include **resale**—that is, favorable talk about the item that has already been ordered. Resale confirms the customer in the wisdom of his or her order and stresses your company's readiness to be of service.

In replying to inquiries about your products, answer all questions clearly and completely, embed negative points, and minimize discussion of prices. Then include sales talk as appropriate (see Chapter 6, "Selling," pp. 224–247).

Motivate Action and Attitude: If you have not done so already, welcome new customers, and for all customers, emphasize service and satisfaction. If your letter has included sales talk, make action easy. In all cases, express your appreciation. In Figure 5.8, the subscription manager for a magazine confirms a gift order and takes the opportunity to reinforce the customer's choice.

A mail-order toy manufacturer accompanies all its toy shipments with a letter such as the one in Figure 5.9. Notice how the letter emphasizes resale, to promote customer loyalty.

REFUSING ORDERS AND REQUESTS FOR INFORMATION

No business wants to, but you will occasionally have to refuse an order or a request for product information. You may not carry the item, you may be out of stock, or you may sell only to distributors or retailers rather than to individuals. You may simply not know the answer to an inquiry. Although these are bad-news situations and require the indirect letter pattern, you can turn them into good news by suggesting an alternative.

For example, in refusing an order or request because you do not carry or know about the item, suggest to the reader another company or source that does. Providing such a referral demonstrates your service attitude and may win you a loyal customer in the future. Meanwhile, you can also use the letter for a brief sales message of your own. But rather than sending the reader to another source, you may be able to sell the reader a substitute.

SELLING SUBSTITUTES

If you believe you can satisfy your reader's needs with an alternative from your own products, don't refer the reader to another source. Instead, use your letter to sell the customer on the advantages of your substitute.

Figure 5.8

LETTER CONFIRMING AN ORDER

The Atlantic

2400 N STREET, N.W. • WASHINGTON, D.C. 20037-1196 • (202) 955-2412

October 16, 199_

Dear Friend of **The Atlantic**,

Thank you for your recent gift subscription order.

The first copy of each subscription will be delivered to the persons shown on the enclosed acknowledgment form, and will start with the January 199_ issue.

We will also send each recipient a gift announcement in your name.

Please take a moment now to check the names and addresses of your recipients carefully, and notify us of any changes immediately.

You are giving the most talked about magazine of public affairs and the arts today: News-making journalism, fiction, poetry, book reviews, humor—the perfect gift for anyone.

The enclosed acknowledgment form shows the amount charged to your account. If you wish, you may return your payment with the top portion of this acknowledgment.

Thank you again for your order.

Sincerely,

Steven C. Pippin

Steven C. Pippin
for **The Atlantic**

Figure 5.9

LETTER ACCOMPANYING A SHIPMENT

Johnson & Johnson
CHILD DEVELOPMENT TOYS

Dear Parent,

Your youngster's new Child Development Toy is here! You'll find CLEAR RATTLE inside this package. It is full of learning opportunities for you and your child to share.

CLEAR RATTLE is sure to be one of your child's favorite toys for many months because it's so versatile. Your infant will find it visually fascinating with its bright blue beads and candy-striped rod.

As baby gets a little older, he or she will learn how to control it by grasping and tilting. Baby will watch in sheer fascination as the beads spin round and round. Baby will discover, too, that by shaking CLEAR RATTLE he or she can create some very interesting sounds. Your baby will love these discoveries!

                Like all Johnson & Johnson Toys
                   Clear Rattle is safety tested
        well beyond standard government regulations.

All toy makers must meet standard government regulations. In addition to passing those, we do some testing of our own.

Johnson & Johnson Child Development Toys are exposed to exaggerated weather conditions. They must pass rigid drop, tension, bit, tumble, flex, pull, flammability, and toxicity testing—to make sure they'll stand up to the most vigorous play. And, to assure that small parts are inaccessible to your baby, whenever needed we design our toys with a double fail-safe sealing system. We do our best to make sure Child Development Toys are safe, reliable, and virtually unbreakable.

                                          Sincerely,

                                          Karen Davis

                                          Karen Davis
                                          for Johnson & Johnson
                                          Child Development Toys

WRITING AND RESPONDING TO REQUESTS 183

Establish Rapport: Buffer the bad news that you don't have the product requested by beginning on a positive note. Refer to the product the customer ordered in terms that apply both to the ordered item and to the substitute you will later propose. If a customer ordered a rocker with curved arms and you have only the standard arm model in stock, you might begin:

> Your choice to purchase solid hardwood furniture means you have chosen the best quality furniture you can buy.

Influence Thinking: Before explaining that the ordered item is unavailable, say something positive about the items you do carry:

> Our rib rockers provide a rare and graceful antique copy with a back that is gently sloped for the utmost in comfort.

Then reveal that the item is unavailable, but de-emphasize this information: mention the ordered item only once and in general terms, then stress what you do carry. Elaborate on the merits of your substitute by stressing those same qualities that probably led the reader to place the original order. But don't refer to your item as a "substitute," since the word connotes inferiority.

> Because our rockers are individually handcrafted by skilled and experienced artisans, the rockers take time to produce. Currently we have a six-month waiting list for our curved arm rib rockers. However, we can immediately ship you the rib rocker with standard arms as pictured in our catalog item 84–B. These arms provide the same graceful slope you are looking for, and they enhance both an Early American or a Contemporary decor. You will also find the price appealing, $38 less than your original order.

Motivate Action and Attitude: Make action easy and emphasize the reader's satisfaction with the product.

> We can immediately ship you the standard rib rocker by motor freight and return you $38. Otherwise, may we put you on our waiting list for the curved arm rib rocker? Please indicate your decision below and return this form in the envelope provided.
>
> Whichever model you choose, we know you will be delighted with your beautiful handcrafted furniture.
>
> Thank you for your order.

A silk clothing mail order house used the letter in Figure 5.10 to suggest a substitute for an item no longer in the house's collection.

Figure 5.10

LETTER SUGGESTING A SUBSTITUTE

15 ST. JAMES AVENUE BOSTON MA. 02116

August 23, 199_

Mrs. Carol Nadimer
21 Bailey Road
St. Paul, MN 55119

Dear Mrs. Nadimer:

Silk blouses can add to your wardrobe that simple elegance that is smart, relaxed, and confident.

RegalSilk sells many shades and styles of blouses, but our Autumn Collection does not include the particular combination you ordered. If you are looking for an off-white, executive style, we can offer you our Pongee Classic. Made of durable 90-gram Soie de Chine, the supple silk from China, it is detailed with a yoked back and box pleat. For an office look or for off-duty hours, Pongee projects self-assurance around the clock.

Enclosed is the catalog describing our most recent collection, with the Pongee Classic pictured on page 18. To receive a size 10 Ivory Pongee Classic for $52.00, please check the box below authorizing shipment, and return this letter with a check for $52.00 in the enclosed envelope.

We are sure you will be pleased with the elegance of our luxurious silk at affordable prices.

Sincerely yours,

Beverly Madison

Beverly Madison
for RegalSilk

Enclosure

WRITING ABOUT PEOPLE: REQUESTING AND WRITING RECOMMENDATIONS

Letters of recommendation help candidates to support their applications for jobs, graduate school, or other positions or honors. In turn, they help employers and other decision makers select the most suitable candidate for the position.

Requesting a Recommendation

As an applicant for a job, admission to a school, or an award, you may need to ask **references**—responsible people who are sources of information about you—to recommend you. As an employer or decision maker, you may have to call on an applicant's references to supply confidential information about that applicant. While you may request these recommendations through a telephone call or in person, a letter of request can be invaluable in eliciting just the information you would like the recommendation to cover.

Since most teachers and supervisors consider writing letters of recommendation part of their jobs, you can use the direct letter plan in requesting a recommendation. But you should keep in mind that you are still asking them to do you a favor. Be courteous, and make their job as easy as possible by providing sufficient information.

Establish Rapport: Begin by stating your request courteously. As an applicant, explain why you need the recommendation and who it is for. As an employer, give the name of the applicant you are considering, the position you are considering the applicant for, and why you are writing. Here's how an employer began his request:

> Cynthia Orsky has told us you are familiar with her work at Metro Archives and that you would provide us with some information. We are considering her for a position in customer relations and would like you to help us determine her suitability.

Influence Thinking: Whether as an applicant or as an employer, provide your references with whatever information you think will help them be specific and convincing. As an applicant for a job, don't assume that your reference remembers all your responsibilities, projects, and accomplishments, even though these may have taken place under his or her supervision. Remind your reference of those activities and accomplishments. If your record shows gaps or apparent lapses, explain why these occurred so that your reference may put these in the best possible light. If you think the information on your resume would be helpful in filling your reference in on your activities, attach your resume to your letter.

As an employer inquiring about an applicant, help the reference give you the information you need. Specify the job responsibilities or other job requirements. Ask specifically what you want to know about the applicant's abilities, experience, or qualifications. (Exclude, of course, inquiries about race, color, religion, sex, national origin, age, handicap, marital status, or parental status.) Notice how specific this employer's questions are about the candidate:

The person we hire will be responsible for handling customer inquiries and complaints. Therefore we require a person with initiative, the ability to think on her feet, and very strong communication skills, both in writing and in speaking.

We would appreciate whatever specific evidence you can provide, based on your knowledge of Ms. Orsky's current responsibilities and performance, that would help us evaluate her potential here.

Motivate Action and Attitude: Make action easy by stating clearly where the recommendation is to be sent and when it is needed. If relevant, assure the recipient of your letter that the information will be kept confidential. Finally, state your appreciation.

I will be contacting you early next week to find out if you would be willing to discuss Ms. Orsky's qualifications. All information will, of course, remain confidential.

Thank you very much.

In Figure 5.11, a student requests a recommendation from a professor. The student had previously asked the professor in person for the recommendation, and when the professor consented, the student sent this letter to follow up on his request. Notice how he explains what information his potential employer is looking for. He also helps the professor remember specific details about his accomplishments in the professor's class, especially concerning his class participation, since he was a quieter member of the class. By summarizing his achievements, he is providing his professor with specific information that can be included in the letter of recommendation to support his application effectively.

Figure 5.11
LETTER REQUESTING A RECOMMENDATION

Box 517
University of Notre Dame
Notre Dame, Indiana 46556
February 11, 199_

Professor Dennis Garner
312 O'Shaughnessy Hall
University of Notre Dame
Notre Dame, Indiana 46556

Dear Professor Garner:

Thank you for agreeing to be a reference for me. As I explained on the phone, I am applying through the Summer Interns in Business Program (SIBP) for an internship with the New York City Engineering Division, and I would appreciate your filling out the attached recommendation form for them. Since you were my professor for both micro-and macroeconomics, I think the Engineering Division would be especially interested in hearing from you about my analytical and problem-solving abilities, my initiative, and my ability to work under pressure.

I took micro with you in the fall of 199_ (grade earned: B) and macro in the spring of 199_ (grade earned: A-). Each class required a major term paper and two small group case analyses. I am enclosing copies of your final comments on the term papers. For the first paper you were enthusiastic about the way I applied micro theory to an unusual problem, and for the second you thought my analysis was excellent and my recommendations would be very effective.

Although I was one of the quieter members of the class, you commented very favorably on two of the presentations my groups were involved in: one on venture capital funding of small businesses, and the other on national unemployment. Both presentations demonstrated what I believe is my strong point—grasping theoretical principles and finding ways to make them practical.

Currently I am a junior majoring in finance with a 3.0 GPA. This summer internship is exactly what I would like to do to get hands-on

(continued)

> Professor Garner
> page 2
> February 11, 199_
>
> work experience in a large organization. The internship should help me decide what kind of job I'll be looking for once I graduate. If I know that, I can make the best use of my last year here at school.
>
> The recommendation form goes directly to SIBP in the enclosed envelope. It must get there before March 1st if it is to be considered.
>
> Thank you very much for helping me.
>
> Sincerely,
>
> *Dan Reiter*
>
> Dan Reiter, Junior

Writing a Recommendation

If you supervise others' work, you are likely to be called on as a reference should they apply for further training, promotion, or another job. As a reference you must represent applicants fairly and honestly. You have an obligation to the applicants, to allow them the opportunity for positions they are best qualified for, and you have an obligation to the inquirers, to provide them with information that will help them make a fair decision.

Being fair and honest may mean including information unfavorable to the candidate. You may do so legally and morally if (1) the information has been requested by someone with a right to know, and (2) you tell the truth in good faith and without malice. But if you feel that on balance your letter will be unfavorable, it would be preferable to tell the candidate you cannot write a favorable recommendation.

Establish Rapport: Begin directly. The following information is usually included in the first paragraphs:

1. The applicant's name, relationship to you, and length of time you have known or worked with this person.
2. The fact that you are writing confidentially if you are permitted to do so (this may be included in a subject heading).
3. A general statement expressing your pleasure or previewing your recommendation.

You will be making a wise choice in selecting John Peters for your MBA program.

In the past year and a half, I have had the opportunity to know John in two capacities: first, as an "end-user" of his department's services, and second, as his manager. From both perspectives, John is a very professional and hard-working individual.

Influence Thinking: Organize your evaluation around the questions the inquirer wants answered. Consider the qualifications important to the job the applicant is applying for, and discuss the candidate in those terms. If you must include negative material, embed it in and subordinate it to positive information.

Don't rely on generalities. If you say a candidate is "good," "outstanding," or "superior," include specific facts about job performance that demonstrate these qualities. Notice that John Peters's manager discusses those qualities he considers important to graduate work.

One of the major tasks facing a high-growth software company is keeping pace with change. To work in this type of environment, an individual needs to develop new methods and tools for doing daily tasks as well as to have the ability and insight to plan for the future. John not only has the capabilities to meet these challenges, but he also has a very positive attitude. In addition, he is responsive to the people he manages and works exceptionally well on projects with people from other departments.

In January 199_, the company honored John with our "Chairman's Medal" for outstanding performance. This honor is given to a select few and is awarded on the basis of dedication to company goals, adherence to professional standards, and demonstration of creativity and initiative in getting a job done. John was felt to be outstanding in all these areas.

Motivate Action and Attitude: End with your overall judgment about the candidate's fitness for the position or award. Express your willingness to cooperate further.

John is a dedicated young man who will make a commitment to doing a job and doing it well. He is an ideal MBA candidate who has a very strong future at Williams and Williams.

Please review his credentials carefully and if I can provide further information to you, please call me at 555–6100, ext. 7235.

In Figure 5.12, notice how a professor embeds discussion of a few of the candidate's less favorable qualities in an otherwise highly supportive recommendation.

Figure 5.12

LETTER OF RECOMMENDATION

COLLEGE OF PORTLAND
DEPARTMENT OF ECONOMICS, PORTLAND, OREGON 87208

December 5, 199_

To Whom It May Concern:

    I feel confident in recommending Ms. Hughey as a responsible and well-trained candidate for a management position. I have known Ms. Hughey for the past two years, during which she has taken my economic statistics course and has served as my research assistant. She has been a serious, motivated student who has consistently performed in the top 25 percent of her class. She is also an independent and effective worker.

    Ms. Hughey has not refrained from taking "hard core" science and mathematics courses, and she has done well. As a result, she is well trained analytically and feels comfortable operating in analytical situations. In interpreting her academic record, I feel compelled to say that her transcript tends to underestimate her true potential. Ms. Hughey has been penalized by the nature of our grading system. She has a tendency to perform close to the A-B borderline. Since we don't have half-grades, the average observer of her academic record may incorrectly infer that Ms. Hughey is a mediocre student. This definitely is not the case.

    In my statistics course, Ms. Hughey performed in the top 15 percent of the class. She readily mastered the analytical components of the course and was an innovative leader in her small-group final project.

    As my research assistant, Ms. Hughey has performed all research tasks responsibly and efficiently. Although she does not do computer programming, she works well with "canned" statistical programs. Most important, she is an independent worker.

> Bacon Associates
> page 2
> December 5, 199_
>
>   Ms. Hughey is personable and easy to work with. Although initially as my research assistant she seemed shy, she has since acquired assertiveness. She is now confident and takes demonstrable pride in her work.
>
>   I enthusiastically recommend Ms. Hughey as a promising candidate.
>
>   Sincerely,
>
>   Jose Garcia
>
>   Jose Garcia, Ph.D.
>   Assistant Professor of Economics
>
> JG/np

WRITING ABOUT CLAIMS AND ADJUSTMENTS

Although we may aspire to perfection, no business can provide perfect products and services to all its customers all the time. That is why writing about claims and adjustments is an important component of business correspondence. Whether you are writing to your suppliers to request an adjustment from them, or you are dealing with a customer's request for a refund, being polite and factual can help you succeed in these bad-news situations with company goodwill intact.

Making Claims or Requesting Adjustments

If you have the job of purchasing products and services for your company, orders may occasionally turn out unsatisfactory: merchandise may be incomplete, faulty, or damaged; shipments may arrive late or get mixed up; all the services contracted for may not be rendered. You must then write a claim letter—for example, to request a whole or partial refund, to correct a billing, or to ask for a free repair or replacement.

    In assessing the reader of your claim letter, assume that companies know it is good for business to respond promptly and favorably to reasonable claims. First, a prompt and favorable response means a satisfied customer. Second, claim and complaint letters provide valuable information on a company's quality control. Third, prompt and favorable replies encourage customers to write. If your letter can demonstrate that your claim is reasonable, you should win a refund or adjustment.

But besides winning, you may also want your letter to express your frustration or anger at the inconvenience caused you. Restrain yourself! Bear in mind that a certain percentage of defects is normal in the best-run operations. Most companies recognize this and are prepared to respond to your claim quickly. Remember, too, that the reader of your claim is not likely to be the person who made the mistake. Instead, your reader will be the claims adjuster, a person the company has selected to evaluate the merits of complaints like yours. If you sound reasonable and can justify your complaint with evidence, the adjuster will be likely to trust your account of the matter.

DIRECT CLAIM

To make a routine claim explicitly covered by a company's guarantee, you should use the direct letter plan.

Establish Rapport: Begin with a statement of the problem.

Influence Thinking: Continue with complete details to provide evidence for the claim.

Motivate Action and Attitude: Be explicit about what you are asking for, and close in the expectation that the company will honor your complaint.

In Figure 5.13, a building supplies company uses the direct approach to request a routine adjustment from its shipper.

INDIRECT CLAIM

The direct approach should be sufficient for most claims, but occasionally a more persuasive claim is in order—for example, when the adjustment requested is not specifically covered but you feel your claim is justified, or when you have tried before but received a negative reply. In these cases, the indirect letter plan is in order.

Establish Rapport: Appeal to your reader's desire to protect the company's reputation. Most companies provide explicit warranties, guarantees, or other adjustment policies that underscore their concern for customer satisfaction. This concern for the company's reputation is a principle both you and the company can agree on.

> Your company can compete with those much larger than itself because of your excellent reputation for quality products and dependable service. You will be concerned, then, when I tell you the serious difficulties I have been having with your billing department.

WRITING AND RESPONDING TO REQUESTS 193

Figure 5.13

LETTER MAKING A CLAIM USING THE DIRECT APPROACH

---

bernstein products
2911 Berkeley Street
Fullerton, CA 92631

May 3, 199_

Cincinnati Supply Co.
1712 Gilbert Avenue
Cincinnati, OH 45202

Claims Department:

Our customer, Close Building Materials in Hayward, refused to accept a portion of the referenced shipment due to damage. We are filing claim with you to recoup the loss for the six cartons of 10′ CornerAid and enclose the following paperwork to support our claim:

1. Copy of Freight Bill #4424205 indicating shipment.
2. Photocopy of Delivery Receipt indicating damage.
3. Copy of our Price List No. 2 substantiating price for our 10′ CornerAid as $112/carton.
4. Original Bernstein Products Invoice No. 23123: 6 cartons CornerAid @ $112 = $672.
5. Photocopy of initial Bernstein Products Invoice No. 23043 to Close Building Materials to further substantiate material charges.

Our invoice to you (#23123) includes a charge for a portion of our out-of-pocket freight expense, as well as the cost of the six cartons of 10′ CornerAid calculated as follows:

Freight expense for 10′ CornerAid = 49 lbs./carton × 6 = 294 lbs. × $9.50/cwt:	$ 27.93
Damages for 6 cartons of 10′ CornerAid	672.00
Total	699.93

We think this documentation will enable you to handle our claim for $699.93 as expeditiously as possible. But if you have any questions, please contact me.

Yours truly,

Burt Smith

Burt Smith, Operations

enc.

Influence Thinking: Provide the information about your claim: date, invoice numbers, warranties, contracts, nature of the problem, and so on. Explain what went wrong, when, why, and how, but avoid making accusations or showing anger. Instead, try to be firm and clear in presenting your version of what happened. Your aim is to provide proof for the merits of your claim.

Rather than in anger writing, "It's absolutely impossible for our office to have made calls amounting to more than $500 for the month in question. This exorbitant bill is way out of line," provide proof for your claim:

> From June 15 to July 15, our company (account no. 452-34-88731) was charged $1,453.45 for phone calls. According to our records, however, our actual calls amount to $456.80, including tax and local service charges. The remainder, $996.75, has been erroneously billed to our account.
>
> We have checked our records and are confident we have recorded all calls. We have never done business with several of the locations in area codes billed to us. And as you will see if you check your records, we have been your customer for over six years and have never had a bill that exceeded $550. At your service representative's suggestion, I am enclosing a photocopy of your invoice with all our calls circled in red.

Motivate Action and Attitude: Request the specific action you want the reader to take in order to satisfy your claim. Instead of, "Please resolve this problem immediately," try:

> We have discussed this error with your billing department three times now and still we receive "past due" notices. On the basis of the information we are providing, we expect the bill to be corrected to show no debits. Thank you for your prompt attention.

In Figure 5.14, a buyer tries to persuade the seller to back up a product that gave poor service, even though the product is not covered by a guarantee.

Responding to Claims

When a claim is involved, something has gone wrong. Whether you grant the claim or deny it, take care to explain your viewpoint tactfully.

YES TO CLAIMS: SELLER AT FAULT

If you can grant a claim or request for adjustment, this is good news to your reader and you can be direct in your approach. Yet you still must deal with a negative element:

Figure 5.14

LETTER MAKING A CLAIM USING THE
INDIRECT APPROACH

EMERY
TURBINE CORPORATION
3237 DOUGLAS AVENUE DES MOINES IA 50310

July 7, 199_

Quality Lawn Products
9005 Hiokman Rd.
Des Moines, IA 50322

Dear Mr. Thompson:

    Three years ago we decided to buy sprinkler valves from you for our new headquarters because we knew of you as a neighborhood business that lives up to the reputation of its company slogan: "Quality is the word for all the work we do."

    As you may recall, your sales rep Carl Taber spoke to me at length about our needs. I told him that we were more interested in durability than in saving a few dollars. Carl said that you carried both brass and plastic valves, brass for $65/each and plastic for $15 less. We knew the brass are usually good for six years. Carl assured us the platic would hold up as well, if not better. He said that plastic would definitely withstand the stress of the water pressure through our main pipes.

    On Carl's recommendation the company purchased 48 plastic automatic sprinkler valves (code 19-3-58) from you. Over the past three months the sleeve connecting the top of the valve to the main water pipe has burst or cracked in twelve of the valves. Last Sunday, one-fourth of the lawn was flooded for a full day, since two valves broke while our small maintenance crew was out handling a problem in another building across town.

    The result is that besides repairing considerable damage to the lawn (estimates run about $500), we will need to replace the twelve valves.

(continued)

(LETTER MAKING A CLAIM USING THE INDIRECT
APPROACH continued)

Mr. Thompson
page 2
July 7, 199_

    Our warranty with you expired two years ago, but we trusted your recommendation on the plastic valves. When we rechecked our water pressure, we found that it was still well under the limit the valves should withstand.

    Since we bought plastic valves only on your recommendation, we think you should be willing to stand behind your work and provide the labor to replace the plastic valves with brass ones. We are willing to pay for the new valves.

    Our intention today is what it was three years ago. We want to own a durable product backed by a company with a reputation for quality. Except for this incident, you have provided us with excellent advice and service in the past, and we want our good relations to continue.

                              Sincerely yours,

                              Nancy Simmons

                              Nancy Simmons
                              Maintenance Dept.

NS/rr
cc: B. Emery

Someone has been at fault. If you, the seller, are at fault, you have been responsible for the buyer's inconvenience. In this case, acknowledge your fault and apologize, but at the same time assure the reader that the error is the exception in your operation and not the rule.

Establish Rapport: Begin with the good news. If the customer is most interested in receiving the refund, credit, exchange, or whatever was requested, announce that you are making the adjustment requested. In doing so, avoid an imperious tone created by such phrases as "we are granting," "we will allow you," "we want to keep you satisfied."

If on the other hand the customer most wants an apology for inconvenience you caused, begin by first apologizing for the inconvenience. In referring to your fault, avoid specific images that would too vividly recall the customer's inconvenience.

    We are sorry for the problem you have encountered and have processed an order for a new replacement stroller to be sent to the above address via UPS at no charge.

Here or in your closing, thank the customer for pointing out your error.

Influence Thinking: Explain enough about what caused the mistake to assure your reader that you now have the problem solved and that the error will not happen again. But you do not need to give a detailed analysis of your operations and the competence of your employees. If you need to investigate the cause of the problem, assure your reader you will do so.

> When UPS delivers the new stroller, we request that you give the driver the defective one. He will have return authorization papers with him. If you no longer have the carton that the original stroller was in, have the stroller put into the new carton and the driver will return it to us here at the factory. Our engineering department would like to inspect the defects so that they may be prevented in the future.

Motivate Action and Attitude: To promote a positive attitude, don't end with apologies or tentative phrases such as "we hope you will be satisfied." Instead, thank the reader for understanding and, if appropriate, encourage future transactions.

> Thank you for your understanding and cooperation. Komfort stands behind all its products. Our reputation is your guarantee of satisfaction.

YES TO CLAIMS: BUYER AT FAULT

If you are granting the claim even though the buyer was at fault, somewhere in your letter you must make clear how the buyer was at fault so that the mistake will not be repeated and the claim made again. In explaining the buyer's fault, take special care to avoid accusatory phrases such as "you failed to," or "if you had read the instruction manual." Even though the buyer was at fault, once you have decided to grant the claim, grant it ungrudgingly and avoid such phrases as "in order to keep you satisfied," or "because you have insisted."

Establish Rapport: Begin directly by announcing that you are granting the claim. Or begin indirectly with an agreeable statement, withholding the best news until you have explained why your company is not at fault.

> When you told us of the difficulties with your MadeRite Food Processor, we immediately checked into it. Your satisfaction with our products is our primary concern.

Influence Thinking: Explain the cause of the problem tactfully. Remember that your purpose is educational rather than judgmental. You want to help the buyer avoid such problems in the future. If appropriate, take this opportunity for sales promotion.

> Our repair department has discovered that the machine's malfunction was caused by excessive debris choking the motor. Malfunction caused by debris is not covered by the machine's warranty. However, to ensure that you have a positive experience with our products, we are providing a one-time service: complete cleaning and overhaul of the motor.
>
> If properly cared for, the repaired motor will give you many years of service. Please read the instruction manual carefully. The manual explains that in order to preserve the life of the motor and remain covered by the one-year warranty, the user should always place the MadeRite on a clean surface, away from crumbs or debris that might be sucked into the motor.

Motivate Action and Attitude: End with sales promotion or anticipate future business relations.

> Your MadeRite Food Processor should be arriving at your home within two weeks, and you can begin again to enjoy the ease of preparing foods with MadeRite.
>
> Don't forget that in major department stores you will find the complete line of MadeRite accessories. These can help make delicious meals even easier to prepare.

NO TO CLAIMS

Most people who make a claim believe their position is reasonable. But if, on reviewing the situation, you decide that in all fairness you cannot grant the request, you must write a letter saying no. To avoid any offense, pay special attention to the reader's point of view.

At first it may seem very polite to begin, "We are sorry, but we cannot"; or "We regret, but our policy demands"; or "We wish we could grant your request, but." If you keep your reader in mind, however, you will recognize that these phrases sound about as comforting as when our parents turned us over the knee and said: "This is going to hurt me more than it does you." Although you will be sorry to have to displease the reader, avoid emphasizing your own response or sounding condescending. Instead, focus on helping the reader understand the reasons for your decision. To do so, use the indirect pattern: First give your reader the reasons for the refusal, and only then announce the refusal.

Establish Rapport: Since above all you want to persuade your reader that you have given the request a fair hearing, establish rapport by indicating you understand the reader's needs and have taken them into consideration.

> Hot water is important to every household, so when we heard you were having trouble with your new QuikFlow electric water heater, we sent our repairman, Al Briskowski, immediately to check out the difficulty.

Influence Thinking: Help your reader understand your decision by first explaining as fully as necessary the facts and reasoning that led to it. If you can, show that your reasoning is, if only in the long run, in the reader's best interest.

Then announce your decision, subordinating the bad news to positive information. If possible, suggest an alternative course of action or make some other constructive suggestions. This will indicate your respect for the reader's interests.

> Al told us that the thermostat controls on your heater had shorted out because of a loose connection in your circuit board. He told us you agreed that it would make most sense not to replace the thermostats until the wiring in the circuit board was replaced. Otherwise the thermostats would probably short out again very quickly.
>
> Since the burned out thermostats were not due to a defect in the material or workmanship of your new heater, they are not covered by the QuikFlow warranty. This explains why you have been billed $40 for Mr. Briskowski's service call.
>
> Now that you know the source of your electrical problems, it should be easy for you to have an electrician repair your wiring. Just as soon as the wiring is repaired, we can replace the QuikFlow thermostats and have your heater working smoothly. The new thermostats will, of course, be covered by our one-year warranty.

Motivate Action and Attitude: Close on a positive note and avoid the tentative phrases "we hope" or "we trust." If your alternative suggestion requires action, ask for it positively. Otherwise, end with suggestions for resale, future orders, or service.

> We can have your heater working properly within 24 hours of the time we get your call. We look forward to hearing from you.

In Figure 5.15, a company refuses an adjustment to a buyer who claims that his new flooring is defective.

Figure 5.15

LETTER REFUSING A CLAIM

DIAMOND FLOORS
9 BURTON ROAD DALLAS, TX 75227

July 27, 199_

Mr. John Washburn
519 Burton Road
Dallas, TX 75227

Dear Mr. Washburn:

The purchase of a new floor is a large investment today, and it can be frustrating when the product appears to be defective. That is why at Diamond we make it a policy to respond quickly to all questions and claims. When we heard about your floor discoloration, we sent a representative out immediately.

After careful inspection, our representative found the discoloration to be confined to traffic areas, such as in front of the kitchen sink and between the table and counters. He also noticed a similar brown discoloration on the carpet going out the back door. When he looked out the back door for a possible source of staining, he discovered that your driveway had recently been covered with an asphalt driveway sealer.

With the staining only in the traffic lanes and on the back stairs carpet, it appears that the driveway sealer was tracked into the house and caused the discoloration of your floor. As a petroleum-based product, driveway sealer will stain any vinyl-surfaced floor.

Staining is not covered under the Diamond guarantee, but the information our representative gave you on solvents and other cleaning agents should help you return some of the original color to your floor. If there is any other way we can be of service to you, please let us know.

Sincerely,

Thomas D. Giovanni

Thomas DiGiovanni
for Diamond Floors

TG/sn

WRITING ABOUT CREDIT

For buyers, a credit account can be not only a convenience but, when cash is short, a necessity. That is why a company that sells on credit offers its customers an important service that can make its business more competitive. But offering credit terms means taking a risk, and to minimize that risk, companies must know a customer's credit record. On the basis of that record, they can reasonably grant or refuse credit terms.

Checking Credit References

When customers apply for credit, they offer **credit references**—that is, businesses with which they have established a good credit record. You may check these references yourself either by telephone or a form letter, requesting such information as length of time sold on credit, credit limit, paying habits, and so forth. Figure 5.16 illustrates a form that one business uses to request credit information.

Rather than checking for yourself, however, you may subscribe to one or more credit rating services. These services can immediately supply current credit ratings to their subscribers through a computer connection to their data banks. You may also choose to rely on your customers to obtain bank credit cards such as American Express, MasterCard, or Visa. If you honor these cards, you pay the bank credit card fee of 1 to 3 percent of each credit card sale, and the bank guarantees that you will be paid for the sale.

Replying to Credit Checks

You may be on the receiving end of calls or letters requesting credit checks. Such exchange of information is routine among businesses. In giving out credit information, be sure to state that the information you provide is confidential. Answer only the questions you are asked, and provide only information derived from your own business, not from any investigation you may have made. Since an applicant who has been refused credit has the right to know why he or she was denied, be prepared to justify the information you report.

Approving Credit

You bring good news to a credit applicant when you announce that his or her application has been approved. In these instances, use the direct letter pattern.

Figure 5.16

REQUEST FOR CREDIT INFORMATION

```
                              ┌─────────────┐
                              │ CREDIT ✓    │
                              │      CHECK  │
                              └─────────────┘
                              An Inspection-Reporting Company

      306 High Street                                    (617) 326-3464
      P.O. Box 4160,                                     Dedham, Massachusetts 02026


      ---                              ---
                                        Date
                                        _____

      ---                              ---


                              REQUEST FOR REFERENCE

      We are completing a credit report on the below named person(s) in connection with
      processing an application for credit. We would appreciate your providing us with
      a reference on your experience, where applicable. Please return the completed form
      in the postage paid, addressed envelope that accompanies this form. Thank you.


      Applicant(s)_____  Soc. Sec. No._____
      Address_____               _____


      EMPLOYMENT
      Position_____   Date(s) Employed_____
      Salary/Wage_____  Per_____  Permanent or Temporary (circle one)
      Remarks_____

      CREDIT
      Type of Account_____  Account No._____
      Opening Date_____  High Credit_____  Bal. Due_____  Past Due_____
      Terms_____  Paying Record_____  ECOA Des._____

      DEPOSITORY ACCOUNT
      Checking Account No._____  Average Balance_____
      Opening Date_____  Number of NSF Checks_____  ECOA Des._____
      Savings Account No._____  Open Date_____  Bal._____  ECOA Des._____
      Certificate No._____  Open Date_____  Bal._____  ECOA Des._____

      REMARKS_____
              _____
              _____


      Signed_____  Title_____  Date_____
           (employer or creditor)
```

Establish Rapport: Open the letter by announcing the credit approval and welcoming your new credit customer.

> Your credit application has been approved. Enclosed you will find two McCord's credit cards for your shopping convenience. Welcome to our list of most valued customers!

Influence Thinking: If necessary, include specific information about the payment schedule and credit terms. If the terms include a credit limit, avoid making the limitation seem a penalty by phrasing the limit in a positive way.

> You can now charge up to $500 in McCord's merchandise. Once you receive your monthly bill, you can take up to 30 days to pay.

Motivate Action and Attitude: Take the opportunity in the final paragraphs to invite sales by highlighting the goods and services that your company can provide the applicant.

> McCord's offers you 23 departments with the latest in merchandise to meet all your clothing and home decorating needs.
>
> Please come by soon and see how convenient credit card shopping at McCord's can be. We look forward to offering you the finest goods and services.

Refusing Credit

Refusing a request for credit requires tact, because you are passing judgment on the applicant's ability to keep promises to pay debts. Since your reader may feel that his or her character and ability to honor financial commitments are on the line, demonstrate that you understand and respect the reader's position. At the same time, sell the reader on your position. In these cases, use the indirect letter pattern.

Establish Rapport: Begin with a buffer opening, such as one of the following:

- Express appreciation for the reader's application and interest in your company.
- If relevant, point out the positive aspects of the applicant's situation or credit record.
- Suggest that you have given the application careful consideration.

> Your order for our top-of-the-line marine paints tells us you will be having a busy summer at the harbor. We wish you a successful season.

Influence Thinking: Explain the reasons for your refusal. If, because of the volume of credit applications your company receives, you must use a less personalized credit refusal, you may simply list several factors that are considered in all credit refusals without identifying the particular shortcoming of the applicant. The refusal might then invite the reader to reapply when circumstances change:

> In reviewing credit applicants, we take into consideration a number of factors: length of residency and employment, income, assets, number of dependents, paying record, . . .

A more helpful refusal explains why the application was refused and offers specific suggestions the applicant can follow to qualify for credit in the future. These may include establishing a credit relationship, reducing inventory, building sales, or obtaining local financing.

While you must make your refusal clear, embed the refusal in positive information. Better yet, imply the refusal by stating a counterproposal. This usually takes the form of offering sales on a cash basis, pointing out current sale items, offering a cash discount, or suggesting smaller orders.

> We have analyzed the financial statements you have provided us, and we anticipate that when the summer season gets fully under way, you will be able to achieve the 2:1 ratio of assets to liabilities that provides a sound foundation for credit. At that time we would like to ship your orders on a credit basis.
>
> Meanwhile we can offer you the substantial savings of a 7 percent cash discount on orders of the size you requested. Or, if you prefer to order in smaller quantities, may we introduce you to our Frequent-Delivery Plan? It is designed to help our dealers buy low quantities and still maintain adequate inventory even during high-turnover periods.

Motivate Action and Attitude: If you have suggested an alternative action, make action easy. End by encouraging future relations.

> We can have your order at your door within four days of the receipt of your check. Just fill out the enclosed order form and attach your check. The quality paints you are buying, backed by our fast delivery and advertising support, can help you to a prosperous season.

In Figure 5.17 a department store refuses credit to a young newcomer to town who currently holds a part-time job while looking for full-time work. He has provided no credit references from his hometown.

Figure 5.17

LETTER REFUSING CREDIT

JENSEN'S
2447 34TH STREET SOUTH
ST. PETERSBURG FL. 33711

March 9, 199_

Mr. Andrew Warman
301 Crystal Drive
St. Petersburg, FL 33708

Dear Mr. Warman:

Welcome to St. Petersburg! And thank you for choosing Jensen's as your place to shop.

In order to maintain fair prices for all our customers, we analyze closely the employment and credit records of all our credit applicants. Since you have just moved to St. Petersburg and, understandably, have yet to establish a credit record here, we feel we can best serve you on a cash basis. Many longtime St. Petersburg residents have found that our sale items and easy layaway plan make Jensen's the best shopping location in town.

We would be delighted to review your application once you have finished your job search. We feel certain you will prosper in St. Pete's!

Sincerely,

Nikki Lindley

Nikki Lindley,
Store Manager

WRITING TO REFUSE REQUESTS FOR FAVORS

Conscientious business people know that the prosperity of their business depends on the good opinion of the public and the well-being of the community at large. They make concerted efforts to respond to individual and community requests for favors. Such favors may include giving money to a charity, heading up a community project, serving as a speaker, or offering other business services to support individual or community projects. But as a conscientious business person you will not always be able to do as much as you or others would like. You may have to refuse requests for money, time, services, or expertise.

People usually make reasonable requests and hope for a favorable reply. They deserve a considerate response. Even those who make what may seem ill-considered or outlandish requests will be impressed and perhaps chastened by a courteous response. To show consideration, cushion the disappointing news by using the indirect letter pattern.

Establish Rapport: Begin with something both you and the reader can agree on. This may be some statement in the request letter, or simply saying that you have considered the request carefully. Although you want to be agreeable, don't say anything which might imply that you are going to grant the favor—such as, "Certainly every Galveston business has the obligation to support the Community Fund."

> We appreciate your interest in the Xylo Company's manufacturing process and can understand how an introduction to the manufacture of new products would be of educational value to your third-grade music students.

Influence Thinking: First give reasons for your refusal, and only then announce the refusal. In providing your explanation, avoid apologizing or appealing to "our policy." If you explain your reasons clearly, the reader should see that your refusal logically follows from your explanation.

> The Xylo Company is proud to be the leader in cymbal sounds. As you may know, generating a constant flow of new products and new ideas is a demanding task. In addition, it is difficult to bring these new products to market before the competition has an opportunity to copy our innovation.
>
> Over the past few years, the Xylo Company has suffered as a result of having extended manufacturing tours to the public. Unfortunately, the company's open tour policy provided a vehicle for one of our competitors to learn of our new product line three months prior to its introduction. As a result, our competition was able to come out with substantially the same new product as ours within weeks of our introducing it. As you can well

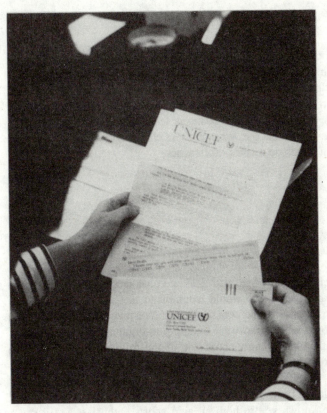

Business people make concerted efforts to respond to requests.

understand, such a situation demoralizes our Research and Development staff, and precludes us from attaining our corporate goal of providing musicians with innovative sounds.

As with any bad-news message, the refusal may be implied rather than stated. Emphasize the positive—that is, what you can do or are doing—and avoid negative statements such as ''we cannot,'' ''we are unable to,'' or ''we are sorry,'' if it is possible to do so while still making your decision clear.

It is critical for the Xylo Company to safeguard its new ideas, products, and manufacturing methods from the view of the general public. Only in this way can the company fulfill its responsibility to its customers.

Motivate Action and Attitude: End on a positive note—for example, by suggesting a counterproposal or by extending your good wishes for the success of the project.

We do hope that your third graders will enjoy the enclosed pictures and text describing the company's manufacturing process.

SUMMARY

The routine business correspondence discussed in this chapter offers you the opportunity to create positive relationships with your readers. Good-news messages written in a direct and positive style help cement good relations, and even bad-news messages, if you are sensitive and show respect for the reader, can build goodwill for your firm. You can adapt the RTA formula to handle several business letter situations: writing about products and services, writing about people, writing about claims and adjustments, writing about credit, and writing to refuse requests for favors.

EXERCISES

See "The Good-News Direct Letter Pattern," pp. 160–167, for Exercises 1–3.

1. A senior at the high school from which you graduated has written the letter shown in Figure 5.18, asking whether or not you would recommend that she attend your college or university. Write a response to the senior's letter. You may want to circle the senior's questions and jot down a list of answers to help you organize your response.

2. The same student would like to know about one of the following policies: dorm rules, class attendance, scholarships. Write a letter of response to her on one of these topics.

3. You have received a letter from a close friend concerning the purchase of some sports equipment. Since she knows you're both an avid sports enthusiast and a smart buyer, she wants your recommendation before she speaks to sales people about purchasing the item in question. She expects that you'll be able to recommend a good but moderately priced pair of skis (for skis you may substitute jogging shoes, sailboat, tennis racket, golf clubs, bowling ball, or equipment for a hobby). Write her a letter informing her of her "best bet" and her options.

See "The Bad-News Indirect Letter Pattern," pp. 167–171, for Exercises 4–6.

4. You are assistant manager of Dydee Diaper Services. Last week your boss asked you to ghostwrite a bad-news letter announcing a price hike. In the past few days you have collected the following information to help you write your letter:

- If increase number of diapers rented weekly, rate reduced
- If continue with same number, price increase of 60 cents a week as of April 1
- Compare price of disposables, increased last week (e.g., Pampers small-sized diaper: 12/box is $3.69, 48/box is $7.79, 66/box is $9.99)

(turn to page 210)

Figure 5.18

A HIGH SCHOOL SENIOR'S REQUEST FOR ADVICE

Dear _____,

   I am a high school senior interested in applying to your college. The guidance office gave me your name since you are currently attending _____ and are a graduate of _____ high school.

   As you probably know, selecting the right college is a difficult choice. Since you are a junior at _____, I wonder whether you would answer a few questions to help me evaluate whether your college is the right one for me.

   I'd like to pursue a career in business on graduating from college. Does your college offer a strong major in business or economics? Can I major in another field and minor in business?

   I think I'd enjoy taking elective courses. Have you found room in your schedule to take courses outside your major?

   What's the social life like? Do people party on weekends? During the week? Does the campus close down on weekends or is there a lot to do on campus?

   What would you say is the best thing about going to your college? What's the worst?

   I realize that I've asked you a lot of questions and you're probably very busy. But if you'd just take a few minutes and jot down some quick responses, I'd really appreciate your help. I value your experience at _____ and know that you could give me a better sense of the school than any of the brochures it sends out and any meetings I might be able to set up with your admissions office.

Yours truly,

Leslie Brown

Leslie Brown

- Dydee new prices for set sizes:

190 –	$14.95	100 –	11.35
180 –	14.55	90 –	10.95
170 –	14.15	80 –	10.55
160 –	13.75	70 –	10.15
150 –	13.35	60 –	9.75
140 –	12.95	50 –	9.35
130 –	12.55	40 –	8.95
120 –	12.15	30 –	8.55
110 –	11.75	20 –	8.15

Group and order the relevant information and write the letter.

5. As a management trainee in the credit card division of Hartford Cooperative Bank Company, you have been asked to revise the bad-news letter shown in Figure 5.19. What changes would you make?

See "Orders for and Inquiries about Products and Services," pp. 173–177 for Exercises 6–9.

6. During a recent trip to Seattle, you bought a brand of spice tea you like very much—Chamomint Cinispice—and have subsequently found it to be unavailable in your area. Since you know the address of the store where you bought the tea, write to the store requesting that the owner tell you either where to buy the tea in your area or how to get in touch with the manufacturer.

7. As manager of a hardware store, you need to stock electric fans for the summer season. You want window fans, floor fans, and table fans in a variety of sizes and with adjustable speeds. Write a form letter to go to several manufacturers requesting all the information you need.

8. As the hardware store manager mentioned in Exercise 7, you have decided to order Patton fans. From the information on how to order printed in the Patton brochure (Figure 5.20), decide on five models you want to stock and the store displays you would like to use. Write a letter requesting the fans and displays. Stress that you need to receive the fans by early May.

9. You are Janet Halpern. Three years ago last October, your mother loaned you $40,000 at 10 percent for twenty-five years, so that you could make a down payment on a house. The money came from a trust fund (# 3797) she had with her local bank, Utah National, 2112 State Street, Salt Lake City, UT 84115. You have been paying $364 to the trust fund every month. Now, however, you think you could handle larger payments and would like to have the loan paid off fifteen years from now. Write the bank requesting information about what your payment amount would be if you were to pay off the loan in fifteen years.

See "Yes to Orders and Inquiries," pp. 176–180, for Exercises 10–12.

10. As an administrative assistant for the Trust Department of Utah National, you received the letter from Janet Halpern (exercise 9) about six weeks ago. You have not responded to the letter yet. The reason for the delay is that you are not in the Mortgage Department and have never had to do an amortization schedule before. (An amortization

Figure 5.19
LETTER REGARDING CREDIT CARD CHARGES

                                                                        Hartford Cooperative Bank
                                                                         4007 Wethersfield
                                                                         Hartford, CT 06109
                                                                         August 5, 199_

Megan Greenfield
609 N. Windham St.
Willimantic, CT 06256

Dear Megan Greenfield:

    Unfortunately from time to time we write letters that do not "cheer up" our customers, and we guess this is one. Like everything else, the costs of administering the MasterCard program are increasing, and therefore, we are making the following changes, which will affect the FINANCE CHARGE and Annual Fee as follows:

1. The FINANCE CHARGE on your Merchant Advances will be computed on the average daily balance method, beginning with the statement you receive in October 199_. Currently, the FINANCE CHARGE is computed on the balance of your Merchant Advances at the end of a billing cycle.
2. The Annual Membership fee for the year beginning January 1, 199_ and each subsequent year will remain at $18.00 for SINGLE ACCOUNT CARDS ONLY. All other accounts will be charged $18.00 for the first card, plus $12.00 for the second and each additional card for cardholders who have more than one card.

    Hopefully the above will not be too disturbing to you as we do realize we are the bearers of "bad news."

                                                                           Very truly yours,

                                                                           MASTERCARD DEPARTMENT

Figure 5.20

PATTON PRODUCT MODELS

Patton merchandising makes the sale

Only Patton has a complete merchandising program to move product and build profits. Just look at the self-sell packaging — dramatic, beautiful, but most important — effective. Based on 40 years of research and experience, Patton's silent salesmen tell the story and close the sale.

Build your own sell-out crowd.

Patton's complete merchandising package includes:
- National and regional television advertising
- Full-color, self-sell packaging
- On product, P.O.P. labels
- Beach Ball display sell kits
- Colorful stand-up header cards
- Co-op advertising allowances
- Radio scripts
- Window + Fan™ display
- Ad slicks, line art, photographs
- 30-second television commercials

Displays

BBSK	Beach Ball Display Kit	Includes beach ball BB-1 and header card HCAC for use with U2-1885, WF-1885 and R-1885.
WFDS	Free Standing Display Stand	For use with all W and WF models.
HC20	Whole-House Window Fan Header Card	For use with 20" Models W-2084 and W-2085T.
HCAC	4-Color Header Card	For use with Whole-house Air Circulator Models U2-1885, WF-1885 and R-1885.
BB-1	Colorful Imprinted Beach Ball	For use with U2-1885, WF-1885 and R-1885.
HCWF	Window + Floor Fan™ Header Card	For use with WF-1285, WF-1485 and WF-1885.

Purchasing Specifications

Model	Description	CFM	Watts	Speeds	Pkg. Wt.	Cubic Ft.	Minimum Window Size
Air Circulators							
U2-1285	Whole Room 12"	4,000	65	3	10#	1.5	N/A
U2-1485	Multi-Room 14"	6,000	80	3	12#	2.0	N/A
U2-1885	Whole House 18"	10,000	241	3	19#	3.0	N/A
Pedestal Air Circulators							
R-1885	Whole House Rollair 18"	10,000	241	3	27#	4.5	N/A
P-2486	Adjustable Pedestal 24"	22,000	338	2	45#	10.5	N/A
P-3086	Adjustable Pedestal 30"	26,500	335	2	64#	10.5	N/A
OS-3000	Oscillator Pedestal 30"	26,500	335	2	68#	10.5	N/A
Window + Floor Fans							
WF-1285	Whole Room 12"	4,000	65	3	11#	1.9	16" x 13½"
WF-1485	Multi-Room 14"	6,000	80	3	16#	3.35	19" x 17½"
WF-1885	Whole House 18"	10,000	241	3	21#	4.35	22" x 19½"
Whole House Window Fans							
W-2084	Whole House 20"	2,300*	208	2	25#	3.9	22" to 35" wide
W-2085T	Deluxe Whole House 20"	2,300*	208	3	30#	3.9	22" to 35" wide
W-2485T	Whole House Exhaust 24"	4,020*	448	3	41#	5.8	24" to 36" wide
Rotating Louver Fan							
CA-1284	Rotating Louver 14"	1,750	80	3	9#	1.6	N/A

*@ 0" Static Pressure

FIVE YEAR WARRANTY
MADE IN THE U.S.A.

PATTON®
When your comfort demands the best.

Patton Electric Company, Inc., P.O. Box 128, 15012 Edgerton Road, New Haven, Indiana 46774, 219/493-3564

schedule tells you what your equal monthly payments have to be in order to pay off a loan in a given period of time. It also tells you how much of each payment will be applied to the principle and how much will be paid as interest.) You had to learn a computer program before you could get the information. Now you have mastered the program and have learned that if Janet starts with today's date, this month's payment having not yet been received by the Trust Department, her monthly payments will amount to $420.08. Since you don't know whether Janet wants to start immediately with the new payment amount or wait a month or more, you want her to call or write you whenever she is ready to change payment amounts. At that time you can determine the exact payment amount. Write the letter responding to Janet's request.

11. You have started a safety lock business with two of your classmates and are delighted to have received your first order for twenty-four from a local sports store. You are about to send out the shipment. Write a letter to accompany your shipment.

12. As manager of a sports store, confirm the local high school's order of thirty football uniforms. (You can substitute for football uniforms a product you know more about.) Be sure to reinforce the selling features of the uniforms.

See "Refusing Orders and Requests for Information," pp. 180–184, for Exercises 13–14.

13. You are an assistant manager for a wholesale nursery. Your customers are either retailers or individuals who buy plants and flowers in large quantities. A family moving into your area has written to you inquiring whether you could provide flowers for a small wedding they are planning. Your company had been recommended to them by a friend who is a local customer of yours. Write a letter to the family refusing their order.

14. As student president of your dormitory, you are in charge of assigning rooms to incoming freshmen. There are 100 rooms in your dorm: 40 singles, 40 doubles, and 20 suites (two rooms with private bath shared by four students). Assignments are made in order, by date of dorm application. By now you have reached the February letters, and you have run out of suites. Several freshmen have requested suites. They may apply to another dorm requesting their preference. Write a form letter refusing their request and suggesting a substitute.

See "Requesting a Recommendation," pp. 185–188, for Exercise 15–17.

15. Write a letter to one of your instructors asking for a recommendation to a graduate school of business. Check the college catalogs in your library to learn the qualifications for the MBA program to which you might apply. Include in your letter any relevant information about your academic experience and background that might assist your instructor in writing the recommendation. Be sure to refer to the work you did for this instructor's course.

16. Write a letter to one of your instructors asking for a letter of recommendation to be sent to a company which has interviewed you for a job that interests you. Be sure to specify what information the company will be interested in.

17. Comment on the strengths and weaknesses of the letters of recommendation shown in Figures 5.21 to 5.24.

Figure 5.21

SAMPLE 1

> Union Packaging
> 49 Broadway
> White Plains, New York 10601
> July 7, 199_
>
> Director of Admissions
> Circle College
> 1000 Crescent Rondalsa
> Madison, New Jersey 07940
>
> Dear Director of Admissions:
>
> I have known Ron for fifteen years and have supervised him at various times for a total of about ten years. He should prove himself a fine MBA candidate.
>
> He is a self-starter who needs little or no direction. He sets aggressive goals and then achieves them. He can follow tasks through to completion and critique his own performance. He has shown the ability to work well with people. Ron is clearly a leader and has excellent potential for promotion.
>
> I am happy to see that he is continuing his education, and I am sure that he will be a credit to your institution.
>
> Sincerely yours,
>
> *Martin Weiss*
>
> Martin Weiss
>
> MW/bd

Figure 5.22

SAMPLE 2

Admissions Office
University of New Hampshire
Durham, NH 03824
December 14, 199_

Director of Admissions
Raymond Casswell Graduate School of Business
Lawrence College
Lancaster, PA 17603

Dear Director of Admissions:

Marcia Jones has asked me to write her a letter of recommendation and I am pleased to do so. I am supervisor of a student organization to which Marcia belongs: the Student Admissions Representatives. This organization comprises approximately forty students who volunteer between five and ten hours of their time each week to interview prospective students and their parents, conduct tours of campus, participate in large group information sessions, and generally help us in the many facets of our public relations work. Each year well over one hundred students apply for the twenty to twenty-five openings in this program. Consequently, our student "reps" represent UNH's finest, most well-rounded undergraduates.

Marcia's greatest attributes are her diligence, determination, and concern for people. She is extremely conscientious, and throughout her two years in our program, she has never missed an interview or tour. This kind of reliability and punctuality will surely stand her in good stead in any business environment. Moreover, Marcia is not one who draws a well-defined line on her commitments; she is often willing to help us out when we need extra interviewers or tour guides. In fact, Marcia is one of two "reps" chosen for a special three-week internship in our office during this semester break.

The interview comments that Marcia writes about each student whom she interviews are done in an objective, fair, and articulate manner. Her sensitivity and concern for others definitely show through in these interview write-ups. Marcia does not stereotype people; she gives each person whom she interviews her full attention and understands the importance of setting aside personal concerns and of approaching each interview with a positive attitude.

(continued)

(SAMPLE 2 continued)

Director of Admissions
page 2
December 14, 199_

Marcia is very personable, while at the same time treating her commitment to our office in a very professional manner. She holds herself and others to high standards. Last year, for example, she felt that our meeting attendance was not up to par and made that known not only to myself but to the other students in the program. This year when she and a small group of "reps" were in charge of one of our early meetings, I was impressed with Marcia's effort to make sure that the meeting was a constructive one. She organized her group very well and assumed the primary leadership role.

I have observed considerable growth in Marcia since she began in the student rep program over a year ago. She is by nature a somewhat shy person, but she has made great strides to ensure that her inherent shyness does not prevent her from assuming a very full and active role in life. Her participation in our program is a good example of this in that she deliberately places herself in situations where she has to speak to large groups of people. Marcia is poised and competent whether in a one-to-one interview situation or before a group of over one hundred people.

Whoever employs Marcia can be assured that he/she is employing a person who will give more than 100 percent to that company or institution. She strikes me as a personable, determined, and ambitious young woman who is willing to work hard. What more could one ask? We will miss Marcia in our offices next year, since she has become a truly valued member of our paraprofessional staff. If I can be of further help in answering questions about Marcia's performance in our office, please do not hesitate to call me.

Sincerely,

Martha Foley Jackson

Martha Foley Jackson
Assistant Director of Admissions

KC/oc

Figure 5.23

SAMPLE 3

Advanced Systems, Inc.
1500 N.E. 25th Avenue
Hillsboro, OR 97123
January 25, 199_

Atlantic University
872 Harrison Ave.
Boston, MA 02118

To Whom It May Concern:

I am truly pleased to have been asked to provide a recommendation for Mr. Carl Brown for I feel he is an exceptionally able professional. I have known Carl Brown since about 1979 when I was the chief person responsible for hiring him as a programer at Advanced Systems, where he worked with me and others on several projects. At that time we reviewed his academic record at North College as well as several recommendations. These were all excellent and spoke well for his academic capabilities. Our estimations of his potential were well justified over the several subsequent years he spent with us.

Mr. Brown proved himself as a careful and able programer. The job required him to operate several computer and software systems that were entirely new to him; he learned rapidly and seemed always to enjoy learning. More than once his careful documentation and sensible approaches saved important data. He rapidly acquired the background he needed to operate in a diverse, multidisciplinary environment. One especially commendable trait was that he always knew when to rely on his own judgment and when to seek help. He rapidly increased his responsibilities and in a few years was operating at a level significantly beyond his job position. He was skillful in his interpersonal relationships too, able to interact well with a variety of professionals, all of whom liked him, and capable of balancing the various pressures, demands, and priorities placed on him. Subsequent to his work here, Mr. Brown left for a more responsible position: he is performing again excellently in a senior and managerial role at Lyndon and Ford as an installation supervisor.

(continued)

(SAMPLE 3 continued)

Atlantic University
page 2
January 25, 199_

Mr. Brown has the personal tools to become an excellent manager. He is bright, sensible, careful, diligent, good with others, pleasant, and well-spoken. My only negative comment is that he is so unassuming that he seems to underrate his own abilities; I think he has in the past set his sights too low. I am thus pleased to hear that he has decided to return to school and feel that the choice of a management degree is an excellent one for him. His personal, analytic, and technical skills will, I am sure, make him one of the best students in any school. I can fully recommend him to your attention without reservation.

Sincerely,

David Berendes

David Berendes, Senior Systems Engineer

DB/fg

Figure 5.24
SAMPLE 4

Bay Colony Industrial Products
11150 Picard Drive
Rockville, MD 20850
August 5, 199_

Admissions Office
Century University
6000 N. 15th Street
Phoenix, AZ 85014

To Whom It May Concern:

    Bob exemplifies the qualities of commitment, integrity, and perseverance. These become apparent whenever Bob decides to complete a task or project. This is the overriding theme in Bob's application to your program. The decision is the end result of a very organized and methodical search to fulfill his career aspirations based on five years of experience in the marketing and business field.
    Bob will work extremely hard at mastering the tasks of graduate school; whatever the necessary commitment, Bob will succeed.

Sincerely yours,

Mary Rodi

Mary Rodi

See "Making Claims or Requesting Adjustments," pp. 191–194 and "Responding to Claims," pp. 194–200, for Exercises 18–26.

18. Think of a product or service you have been unhappy with. If you can't think of such a product or service, ask friends or relatives if they have purchased something within the last year with which they were unhappy. Write a letter of complaint that explains to the seller the problem with the product or service, describes the inconvenience, and asks for an adjustment.

19. As director of special events for a college business club, you are in charge of ordering the buffet and drinks for guest lectures. Last week the catering service you use delivered stale bread for the sandwiches. Write a letter to the service requesting a refund for the money you paid them for the sandwiches.

20. The Blackwell Hotel offers discount rates to its corporate clients who belong to the Blackwell Club. Corporations can accumulate points based on the number of nights corporate employees stay at the hotel, and they can redeem these points for free benefits such as the following: for 15 room nights, lunch for two in Cafe Alfredo; for 20 room nights, one night's complimentary stay at the Blackwell; for 30 room nights, dinner for two at Pierre's.

As Blackwell Club manager, you have received a letter from one of your Club members, Andrew Perry of Midstreet Bank, who wants to redeem 56 points he believes his company has earned for the current year. After examining your records, you conclude that Midstreet has earned only 14 points, for stays from 1/20/9_ through 1/22/9_. Guests from Midstreet did stay at the hotel 5/25/9_ through 5/27/9_ and 9/30/9_ through 10/2/9_, but the reservations were made through Village Travel and so you awarded Village the points. Midstreet also sent guests 11/16/9_ through 11/18/9_, but since the party exceeded ten, Midstreet was charged a special discount group rate of 20% off the average room rate of $80/night. Guests charged the group rate are not eligible for Blackwell Club points. As the Blackwell Club Manager, write to Mr. Perry refusing his request.

21. As Mr. Perry (Exercise 20), re-request the full 56 points because the Club did not make clear in advance that some room nights might be ineligible.

22. You asked a new assistant in your firm to write a claim letter about a delay in receiving a shipment of raincoats to your Cincinnati stores. The delay resulted in a great deal of embarrassment and financial loss for you. You had featured the raincoats in your March sales and were forced to turn away several customers who came to the sale exclusively to purchase the coats. You were also very surprised about the delay because you have done business with this manufacturer for over fifteen years. Your assistant shows you the following letter:

> Because of the intolerable delay in receiving a shipment of raincoats, action must be taken at once to remedy this problem. The order number of the coats with which reference is to be made is 90–87–3290.
>
> This incident of having waited over two weeks to receive an order is most definitely a lack of responsible service and will not be tolerated. Therefore, immediate action to resolve this problem will be greatly appreciated.

Suggest to your assistant how to revise the letter.

23. Your company manufactures swimming pools and saunas and sells them to department stores and other retail outlets. You have just received a letter from one of your customers complaining about cracks in one of your saunas and requesting a refund or a new sauna. Write a letter granting his request.

24. Four months ago you spent $75 on a pair of leather sandals by Berkshire, a company whose shoes are known for their quality, comfort, and durability. You have worn the sandals only in the house so that the soles still look practically new. But yesterday one of the leather straps on your left sandal broke just above the buckle. When you took it to have it repaired, the leather worker showed you that the leather on the broken strap was much thinner than the leather elsewhere on the uppers. He said it wasn't possible to sew up the old strap and he did not have matching leather to replace it. Write a letter to the manufacturer requesting a new pair of sandals.

25. You are a student intern for the local outdoor music festival. Your boss has received a claim from one of the patrons asking for reimbursement for four tickets at $20 each because the concert was rained out. The tickets state clearly that there are no refunds in the event of rain, but the patron claims that he was unaware of the policy. Write the letter for your boss refusing the patron's claim.

26. As a claims adjuster for the BCB Automobile Club, you are breaking in a new trainee. You have received a call from a disgruntled member, Karen Kristoferson, who complained about your club's towing service. Your club promises a free tow whenever a member's car won't start. Karen told you she called one morning because her car wouldn't start and she wanted her car towed to her mechanic's garage. She said that when the tow truck came, the attendant jump-started her car, so that it was running, and then refused to tow the car to the mechanic's. The attendant explained that it was BCB policy not to tow a car that could be started. Karen said she was very surprised to hear this since over the phone she had only requested a tow, and BCB had promised to have someone out within the hour. She had not asked for a jump start and didn't realize it would be tried. Since she had a small child in the house, and therefore couldn't drive the car herself to the mechanic's once it was started, the jump start was a waste of time. She knew the car wouldn't start up again when she could finally arrange for child care and drive the car herself. She was angry with BCB for not making its policies about starting and towing clear to her over the phone when she first called in to request a tow. In addition, Karen complained that the attendant, when he realized that she couldn't use the jump start, was rude to her for bringing him all the way out to her house for a jump start that she couldn't use.

Here is the letter your trainee wrote in response to Karen's call. What suggestions would you make for revising it?

Dear Ms. Kristoferson:

Thank you for your telephone call.

We have reviewed your service call and have gathered the following information:

On your printout it states that you did ask for a jump start with a possible tow.

Enclosed please find our dues-paying check in the amount of $10 for your inconvenience.

We certainly understand your feelings, but we can honestly say that the problem you encountered happens very infrequently. We feel sure that, in the future, you'll be pleased with the service we provide.

                                        Sincerely,

                                        Deirdre M. Brufee
                                        Member Relations

See "Writing About Credit," pp. 201–205, for Exercises 27–28.

27. A student-run car wash service has requested a line of credit ($500) from your stationery store. You check your records and their bank references and find that in the past three years they have paid their bills on time and have established a profitable business. Write a letter to the company approving credit.
28. Another student-run business, a catering service, has also applied for credit from your stationery store. But since the business is only a few months old and has not established a credit rating, you decide to refuse them credit. Write this letter.

See "Writing to Refuse Requests for Favors," pp. 206–207, for Exercises, 29–30.

29. For the past few months you have been a member of your chamber of commerce's task force for studying the restoration of historical buildings in the business district. The group would now like you to take over its leadership, but your family and work responsibilities will make it impossible for you to accept the appointment. Write a letter to the task force refusing their request.
30. Your local symphony has requested a contribution, but you are not in a position to donate money even though you would like to support the symphony. Write a letter refusing their request.

6
LETTERS THAT PERSUADE

PREVIEW

This chapter should help you to

1. Write sales letters by
   - Determining your proposition
   - Establishing a mailing list
   - Determining your sales appeals
   - Using the RTA formula to organize your letters
2. Write requests for favors by
   - Emphasizing how the reader benefits from doing the favor
   - Using the RTA formula to generate ideas and organize them for your requests
3. Write collection letters by
   - Emphasizing the benefits that prompt payment has for the debtor
4. Write letters that respond to public controversy by
   - Understanding the situation from the public's point of view
   - Building a bridge between your company's position and the public's

Any letter that goes out in your business's mailbag must promote your company's reputation. We could claim, then, that all business letters are persuasive. They persuade readers to have a positive attitude toward your organization. Almost all the letters we have looked at so far, however, were written to people who had demonstrated an interest in your company. They had, for example, requested information, ordered products and services, claimed adjustments, or applied for credit with your company.

But suppose you wish to gain the favor of people who are indifferent to your company. For example, you may wish to write a sales letter to someone who has never heard of you, your company, or its products. Or you may want to write to someone you have only heard of but never met, to ask for a favor—perhaps to give a talk, to become a member of an organization, or to donate some time or money to a cause.

Or suppose you wish to gain the favor of someone actually hostile to your company. You may have to write letters persuading a customer to pay a long overdue bill. Or perhaps a special interest group is protesting a company policy, and you must write to persuade the group that good reasons stand behind your policy.

In these cases you must write letters that move people to do or think something that they would not do or think without your encouragement. This is persuasion. As with other letters, persuasion requires that you consider exactly what you want to accomplish with your letter. More important, it requires that you understand your reader's needs. For in order to persuade effectively, you must be able to build a bridge between your own goals and those of your readers.

In this chapter we will look at four business situations that require persuasion and the strategies for writing letters to deal with these situations.

SELLING

Dirk Smith, a recent business graduate, felt excited about having a chance to get started in his own business. During college he had worked part-time with a hotel conference center, scheduling business meetings. At the center, he had learned firsthand how harassed many business people get when they have to organize conferences and seminars. While they are trying to concentrate on their sales message, they are annoyed with questions about seating arrangements, media services, luncheons, and directions. As Dirk put it, "They want to keep their mind on conducting a dynamic seminar, not on giving directions to the bathrooms!"

As a result of his part-time work, Dirk and his partner decided to offer their services for complete seminar arrangements. Dirk had already made several good contacts from his part-time work. But the partners knew a strong sales letter would spread the word about their new service even more effectively. Since both had worked primarily with financial consulting firms, they decided to concentrate on that market. Dirk's partner compiled a list of 300 financial service companies in the area, companies that, the partners figured, would want to offer sales seminars regularly.

It is now Dirk's job to draft the letter that will—as in his most optimistic moods he likes to think—make his name as an entrepreneur. But so far he is not happy with his rough drafts: "I have long lists of all the things we can do for our clients. I know my letter has to explain all that, at least. But I don't know how to start. How do you make a great sales pitch?"

Most businesses and households receive dozens of sales letters every week asking them to buy, subscribe, inquire, visit, renew, mail, or enroll. Why? Because sales letters, if they are well written and sent to the right people, can be a business's most economical and effective means of advertising. In writing a letter to sell their services, Dirk and his partner were joining thousands of businesses who rely on direct mail to market their products. Direct-mail advertising has one great advantage over television and newspaper advertising: It sends its message only to the people most likely to be interested. Whereas twenty years ago it was considered advertising's poor relation, recent statistics reveal that direct mail now accounts for over 17.1 billion ad dollars, almost as much as television.[1]

Of course direct mail is not all magic. The disadvantages can be summed up in one phrase: "junk mail." The more unsolicited advertising people receive, the less interested they become in reading it. Envelopes go into the wastebasket unopened. On the other hand, if advertisers select their addressees with care, people receiving the sales message will be more inclined to read it; so the letter will get read, and often enough a sale will be made.

Although many companies hire letter-writing experts to formulate their sales letters, for several good reasons every business person should know how to write effective sales messages. A national survey published by the Association for Business Communication showed that almost 50 percent of business people have to write some form of advertising or promotional material on the job.[2] Many companies do hire letter-writing experts, but many more rely on their own expertise to spread the word about their goods or services: bankers, real estate agents, consultants, financial planners, special tool manufacturers, health care services, insurance agents, and thousands more rely on letters they write themselves to communicate directly with their market. It is quite possible, then, that in the course of your career you will write sales letters. But even if you never actually write a sales letter, knowing sales letter strategies can help you promote your company and its products.

The process of writing sales letters involves the familiar activities of writing: setting the goal, assessing the reader, gathering information and generating ideas, organizing, writing drafts, and revising; and the RTA formula can help you as you write. But before we look carefully at some strategies involved in writing for sales, let's consider Dirk Smith's writing process and the letter he finally mailed. How did he get from his initial frustration to the published sales letter that eventually brought in several large company contracts?

> I knew the main point I wanted to make. That was easy. But I just didn't know how to get started. You should've seen how I started out my first draft: "I am pleased to inform you of a unique, new seminar promotion and management service provided by my company." I am totally comfortable talking to these people in person, but here I started sounding like a stuffed shirt. I know I'm not that kind of person, but I felt uncomfortable writing the letter. I think I felt like I was asking them to do me a favor and had to come on as very official. I didn't like this draft at all, so I talked it out with my partner. That was a big help, because while we were talking I realized, "Hey, they're not doing *me* a favor, I'm doing *them* one. I'm solving their problem." I was on my way after that. I just had to remind them they had a problem and then show them we're the guys to solve it.

Dirk's analysis of his own writing process showed that three things were essential: having a clear sense of what he wanted to accomplish, understanding the people he was writing to, and knowing precisely how the service he offered would help those people. He also knew when to stop writing and try to generate some fresh ideas by talking things out with his partner. These are writing activities we are by now very familiar with: setting the goal, assessing the reader, and generating ideas. Dirk also organized his letter in a way that conformed with the RTA pattern. Figure 6.1 (on page 226) shows the letter Dirk and his partner finally felt was worthy to launch their business.

Figure 6.1

DIRK'S SALES LETTER

THE ALEXANDER GROUP
10 UNION SQUARE WEST SUITE 101 NEW YORK, N.Y. 10003

Dear [prospect]:

You know that seminars provide an excellent forum for marketing your business. But you also know how distracting all the chores of putting on a well-planned seminar can be. Petty details demand your attention just at the time you want to focus on making a dynamic sales presentation.

That's where we can help. Let the Alexander Group plan, promote, and manage your entire seminar. We can worry about the details while you focus on selling.

We offer complete seminar planning, including all of the following services:

<u>Planning</u>

- Organizing company formats and objectives, and planning the most effective presentation media

- Researching and selecting qualified lecturers

- Preparing all arrangements with convention site, hotel, and seminar facilities

<u>Promotion</u>

- Designing, copyrighting, and executing all graphic materials, including

    invitations
    brochures
    slide presentations
    signs
    leave-behind pieces

- Recommending the most effective media, such as local advertising and public relations releases

page 2

Management

- Supervising convention center staff
- Operating all audiovisual equipment
- Providing convenient, complete estimate of billing

For a no-obligation estimate of services, please check the enclosed card and drop it in the mail, or call our office collect (212-555-8390). We will be happy to explain our service in greater detail.

Sincerely,

Dirk A. D. Smith

Dirk A. D. Smith
Senior Promotional Consultant

To get to this successful version of his sales letter, Dirk had to go through the stages of the writing process. Let's consider how these stages can help you write a successful sales letter.

A sales letter must compete successfully with many demands on the reader's attention.

Setting the Goal: Your Proposition

When you begin creating a sales message, the central component is the sales proposition. In other words, what have you got to offer? A great invention? The best price? The best quality? A free trial? Complete service? As top Toronto sales writer Susan Park points out: "Offers that work involve gifts, trials, installment terms, and price savings. And remember, the most powerful word in mail order is 'free.'"[3]

Only when you have an attractive proposition can you decide how your sales letter can fit into your overall sales strategy. Is this a sale you can clinch in one letter, or should you plan to follow up, either with a sequence of letters or by the same letter again? For inexpensive, simple products or services, the letter itself can be expected to motivate the reader to buy. But for expensive and complex items, the sales letter will only introduce your product or service. You can ask the reader to respond by indicating interest in knowing more, and then follow up the letter with printed information, phone calls, or visits from sales representatives. For some companies, the most effective goal for the letter may be to offer the reader some incentive to come into the store or showroom.

Dirk and his partner, for example, knew that what would sell their service was the experience and confidence in their abilities that they could personally convey to their clients. They decided to use their sales letter, then, simply to encourage the prospect to indicate interest in their service. They planned to follow up all responses with a sales call or visit.

Assessing the Reader: The Mailing List

Direct-mail advertising works only if the sales letter gets to the people likely to be interested. Mailing-list broker Roger Logan of Herbert A. Watts Ltd. asks: "Would you mail a chocolate-recipe-book offer to members of WeightWatchers? No. It could be done, but it just wouldn't work. The mailing list is the key to the successful mail-order sale."[4] Large companies have sophisticated market research teams that work to define the best target market for a particular product. Other companies can buy a mailing list already compiled for businesses such as theirs, or they can compile their own. But any direct-mail advertiser, whether large or small, must have a good mailing list of prospective customers.

Hundreds of companies make mailing lists their business. These services compile lists of consumers who recently made purchases in various categories, or lists of companies categorized according to their type of business. Suppose, for example, you wanted to market a device you had developed that, when attached to a garden faucet, automatically switched a sprinkler on and off at programed intervals. You could buy a mailing list of people who had recently purchased garden equipment—for example, lawn mowers or hedge trimmers. Or you might be able to buy the mailing list of a mail-order garden supply company. Such companies would be likely to sell you the use of their list if your product did not duplicate one of their offerings. As a third alternative, you could buy a list of garden-supply retailers, businesses likely to be interested in stocking your device.

Mailing-list services charge anywhere from $45 to $100 per thousand addresses for a minimum of five thousand, and with an additional charge for preprinted labels. For a one-time mailing, this can be well worth the price. But you may want to begin your own list for repeated use, updating it regularly. (One in four Americans changes address every year.) Your library has resources that may help you compile a useful list. For likely retailers of your garden faucet device, for example, local chambers of commerce and county business directories would be excellent sources. To create a list of their prospects, Dirk and his partner used the library to find the names of officers of financial companies and then typed this information into their computer mail program. As another source for lists, many companies maintain addresses of their previous customers, intermittently sending these patrons sales promotions.

Whatever the source of your list, direct your sales message to those specific readers. Can you show your understanding of the garden supplier who is in the midst of the annual spring rush? Can you congratulate the parents on their new arrival? Can you share a new car owner's pride of possession? Knowing just one or two characteristics of your readers can help you establish rapport and personalize your sales message.

Gathering Information and Generating Ideas: Determining the Sales Appeals

Advertising's Elmer Wheeler long ago advised: "Don't sell the steak, sell the sizzle." In other words, it is not enough simply to describe the product or service you want your reader to buy. Your reader must be able to imagine the experience of using it—the sound, the smell, the taste, the entire psychological experience. Charles Revson of Revlon cosmetics put it another way: "In our factory we make cosmetics; in the stores we sell hope." Sales letters must persuade the reader to want the product, usually on an emotional or psychological level; readers must be given a strong feeling for how the product will benefit them.

This does not mean, however, that the psychological appeal of the product is all that readers want to know about. They also want logical appeals—the evidence to back up your claims. In addition, they may want to know how trustworthy you are—that is, your authority to make business claims. They may also be interested in testimonials— what others have to say about you or the product.[5]

But all these appeals become relevant only after you have created in the reader the desire to know more about the product.

PSYCHOLOGICAL APPEALS: THE CENTRAL SELLING POINT

Get in touch with us now about our lawn care services! Our liquid fertilizer includes ammoniacal nitrogen, chlorine, ammonium phosphate, urea, and muriate of potash. Our pesticides include methoxychlor, trychloromethyl cyclohexene, and dicarboximide.

What would you think of a letter selling lawn care services that started out this way? Certainly it would not get very far. Prospects don't want to know all the chemical compounds in your fertilizers and weed-killers. What they want to know is, How will my lawn look? When can I expect results? How will the results compare? When you ask a building supply store to stock the insulation windows you manufacture, of course the store will want to know dimensions and features. But what about the other questions? How quickly will these windows sell? What will be the overhead? What kind of advertising support can you give? The auto repair shop does not need to know all about the insides of a computer to be convinced they need a computerized tune-up machine. Instead: How much time and labor will it save? Can it do the job more accurately? Will it be a selling point for customers?

A good sales letter begins not with the physical description of the product but by emphasizing the product's psychological appeal. It lets the reader experience what it is like to be the owner of the product or to enjoy the service.

When Dirk formulated his sales letter for the service he wanted to offer, he discovered he could come up with his sales pitch only after he had thought carefully about how his service would benefit his readers. His service would rid executives of the bothersome details required to set up a sales seminar. What he was selling was a kind of relief, and he realized that once he got readers to recognize this, he could spend the rest of the letter providing the details to back up his claim.

Like Dirk, when you formulate a sales letter, first think about how your product or service will benefit the reader. This will help you imagine the "sizzle," or psychological appeal. After you have decided on that, you can consider other appeals to the reader.

The Central Selling Point.   Most products and services can appeal to buyers in many ways. But you can best focus your reader's attention by developing a central selling point. One direct-mail professional put it this way: "Some advertisers give many reasons why consumers should buy, but usually one reason is more compelling than all the others. We try to identify that one reason, then concentrate our energies behind it."[6]

Three steps constitute a good strategy for generating ideas that will help you determine your central selling point:

1. *Analyze the product features:* Of course you know what you are selling. Anybody who sells knows that. But have you looked at it closely? How does it work? Why does it exist? How do you use it? If you are selling a service, exactly what will be done? When and how? By whom? Why are you better? What is the story behind it all? As you answer these questions, write a list of all your product features. The more you know about your product or service, the more you will be able to understand how it can benefit the reader.

2. *Determine reader benefits:* Once you have listed all your product features, next to each describe how the reader can benefit from that feature. What need will it satisfy? What benefit will the user enjoy?

   As an example, let's consider the situation of a manager whose hardware store lies close to a large university. He wants to send a letter to the college's dorm students promoting the popcorn poppers he has just stocked in large quantity. Figure 6.2 shows how he might analyze the product features and the benefits they have for readers.
3. *Select the central selling point:* Once you have compiled your list, review the reader benefits you have identified. Is there one selling point above all others that you think most likely to appeal to your reader? Do the benefits seem to cluster around one major idea?

In the popper case, the readers are college students. If you look at the list of benefits, you will notice that several features suggest that the popper makes popping easy and results in perfect popcorn every time. Other features suggest that it is possible to vary the kinds of popcorn the user can serve—buttered or not, popped with oil or not. Still other features suggest that the popper attracts gatherings of friends. Would one of these benefits appeal to college students more than others?

The store manager decided that what college students wanted above all was easy, perfect popcorn every time, but that the options in the kinds of popcorn produced would be important to distinguish this popper from others. He decided on a letter that would emphasize "quick and easy" but also "perfect popcorn for every palate," Do you agree with his selection of the central selling point?

Figure 6.2

DETERMINING A PRODUCT'S BENEFITS:
A POPCORN POPPER

Feature	Benefit
2 lbs., 7¾″ tall, 13″ diam.	Easy to handle, easy to store
4-quart capacity	Generous serving for a whole suite full of friends
Totally electric	Easy to operate in a dorm room; no special equipment required
Container inverts to become serving bowl	No extra dishes
Options: pops without oil	Good for weight watchers
Automatic butter melter and dispenser	No risk of burning butter; evenly buttered every time
Pops 4 quarts in 4 minutes	Great for spur-of-the-moment study breaks; for TV commercial breaks

LOGICAL APPEALS

A look at effective sales letters will show that while they emphasize the psychological appeal of the product, they spend a great deal of time backing up that appeal with logical appeals. They provide evidence for their claims because they know readers are too sophisticated to be persuaded by a handful of generalities: "the best performance," "the easiest to use," "tremendous cost savings," "fast and reliable." All these may be understood as empty claims unless you can provide the evidence to back them up. To demonstrate the authenticity of your claims, describe, compare, and offer samples or free trials.

Describe. If your product is "sturdy and good looking," what is it made of and how is it constructed? If installation is "quick and easy," how many hours will it take? How many tools? If you claim "fast service," how long will it take?

Compare. What, precisely, makes your repair service better than others'? Can you use statistics to prove your product is more energy efficient? If your color prints are sharper and clearer, can you provide reprints for the reader to see firsthand?

Offer Samples and Trials. In the envelope, can you include a sample of the fabric, a free seed packet, or the embossed letterhead just as it might appear when an order is filled? How about a coupon for a free sample redeemable at a retail outlet? Can you offer a free 45-day trial period?

APPEALS BASED ON YOUR AUTHORITY OR TRUSTWORTHINESS

Establish your authority by referring to your years in the business and by offering guarantees.

Years in the Business. Customers know a well-established business wants to maintain its reputation and will stand behind what it sells. Can you reinforce your credibility by discussing your years in the business? When were you established? How long have you been in the same community?

> Maley's Dry Cleaners. Serving St. Cloud for three generations.

Guarantees. You can also prove your willingness to stand behind what you sell by offering guarantees:

> Guaranteed to remain 100 percent accurate for as long as you own it.

> One-year guarantee on parts, and our exclusive 90-day full-service warranty.

TESTIMONIALS

Testimonials allow you to draw on the authority of other people to reinforce both the psychological appeal of your product and your logical appeals.

Testimonials for Psychological Appeal. We are all familiar with high-cost ads that pay famous people to endorse products. But a low-budget sales message can capitalize on the same principle by using endorsements from satisfied customers. Sometimes customers will write spontaneously. Other times you may solicit responses through phone calls, suggestion boxes, or surveys. (If you want to use the name of the customer, be sure to get the customer's permission first.)

> My recent experience trying your connector kit was such an outstanding example of quick, uncomplicated service, I had to write and compliment everyone involved.

Testimonials for Logical Appeal. Besides using testimonials from satisfied users to back up your psychological appeals, you can use testimonials from experts and customers to back up your logical appeals. If, for example, you claim leather shoes are better for kids than sneakers, back up your claim with expert testimony:

> "We found properly fitted leather shoes not only better, but safer"—
> Nathaniel Gould, M.D., University of Vermont, Department of Orthopedics and Rehabilitation

Testimony from customers can also be used as a basis for statistical evidence:

> In a recent survey, nine out of ten TIAA policy owners interviewed had compared prices before buying from TIAA.

> Eighty-five percent of our new business comes from people who have been referred to us by satisfied customers.

To generate ideas for your sales letters, keep in mind that an effective letter reinforces the psychological appeal of the product or service, and then backs up any claims with logical appeals and perhaps testimonials.

Organizing the Sales Letter: Using RTA

If you have a good sales proposition, the right mailing list, and well thought-out appeals, you are ready to organize and draft an effective sales letter. The RTA formula can help you select from and organize the ideas you have already generated and can also help you think of new ideas. Let's see how.

Establish Rapport: According to one study of advertising, Americans encounter 1,600 messages on an average day, but only 80 are consciously noted, and fewer than 15 evoke some reaction.[7] The increase in advertising has resulted in consumers becoming more sophisticated and skeptical, which in turn makes them harder to sell. Certainly, then, the opening sentences of your letter are extremely important. They must "hook" readers and give them a reason for reading on. At the same time they must tie into the sales message you develop in the body of the letter. Your opening must

1. Establish rapport with readers by gaining their interest and giving them a reason for reading on
2. Begin to develop your central selling point

Beyond these two major requirements, there is no set formula for establishing rapport. Below are several well-tested ways to begin. Consider which opening strategies would be most appropriate to your sales situation.

1. *Begin with a surprising fact.* The following "opener" constituted the entire sales message of a letter that resulted in a large number of inquiries for a new Xerox product:

> In just six months, 137 of the Fortune 500 have switched to our new scientific system of selling. Shouldn't you find out why?[8]

2. *Make an emotional appeal.* A company selling film development services began this way:

> Pictures are memories captured forever . . . the child's first step into the unknown world, the first bicycle, a best friend.

3. *Create a scenario.* Put your reader in a hypothetical situation. A computer training consultant used this opener to generate interest in his seminar, "Developing Effective User Support":

> The word comes down from management: "We want the documentation for the new system to be on-line." What does this mean to the system developers and technical writers who must carry out this decision? How will it affect training? What impact will it have on user performance and user acceptance of the system?

4. *Begin with a story or anecdote*. ATRON, "the debugger company," introduced its latest product this way:

A Bugbuster Story

Brad Crain, a project manager at Software Publishing, relates the following: "On Friday, March 22, 199_, I was about to get on an airplane with Jeff Tucker, my co-author of PFA:WRITE, and fly to IBM's Boca Raton, Florida, facility. For a week, we had been unsuccessfully trying to isolate a bug in a new software product. In a last, desperation move, I set up an early Saturday morning appointment with ATRON.

"Three of us walked through ATRON's door at 8:00 the next morning. Using ATRON's hardware-assisted debugging tools, we had the problem identified and fixed by 10:30 AM."

Mr. Crain concludes: "We'd never have found the bug with mere software debuggers."[9]

5. *Offer testimonials*. A trade association promotes its product by referring to other satisfied customers:

What did Birds Eye use to heat up sale of its frozen vegetables?

What did Maxwell House Coffee use to stay good to the last drop?

What did CIBA Pharmaceutical use to protect its motion sickness medication?

What did Borden's use to keep its snack in Cracker Jack condition?

What did Johanna Farms use to keep its juice fresh without refrigeration?

Aluminum

6. *Suggest a problem you will solve*. An insurance company offers a new policy:

Clark Kent has an advantage the rest of us don't have. He is Superman.

If he's hit by a truck, the truck might be bent out of shape but all he has to do is go into a telephone booth, Superman comes out, and he flies to the nearest dry cleaners to have his suit pressed.

If you or I were hit by a bicycle, we could have a broken ankle that would put us out of commission for a month.

Clark Kent doesn't need *Lossguard*. But we do.

7. *Identify with the reader*. The publisher of a popular mechanics magazine invites subscriptions:

This invitation isn't for dead-beats, rip-off artists or "gentlemen" who hate to get their hands dirty. It's for the rest of us. It's for the guys who aren't afraid to get down under the sink with a pipe wrench. Guys who don't mind sticking their hands in the toilet tank to adjust the ball cock (because they know it's going to save a $16 plumber's bill).[10]

8. *Compliment the reader*. An automobile association offers new insurance coverage.

We think you're important! And because we do, we want you to have the opportunity to enroll for a service which has already paid over *$53 million in benefits* to thousands of our members nationwide.

9. *Ask a question*. A pool-cleaning service invites inquiries:

What has four feet, climbs walls, and walks circles around other automatic pool cleaners? Poolvac.

10. *Use a command*. A discount travel service invites new members:

Fill in unfilled space and save up to 67% on travel!

11. *Offer a gift*. A developer of vacation homes encourages prospects to view the property:

Congratulations!

Your name as a local homeowner was included in our Grand Giveaway, and your Official Entry has been drawn, making you eligible to receive one of the following gifts. [Reader can pick up gift at site of vacation home development.]

12. *Show how to save money*. A long-distance service solicits new accounts:

Tired of the high price of long distance calls? You can save up to 50%—and call any day, any time, anywhere out-of-state in the continental U.S.

Let these suggestions help you come up with an opening for your sales letter that will immediately establish rapport.

Influence Thinking: After establishing rapport, influence thinking by developing your central selling point and presenting your other appeals. There is no set pattern of organization. As a general rule, first create the reader's desire for your product or service by focusing on the benefits, then provide evidence and testimonials to support your claims. Frequently a letter may move back and forth among benefits, evidence, and testimonials. (For examples, see letters in Figures 6.3 to 6.5.)

Two questions may concern you as you write the body of your sales letter: How do I talk about price, and how long can my letter be?

How Do You Talk About Price? It is the rare reader indeed who can ignore cost. Regardless of how much you can persuade readers to want the product, they must feel that the price is reasonable, one they can afford. But unless price is your central selling point, subordinate discussion of money by putting it at the end of the letter. Introduce price in terms of the benefits it buys, and break down the amount into manageable sums.

1. *What benefits does the price buy?*

   For only $11.95, enjoy all 10 Disney classic stories, plus your free bonus.

   The Whistling Cleaners service charge includes all transportation, equipment, materials, and only the finest quality products. We guarantee our performance, and we are fully insured.

2. *Compared to similar items, is it a bargain?*

   Sells for $15.95 in retail stores. Our price is just $7.95.

   Buy direct and save 50% or more!

3. *How does the price work out in monthly payments?*

   The annual fee is $60. Just $5 per month covers you and all the members of your household.

4. *How does the cost break down* based on a daily, monthly, or yearly rate over the life of the product? Is there a point at which the item pays for itself?

   That's 17 cents per day to help ensure your child stays healthy and strong.

   You can see that in four seasons the carts will be practically paid for by the golfers.

5. *If the product comes in quantity, what is the price per item?*

Only $12.75 net for a box of 50. That's less than 26 cents for each note pad.

Just $48 for 12 full issues. That's just $4 an issue . . . pennies an idea. And the cost is fully deductible.

6. *What does the product cost in comparison with some other purchase?*

Your swim club membership offers you fun and exercise every week, for less than you might spend at the movies.

How Long Can Your Sales Letter Be? One direct-mail professional put it simply: "Who says people won't read long copy? What they avoid is long, dull copy."[11] In other words, as long as your letter remains lively and engaging, the reader will read on. Although most sales letters do not go over a page or two, some are as long as six or eight pages.

Motivate Action and Attitude: The goal of the sales letter is to get your reader to act: either to purchase your product or to indicate an interest in hearing more about it. Since readers who respond to sales letters almost always do so very soon after they have read the letter, it is important to provide incentives to act as soon as possible. To do this, close the letter by making action easy and emphasizing reader benefits.

Make Action Easy. Encourage the reader in any of the following ways:

1. *Ask the reader to act within a limited time to earn a special discount or free offer:*

The enclosed coupon is good for a $25 rebate if you arrange for a free demonstration within 30 days.

You must call within 72 hours to make your reservation to pick up your prize.

If you order before October 15th, our quoted prices will include free delivery.

2. *Ask the reader to act now because of limited quantity:*

We have only 300 copiers to sell at this low clearance price. Don't be left out. Order today.

LETTERS THAT PERSUADE 239

3. *Offer a free trial period:*

You have a *Ten-Day Right to Examine Your Lossguard Certificate.* If you are not competely satisfied with it, return it to American Bankers for cancellation and a complete refund of any premiums you may have paid.

Emphasize Reader Benefits. Close by reminding readers of the benefits they will enjoy.

To ensure uninterrupted Check Guarantee Service, mail the form below *today.*

Art is a truly universal language, one that transcends all boundaries. Your tickets will serve as your personal key to the world of discovery that awaits you at the Brandywine Arts Festival. We know your experience will be exciting, enlightening, and memorable.

Sometimes, to remind readers of the benefits they will obtain, a letter can close by recalling the letter opening. Here is the closing paragraph of the letter whose opening referred to Clark Kent (pp. 235–236):

Peace of mind is worth the few dollars you invest in this sensible protection. Who else besides Clark Kent can take the risk of saying, "Nothing will happen to me"? You and I aren't indestructible but we *can* take this logical step to protect our mortgage payments if something *should* happen.

Now that you have considered the ideas for the main parts of the sales letter, look at the letters in Figures 6.3 to 6.5 and notice how the parts work together as a whole. The letters demonstrate a variety of ways to establish rapport in the opening, to weave together benefits and evidence in the body, and to motivate action in the closing paragraphs. In Figure 6.3, a computer manufacturer makes a claim and then offers an incentive for customers to come in and judge the evidence for themselves. In Figure 6.4, a company in the business of writing sales letters for others uses the sales letter itself as evidence for its claims. The writer in Figure 6.5 begins first with evidence and only later discusses benefits more fully. Do you think he uses the most effective order?

The great advantage of direct mail is that you can analyze the sales results more easily than those of broadcast advertising. According to advertising executive Max Roujeon, "Direct mail is cost effective, accurate, and above all, testable. Before a company commits itself to a major campaign, it can do a small test to find out what the economics of the effort are. That's its great power."[12]

Figure 6.3

SALES LETTER 1

TEXAS INSTRUMENTS

July 12, 199_

Dear [business person]:

If you're like most people, shopping for the right business computer can seem like hacking your way through a jungle of specs, claims and counter claims, and just plain chaos.

Establishes rapport by suggesting a problem the writer will solve

You might end up feeling like you need a computer just to help you choose a computer.

At Texas Instruments, we couldn't agree more. So we're making not one, but two computers available to help you decide.

Influences thinking by logical appeal: offers evidence by inviting reader to try product and compare

We call it "Dare to Compare." It lets you come down to a participating dealer and match our remarkable Texas Instruments Professional Computer directly against the IBM Personal Computer.

Compare the sharpness of the display, the amount of data on screen, the number of available colors, the ease of keyboard use, the speed—in short, you can compare them side by side and put them through their paces with the same software titles.

We think it will make your choice of a computer clear.

We're so sure, in fact, that when you come down and "Dare to Compare," just give the dealer your business card (no obligation), and we'll give you a TEXAS INSTRUMENTS SOLAR POWERED CALCULATOR—free. The offer is good till July 31st.

Motivates action by offering free gift

So come on down to your participating dealer, see the dramatic demonstration for yourself, and take home your free TI solar powered calculator.

> page 2
>
> If you're in the market for a personal computer, you owe it to yourself—and to your business—to "Dare to Compare."
>
> Sincerely yours,
>
> *Eric L. Jones*
>
> Eric L. Jones
> President, Data Systems Group
>
> P.S. The literature enclosed will give you a more complete picture of our remarkable TI Professional Computer. And you'll see why we're confident enough to be staging this dramatic country wide challenge. Also enclosed is a current list of the software available for the TI Professional Computer. We say "current" because programmers are so excited about the TIPC they're writing more software every week.
>
> TEXAS INSTRUMENTS INCORPORATED · POST OFFICE BOX 2909 · AUSTIN, TEXAS 78769
> 12501 RESEARCH · AUSTIN · 512 250-7111

Emphasizes benefit to company

Postscripts can make sales letters more effective. This one emphasizes company's authority and product features

Testing the Sales Letter

If you are doing a very large mailing, 5,000–50,000, it will pay to test at least two versions of the same package. You may experiment with the offer, the letter copy, the envelope, or the enclosures. (To be strictly scientific about it, you would test only one of these variables at a time.) Select a representative cross section of your mailing list (between 5 percent and 10 percent of the names), send different versions to each half, and see which version results in the most sales.

Once the test is completed, send out the whole mailing as soon as possible. Time your mailings carefully. Studies have shown that your letter's "pulling power" can be affected by the season of the year (Christmas and tax time are said to be the worst) and even the day of the week your letter arrives (Mondays and Fridays seem to get least response).

What kind of return can you expect? Although your success will depend on many variables, an appropriate mailing list and an effective sales package can be expected to draw anywhere from .5 percent to 10 percent responses. To determine whether it is

242 THE RANDOM HOUSE GUIDE TO BUSINESS WRITING

Figure 6.4

SALES LETTER 2

CINAMON
ASSOCIATES INC.

August 23, 199_

Ms. Nancy Gust
Stage One Press
149 Larch Road
Boston, MA 02138

Dear Ms. Gust:

Your success in marketing your company's products depends on your ability to grab the attention of your prospective customers. And then to motivate them to act. — *Establishes rapport by identifying with reader and suggesting a reader problem*

But with all the competition in the marketplace and the corresponding glut of advertising and promotion, can you be certain your message is getting through? (For example, leaf through your trade and consumer magazines, and you'll see that they're so filled with advertising, none stands out.)

High-quality direct mail, though, gets right to *your target audience*. What better example could I show you than the letter you're reading right now? — *Influences thinking by offering solution*

Clients like *Computerworld, PC World,* Digital Equipment, Polaroid, Provident Institution for Savings and many others nationwide use the direct mail/marketing services of Cinamon Associates as part of their marketing mix . . . for new-customer acquisition, for cultivating customer loyalty, for corporate identity programs, for qualified sales-lead programs, and for every other aspect of consumer and business marketing. — *Gives evidence of effectiveness by listing satisfied customers*

We would like to work with you in fully developing *your company's direct-mail business potential*. We can show you how best to invest your advertising dollars in a targeted marketing program to maximize your return for each advertising dollar invested. (Our purpose is not to replace an existing ad agency relationship, but to provide a different service that can complement and strengthen the impact of other advertising.) — *Shows how reader will benefit*

> Ms. Nancy Gust
> page 2
> August 23, 199_
>
>   Call me today at 617-555-2400 to discuss how we can work together to achieve your marketing and sales objective. Or, return the enclosed reply form for more information. Find out what we can do for you!
>
> Sincerely,
>
> *Marcia Cinamon*
>
> Marcia Cinamon
> President
>
> MC:hd
> Enclosure
>
>   **DIRECT MAIL/MARKETING**
>   **DIRECT RESPONSE ADVERTISING**
> **29 HARVARD STREET, BROOKLINE, MA 02146 (617) 739-2400**

Motivates action by making action easy and suggesting reader benefit

profitable, measure returns against costs. But keep in mind that such a measure will not necessarily tell you what your letter may have achieved in name recognition for your company or product.

Envelopes for the Sales Letter

Clear, powerful graphics, in both accompanying brochures and envelopes, can be especially important to the pulling power of your sales letter. This is especially true of envelopes, since often the reader determines with just a quick glance, whether to open the envelope or toss it out. That glance is all the time you may have to begin to get your message across.

    One successful direct-mail consultant, William Jayme, has made his trademark the mailing envelope. He emblazons it with a bold, one-word, tease headline that crystallizes the sales appeal. For example, his "Mousetrap" (shown in Figure 6.6 on page

THE RANDOM HOUSE GUIDE TO BUSINESS WRITING

Figure 6.5

SALES LETTER 3

RECRUITER'S VIDEO NETWORK, INC.
100 N INTERREGIONAL · SUITE 300 · AUSTIN, TEXAS 78701 · 512/477-3014

March 9, 199_

Mr. Ronald Young, Human Resources Manager
Bentley Oil
P.O. Box 2000
Tulsa, Oklahoma 74102

Dear Mr. Young:

Since introducing video interviews in 1982, we have found that | *Establishes rapport by beginning with surprising facts*

- Those companies who use our services are so satisfied that they use them again and again.

- Those companies who view our video brochure, a demonstration tape, are impressed with the possibilities and advantages video interviews will add to their recruiting program.

Right now your company is probably reviewing its fall and spring college recruiting program. Would you be interested in exploring new ways to capture the top graduates, enhance your campus image, and reduce costs? Video interviews can do all of these things for you. | *Influences thinking by listing reader benefits*

Video interviews

- Give Human Resource Departments a screening tool that maintains your control, yet is applauded by operating managers.

- Save staff and operating managers valuable time, yet provide more candidate information for more confident selections.

- Save recruiting dollars by reducing travel expenses dramatically (a tape can be mailed anywhere in the country for under $5.00).

- Give graduates an opportunity to demonstrate to your company a more complete picture of their potential.

> Mr. Ronald Young
> page 2
> March 9, 199_
>
> We would like to send you our video brochure, which contains portions of actual interviews. There is absolutely no obligation, and viewing requires only 10 minutes of your time.   *Offers free trial*
>
> We welcome the opportunity to introduce you to the benefits that video can add to your college recruiting program. Call us or return the enclosed postcard and we will send you a video brochure at no obligation.   *Motivates action by making action easy*
>
> We look forward to working with you.
>
>   Sincerely,
>
>   William B. Reese
>   President
>
> **VIDEO TAPED INTERVIEWS AND RESUMES
> COMPANIES AND INDIVIDUALS**

246) was long a winner for *Inc.*, a magazine for small entrepreneurs. Jayme explained his philosophy this way:

> What always works for us is that outer envelope that doesn't pretend to be anything other than what it is—advertising mail. We develop an outer envelope that orients the prospect to the product and even the offer right away. We spend about a third of our time conceptualizing the outer envelope. It determines the direction of the rest of the package.

Compare the three sample envelopes in Figure 6.6. Since the offer and the letter copy, as well as the envelope, differed with each package, we cannot be sure just how much the envelope affected the sales results. What would your guess be?

You can use the checklist on page 247 to judge the effectiveness of your sales letters.

THE RANDOM HOUSE GUIDE TO BUSINESS WRITING

Figure 6.6

PRIZE-WINNING DIRECT-MAIL ENVELOPES

The Pulling Power of Three Throw-Aways

The Favorite
This envelope stands out in a pile of mail because of its size. The envelope also gives the impression of a strong offer by prominently displaying the word "free" — a key word in direct mail. The enclosed letter also proved enticing. The package generated 48 percent more subscription orders than its nearest competitor.

Second-Best
With a bright orange circle, this envelope boasts a catchy phrase in a splashy graphic display. Once again, "free" is an inducement to open the package and read the letter. This package generated 56 percent more subscription orders than the third promotion.

So you've got a better one. Now what? PRESENTING *Inc.* the new magazine about you and your company.

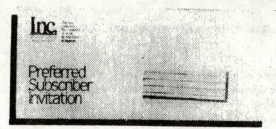

Last Place
This envelope does not convey the promise of a strong offer since it does not use the word "free." Also, the envelope is easier to overlook in a pile of mail than the other two. It is considered a standard direct-mail package.

RTA CHECKLIST FOR WRITING THE SALES LETTER

R: Have you
- Gained the reader's interest?
- Given the reader a reason for reading on?
- Begun to develop your central selling point?

T: Have you
- Created in the reader a desire for your product by focusing on reader benefits?
- Backed up your claims with evidence and testimonials?
- Mentioned, if you discuss price, benefits the money buys and broken down the amount into manageable sums?

A: Have you made action easy and emphasized reader benefits?

To promote your business, you may decide that direct mail is the best way to get in touch with potential customers. By following the suggestions in this section, you can write the letter that will get your business going and keep it going.

REQUESTING FAVORS

Rachel Bayer knew that if she could only persuade Mr. Rosen to give a talk next fall at the Career Advisory Night of the Society for the Advancement of Management (SAM), she would have managed one of the most successful events of her upcoming senior year. In the first semester of her freshman year, she had roomed with a senior, Heddy Rosen, and so had a few chances to meet Heddy's father. Mr. Rosen had impressed her with his remarks about his position as Overseas Operations Manager for Cosmetics Plus. Getting him to speak at the school would mean he would be one of the first company representatives SAM had been able to attract who was extensively involved in international business.

But Rachel found the letter of invitation difficult. She had not had any contact with the Rosens since Heddy graduated almost two years ago, so Mr. Rosen would hardly remember her. She did not feel comfortable asking him to appear as a personal favor to his daughter's old roommate. What could she say in a letter that would persuade him to come?

Although still a student, as a member of a college organization Rachel found herself in a situation many business people face. Whether it is on behalf of their company, other business organizations, or community organizations, business people often have to request favors of others. Many business people get much more involved in their community than simply by working at their jobs. They become involved partly because they know it is good for business. But they also take satisfaction in using their business and personal talents to promote community goals—through religious, civic, or professional clubs and organizations. In the course of such work, business people are frequently called on to donate—and in turn ask others to donate—their time, talents, or money. Thus, knowing how to write letters requesting favors becomes an important business writing skill.

We will look more closely at the stages in writing the request for a favor, but first let's find out how Rachel Bayer wrote the letter that brought Mr. Rosen to Ohio State to speak at SAM's Career Advisory Night.

Rachel explained to us that she worked through two major drafts of her letter. When she wrote the first draft she was mainly concerned about getting all the facts straight.

> As I look back at my first draft, I can see I felt embarrassed asking a top executive for a favor. My letter ignored the problem by focusing on the details. I just got all the information together on Career Advisory Night, accommodations, and so on. Then I sat down and wrote.

Here's the beginning of her early draft:

DRAFT

Dear Mr. Rosen,

My name is Rachel Bayer, and I am writing to you on behalf of the Society for the Advancement of Management (SAM) at Ohio State. On September 22, 199_, SAM will be sponsoring its semiannual Career Advisory Night. This program is designed to help students in their job search. In the past, SAM has invited business people who have positions in finance, accounting, and marketing, but this year, due to the increased interest in international business, we have decided to invite a panel of representatives from the international business environment.

> Obviously I wasn't crazy about this letter. It sounded very polite, sure. But really, why should Mr. Rosen care about Rachel Bayer and Career Advisory Night? I didn't know how to change it.
>
> Finally, I took it to Carol, the head of the Graduate Student Organization and a friend of mine. I know GSO asks for speakers all the time, and I figured the grad students might know better. She and I read over several letters in the GSO files. The best letters, we thought, always emphasized the same thing: what the speakers would get out of coming—like getting top students interested in working for their company. I noticed a couple of letters, too, that emphasized how much students get out of the chance to meet top executives. I thought that was good too—it would make the speaker feel like he or she was doing some good. I took a lot of notes from those letters and then went back to the drawing board.

Rachel explained that she showed her next draft to Carol, who had a few further suggestions. After revising, Rachel sent off the letter shown in Figure 6.7 to Mr. Rosen. He, by the way, graciously accepted her invitation.

Figure 6.7

RACHEL'S LETTER TO MR. ROSEN

> 60 East Norwich Avenue
> Columbus, Ohio 43201
> March 5, 199_
>
> Mr. Burt Rosen
> Cosmetics Plus Corporation
> 20 West 13th Street
> New York, N.Y. 10011
>
> Dear Mr. Rosen:
>
> Would you be able to contribute some of your expertise to the education of enthusiastic business students? Ohio State management students want very much to know more about the international business environment from important executives in the field. We think you might enjoy the opportunity of personally explaining your company's position in the international market.
>
> As head of international divisions for Cosmetics Plus, you could, I know, provide us with valuable insights. Your speaking at Ohio State would offer students the opportunity to hear more about your work and Cosmetics Plus's international operations. And perhaps meeting Ohio State students might introduce you to promising job candidates. Past speakers have been very impressed with Ohio State students and the Ohio State program, and many of them have returned to recruit students for employment after graduation.
>
> We would like to have you speak at the Society for the Advancement of Management's semiannual Career Advisory Night, September 22, 199_, 7:30 p.m. Due to increased interest in international business, this year, for the first time, we are featuring a panel of three representatives from the international business environment.
>
> We would like you to be one of those representatives. Panel members will each make a 20-minute presentation, and there should be at least 150 students in the audience. After the presentations, the panel is invited to talk informally with students at a reception. We anticipate that the reception will be over by 10 p.m.
>
> *(continued)*

(RACHEL'S LETTER TO MR. ROSEN continued)

Mr. Burt Rosen
page 2
March 5, 199_

As I am sure you know, student activities budgets are slim. We can, however, offer you excellent campus accommodations at the Alumni Suite, should you wish to stay the night of September 22nd.

Your appearance at our Career Advisory Night would give Ohio State students a wonderful opportunity to learn more about Cosmetics Plus. Having met you a few times (remember Heddy's senior-year roommate?), I know you would be a dynamic speaker who would make students eager to know more about your company. And as the father of an Ohio State alumna, you might be very pleased to find that students' awareness of international management and their enthusiasm for it have grown considerably in the past two years.

I will be calling your office in two weeks to find out whether I can provide you with any more information. But if you have questions before then, please call me at 614-555-1667. I would be delighted to hear from you.

Very truly yours,

Rachel Bayer

Rachel Bayer, for
The Society for the
Advancement of Management

Notice that Rachel's letter begins by picturing enthusiastic students waiting to hear what Mr. Rosen has to say. It then goes on to describe how Mr. Rosen might benefit from the exposure to good management students. In other words, Rachel focused on two ways the reader would benefit from accepting the speaking invitation. Only after she has mentioned benefits does she explain the details of the favor she is asking.

Rachel's experience illustrates an important principle for requesting favors. Every reader is busy. All readers already have more plans for their time, energy, and money than they can possibly carry out. Therefore, your request must above all demonstrate what they will get out of doing a favor for you. A look at the stages in the writing process can help you understand and appeal to your reader.

Setting the Goal: Know What You Are Asking

In requesting a favor, your goal is of course clear. You want the reader to agree to do the favor. But examine your goal more carefully. Have you figured out precisely what you want your reader to do? If you are requesting time, how much time? Is this a reasonable request? If you are requesting the reader's talents, for example as a speaker or manager, what precisely are the skills required? You may be able to persuade your reader to be willing to do a favor, but is your reader *able* to do it? Have you checked to be certain you can provide all the support services necessary? If you are requesting money, is there some likelihood enough readers will be able to respond positively so that returns outweigh costs?

No one wants to be part of an ill-conceived or poorly managed venture. Only if your readers perceive that your request is well thought out and reasonable will they be likely to respond. Only after you have examined your goal carefully can you be sure you are asking the right favor of the right person.

Assessing the Reader: Understanding Reader Benefits

Writing a letter that asks someone to do a favor is somewhat like writing a sales letter. Just as a good sales letter must focus on how the reader can benefit from the purchase, so the request for a favor must focus on how the reader will benefit from doing the favor. This is not to say that all people are only out to benefit themselves. But even altruistic people want to know what their contributions have accomplished, not for themselves but for others.

The benefits the reader will experience by granting a favor are frequently far less tangible and direct than those resulting from a purchase. The good request for a favor persuades by demonstrating that the favor will be appreciated and rewarded—if not directly and tangibly, then certainly indirectly and in personal or social terms.

In assessing the reader, consider how he or she might best feel rewarded for doing the favor you request. When Rachel Bayer first wrote her request to Mr. Rosen, she neglected to consider how he could benefit from speaking at Career Advisory Night. But her final draft showed she had learned how an executive might feel rewarded from talking to students.

Gathering Information and Generating Ideas

To generate ideas that may persuade your reader to grant the favor you are requesting, use the same technique that you learned for developing the central selling point in the sales letter. First, in one column list all the activities involved in doing the favor and the results that doing the favor will accomplish. Then opposite each activity and result, list the benefit that the reader might get out of each activity and result. Frequently, granting favors will provide some or all of the following opportunities for the reader:

- To make contacts
- To create goodwill for the company and to be remembered, as an individual, for generosity
- To belong to an important group effort that many people have already joined
- To benefit the welfare of the organization and community to which the donor belongs

Once you have generated your list of benefits, focus on those you think will be most persuasive, as when developing the central selling point in the sales letter. Rachel, for example, concentrated on convincing Mr. Rosen that his audience would be very interested in what he had to say, implying that he would be greatly appreciated for his generosity.

Remember, the more convincingly you can illustrate these intangible yet significant benefits, the more persuasive your letter will be.

Organizing: Using RTA to Request Favors

Let's see how the RTA formula can help you organize the ideas you already have for making your request, and perhaps help you generate some new ones.

Establishing Rapport: Since readers are often not readily able to grant favors and must be "sold" on doing them, many of the strategies used for beginning sales letters can be useful in requests for favors. As with a sales letter, the opening sentences of a letter requesting a favor not only must establish rapport by gaining the reader's interest. They must also lead into the central benefit you are emphasizing. As you look at the following suggestions for opening strategies, can you discern the central benefit being emphasized?

1. *Begin with a story or anecdote.* A senior citizens organization asks for support:

   To get from the airport to my home in Philadelphia, I have to pass a junkyard, where old cars are thrown on a heap, left to rust and disintegrate, and finally smashed to smithereens by a society that wants everything shiny-new. . . . That junkyard haunts me because America does the same thing to people. When we turn 65, we are trashed.

2. *Compliment the reader.* A student organization requests a speaker:

> Union Oil is generally regarded as unique in its industry, not as a maverick but as a company that marches to a different drummer—successfully. And the personality of its chief executive officer is certainly a major factor! You could provide a group of eager students with important insights into corporate opportunities and challenges.

3. *Suggest the problem and what your organization is doing about it.* An auto safety consumer group solicits members:

> What you are about to read is going to shake up a few vice presidents in the auto industry. Maybe it will jar them enough to make them realize that you and many other Americans are no longer going to sit back and let car and tire manufacturers put your lives and safety in jeopardy for the sake of cutting corners and amassing higher profits.

4. *Describe your organization's major accomplishments.* A public television station requests corporate funding:

> Once again, KQED/Channel 9 will present some of the most exciting, entertaining, and varied television programs and series in the coming 199_ season. Once again, we believe, the 2 million households in the Bay Area and beyond in Northern California will be tuning to Channel 9 for television out of the ordinary . . . television that respects one's intelligence, that stimulates and provokes one's curiosity about the complexities and wonders of today and the world around us.

5. *State a shared goal.* A girls' organization requests volunteers:

> We both have a vested interest in women and girls who will be tomorrow's employees, customers, and leaders. That's why this year your membership in our growing roster of volunteers is more important than ever.

6. *Use testimonials and give statistics to show support already gained.* An alumni magazine begins its request for donations with quotes from alumni:

> "You have an excellent publication and I look forward to each issue. Happily I send you $10."—Sue Ellenberger Shields, '70.
>
> "I am more than pleased to contribute to help maintain production. The alumni magazine keeps me in touch with my friends."—Pat Nelson, '82

Last year 1,640 alumni contributed $17,556 to the annual <u>Courier</u> voluntary subscription campaign. These funds, which were used to offset the rising cost of publishing your alumni magazine, covered expenses for about one issue.

7. *Ask a question.* A professional organization solicits new members:

   Looking for fresh ideas? Want a pleasant way to keep current in your field? The STS Educational Activities Stem sponsors interesting noontime lectures and conferences completely free of charge to its members.

8. *Frankly admit you are asking a favor.* A health organization requests contributions:

   I really need you to join me as a Red Cross "Life Giver."

Influence Thinking: After your first sentences have established rapport, readers want to know four things:

1. What are the benefits of granting your request?
2. What precisely is the request?
3. What is your organization, its purpose, members, activities, and goals?
4. How will you answer their objections to doing the favor?

Let's take a closer look at each of these.

Benefits, the Request, Your Organization. In discussing benefits, the request, and your organization, you need not follow a fixed order. Your opening, in establishing rapport, may already have shown a benefit, frankly made your request, or mentioned accomplishments of your organization. The body of your letter must follow upon your opening statement and include all necessary additional information. Although the order in which you discuss this information is up to you, make certain that reader benefits receive the primary emphasis.

Rachel's letter, for example, emphasized to Mr. Rosen the benefits of speaking at SAM's Career Advisory Night at the same time that she made her request and explained her organization's activity. Her request implied the personal reward of speaking to an eager audience:

   Would you be able to contribute some of your expertise to the education of enthusiastic business students? . . . We think you might enjoy the opportunity of personally explaining your company's position in the international market.

Rachel immediately followed up on her request by making reader benefits explicit:

> Your speaking at Ohio State would offer students the opportunity to hear more about your work and Cosmetic Plus's international operations. And perhaps meeting Ohio State students might introduce you to promising job candidates. Past speakers have been very impressed.

Answering Objections. In specifying the favor you are requesting of the reader, frequently you must ask what may seem difficult for the reader to grant. Try to make the request while maintaining as favorable an image of the activity as possible.

1. If you are requesting a speaker and your honorarium or other reimbursements are inadequate, *emphasize what you can do for the speaker:* Arrange accommodations and transportation? Provide an enjoyable banquet or sightseeing guides? Be flexible in scheduling dates and times? Recall how Rachel Bayer handled the fact that her organization could not offer an honorarium or transportation expenses. Rather than saying what she could not do, she emphasized what she could do.

> As I am sure you know, student activities budgets are slim. We can, however, offer you excellent campus accommodations at the Alumni Suite, should you wish to stay the night of September 22nd.

2. If you are asking readers to do something that requires time, *suggest what might make the task easy, and emphasize reader benefits*. If you are asking readers to fill out a questionnaire, will it take only a few minutes? If you are requesting blood donations, how little time will a donation require? If you are encouraging readers to participate in a lobbying effort, can you offer suggestions for what a letter to a congressional representative might include? If you are requesting a speaker, have you suggested what the talk could cover that would clearly be within his or her range of expertise?

3. When you are requesting what may seem like a large contribution, try one of the following techniques:

    a. *Break the amount down* into smaller monthly payments:

    > For contributions over $60, you can donate monthly amounts of $5 or more. We will provide convenient envelopes.

    b. *Compare the amount* to what is spent on other items:

    > Right now we urgently need your support. I realize the cost of living is high and money is tight . . . but we're working for you. Look at it this

way: the consumer membership support we ask for—$15 a year—can be returned to you many times over in the money we might save you in repair costs alone. More important, that $15 will be put to work to keep you and those you love safe and free from accidents on the highway.

c. *Show what the money will accomplish:*

Your special gift of $50, $100, $150—or whatever you can send—will help provide nutritious food, a warm bed, clean clothing, medical treatment, counseling, and therapy to battered children in your community.

Motivating Action and Attitude: As in any good business letter, the closing of a request letter makes action easy and reemphasizes reader benefits. To encourage prompt response, set a time limit and explain the reasons for it. Or say you will follow the letter up with a call within a specified time, and then do so. Postpaid envelopes and easy check-off boxes for contributions also make response easy.

Consider these action closings:

Join me as a fellow member today—right now—before the press of your own business takes you away from one of the most truly significant contributions you, as an executive, can make to a safer world.

We have a big job ahead of us, and I hope we can look forward to your help in meeting the challenge of an inner-city major medical center. With your support you will be participating in the exciting redevelopment of the Central City.

May I look forward to a call from your office? I would consider it a privilege to meet with you to pursue this matter and bring additional information for your consideration.

A speaking engagement at the University of Florida could offer great exposure to your company. Can we look forward to your appearance? I will be contacting you by phone sometime next week, to answer any questions you may have and so that we can arrange plans for your visit. I hope to meet you in the near future.

Sometimes, when I am kneeling in my garden to pick vegetables, or sitting with my family at the dinner table, or simply when I open my eyes in the morning and see the sky through my window, I remind myself of how fortunate I am—to have a garden, to have a family I can share things with, to have a window I can see from.

Then I think of those who don't.

Please help.

P.S. Your contribution is **tax deductible**.

Now that you have some ideas for writing the beginning, middle, and end of the request for a favor, look at the three letter examples in Figures 6.8 to 6.10 to see how the parts of the letter work together as a whole to create a persuasive appeal. In Figure 6.8, a company specializing in technology for industrial fire protection requests the deputy administrator of the U.S. Fire Administration to speak at a conference. Figure 6.9 illustrates how one corporation encouraged others to contribute to a civic organization. In Figure 6.10, a charity requests funds from individuals. Notice that especially in requests for charity, the reader benefits may be indirect rather than direct. That is, what benefits the community as a whole indirectly benefits each member.

The accompanying checklist can help you review your letters requesting favors.

RTA CHECKLIST FOR REQUESTING FAVORS

R: Have you gained the reader's interest? Have you begun to develop the central reader benefit?

T: Have you
- Made the benefit of granting the request clear?
- Precisely stated the request?
- Identified your organization, its purpose, members, activities, and goals?
- Answered any objections the reader might have to doing a favor?

A: Have you made action easy, for example by setting time limits, including postpaid envelopes, or promising to follow up with a call or visit?

As a member of the business community, you may frequently be called on to promote worthwhile projects, both for your own organization and for the community it depends on. Doing your part and knowing how to encourage others to contribute their efforts can be doubly satisfying. It can promote goodwill for your company, and it can provide you with considerable personal satisfaction.

Figure 6.8

LETTER REQUESTING A SPEAKER

moore research associates industrial safety division
1300 NORTH LUDLOW ST. DAYTON, OH 45402

September 12, 199_

Mr. Edward Wall
Deputy Administrator
United States Fire Administration
Federal Emergency Management Agency
Emmitsburg, MD 21727

Dear Mr. Wall:

As USFA director, you know that the USFA can be proud of its contribution to the recent significant decrease in our nation's fire losses. Because of USFA support and promotion, residential sprinkler technology realized the fast-response time that has made it so effective in decreasing losses.   *Establishes rapport by complimenting the reader and stating a shared goal*

We at Moore Research Associates feel sure that you will want to continue promoting sprinkler technology, now at the industrial level, so that the benefits of fast response can be realized there. That is why we would like to ask you to be the keynote speaker at our upcoming conference.   *Influences thinking by making request and emphasizing reader benefit*

Two years ago we initiated several research programs to develop a fast-response industrial sprinkler. We have now achieved very promising results. In order to share our research outcome with the fire protection community and promote its use in industrial fire protection, we have planned a national conference on industrial sprinkler technology. Your experience in promoting the residential sprinkler would be extremely helpful in guiding our promotion efforts for the new industrial sprinkler. We believe that once our technology is widely used, USFA will again be able to boast of significant declines in fire losses, this time at the industrial level.   *Describes organization and again emphasizes reader benefit*

Mr. Edward Wall
page 2
September 12, 199_

The conference will be held at Moore Research Associates' Conference Center on Monday, January 27, 199_, 9:30–3:30. We expect about 100 people to attend. After our president welcomes the conference participants, we would like you to present your keynote speech for approximately thirty minutes. Of course we will handle all your expenses and arrange for convenient lodging. *Gives details about the favor requested*

Your favorable reply will ensure the success of our conference. I will be in touch with you before the end of the week to explain our conference more fully and to answer any questions you might have. Because the conference bulletins will be mailed out in four weeks, we hope you can make your final decision by October 1. *Motivates action and reaffirms benefit (appreciation)*

The members of our fire protection community will sincerely appreciate the contribution you can make to our common endeavor to reduce the nation's fire losses.

Sincerely yours,

H. C. Kung
Manager, Applied Mechanics Section

HCK/jt

Figure 6.9

LETTER REQUESTING CONTRIBUTIONS TO A CIVIC ORGANIZATION

La Fortuna Enterprises 28 LUZERNE ST. PHILADELPHIA, PA 19124

April 9, 199_

Paul Fenster, President
American Engineering Corporation
1500 Harvard Ave.
Seattle, WA 98122

Dear President Fenster:

The future of a corporation can rest with the decision of a single judge. The decisions made in the courts on such subjects as product liability, government regulation, antitrust, and commercial disputes have direct and immediate impact on the corporate community. — *Establishes rapport by suggesting a common problem and what the organization is doing about it*

That is why I am asking your support for the American Judicature Society (AJS). The AJS works to find ways of assuring the quality of our judges and the justice they deliver. At La Fortuna Enterprises, we believe that AJS has made significant strides toward building a stronger, more effective, more efficiently managed judicial system. I personally believe strongly in the goals of the society and have been impressed with their accomplishments—some of which are outlined in the enclosed report. — *Influences thinking by showing how organization works to solve problem*

More than 90 corporations have already invested in AJS. Their contributions, together with those of 30,000 concerned citizens, help the society in its quest for a more effective system of justice. Because the quality of our system of justice should be the concern of every member of the business community, I am requesting your company's support. — *Shows many other companies support organization's goals*

I hope you will encourage your company to join with La Fortuna Enterprises and the other corporations who support the efforts of the American Judicature Society. We believe it is a worthwhile investment. — *Encourages action by emphasizing benefit: investment*

Sincerely yours,

Michael Lansing

Michael Lansing,
President

ML/hd
enc.

LETTERS THAT PERSUADE 261

Figure 6.10

LETTER REQUESTING A CHARITABLE CONTRIBUTION

American Friends Service Committee
1501 Cherry Street, Philadelphia, Pennsylvania 19102 • Phone (215) 241-7000

Stephen G. Cary
Chairperson

Asia A. Bennett
Executive Secretary

Colin W. Bell
Executive Secretary Emeritus

Dear Friend:

The smile on the face of a Cambodian child who has enough to eat for the first time in years . . .

The pride in the eyes of a working mother in North Carolina who has struggled for her rights on the job—and won . . .

The determination on the faces of the men and women demonstrating at the United Nations for an end to nuclear madness . . .

The relief on the faces of a family in Beirut that has located relatives on a list of captured prisoners . . .

Although they are thousands of miles apart, all these people share something in common. They are living with new dignity and self-respect with the help of the American Friends Services Committee (AFSC).

You will find AFSC volunteers and professional staff in Lebanon, East Africa, Cambodia, and other troubled regions you've read about in the headlines. But you are just as likely to find them in places few outsiders ever visit—remote farming communities in Asia, American Indian reservations, impoverished villages and urban neighborhoods in Mexico, and in other parts of the developing world.

For the hungry, AFSC offers seeds, tools, and new methods of agriculture for self-sufficiency.

For victims of oppression and the threat of war, AFSC promotes effective means for peaceably resisting violence and building community.

Establishes rapport by describing organization's accomplishments with specific descriptions

Influences thinking by explaining organization's activities and goals

Lists more accomplishments

(continued)

(LETTER REQUESTING A CHARITABLE
CONTRIBUTION continued)

For those living in the shadow of fear and hatred—both the perpetrators and the victims of prejudice—AFSC works to heal divisions through gentle but powerful programs for replacing mistrust with reconciliation.

But the most special thing about AFSC's work is not *what* we do, but *why* we do it.

As a Quaker organization, we believe that all people, whatever their age, race, faith or nationality, can be guided by an "inner light" of love and peace—and that eliminating the evils which oppress people will help them discover that light on their own.   *Shows benefits to all humanity*

The enclosed brochure will tell you more about AFSC's efforts to seek ways of promoting the peaceful, the just, and the compassionate in our world. I hope you'll take a moment to read it. You'll learn that it doesn't take a violent revolution or an earth-shaking political change to improve people's lives. Sometimes all it takes is a textbook, a meeting place, a shovel, a packet of seeds—small things with profound impact that can be provided by generous Americans like you.

I hope the importance of AFSC's goal will, as the Quakers say, "speak to your condition," and that you will find it possible to send a tax-deductible gift of $25, $50, $80, $100, $500—as much as your circumstances permit— to the American Friends Service Committee today.   *Motivates action by urging prompt response and reemphasizing benefits*

Thank you for sharing the faith that we must struggle to free our world from the evils that prevent us from being as loving and human as we possibly can.

Sincerely,

Asia Bennett

Asia Bennett
Executive Secretary

AB/tp
enc.

An Affirmative Action Employer

COLLECTING

Paula Hatfield was irritated. After three months and three follow-up letters, she still had not gotten a dime out of Jim Busey at Martin's Manufacturing. "I know Jim is hoping I'll forget about this because it represents a big mistake for him. But just because he ordered us to install the wrong soft drink dispensers, and then we had to take them out, that doesn't mean we should be left holding the bag. I think he's just trying to see if he can get away without paying."

Paula wanted to let Jim know she had waited about as long as she was going to. She figured she had a right to be irritated. But what was the best way to get her money?

Like Paula Hatfield, any business that sells its products or services on anything but a strictly cash basis is likely to find itself with at least a few **delinquent accounts**—that is, customers who have not paid their bills. While most customers conscientiously fulfill their agreements, some customers need to be persuaded to pay. Perhaps because they have fallen on hard times, perhaps because they took financial risks that were too great, perhaps simply because of compulsive credit card spending, these customers avoid paying their bills.

Offering customers the convenience of credit buying encourages sales. That is why most businesses think that extending credit is worth the trouble, even if it means having to collect delinquent accounts. Firms try to ensure that they extend credit only to good-paying customers by screening applications. They accept accounts only from those whose past credit records and current financial status indicate they are good credit risks.

Yet past performance cannot always predict the future, and some credit risks may seem worth taking. If a business has an effective collection policy, it can keep credit losses to a minimum. After the careful screening of credit applications, the most important component of a credit system is the series of messages sent to debtors to persuade them to pay. This is often called **the collection series**.

Setting the Goal of the Collection Series

The collection series offers a special challenge in persuasion for two reasons. First, the debtor is likely to have other bills to pay besides yours, so your messages must influence him or her to give your bill priority. Second, since most debtors do not remain debtors forever, and since they have friends who may be your potential customers, you want to retain the debtor's goodwill. Debtors who believe they have been treated fairly, even if they are not able to remain your customers, can be important for your business's image.

THE RANDOM HOUSE GUIDE TO BUSINESS WRITING

Thus collection messages have two goals:

1. To collect the debt as soon as possible
2. To retain the customer's goodwill

The collection letter does not have as its goal to express your annoyance and frustration at not being paid. When Paula Hatfield had written three letters to Jim Busey, trying to collect for work her company had done, she was irritated, and her first notes for her letter (shown in Figure 6.11) showed it. Paula thought twice about this draft. She wondered whether it would really persuade Jim to pay. Could she be sure why Jim hadn't paid? If she was wrong, she would almost certainly lose Jim's goodwill.

Paula was right to think twice. While a tone of righteous anger may make you, the writer, feel better, it risks offending the reader. Keep your primary goals in mind—to collect the debt and to retain goodwill. Often enough, it is only by being careful to retain goodwill that you are successful in collecting the debt.

Figure 6.11

PAULA'S FIRST NOTES

> I know you are trying to avoid paying this bill because you made a mistake. You ordered the wrong dispensers and had to have them taken out. But we can't be expected to absorb this loss for you. You have had three months to pay and that's long enough.

Offering customers the convenience of credit buying encourages sales.

Assessing the Reader of the Collection Series

The collection series normally follows five stages, each stage representing a different assumption about the reader. The stages are shown in Figure 6.12. While the sequence of messages is usually the same, the timing and number of mailings at each stage will depend on how much understanding and leeway the debtor merits.

It would be a foolish collection department indeed that would send out the same collection notices at the same intervals, without discriminating among debtors. What is said to customers should depend on their past relations with the company. Is this a customer of long standing who has for the first time fallen behind in payments? Or is this a more recent customer who has missed paying the first bill? Or is this a steady customer who always needs reminding before paying? Obviously a longstanding, good-paying customer deserves more time to pay, and more understanding terms of payment, than a new customer or a customer whose payments you have always had to ask for several times.

Figure 6.12

THE COLLECTION SERIES

> 1. **Reminder:** Assume the reader has overlooked the bill.
>
> 2. **Inquiry:** Assume something unusual has happened to make payment difficult. You inquire to find out whether you can make special arrangements to make payment easier.
>
> 3. **Appeal:** Assume the reader needs to be persuaded to pay.
>
> 4. **Urgent appeal:** Assume the reader needs to know you are not willing to wait any longer.
>
> 5. **Ultimatum:** Assume the reader must be made to pay but may respond to a last-chance appeal.

Thus, although most collections go through standard letter stages, these standard letter messages cannot be sent out automatically to every debtor. Some companies find it convenient to classify their debtors into three categories and then to follow more or less standard procedures within each category. The following classification is common:

Good-paying: These customers consistently pay their bills promptly. When they fall behind in payments, they deserve understanding terms and lenient time constraints.

Fair-paying: These customers always pay but need continual reminders. They are treated more firmly, with stricter terms and tighter time constraints.

Poor-paying: These customers seem intentionally to take advantage of lenient credit policies and can be persuaded to pay only with urgent appeals or ultimatums.

When Paula had set aside her angry collection letter, she thought about her reader. She knew of Jim through her town's Better Business Association, and he had a good reputation in the community. Perhaps he was experiencing some hardship. Yet she had given him plenty of time to explain his situation. She decided that Jim needed to know she was not willing to wait any longer. "I know some people are like that about paying bills," she explained to us. "They have to be told, this is the last chance. I think Jim may be waiting for the ultimatum, especially since he has nothing to show for the expenditure. The dispensers had to be taken out."

As we discuss the five stages in the collection series, bear in mind that each letter in the series must be adjusted to the type of customer you are dealing with. Before we look at specific examples of letters in each stage, however, let's look at how RTA can help you write the typical collection letter.

Generating Ideas for and Organizing the Collection Letter: Using RTA

As we have seen, every collection letter attempts to collect the debt as soon as possible while at the same time retaining the customer's goodwill. The collection letter must, therefore, be a combination of firmness and courtesy. RTA can help you achieve this balance. Since the collection letter will usually be perceived as bad news, use the indirect letter pattern.

Establish Rapport: In the early stages of collection, begin on a positive, understanding note:

> We are grateful for your business and have always appreciated your
> promptness in paying your credit account. That is why we are concerned
> that we have not heard from you about the enclosed invoice. Is there any
> reason why payment is past due?

In the later stages, when more firmness is in order, you should still begin on a positive note, but your remarks may include a review of the facts, and they should also lead into your persuasive appeal. Here's how Paula opened her fourth appeal to Jim Busey:

> In good faith we installed your cold drink dispensers on your premises,
> only to have the installation countermanded.
>
> Your company was sent an invoice dated December 30, 199_ in the
> amount of $212.00 to cover labor expenses and two trips made by Mr.
> Byerly. That invoice was followed up by three reminders.

Influence Thinking: In the early stages of collection, a reminder is usually all that is needed to encourage a customer to pay:

> Your mortgage payment was due on the first day of this month and we
> have not received it.

If, however, the debt remains unpaid, then your letter must persuade by appealing to the debtor's concern for one of the following:

- A good credit rating
- A sense of fairness
- A sense of self-esteem

In making your appeal, avoid the accusatory phrase "you are delinquent," and instead refer to the "delinquent account" or "unpaid balance."

> We know the pride you take in providing your customers the finest wines and cheeses available anywhere. We feel sure that you take the same pride in your reputation as a good paying creditor. That is why we are concerned about your delinquent account.

Paula appealed to Jim Busey's sense of fair play and self-esteem:

> I know that your company, as a longstanding member of the Tacoma business community, must be concerned with fairness in business. I simply can't believe that your company would reject the validity of the rather meager bill we sent, which barely covers our costs.

Motivate Action and Attitude: As with any business letter, make action easy. Make clear the action you expect the reader to take, including amount to be paid and when due. Reinforce the benefits to the reader of paying promptly.

> In fairness to yourself, as well as to us, please send your $485.80 payment today, and return your account to most-favored-customer status.

Paula's letter urged Jim Busey this way:

> Since our fiscal year ends on March 22, and auditors will be in to do the yearly audit, we are acting to clear outstanding invoices like yours from the books. I am sure you too would like to get this matter resolved without legal complication.
>
> Please send payment immediately.

Now let's look more closely at the five stages in the collection series, bearing in mind that each letter in the series must be adjusted to the type of customer you are dealing with.

The Collection Series

REMINDER

When a bill first becomes overdue, it is likely that the customer has simply overlooked it. Remind the customer by reissuing the statement of account, including the date pay-

LETTERS THAT PERSUADE 269

ment is required and any finance charges. A second and third reminder might also consist of reissuing the bill, but this time it may be stamped with a short message—such as "Notice of Overdue Account" or "Please Pay Promptly." Or a short note such as the one shown in Figure 6.13 can be included with the bill.

Some companies include a resale message with their reminders, usually in the form of a printed advertisement. This demonstrates confidence in the customer as well as encouraging future sales.

How many reminders you send before moving on to the next stage will depend on how you have assessed your customer in terms of being good-, fair-, or poor-paying. As for timing, after the first statement a company will frequently wait 30 days, send the first reminder, wait 15 days, send the second reminder, and then follow up with firmer appeals. But of course the pattern varies with company and customer.

INQUIRY

If customers do not respond to reminders, they require more energetic persuasion. Again, discriminate among the customers you are dealing with. For a customer of long standing, if you have not heard anything after several reminders, you can assume something unusual has happened and you will want to inquire. Your objective is to get a response that will explain the delay. Your inquiry, in turn, can offer helpful options for how payment might be made. Your tone is understanding, but at the same time it makes clear the debtor must take some action.

Figure 6.14 is a simple inquiry sent out to mail-order customers and accompanied by a statement and return envelope. Figure 6.15 shows one manufacturer appealing to another. Figure 6.16 shows the personalized form letter a department store sends to its good-paying delinquent customers. These letters all assume that the debtor wants to pay, but has encountered something that makes payment difficult. Because the companies have good prior relations with the debtor, they offer easy terms, but they make clear that they expect either payment or an explanation. For customers without longstanding credit records, the offer of easy terms and an appeal for explanation are usually considered optional, since the company knows less about the character of the debtor. Debtors who have ignored your reminders and inquiries require strong appeals.

APPEAL

If you have received no response from reminders or inquiries, you can issue more persuasive appeals. The goal is still to retain the customer's goodwill by remaining friendly but to become increasingly firm. And whereas reminders and inquiries may have been form letters, appeal letters should be tailored to the particular customer. This gives the debtor a clear sense that he or she has become a special case.

The letter in Figure 6.17 appeals to the reader's concern for his good credit rating. The one in Figure 6.18 appeals to a sense of fair play.

Figure 6.13

REMINDER NOTE

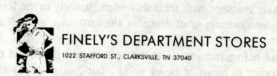

FINELY'S DEPARTMENT STORES
1022 STAFFORD ST., CLARKSVILLE, TN 37040

March 3, 199_

Stephen Fowler
6450 Brownlee Drive
Nashville, TN 37205

Dear Customer:

    Your purchase, as reflected on the enclosed statement, is sincerely appreciated.

    If you haven't paid this bill, will you please do so now?

    If you recently sent your payment, we appreciate your promptness.

    Please be sure to enclose our bill with your check. Thank you.

FINELY'S DEPARTMENT STORES

Enc.

Figure 6.14

INQUIRY LETTER 1

4105 W. Greenfield Ave. Milwaukee, WI 53215

June 3, 199_

Joseph R. Finch
6 Doubletree Lane
St. Louis, MO 63131

Dear Customer:

Subject: Payment for Basketball Uniforms

Since you have had several opportunities to process our invoice for payment, perhaps there is some problem.

If you have withheld payment for any reason, please let us know. For our part, we will promptly correct any errors or omissions.

But if, for some reason, you cannot make your payment immediately, please let us know so that we can work out terms that will be most convenient for you.

Sincerely yours,

Maureen Berenson

Maureen Berenson,
Credit Manager

MB/mf
enc.

Figure 6.15

INQUIRY LETTER 2

OWENS CONSTRUCTION SUPPLY CO.
2762 CALDER ST. BEAUMONT, TX 77702

June 9, 199_

Richard Ablewood
Ablewood Builders
424 Austin Avenue
Port Arthur, TX 77640

Dear Mr. Ablewood:

Subject: Payment for Kordex Wiring

Since you opened your account with us two years ago, we have appreciated the opportunity of providing you with our top-of-the-line wiring products. We have genuinely enjoyed dealing with you and have always been thankful for the way you have paid your accounts so promptly.

That is why I am concerned about the delay in paying your current invoice for Kordex light-weight insulated wiring.

We know you want to settle this account as soon as possible. We'd like to help you. Would spreading payments out over the next six months help you? Can we arrange to have the wire shipped back to us for resale?

An envelope is enclosed to make your reply easy. Or you can use it to drop off a check for the balance owed.

Please let us hear from you by mail, or call us collect: 555-1200.

Sincerely yours,

Matt Wilson

Matt Wilson for
Owens Construction Supply Co.

MW/na
enc.

Figure 6.16

INQUIRY LETTER 3

Hilliard's
TWELVE-HUNDRED FIFTY-ONE HOGAN ROAD, BANGOR, MAINE 04401

August 23, 199_

Jean Radcliffe
39 James St.
Bangor, ME 04401

Dear Ms. Radcliffe:

    Serving you has been our privilege and our pleasure. We thank you for shopping at Hilliard's.

    We have noticed that you have always been prompt in paying your account with us, and we value your continued patronage.

    Your most recent bill is 90 days past due. Do you have some question about the amount owed? Is there some other reason why payment has been delayed? Perhaps we can work out arrangements for monthly payments that will make clearing your account easier for you.

    If you would please write a note at the bottom of this letter explaining what we can do to help expedite your payment, we will respond promptly.

    Thank you for your cooperation.

Sincerely yours,

Beverly Hilliard

Beverly Hilliard

Figure 6.17

APPEAL LETTER 1

COLBY AIR SYSTEMS AND SUPPLIES
4020 LINGLETOWN ROAD
HARRISBURG, PA 17112

February 3, 199_

President Howard Perlin
Perlin's Home Centers
3240 Hempland Road
Lancaster, PA 17601

Dear Mr. Perlin:

You know how important a good credit rating can be to your business. Credit allows you to stock the latest and most popular models so that you have what your customers want, when they want it.

We extended you credit on the basis of your reputation for prompt payment. Please do not let the balance you owe us threaten that good reputation.

To protect your competitive edge, send us your payment of $1,259.85 in the enclosed envelope immediately. That way, when asked about your credit standing, we can gladly give a favorable reply.

Sincerely yours,

Michael Colby

Michael Colby,
Vice President

MC/bt
enc.

LETTERS THAT PERSUADE

Figure 6.18
APPEAL LETTER 2

BENNETT PROPERTIES, INC.
5400 WILSHIRE BLVD. LOS ANGELES, CALIFORNIA 90036

July 17, 199_

Mrs. Martha McClellan, Purchasing
Kormanik Industries
1692 Flower Street
Glendale, CA 91202

Dear Mrs. McClellan:

Subject: Lampoc Rent

I'm writing again about the matter of rent at Lampoc.

You may recall that when you and I worked out a rental agreement last year, we found that the price for storage space in buildings comparable to mine ran between 35 cents and 80 cents per square foot. But because of our longstanding relationship, I settled with you for 28 cents. At that time you agreed that this offer was more than fair.

Currently, three month's rent from you is still outstanding on my accounts. Could you continue to do business if your customers didn't pay you what they owed? I don't think so, and neither can I.

Please pay the balance due today: $4,830.00. Or contact me at 555-1200 to make arrangements.

Sincerely yours,

Larry Garcia

Larry Garcia for
Bennett Properties, Inc.

P.S. I hope to hear from you soon because I am very reluctant to have to take stronger action.

LG/as

URGENT APPEAL

If the debtor has not responded by this point in the collection series, you need to convey a sense that you are not willing to wait much longer. The appeals are the same as for earlier messages, but more insistent. Frequently they are signed by an executive higher in the company, to convey a sense that strong action is about to be taken. You still want to retain the goodwill of the customer, whom you might deal with again, if only on a cash basis. But you want to make clear (as in Figure 6.19) that this is close to the last chance you can reasonably be expected to give.

ULTIMATUM

If the strong appeals of the previous letters have had no effect, you assume the customer must be made to pay, but you give one final chance before recourse to a lawyer or a collection agency. From your point of view, it is better to settle the matter between yourselves than to go to an outside agent, since agencies will be concerned neither with your company's image nor with retaining goodwill. They are concerned solely with collecting the account (for which they get paid between 25 and 50 percent of the collected amount).

Although the ultimatum is your strongest letter, keep in mind that you want to retain the customer's goodwill. Even though your tone is firm, show that you are fair-minded, reasonable, and considerate. Review the facts of the case to make clear why the ultimatum is necessary, despite your reluctance. Appeal once again to the debtor's sense of fairness and concern for a good credit rating. Make the ultimatum clear, and stress the benefits of responding quickly.

The letter in Figure 6.20 attempts to collect past due installments on a student loan. Notice the letter's appeal to a sense of fair play, even as it makes clear that legal action will follow. The letter in Figure 6.21 makes a strong appeal to the customer's desire for a good credit rating.

The accompanying checklist can help you review your collection letters:

RTA CHECKLIST FOR WRITING THE COLLECTION LETTER

R: *Early stage:* Have you begun on an understanding note—for example, by showing appreciation for the customer's business or by showing understanding for the debtor's problem?

Later stage: Have you included a review of the facts, and do you then lead into your persuasive appeal?

T: *Early stage:* Have you included a simple reminder or request for explanation?

Later stage: Have you appealed to the debtor's concern for one of the following:
- A good credit rating
- A sense of fairness
- A sense of self-esteem

A: Have you made action easy by making clear what action you expect the reader to take—for example, the amount to be paid and when due? Have you reinforced the benefits of paying promptly?

Figure 6.19

URGENT APPEAL LETTER

Tulane Paints, Inc.
3043 S. PARKER ROAD AURORA, CO 80014

October 23, 199_

Mr. Ryan Danielson
Gillis Ladder Co.
218 No. Cascade Ave.
Colorado Springs, CO 80903

Dear Mr. Danielson:

As the owner of a successful business for over 20 years, you know the value of a good credit rating. That is why, when you ordered $2,081.45 worth of supplies on January 14, we shipped them to you on credit, without delay. We assumed you would stand behind your word.

It has been nine months and seven letters since we first requested payment, and still we have received no word or payment. Does this mean that you no longer are able to stand behind your word? Are you ready to lose your good credit rating?

I cannot believe you want us to turn your account over to our attorney. Yet that is what we must do if we do not hear from you. Should this go to court, you will be liable not only for your outstanding balance but also for court costs.

Please protect your own reputation and save yourself legal costs. Let us hear from you immediately, in the form of a check for the amount owed.

Sincerely yours,

Benjamin Chung

Benjamin Chung, Credit Manager

BC/de
cc: R. Waters

Figure 6.20

ULTIMATUM LETTER 1

Paxton University
TWO-HUNDRED ONE ADMINISTRATION BUILDING, SYRACUSE, NEW YORK 13224

September 9, 199_

Victor Toulmin
174 Scott Avenue
Syracuse, NY 13224

Dear Mr. Toulmin:

FINAL DEMAND LETTER:
OUTSTANDING LOAN BALANCE $1,005

Your account is now seriously past due and, according to our records, you have not responded to our previous notices. You must settle your account immediately to prevent further collection action, including the possibility of contacting any co-signers.

As you may recall, the money collected from student loans is used to fund new student loans. When you do not pay your loan as agreed, you deny current students the same assistance that you received while in school.

We urge you to send your check or money order for the above amount. Otherwise we will be contacting co-signers or else referring your account to a collection agency.

If further action is necessary, it will be in accordance with the terms of your promissory note. Please send your payment immediately. We will expect to hear from you within seven days.

Sincerely,

Steven Bender

Steven Bender
Director of Financial Services

Figure 6.21
ULTIMATUM LETTER 2

COMPUTERSAFE
SECURITY SYSTEMS
1960 PEACHTREE ROAD N.W. ATLANTA, GA 30309

January 2, 199_

Harriet Rowley
1635 Clifton Road N.E.
Atlanta, GA 30329

Dear Harriet Rowley:

For the past five months you have been enjoying the protection of a Computersafe Security Alarm System. You no longer need be concerned about the safety of your home and valuables. But shouldn't you be concerned about the protection of your credit reputation?

Your account of $1,243 is now seriously past due. Although you have made several promises to pay, we have yet to receive a check. Unless we receive payment from you within the next five days, we will refer this account to our lawyer.

Please consider carefully the consequences of delaying payment any longer. It means that you will lose your good credit standing. Besides enabling you to enjoy your standard of living, credit is an asset that can be essential in times of emergency.

We still want to offer you an opportunity to resolve this matter and retain your credit standing. Please let us hear from you in the form of a payment. We will accept half the amount owed now and expect the balance in thirty days. Otherwise you may expect to talk to our lawyer.

Thank you for your cooperation.

Sincerely yours,

Leslie Gazley

Leslie Gazley for
Computersafe Security Systems

LG/jy

To prosper, your company must not only retain the goodwill of its customers but also maintain good-paying customers. Use the collection series to urge debtors to pay without losing goodwill.

COMMUNICATING IN CONTROVERSY

At 1:30 in the morning, in a sparsely populated rural area about three miles from the little town of MacGregor, Manitoba (population 1,100), a raging snowstorm derailed twelve cars, and two of them began leaking vinyl chloride monomer (VCM).[13] As the spokesperson for Sun Chemical, Judith Rysdale thought she had handled inquiries from the media and concerned citizens very well. The greatest hazard VCM creates is the danger of fire, but there was no chance of fire connected with these leaks, nor any other significant public health or environmental hazard. Since expert crews quickly had the leaking tank cars under control, Judith decided communications about the incident should be brief. By publishing only the scientific and technical data on VCM that she judged relevant to this incident, she felt she would avoid needlessly confusing or alarming the public.

Her view quickly changed two days later, however, when a New York professor of environmental science visiting the nearest university issued a public statement. It said that if this type of derailment had occurred in his state, an immediate evacuation of the area within at least a ten-mile radius would have been ordered, because VCM has been proven to cause cancer.

Every newsperson in Manitoba jumped on the story and created a crisis for Judith. She needed to get the technical facts across immediately, clearly, and persuasively. What should she do?

Thus far in the letter chapters, we have been discussing writing situations that are routine to most business organizations: filling orders, handling adjustments, promoting sales, or collecting bills. But occasionally a company must deal with an extraordinary situation such as the one Judith Rysdale confronted. Perhaps one of your products must be recalled. Perhaps a consumer interest group has targeted your company for protest. Perhaps an explosive gas has been discovered leaking from a drum case in your company's manufacturing plant. Increasingly in recent years, companies have had to respond to questions and controversies over their responsibilities to consumers, the environment, and the public. No matter how ethical and socially responsible a company might be, controversy may arise—and a company's activities may be endangered—for two reasons:

1. *Public misperception:* Although the company's activities are not harmful, the public misperceives them as harmful.
2. *Changing social values:* A company activity that the public once perceived as acceptable and ethical is now considered questionable.

Whether these issues are brought home to the company by shareholders, by the news media, by special interest groups, or by government agencies, the company must be prepared to respond quickly and persuasively.

In large companies, a public relations department often handles these communications. But even with good public relations departments, managers from several functional areas may be involved in deciding communications policy. Especially in crisis situations, even local plant managers must be prepared to respond to public inquiry. Thus in the midst of public controversy, how a company handles its communications with the public becomes every manager's concern.

If you find yourself in the midst of controversy so that you must explain your company's position to the public persuasively, you may very well make use of several different media—television, newspapers, and meetings with community groups and government officials. Here we offer strategies for responding in writing to inquiries and concerns expressed by the public, but these strategies may be modified for use with any media. Let's consider first what can be done at each stage of the writing process to communicate effectively when public misperception is involved. Later we will discuss controversy created by changing social values.

Public Misperception

SETTING THE GOAL

What are the company goals when communicating in controversy? Although the specific goal of a communication will depend on the situation at hand, the general goal will be twofold:

1. To present the company's position in as clear a light as possible
2. To promote a credible, favorable image of the company

This means telling the truth and nothing but the truth. And although it does not mean that a company must advertise its faults—other social institutions, such as the media and government agencies bear that responsibility—it does mean never suppressing information so as to distort the truth.[14] Your company's credibility as well as your own integrity can be sustained in the long run only by your being able to stand behind what you say. If the controversy is caused not by company error but by public misperception, spokespersons attempt to correct those misperceptions. (If, on the other hand, company error is involved, company spokespersons aim to minimize company error primarily by maximizing the actions the company is taking to correct the situation.)

These goals—presenting the company's position in as clear a light as possible and promoting a credible image—must be accomplished while bearing in mind that in controversy both parties may frequently learn valuable lessons, grow in understanding, and end up compromising. Many company policies have been changed as a result of public and shareholder concerns. In other cases the public has learned to understand better the position of companies that often have to act in a situation where an action can produce at the same time both good and evil, a desirable and a negative result.

What was Judith Rysdale's goal in responding to the crisis created by two derailed tank cars leaking VCM? You recall that although her company's crew had the cleanup under control, a professor's public statement had caused havoc. The statement claimed that the area within a ten-mile radius should have been evacuated because exposure to the VCM leak could cause cancer.

The media, politicians, and citizens naturally wondered why the company had not informed them of the danger, and accusations of cover-up were heard. Why had the company needlessly endangered the lives of citizens? In order to conceal their gross negligence? Hadn't the company provided only irresponsibly incomplete and misleading information? Meanwhile, several distraught MacGregor residents had evacuated their homes, and a public school principal had begun readying his entire school for mass evacuation. Apparently no one had thought to question the professor's statement or credentials.

But Judith knew the facts were these: It is true that VCM was discovered in 1974 to cause a rare form of liver cancer, but only in plant workers who had been exposed to *high concentrations* of VCM gas *over a working lifetime*—what scientists call a chronic exposure condition. These exposures were hundreds—indeed, thousands—of times greater and of a far longer duration than those occurring at the derailment site or in the town of MacGregor.

Obviously the public had misperceived the danger in the situation. Judith's goal, then, was to correct as quickly and persuasively as possible the public's misperception.

ASSESSING THE READER

Communicating in controversy usually means that you are communicating with elements of the general public. To understand your reader, then, you must understand the public's attitude toward business and business's relations with the community. Obviously no single, homogeneous attitude prevails, and a thorough coverage of business's relations with society is outside the scope of this book. Nevertheless, we can make some generalizations.

Current thinkers on business ethics[15] see essentially two attitudes toward business's social responsiblity: the "moral minimum" and the "affirmative duty." The **moral minimum** demands that a business merely avoid and correct any social injuries that accompany its activities. Business managers, according to this attitude, should be required to do only the moral minimum—that is, avoid hurting others—while they turn out products necessary for individual and social well-being. Solving the nation's social problems should be left to community groups, political parties, and government bodies.

Those who believe in the **affirmative duty,** on the other hand, demand that business go beyond the minimum to attack social problems such as poverty, discrimination, or urban decay. These thinkers believe that the moral minimum too readily allows businesses to take advantage of operating in a healthy society while ignoring their responsibility to contribute to that health.

Judging from this analysis, you can assume that in controversy the public will demand at the very least that a company abide by the moral minimum. But bear in mind that a significant element in the public may expect the company to act more affirmatively. In controversial situations, then, the business that can draw on a record of social concern and high credibility is at a great advantage in communicating with all elements of the public.

You might well ask: Is it possible for a company to create a record of social concern and still remain competitive? Many managers believe that what is required of them is merely to comply with the law. They will refrain from questionable, if still legal, activities only if forced by the government or public pressure to do so. Other companies take the lead in socially beneficial activities above and beyond strictly legal requirements. Which policy is best?

Careful observers have been able to distinguish between corporations that have performed well and those that have performed poorly in responding to larger societal needs. Their research has concluded that firms ranking high in social responsibility also rank high in earnings per share. According to economist Harold L. Johnson, "Corporations in both 'honorable mention' and 'best' categories [in social responsibility] outperformed the rest of their industries in profits, while 'worst' companies fell below average."[16]

Similar distinctions can be made among small businesses. Although comparative data on profits are not available, interviews with small business managers suggest that they perceive going beyond the moral minimum to be important both to profits and to their personal satisfaction. A study published in the *Journal of Small Business Management* revealed that while most managers were basically profit-oriented, they were also interested in social responsibility—if only as a means to higher profits.[17] In addition, 12 percent of the businesses surveyed actively pursued socially responsible values, regardless of the profit motive. These values included taking pride in providing quality goods and services, having that "personal touch," encouraging employee development, helping minority employees and entrepreneurs, being involved in political and religious activities, and helping others.

The owner of a sports equipment store explained his community interest this way: "I come in contact with a lot of kids in this neighborhood, and I like to feel that I'm a positive influence on them. I try to teach them sportsmanship, to work in helping each other, and to think for themselves."[18] A mom-and-pop grocer explained his attitude: "I sell good merchandise with quality, so I, as a businessman and also as a member of our society, am able to get respect and some kind of prestige. And then I am happy. Of course, I've got to make some money. That's for sure. But I never sold spoiled milk, you know. They need me around here. And I need them."[19]

Whether a business takes a minimal or a more affirmative approach to social responsibility, studies show that profitable business is by and large ethical business.[20] Society punishes unethical businesses through prosecution, adverse publicity, low employee morale, loss of sales, or government intervention. In the long run, society's power to exert pressure on businesses to conform to its standards is an advantage to businesses. Society's pressure prevents unethical businesses from forcing their competitors into the lowest common denominator of ethical behavior in order to survive. To act ethically within a society, then, businesses must follow at least the moral minimum—that is, they are required at the least not to injure others.

Public perception of whether a company is acting ethically is important. In her situation, Judith Rysdale had to deal persuasively with a public that perceived her company's activities as harmful and unethical when in fact they were not. Since newspapers across Manitoba had covered the story, she knew she had to reach as many people as possible with her message, and as quickly as possible. She immediately scheduled a press conference for the following day, and she planned to appear at a public meeting arranged by the mayor. Meanwhile she decided to prepare a full-page, full-disclosure newspaper statement to be published in several Manitoba dailies and weeklies, and to be sent in letter form in response to inquiries.

As Judith prepared to write her statement, she thought carefully about her readers. Since they believed VCM to be harmful, she had to provide the technical information that would demonstrate the truth about VCM's effects. But she also knew an "expert" had already told them that VCM was a proven cause of cancer, and she knew her readers would not necessarily be familiar with scientific terms. Judith determined that her statement would have to make clear what VCM is, the health risks involved at MacGregor, and how chronic exposure differs from the conditions existing in MacGregor. She would have to explain all this simply, in lay language.

GATHERING INFORMATION AND GENERATING IDEAS

To respond effectively to public controversy, you must understand two things thoroughly: the public's position, including the reasons and motives behind that position, and your company's activities, including the facts and reasons behind those activities.

To become as sensitive as you can to the public's position, use all the sources available to find out what the cause of the controversy is and why, as well as which interest groups or segments of the public are most concerned or most affected by your activities. This may mean consulting the media, talking with the public, communicating with shareholders, and using whatever other sources and contacts are available.

To understand your own company's position thoroughly, talk to as many people who are involved as possible, and consult company archives for necessary background information.

When Judith had determined what she had to do and who her readers would be, she immediately consulted with her company's chemical engineers to make certain she thoroughly understood the nature of VCM, its uses, properties, and effects. She then translated this information into lay language and had that translation checked again by her technical experts. Meanwhile, she monitored the media, TV news, and newspapers from across the state, to make certain she understood precisely what the public had been hearing about VCM and the leak at MacGregor.

ORGANIZING: USING RTA

You know what you want your statement to accomplish, and you understand the public's and your own company's position. How, then, do you bring all this together in a statement that will persuade the public of your company's ethically sound position and promote a favorable image of your company? The strategy is similar to that of any bad-news message in which the reader is likely to resist your communication. Take the indirect approach. First demonstrate your empathy with the reader, then explain your own position. The RTA formula can suggest guidelines.

Establish Rapport: Begin by showing that you understand your reader's concerns or point of view. State those concerns or that point of view, and show in what ways you think it is valid. Figure 6.22 shows part of the statement Judith published to allay readers' fears about VCM. Notice how the statement begins by stating her readers' questions and concerns, and demonstrates that her company understands those concerns and is addressing them vigorously.

Influence Thinking: Once you have shown readers that you understand their point of view, they may be more receptive to understanding your point of view. At this point, you can explain your position. In doing so, whenever possible demonstrate that you share concerns and values with the reader and emphasize those shared concerns. In each phase of your statement, be scrupulous to avoid sounding defensive, accusatory, or condescending. For best results, use simple, nontechnical language and respond to the readers' concerns.

Notice in Figure 6.22 how Judith influences her readers. She uses the information she has gathered to disprove the danger of VCM, calm her readers' fears, and demonstrate that her company acted responsibly.

Promote a Positive Attitude: End by reinforcing the values and concerns you share with the reader, and by emphasizing what your company is doing to promote those values and concerns. Judith ended her statement in this way:

> Sun has always had one of the best safety records in the industry because we have always put people's health and safety first. We believe the facts about VCM will reassure you that the recent derailment at MacGregor posed no health or safety threat. We appreciate the community's concerns and we are always ready to respond immediately.

As mentioned earlier, in controversy both parties may learn valuable lessons, grow in understanding, and end up compromising. Judith's company did change as a result of the public's serious concerns over the VCM leak. Certainly it is now better prepared to meet such crises with information packages and crisis communication plans. But more important, by its own account Sun became much more socially aware and has made the following postulate a guideline for the corporation:

> The business community's efforts to solve social problems must be integrated with long-term profit growth. If done properly, solving social problems is both good business and good citizenship, for the two are wholly compatible.[21]

Figure 6.22

JUDITH'S PUBLISHED STATEMENT

The Facts About
Vinyl Chloride Monomer (VCM)

The recent train derailment near MacGregor, Manitoba, involving 12 tank cars carrying Sun's vinyl chloride monomer (VCM), has raised many questions in people's minds.

Many are concerned that their health may have been affected by breathing air containing trace amounts of VCM gas. Others are concerned about the safety of the work crews clearing up at the derailment site. Still others are concerned about possible environmental damage.

We understand these worries. We believe people have a right to know the facts about this chemical and the part Sun is playing in helping to protect people's health and the environment.

Our technical experts arrived on the derailment scene Monday morning, March 10th (the accident occurred about 1:30 a.m. Monday). Their role from the outset was to provide scientific advice to the railway and to local officials on the safe and proper handling of the chemical and the tankcars involved. They brought specialized air monitoring equipment with them, plus other gear. More has been flown in since. More than 10 Sun experts are at the site. Leaks have been sealed. Off loading the derailed VCM cars is proceeding as quickly as possible in a manner which reduces hazards as low as humanly possible. It is not an easy task nor a simple one. We expect the job will take several weeks before all cars are removed and all traces of VCM disappear.

On Wednesday, March 19th (when this ad was written) crews at the derailment site transferred 3½ tankcars of vinyl chloride to waiting empty cars. This brings the total number of derailed vinyl chloride cars emptied to this point to 6½ out of a total of 12. The off-loading procedure has progressed faster than originally expected. Air monitoring at the derailment site indicates a continual improvement.

Transport Minister Jean-Luc Pepin announced Wednesday that the Canadian Transport Commission will hold a public inquiry into this incident. The inquiry is expected to report its findings in two months. Both CN Rail and Sun Chemical have indicated they would welcome such an inquiry and will cooperate to the fullest.

The public meeting Wednesday in MacGregor, attended by about 150 townsfolk, was orderly. Experts from CN, Sun, the Manitoba and federal environment ministeries, and the University of Montreal responded to numerous questions from residents, quelling their fears of possible human and animal health hazards. The meeting ended with one elderly resident proposing a commendation to all workers at the derailment site. He was loudly applauded.

What is Vinyl Chloride?

Vinyl chloride monomer is a synthetic organic chemical. It is called a "chemical intermediate" because it is entirely consumed to produce another end product and is never employed as an end product itself. It was first synthesized in 1837.

At normal temperature and pressure VCM is a colorless gas with a pleasant ethereal odor. It can be smelled at concentrations above 400 to 2000 ppm (depending on your sense of smell). The gas is 2–15 times as heavy as air. At room temperature VCM gas will form a liquid when under a pressure of about three times normal atmospheric pressure. It is stored and transported in a refrigerated state under slight pressure.

VCM is slightly soluble in water. It is flammable when the concentration in air is in the 3.6 percent to 33 percent range. (levels of 36,000 ppm to 330,000 ppm). Liquid VCM's boiling (i.e. vaporization) point is about -14°C (about 7°F). Exposure to liquid VCM may cause a frostbite-type burn similar to many gases under pressure, such as liquified carbon dioxide in fire extinguishers.

The Risks Involved

In a transportation accident, the main VCM hazard is from fire, caused by an open flame or spark. Occasional exposure to relatively high concentrations of VCM gas (termed "acute exposures" in scientific parlance) **represents neither a short nor long term hazard for people or animals.** In fact, at one time VCM was considered a promising anaesthetic, but was never employed for this purpose. In high concentrations, VCM gas will cause dizziness and unconsciousness (not permanent).

The risk to human health from short term exposures to VCM is minor indeed. For example, if the people of MacGregor, Manitoba were exposed to 1 ppm of VCM in the air (a level which far exceeds the highest level monitored only 250 yards away from the recent derailment site) for about 3 months, the risk of anyone contracting cancer as a result would be about equal to the cancer risk involved in smoking 1/25th of a cigarette during one's lifetime.

Thus, it is extremely unlikely evacuation of nearby homeowners or townsfolk will become either necessary or deemed a precautionary measure. That is soundly based on scientific fact.

Moreover, the health hazard for crews working at the derailment site is minor too. The risk of contracting cancer from 24 hours continuous exposure to air containing 25 ppm of VCM is also equal to the cancer risk one would incur by smoking 1/25th of a cigarette during the worker's lifetime, or eating 1/2 tablespoon of peanut butter in a lifetime. Such a VCM exposure would be well in excess of levels at the derailment site, except immediately adjacent to the two VCM cars that were leaking until patched Wednesday and Thursday, March 12 and 13. Men working there wore full respirators or self-contained breathing apparatus.

Because of the physical properties of VCM (low boiling point), it tends to rapidly disperse in air, not concentrating to any significant extent in water or soil. Once in the air it is broken down rapidly into hydrogen, disassociated chlorine (not the kind that is harmful to people), and carbon oxides by the action of the sun's rays. Half of a given volume of VCM breaks down in the atmosphere in about 6 hours, half of the remainder in another 6 hours, and so on. Only about 3 percent of the VCM would be left after about 22 hours of daylight, a small fraction of 1 percent after 44 hours.

Workplace Risks Different

Repeated exposure of workers to high concentrations of VCM gas over a working lifetime was reported in 1974 to cause a rare form of liver cancer. Often workers in plastic factories were exposed to concentrations of 1000 to 4000 ppm. In the same year, an Italian researcher demonstrated that exposure of rats to VCM caused the same type of cancer. Even prior to these reports, there existed some concern about the health effects of repeated daily exposure to VCM. In 1962, the American Conference of Governmental Industrial Hygienists adopted a concentration standard for a 5-day week (8 hours per day) of 500 ppm for a working lifetime. Later information resulted in this value being reduced to 1 ppm maximum in 1974 in accordance with the U.S. Occupational Safety & Health Act. This standard is in effect today. Of the well over one million chemical and plastic plant workers exposed in years past in the world to levels of 200 ppm and greater, somewhat less than 80 have developed this rare liver cancer, angiosarcoma.

The risk estimates for individuals exposed to 1 ppm of VCM 8 hours a day, 5 days per week for a working lifetime indicate the possibility of developing cancer ranges from 1 per 100 million to 2 per 100,000. Even using the higher estimate, the risk is over 100 times less than that of smoking, or 20 times less than that of being an airline pilot. Data from studies of workers exposed to lower levels of VCM and of animal studies support the lower estimate of risk. For example, Sun controlled exposures to 50 ppm or less in its VCM plants starting in 1961. Assessment of the mortality experience in this work force indicates an incidence of death and cancer less than that expected for the population at large.

It can not be scientifically unequivocally stated that there is absolutely no risk to the public whatsoever as a result of the recent derailment near MacGregor, any more than it can be stated that there is no risk in walking across a quiet residential street or indeed, sitting in your living room. However, it should be obvious that the risk is far less than has been previously suggested.

Not an Environmental Hazard

VCM is regarded by scientific and regulatory people as mainly an occupational rather than an environmental hazard. In the workplace, allowable levels of VCM vary from province to province. In Ontario the 8-hour time-weighted average maximum exposure level is 1 ppm. with a fifteen minute peak maximum of 25 ppm. Beyond these levels workers must wear respirators. There are corresponding exposure limits of 5 ppm and 10 ppm in Alberta, 1 ppm and 5 ppm in British Columbia and Quebec and 1 ppm and 5 ppm in the U.S. These standards employ a substantial safety factor many times below the no-effect level in chronic exposure conditions (i.e. daily exposures over a working lifetime).

What is VCM Used For?

Virtually all the VCM manufactured is used in the production of polyvinyl chloride (PVC) plastic resin, known commonly as "vinyl" (pronounced vie-nil). In the United States there are nine major producers of VCM, but only one in Canada, Sun Chemical. Sun makes VCM at Fort Saskatchewan, Alberta, and at Sarnia, Ontario.

In Canada there are three PVC producers—Esso Chemical, Diamond Shamrock Alberta Gas (DSAG), and B. F. Goodrich—who supply hundreds of fabricators, molders and extruders in every province. These businesses turn out such vinyl products as garden hose, pipe, electrical fittings, wire and cable insulation, housewares, house siding material, fabrics, luggage, garments, medical supplies, phono records, packaging, auto upholstery, food wraps, and many others too numerous to mention.

Any Questions Unanswered?

Should anyone need any information on vinyl chloride monomer additional to this summary, you are invited to write to Sun Chemical of Canada at either of the following addresses: P.O. Box 759, Fort Saskatchewan, Alberta, T8L 2P4, attention Mr. Gordon Butte; or to P.O. Box 1012, Sarnia, Ontario N7T 7K7, attention Mr. D. R. Stephenson. We can assure you a detailed response promptly.

Footnote #1: A part per million (ppm) is roughly equivalent to a pinch of salt in a large residential swimming pool.

Changing Social Values

Besides controversies created by public misperceptions, companies can also suffer from changing social values. For example, what had earlier been considered safe and acceptable smokestack emissions are now—because of population expansion, industrial concentration, and greater health awareness—considered dangerous. Premarket tests of a drug may have "improved" it to be safe, but more extensive public use may reveal dangerous side effects. Cured meats, sugar, and white bread, the staples of many a pantry, are now thought by some to be unhealthy. Companies have had to respond to these and similar changes in the values of the people they serve. Frequently this leads to changes in company policy—to recalling a product, to installing extensive pollution control equipment, to changing the way a product is produced.

During this process of adapting to social change, it is especially critical for companies to communicate effectively with their communities. Let's consider, for example, the case of Prima, a major cosmetics manufacturer.[22]

Prima had been an international name in cosmetics for over forty-five years when, one summer, they were confronted by protest marchers and full-page *New York Times* ads opposing one of their laboratory practices. Specifically, animal protection groups were attacking Prima's use of the Draize eye-irritancy test, which uses rabbits to test for toxins in eye cosmetic ingredients.

Although many other cosmetic companies, as well as the makers of hundreds of noncosmetic products, also use the test, a coalition of animal protection groups targeted Prima for a protest. (In Figure 6.23, one such group encourages opposition to the Draize test.) The coalition spent $122,000 and bought full-page newspaper ads headlined, "How Many Rabbits Does Prima Blind for Beauty's Sake?" The groups urged consumers to boycott Prima products. Consumers were called on to write to the company president, James Merritt, that they "will not use Prima products until Prima funds a crash program to develop nonanimal eye-irritancy tests." Besides placing these ads, protesters marched on company headquarters and on major retailers of Prima products. Subsequently the company received over 500 letters either inquiring about or protesting Prima's "cruelty to animals." A typical letter is shown in Figure 6.24.

Obviously Prima faced a crisis. Although researchers have long relied on animal testing, and although animal testing has led to hundreds of medical and pharmaceutical advances without public oppositon, a special interest group had now placed this question to the public: Does animal testing for cosmetics constitute cruelty to animals? Many Prima customers agreed that it does.

With protesters at the door of headquarters and retailers, Prima had little time to debate the ethics of the Draize test. The company immediately began investigating protest claims and whether alternative testing methods might be available. The Consumer Product Safety Commission, for example, proposed that a local anesthetic be used in test rabbits. Company scientists, however, concluded that this would invalidate results, since an anesthetized animal does not respond to acute toxicity as it normally would.

While the company debated what to do about developing new procedures, they had to communicate their present position clearly, and in as favorable a light as possible. In response to protests, they composed a statement (shown in Figure 6.25) to be adapted

Figure 6.23

SPECIAL INTEREST AD TO AROUSE PUBLIC OPPOSITION TO THE DRAIZE TEST

Figure 6.24

LETTER PROTESTING PRIMA'S "CRUELTY TO ANIMALS"

Route 3
Bar Harbor, ME 04609
November 17, 199_

Mr. James Merritt
Prima, Inc.
400 South Wright Street,
Urbana, IL 61801

Dear Mr. Merritt:

   This letter is for the purpose of telling you I will no longer be purchasing <u>any</u> of your products and my reason for this discontinuance.

   I've recently learned that you are among the companies exploiting animals in research. Not only am I opposed to contributing money to promote cruelty to animals, but the fact that you seem to feel such experimentation is warranted makes me feel you must be using ingredients you believe are questionable.

   You might be well advised to realize that as the public becomes more educated, they are getting more turned off by products "animal tested" and more and more inclined toward going back to the use of good, clean ingredients provided by nature.

   Incidentally, it might well prove worth your while—financially if for no other reason—to contact <u>Beauty Without Cruelty</u>, 175 West 12th St., New York, N.Y., 10011.

                              Yours truly

                              Harriet Jones
                              Harriet Jones

Figure 6.25

PRIMA'S RESPONSE STATEMENT

Recently animal protection groups have begun to question whether the use of animals to test products for human use does not constitute cruelty to animals. In particular, they have been concerned with cosmetic eye products, and the use of the Draize eye-irritancy test. The Draize test uses rabbits to discover toxins in potential product ingredients, toxins that cannot be detected any other way.

Establishes rapport by showing understanding of reader concerns

Prima strongly opposes cruelty to animals whenever human safety is not at stake. But Prima is also committed to protecting the consumer from unsuspected hazards. For that reason, we would like to review with you the facts about the Draize eye-irritancy test and let you know what we are doing to protect consumers.

Influences thinking by stating company position and emphasizing shared concerns

You can be certain that any Prima eye cosmetic available in your stores is nontoxic and perfectly safe for use on the sensitive areas surrounding the eyes. In order to be certain of our product safety, Prima follows the requirements of the Food and Drug Administration (FDA), which requires the Draize eye-irritancy test.

This test requires that cosmetic ingredients be tested by applying them to the eyes of rabbits. If, after a few hours, the rabbits show no signs of irritation or inflammation, the rabbits' eyes are rinsed and the product, having passed several tests prior to this one, is ruled safe for human use.

If, on the other hand, the animal responds with signs of irritation or inflammation, the test ingredients are washed from the eye and rejected as unsafe.

The Draize test is the only test known that can effectively indicate harmful irritants in eye products. The FDA has said that before the Draize test became mandated, "Numerous case histories involving products found to produce, or strongly suspected of producing, adverse effects have been documented. . . . These adverse effects could have been predicted if the appropriate animal tests had been done and correctly interpreted beforehand. . . ."

LETTERS THAT PERSUADE 291

> Because Prima puts product safety first, we have no choice but to use the Draize test to protect consumers. Currently, however, Prima is investigating opportunities for developing alternatives to the Draize test. But Dr. Goldberg of the Johns Hopkins School of Hygiene & Public Health has warned, "As a practical matter, there *will be* a need to rely on animal tests for some time to come to protect the public and to advance the frontiers of medical knowledge."
>
> Prima appreciates the concerns of animal protection groups and will continue to monitor developments in testing procedures. Meanwhile we remain proud of our perfect safety record in the products we deliver to consumers.
>
> Thank you for your concern.

Encourages a positive attitude by emphasizing shared values

to letters and other public statements. Notice how the statement begins by acknowledging the reader's concerns, shows in what sense those concerns are valid, and then clarifies the company's own position and the reasons for it.

With carefully planned messages such as these, Prima was able at least to make the reasons for its policies clear and to indicate that it currently has no other choice but to continue using animal tests. Eight months after these protests, however, the company contributed a $750,000 grant to a major research institute to investigate other means of evaluating the eye damage potential of cosmetic ingredients. Said Prima president Merritt: "Prima wants to keep the trust of the customers sympathetic to animal rights advocates."

The accompanying checklist can help you evaluate your communications in controversy.

CHECKLIST FOR COMMUNICATING IN CONTROVERSY

R: Have you demonstrated that you understand your readers' concerns by stating those concerns and indicating the ways you think they are valid?

T: Have you explained your position, making it clear whenever possible that you share concerns with the reader? Have you avoided sounding defensive, accusatory, or condescending?

A: Have you ended by trying to promote a positive attitude? Have you reinforced the values and concerns you share with the reader and emphasized what your company is doing to promote those values and concerns?

If you find yourself in an extraordinary situation in which you must deal with a public concerned and even angry with your company's actions, first prepare yourself well. Find out as much as you can not only about your company's position, but also about the public's concerns. Then be ready to respond to the public with both understanding and fairness. Figure 6.26 presents a succinct list of crisis do's and don't's.

SUMMARY

As a business person you will often find it necessary to persuade people through the letters you write: to convince them to buy, to do you a favor, to pay a bill, or to change their attitude toward your company. These people may be indifferent or even hostile to what you have to say, but you can succeed in persuading them: The RTA formula can help you generate and organize ideas for any of your persuasive letters. But, more specifically, to write a persuasive sales letter, determine your proposition, establish a mailing list, determine your sales appeals, and use RTA to organize your letter. For the letter requesting a favor, persuade your reader by emphasizing how the reader benefits from doing the favor and use RTA to generate and organize ideas. For collection letters that collect the debt while maintaining goodwill, emphasize the benefits to the debtor for prompt payment. For letters that respond to public controversy, understand the situation from the public's point of view and then build a bridge between your company's position and the public's.

EXERCISES

See "Setting the Goal: Your Proposition," p. 228, for Exercise 1

1. Decide on an attractive proposition for a sales letter that will persuade students at your school to (choose one):

- Eat in the school cafeteria or at one of the snack bars
- Attend a sports event, film, or lecture
- Take a particular course

Figure 6.26

CRISIS DO'S AND DON'T'S

Crisis "Do's"

- Before a crisis takes place, do let the press know who is the best source of information relating to company activities and opinions. Then, during a crisis indicate again that the company is willing to cooperate with the press.
- Do try to meet press deadlines.
- Do attempt to comment on a topic if you believe that incorrect or misleading statements are being made to the press by persons outside the company.
- Do monitor the news coverage, and make a courteous effort to bring inaccuracies to the attention of the media.
- Do accentuate positive aspects—e.g., the company's safety record, plans for rebuilding, continuing precautions, acts of heroism, concern for employees, etc. But do so *without* glossing over the negative aspects of the situation.
- Do express gratitude to the community, employees, outsiders for whatever help they may have given during the crisis.

Crisis "Don't's"

- Don't attempt to blame anyone for anything.
- Don't speculate on anything; release only confirmed facts. This includes speculative statements about the cause of a crisis, the extent of damage, resumption time of normal activity, or possible outcome.
- Don't release information about people. Respect their individual rights to privacy and confidentiality.
- Don't release damage or loss estimates without confirming their accuracy.
- Don't try to mislead or cover up facts. Never lie.
- Don't make "off the record" statements. During a crisis situation, such promises are likely to be forgotten.
- Don't play favorites to the media. Release the same information to all media.
- Don't repeat negative or inflammatory words used by a reporter. It might end up as part of *your* quote.
- Don't demonstrate a great deal of emotion with the press. It may cause panic, particularly if on television.

Source: Copyright *Public Relations Quarterly*, Fall 1982, "Crisis Communications," by Judith A. Ressler, president, Ressler Communications.

See "Gathering Information and Generating Ideas: Determining the Sales Appeal," pp. 229–233, for Exercises 2–4.

2. Generate some ideas for writing the sales letter you chose to write in exercise 1. Remember to consider psychological and logical appeals. Would it be appropriate to use appeals to your authority? How about testimonials?

3. Choose a product you like, and suppose that you are to write a sales letter for it. Analyze the product, determine reader benefits, and select the central selling point.

4. Analyze a sales letter that succeeded in convincing you to buy a product or service. How did the letter appeal to you?

See "Organizing the Sales Letter: Using RTA," pp. 233–241, for Exercises 5–7.

5. As a college student, you have begun a graphics and marketing service. You would like to sell your services to the administration, student clubs, and faculty at your college. Write a sales letter addressed to your potential customers. Here is some information you have generated that you may want to include in your letter:

- You distribute fliers and posters on the campus and at other local colleges.
- You draw and print fliers that can increase attendance at meetings and social gatherings.
- You design and create posters.
- You need nine workdays to design posters and fliers.
- You need five workdays to do a graphic design (good for clothing such as shirts, hats, and sweatshirts; letterheads; and pamphlets) two days are for preliminary drawings (an unsatisfied customer is not obligated to use service).
- You can use offset printing or photocopying for graphics.
- You designed a successful logo for a college sweatshirt that sold 200 sweatshirts.
- You printed a brochure for the college playhouse.
- You designed fliers and posters for the computer club's speakers forum.

6. Suppose you have started a small moving company. Since you own a large van and have employed two professional movers, you are able to pack and move small households and businesses within a fifty-mile radius. Write a sales letter to publicize your new company. First choose your potential customers; then, think about the best kind of appeal to make to them; finally, write your letter.

7. The director of Public Television Sales for Time/Life does not write many letters. But the ones she does write are never routine. Her job is persuasion. As she explained to us,

> The job I have is a difficult one—gaining financial support for public television. Corporations decide to fund programs for a variety of reasons, and the decision that is made is made on the highest level—the chairman of the board. So my sales letters are addressed to the top of the company.

She once launched a campaign to request a number of corporations to sponsor a new series of shows. Read the letter (shown in Figure 6.27) that she sent to Mark Simmons, the head of a leading corporation. Then decide how you would react to the letter if you were Simmons. Be prepared to identify the specific strategies the writer used that caused you to respond as you did.

See "Requesting Favors," pp. 247–262, for Exercises 8–11.

8. The local private swimming club you belong to has established a policy that permits members twenty coupons a year to bring in one guest free of charge on Wednesdays and Thursdays. You are well below your guest quota, for you have brought in only five guests in a nine-month period. But a problem has arisen: three friends will be visiting you for a week and you would like to bring all three of them with you to the pool on the same day. You have decided to write a letter to the director of the swimming club. Set the goal and analyze the reader of your letter.

9. As an enthusiastic business sponsor of your local high school's athletic program, you have become concerned that the high school is having trouble finding volunteer assistant coaches. In particular, the wrestling squad (or fill in the sport of your choice) has been without an assistant coach for six weeks, and the squad has been performing very poorly. You know the squad could do much better with a coach working with them regularly. Although you were never active in wrestling yourself, you know several alumni members who might make helpful assistant wrestling coaches. Write a letter requesting one of the alumni to volunteer.

10. As a marketing agent, you represent manufacturers of flooring, including Fine Floor products. Your company has been aggressively supporting the do-it-yourself market by giving product demonstrations at large retail outlets of home building supplies. Recently you scheduled a series of consumer clinics for a large chain of Home Center stores. The purpose of the clinic is to demonstrate how easy it is to trim and fit any floor using Fine Floor's new product, the "Trim and Fit" kit.

But now you are in a bind. You have discovered that you have agreed to run several clinics on the same night and you do not have enough qualified people to do the demonstrations.

You remember, however, that Bob Sansone of Fine Floor did a nice job demonstrating several of his company's products at your last sales meeting. You have decided to write him a letter asking if he would run clinics for you on the evenings of Tuesday, April 8, and Thursday, April 10. He may choose from among four possible locations each night the one that is most convenient for him.

11. The Peabody Institute, a well-known musical conservatory in Baltimore, sent the letter shown in Figure 6.28 to convince patrons to renew their support of the conservatory. Discuss its effectiveness.

See "Collecting," pp. 263–280, for Exercises 12–16.

12. For the senior class gift, the Senior Committee is planning to present a chiming clock for the tower of the school library. As chairperson of the gift fund, you must write a letter to twenty-seven of your classmates who have yet to pay the pledges they made during the campaign. Graduation is in four weeks. During the ceremonies, the senior class will present its gift. If all twenty-seven of the students pay you their

Figure 6.27

SALES LETTER

February 7, 199_

Mr. Mark Simmons, President
Bradley Toys, Inc.
253 Park Ave.
New York, NY 10017

Dear Mr. Simmons:

I'm sure you have considered funding programs on Public Television but probably have never found just the right one. I think our BBC coproduction, ALL CREATURES GREAT AND SMALL, might be just the vehicle to allow you to reach your key publics through PBS. Let me explain.

ALL CREATURES GREAT AND SMALL is based on the best-selling books by James Herriot. These books have sold over 2 million copies in America alone. The warmth and good humor of Herriot's memories of his veterinarian days in Yorkshire in the 1930s have been translated into delightful television fare. The series has wit, charm, and superb acting, and is beautiful to look at. In England, ALL CREATURES GREAT AND SMALL has been at the top of the ratings for the past two years—even outshining THE MUPPET SHOW! The critical acclaim it received is unprecedented.

There is no question in our minds that ALL CREATURES GREAT AND SMALL will be a major hit on PBS. The originating station will be WGBH in Boston, which has put together the enclosed proposal. As the series is ideal for family viewing, WGBH hopes to get an 8 P.M. national broadcast. We plan to release the first series of 13 programs in 198_, the second 13 in 198_, and to repeat all 26 in 198_.

There is a possibility of splitting the funding with another major U.S. corporation. This means that for a very low price, Bradley would have a three-year association with an outstanding dramatic series guaranteed to be a hit.

Mr. Mark Simmons
page 2
February 7, 199_

After you've had a chance to read the enclosed materials, I'd like to show you one of the programs and discuss with you the details of pricing, placement, and why we think Bradley should take advantage of the audience PBS can deliver.

Yours truly,

Sarah Frank

Sarah Frank
Director of
Public Television Sales

SF/hw
enc.

pledges, you will have 98 percent participation from the class, the best record for a senior class in the last six years. Write the letter you will send to the twenty-seven students.

13. Figure 6.29 shows several collection letters written by a major city bank. Consider when the bank would send each of these form letters. Can you suggest any improvements?

14. You are the manager of an office supplies and equipment store. In June, you sold to the Wine Cask $6,619 worth of cash registers and office machines, in time for the opening of their new branch store in a fancy suburban shopping center. The owner agreed to 12 percent down and $660 per month for ten months. You received the first three payments on schedule, but nothing for the October 15 payment date, in spite of reminders sent November 1 and 15. You read in the newspaper that the store's grand opening was a great success and that the Wine Cask now stocks more selective vintages than any store in your half of the state. You suspect the store has become short on cash because of the huge inventory it keeps. Write the collection letter you would send.

15. As a distributor of children's toys, you have had good business relations with Sylvia Owens, owner of Mrs. Mcgoofintosh's Childrens House, a children's specialty store. Ms. Owens has been a steady, if slow-paying, customer for over three years. Now, however, she has owed you $347.53 for two months and has not responded to

Figure 6.28

THE PEABODY INSTITUTE'S LETTER TO PATRONS

Dear _____,

I am seeking your renewed participation in a venture that holds the promise of great dividends to our society.

All of us who have become part of it know how deeply we feel about the Peabody Institute of Music. I know I do not have to tell you and other close friends of the Music Conservatory about this extraordinary institution—after all you are part of the Peabody family, having participated in last year's record-breaking Annual Giving Campaign. However, your continued support is crucial in order to strengthen the Peabody.

Elliot Galkin and the Board of Trustees are determined to maintain the high standards by which the Peabody is so widely recognized. In fact, we are committed to new and even more innovative and striking thrusts in music education, now and in the immediate future.

Your participation in this year's Annual Giving Campaign will be your reaffirmation of the goals and aspirations of this remarkable institute and will indicate your continuing appreciation now and in the immediate future.

I hope that you will be able to increase your contributions this year since, as you must know, our operating expenses have risen due to inflation.

You will be contacted shortly by a member of our Peabody solicitation committee, who will talk to you about the plans for the Peabody and answer any questions you might have.

I thank you for your interest, and hope you will participate in giving the Peabody a much needed boost at this critical time in its long and illustrious history.

Very truly yours,

John C Moore III

John C. Moore, III
Vice Chairman
Annual Giving Campaign

LETTERS THAT PERSUADE

Figure 6.29

A BANK'S SERIES OF COLLECTION LETTERS

FIRST LETTER

Dear _____:

Overdrafts are an unnecessary expense to many customers and, in the event of a returned check, a source of embarrassment.

In light of a recent overdraft on your account, Greater City Bank would like to offer you the opportunity to avoid future overdraft charges and the embarrassment of returned checks by applying for our Quick Credit line.

Quick Credit is a line of credit that is linked to your checking account. Having it available creates an automatic loan in your checking account to cover checks presented against an insufficient balance. You can also borrow directly from Quick Credit simply by transferring funds from your Quick Credit to your checking account.

The finance charge for Quick Credit is 1½ percent per month (18 percent annual percentage rate) on the average daily outstanding balance. If the line of credit is not used, no charge will be incurred.

I have enclosed a brochure and application that further explain Greater City's Quick Credit. If your account is in two names, both parties should complete and sign the application. A self-addressed envelope is also provided for your convenience.

I look forward to receiving your completed application in the hope that we will be able to provide you with available credit as well as spare you the inconvenience of future overdraft problems.

(continued)

(A BANK'S SERIES OF COLLECTION
LETTERS continued)

SECOND LETTER

Account No.:

Dear _____:

We wrote to you several days ago regarding the overdraft status of your account mentioned above. At that time, we offered you an opportunity to review your records and discuss with us a satisfactory method of payment of the outstanding debt. To date, we have not received any communication from you.

Accordingly, you may consider this letter a final demand for satisfaction of the claim against you. Unless a suitable schedule for repayment of the debt is worked out with this office by calling me at 555-8760, ext. 5451, within ten (10) days, you will leave us no choice but to present this matter to our legal counsel for disposition.

THIRD LETTER

Dear _____:

This letter is in reference to your account # _____, which has been overdrawn for the past 30 days. During this period of time, you have made no attempt either to contact us or to correct this overdraft status. Because of this, we have decided to close your account with us as it is not our policy to allow accounts to remain overdrawn for this length of time.

If you wish to avoid having your account closed, you can contact me at 555-8760, ext. 5451, to arrange a repayment schedule. If I do not hear from you in 10 days, I will assume that you do not wish to maintain your account with us, and I will be forced to charge off your account. This charge-off will result in your account being reported to the National Check Protection Service, severely affecting your ability to open a new account at any bank.

I look forward to hearing from you so that we can arrange to have this problem remedied.

(continued)

(A BANK'S SERIES OF COLLECTION
LETTERS continued)

FOURTH LETTER

Dear _____:

Your checking account # _____ is being handled in an unsatisfactory manner. Your account has been in an overdraft status for 30 days and now maintains an overdrawn balance in the amount of $550.

Please forward that amount to cover this overdraft on receipt of this letter. If a deposit is not received shortly, the account will be closed and reported as unsatisfactory.

Should you have any questions regarding this overdraft, kindly contact me at 555-8760, ext. 5451.

your reminder. Last month, you began applying a 1.25 percent monthly interest charge. You think that possibly the recent recession has hit her store hard. Write the inquiry. Then write the appeal you would send next.

16. As Master Kim Do of the Kung Fu Training Center, you want to collect $100 owed by Adam Severill. Mr. Severill registered for your twelve-week, Tuesday/Thursday 7:00 P.M. session and paid $50 to reserve his place in a class limited to fifteen. A second $50 was to be paid on the first day of class, and the third and final installment was due the fourth week. When Mr. Severill came to your first class, he did not have the payment but promised the entire $100 at the next class. However, he came to no more classes. He responded to your bill for $100 by saying that since he had become ill, he would not be able to attend any classes and did not expect to have to pay for lessons he was not taking. Although your class had a waiting list, you do not believe it is instructionally sound to start new students after the second week of classes. You have already sent Mr. Severill the reminder, inquiry, and appeal. Write the urgent appeal, ultimatum, and final demand.

See "Communicating in Controversy," pp. 280–293, for Exercises 17 and 18.

17. As corporate communications director for Union Oil, you have your hands full. Ten days ago an accidental oil spill spewed 15,000 barrels of oil off the Santa Barbara coastline. Two days before the spill itself, the coastline suffered one of the heaviest storms in decades. (People were killed, tons of debris were scattered along the shore, and property damage was estimated in the multimillions of dollars.) Seven days after the spill, heavy winds and rains coated sea walls, cliffs, homes, and the debris already accumulted from the storm, with oil and more debris. You have received hundreds of calls and letters from journalists, homeowners, and environmentalists, accusing your company of destroying the environment, especially fish and fowl; of irresponsible technical control over your rigs: and generally of "ripping off" the public in order to make inordinate profits. You have to write a statement that will serve as a general response to individuals concerned with your company's actions. Here are some of the details you may want to include in your letter.

- The accident occurred on a drilling platform five miles off the Santa Barbara shore. The platform belonged equally to four oil companies, but Union was operating the platform at the time.
- So far, no human lives have been lost.
- In February 1968, Union Oil and its three equal co-lessees paid $61.4 million to the federal government to drill in a 5,400-acre block, number 402, off Santa Barbara.
- From November to January, four successful development wells were drilled under procedures approved by federal regulatory authorities. The fifth well, A-21, was being drilled under the same procedures and circumstances as the other four.
- By January 28, A-21 had reached its targeted depth, almost 3,500 feet. A routine "wiper" trip (withdrawal of drill pipe to the surface) was started off the bottom of the hole. Suddenly an uncontainable and powerful stream of drilling mud and gas

shot through the drill pipe high into the derrick, roaring as it went, and platform visibility was reduced to almost zero.
- The well head was sealed 13 minutes after the trouble started. But below the surface, pressure from the well bore caused an eruption of brownish-colored oil and gas. This eruption reached the surface through shallow open fractures and seams as a result of sub surface pressures.
- Specialists were immediately called to control the blowout.
- Ten days [that's today] and 15,000 barrels of oil later, cementing operations have stopped the flow. Now any oil reaching the surface will be coming from fractures and seeps other than from A-21.
- Immediately after the accident, the company began a massive companywide mobilization to deal with the spill problems. The company is taking full responsibility for the new cleanup.
- Construction managers are setting up deflecting devices, commonly referred to as tents, to collect seeping oil and carry it to surface containers.
- A bird cleaning and care center with sixteen top people has been established. In teams of two, one person holds the bird and the other washes. Volunteers are asked to bring birds from the beach. Each team washes ten birds per hour. So far the survival rate is 10 percent.
- Environmentalists are especially concerned about fish, seals, and whales. Several federal government and California state agencies are looking into the possible damage.
- The company is employing skimming devices, booms, and a variety of dispersants (these latter with the U.S. government's permission) to break up oil patches headed for beaches.
- The cleanup will go on for several months.
- Straw is the best absorbent. Each rock in the breakwater will be individually cleaned. Several hundred people are being assembled to work on this job, which can be accomplished only by hand labor.
- Homes, piers, and boats will be meticulously cleaned. Insurance claims will be quickly handled.
- Further drilling is being done to reduce the pressure and to deplete the reservoir, as recommended by the Secretary of the Interior.

18. It is summer, and as head of a large corporation called Quick Can,[23] you are facing a crisis. Quick Can started out in 1894 as a home canning supply manufacturer. Right now, glass containers and consumer products amount to 30 percent of your sales dollars, with home canning supplies making up 15 percent of total sales dollars. These supplies are produced in two of your plants. You control almost half the market for replacement canning lids.

This year your two plants produced approximately 3 billion replacement lids, compared with approximately 1.4 billion the previous year. You did this because last year the company was not able to meet the consumer demand for replacement lids and caps. Both an unprecedented increase in consumer demand (the dollar amount of replacement lids and caps sold was more than thirty-four times what it had been during the previous year) and a shortage of soda ash and tin-plated steel (essential ingredients for manufacture of the product) made meeting the demand impossible.

This spring, with production up, you were hopeful but not absolutely certain you could meet the expected increase in demand for this year. Your consumer affairs office held a press conference and announced: "It looks as though we should have enough jar and lid units, but the supply outlook for replacement lids is tighter." By midsummer it became clear. Not only was there a severe shortage of replacement lids but there was a severe nationwide shortage of jar and lid units as well. Consumers were crying foul play, accusing your company of collusion, favoritism, and hoarding lids to drive prices artificially high.

In fact what had happened was a combination of a huge increase in the number of home canners and a "hoarding psychology," whereby consumers scooped up whatever supplies were available whether they needed them or not.

The consumer outcry led to a congressional investigation by the Subcommittee on Commodities and Services of the House Committee on Small Business and a second investigation by the Federal Trade Commission. Their findings completely exonerated your company.

Meanwhile, your officials have placed orders for a new lid manufacturing line. But, because of the technical sophistication and lead time for equipment, the line will not be opened for six months. Your other plants have been working three shifts, seven days a week.

Company officials are now very concerned about getting the word out to angry consumers. The officials have been issuing press releases, doing media interviews, and answering all phone calls and letters. Despite a special public relations staff, however, it has become impossible to answer every letter separately. (Over 120,000 letters would come in by the end of the year.) Now at the height of the shortage, you have been asked to write a letter for the Consumer Products Division that can be used as a form letter to respond to the most common consumer concerns. Your objectives are

- To convince the public there is no conspiracy among canning lid manufacturers and suppliers causing the shortage, and no gouging to increase the profit for manufacturers and suppliers
- To transmit to the public as much information as possible about the situation and the reasons for the shortage
- To convince the public that your company is doing its best to meet the public's needs
- To let consumers know politely that certain actions, such as hoarding, contribute to the problem
- To tell the public what you are doing to prevent shortages in the future and to alleviate the fear that a shortage will occur again

7
GOODWILL LETTERS

PREVIEW

This chapter should help you to

1. Write goodwill letters that demonstrate your genuine interest in the people you do business with
2. Decide on the appropriate occasions for expressing business goodwill
3. Use the RTA formula to generate and organize information and ideas for your goodwill messages
4. Become acquainted with goodwill letters that express
   - Congratulations
   - Appreciation
   - Sympathy
   - Season's greetings
   - Welcome

As coordinator of the American Engineering Institute (AEI) conference this year, Max Astin had many reasons to be thankful. He had had his problems: several last-minute changes in the schedule, stormy weather, which had made many conferees late, and a speaker cancellation. Yet several attendees had told him that in their years of attending AEI conferences, this one was the best.

Max knew, however, that he should not be the one to get all the credit. John Robinson was at the top of his list of people to thank. As convention coordinator at the hotel, John had arranged one of the banquets and several meetings, as well as providing accommodations for all the participants.

Max thought about the letter he wanted to write to John: "I want this to be more than just the usual thank you. John did so much more than just a good job. Because of him, we untangled several snafus before anyone even noticed. I've received many comments about how well coordinated the events were. I know it was John's experience and input that made the big difference. I want him to know that I noticed."

307

In the letter chapters so far we have been discussing letters that are necessary for ordinary business dealings—letters about buying and selling. But the people you deal with appreciate being recognized as people, regardless of business relations. We all like to be acknowledged for our accomplishments, for our generosity, on occasions for celebration, and during hardships. Managers who are genuinely interested in the people they deal with take special care to recognize people through goodwill messages.

Some business people find the goodwill letter easy to write. The effective letter is usually short, simple, and direct. In it, you are not asking anything from the reader, and the reader welcomes your message. Yet many business people who are able to dash off a business report without a qualm find goodwill letters difficult. They don't know what to say. They feel stilted and awkward, and their writing shows it. Fortunately, the solution can be simple. Let's consider the stages in writing the goodwill message and the situation in which Max Astin found himself.

SETTING THE GOAL

Whether you are congratulating, showing appreciation, or offering sympathy, the goal of your goodwill message is simple. You want your readers to know that their efforts, their sorrows, and their special occasions are important to you. You want them to know that you value knowing them not just as business associates, customers, or clients, but as human beings.

As a busy manager, you may find yourself questioning the goal of communicating on matters seemingly unrelated to business while so many pressing things need doing. But don't be caught in a trap like those managers who pay lip service to the idea that people are important and then complain, "People issues take up all my time." In their book *In Search of Excellence,* management consultants Thomas Peters and Robert Waterman have warned of this pitfall. They show that in successful companies, "caring runs in the veins of the managers of these institutions. People are why those managers are there, and they know it and live it."[1]

This attention to people is necessary not only in dealing with employees but also in dealing with customers and suppliers. Frequently, human relations will make the difference between a customer's choosing to do business with you rather than with a competitor. Suppliers will be much more likely to go out of their way to serve your special needs if you have shown appreciation for their services in the past. Max Astin, for example, knew how much more John Robinson, as hotel coordinator, had done than simply to fulfill his contractual obligations. While Max could not be sure he would ever need John's services in the future, thanking John now would demonstrate Max's appreciation and ensure their good relations.

Since your goal in the goodwill letter is to show your genuine interest in the reader, don't defeat your purpose by sending mixed messages. For example, if in order to establish good business relations, you send a message welcoming newcomers to town or congratulating new parents, don't destroy the goodwill you create by tainting your message with advertisements. If you thank a company for the extra effort put into a job done for you, don't ruin the effect by going on to list the items you think still need attention. Keep your goodwill messages and your business transactions separate.

Goodwill letters, precisely because they are not required for transacting business, help establish friendly relations between you and the people you deal with. Good managers "keep the channels open" by demonstrating their concern for others.

ASSESSING THE READER

Most of us are glad to receive goodwill letters. If they are written appropriately, they let us know we are thought of and valued. But although we appreciate receiving these letters, as writers we may sometimes imagine that readers expect nothing less than literary masterpieces.

Not so. What readers do expect is that you demonstrate a sincere interest in their situation. When Max Astin wanted to thank John Robinson for his excellent work as convention coordinator, he tried to think about it from John's perspective. "When I do a great job at something, sometimes my boss doesn't notice. Either he's too busy, or he's just not aware of what I had to go through to accomplish what I did. I want John to know I haven't overlooked the extra effort he put out for us. I want to let him know that I noticed."

How do you let your readers know you take notice of them and are sincere? Let's look at some ideas for what can go into the goodwill letter.

GENERATING IDEAS AND ORGANIZING FOR GOODWILL

Effective goodwill letters demonstrate that you are concerned enough about readers to be familiar with the details of their situation—for example, their accomplishment, their special occasion, or their hard work.

People who have been told you care about their actions and feelings like to know why you do. When business people have trouble writing goodwill messages, it is often because they have trouble figuring out what to say after they have said "congratulations," or "good work." But by explaining exactly why you are offering the praise, thanks, or sympathy, you can let readers know that you have indeed understood and are genuinely interested in their situation. You should give details or comments about their accomplishments or situation that show you have thought about it carefully.

For example, to show John he noticed, Max simply listed all the things he could remember that John had gone out of his way to do (see Figure 7.1). Once Max had his list, he knew he could write the thank-you letter that would show he genuinely appreciated the excellent job John had done.

Max used a list to generate the ideas that would demonstrate his appreciation. Other writers like to imagine what they would say if they were speaking to the person face-

Figure 7.1

MAX'S LIST OF JOHN'S CONTRIBUTIONS

> — Suggested revisions in banquet and meeting schedule, especially a free night that turned out to be crucial.
> — Provided directions to late arrivals; made the first sessions work
> — Rearranged seating on extremely short notice
> — Put in four 18-hour days to provide continuity with staff
> — Was very helpful at the personal level, especially in providing information about the local area: helped several conferees find just the right place on their free night

to-face; they like to do some nonstop writing or tape their ideas. Still others find that dictating a draft of the letter helps them talk less formally and more naturally. Whatever strategies they use for generating ideas, successful writers know that the goodwill letter is easy once they are able to show how much they understand the reader's situation.

Generating Ideas and Organizing: Using the RTA Formula for Goodwill

Once you have thought about your goal and your reader, and you have some ideas for expressing your goodwill, consider the RTA formula. It can help you organize the ideas you already have and perhaps come up with more. Max, for example, grouped and ordered the ideas he had already come up with for his thank-you letter. Then, when he thought about establishing rapport in his opening and about closing on a positive, forward-looking note, he thought of more ideas. Let's see how Max's finished letter illustrates use of the RTA formula for the goodwill letter.

Establish Rapport: Since people welcome genuine goodwill messages, establish rapport simply by getting directly to your message:

> Your contribution is in large part responsible for the enormous praise I've been receiving ever since our AEI conference wrapped up last week.

Influence Thinking: Demonstrate you care by giving the details that show why you are praising, thanking, or showing interest.

> Late arrivals told me they had no trouble finding our conference site because everybody at the front desk knew directions and had schedules. As for the conference sessions you hosted, you and your staff provided perfect seating arrangements and media support, especially considering the crowd. I'm especially grateful that you personally oversaw the last-minute change in seating arrangements for our formal banquet.
>
> The free night you advised me to include turned out to be just the break everyone needed. Several people mentioned they had a great time in town because they got such helpful tips from you and your staff.

Reinforce a Positive Attitude: End your message by reinforcing your positive attitude toward the reader. Either use a forward-looking message, or restate your goodwill.

> In all my years of conferences, I have rarely experienced such attentive service. I was fortunate to have your help coordinating this one. I certainly plan to tell anyone I know looking for a Charlottesville convention site that yours is the one.
>
> Thank you for your superb service.

Above all, let your goodwill messages be direct, sincere, and brief. What is most important is that you sound natural and genuinely interested in the reader.

A Note About Stationery. Because goodwill messages are more personal than routine business messages, they can be handwritten on personal stationery. But they may instead be typed on the company letterhead or printed for the occasion. Your choice will depend on the occasion and on how well you know the reader. Even goodwill messages sent *within* the company are often written on the company letterhead, rather than in memo format, to emphasize the special nature of the message.

The accompanying checklist will help you review your goodwill letters.

RTA CHECKLIST FOR WRITING THE GOODWILL LETTER

R: Have you gained interest by announcing your goodwill immediately?

T: Have you influenced thinking by explaining exactly why you are offering praise, thanks, sympathy?

A: Have you closed by reinforcing your positive attitude toward the reader with a forward-looking message or a restatement of your goodwill?

Now that we have looked at the process of writing for goodwill in general, let's consider some specific types of goodwill letters.

LETTERS OF CONGRATULATION

"The senior McGarvey loves to tell us how in his day he knew every customer by name," Jim Seward explained. As head of customer relations in McGarvey's downtown department store, Jim was explaining to a visitor the importance the company placed on his department. "He used to deliver fruitcakes free on Christmas, and he sent a present for every new baby. Of course that's impossible now. But we built our reputation on personal service, and we do everything we can to keep it that way."

Jim was in the process of signing several letters of congratulations that his staff had prepared by combing local newspapers for names of people deserving commendation—volunteers doing community service, people winning civic awards, and college and high school students earning scholastic honors or doing well in sports.

"We're not counting dollars and cents here. That's not the point. We just want to maintain our reputation for personal service and civic pride."

Letters of congratulation can extend your good wishes to business friends, acquaintances, and customers on important business and personal occasions. Business occasions include

- Promotions
- Elections to office
- Honors
- New partnerships
- Plant openings
- Company anniversaries

Personal occasions include

- Marriages
- Births
- Graduations
- Athletic achievements
- Civic awards

Let your congratulations sound enthusiastic; avoid the stiff and formal. Be as specific as you can about why you believe the reader deserves congratulations, and send the letter promptly.

When Jim Seward read in the paper that high school students who had spent a summer as volunteers in a community halfway house were being awarded a Certificate of Merit, he knew this was the kind of civic responsibility his company's president, Ed McGarvey, admired. He knew, too, that Mr. McGarvey served on the Patterson Halfway House's board of directors and so had a particular interest in the house's work. This was an occasion for McGarvey's to extend congratulations. But before Jim wrote, he wanted to understand more precisely the role these students had played in the halfway house's service. To learn more, he made a quick call to the Patterson House director and got the details. Then, with his notes beside him, he was ready to say congratulations. Since he had a lot of experience writing letters of this kind, he required only one draft on the word processor, making several sentence-level revisions. His letter is shown in Figure 7.2.

Jim's letter showed that he was familiar with Bob Moffett's accomplishment and that McGarvey's understood how important community service such as Bob's was to the town and to the company. As a manager, you will have many different occasions for congratulating people outside the company, as well as employees within the company. Let's look at letters written in response to some typical situations.

When a computer hardware manufacturer heard that one of his customers had won a major contract, he knew the customer would be extremely pleased. He wrote the letter shown in Figure 7.3 to extend congratulations.

Congratulations can be brief and still convey enthusiasm. In Figure 7.4 a wire products wholesaler congratulates a contractor on a technical article she wrote.

Your congratulations and praise may be important to your reader not only because they express your good feelings toward him or her. Sometimes your letter can also be used as an endorsement to help the recipient promote his or her business. For example, Littlewood Communications, with permission from the Augat Corporation, reproduced the letter shown in Figure 7.5 in a full-page ad for its media services.

Besides congratulating associates outside the company, as a manager you will have many opportunities for congratulating employees—on awards, employment anniversaries, promotions, and the like. Although most correspondence within an organization uses the memo format, using letter format can convey the special nature of the goodwill message. In Figure 7.6, a vice president of Sales for a major pharmaceuticals firm congratulates an employee.

Figure 7.2

McGARVEY'S LETTER OF CONGRATULATION

1478 WILLOW AVENUE PHILADELPHIA, PA 19126

May 7, 199—

Mr. Robert Moffett
4790 Pine Street
Philadelphia, PA 19143

Dear Mr. Moffett:

We heard from the director about your help at the Patterson Halfway House this summer. Congratulations on a well-deserved award for an important contribution.

We understand that work at Patterson House is demanding, both physically and emotionally. You have been helping residents who have for many years relied on institutions to learn to lead independent lives. Your willingness to reach out to others, giving friendship and emotional support to those in need, deserves the highest praise. It is not only those people at the Halfway House who benefit from your help. It is the community as a whole. When you give your time and energy for others in need, the entire community enjoys strength and harmony.

McGarvey's Ltd. extends warm congratulations to you. We know such work has its own rewards, but as a token of our appreciation for your contribution to our community, we are enclosing a gift certificate that you may redeem any time at McGarvey's. Citizens like you make Philadelphia a good place in which to do business.

Sincerely yours,

Jim Seward

Jim Seward,
Head of Customer Relations

Figure 7.3

LETTER OF CONGRATULATION 1

TRANSACT INTERNATIONAL INC.
98 SOUTHGATE PARKWAY
MORRISTOWN, NJ 07960

March 12, 199_

Michael Sherr
Data Directions Inc.
28 Old Kings Highway
Darien, CT 06820

Dear Michael:

Congratulations on getting the Apple III project. I read about it in *DAT Newsletter* and I know this huge project must mean a major expansion for you.

Your reputation for sound program design and readable documentation no doubt had a lot to do with getting the contract.

Good luck in the enterprise. When I'm in the area next month I'll be dropping in on you. I'd like to hear more about how you put the proposal together. Maybe I can put you on to some good programmers.

Yours truly,

Jay Peters

Jay Peters, Senior Engineer

JP/pd

Figure 7.4

LETTER OF CONGRATULATION 2

EASTSIDE ELECTRONICS
2387 S. WEINBACK AVE. EVANSVILLE, IN 47714

February 17, 199_

June Lemus
Condra Industrial Designs
1748 Deer Run
San Antonio, TX 78232

Dear June:

Terrific article in the February *Construction Dimensions* magazine. Three cheers for your accomplishment and style.

I look forward to learning more from your designs.

Best wishes,

Ray Goss

Ray Goss, Marketing Director

Figure 7.5

LETTER OF CONGRATULATION 3

 Corporation
Designers and Manufacturers For The Electronics Industry

June 5, 199_

Mr. John W. Littlewood
Littlewood Communications
Woodsville, Massachusetts 01784

Dear John:

You and your people deserve some very big congratulations. The nine-projector slide presentation you recently completed for Augat keeps drawing high praises.

The 140 executives of our major distributor who saw the presentation debut in Palm Springs last week gave it a standing ovation. After four days of viewing a variety of shows, they rate ours the best.

That's an excellent testimonial to your ability to create an impressive presentation under such a tight deadline.

Your slide show captured the "quality and innovation" theme of our company and demonstrated the breadth of our product line. It also demonstrated Littlewood Communications' capacity to absorb quickly and understand an enormous amount of product, marketing, and technical information and translate it into a successful audiovisual production.

We'll continue to use the show to highlight Augat's strengths and capabilities to a wide range of audiences, including the financial community, customers, and our personnel.

Sincerely,

Richard M. Grubb

Richard M. Grubb
Corporate Senior Vice President

Figure 7.6

LETTER OF CONGRATULATION 4

January 23, 199_

Harvey Pletcher
9 Rickenbacker Rd.
Columbia, SC 29205

Dear Harvey,

Congratulations on the Go-Getter Award! Your outstanding sales performance is a credit to your energy and character. You got a considerable amount of competition from the New York crew this year, but you outdid them all.

You already know how happy you made me winning back the MedTech account.

Middlesex District has always been one of the toughest markets. Your superior results show that you can move into the competition's strongholds.

Orson's is proud to have you on its team. Keep up the great work!

Best wishes,

Craig Mazur

Craig Mazur
Vice President of Sales

LETTERS OF APPRECIATION

It's just plain good manners to show appreciation for favors and kindnesses, and the workplace provides ample occasions for expressing thanks. You know yourself that when your extra efforts are understood and appreciated, you feel good about the work you did and are more willing to go the extra mile the next time. Such good spirit is essential to a well-managed organization and to customer relations.

Send letters of thanks to people who have donated time, effort, expertise, or money. They may have granted an interview, made a presentation, written a letter of recommendation, sent you a referral, or critiqued your work-in-progress. Also, take the time to show your appreciation for a job well done or for exceptionally good service. In dealing with customers, many companies find it appropriate to offer thanks for opening or renewing an account, for consistently paying bills promptly, or for placing especially large orders.

In expressing your appreciation, be specific about what the reader has done for you. For example, rather than general praise such as "you are a good worker," show that you understand what that worker has accomplished and what it has meant to you: "The extra hours you put in to get the supplies to us before our deadline meant that we could finish our contract on time. Thanks for your hard work."

Doing business offers a variety of occasions for saying thank you. In Figure 7.7, a manager thanks a sales rep from another company for an act of thoughtfulness that led to important savings.

After a real estate developer had interviewed several printers' representatives, she decided that one printer would be most likely to do the best job for her. Her letter in Figure 7.8 follows up a dinner meeting in which she discussed brochures with the printer.

Besides ensuring good relations with employees and associates, thank-you letters are a way of giving your customers the VIP treatment. In Figure 7.9, a tailor thanks his customer for making a referral.

When customers offer criticism or suggestions for improving your business, they are doing you a favor. Be sure to acknowledge their help with thanks. The editor in Figure 7.10, for example, replies to a banker who pointed out an error in an issue of her publication, *Bank Notes*.

Retail organizations take special care to encourage good customer relations. In the form letter shown in Figure 7.11, a subscription clearing house thanks customers for paying overdue accounts and takes the opportunity to assure the reader of its willingness to be of service.

When customers or clients write thanking you for your service, they don't require a reply. In Figure 7.12, however, a manager shows how you can take this opportunity to strengthen good relations by showing your appreciation.

Of course any contribution or donation must be promptly and graciously acknowledged. Show your appreciation, as in Figure 7.13, by demonstrating what the contribution will help accomplish.

320 THE RANDOM HOUSE GUIDE TO BUSINESS WRITING

Good managers show their appreciation through both ceremonial occasions and written messages.

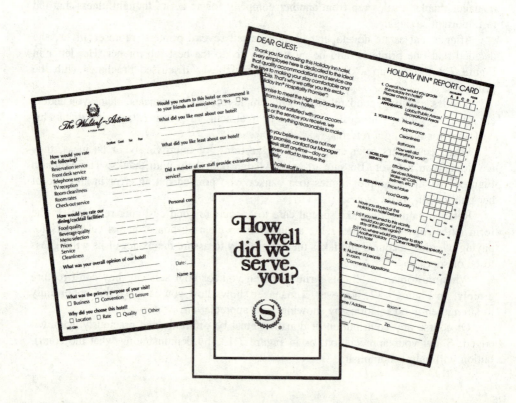

Figure 7.7

LETTER OF APPRECIATION 1

208 WOODLAND ST.
NASHVILLE, TN 37213

August 23, 199_

Jan Perez
Imports Inc.
5084 Poplar Ave.
Memphis, TN 38117

Dear Jan:

You know that tip you passed on to me about JIL modernizing their conference room? It paid off for me splendidly. I called last week and volunteered to take the old furniture off their hands if we could strike a bargain. I ended up saving over 50 percent on almost everything I was looking for. And you were right. It's all in very good condition.

Besides helping me find a bargain, you saved me a lot of time.

Thanks for keeping me in mind. Next time you make your visit, lunch is on me.

Sincerely,

Valerie

Valerie Briscoe,
Senior Manager

Figure 7.8

LETTER OF APPRECIATION 2

Gruss Industries
235 SOUTH 70TH STREET LINCOLN NE 68510

June 14, 199_

Ron Hensley Printers
4310 Progressive Ave.
Lincoln, Nebraska 68510

Dear Ron:

Thank you for a delightful dinner on May 18. I enjoyed the opportunity to look over your brochures. They reflected an impressive group of diversified services and conveyed an unusual and refreshing sense that you take responsibility for your projects.

The photographs were sharp, with a pleasing abundance of white space, and they outlined some beautiful design shapes and curves. These designs and your distinguished resume attract me as a client.

I strongly preferred the white Crowell brochure format because, except for the real estate development and property management, the interconnections among the areas of responsibility appeared easy to comprehend.

I look forward to seeing you again.

Yours truly,

Shawn O'Hare

Shawn O'Hare
Real Estate Developer

SO/vs

Figue 7.9

LETTER OF APPRECIATION 3

SCT
stanton's custom tailor
1478 WILSON BLVD. ARLINGTON, VA 22209

September 15, 199_

Mr. Henry Renquist
2650 Round Hill Rd.
Arlington, VA 22207

Dear Mr. Renquist:

Thanks to your recommendation, Mr. Arthur Quinn ordered a custom-tailored suit from Stanton's Custom Tailor. I am grateful for your recommendation.

To show my appreciation, I have enclosed a coupon worth $30 toward your next order of any suit, slacks, or shirt. It will be my pleasure to redeem your clothing credit either on your next visit or through the mail. Remember that your measurements are on file and we can tailor and ship to you directly.

Your friend's complete satisfaction—and your own—are fully guaranteed.

I look forward to your next visit.

Sincerely,

Jeff Stanton

Jeff Stanton

Figure 7.10

LETTER OF APPRECIATION 4

NATIONAL

COOPERATIVE PUBLICATIONS
748 5TH AVENUE
NEW YORK, NEW YORK 10022

August 5, 199_

Mr. Gordon Johannsen
23925 Commerce Park Drive
Cleveland, Ohio 44142

Dear Mr. Johannsen:

Thank you for your letter of June 9 about the *Bank Notes* article on Equal Credit Opportunity requirements. You were concerned about our explanation of the requirement for notifying married customers about separate credit histories.

Your understanding is correct concerning the ECOA and Reg. B notification requirement—as you can see by the clarification in the June 14 issue of *Bank Notes*.

Careful and demanding readers are essential to a quality publication. Thank you for taking the time to ensure our accuracy.

Sincerely yours,

Susan Bannister

Susan Bannister, Editor
Bank Notes

SB/je

Figure 7.11

LETTER OF APPRECIATION 5

SUBSCRIPTION SERVICE
58 BOWEN ST. PROVIDENCE, RI 02903

May 7, 199_

Michael Henderson
4153 McCain Court,
Kensington, MD 20895

Dear Michael Henderson:

    Thank you so much for sending your payment, and for taking the time to explain the delay.

    We're delighted to have you as a customer and are always here to serve you. Whenever you have a question about magazines, just let us know.

    If you move, we'll make sure your subscriptions follow you to your new home. Simply send us a list of your magazines—whether or not you ordered them here—six to eight weeks ahead of time, if possible.

    We want Subscription Services to be the kind of place where you feel comfortable and easy doing business, so call on us whenever we can be of service. We'll always try to be helpful.

Yours truly,

Brian Platt

Brian Platt,
Customer Relations

Figure 7.12

LETTER OF APPRECIATION 6

CRAGAR OUTDOOR SUPPLIES
834 SW Adams St. Peoria, IL 61602

March 23, 199_

Marjorie Shannon
1673 Asbury Ave.
Winnetka, IL 60093

Dear Marjorie Shannon:

    How nice of you to take the time to write to use expressing your gratitude for the way in which your order was handled. We are always available to provide you with quality service.

    Do stop in at our Peoria retail store when you are in the area. We can guarantee you the same personal service there that you have experienced from our mail-order department.

    We look forward to serving you again.

Sincerely yours,

Michelle Simmons

Michelle Simmons
Vice President

MS/er

Figure 7.13

LETTER OF APPRECIATION 7

Saint Mary's College
NOTRE DAME · INDIANA

Dear

Thank you for your gift of   to Saint Mary's College. We received your gift on   ; this letter will serve as the official receipt for your records.

As a member of the Tower Club you demonstrate your concern for Saint Mary's and your pride in the College's accomplishments. Our future strength is in the hands of donors like you who give generously to guarantee the College's vitality. We would like to show our appreciation by listing your name with other members of the Tower Club in the annual Honor Roll of Donors.

Your gift has made possible the commitment to excellence that is Saint Mary's heritage. Thank you again.

Sincerely,

Becky L. Drury

Becky S. Drury, Ph.D.
Director of Development

BSD:dp

Office of Development
Notre Dame, Indiana 46556-5001/(219) 284-4588

LETTERS OF SYMPATHY

In dealing with the human dimension of business relations, we must deal not only with occasions for congratulations or praise but also with times of sorrow. A helping hand and message of sympathy extended to persons suffering misfortune can be very meaningful. We have probably all had the experience of feeling less isolated in our sorrow because people have shown their concern, and we especially remember these acts of kindness.

Convey your sympathies to employees, customers, and business associates in situations involving death, sickness, accident, serious loss, or other misfortune. Handwrite your message, or if the relationship is purely business, type it on the company letterhead.

The message of sympathy may require special thought because the circumstances for your reader are difficult. Just remember to begin directly, identifying the event and expressing your sympathy. Then concentrate on the positive details appropriate to the situation.

Finding something positive to say in the case of a terminal illness or death is understandably difficult. In the case of a serious illness, the "get well soon" message is obviously inappropriate. Instead, let the patient know he or she is in your thoughts, and consider the positive aspects of the patient's care and situation.

In the case of a death, rather than mentioning the sorrows of the survivors, show your sympathy by concentrating on the good qualities of the deceased. End on a positive note, perhaps by suggesting that these good qualities will be remembered or by offering your help.

In Figure 7.14, a company president extends sympathy to the wife of an employee. Because he does not know her personally, and because he is speaking for the company as a whole, his remarks are more formal, and they are typed on the company letterhead.

Writing to a business associate can be more personal. When a manager was taken ill, he received the letter in Figure 7.15, handwritten by one of his associates.

If a friend or acquaintance suffers a business loss, there may be ways, small or great, in which you can lend a helping hand, as shown in Figure 7.16.

SEASON'S GREETINGS

Traditionally companies send season's greetings to their employees, and many firms also choose to send holiday messages to customers and other associates. Holidays are a good time to demonstrate your community spirit and to express appreciation in general for the contributions people have made to your organization.

Season's greetings sent to customers can be specially designed and printed in a variety of ways: handwritten messages on colorful holiday letterheads, traditional

Figure 7.14

LETTER OF SYMPATHY 1

INGARD

January 12, 199_

Mildred McKenzie
6842 Snowshore Trail
Evergreen, CO 80439

Dear Mrs. McKenzie,

    All of us at Ingard were shocked and saddened to hear of Tim's sudden death. We extend to you our deepest sympathy.

    Tim's value to us as an employee went far beyond his expertise as an engineer, though he was among the very best we've known. His patience, his dry wit, and his good nature made him many friends here.

    We will always remember Tim as a valuable employee and a fine human being. We hope these thoughts comfort you during this difficult time.

                                          Sincerely yours,

                                          Bert Applebee

                                        Bert Applebee,
                                        President

1568 CLARKSON ST. DENVER, CO 80218

Figure 7.15

LETTER OF SYMPATHY 2

May 14, 199—

Dear Bill,

Get well soon!

We miss you here, you know. It's hard to enjoy lunch without your choice comments on office politics. Evie says your clients have all expressed concern for you. They wish you well and want you back in time to give them the insider's dope on the election.

We hope you'll take it easy and keep doing what the doctor says. While you work on getting well, we'll try to muddle along without you.

Let us know if there's anything we can do for you. We wish you a very quick recovery.

Best wishes,
Harry

Figure 7.16

LETTER OF SYMPATHY 3

ANDERSON DEVELOPMENT CO.
17983 COWAN ST. IRVINE, CA 92714

February 15, 199_

Kyle Bauer
Kyle Bauer's Instrument Store
2218 Martin St.
Irvine, CA 92715

Dear Kyle,

    I was very concerned when I read about the theft and vandalism at your store. I know several of those instruments were collector's items and meant very much to you.

    Please get in touch with me if I can give you any help with plans for building renovation. I know an expert contractor who should be excellent at the kind of restoration your building probably requires.

    Meanwhile, I will follow the paper to see what the police find out. Do call if I can give you a hand.

Sincerely yours,

Mary Hunter

Mary Hunter

holiday cards with the executive's signature, or cards with artwork integrating representations of the company in a seasonal setting. The messages can be short and straightforward, or more playful and inventive, depending on the image you want to project for your company. Frequently the message can be related to the nature of the company business. A center for dance and physical fitness sent the holiday message in Figure 7.17 to its customers.

Season's greetings within the company may be expressed in memo form or on letterhead and sent through office mail. Many companies, however, believe it is in the spirit of the occasion to send specially printed cards, personally signed if possible. Figure 7.18 shows a letter that a president sent on company stationery to each employee's home.

Figure 7.17

SEASON'S GREETINGS 1

On Dasher! On Prancer!

Dear Patron:

While we don't expect you to be hopping over rooftops or sliding down any chimneys, we do hope you'll be enjoying the holidays with a sense of vigor and spirit.

Best wishes for a harmonious holiday season. And may you enjoy a healthy and prosperous new year!

THE DANCE AEROBICS COMPANY

Figure 7.18
SEASON'S GREETINGS 2

WILLY'S WAREHOUSE

205 WEST MONROE
CHICAGO, IL 60606

November 21, 199_

Leslie Adams
1542 Astor St., Apt. 22W
Chicago, IL 60610

Dear Leslie,

Let me take the occasion of the upcoming holidays to express my great pride in the work you are doing for Willy's Warehouse and to offer you my season's greetings.

In my recent business travels, I have met with a number of people whom our organization has served, new accounts and old, and the opinion expressed overwhelmingly is that the efficiency and quality of our service is unmatched. Only your expertise and efforts have enabled us to maintain our high standards.

With your efforts in mind, and your spirit and goodwill for the company, I extend to you my heartfelt appreciation and my sincere good wishes for the holiday season.

May you and your loved ones have warm and wonderful holidays, and a most happy and fruitful new year.

Best wishes

Will Smith

Will Smith,
President

LETTERS OF WELCOME

Welcome messages let people know their presence is appreciated. Businesses can welcome newcomers to town, new accounts, and account renewals. Within the company, managers can welcome new employees.

Many local businesses make it a practice to welcome newcomers to their city. A letter making contact with the newcomer can introduce your business at a time when the potential customer is likely to be very receptive to information about local businesses. Your being the one who comes forward with a greeting can be reason enough for a new arrival to choose your business over another's. Because you are introducing yourself as a business, these welcome letters, unlike other goodwill messages, can lend themselves to a sales message—but only a very *low-key* one. Many businesses, for example, offer the newcomer some incentive to come into the store.

One way of extending a welcome is to offer a gift in some way suggestive of your business. One insurance company, for example, gets together with a few other area businesses to send a telephone-address book to community newcomers. Already inserted in the address book are the names and telephone numbers of those businesses. The insurance company then sends the letter shown in Figure 7.19 as a follow-up.

A health maintenance organization (HMO) sends the letter in Figure 7.20 to new residents of the community it serves; and a lumber and hardware company sends the postcard shown in Figure 7.21.

Besides welcoming newcomers to town, many businesses welcome customers who open a new account or who renew an old one. In Figure 7.22, an office supply store welcomes a new business account.

An important ceremonial function that managers carry out is welcoming new employees to their company. Besides being a matter of common courtesy, timely recognition of new employees demonstrates to newcomers that they are valued members of the organization. Managers who instill in workers a strong sense of self-esteem are more likely to gain their full cooperation.

As Figure 7.23 illustrates, a welcome letter is simple and direct, and usually emphasizes the assets the newcomer brings to the organization.

SUMMARY

Your business career will present you with many and various occasions for showing your goodwill, whether by way of congratulations, appreciation, sympathy, season's greeting, welcome, or some other form. Seize the opportunity. The goodwill you express toward others gets returned in good feelings toward you.

Figure 7.19

LETTER OF WELCOME 1

MURPHY & CUMMINGS INSURANCE CO.
784 ROOSEVELT RD. GLEN ELLYN, ILLINOIS 60137

September 24, 199_

The Grant Family
256 Merton Ave.
Glen Ellyn, IL 60137

Dear Mr. and Mrs. Grant:

Welcome to your new home! We hope that by now you have received an attractive new address book that we, along with other businesses in Glen Ellyn, sent you in the hopes that you would find it useful.

Murphy & Cummings has been providing quality insurance coverage and service to this community for over 69 years. We have modern computers to save you time and to provide accuracy in account handling.

Again, we welcome you and hope you enjoy this fine town.

Sincerely yours,

Dave Cummings

Dave Cummings,
Vice President

Figure 7.20

LETTER OF WELCOME 2

Midwest HMO
4 WEST 26TH STREET, INDIANAPOLIS, IN 46208

October 5, 199_

Marilyn Becker
7483 N. Pennsylvania St.
Indianapolis, IN 46240

Dear Ms. Becker:

Welcome to the neighborhood. May we offer you a gift for your new home?

Accidents can happen, especially when changes occur in your household routine. And while you're settling in, your medical supplies may not be right at your fingertips. So we've organized into a compact kit the supplies and information you need to handle first-aid emergencies in your new home. (You may also find it's just the right size to fit into the glove compartment of your car when you want to take it with you on the road.)

Just fill in the enclosed coupon and bring it with you when you come in to the Hoosier Center to pick up your free first aid kit. We're located at 4 West 26th Street, just off Route 9, 7/10th of a mile west of Route 123.

Drop by at your convenience. We look forward to meeting you.

Sincerely yours,

Mark Barrera

Mark Barrera,
Assistant Manager

MB/bh
enc.

GOODWILL LETTERS   **337**

Figure 7.21
POSTCARD OF WELCOME

235 70TH STREET BAYONNE, NJ 07002

To Our New Neighbor:

The welcome mat is rolled out and our friendly staff is waiting to greet you personally. Please come by soon and bring this card for two complimentary keys.

It will be our pleasure.

Farradyne Lumber

Figure 7.22

LETTERS OF WELCOME 3

PIERCE OFFICE SUPPLIES
**2478 NEVADA AVE. N
MINNEAPOLIS, MN 55427**

November 21, 199_

Mrs. Doris Chen
Kramiz Investment Corporation
784 Aldine St.
St. Paul, MN 55104

Dear Mrs. Chen:

    Thank you for opening an account with Pierce Office Supplies. Whenever you think of ordering quality office supplies, give us a call. We can serve you quickly and efficiently.

    But fast efficient service is only part of the Pierce Company story. Our frequent Customer Bulletins will keep you posted on the many new products, exclusives, super discounts, gifts, and much more. And with every order you'll be adding credit to your earnings in our Executive Discount Club, which entitles you to free merchandise.

    So thanks again for your order. You'll be glad you welcomed the Pierce Company into your business. We look forward to serving you again in the future.

Sincerely yours,

John Noland

John Noland
for Pierce Company

Figure 7.23

LETTER OF WELCOME 4

Yorktown Commerce Center
228 NORTH LYNNHAVEN ROAD   VIRGINIA BEACH VA 23452

May 16, 199_

Alice Meyers
684 Heron Point Circle
Virginia Beach, VA 23452

Dear Alice:

It is a pleasure to welcome you to our staff. As you know, we are an expanding company committed to promoting from within. Your strong background in training and development, and in affirmative action, is just what we need to achieve our goals. We know you will find your job rewarding and challenging. If there is ever anything I can do to help you achieve your job objectives, my door is open.

Welcome aboard! I am delighted that you are joining us.

Sincerely yours,

Steve Johnson

Steve Johnson,
Store Manager

THE RANDOM HOUSE GUIDE TO BUSINESS WRITING

EXERCISES

See "Setting the Goal," pp. 308–309, for Exercise 1.

1. Figure 7.24 shows the draft of a letter the representatives of a tenant association want to send to their landlord. The goal of this letter is to thank Mr. Reynolds. What changes would you suggest the tenants make before sending the letter?

See "Generating Ideas and Organizing for Goodwill," pp. 309–312, for Exercises 2 and 3.

2. Think of a goodwill situation you have been in, or choose one of the following situations, and generate some ideas for a goodwill letter. Consider making a list, doing nonstop writing, or using a tape recorder.

- A family friend has helped you get a good summer job.
- An acquaintance of yours has received a special award.
- A business has donated money to a campus club you belong to.
- A co-worker has visited you while you were recovering in the hospital.

3. Continue with the ideas you generated for Exercise 2, and use the RTA formula to generate more ideas and organize your goodwill letter. Then write the letter.

See "Letters of Congratulation," pp. 312–318, for Exercises 4 and 5.

4. As sales manager of a sports store called "Roller Skating Pro," write a letter congratulating sales rep Harold Shaneson for his excellent sales record. The sales report for the winter season indicates that Harold has sold 14 percent more roller skates than anyone else in the company. He has also helped create a new market for skates by suggesting that the store offer five free private skating lessons to any adult who purchases a pair of genuine leather, individually fitted skates that costs over $125.

5. You are an engineer and manager for a telecommunications company. You have learned from the company newsletter that Jack Ackermann, one of your subordinates, has just received a promotion to senior management. According to the article, Jack's recent promotion has resulted from his excellent performance on a government contract that the two of you had worked on together. He had successfully managed the activities of three subcontractors and had himself contributed significantly to the technical side of the contract. In particular, he had helped develop the company's special purpose processors and data bases. And finally, he had given a superb briefing to the government. You have admired Jack for his work on several projects and have worked with him four or five times over the past two years. Write him a letter of congratulation for his promotion.

See "Letters of Appreciation," pp. 319–327, for Exercises 6–10.

6. As chairperson of your college's fall program for student internships in local businesses, write a letter thanking the president of the local bank for setting aside a position in the computer division for a student intern.

7. You are the head of new series development for a national TV network. Two hundred volunteers recently reviewed the pilots for three new shows: a western, a situation comedy, and a science fiction film made for TV. The volunteers also filled out a three-page questionnaire after each show. Write a letter thanking these viewers for their work. Include in your letter some of the suggestions the viewers had made that you are planning to incorporate in next fall's offerings.

8. Yesterday the computer at your travel agency broke down, and it cannot be repaired until early next week. As a result, all your agents are working long hours scheduling flights without computer assistance. Write a letter thanking the agents for their patience, hard work, and good spirits during this computer crisis.

9. You interviewed Gloria Cliss, director of consumer affairs at a national TV network, in order to write a report on private agencies that protect consumers' rights. She explained how TV's exposure of false claims for a product can affect sales. She also showed you complaint letters that her office has received from consumers. Write a letter thanking her for her time and effort.

10. Publishers Clearing House is a company that distributes magazines. Due to the large number of thank-you notes it has received from customers, the company has decided that it needs to develop a form letter that expresses its appreciation to customers for taking the time to write.

Figures 7.25 through 7.30 show some of the letters Publishers Clearing House has received. After reading them, write the form letter.

See "Letters of Sympathy," pp. 328–331, for Exercises 11 and 12.

11. Joan Macksey, a business associate of yours, has been in the hospital for two weeks. You have known Joan for several years. The two of you were college roommates and then went to work for the same company as sales reps. You have recently moved on to a firm that is competitive with Joan's. Write her a letter expressing your concern that she has been ill.

12. A fire has gutted the bicycle shop owned by a family friend of yours. Over the past ten years, he has given you and your family generous discounts on bicycles and service. Write him a letter expressing sympathy.

See "Season's Greetings," pp. 328, 332–333, for Exercise 13.

13. You work for a store that sells (choose one) chocolates, pets, computers, CD's sports cars, clothes. Your boss would like you to draft a holiday message that somehow incorporates the company's product in the message. Write the letter.

Figure 7.24

A TENANT ASSOCIATION'S LETTER OF THANKS

> Dear Mr. Reynolds:
>
> We would like to take this opportunity to thank you for your quick response to the increased safety needs of our apartment building at 19 West 13th Street.
>
> As of this date, the following improvements have been made:
>
> 1. Placing brighter bulbs in the lobby.
> 2. Closing the 14th Street door so that it is now an emergency exit only.
> 3. Placing two large mirrors in the South and North lobbies.
>
> We would also like to thank Charlie Johnson, our super, for his help. Finally, we want to praise our weekday doorman, Bob, for the excellent job he is doing.
>
> To complete the task of improving the safety of the building, we would appreciate your quick attention to the following:
>
> 1. Change the 13th Street lock.
> 2. Place a third large mirror in the mailroom.
> 3. Reposition elevator mirrors to the corners so that blind spots can be viewed when one enters the elevator.
> 4. Put a fence of some sort adjacent to the first-floor windows on the 14th Street side. As urged by Detective Kerney, this would serve as a major deterrent to crime via our fire escapes.
> 5. Place a brighter bulb outside the 14th Street door.
> 6. Explain to our new weekend doorman that it is his responsibility to question all persons entering the building and to announce all visitors.
>
> We are not aware of any burglaries that have occurred since these initial improvements have been made. This is a good sign. We look forward to hearing from you shortly on the status of the additional safety measures that we believe are required.
>
> Again, on behalf of the tenants, we want to thank you for your help and cooperation.

GOODWILL LETTERS

Figure 7.25
LETTER OF APPRECIATION 1

> My experience in dealing with serious companies nowadays amounts to this — LOUSY service! What keeps them in business I will never know!! It is a PLEASURE — I assure you — to deal with your organization and to know I will be treated ~~fairly~~ and ~~promptly~~. Thank you and KEEP UP THE GOOD WORK!
>
> Mrs. Clyde Judd

Figure 7.26
LETTER OF APPRECIATION 2

> We were quite surprised and pleased to receive your complimentary copy of Mother Earth News, which we had requested that our subscription start with. (Our old subscription purchased through you had expired before we realized, and we didn't want to miss an issue.)
>
> We have used your services for many years and have always appreciated your low prices and prompt service, as well as your handling of change of address at moving time.
>
> But this complimentary magazine made us really glad we're doing business with you. It's actions like that that build your reputation as a customer-centered company. We're glad to tell our friends. Thank you!
>
> Sincerely,
>
> Carol Fischer
> Carol Fischer

Figure 7.27

LETTER OF APPRECIATION 3

> Dear Sir,
>
> Thank you so much for your quick response to my letter. But I am not surprised. I have yet to be unhappy with your service at any time through all the years I've been your customer.
>
> Sincerely
> Ruth B. Brittain

Figure 7.28

LETTER OF APPRECIATION 4

> Dear Publishers Clearing House,
>
> I would like to say that ordering these magazines was the best thing to happen to me for the start of '8_. I was looking for this for a long time, and I'm glad you found me. Thanks a million for the thousands of enjoyable times that I know I will have with these wonderful magazines.
>
> Barry White
> Barry White

Figure 7.29

LETTER OF APPRECIATION 5

> Dear Publishers Clearing House:
>
> Just a note to tell you that I have started receiving the magazine that I ordered through you.
>
> Thank you for your timely processing of my order.
>
> In a day and time when everybody is very quick to complain, I want to compliment your organization on your handling of my order.
>
> *George Markland*
>
> George Markland

Figure 7.30

LETTER OF APPRECIATION 6

> Dear Sir:
>
> A hastily written note in my car to tell you that Publishers Clearing House has given us better service on orders and cancellations than dealing directly with the magazines. You people helped us when we were transferred in the Navy every two years.
>
> We thank you.
>
> *Millie White*

See "Letters of Welcome," pp. 334–339, for Exercises 14 and 15.

14. As a member of the student council at your college, you have been asked to write a letter welcoming freshmen to the college. Discuss a draft of the letter with several classmates before submitting it to your instructor.

15. As an assistant manager at Security Savings and Loan, a local bank, write a letter welcoming a new dry cleaners to the shopping mall, located one block from the bank. Although the bank offers lower interest rates than large national banks located in the area and has not yet installed computerized service, Security Savings can offer personalized service to the dry cleaners.

8 MEMOS

PREVIEW

This chapter should help you to

1. Write a memo by
   - Setting the goal
   - Assessing the reader
   - Gathering information and generating ideas
   - Organizing by either a direct or an indirect approach
   - Writing a draft
   - Revising
2. Choose an effective format for your memo
3. Write memos that
   - Announce
   - Give instructions or explain a procedure
   - Make a routine request
   - Confirm an agreement
   - Clarify
   - Remind
   - Promote goodwill

Memos are brief written communications circulated *within* an organization. They communicate information about operations and influence decisions.

Memos handle the flow of information *up*, *across*, and *down* in an organization. You may need to write

- *Up* to a superior (e.g., to make a routine recommendation)
- *Across* to an associate (e.g., to confirm an agreement)
- *Down* to subordinates (e.g., to remind, to announce, to give instructions, or to explain a procedure)

No other kind of written communication reaches so many people at so many levels of an organization. The larger the organization you work for and the more levels of authority it has, the more inefficient phone calls and face-to-face discussions become. A memo is a good way to reach many people at once.

Since you may communicate with your co-workers more often in memos than face-to-face, your memos also make you visible within your organization. Reputations are rarely made or lost on the basis of a single memo. But over time an impression of your ability is bound to be based, at least in part, on your memos. Not only will memo

347

writing be built into your daily tasks, but a well-timed and well-written memo can do wonders for your working relationship with others. For these reasons, you need to master the basics of memo writing.

In this chapter we take you through the process of writing memos. We also show you how to write a variety of memos that perform specific functions.

Manager Susan Long needs to handle a problem with her staff's lateness, which has recently increased. Although employees are supposed to be on the job by 9 A.M., many of them don't show up until 9:30 or 10.

Susan decided to put a stop to her employees' lateness by sending the memo shown in Figure 8.1.

SETTING THE GOAL

Memos can achieve a broad range of goals. Memos can announce, give instructions, request, confirm, clarify, remind, and promote goodwill. They may also be used to give bad news and to persuade. The goal of Susan's memo was to remind employees about company policy regarding work hours.

ASSESSING THE READER

Readers generally have two attitudes toward memos:

1. They are receptive to memos that give information to help them do their work or that request information they are willing to give or action they are willing to take.
2. They may be resistant to memos that give bad news or make a recommendation they are reluctant to follow.

Susan's readers fall into the second category. They will not be happy with the news they are about to receive. Let's consider in more detail some of Susan's concerns in writing to her readers, since you will need to assess your readers similarly when writing memos.

Your Readers' Business Relationship with You. As a superior writing to her staff, Susan has authority over them, but at the same time, she needs their cooperation. If you take into account whether your reader is your superior, peer, or subordinate, you can realistically assess how best to get your message across. You can influence and

Figure 8.1

SUSAN'S MEMO TO HER STAFF

DATE: March 9, 199_
TO: All Employees
FROM: Susan Long, Division Manager
SUBJECT: Work Hours

Let me remind you that the official working day is from 9:00 A.M. to 5:00 P.M. Exceptions must be cleared with your supervisors.

If you are consistently late, it is unfair to your fellow employees who are prompt. We all have trouble getting up in the morning. But 9:00 A.M. is not only "do-able," it is also company policy.

Thanks for your cooperation.

SL/bt

persuade superiors and peers, but you cannot give them orders. On the other hand, you have authority over your subordinates, but you cannot simply command their cooperation.

Your Readers' Knowledge of the Subject. Susan's workers know that company policy requires them to be on the job by 9 A.M., but they are perhaps unaware of how strictly this rule is enforced. Your readers frequently know something about the subject of your memo, perhaps because it is related to work responsibilities or an ongoing project.

Your Readers' Expectations About How the Memo Should Be Presented. Susan's readers expect her to follow standard memo *format* (see Figure 8.1, p. 349), to be brief, and to use a cordial, informal tone that is in keeping with her management style in supervising them.

Like Susan's staff, your readers may have expectations about the *length* of memos (e.g., no more than one page, one or more pages with supporting data appended). At Procter & Gamble, for instance, it is standard practice for memos to be no more than one page.

Your readers may also have expectations about *content*. Some expect you to fill in all the details of a decision. Others want your recommendation and a minimum of supporting evidence.

As for *structure,* most readers want you to put the recommendation up front and supporting material below. A few want to be led through the process of your investigation before you identify your conclusions and recommendations.

As regards *style,* your organization and your relationship with your readers suggest the degree of formality or informality you should adopt in your memos. In some companies, a formal style is expected; in others, a handwritten note, informal in style, is the rule. Some bosses—those who believe in the importance of upholding status distinctions—want your memos to sound formal and distant in a way that is appropriate to your subordinate position. Others—those who have an open and participative approach to managing—want you to use the first person, contractions, and even sentence fragments to create an informal, conversational style.

Your Readers' Attitude Toward You and Toward the Subject of the Memo. Susan knew she had a good relationship with her staff. As she expressed it, "My staff's a friendly and cooperative bunch, and I don't like to be demanding or commanding. It's just not successful in the long run. I believe in honey rather than vinegar." Concerning this memo, she felt that her staff would be unhappy receiving her reminder, so she decided on a strategy that would show firmness but would not alienate them.

Your readers will develop an attitude toward you from working with you every day or from participating with you on various projects. As for their likely attitude toward the subject of your memos, you will have to anticipate in every case how they will react.

If you are uncertain about any of these questions concerning your readers, ask them for clarification. Remember that when the readers of your communications are people within your company, you are in a good position to find out about their needs, expectations, and attitudes.

GATHERING INFORMATION AND GENERATING IDEAS

If you keep your goal and your readers in mind, often all you need to write a memo is in your head or easily available. If, for example, you want to announce the hiring of a new staff member, all you may need to do is look at his or her resume and your company's job description. Or if you get a request for monthly sales figures, you may just need to check your computer print-out listing the figures.

If you require further information or need to develop ideas for your memo, you can rely on the techniques described in Chapter 2 to assist you: taking notes on sources, talking to associates, using a tape recorder, writing nonstop, and making a list.

ORGANIZING MEMOS THAT GIVE OR REQUEST INFORMATION

When you write memos to give information that will help your readers do their work or to request information they are willing to give, your readers will be receptive to your message. For this reason, you don't have to spend time assessing your readers beyond considering their knowledge of the subject and their expectations about the format, length, and style of the memo. In fact, you should be able to write several routine memos at one sitting, in contrast to the extended time you may need to write memos that persuade or reports that require research and analysis.

Your major question in writing memos that inform or request information is how to group and order the content in a way that makes sense to your readers. Remember that these messages can contain a lot of information, which your readers will need to sort into major and minor points. Readers can't remember everything; if you want them to take away a few important ideas, give them clues that indicate which are major and which are minor points.

For memos that inform or request information, the best order is usually direct, since your readers are receptive to your message:

- State the purpose of the memo.
- Present relevant facts or examples in subsequent paragraphs.
- Close with a cordial remark and, when appropriate, ask for action.

Inexperienced memo writers or writers working on their first draft may use some kind of order to organize the content. Too frequently, however, it is the chronological order in which they have collected the information, or the order that suits their own priorities but not necessarily those of their readers. For instance, let's see how Richard Durkin, assistant quality control inspector, organized the first draft of a memo, which he dictated to his secretary.

Richard works for Bi-Rite Kids Furniture Company, a wholesale company that sells children's furniture to large department stores. The purpose of Richard's memo is to report to his supervisor, Jack Reilly, the good results of Richard's meeting with a Bi-Rite supplier, Bard-Jones. The meeting concerned defects in the vinyl material used in several of Bi-Rite's leading products.

To compose his first draft, Richard simply read through his notes from the meeting but did not think about helping his reader understand the information. As shown in Figure 8.2, he reported the results of the meeting in the order in which topics were discussed.

After getting the draft back from his secretary, Richard decided to use an analysis tree to group and order the information for his reader. Since Richard could anticipate the positive response of his reader, it made good sense for him to begin with the purpose, or major point, of the memo: to inform his boss about the results of his meeting with Bard-Jones. The major point thus appears at the top of his analysis tree (see Figure 8.3). The results of the meeting could be divided into three parts, each concerning one of three products, "Green Garden Patch," "Plaid Kid," and "Baby Stuff." Each product is handled as a subpoint and appears in the analysis tree as a branch.

Richard's analysis tree enabled him to write the greatly improved memo shown in Figure 8.4. In his revision, Richard first states the purpose of his memo: to inform his

Figure 8.2

RICHARD'S DRAFT

DATE: July 29, 199_
TO: Jack Reilly, Quality Control Inspector
FROM: Richard Durkin, Assistant Inspector
SUBJECT: Defective Vinyl

We had a meeting with Bard-Jones representatives Joseph Renquist (Marketing Manager) and Lou Ambinder (Regional Sales Manager). We first mentioned problems we were having with one of our big sellers, "Green Garden Patch." This product has stained green beyond the border design. Then I reported that another big seller, the plaid high chair called "Plaid Kid," has some discoloration. We need to contact Shipping at Bard-Jones to have the items picked up. Bard-Jones will give us complete credit for all defective items.

The discussion of these two items took about ten minutes, after which we decided it would be useful to define the scope of our responsibility and Bard-Jones's. So we then decided to designate the action each of us had to take for each of these two items before going on to discuss the third item.

For "Green Garden Patch," we need to contact Palmer for replacement. Bard-Jones will give us full credit for all defective material we return and will replace these items immediately. We should have replacements within a week after they receive the merchandise.

Since we don't know the extent of damage to our "Baby Stuff" booster seats, Bard-Jones has asked us to run ten rolls of the seating under standard conditions and to keep track of labor costs for doing this. They'll credit us for all defective material and pay the cost of labor.

As you can see, the results of the meeting were very positive. Bard-Jones is clearly looking to keep us as preferred customers. If you have any questions, please call me at my extension.

Figure 8.3

RICHARD'S ANALYSIS TREE

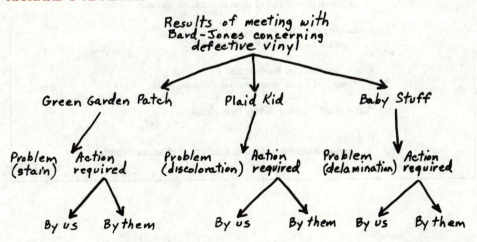

Figure 8.4

RICHARD'S MEMO: FINAL VERSION

DATE: July 29, 199_
TO: Jack Reilly, Quality Control Inspector
FROM: Richard Durkin, Assistant Inspector *RD*
SUBJECT: Defective Vinyl

On July 28, 199_, we had a meeting with Bard-Jones representatives Joseph Renquist (Marketing Manager) and Lou Ambinder (Regional Sales Manager) to resolve quality problems and to forestall future ones. Below are current problems and proposed resolutions:

1. "Green Garden Patch," Tick #2617

    Problem:
    All in-house material has green stains, which appear to have bled through.

    Action Required by Us:
    Contact Palmer for immediate replacement.

    Action Required by Bard-Jones:
    Credit us for all defective material once it has been returned and immediately replace it.

2. "Plaid Kid," Tick #4320

    Problem:
    Approximately 12" of discoloration on one end.

    Action Required by Us:
    Contact Bard-Jones for pickup.

    Action Required by Bard-Jones:
    Credit us for all returned defective material.

3. "Baby Stuff" Booster Seats, Tick #8530

    Problem:
    Delamination on unknown quantity of in-house material.

> Action Required by Us:
> Run 10 rolls of material under standard conditions. Keep track of hours spent on bad material. Notify Bard-Jones for credit on material and labor.
>
> Action Required by Bard-Jones:
> Credit us for all defective material.
> Credit us for labor spent on defective material up to ten (10) rolls.
>
> As you can see, the results of the meeting were very positive. Bard-Jones is clearly looking to keep us as preferred customers. If you have any questions, please call me.
>
> RD/et

boss about the meeting with Bard-Jones about quality problems. He then systematically discusses each of the three problems. He concludes on an upbeat, affirmative note that summarizes his main point and tells his reader how to get further information if needed.

Richard also made good use of formating to organize the wealth of information he wanted to present to his boss. The three products he considered appear as subpoints, which are numbered and indented from the body of the text. Within each subpoint, the important categories discussed at the meeting (problem, action required by us, action required by Bard-Jones) are treated as sub-subpoints; they are further indented and underlined. His effective use of visual design makes the information much easier to understand than did the earlier draft.

Use the accompanying checklist to ensure that your memos are effective.

CHECKLIST FOR WRITING MEMOS THAT GIVE OR REQUEST INFORMATION

1. Do you present the purpose of the memo at the beginning?
2. Do you present relevant facts or examples in subsequent paragraphs?
3. Does your memo close with a cordial remark, and when appropriate, does it ask for action?
4. Does visual design help to convey the message?

Checking for Completeness

Usually you will need not only to organize information in a way that makes sense to your readers but also to check your memo for completeness. To make sure that your memo covers everything it should, we suggest you check it to see if you have answered all of the following questions that apply to the communication: *who? what? when? where? how? why?* Let's look at a situation that called for using this technique.

Bob Gaynes, assistant to Personnel Manager Larry O'Keefe, was asked by his boss to draft a memo announcing a workshop on career development for the Management Development Group, a club sponsored by the company for employees interested in career development. The memo was to go out under Larry's signature. Figure 8.5 shows the first draft of Bob's memo, based on his notes from a discussion with Larry on the details of the workshop.

What do you find missing from Bob's draft? When reviewing the draft, Larry jotted down the questions who? what? when? where? how? and why? and checked the draft for completeness. He found two empty slots:

When: Saturday, October 1, from 9:30 A.M. to 4 P.M.
Where: Conference rooms on the 37th floor of the Franck building

Clearly, sending out this draft to their membership of 350 employees would have meant time and money wasted, and would have resulted in frustration among the employees interested in the workshop. The memo that Larry actually sent is shown in Figure 8.6.

The accompanying checklist can help you review your memo for completeness.

CHECKLIST FOR ASSESSING COMPLETENESS

Have you answered all of the following questions that are relevant?

- Who is involved?
- What is to take place?
- When will it occur?
- Where will it occur?
- How is it to be done?
- Why is it to occur?

In the examples in this section, memo writers chose to organize the content of their messages using a direct approach because they thought the reader would readily accept what they had to say. For this reason, their memos gave the main point first and then

Figure 8.5

GIVING INFORMATION: BOB'S DRAFT

DATE: May 9, 199_
TO: All MANAGEMENT DEVELOPMENT Members
FROM: Larry O'Keefe, Personnel Manager
SUBJECT: "Managing Stress": The Second Annual Career and Personal Development Workshop

The MANAGEMENT DEVELOPMENT GROUP is pleased to announce the Second Annual Management Development Career and Personal Development Workshop.

Sponsored by the Education Committee, the workshop is <u>free to MANAGEMENT DEVELOPMENT members</u>, with a $10.00 charge for guests. The fee covers both the workshop and an informal luncheon.

The keynote speaker at the luncheon is special guest Dr. Nancy Plummer, an expert in sports medicine, a consultant to Fortune 500 companies, and a former world-class gymnast. Dr. Plummer, who is an enthusiastic and eloquent speaker, will discuss "Aerobics Exercise: Key to Health and Achievement."

Because space is limited, registration will be on a first-come basis. Please complete and return the form below no later than Monday, <u>May 26</u>. If you have any questions, please contact Education Chair Barbara Jamison at Ext. 6-6046.

Figure 8.6

GIVING INFORMATION: BOB'S REVISED MEMO

DATE: May 9, 199_
TO: ALL MANAGEMENT DEVELOPMENT Members
FROM: Larry O'Keefe, Personnel Manager LOK
SUBJECT: "Managing Stress": The Second Annual Career and Personal Development Workshop

The MANAGEMENT DEVELOPMENT GROUP is pleased to announce the Second Annual Management Development Career and Personal Development Workshop to be held Saturday, October 1 from 9:30 A.M. to 4 P.M. in the conference rooms on the 37th floor of the FRANCK tower. An informal luncheon is included.

Sponsored by the Education Committee, the workshop is <u>free to MANAGEMENT DEVELOPMENT members</u>, with a $10.00 charge for guests. The fee covers both the workshop and the informal luncheon.

The keynote speaker at the luncheon is special guest Dr. Nancy Plummer, an expert in sports medicine, a consultant to Fortune 500 companies, and a former world-class gymnast. Dr. Plummer, who is an enthusiastic and eloquent speaker, will discuss "Aerobics Exercise: Key to Health and Achievement."

Because space is limited, registration will be on a first-come basis. Please complete and return the form below no later than Monday, <u>May 26</u>. If you have any questions, please contact Education Chair Barbara Jamison at Ext. 6-6046.

LOK/de

supplied necessary supporting details. But sometimes you will find it preferable to use an indirect approach, building a case for your point of view first and then identifying it or, at a minimum, "softening" the message before stating it.

ORGANIZING MEMOS THAT GIVE BAD NEWS OR PERSUADE

When the purpose of your memo is to give bad news, an indirect approach may make the news more palatable to your readers.

Bad-News or Persuasive Memos to Subordinates

Complaints from nonsmokers had reached Personnel Manager Sandra Peterson: People were continuing to puff away in the off-limits area, the left side of the main office. She had already held two staff meetings on the rights of smokers and nonsmokers and had thought that the topic was exhausted. But each group continued to complain. "What do I do next?" she wondered. "How can I make the staff comply with the company's decision?"

To solve the problem, Sandra decided to send the memo shown in Figure 8.7. Notice that she addresses her readers as fellow human beings who share a common problem. Only then does she restate company policy. By showing that they are all in the same boat, she softens the effect of her order.

As in Sandra's case, you will find that because of the strength of your formal status in an organization, you won't need to *persuade* subordinates to do something. But, as a business person with authority over others, you will still want to acknowledge people's attitudes, as Sandra did ("Some people like to smoke, some people like to complain about others smoking"), even as you tell them to do something they may dislike doing.

To organize memos that convey bad news to subordinates, we suggest you do the following:

- Establish a shared goal or common frame of reference with your readers.
- Provide them with information that will support the unpopular news you have yet to supply or that will help them to think or act as you want them to.
- Give the bad news.
- Close with a cordial remark, and when appropriate, ask for action.

Figure 8.7

SANDRA'S PERSUASIVE MEMO TO HER SUBORDINATES

```
DATE:    July 8, 199_
TO:      The Staff
FROM:    Sandra Peterson, Head of Personnel  SP
SUBJECT: Complaints About Smoking
```

We all have our vices—some people like to smoke, some people like to complain about others smoking. Since your management does not purport to be infallible, we've decided to follow the solution of the state and federal governments. That is, SMOKERS ON THE RIGHT, "NONS" ON THE LEFT.

We'll begin enforcing this policy Monday morning. Please cooperate so that working here will be more pleasant for all of us.

SP/nt

Bad-News or Persuasive Memos to Peers or Superiors

When you are writing across or up, rather than writing down as Sandra was doing, you obviously won't be giving orders. You don't have the authority to do so. You may, however, have unpleasant news to convey or an opinion to voice that may not at first be well received. In these instances, use an indirect approach to organize your message, since your task is to persuade. Let's look at an example.

Suppose that your secretary, Jan Corbett, asks to be given an extended leave of absence so she can go on a round-the-world cruise with her husband. You would like to grant her the leave because you don't want to lose her.

In the five years that Jan has worked for you, she has always worked overtime whenever you needed her and has consistently done an excellent job on everything from scheduling meetings to greeting clients. You also know that if you don't grant her a leave of absence she will go anyway. You have decided that you don't want to lose her even if it is inconvenient to work with a temporary secretary until she returns.

Your superior has already refused to grant Jan's request because a company rule states: "Extended leaves of absence will be given only in cases of emergency."

Your strategy in writing a persuasive memo involves a similar indirect approach you would use to convey bad news to subordinates:

1. *Establish a shared goal or common frame of reference*. In this case, you choose a common frame of reference by appealing to your boss's values—the importance he places on his staff's loyalty and productivity.

2. *Provide readers with information that will support the request you have yet to make and that will persuade them to think or act as you want them to*. In this case, your bad news is your request that your secretary be granted a leave of absence. The information you use to support this request includes everything that demonstrates Jan's exceptional productivity and loyalty—her exemplary completion of tasks, her willingness to work long hours, and so on. You also support your case by bringing in two other facts: Her absence affects only your office, and a permanent replacement who can equal her performance will be immensely difficult to find.

3. *Give the bad news*. Once you have established Jan's value, you can say that she deserves an extended leave.

4. *Close with a cordial remark*. You make your request courteously and respectfully, so that your boss knows you respect his authority and that you are asking him to grant a special favor.

Figure 8.8 shows how your memo to your boss might read.

THE RANDOM HOUSE GUIDE TO BUSINESS WRITING

Figure 8.8

A PERSUASIVE MEMO TO A SUPERIOR

DATE:
TO:
FROM:
SUBJECT: Leave of Absence for Jan Corbett

As you may know, my secretary, Jan Corbett, is requesting a leave of absence. Her work has been uniformly excellent since she began with us five years ago. She has demonstrated exceptional productivity and loyalty to the company—the kinds of qualities all of us value in our staff. I support her request because of her performance.

Let me outline for you in some detail just how Jan has assisted my division. First, she has volunteered to work overtime whenever we had to meet important deadlines; e.g., during last spring's rush to complete our quarterly report, she gave up a vacation she had been planning and helped us get the report out on time. Jan has also successfully taken on tasks that I normally assign to administrative assistants. For instance, she has done an excellent job of scheduling meetings for my staff and greeting important clients. In sum, Jan is an exemplary employee who's been invaluable to me and my division.

Last week Jan requested that I grant her a six-month leave of absence to take a round-the-world cruise with her husband. Since her absence would affect my office only, I would prefer finding help during her absence to losing her permanently, which will happen if we are forced to deny her request.

Although Jan's is an exceptional request, I think she's an exceptional employee who deserves special consideration due to her outstanding productivity and loyalty over the past five years. I hope you'll agree. Please authorize me to grant Jan's request.

The accompanying checklist can help you review your memos that give bad news or persuade.

> ### CHECKLIST FOR WRITING MEMOS THAT GIVE BAD NEWS OR PERSUADE
>
> 1. Have you established a shared goal or common frame of reference with your readers?
> 2. Have you provided them with information that will support the unpopular news you have yet to supply or that will persuade them to think or act as you want them to?
> 3. Have you given the bad news?
> 4. Have you closed with a cordial remark and, when appropriate, asked for action?

WRITING A DRAFT

If you have organized your memos with your purpose and reader in mind, you will be able to write several memos at one sitting. Especially if they are routine memos that you frequently write to the same people, the first draft of such memos will usually be your final draft. Nonroutine memos and those presenting particular challenges in organization, completeness, persuasiveness, or tone may have to be revised.

REVISING: CHECKING FOR TONE

As we have seen, writers may have trouble organizing memos in a way that makes sense to the reader, ensuring that their memos are complete, and persuading the reader to go along with their message. In addition, writers may discover a problem with tone. For instance, they may sound arrogant, insensitive, or angry when they want to come across as cordial and respectful. Let's look at an example.

Carol Wilson is an assistant manager in publications for a cosmetics company. She is in charge of photography for company publications. At a recent staff meeting, one of Carol's associates, Brian Cooperman, mentioned that while Carol was on vacation he had spent two weeks working on the photographs for their new sales brochure because the ones she had done were unsuitable. Carol was surprised by Brian's remark because she had, in fact, completed all her work satisfactorily before leaving on vacation and because Brian had not bothered to tell her of this problem before making a public announcement of it. Later that day, Brian told her that in her absence the department had developed a new concept for the brochure, so the photos she had done were no longer appropriate.

Carol decided to write a memo to Brian (and to send a copy to the boss to whom both she and Brian report) to clarify the reasons for the problem with the photographs and to ensure that, in the future, Brian would discuss such problems with her in private. Figure 8.9 shows the draft of Carol's memo.

When Carol reread her memo, she could see that she had allowed her anger and self-righteousness to take over. She also knew that although getting angry might feel good in the short run, it would only succeed in alienating Brian and might reflect poorly on her in her boss's eyes. Carol's revision is shown in Figure 8.10. How successful do you think she is in making her point fairly and courteously?

Figure 8.9

CHECKING FOR TONE: CAROL'S DRAFT

DATE: May 19, 199_
TO: Brian Cooperman, Assistant Manager of Publications
FROM: Carol Wilson, Assistant Manager of Publications
SUBJECT: Photographs for the New Sales Brochure

During your review of progress on the sales brochure at last week's all-staff meeting, you mentioned that you had spent about fifteen hours retaking photographs for the brochure while I was off on vacation.

Frankly, I was outraged by your statements, because this meeting was the first time I was informed of your problem with the photographs. Your remarks were especially annoying to me because, after reviewing my records, I find that you sent me a note several weeks ago saying how much you liked the photos. It seemed unprofessional to me that you were mentioning at a full staff meeting a situation that is exclusively the concern of the two of us without having discussed this matter with me first. Later that day, you told me that the concept for the brochure had changed during my absence and that the photographs I submitted to you several weeks ago were no longer appropriate.

As you know, it is not possible for me to supply new photographs at the last minute. Nor is it my responsibility. You owe me an apology. I met my responsibilities, and you're blaming me for something you may have caused.

Last week was the first time I heard of your problem with the photographs. Should you have problems with photographs in the future, you must check with me first and in private.

cc: M. Wright

Figure 8.10

CHECKING FOR TONE: CAROL'S REVISED
MEMO

> DATE: May 19, 199_
> TO: Brian Cooperman, Assistant Manager of Publications
> FROM: Carol Wilson, Assistant Manager of Publications *CW*
> SUBJECT: Photographs for the New Sales Brochure
>
> During your review of progress on the sales brochure at last week's all-staff meeting, you mentioned that you had spent about fifteen hours retaking photographs for the brochure while I was on vacation.
>
> I was surprised by your statement, because this meeting was the first time I was informed of your problem with the photographs. Your remarks were especially surprising to me because, after reviewing my records, I find that you sent me a note saying how much you liked the photos I submitted to you several weeks ago. It seemed inappropriate to me that you were mentioning a situation that is exclusively the concern of the two of us at a full staff meeting without having discussed this matter with me first. Later that day, you told me that the concept for the brochure had changed during my absence and that my photographs were no longer appropriate.
>
> As you know, it is not possible for me to supply new photographs at the last minute. Nor is it my responsibility.
>
> Last week was the first time I heard of your problem with the photographs. Should you have problems with photographs in the future, please check with me first in private. By doing so, you'll ensure receiving the photographs you need on time.
>
> CW/mf
> cc: M. Wright

To revise her memo, Carol eliminated expressions that showed her anger and her sense of being wronged: "I was outraged"; "Your remarks were especially annoying"; "It seemed unprofessional to me"; "You owe me an apology"; "you're blaming me"; "you must check." She also withdrew her demands, replacing them with a request for cooperation and stating the benefits of cooperating.

Check the tone of your memos before sending them out. Especially for memos that convey bad news or persuade, be sure you sound cordial and respectful to your readers.

The accompanying checklist will help you revise your memos for tone.

CHECKLIST FOR REVISING MEMOS FOR TONE

1. Have you removed negative expressions and statements that will anger or alienate your reader?

2. Have you chosen language and information that stresses the reader benefits of your message?

MEMO FORMAT

From the memos you have seen so far, you have some idea of how memos ought to look. All memos have certain features in common. Let's look at those features, in Figure 8.11, a sample memo.

Memos Have a Similar Heading Format

The heading of a memo includes the date, the recipient, the writer, and the subject. All four of these items must appear, but they can be sequenced differently at the top of the page. Most companies have standard memo forms.

"From" is followed by the full name (and title if appropriate) of the writer: for example, "S. V. Bainton, Head of College Relations."

"To" is followed by the name(s) and title or function of the recipient(s): for example, "Richard Lane, Paul Manning, and Jane Singleton, Recruitment Committee."

Figure 8.11

A SAMPLE MEMO

DATE: September 23, 199_
FROM: S. V. Bainton, Head of College Relations *SVB*
TO: Richard Lane, Paul Manning, and Jane Singleton, Recruitment Committee
SUBJECT: BA Recruitment Meeting

The 199_ recruiting season will begin in November. In order to understand our responsibilities and objectives, I'd like you to attend a meeting on recruitment.

The meeting is scheduled for 10:00 A.M., Wednesday, October 20, in AP-631 and will take approximately 45 minutes. Topics that will be discussed include:

- Participating schools
- Hiring objectives
- Rating system
- Scheduling procedures
- Interviewing
- Transcripts
- Secretarial support

We'll set aside about twenty minutes for general discussion, so please come prepared with suggestions of topics we might consider. Your participation is extremely important to the overall success of our recruiting efforts.

SVB/de

cc: B. Fainstock
    R. Young

The writer's initials should appear after his or her typed name and title. Alternatively, the typed name and signature can appear at the end of the memo after a complimentary close:

Thank you

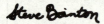

Steve Bainton

Adding your initials or signature to a memo tells the reader that you have authorized what is being sent out under your name.

"Subject" is followed by a succinct identification of the memo's topic: for example, "BA Recruitment Meeting."

The body of the text of the memo follows this heading.

At the bottom of the memo may appear two or three capital letters followed by a slash and then two or three small letters, for example,

SVB/de

The capital letters stand for the author's initials. The small letters stand for the initials of the person who has typed the letter.

Below these initials can appear the abbreviation "cc" (which stands for carbon copy), followed by a colon and the full names or initials of people who are to receive copies of the memo, for example,

cc: B. Fainstock
R. Young

As for stationery, most companies have standard memo forms that may include the company **logo**, a graphic design that conveys the image the company wants to project (see Figure 8.12).

Memos Are Short

Memos are limited to a single subject that is identified in the heading. The body of our sample memo has three short paragraphs and is limited to one subject, the BA recruitment meeting. The meeting appears as the subject heading. Memos are typically not more than one page and contain short paragraphs.

The subject heading indicates briefly but clearly the main point of the memo so that readers can grasp it quickly. If the heading is accurate, it can provide the key word or phrase by which to file the memo for later reference.

Figure 8.12

SOME STANDARD MEMO FORMS

RANDOM HOUSE, INC.

TO: DATE:

FROM:

SUBJECT:

Interoffice Correspondence
TRW Defense Systems Group   **TRW**

Subject   Date   From

To   cc   Location/Phone

Memos Use Page Layout to Reinforce Their Messages

To emphasize ideas and to reveal their structure, memos use

- White space
- Paragraphing
- Underlining
- Capitalization
- Numbers
- Bullets (A **bullet** is a heavy dot used to draw attention to a point. Bulleted items are set off from the body of a paragraph by indentation and spacing in a memo.)

Consider how much visual design contributes to the ease with which you can understand the body of the sample memo.

PARAGRAPH STYLE

When paragraphs are set flush left with extra space between them, this is referred to as **block paragraph style.** In the sample memo (see Figure 8.11), the first paragraph announces the meeting and its purpose, the second gives the topics, and the third encourages the staff's participation at the meeting. Instead of the block style, you can use **paragraph indentation** to show where each unit of thought begins and ends.

CAPITALIZATION AND UNDERLINING

When you want to tell readers that certain words and phrases are especially important and help them remember this information, you can use capitalization and underlining. In the sample memo, underlining helps readers to remember the time, date, and location of the recruitment meeting.

BULLETS AND NUMBERS

To set off a series of specific, related items, you can use bullets or numbers. In the sample memo, the topics to be considered at the meeting are bulleted for easy reference. Bullets highlight each of the topics on the agenda. Like bullets, numbers highlight discrete points; unlike bullets, numbers also suggest the relative importance or the sequence of items.

Memos Often Have a Conversational Tone and Style

As in business letters, a friendly tone and style are needed to show courtesy and sympathy toward the reader. (See Chapter 4, "Local Revision: A Friendly Tone and a Conversational Style.") Since memos may go to people whom you don't know personally, a courteous and sympathetic tone are especially important. To achieve this tone, say things positively and emphasize reader benefits. You can also

- Strive for a balance of "I" and "you"
- Use short paragraphs and sentences
- Use words and phrases you would use in conversation
- Use contractions

The tone of the sample memo is matter-of-fact and informal. The writer gives lots of information, but that does not mean he forgets that he is dealing with people. Notice the good balance between "I" and "you," the use of contractions, and the cordial close inviting people to participate in the meeting.

Memos may sometimes be more formal in tone—if, for instance, the seriousness of the subject warrants this tone or if they are written to a superior who expects you to maintain a respectful distance.

The accompanying checklist can help you review the format of your memos.

CHECKLIST FOR REVIEWING FORMAT

1. In the heading of your memo, have you included the date, your name, the recipient's name, and the subject?
2. Is your memo short and limited to a single subject identified in the heading?
3. Have you used page layout to reinforce your message?
4. Have you used a conversational tone and style, and shown courtesy and sympathy toward the reader?

THE FUNCTIONS OF MEMOS

Memos serve several different functions, some of which are discussed below.

Memos That Announce

When an announcement is clearly in the best interests of your readers, you can begin your memo with it. In Figure 8.13, the writer begins immediately with his message, since he knows that Purchasing expects to have policy come from his office. (If your reader needs reasons or other details to understand the announcement, give these first.) He then reinforces the positive side of the announcement by describing its benefits.

Memos That Give Instructions or Explain a Procedure

Since much of a company's business depends on people properly carrying out routine tasks and procedures, many memos are written to give instructions or to explain procedures. People expect and even welcome such memos because well-written instructions help make a job easier. These memos can begin with a statement of their purpose and reader benefits and then give step-by-step instructions, sometimes by grouping information, as in Figure 8.14. Because she knew that her readers would be receptive to the

Figure 8.13

MEMO ANNOUNCING POLICY

DATE: February 10, 199_
TO: Ron Orpeza, Head of Purchasing
FROM: Ben Fromkin, Vice President of Finance *BF*
SUBJECT: Vendor Price Increases

As a matter of policy, instruct your purchasing people not to accept price inceases from existing vendors unless you personally review the increase with the vendor's representative. — *Tells Purchasing reasons for policy*

This approach will put pressure on the vendor to hold back on increases. The vendor's major concerns in the current economic climate are twofold: — *Gives benefits of policy*

1. To keep customers
2. To secure orders

Let's force these conditions to work for us.

Thank you!

Ben Fromkin

BF/ds

Figure 8.14

A MEMO GIVING INSTRUCTIONS

DATE: August 31, 199_
TO: All Panelists
FROM: Victoria Wells, Conference Coordinator
SUBJECT: Preparation of Visual Aids

VW

The following information will help you prepare high-quality and effective visual aids:

Announces memo's purpose and its benefits to the reader

SLIDE CONTENT

Following are a list of points to consider when preparing slides:

Breaks down instructions by category and gives details under each category

1. Have an introductory and summary slide stating goals, overview, and conclusions of the presentation.

2. Provide continuity as much as possible from slide to slide.

3. Give each slide a "thesis."

4. Cover one basic idea in each slide. Several simple slides are more effective than one that is complex.

5. Use a maximum of six facts per slide. If one idea requires more, use several slides. In particular, do not use listings, detailed flowcharts, or circuit diagrams on slides.

6. Don't crowd information. A slide that is overloaded will bore or annoy your audience.

(continued)

(A MEMO GIVING INSTRUCTIONS continued)

> 7. Include only basic points in your slides. Detailed information should be covered orally. If such information is essential to your audience, provide it in a handout.
>
> 8. Use pictorial or graphic representation wherever possible, instead of phrases or tables.
>
> **EQUIPMENT**
>
> A viewgraph projector and a 35mm carousel projector will be supplied to you at the time and place you designate by calling Audiovisual at 9-8651.
>
> If you have further questions about how to prepare your visual aids, please call me at extension 5-9541. I have several books you may consult that contain detailed instructional guidelines and illustrations. My assistant, George Lowie, who has worked as a graphics designer, can also help you plan your visual aids.
>
> VW/sp

information, the conference coordinator began immediately with the purpose of her memo. She followed up with detailed instructions, by category, and closed courteously with an offer of further assistance.

Because readers of the memo in Figure 8.15 may feel unconvinced as to the need for the procedure it announces, the writer has chosen to explain briefly the reason for the procedure.

Memos That Make a Routine Request

Taking care of routine business involves requesting as well as giving information. When you want to make a request for which you know you will receive a positive response, use a direct approach. Begin immediately with your request and follow up with details—as in Figure 8.16.

Figure 8.15

A MEMO EXPLAINING A PROCEDURE

DATE: April 12, 199_
TO: All Employees
FROM: Jerrold Owens, Accounting Department
SUBJECT: Expense Report Preparation: New Procedures

    Due to the increased amount of travel, we have a new procedure for filling out expense reports. Please remember to do the following: *Names procedure and justifies need for it*

- Break down your trip by days.   *Explains how to follow it*
- Identify the purpose. If your trip is multipurposed, identify the days specifically spent on each activity.
- If your hotel bill includes miscellaneous items such as food or telephone, identify them under the miscellaneous column. If the form doesn't have enough room under "miscellaneous," use the space at the bottom.
- Be sure to identify those charges that are either paid by company credit card or prepaid.
- Fill out the report in ink.

    Your assistance will save time for your office and mine. Spending five minutes on this form will greatly reduce the amount of paperwork we all have to do.

JO/es

Figure 8.16

A MEMO MAKING A ROUTINE REQUEST

DATE: October 9, 199_
TO: R. L. Merkin, Manager
FROM: Stan Lewison, Project Green Manager *SL*
SUBJECT: Management Support for Project Green

Because we want to comply with the new scheduling procedures instituted in your department several weeks ago, we hereby request 16 days of Mindy Crocker's time to assist us in Project Green: *Makes request*

- 3 days to design the experiment procedures of request (i.e., setting up files and getting into the system) *Gives details*
- 11 days to run the model using various predictor variables and analyzing correlation relationships
- 2 days to edit the materials and present the data to Van

Thanks.

SL/pw

Sometimes you will need to recall for your readers the circumstances of your request before making it. This is the case in Figure 8.17.

Figure 8.17

A MEMO REQUESTING INFORMATION

DATE: October 14, 199_
TO: Bill Ishimine, Sales Manager
FROM: Arlene Williamson, Assistant Director of Accounting Services *aw*
SUBJECT: Policy for Charging Returned Equipment from New Brunswick Children's Hospital

You called me a couple of weeks ago questioning whether a sales rep's performance against 199_ quotas should be burdened with the returned equipment sold the previous year. Specific reference was to customer number 01261 New Brunswick Children's Hospital.   *Recalls situation for reader*

Can you give me more information on this situation? I find nothing in the files to indicate shipment of a unit to this hospital.   *Makes request*

I would appreciate your prompt response. Thank you.   *Gives courteous close*

AW/cj

Memos That Confirm an Agreement

Anytime an important verbal agreement is made, follow up with written confirmation to clarify the scope and details of the agreement. You can begin such a memo immediately with a statement of the agreement and then provide the reader with the necessary details. In Figure 8.18, the writer begins with the topic, criteria for evaluating staff, which had been discussed at a meeting with all section heads. She then follows up with her understanding of those criteria.

Figure 8.18

A MEMO CONFIRMING AN AGREEMENT

DATE: May 9, 199_
TO: All Section Heads
FROM: Mary Reynolds, Director of Human Resources *MR*
SUBJECT: Criteria for Evaluating Staff

In the next month you will be asked to submit a performance evaluation for each of your staff, using the rating system we developed at our last meeting. To assist you in making your assessment, here are the definitions of terms you are asked to use in your evaluations:

Confirms oral agreement on performance requirements

SUPERIOR:

Consistently performs above job standards. Consistently makes contributions beyond the responsibilities of current position. Requires minimum supervision, and when direction or supervision is needed, knows it.

Gives performance requirements

ABOVE AVERAGE:

Frequently performs above job standards. Occasionally makes contributions beyond the responsibilities of current position. Requires less than normal direction or supervision, even on nonroutine assignments.

SATISFACTORY:

Consistently meets all job standards. Requires normal direction and supervision on assignments. Requires assistance on nonroutine assignments.

> NEEDS IMPROVEMENT:
>
> Sometimes performs below job standards. Cannot always be relied on to fulfill job responsibilities. Requires more than normal supervision to complete routine assignments.
>
> UNSATISFACTORY:
>
> Frequently performs below job standards. Cannot be relied on to fulfill job responsibilities. Requires excessive supervision to complete routine assignments.
>
> It is important to maintain objectivity in assigning ratings. Remember that there are truly superior people, and that above average or satisfactory people should not be upgraded for purposes of salary increases.
>
> MR/jb

Memos That Clarify

Sometimes oral instructions and requests need further explanation or are so detailed that they need to be written down so the reader can understand them fully. Memos can give such clarification. In Figure 8.19, a supervisor gives his subordinate the detailed instructions he had mentioned to her over the phone. Notice that he gets immediately to the main point of his memo—contacting the distributor for delivery—then fills in all the necessary details that will allow Joni to accomplish her task.

Memos That Remind

Sometimes people need a written reminder to get them to do an assigned task. Perhaps because of other responsibilities, they have simply forgotten or ignored your message. If your reminder does not prompt them to comply, it can serve as evidence of your attempt to get them to complete the task if the issue is taken up at a higher level. Figure 8.20 is such a reminder.

THE RANDOM HOUSE GUIDE TO BUSINESS WRITING

Figure 8.19

A MEMO CLARIFYING INSTRUCTIONS

DATE: June 28, 199_
TO: Joni Hawkins, Assistant Manager
FROM: Craig Bower, Manager CB *CB*
SUBJECT: Ice Cream Disc inventory

Please ask Jay Chesterham at Deluxe Freezer, Inc., to deliver 80 cases of ice cream discs, as we agreed on the phone yesterday. This memo is to clarify my oral instructions on how delivery should be made. — *Announces main point of memo*

Delivery should follow this schedule: — *Gives details*

    July 14: 30 cases
    July 28: 45 cases
    August 7: 5 cases

Let Jay know that we may be ordering more cases for August 7 delivery if we use up our inventory by July 20. If we need an additional order, we can let him know by July 30. If that's not sufficient lead time for him, would you please let me know as soon as possible. We would expect to receive the extra cases with the August 7 shipment.

Please coordinate delivery of the discs with Jay and with Wally, our shipping clerk.

CB/ta

Figure 8.20

A MEMO OF REMINDER

DATE: March 22, 199_
TO: All Staff
FROM: Reggie Hines, Director of Personnel   *RH*
SUBJECT: Completing Time Sheets

    Since there has been some confusion about filling out time sheets, this is to remind you that they are to be submitted to the Business Office at the end of each week and by 10 A.M. on the last working day of a pay period for onsite operations. Offsite, they are to be submitted as determined by the Business Office on a location-by-location basis. Time sheets are vital to the company's operations and accounting system, and must be submitted on time.

RH/es

States reason for memo

THE RANDOM HOUSE GUIDE TO BUSINESS WRITING

Memos That Promote Goodwill

Sometimes the major purpose of a memo is to build good business relations with superiors, associates, or subordinates. People like to be congratulated for their accomplishments, appreciated for a job well done, or recognized during times of sorrow. If you show genuine interest in the people you deal with, such consideration is bound to be rewarded by their respect for you and their willingness to cooperate.

Often goodwill messages sent to people within the organization go out as letters (see Chapter 7, "Goodwill Letters"). If you want to be less formal, send these messages in memo form, organizing them as follows:

- Begin the memo by announcing your message, since people will welcome it.
- Give some significant details or explain why you are offering praise, thanks, or sympathy.
- End by reinforcing your positive attitude toward the reader.

A manager wrote the memo in Figure 8.21 to let his staff know how grateful he was for their extraordinary efforts in helping him complete a difficult project. Notice

Memos can be used to summarize or clarify an understanding reached over the phone.

that he thanks the staff as a group but also singles out individuals for special appreciation. Don's staff will not only feel acknowledged; they will also feel good about helping him on the next project. Keep in mind that memos can perform more than routine business tasks; they can also be a great way to build good relationships between you and other members of your organization.

Figure 8.21

A MEMO PROMOTING GOODWILL

DATE: 4 March 9_
TO: The Staff
FROM: D. Brabant
SUBJECT: Briefing Awards

I want to thank all of you who helped to put together the RDS Upgrade Study Midterm briefing. Although this was a very difficult and frustrating briefing to create, the response from the government has been very favorable. Our success is due to an outstanding effort by all who participated in creating the briefing. Special thanks go to: *— Announces message*

- Barry Lindsey, who worked late nights away from home and contributed many of the ideas that made the briefing a success. Much of the sweat that went into the briefing was his. *— Gives significant details*

- Dan Polk, who provided much of the focus and several of the key concepts.

- Tim Darden and Valerie Peters, who did a lot of the homework needed to show our "understanding of the problem."

- Bonnie Sylvan, who stayed late, did beautiful work, and never threw the charts back in our faces, no matter how many times or how late we said, "Just one more minor change."

- Red Olson, who gave the briefing its only (much needed) light moments.

(continued)

(A MEMO PROMOTING GOODWILL continued)

- Joan Mikawa, Barbara Greene, Dick Soto, and Blanche Ohano, who made the briefing look professional no matter what we gave them to work with.

- Joe Davis and Mark Whitsitt, who moderated our "discussion" of how and why the briefing should be organized.

- All the reviewers (who wound up working as much as reviewing), including, especially, May Reilly, Bart Ling, and Jessie King.

The efforts of all of you made this briefing a success. Thank you.   *Reinforces positive attitude*

Don Brabant

Don Brabant

SUMMARY

Business people frequently use memos to communicate information and to make recommendations in an organization. Memos routinely announce, give instructions or explain a procedure, make a request, confirm an agreement, clarify, remind, and promote goodwill. By keeping your purpose and reader in mind and by giving careful consideration to your memo's organization, completeness, and tone, you can be assured of writing effective memos.

EXERCISES

See "Setting the Goal," p. 348, and "Assessing the Reader," pp. 348–351, for Exercises 1 and 2.

1. As the junior staff member of your company's operations division, you need to write a memo to all part-time employees who formerly worked full-time. The memo is to request that they return their portable computers to Purchasing by Monday, April 18, 199_. Use of the portable computers is a privilege of the full-time staff, and the supply of these computers is limited. Shipping can pick up the computers anytime during the day at the employee's convenience.

    Your problem is that several of the part-time employees prefer to keep their computers. Because your company is small (seventy-five employees) and close-knit, you know most of the employees, full- and part-time. Write the goal statement and assess the readers of your memo.

2. You are an entry-level manager in an accounting department. In checking the expenses of the second-floor sales staff over the past six months, you have discovered that two of the salespeople, Lesley Tippett and Bob Swanson, each sent out 1,000 sales brochures last month. Each brochure costs the firm over $5 because of paper quality, color photographs, and mailing expenses. Lesley and Bob work with over one hundred accounts. But so do the five other salespeople on the second floor, and the other salespeople never use more than 250 brochures a month. From speaking to Lesley's and Bob's bosses and from reviewing their sales reports, you have discovered that they bring in approximately the same amount of business as do the other salespeople.

    Your boss has told you to write a memo to go out under his name to the second-floor sales staff. The memo is to concern the high cost of brochures and to tell the salespeople that company policy requires them to justify use of the brochures beyond the quota of 250 per month. Write the goal statement and assess the readers of your memo.

See "Organizing Memos That Give or Request Information," pp. 351–355, for Exercises 3 and 4.

3. You are a member of a human resources department. Last week the vice president of your department announced the opening of a new physical fitness center. Do an analysis tree for a memo that will follow up this announcement with details about the center. Here is the information that should be included in the memo:

- The center features a heated swimming pool, a sauna, exercise machines, a dance studio, and an indoor track (an eighth of a mile).
- Hours are lunchtime (11:30 to 1:30 P.M.), early mornings (6:30 to 7:30), evenings (7 to 9:30 P.M.), and weekends (9 A.M. to 8 P.M.).
- Several classes are currently being offered and several more are being planned.
- The center is located on the twelfth floor of the main office building.
- Family memberships are available ($30 a year for the employee, $20 for a spouse,

and $10 for each child), and employees are entitled to five guest passes each year, which can be used at any time except lunch hours.
- Each class runs for 10 weeks, one hour per week.
- Sign-up sheets will be circulated on the Monday before classes begin, and enrollment is limited to those who sign up in advance.
- The classes that are now being offered include aerobics for beginners (three sections: Monday and Wednesday at 7 A.M. and Tuesday at 6:30 A.M.); intermediate aerobics (Tuesday and Thursday at 6:30 P.M.); advanced aerobics (Friday at 7 A.M.); jazz dance (Monday at 12 noon); beginning karate (Tuesday at 12 noon); modern dance for beginners (Wednesday at 12 noon); intermediate modern dance (Thursday at 12 noon); synchronized swimming for beginners (Monday and Wednesday at 7 A.M.).

4. You work for the research and development unit of a computer software firm. You have just informed Marketing that your unit's work on a new spelling and grammar software package is now complete. The software has passed all tests and is on schedule and ready for production. Marketing may now begin designing brochures that feature the software in the company's line of products for the coming year. Write a memo to Marketing confirming your phone conversation and adding any details you think might help in preparing the brochure. These details might include the following:

- The software can be used on any personal computer.
- The grammar software contains special sections on common errors made by business writers and how to correct them.
- The spelling software not only helps writers identify errors; it also gives them the correct spelling.

See "Organizing Memos That Give Bad News or Persuade," pp. 359–363, for Exercises 5–7.

5. You want Andrew Quinn, the illustrator in publications, to handle all arrangements for the company Christmas party (December 21 from 4 P.M. to 9 P.M.). Because you were the most recently hired member of your company's publications division last year and wanted to meet new people, you had managed the event at that time. The task has fallen on you to persuade someone else in the company to plan the party; otherwise you will have to do it again.

Planning the arrangements was time-consuming, but you had met people in every division of the company. Some of them were several levels above you. In fact, everyone from the president to part-time clerks attends this annual event.

Andrew joined the company eight months ago, and you have been helping him informally to learn about his job and the company. As coordinator of the party, he will be responsible for arranging publicity, decorations, and refreshments. In all, 200 employees are expected to attend, and $1,500 has been budgeted for the occasion.

You will be out of the country on a two-week vacation beginning tomorrow so you won't have time to discuss the party with Andrew until you return. Write him a memo that persuades him to volunteer.

6. As assistant to President M. G. Brown of Alabama Claytime, a family-owned company, you often ghostwrite his speeches and memos. Three years ago, he decided that the best way to reward and encourage workers was to give them an annual bonus at Christmas based on their increase in productivity during the year. Last year the increase was 8 percent, and people received an 8 percent bonus in their Christmas pay-envelopes.

This year productivity has not increased. Although your company's sales have held, President Brown will not be paying any bonuses at Christmas. He has asked you to prepare a memo on this subject to go out under his name.

7. As the head of a project for your company, a satellite communications firm, you have concluded that the report due at your customer in three weeks cannot be completed unless you and your staff work overtime nights and weekends. If you don't, you will either not meet the deadline for the report or its quality will suffer significantly. The contract is worth $1 million to the company.

For your staff to work nights and weekends, the company will need to pay overtime to three secretaries and to the receptionist at the front desk. Overtime will cost the company approximately $6,000. Top management at the firm has been trying to keep expenses down. Write a memo to top management arguing for the money.

See "Revising: Checking for Tone," pp. 363–366, for Exercise 8.

8. Brad Fillmore is president of his own consulting company, Brad Fillmore Associates (BFA). The firm specializes in training business people to use computers. Most members of his staff are highly educated consultants who work on commission. They receive 25 percent of the fees the company charges for its services. For instance, if BFA charges a company $800 for providing a consultant, he or she makes $200.

Until now Brad has encouraged his consultants to pursue new business. Most of them took advantage of opportunities to be interviewed on radio and TV. They also granted interviews to trade journals and newspapers, since media coverage gave them free publicity. But Brad now finds that he needs to limit such interviews to the four senior managers. Because the company's services are changing and expanding so rapidly, he wants to be certain that a consistent, accurate picture of the firm gets communicated to the media. He also wants to funnel most of the new business through these four managers. Brad anticipates that the other consultants may be unhappy with his decision, because they enjoy pursuing their own business for the firm as they see fit. Most of them enjoy using the media to build business.

Brad wants to send a memo to his professional staff to tell them about the new company policy concerning the media. From what you know about the consultants, what changes does he need to make in the draft of his memo shown in Figure 8.22 so as not to alienate his staff?

Figure 8.22

BRAD'S DRAFT

TO: All Consultants
FROM: Brad Fillmore, President
DATE: March 28, 199_
SUBJECT: Press/News Media Interview Policies

As our rapid growth continues, we will receive added attention from trade and business publications. To ensure that the information we are presenting to the media is accurate and in the best interests of all of us, we are establishing a new interview/contact media policy.

To this end, only four managers will give interviews or contact the media: Joel Babcock, Barry Lewis, Dave Ferguson, and me. Exceptions will be made on a very selective basis, but all such interviews MUST be cleared beforehand with Dave Ferguson in Marketing.

If you receive a telephone call or are contacted in person (such as at a trade show) by an editor, reporter, or other news media representative, please tell the person politely that you are not the right person to answer the questions. Then transfer the call or direct the person to me or, in my absence, to Dave Ferguson. If neither of us is available, please get the person's name AND DEADLINE and inform Dave. He will then take care of the interview request.

This policy, effective immediately, applies to calls both from and to the media, including newspapers, magazines, and radio and television stations.

Your cooperation will be most appreciated.

See "Memos That Give Instructions or Explain a Procedure," pp. 371–374, for Exercises 9 and 10.

9. In a memo, explain a procedure you know well to a group that might need to use it. You may draw on your part-time work or summer job experience to choose a procedure.

10. As a manager of the plant maintenance department of your company, write a memo to all employees concerning the use of electrical outlets. Instruct employees that they must use long cords of at least six feet and no more than a six-foot extension. These must meet Underwriters Laboratory (UL) standards. All plugs must be three-pronged. With supervisory approval, an employee may use extra extensions, but they must have no more than three outlets.

See "Memos That Make a Routine Request," pp. 374–377, for Exercise 11.

11. You are the editorial assistant for the company newsletter of a large auto company. Write a memo to Lauren Frommer, winner of the 199_ award for best auto sales record, asking her to send you two or three sentences about her educational and work background to be included in next week's issue of the newsletter.

See "Memos That Confirm an Agreement," pp. 377–379, for Exercise 12.

12. Write a memo confirming an agreement about an assignment for school or about a project for a summer or part-time job. Be sure to take into account the reader (e.g., your instructor, your boss) and spell out the important details.

See "Memos That Clarify," pp. 379–380, for Exercise 13.

13. You are assistant manager of food services at a large oil company. Last month Mark Dubrow, the head of advertising, ordered the chicken special for a 100-person banquet to be given three days from today. This morning Mark called you to tell you that he now wants roast beef served at the banquet, but he is unhappy with what he perceives to be a huge, unwarranted increase in the price of banquet meals since he ordered the chicken specials. He has reluctantly agreed to pay the difference. The chicken specials cost $4.95 each; if roast beef is substituted for chicken, the cost is $7.95. The increase is due both to differences in cost between chicken and beef and to the lateness of Mark's request. (With advance notice, you can buy meat at significant discounts.) Write a memo to Mark clarifying the reasons for the increase in price.

See "Memos That Remind," pp. 379–381, for Exercise 14.

14. You are in charge of seeing that a marketing report outlining your major competitor's product line is finished by the end of the month. Several people need to contribute their efforts for the report to get done on time. Recently you met an early milestone in the project: the creation of an outline of the report's content. In reviewing the outline,

you saw a need to make a few changes in deadlines and personnel. You presented these changes at a recent meeting and drew up the following schedule for completing the report:

- All research must be completed by the end of week 1.
- The methodology has to be drafted three days later by marketing analysts Gail Manville and Rory McQuire.
- You must see the methodology section and the introduction, conclusions, and recommendations, which Gail and Rory are also responsible for, by the end of week 2.
- You will meet with Gail and Rory at the beginning of week 3 to discuss your comments and suggested revisions of the draft. On the basis of their responses, you will put together another draft and have it ready for Stuart Gormely of word processing by the end of week 3.
- You will meet with Cindy Liu of graphics Monday of week 4 to discuss the design of charts and graphs.
- The complete typed report must be in your hands by Tuesday of week 4.
- Word processing and graphics must make final changes by Thursday of week 4 so that you can take a last look at the report before it goes out.

After grouping and ordering this information, write a memo to the concerned parties reminding them of the revised schedule.

See "Memos That Promote Goodwill," pp. 382–384, for Exercise 15.

15. Imagine someone you have worked with over a period of time. Put yourself in the place of this person's boss, and write a memo expressing your appreciation for this employee's high record of accomplishments in his or her ten years with the company.

9
THE BASICS OF REPORT WRITING

PREVIEW

This chapter should help you to

1. Write a problem-solving report by
   - Using a systematic approach to solving the problem
   - Deciding on the recommendation you want your reader to go along with
   - Assessing your reader's
     — Business relationship to you
     — Knowledge
     — Attitudes
     — Expectations of how the report should be presented
   - Gathering the appropriate information
   - Using an analysis tree to organize ideas and information in a way that convinces your reader to go along with your recommendation
   - Using an analysis tree to write a draft
   - Choosing an effective format for your report
   - Identifying weaknesses in your draft in order to revise it
2. Write other kinds of short reports, including
   - Meeting and trip reports
   - Progress or status reports
   - Reports on procedures
   - Proposals

Chris Campbell, a computer buff and a travel agent at the Wide World Travel Agency, had a strong hunch that his five-person company could improve customer service and save money. Wide World just needed to buy a computer system to do the company's client accounting, rather than leasing time from a computer time-share service as they currently did. Chris also knew that his knowledge of computers would help him back up his hunch.

"Everything's working pretty well now, so the big task," Chris thought to himself, "will be to get my boss to *see* there will be problems in the future if we continue to use the time-share service. Unless I can show her the potential problems from the start, my recommendation's going to seem as though it's come out of the blue. I've also got to make a good case to get her to see that a computer system will solve more problems than it will create.''

PROBLEM SOLVING AND REPORT WRITING

Do you need to advise your boss about whether or not to purchase new equipment? A **problem-solving report** is a response to a business problem that requires you to do some analysis and investigation to find the best solution.

In the first part of this chapter, we look at a systematic approach to solving a business problem and then consider how to present conclusions and recommendations in a short report. In the second part of the chapter, we look at four other kinds of short reports: meeting and trip reports, progress or status reports, reports on procedures, and proposals. (All of these reports are usually short; occasionally they are lengthy.)

In today's business curriculum, more and more emphasis is being placed on understanding how business people come up with good ideas. The ability to identify and solve problems in a systematic way is a tremendous asset for a business person. Few of us can rely on flashes of insight to handle business problems. Even in those rare instances when our intuition seems to give us a solution, in a business environment, intuition needs to be tested against information and through analysis for hunches to be credible to others. For this reason, we present a systematic approach to problem solving that breaks down the process into three stages:

1. Determining the question the reader wants answered
2. Analyzing the problem and doing research to determine the sources of the problem and to uncover possible solutions
3. Establishing criteria for selecting the best alternative among possible solutions, and evaluating and choosing among alternatives

Determining the Question the Reader Wants Answered

When you are presented with a business problem that you have to solve, first define the problem in terms of a question the reader wants answered. Most often, the problem you need to solve is identified by the person who is requesting the solution and has the authority to ask you to investigate the problem. Occasionally, you will identify a problem yourself that needs to be solved and brought to the attention of appropriate decision makers. This was Chris Campbell's situation. Since Chris is both a computer buff and a travel agent, he guessed that his company could improve customer service and save money by using its own computer system. Because he wanted to seize the opportunity to improve the business and to demonstrate his value to his boss, Chris took it on himself to investigate the question, "Would Wide World's owning its own computer system improve customer service and save money?"

Whether your boss gives you a problem to solve or you identify the problem yourself, begin investigating it by stating the problem as a question that the reader wants answered.

Analyzing the Problem

Whatever the problem you face, state it as a question and see if it can be divided into subquestions. Your training in business courses will give you ways to break down the question. Your subquestions will help you in your research if they are specific and limited enough in scope to allow you to search systematically for solutions that your thinking or other sources can provide.

USING AN ANALYSIS TREE

To formulate subquestions and to do a systematic search for answers, we suggest that you use an analysis tree. You are already familiar with how an analysis tree can help you group and order ideas in your writing. An analysis tree can also help you answer the reader's question by providing you with a visual representation of the subquestions. Finding answers to these subquestions becomes easier when they are laid out before you. Put your main question at the top of the page, and place the subquestions below it. Alternatively, put the main question on the left and the subquestions to the right of it. Figure 9.1 shows how Chris used an analysis tree to investigate his reader's question.

Chris began his investigation by asking himself the question his boss would ask and then breaking it down into two parts:

1. Would owning our own system help us improve customer service?
2. Would it save money?

To answer his first subquestion (Would owning our own system help us improve customer service?) Chris consulted his own experience as a computer buff and as a travel agent. First, he reviewed in his mind Wide World's uses of computer assistance. They used it to keep track of clients' travel plans and interests and to do client billing. To perform these functions, Wide World currently used two computer terminals and a printer linked to a remote time-share computer service. The time-share service charged them for leasing the terminals and printers and for storing client data files.

Figure 9.1
CHRIS'S ANALYSIS TREE FOR FORMULATING SUBQUESTIONS

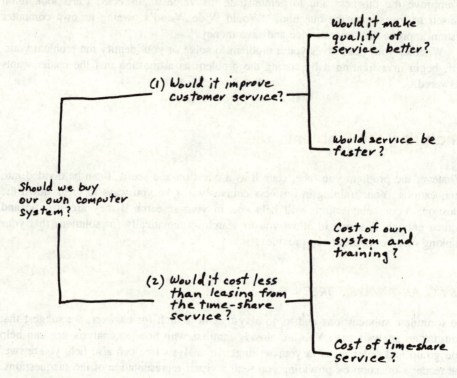

Chris knew that with the current system, the response time to customer inquiries about their accounts could be slow, because the computer service had limited capacity and was used simultaneously by several other companies during Wide World's peak business hours. Some of Wide World's customers became annoyed by these delays; Wide World probably appeared to them to be inefficient.

If Wide World used their own equipment rather than relying on the time-share service, response time would improve. And so would the travel services provided by Wide World. The time-share service provided only limited ability to tailor the kind of information Wide World stored for each client. By having their own system, Wide World would be able to specify relevant information (e.g., preferred hotel class, plane seating, and choice of airline) to be stored for clients. Attention to little details such as these could make clients feel that the company was personally involved in their travel comfort. From his experience as a travel agent in a five-person company, Chris knew how the "personal touch" could translate into more dollars for a firm.

To answer his second subquestion (Would it cost less than using the time-share service?), Chris had to do further analysis. The cost of a computer system depended on the features Wide World required. Only after determining Wide World's requirements could he project the cost of owning a computer system and compare it to the company's expenses for the time-share service. After reviewing the agency's needs, Chris figured that its computer system should have four terminals (one for each agent); a printer; a large, fast disk for data storage; and a flexible data management system to store and retrieve client data. In addition, the system should have good documentation, good training and user support, and good maintenance service. Finally, the system should be expandable to add more storage and terminals as the business grew.

Once Chris had identified Wide World's requirements, he visited several retailers to determine the cost of specific computer systems that met Wide World's needs. From speaking to their sales representatives and reviewing their brochures and manuals, he was able to select and price three systems for fuller investigation:

Big Blue BC AT	$7,240
Cherry II F	$5,730
Okifuji 32S	$4,270

According to Chris's review of Wide World's budget, the agency could afford to spend approximately $6,000. Added to this cost would be the cost of training the company's travel agents to use the new system, which Chris estimated to be about $2,000. To compare the costs of a computer system against those of using the time-share service, Chris consulted Wide World's financial records for the past year. He found that the company had paid $4,800 for the time-share service. If a computer system costs $6,000 (including a warranty for maintenance) and training costs $2,000, the system would pay for itself in about a year and a half.

As Chris did his research, another question came to mind. What would a used computer system cost? He added the question to his analysis tree. Chris checked the cost of used systems and found them to be almost as expensive as new equipment and virtually unavailable.

Purchasing a computer system would save Wide World money. Certainly, even if they bought the most expensive of the three systems, it would pay for itself in less than two years.

ESTABLISHING CRITERIA

As you discover answers to the questions that will help you solve your business problem, begin considering criteria by which to judge alternative solutions. **Criteria** are the standards your reader will use for making a decision. To determine your reader's criteria, you must either work closely enough with the reader to know the standards he or she uses to make business decisions, or you must consult with people who have this knowledge. Chris, for example, knew her boss would choose to buy a system if it would improve customer service and cost less than using the time-share service. These were her first criteria. But then how would she choose among alternative computer systems?

Chris had worked with Wide World's boss on several projects, so he could draw up a list of criteria by which she would judge a computer system: cost, quality of equipment (e.g., fast disk drive, flexible data management software, small and durable terminals, fast and high-quality printer), quality of documentation, availability of training and support, quality of service, and expandability.

Rarely will a possible solution meet all of your reader's criteria. Chris's case was no exception. The three systems he found promising varied in fulfilling his reader's criteria. Because of this, he created a chart (Figure 9.2) to enable him to compare each system against the others.

With the exception of each system's cost, which could be established in precise terms, Chris made qualitative judgments about each system. These judgments were based on discussions with sales personnel and other owners of these systems and on his own personal knowledge of computers. Big Blue and Cherry II-F met most of the criteria, although Big Blue exceeded the budget. The Okifuji line of computers was quite new and so had not established a reputation for service.

When one solution meets some criteria and another (or others) meets other criteria, you need to decide which criteria are most important and give more weight to the solution that meets those criteria. In Chris's case, all systems contained the necessary equipment. Of the remaining criteria, "cost" and "service" were more important to his boss than were any other criteria. Based on the system's cost and reputation for very good service, Chris's choice was the Cherry II-F.

Sometimes your decision will require you to decide which criteria are most important before a solution becomes evident. At other times, your decision will be clear-cut; one alternative will stand out from the rest.

Figure 9.2

USING CRITERIA TO EVALUATE ALTERNATIVES

Criteria	Big Blue BC AT	Cherry II-F	Okifuji 32S
Cost	$7,240	$5,730	$4,270
Equipment	yes	yes	yes
Documentation	good	good	fair
Training/support	good	good	good
Service	excellent	very good	unknown
Expandability	good	good	fair

THE BASICS OF REPORT WRITING

Use the accompanying checklist to evaluate your analysis of a business problem.

CHECKLIST FOR SOLVING A BUSINESS PROBLEM

1. Have you determined the question the reader wants answered?
2. Have you analyzed the problem and done research to determine the sources of the problem and to uncover possible solutions?
3. Have you established criteria for selecting the best alternative among possible solutions and evaluated and chosen among alternative solutions?

WRITING THE PROBLEM-SOLVING REPORT

Once you have found the solution to a problem, you are ready to write a report that convinces your reader to go along with your solution. As with any writing assignment, report writing involves all the activities of the writing process. Let's look at one representative writing process, Chris Campbell's, to get a better understanding of what you will need to do to write a problem solving report.

Setting the Goal

Your goal is to get your reader to agree that the solution you have found is the best among the alternatives you have considered. Chris Campbell, for example, wanted his boss to agree to purchase the Cherry II-F.

Assessing the Reader

Convincing your reader to go along with your recommendation depends in part on how well you assess your reader.

The checklist on the next page summarizes what was said in Chapter 2 about assessing your reader, but it focuses especially on readers of reports.

CHECKLIST FOR ASSESSING READERS OF REPORTS

1. Who is your primary reader—the person who can make a decision as a result of reading the report? Who are your secondary readers—persons who may receive the report and may act on the message?
2. What is your reader's business relationship to you?
3. How much does your reader know
   a. About the particular topic discussed in the report?
   b. About the general subject area of the report?
4. What is your reader's likely attitude
   a. Toward you?
   b. Toward your recommendation?
5. What is your reader's expectation about how the report should be presented?

Here is how Chris's reader can be considered according to these questions:

1. *Primary and secondary reader:* Chris's *primary reader* is his boss. She is the only one in the firm with authority to allocate funds for the system and to order a change in the way Wide World maintains information about client accounts. His secondary readers include the other three travel agents, who report directly to his boss.
2. *Reader's business relationship to Chris:* Obviously Chris's boss is his superior, so he must explain and support the rationale for his recommendation.
3. *Reader's knowledge*
   a. *Of particular topic:* His boss is unaware of problems Wide World may face if it continues to use the time-share service, so Chris will have to make her aware of potential problems.
   b. *Of general subject area:* Since his boss lacks expertise in computers, Chris will have to avoid a technical discussion. But since she herself uses the time-share computer service, she does know something about its capabilities.
4. *Reader's likely attitude*
   a. *Toward Chris:* His boss has a receptive attitude toward Chris's advice because he has a good record as a travel agent and as a computer expert. On several occasions, she has deferred to his judgment on a technical matter about the time-share service.
   b. *Toward Chris's recommendation:* Chris knows that his boss will be receptive to the message. Even though she is a novice, she enjoys using the computer and appreciates what it can do for her firm. More important, she is always interested in cutting costs and improving service. However, Chris must present good arguments for purchasing a computer system, since this is a need only he recognizes, not his boss.
5. *Reader's expectation about how the report should be presented:* Generally Chris's boss likes to see his recommendations up front and then supporting material. But because she is unaware of the problem Chris has solved, he decides he will have to depart from this format and give reasons before presenting his recommendation.

THE BASICS OF REPORT WRITING

Gathering Information and Generating Ideas

Often your work in solving the problem provides you with the information necessary to your report. However, you may find that you need additional information for convincing your reader, information that you did not come upon in solving the problem. You can gather such information through library and other research. (Chapter 10, "The Formal Report: Goal, Reader, Ideas, and Information," discusses these data-gathering activities in detail.)

Organizing

Once you have gathered information and generated ideas, you must organize this information in a way that allows you to achieve your goal—convincing your reader to go along with your recommendation. By understanding the psychology of your readers—what he or she judges to be most important—you have the best chance to organize your report effectively and to include information the reader will find convincing. The information that persuades your reader to go along with your recommendation comprises the main point and the subpoints of your report. Use an **analysis tree** to arrange these points, as Chris did (see Figure 9.3).

Figure 9.3

CHRIS'S ANALYSIS TREE FOR WRITING HIS REPORT

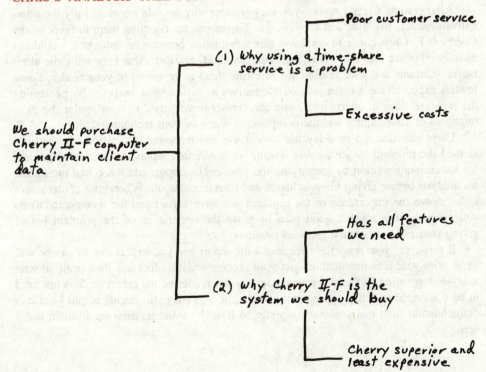

Chris began the analysis tree by thinking about what would convince his boss that Wide World needed to purchase a computer system. Since he knew that saving money and improving customer service were vital concerns of his boss, he thought he should stress these as the main reasons for purchasing the system. Because he had to establish the need for the new computer system first, he decided that he should begin by explaining Wide World's current needs and expenses. Making a case for a new system was his biggest challenge. It was essential that he first show his boss the benefits of owning a computer system. Only then should he present his reasons for recommending the Cherry II-F. These reasons would be drawn from the criteria he had established for choosing among the three computers.

Writing a Draft

If you have kept your purpose and your reader in mind, your analysis tree should make evident to you the main points of your argument and how to structure them. Use the analysis tree as a guide in putting together a draft of your report. Notice in Chris's report (Figure 9.4) that the two large branches of his analysis tree (see Figure 9.3) become the two major sections of the body.

Once you have chosen the sequence of ideas for your report by using an analysis tree, write a draft. Then choose a format that best allows you to present your recommendations and supporting arguments to your readers. (Report formats are discussed on pp. 405–407.)

After reading Chris's report, you may wonder why he didn't present fully the alternative systems, Big Blue and Okifuji, and his reasons for rejecting them in favor of the Cherry II-F. Chris chose to condense this information because he thought it would not heavily influence his boss's decision. You may find, however, that presenting the alternative solutions and your reasons for rejecting them is important to your reader. Some readers expect to see a discussion of alternatives as part of your analysis. By presenting the pros and cons of alternatives, you can further demonstrate to your reader the thoroughness of your inquiry and the comparative worth of your recommendation.

Chris also decided to delay his conclusion and recommendation until he had described the problem. Since he was writing an unsolicited report, he needed to prepare for his recommendation by identifying the problem his report addressed and presenting his analysis before giving his conclusion and recommendation. When your reader needs to be shown the importance of the problem you have solved and the recommendations you propose, it is often a good plan to prove the importance of the problem before giving your conclusions and recommendations.

If however, your reader has requested the report and you expect that he or she will agree with your recommendation, put your recommendation first and then bring in your analysis supporting it. Even if your reader has not requested the report or does not need to be convinced to follow your recommendation, you may still decide to put your recommendation first; many managers prefer to have recommendations up front in every case.

Figure 9.4

CHRIS'S REPORT

DATE: April 11, 199_
TO: Jean Warren, Manager
FROM: Chris Campbell *CC*
SUBJECT: Reducing the Costs and Improving the Management of Our Client Accounts

    In arranging travel for our clients, I have noticed a problem with our current method of handling their accounts. We have paid an excessive amount ($4,800 last year alone) for handling the accounts because we use an outside time-share service. In addition, we are severely limited in the type of information we can store on each client, and we frequently have to wait several minutes for computer response to customer inquiries about their travel plans or billing. Limitations in the data we can store on clients and delays in returning information reduce customer satisfaction and can result in lost sales.

    Since you have consistently stressed our need to provide quality service at a reasonable cost, let me first outline for you the problem with our continuing to use a time-share service. Then I will suggest a solution that will help us better achieve our goal of excellent service at minimum cost.

Why Using a Time-Share Service Results in Poor Customer Service and Excessive Cost

    A time-share service is used by many people simultaneously. Our business hours are also the peak hours for others' use of the service. During peak hours, the increased number of users and the limited capacity of the time-share system lead to delays in retrieving information about clients' accounts. Meanwhile, our clients are waiting for answers to their questions. And since the current system can be slow and doesn't allow us to store more than a small amount of relevant

1

Annotations:

- *Chris chooses a title that gains his reader's attention by telling her the report is based on criteria that are important to her—reducing costs and improving services.*
- *Since the report is unsolicited, Chris includes a brief introductory section that gives his reader an overview of the problem and an incentive to read the report.*
- *The incentive is based on criteria that are important to his boss—costs and customer service.*
- *If Chris wanted to state his recommendation first, he would have put it here.*
- *Chris analyzes the problem so that his boss will feel a need for the solution. This section corresponds to the first branch of his analysis tree on "Why using a time-share service is a problem."*

(continued)

CHRIS'S REPORT (continued)

2

information on their travel plans, clients may find our services less appealing then those offered by agencies that can store such information. Delays can make us appear less efficient and less professional to clients, and can be very frustrating both for us and them. On the other hand, use of our own computer system would result in a response time of seconds instead of minutes and would enable us to store information tailored to each client.

In addition, by using our own system, we could reduce costs. We are currently one of the smaller users of the time-share service. As a result, we are paying for more than our share of the service's operations. Last year the charges for the service were $4,800. If we bought our own computer system, these charges for the time-share service would be covered in about a year and a half.

Why We Should Purchase the Cherry II-F

I investigated our computer needs in detail, followed up on three systems that could serve us well, and looked at the possibilities of buying used equipment. Used equipment is a poor choice. Of the three systems I reviewed, the Cherry II-F is the best choice because it meets more of our needs than do the other two.

Chris presents his recommendation and the method of investigation he used to decide on it. This section corresponds to the second major branch of his analysis tree "Why Cherry II-F is the system we should buy."

Our Computer Needs

<u>We need four terminals</u>, one for each of the travel agents. With four terminals, each agent could be displaying or entering client information at his or her own desk, rather than moving over to use a terminal at another desk, as is now the case.

3

We need a printer and a disk that processes information quickly and can store a large amount of client information (e.g., travel plans, interests, and billing information). The disk should be fast in order to respond quickly to customer inquiries. The printer should be fast and should produce high-quality copy.

We need flexible data management software to handle the storage and retrieval of client data. Without this software, the computer is essentially useless to us. In addition, we need good documentation, good training and user support, and good maintenance service. The system should also be able to add more storage and terminals as the company expands. Finally, and perhaps most important, we need the least expensive system that meets our needs.

I examined three computer systems that might suit all our requirements:

- Big Blue BC AT
- Cherry II-F
- Okifuji 32S.

In evaluating each system, I considered the features that we require in a system and compared each system in the following chart:

Criteria	Big Blue BC AT	Cherry II-F	Okifuji 32S
Cost	$7,240	$5,730	$4,270
Equipment	yes	yes	yes
Documentation	good	good	fair
Training/support	good	good	good
Service	excellent	very good	unknown
Expandability	good	good	fair

(continued)

(CHRIS'S REPORT continued)

4

The Cherry II-F: Our Best Choice

The Cherry II-F is the least expensive of the three models that fulfill our needs. We can purchase it for $5,730, including the data management software. Among its assets, the Cherry II-F provides excellent training and service. This is especially important for us since we will be depending heavily on the computer. Those I talked to told me that Cherry's professionals are available on a 24-hour hotline to answer questions regarding the use of the system. The documentation and manuals I read were adequate for our use. The computer system is also easily expandable: it can double its current capacity to handle our growing business.

In addition to the purchase of the computer, I expect that each of our agents will need to take the Cherry training course. This will cost a total of about $2,000, including the cost of our agents' time. We must also purchase computer paper and printer ribbons. Cost of a year's supply is approximately $375.

How Using the Cherry II-F Will Help Reduce Costs and Improve Customer Service

It costs us significantly more money to use an outside time-share service than it would to use our own Cherry II-F computer system. Purchasing the Cherry II-F would allow us to give our clients much faster service and to store more specific information about each of them.

Chris gives conclusions and recommendation

To reduce costs and to improve customer service, I therefore recommend that we buy the Cherry II-F system and have each of our travel agents attend the Cherry training course.

I look forward to hearing your response to this report.

THE BASICS OF REPORT WRITING 405

Use the accompanying checklist to review your own writing process for problem-solving reports.

CHECKLIST FOR WRITING A PROBLEM-SOLVING REPORT

1. Have you decided on the recommendation you want your reader to go along with?
2. Have you determined who your primary reader is and assessed your reader's
   - Business relationship to you?
   - Knowledge?
   - Attitudes toward you and your message?
   - Expectations about the order and appearance of the report?
3. Do you have the appropriate information?
4. Have you used an analysis tree to organize your ideas and information so that they are accessible and convincing to your reader?

Choosing a Format

Reports should be formatted to highlight the logic of your argument. For example, inaccurate or vague headings and subheadings can obscure meaning. On the other hand, good headings can motivate a reader to read on because they provide guideposts that focus the readers' attention on the report's main points and subpoints.

Many companies require their employees to follow a standard format, or your boss may tell you his or her preferred format. Some companies will allow you to choose how to present your work. Whatever format you use, be sure to design the subject line, headings, and subheadings of your reports with the reader in mind. Consider the following points:

1. *Choose a title that gains your reader's attention.* Your title will appeal to your reader if it addresses his or her needs and values. With his title, "Reducing the Costs and Improving the Management of Our Client Accounts," Chris gained his boss's attention by mentioning two goals he knew she valued—reducing costs and improving service.

2. *Use headings to divide your report into main blocks of thought.* You can help your reader quickly grasp the main ideas of your report if you choose headings that are good generalizations of the material they introduce and if you identify the sequence of your ideas. If you have worked with an analysis tree to draft your report, the main branches of the tree can suggest to you the headings of the report. Chris had three headings in his report: "Why Using a Time-Share Service Results in Poor Customer Service and Excessive Costs," "Why We Should Purchase the Cherry II-F," and

"How Using the Cherry II-F Will Help Reduce Costs and Improve Customer Service." Notice that the first two headings correspond to the main branches of his analysis tree (see p. 399) and summarize the information they introduce. The third heading recapitulates his argument and invites his boss to respond to the report.

3. *Divide the report into sections and subsections and use a heading or subheading to label each.* Your reader will be better able to assimilate a large chunk of information if you divide it into smaller sections. The larger and more complex the report, the more your reader will appreciate subheadings. To divide the central section of his report, Chris used two subsections, introducing each with a subheading:

> *Heading:* "Why We Should Purchase the Cherry II-F"
> *Subheading:* "Our Computer Needs"
> *Subheading:* "The Cherry II-F: Our Best Choice"

4. *Make headings understandable without reference to the body of the report.* Because your reader will most likely skim the headings first to get an overview of the report, headings should make sense detached from the body of the text. Whether or not the reader goes on to the details of the report, he or she will want to discover in the headings and subheadings the report's main ideas.

5. *Use action headings.* Rather than using general headings—such as "Problem Statement," "Analysis," "Conclusion," and "Recommendation," use headings that name the *specific* problem, analysis, conclusion, and recommendation. General headings give the reader some feel for the sections of the report but no sense of its content or the sequence of ideas. Instead of introducing his analysis of Wide World's needs with the heading "Analysis," Chris used an action heading: "Why Using a Time-Share Service Results in Poor Customer Service and Excessive Cost"; it told his reader specifically what he was building a case for.

6. *Make headings consistent.* Making headings consistent in form can help your reader see the logical structure of the report. For instance, all Chris's headings were full statements: "Why Using a Time-Share Service Results in Excessive Costs and Poor Customer Service," "Why We Should Purchase the Cherry II-F," "How Using the Cherry II-F Will Help Reduce Costs and Improve Customer Service." All his subheadings were phrases: "Our Computer Needs" and "The Cherry II-F: Our Best Choice."

7. *Make headings succinct.* As with all business writing, use the fewest words possible for conveying your meaning.

Use the accompanying checklist to review the format of your report.

CHECKLIST FOR REVIEWING REPORT FORMAT

1. Does your title gain your reader's interest?

2. Do your headings divide your report into main ideas?

3. Do your subheadings divide the main ideas into subparts?
4. Are your headings understandable to the reader without reference to the body of the report?
5. Have you used action headings?
6. Are your headings consistent?
7. Are your headings succinct?

Revising

Consultant Joe Aquilo has just been hired by the American Technical School (ATS), an institute that trains technicians to use communications and electronic equipment. ATS wants to know whether to expand its curriculum to include the training of entry-level programmers. Should the company enter this new market or continue to concentrate its efforts exclusively in communications and electronics? Is there a market for training programmers? And if there is a sufficient market for entry-level programers, what specific training should they receive? With these questions in mind, Joe wondered how he would investigate the situation, solve ATS's problem, and report his findings and recommendations to the company within the month.

Since the parts of a report need to work together to make your recommendations clear and convincing, you may discover various weaknesses in your draft. We use the early drafts of consultant Joe Aquilo's report to the ATS to illustrate these weaknesses and to suggest remedies.

FAILURE TO FORMULATE THE QUESTION THE READER WANTS ANSWERED

This failure can result from poor problem solving, poor writing, or a combination of the two.

The difficulty arose in Joe Aquilo's first draft of his report. Because ATS had given him a whole series of questions to research, Joe initially had trouble figuring out exactly what they needed to know. As a result of his confusion, in his first draft he "defined" in three different ways the question his reader wanted answered:

1. ATS has the capacity and administrative structure to open a school for entry-level programmers—but should ATS?
2. Are the government and independent forecasts for increased demand for entry-level programmers in line with expected market needs?
3. How do industries in the Milwaukee area define an entry-level programmer?

The first question oversimplified what he needed to address. Although this question took into account the demand for programmers, it did not consider whether ATS could provide the training, and if so, whether entering this line of business would be profitable. Question 2 was really a research question. To help him determine the need for programmers in the greater Milwaukee area, he had to find out whether government and independent forecasts were accurate. Question 3 really asked him to find out what potential employers in the Milwaukee area meant by the term "entry-level programmer"—something that he needed to do to get on with his investigation but that was not at the heart of the investigation.

Joe saw that different versions of each question ran through his first draft, so when revising the report, he used an analysis tree (see Figure 9.5) to determine the question his reader wanted answered. The real question, he found, was twofold: (1) Is there sufficient demand for entry-level programmers? and (2) Can ATS provide the right kind of training at a profit to the company?

RECOMMENDATIONS THAT DON'T FOLLOW FROM THE QUESTION THE READER WANTS ANSWERED

Occasionally business people present a whole stack of recommendations that are supposed to follow from a two- or three-part question. To help the reader understand recommendations, group and order them as answers to the reader's questions.

To illustrate, let's look at the differences between Joe's original and revised presentation of his recommendations. Recall that Joe had set out to answer a two-part question: (1) Is there sufficient demand for entry-level programmers? and (2) Can ATS provide the right kind of training at a profit to the company?

Figure 9.5

JOE'S ANALYSIS TREE

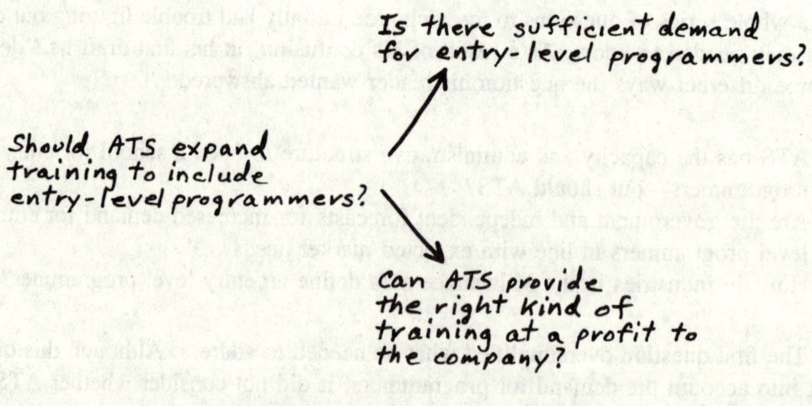

Should ATS expand training to include entry-level programmers?

→ Is there sufficient demand for entry-level programmers?

→ Can ATS provide the right kind of training at a profit to the company?

THE BASICS OF REPORT WRITING

DRAFT

On the basis of my research into the demand within the Milwaukee area, I recommend that ATS <u>not</u> open a programming school at this time. Entering this type of competitive market does not represent a good opportunity for several reasons:

1. ATS has stated that they will not enter the market unless they can enroll at least 100 students and achieve 90 percent placement. This placement percentage seems unachievable under existing market conditions. Since much of ATS's reputation has been built on high placement percentages, its image would suffer if the school could not place graduates.

2. ATS's data on competitive schools show an estimated 18 percent increase in enrollments in 199_. The increase will worsen the current placement problems of already existing schools such as CDI and will make it more difficult for a new six-month school to place graduates.

3. ATS's Arizona Tech curriculum/Prime CPU will not give the company a competitive position in the Milwaukee market. My research indicates that many companies prefer applicants with experience on their equipment, and most companies prefer applicants experienced with their languages. Only IBM equipment and a large emphasis on COBOL, therefore, would give ATS a competitive position.

Notice in the following revision how Joe groups his recommendations under the two-part question his reader wants answered:

REVISION

On the basis of my research into the demand within the Milwaukee area, I recommend that ATS <u>not</u> open a programming school at this time. Entering this type of competitive market does not represent a good opportunity because:

1. There is <u>insufficient demand</u> for entry-level programmers.
   - The demand for entry-level programmer jobs remains constant.
   - Demand for newly trained programmers is on a replacement basis.
   - Only those schools that are not concerned about placement are expanding their enrollments.

2. Even if there were sufficient demand, ATS would be <u>unable to provide the right kind of training at a profit to the company</u>.

ATS's Arizona Tech curriculum/Prime CPU will not give the company a competitive position in the Milwaukee market. My research indicates that many companies prefer applicants with experience on their equipment, and most companies prefer applicants experienced with their languages. Only IBM equipment and a large emphasis on COBOL, therefore, would give ATS a competitive position.

However many recommendations Joe had come up with, he would have had to see how they corresponded as answers to the two parts of his reader's question. He still would have needed two sets of recommendations, each of which might have had several parts.

POORLY ORGANIZED DATA

In a problem-solving report, data should be organized around the reasons that support your recommendations. Too often business people present information in the chronological order in which they did the research, rather than in a logical order that makes the best case for their recommendations.

Joe followed chronological order in the first draft of the section of his report devoted to a discussion of his research. The following paragraphs illustrate his error:

DRAFT

In order to analyze the market, I felt that background research was necessary on the data-processing industry. I wanted to gain insight into the specific entry-level programmer outlook. This background research indicated that widespread growth of the data-processing industry had created unprecedented demand for programming personnel. This growth is a function of increasingly sophisticated equipment, which has created a need for specialized operators. Further, as small businesses have found that data-processing systems are affordable (a function of decreasing hardware costs), the demand for programming personnel has increased even more.

My first method for investigating this problem was a telephone survey of prospective employers of entry-level programmers. Theoretically, this survey was to allow me to collect information from a broad range of potential employers: financial institutions (commercial and savings banks), major insurance companies, medium to large manufacturers (high-technology and industrial companies), hospitals, major retail organizations, and government (local, state, and federal).

A list of company contracts was provided by ATS. The companies represented a population that had had some type of contact with ATS—

THE BASICS OF REPORT WRITING

whether they had hired technical graduates, attended recruiting sessions and career days, hosted industrial tours, or expressed interest in the technical school. From this list, 28 companies were selected for pretesting of my questionnaire.

However, in telephoning to set up appointments I discovered that these companies were not suitable for my study. Some of the contacts provided by ATS were sales offices and used no programmers. Other contacts were satellite offices that did not independently hire programmers. Still others did not use computers. As the sample was not suitable, I extrapolated that the rest of the ATS list was not suitable.

Another information search uncovered a directory of computer executives, the Spring 199_ edition of *The Directory of Top Computer Executives*. It gave an excellent sampling.

Using names provided by *the directory*, I conducted personal interviews before beginning my principal data collection over the telephone. I decided to do so for several reasons. I wanted to gain information that would help me formulate questions for my final questionnaire. I also wanted to gain insights into interviewing and to refine the questions I hoped to incorporate into the final questionnaire. Did the questions follow a logical pattern? Was the questionnaire too long? Were the questions too complex? Did a pattern of likely answers emerge for certain questions? If so, could I design questions with a multiple-choice format for the final questionnaire?

Notice that, in this early draft, Joe discussed his research in the order in which he had done it.

His chronological account reads like a problem solver's trials and tribulations, with its false starts and breakthroughs. But readers of a business report are uninterested in such drama. They want to know how the research supports conclusions and recommendations. In no instance did Joe show in his first draft how the information he gathered supported the recommendation that ATS should not begin a new training program.

In his revision, Joe included the important research he had done but only as it substantiated his recommendation that the company not begin a new program:

REVISION

Both the erratic trends in the computer industry and the responses of computer executives to my questionnaire on entry-level programmers suggest that ATS should not expand its offerings to include training of entry-level programmers:

- *Erratic Trends in the Computer Industry:* Review of several industry publications points to the unpredictable pattern of growth, and a decline in the computer industry over the past three years.
- *Executives' Responses to My Questionnaire on Entry-Level Programmers:* Results of the questionnaire administered to computer industry executives show that the need for entry-level programmers is decreasing. Executives also noted that technical schools in the vicinity provide the new employees that companies seek.

Business people asking for a report want help in making a decision. They do not want to plow through an account of the report writer's painstaking process of investigation. Organize your data around the reasons that support your recommendations.

IRRELEVANT DATA

It is incorrect to assume that including everything you have learned from your research and analysis will strengthen your report. On the contrary, succinct writing is highly valued.

In the section of his first draft (see pp. 410–411), Joe told his reader all about the research he had done even when the research didn't pan out or was redundant. For instance, he used several paragraphs to discuss a telephone survey that was worthless. He also discussed the growth of the data-processing industry. Perhaps his investigation of the industry was the homework he had to do to understand ATS's problem, but his comments about the industry were not relevant to what his reader needed to know.

Doing the survey and gathering information on the industry were obviously important to Joe, but since it was not important to his reader's understanding or acceptance of his recommendations, he had either to eliminate this material or put it in an appendix. (In cases where you need to demonstrate in writing your thought processes and research, as in a report written for a business instructor, relegate the details of your research process to an appendix.) Carefully prune unnecessary facts from your reports by determining what your reader needs to know and excluding everything else.

The accompanying checklist will help you review your draft for errors.

CHECKLIST FOR REVISING A PROBLEM-SOLVING REPORT

1. Have you clearly formulated the question the reader wants answered?
2. Do your recommendations follow from the question the reader wants answered?
3. Are your data presented in support of your recommendations?
4. Have you included only relevant data?

So far we have looked at the challenges in writing a short problem-solving report. But there are several other types of short reports you are likely to be asked to write on the job. These reports are discussed in the next section.

OTHER TYPES OF SHORT REPORTS

Current business practices suggest that you will be writing short reports more frequently than long ones. In fact, an in-depth study of eighty-nine business people who work at varying levels of management in companies of varied size and type revealed that the report they most frequently write is the short report.[1] In addition to the short problem-solving report, at one time or another during your business career you will most likely read and write four other types of short reports: meeting and trip reports, status or progress reports, procedures, and proposals.

Despite the varied purposes of these reports, they have one thing in common: As with the problem-solving report, they should answer a key question (or questions) that their primary readers want answered. In other words, what you choose to say and how you arrange it will depend on what your reader needs to know.

As you read each sample report, consider how the reader's needs shape the report's content and organization. Notice, too, how the format of each report allows the reader to see the answer to his or her question(s) unfold in a sequence that is convincing and clear. Well-constructed subject lines, headings, and subheadings serve as guideposts signaling the major ideas and analysis.

Meeting and Trip Reports

Meeting and trip reports summarize and interpret whatever you have learned from a business trip or meeting that is of interest and importance to your readers. When you go on a business trip or attend a meeting, you are often acting as the eyes and ears of people who need the information you bring back. These are your readers, the people whose questions you need to answer in the report. Let their concerns guide you in determining what to include in the report and in what order.

Although your notes from your meeting or trip will most likely reflect chronological progression (e.g., who spoke first and about what, whom you visited first, what you did first), resist the temptation to pull together the report as a chronological summary of what you observed and participated in. Instead, consider the questions your readers want answered, and group and order the information you have gathered so as to tell readers what they want and need to know.

414 THE RANDOM HOUSE GUIDE TO BUSINESS WRITING

Organizations often require reports from employees on meetings they attend while on business trips.

Figure 9.6 shows a report written by a college junior for an independent study sponsored by her college counseling center. The report was one of several intended to help students learn about job opportunities at businesses within the greater metropolitan area where the college is located. The student spent a day on the job at a corporation's local division. The counseling center asked her to

- Give an overview of the company, focusing on its key products and services
- Identify employees that students can contact for information about job opportunities
- Record her impressions of the firm
- Suggest the kind of student who would be happy working for the firm

Notice that the writer groups and orders information according to these topics and within each topic reports her findings in chronological order.

The next trip report (Figure 9.7) written by business assistant Larry Newman to his superior, B. K. Cross, gives an exploratory overview of the business climate for oil valves in Mexico. B. K., who has over the past several years worked in Mexico for his company, needs timely information on two issues concerning the oil industry: the water well business and petroleum equipment suppliers. Notice how Larry orders his information according to these issues.

Figure 9.6

A STUDENT'S TRIP REPORT

CORPORATION/PRINTING SYSTEMS DIVISION AT DATA
INFODYNAMICS

This report covers four topics of interest to students who may seek employment in the Corporation/Printing Division of Data Infodynamics (DI):   *Introduces report*

1. It presents an overview of the Corporation/Printing System Division.
2. It identifies DI employees who are willing to give students information about employment with the company.
3. It gives my impressions of DI as a work environment.
4. It suggests the kinds of students who would be happy working at DI.

Overview of the Division, Its Major Products and Services   *Uses heading that addresses readers' questions*

The day began with a very comprehensive orientation to the corporation. Jay Reynolds, college recruiter, outlined the functions, products, and organizational structure of Data Infodynamics. He addressed several issues that may be of interest to college seniors:

1. DI does not see itself as solely a copier business. Rather, it defines itself as being in the business of helping other companies to manage their information. A growing aspect of this mission is the improvement of printing capabilities; this is the task of the division located here.   *Numbers essential points*

2. The corporate headquarters are in New Brunswick, New Jersey; DI originated in Cleveland and moved to the New Jersey area ten years ago. Other major U.S. offices are in Houston, Chicago, and Detroit. In our

1

(continued)

(A STUDENT'S TRIP REPORT continued)

2

area, the electronic printing business represents a new major effort. This division views itself as a "rising star" within the corporation.

3. Some stats:

- DI employs a total of 120,000 people (2,200 in the division)
- DI had $78 billion in revenues in 199_

4. The organization

<u>Strengths:</u> Leader in "reprographics"; new products in high-speed printing
<u>Weaknesses:</u> Too early to tell
<u>Opportunities:</u> Rapid expansion in printing—"DI is more than just a copier"
<u>Threats:</u> Japanese electronic industry and smaller U.S. companies

5. The electronic printing business recently came out with several new products. They include a high-speed printer (up to 120 pages/minute) and a somewhat slower (70 pages/minute) but more compact printer. DI just signed a large contract with the U.S. Navy; today, one of its smaller printers is aboard every U.S. ship at sea. The machine can print messages as soon as they are typed at the Pentagon; the information is communicated around the world instantaneously by satellite.

3

<u>Contacts Accessible for
Information and to Job Seekers</u>

Uses heading that addresses readers' questions

College recruiter Jay Reynolds let me know that he regularly schedules on-campus interviews and also invites interested students to call him at his office (555-0084). Other individuals who are accessible for information and to job seekers include:

    Bob Silver Personnel Research (phone: 555-4690)
    Michelle Sanders Manager, Communications for
      Organization Effectiveness (phone: 555-4672)

<u>Impressions of DI as a Work
Environment</u>

Uses heading that addresses readers' questions

My first impressions are that DI is a very large, efficient operation. The high-tech feel is everywhere: secretaries using the latest DI office equipment; very little art on the walls; a stark, cool feel to the environment. The office has the flavor of an engineering firm. The division's location within a rapidly expanding industrial park gives a sense of dynamism and power.

I spent most of my time with people from the Personnel Department. They are energetic, young, and friendly, and spoke enthusiastically of the extensive training seminars offered to all new staff. However, interviews revealed some frustration with "the bureaucracy here." Staff emphasized the importance of learning corporate culture and understanding individual managers' decision-making styles as ways to cope with the bureaucracy.

(continued)

(A STUDENT'S TRIP REPORT continued)

4

<u>Student-Company Fit</u> *Uses heading that addresses readers' questions*

On the basis of the information I gathered and my impressions of the division, I think that a student with both technical and business backgrounds would enjoy working at DI. DI's products are technically sophisticated and the atmosphere of the place is high-tech. As technical as the company is, it is also concerned about the business uses of its products rather than with technology per se.

Students who would like working for a large corporation would also be attracted to DI. Because of its size, the organization offers a range of training programs and opportunities in all areas of management.

Figure 9.7

REPORT ON A TRIP TO MEXICO

DATE: January 24, 199_
TO: B. K. Cross, Vice President
FROM: Larry Newman, Assistant *L.N.*
SUBJECT: Trip to Mexico

The following is a brief overview of last week's trip in terms of the questions you asked about the water well business and petroleum equipment suppliers. I have notes on each conversation and can fill you in with any details you might find interesting or worthwhile.

I spent two days trying to find out about the water well business and petroleum equipment suppliers in Mexico. Any detailed analysis was, of course, impossible in 48 hours, so I tried to get an overview. Acting as your representative, I was able to speak with all the people you had called and sent letters of introduction to on my behalf.

No Readily Accessible Information on the Water Well Business

Answers first question using heading to highlight

Of the two topics, the water well business was the most difficult to tackle. There is no readily accessible list of manufacturers, nor even any information on the number of wells drilled in a given year. If you want to pursue the inquiry, I can give you the names of some people to call and places to do some more hunting.

Petroleum Equipment Suppliers

Answers second question

Thousands of petroleum equipment suppliers who are potential buyers of our products do business in Mexico. We can build our customer base in Mexico in several ways:

1

(continued)

- Review the Registry of Suppliers: The embassy has an old registry of suppliers that I looked through. I photocopied the relevant sections of the registry for you and located the names and telephone numbers of the directors at several of the most prominent petroleum equipment companies.

- Attend the Petroleum Equipment Show: We might consider joining the petrolem equipment show in Mexico City in February, 199_. The total cost of the show would be about $4,000 to the exhibitor and should put us in touch with 2,700 buyers.

- Attend Energetics Committee of the U.S. Chamber of Commerce: Several people strongly urged that our company send senior managers to attend the monthly meetings of the Energetics Committee of the U.S. Chamber of Commerce if we want to make important contacts.

My initial impression is that I am going to need at least three days at the Valve Manufacturers Association to pore over industry statistics. I can draw some conclusions based on the data. If I go back to Mexico for a follow-up visit, I can provide you with more of the information you requested.

Meeting reports summarize and interpret what you have learned from meetings that is interesting and important to your readers.

Progress or Status Reports

Progress or status reports answer your reader's questions about the tasks you have completed during a designated time period. These reports can perform two functions:

1. They may be a routine requirement, built into your job, serving as your superior's periodic check of the work you and the people you supervise have done.
2. They may be linked to a particular long-range project you are doing for your superior, a client, or a customer. In these instances, the report serves as proof of work you have completed according to an agreed-on schedule of tasks.

The progress report in Figure 9.8, written by a subordinate to her superior, is a routine monthly review of work she has accomplished. She covers two issues her boss

Figure 9.8

A ROUTINE PROGRESS REPORT

TO:
Ron Schneider
SUBJECT:
May Activity Report

FROM:
Mary Jones *MJ*
DATE:
May 31, 199_

1. 199_ Staff Projects:

   - Performance Appraisals: Continued monitoring and sent one more round of reminders to the field to maximize the level of policy compliance by May 15.

   - Reorganization: Continued follow-up on department and asset changes.

   - Centralized Billing: Began research on field administrative requirements once the billing was centralized.

2. Administrative Activities

   - Customer Education Billing: Resolved the financial measurement issues for Jim Pepper's group. Jim is to submit data to George Brackden for billing. Revenue will be posted to the proper accounts, and Finance will be splitting out the target to specifically match those actuals.

   - Budgets: Responded to Bob Angler on each of the budget issues raised by the Eastern and Northwestern regions. Provided recommendations on each one. Also resolved remaining reorganization budget transfer.

   - DRO: Resolved the issues between the Eastern Region and TRS on collection activities for TRS clients. The TRS groups will now have its own DRO measurement.

   - Revenue Transfers: Documented current stand on revenue transfers and tried to define issues to Bill Angler.

wanted her to address: staff projects and administrative activities. Notice how she uses headings, numbers, indentation, and underlining throughout to organize information for her reader. (She did not have to define terms and phrases such as DRO, TRS, and "splitting the target to specifically match those actuals" because her reader understands their meaning.)

In Figure 9.9, an inside consulting group reports its progress in introducing sophisticated computer technology and services to a large company. The group's major objective is to demonstrate that it has accomplished its work according to the timetable set in its contract with the company. The report contains four main sections, which constitute the four main activities of the group. The first three sections enumerate areas of activity stipulated in the contract; the fourth concerns supplemental work.

Figure 9.9

A CONSULTING GROUP'S PROGRESS REPORT

DATE: September 5, 199_
TO: Jed Benson, Vice President
FROM: Al Shorter, Manager of Information Systems *AS*
SUBJECT: Work Completed to Date on Introduction of Computer System

WORK COMPLETED TO DATE

We completed the following work activities during the May to August 13 time period in the three areas you stipulated in our contract: conducting interviews, distributing questionnaires, and developing user services. We also completed several tasks outside the scope of the contract.

Groups tasks in three parts designated by company

Interviews

- Prepared interview "script."
- Conducted 82 interview sessions with 172 people.
- Prepared interview notes for all interviews.
- Prepared and tabulated data collection forms that were completed by all interviewers.

Questionnaires

- Prepared and issued follow-up questionnaires for key people not interviewed; there were approximately 6 key people, as determined by the user coordinators, who were not interviewed in our June and July sessions.

1

(continued)

(A CONSULTING GROUP'S PROGRESS
REPORT continued)

<u>User Services</u>

- Developed form to determine service requirements for end users.
- Prepared pilot "Systems User's Manual" to be tested in two subdivisions.

<u>Additional Activities</u>

Some of the tasks that we completed are outside the scope of the initial work program as described in the contract package. Specifically, these tasks include the following:

- Expanded the number of interview meetings and contacts to 172 people in 82 interview meetings.

    —The number and schedule of the interview meetings were controlled by the respective department head for each department; each department was interviewed according to slightly different "ground rules" to accommodate the continuing relationships between individual departments and the Information Systems division.

    —One hundred seventy-two people interviewed amounts to approximately 43 percent of the total head count at Company Staff; this total is about twice the sample size originally intended as outlined in the group orientation sessions.

- Analyzed interview transcripts and put them into a written form that will allow us to monitor the preliminary data results from the end users.

2

Reports on Procedures

Companies routinely need to give instructions to their employees concerning frequently performed operations. These may include company procedures such as evaluating staff, charging expenses, or calculating sick leave and vacation time. If you are assigned to write a report on procedures

- Find out what the purposes of the procedures are, who uses them, and what they should cover.
- Begin your draft of the procedures with an overview and, if necessary, a rationale for the procedures.
- Take the reader through the procedures step by step.
- Once you have a draft, ask several people who will be using the procedures to test them, to ensure that your report is free of gaps or errors. Ask them to perform the task according to your instructions. Observe them as they do so, and find out which points in your report are difficult to follow or confusing.
- Revise the parts of the report that people find difficult or confusing, and continue to test your write-up until people can use it with ease.

To illustrate a report on procedures, let's look at the report Diane Bolger composed on new accounting procedures for the Marketing Department (described at the beginning of Chapter 2). These new procedures resulted from the company's takeover by a larger firm. One group within Marketing, made up of old-timers in the firm, was somewhat resistant to the changes. These people were likely to see the new procedures as symptomatic of a depersonalized, bureaucratic tone that might replace the informal, close-knit atmosphere the group was accustomed to. Other members of Marketing—especially people who came over from the larger firm—were likely to accept the new procedures without question.

Diane's report represents a way to answer the needs of both sets of readers. She didn't need to write a second, persuasive report for the old-timers because she addressed their objections and explained the benefits of the new system to each of them personally before she sent out the report. Diane's report appears in Figure 9.10.

In Figure 9.11, an assistant to the president of a small electronics firm outlines the steps Marketing should take to handle inquiries by potential customers so that the company can build sales from the inquiries.

Figure 9.10

DIANE'S REPORT ON NEW PROCEDURES

DATE: August 22, 199_
TO: All Marketing
FROM: Diane Bolger *DB*
SUBJECT: Filling Out Requisitions/New Chart of Accounts

Since last February our Accounting Department has been reporting to headquarters under the new chart of accounts. This reporting has involved time-costly conversion from our old account numbers to the new ones. — *Puts procedures in context of organizational change*

To save time and money, all departments will begin on September 1 to use this new chart of accounts when filling out requisitions.

Why Using the New Chart of Accounts Is Important

A voucher will no longer be signed before an invoice is paid. For expenses to be properly charged to each department, account numbers must be correct on requisitions to Purchasing. Once you have made a requisition and have been assigned an account number, that account will then be charged with that expense. There will be no opportunity afterward to catch and correct an error. To avoid mistakes, the following procedures will be in effect: — *Stresses importance of procedures*

1. **Filling Out a Requisition** — *Outlines steps*

When you are filling out a requisition

- Make sure that you have used the proper account number.
- Give the number to the support person for your area. It will then be his or her responsibility to

1

2

check and initial the account number and see that it is properly signed off.
- Speak to Sarah, Bob, or me if you have any questions about what account number to use.

2. Handling Purchasing Orders

When you receive a purchasing order

- Sign a copy of the P.O. by Receiving so that they may close out their records and have the invoice paid.
- Mark the blue Marketing copy in our P.O. log closed and date it. This entry will be the only record that a P.O. has been properly closed out.

3. Getting Approval Signatures

When you want approval from Purchasing

- Find out the proper approval signature from your sector head.
- Obtain the signature.

4. Reviewing the Chart of Accounts Procedure

When you want to review the chart of accounts procedure

- Refer to the copy in front of the Purchase Order log.
- Check with me if you still have questions about your account numbers.

Figure 9.11

PROCEDURES FOR HANDLING INQUIRIES

> TO: MARKETING
> FROM: BRUCE WANG *BW*
> DATE: JULY 27, 199_
> SUBJECT: HOW TO HANDLE PEOPLE WHO CALL
> AND WANT MORE INFORMATION
>
> In order to "close the loop" with our reps on the handling and follow-up of telephone literature and demo requests more effectively, we have agreed to establish the following procedures: *Gives reason for procedures*
>
> 1. After you talk to a customer and identify his or her interest and needs, put the information on a Telephone Follow-up form (sample attached).   *Uses numbers to explain procedures step by step*
>
> 2. Give the leads to Paula in Sales. Leave them in a basket under the racing car picture. Paula will divide the leads by Regional Sales groups. The particular Regional Sales manager will then screen the leads to see if any additional call is required that day (either to the appropriate rep or to the customer). Regional Sales managers, please note sales rep at this time, if you can.
>
> 3. Follow up leads about two weeks after the customer has received our literature. (Carolyn will send out literature immediately after she is given the leads by Paula.)
>
> A few general comments:
>
> There are several questions that anyone in Marketing can ask a customer to help determine the urgency of the follow-up for our reps:
>
> 1

2

1. If customers want "just literature" or "price and delivery" info, you can ask if:

   - They are working on a budget proposal
   - They would like a quote sent
   - They are interested in seeing a unit
   - They would like our rep's name and phone number.

2. If callers say they would like a <u>demo</u>, your response should always be that "we can certainly arrange one" for them. Our reps have demos and we can have the rep contact them. Ask them to please leave their name and phone number, and we will take care of it.

3. If callers need <u>technical info</u> or help and you are unable to help them, get their name and other info and assure them that one of our technical people will get back to them <u>within the hour</u>. AND THEN MAKE SURE YOU GIVE THE REQUEST TO SOMEONE WHO WILL CALL THEM BACK.

   It is a good idea to leave your name with callers if you are not sure who will call them back. In this way, if they don't hear from someone and they call back, they can ask for you and at least start with someone who is familiar with the original request. It also tells them you are standing behind the commitment to have their call returned.

Proposals

Proposals are persuasive reports written to sell a product, service, or idea to people within your organization, to the government, or to an outside company. To be effective, a proposal must demonstrate to appropriate decision makers that you can provide a product, service, or idea that meets their needs. Often your proposals will compete with others, so you must show the advantages of what you have to offer over what the competition has to offer.

Proposals are fundamentally selling devices. Therefore, plan to do the following:

BEFORE YOU WRITE

- Learn as much as you can about your potential customers' specific needs and their requirements for content, format, and deadlines.

IN YOUR PROPOSAL

- Use a cover letter to identify what you are selling and to provide readers with the necessary background for understanding and appreciating the worth of what you are selling.
- Make your recommendation(s) and give them a solid rationale (e.g., draw on supporting evidence of past successes, research, testimony of experts).
- Identify costs, scheduling, and the specific results of your recommendation(s).

The cover letter and proposal in Figure 9.12 are written by an advertising executive to Immediate Care Locations, a health care company that is thinking of expanding its home care services to the Seattle area. The goal of the advertising executive's proposal is to sell the health care company on the benefits of using his ad agency's service to test the Seattle market. The cover letter tells the reader about the agency's services and presents arguments for using the services. In the proposal, the executive carefully builds a case for the agency's concept and outlines a plan of action. (Since the ad company does not have any competition in the Seattle area, the executive did not have to address the agency's competitive advantages.)

Figure 9.12

A COVER LETTER AND PROPOSAL

HSR

haniotis, sun, ryan advertising
2211 FAIRMONT AVE., SW SEATTLE, WA 98126

January 4, 199_

Mr. Lawrence Ferguson
Immediate Care Locations
5116 Sheppard Drive
Fort Worth, Texas 76114

Dear Mr. Ferguson:

Your success with the Physicians' Home Care concept in the Dallas/Fort Worth area is well known in the health services industry. We at Haniotis, Sun, and Ryan Advertising would like to assist you in extending your program with equal success to the Seattle area. By using our expertise to market test your concept, you will acquire vital data about the size and demographic characteristics of your target market. This information will help you tailor the concept to suit the unique features of the market here in Seattle.

In our past experience working with over fifty companies, we have found that once a firm is armed with this kind of knowledge, it can realize significant savings in expenses for advertising and operations, avoid investing in unprofitable expansion, and identify a larger market share.   *Draws on past successes*

To conduct a market test that will increase your business, Haniotis, Sun, and Ryan is your best advertising group for two major reasons: *Argues for the worth of the company's services*

(continued)

Figure 9.12

(A COVER LETTER AND PROPOSAL continued)

Mr. Lawrence Ferguson
page 2
January 4, 199_

1. We specialize in advertising medical products and services and have run over twenty successful campaigns for dental groups, chiropractors, medical companies, and doctors in group and private practice.
2. Since our headquarters has been located in Seattle for over ten years, we are a "known quantity" in the business community and have been actively involved in several major local citizens' groups.

To get a better sense of what Haniotis, Sun, and Ryan offers, please review the attached description of our proposed market test plan. I will be calling you during the week of March 2 to answer your questions. If you would like to reach me sooner, please call me at 555-9021 during business hours.

I look forward to talking to you about the prospects for the Physicians' Home Care concept in Seattle.

Sincerely yours,

Charles Haniotis

Charles Haniotis, V.P.
Haniotis, Sun, and Ryan

CH/lb
enc.

1

PROPOSED MARKET TEST PLAN FOR THE PHYSICIANS'
HOME CARE CONCEPT IN SEATTLE

This proposal describes a study designed to assess consumer interest in the Physicians' Home Care concept in Seattle. The study will provide information on consumer reactions to the idea of such a program, which will help in forecasting demand for the service provided by the program.

Announces purpose of proposal

How Your Service Assists Patients

Immediate Care Locations of America has been successfully operating a program called Physicians' Home Care in Dallas. The program has been in operation for about one year. Immediate Care Locations is considering extending this program to Seattle in the summer of 199_. The Physicians' Home Care program makes available to the general public the physician "house call." The program provides a toll-free 800 number over which customers may make an appointment for a physician to visit them at home. The program is designed to appeal to people for whom a trip to a doctor or hospital would be a hardship—for example bedridden elderly people.

Shows knowledge of potential customer's operations

How Our Services Can Increase Your Profits

The method proposed is to call consumers in Dallas and in Seattle, to read a written description of the Physicians' Home Care concept, and to assess reactions to it, including intention to use the service and rating of the service (Dallas only) on a number of relevant attributes. The reactions of the Seattle consumers will be compared to those of the Dallas consumers. The results of the survey will help you capitalize on the current and future demand for your services.

Briefly outlines use of telephone interviews

(continued)

(A COVER LETTER AND PROPOSAL continued)

2

Method

Telephone interviews would be conducted with 150 consumers in Dallas and 150 in Seattle. Telephone interviews (as opposed to shopping mall intercepts) increase the likelihood of reaching the less mobile people this service may appeal to. Respondents would be screened to include only adults between the ages of 18 and 75. A quota of half aged 18–49 and half aged 50–75 would be established in each city, and a maximum quota of 60 percent females would be used. No income criteria would be specified, since one group of possible prospects for the service is retired people with Medicare coverage.

After the screening questions, the respondents would be read a one-paragraph description of the Physicians' Home Care Service. The following paragraph is an example of such a description:

Describes and supports use of telephone interviews

The Physicians' Home Care service lets you make an appointment for a medical doctor to visit you in your home. To use this service, you call their toll-free number and describe your problem. They will make an appointment at a time convenient to you. A doctor will visit you in your home at the agreed-upon time. This service is designed for ill or bedridden people who find it hard to get to a doctor or hospital but are not sick enough to need hospitalization. The basic cost for the service is $40 for a one-half-hour visit. This is about the same as the cost of a one-half-hour appointment at a doctor's office, and about $15 more than a visit at a neighborhood care clinic you go to yourself. Costs of this service may be covered by Medicare or your health insurance.

3

After hearing the concept statement, respondents would be asked their reactions to it. These questions would include:

- Interest in the service
- Likelihood of using the service (and why/why not)
- Use of the service (Dallas only) (and why/why not)
- Likes/dislikes about the concept
- Questions about the service
- Attributes rating (Dallas only)
  - Quality of doctors
  - Reasonableness of cost
  - Speed of response
  - Doctors' personal concern for patients
  - Reliability of service

By comparing the responses in Seattle to those in Dallas, and by then examining the Seattle responses alone, we can make projections about the service's appeal in Seattle. The study will also provide guidance on the aspects of the service that are the most and least attractive to the consumers.

Costs and Timing

The study will cost $4,000. This includes questionnaire design, interviewing, editing, coding, tabulation, and written report. Preliminary results would be available 3 weeks after commencement of interviewing, with a final report 5 weeks after interviewing begins.

Identifies cost and scheduling of output

We are confident that our analysis of the survey results will assist you in determining how best to extend your services in the Seattle area.

SUMMARY

During your business career, you will be writing many kinds of reports. Perhaps the most challenging of these is the problem-solving report, since it requires you to analyze a situation systematically, to pinpoint a central problem, and to come up with a solution before you begin to write. Once your solution is clear, you will then need to focus on how best to present it to your reader. Assessing your reader, gathering appropriate information, organizing your ideas and information in a way that convinces your reader to go along with your recommendation, choosing an effective format, and revising your draft(s) will all contribute to an effective written product.

In addition to the problem-solving report, you may also be asked to write four other types of short reports: meeting and trip reports, status or progress reports, reports on procedures, and proposals. Despite the varied purposes of these reports, they have one thing in common: They should answer a key question (or questions) that their primary readers want answered.

EXERCISES

See "Determining the Question the Reader Wants Answered," pp. 392–393, and "Analyzing the Problem," pp. 393–395, for Exercises 1–5.

1. As part of a graduation requirement, students at a midwestern college work as interns for local businesses. The students help the business solve a problem and put their solutions into a written report submitted to the business. One group of students who are avid sports fans were lucky enough to get a minor league baseball team to take them on as consultants. The students were asked to consider how the team could begin realizing profits. After several weeks of investigation, here is the students' attempt at a problem definition:

> This project presents some very interesting issues and situations that are inherent only to a minor league baseball team. In the past, the existence of a minor league team did not depend on the team's profit and loss statement. This is not true today.
>
> Many minor league teams were formerly owned by wealthy individuals who viewed the team as a hobby. This hobby took advantage of special federal legislation that allowed it to exist and behave unlike any other business. The special tax considerations given to the team and its owners were a major impetus for the existence of the team.
>
> Success for a team is measured by its win-loss record. Some owners believe that a successful team can bring social benefits to a city—such as pride, enthusiasm, and self-respect. For example, the football success of the major league Pittsburgh Steelers during the 1970s added a tremendous amount of self-respect to the city during a depressed period in the steel industry. In the future, minor league teams should be able to contribute as much to the smaller towns that sponsor them.

THE BASICS OF REPORT WRITING

Historically, the minor league we're consulting for was not profit-motivated, since the existence of the team did not depend on the bottom line. However, this train of thought is now changing. The team is now committed to having a successful year both on the playing field and on the income statement. The team wants to increase subscriptions and sell games to local TV and radio.

Teams can derive a tremendous amount of revenue from local broadcasting. We have evaluated the team's practices in handling broadcasting opportunities.

The students are to submit this statement to their adviser. Assume that they have asked you to review and critique their attempt at a problem definition. Write them a memo responding to their request.

2. While finishing up his last few courses as a business major, Ron Lasko was hired by the Lotus Flower Company, a chain of restaurants serving sushi and other Oriental dishes, to help the company develop its business. The company has requested him to put his recommendations and supporting research in a final report. Here is a section of that report, in which Ron thinks he has identified the question the company wants answered:

The Lotus Flower Company is a chain of fast-food restaurants serving sushi and other dishes. The combination of sushi and Oriental hot food was originally designed to get constant sales over the year; sushi sales peak during the summer, whereas hot foods are winter items.

Over the past eight months, the Lotus Flower Company has expanded very rapidly after three years of slow growth. Plans for the next two years entail even more rapid growth in the number of fast-food outlets. This intense rate of growth has put considerable strain on the Lotus Flower organization and its limited managerial staff.

Before rapid growth, everyone from the supervisor of the outlets to the waiters went through an intensive training program to prepare them for their jobs. Now only on-the-job training is available. In the past eight months, new supervisors have been brought in from the outside, whereas previously they were promoted from within. These new supervisors appear to be resented as newcomers by the lower ranks of employees, many of whom have been with the company for years. Turnover in these ranks has increased appreciably (30 percent) over the past eight months.

My assignment is to provide management with recommendations on how best to meet the challenges the company will face in the next few years.

What weaknesses do you see in Ron's definition of the problem?

3. One good way to begin analyzing a business problem is to use concepts you have learned in business courses to investigate it. What concepts can help you investigate the following business problems?

- By how much would word processing speed up the production of company brochures used to recruit entry-level managers?
- How can we ensure enough cash will be on hand to pay suppliers when our bills fall due?
- When should we introduce our new line of cosmetics?
- Why are the official procedures for hiring new sales people ignored?
- What's causing excessive absenteeism in Production?
- Why are the goals of particular units within the company at odds with company-wide goals?
- What impact will changes in computer technology have on the development of new products?
- We're planning to buy a personal computer for all vice presidents so that they can have greater access to information. What's the best personal computer we can buy that's within our budget?
- Will changing our accounting procedures make us appear more profitable this year?
- Why are end-of-year sales reflected in some but not all auditing reports?
- How do we assess the new lines of authority established by the company's recent reorganization?
- Why is turnover high among entry-level engineers?
- Should the new automated equipment be equally distributed among the factories?

4. A secondhand bookstore located in Santa Monica, California, hired four business majors in their senior year to help decide whether to open a second store in Hermosa Beach, a city located fifteen miles to the south of Santa Monica. The store, which specializes in technical publications, has tentatively proposed a site on the main street of Hermosa Beach's central district.

Review the data that the students have collected (see Figure 9.13), and put together an analysis tree that identifies the questions the store wants answered, breaks down the question into subquestions, and when possible, answers these questions.

5. On graduating from college, six members of a student business club for young entrepreneurs considered opening a disco in Guntersville, a resort town on a lake in Northern Alabama about fifteen miles from their campus. Two members were assigned to investigate the site they were thinking about leasing. Review the data they collected (see Figure 9.14), and construct an analysis tree showing the question and subquestions the students want to answer; when possible, give answers to these questions.

Figure 9.13

DATA ON THE PROPOSED BOOKSTORE SITE

DATA ON PROPOSED BOOKSTORE SITE

- Hermosa Beach — high density (1.3 square miles, pop. 18,000+)
- Target market for bookstore — 18 to 64 year olds
- Hermosa Beach — no secondhand bookstore
- Proposed site — considerable pedestrian traffic (approx. 30 people/hr.)
- Hermosa pop. — 80% in 18 to 64 range
- People walk past proposed site on their way to the beach
- All stores on block of proposed site close by 6 p.m.
- Hermosa residents — average education level 12.9 years
- Businesses on block of proposed site — 3 clothing stores, 4 restaurants, 1 hardware store
- City plans — validated parking for city lots near proposed site
- Median family income — high, approx. $35,000
- Jobs of many residents — aerospace industry
- Parking a problem in central business district
    - limited street parking
    - parking garages expensive

Figure 9.14

DATA ON THE PROPOSED SITE FOR A DISCO

> DATA ON PROPOSED SITE FOR DISCO
>
> — Seasonal business in area (heavy in summer, very light otherwise)
> — Metered parking near site and on adjacent streets
> — Market for disco ages 16 to 24
> — In summer nonresidents visit lake mostly during the day
> — No business of this kind exists in this resort or in the region
> — Patrons would need to compete for parking spaces with customers visiting better-quality restaurants and 3 popular bars in area
> — Average age of Guntersville residents is 32.
> — Need to attract patrons from other communities in surrounding areas → big start-up advertising costs
> — Police strictly enforce parking regulations
> — No public transportation to area; access only by car
> — Site formerly used as a theater, which was destroyed twice by vandals after punk rock concerts
> — Neighboring businesses and residents fear influx of "bad elements" causing riots and property damage
>   — may try to prevent licensing of new entertainment place on the site

See "Organizing," pp. 399–400 for Exercises 6 and 7.

6. You are an entry-level manager at Heavenly Donuts. Your boss is responsible for deciding whether or not to close a store opened in Wichita, Kansas. He has asked you to visit the Wichita store and let him know what you think he should do.

For the store to remain open, it has to regain $500 a week in sales within two months and then increase sales to $3,000 a week within six months. With $3,000 a week sales volume, the store would have an annual profit of $50,952.

From reviewing the store's records, you have learned that the store opened in 1977 with sales of $3,800. About three years ago, sales began to decline. Current volume is $1,500. According to your sources, the store is well run, although it is difficult to supervise, being located one and a half hours from the nearest branch headquarters.

Over the last three years, the economy of the area has declined. The greatest source of employment, a meat-packing facility, has permanently closed, and unemployment is running about 11 percent.

Two other donut stores operate in the area, both operated by Pete's Donuts. One is about two miles from Heavenly Donuts and has been there longer than Heavenly Donuts. The second is about 50 steps from Heavenly Donuts and was opened two or three months ago. Sales of Heavenly Donuts dropped $500 per week since the opening of the second store.

The pricing of Pete's Donuts is lower than Heavenly Donuts. For instance, a dozen donuts runs $1.94 there and $3.00 at Heavenly Donuts. However, Pete's Donuts sells only plain donuts whereas Heavenly Donuts sells a large variety as well as brownies.

Heavenly Donuts might consider switching to plain donuts, lowering its prices, and starting a price war with Pete's Donuts. But past experience makes price wars questionable. Or Heavenly Donuts could keep its donut variety and launch an advertising campaign like ones it has successfully held in several other cities. The objective of the campaign would be to gain new customers and to win customers from Pete's Donuts.

Write an analysis tree showing your recommendation and how you would structure your argument for your reader.

7. As a marketing researcher for Florida Sparkling, a regional soft drink and bottled water company, you have been asked by your boss to find out whether consumers in the lower middle income bracket who live in the eastern part of the major city where you sell represent an important enough potential source of sales volume in the bottled water market to justify the company's expanding into this area. If the answer is yes, he wants to know how to price the item. Florida Sparkling currently sells bottled water at 67 cents a gallon. The company can afford to sell as low as 65 cents a gallon for an initial promotional period of two months (with sales volume of 5,000 bottles a week) in addition to covering the expenses for a modest advertising campaign.

Figure 9.15 shows some of the findings you have gathered from checking the bottled water section of six supermarkets located in areas with a large concentration of lower-middle income families. You entered this information in your computer.

Write an analysis tree showing your recommendation and how you would structure your argument for the reader.

Figure 9.15

FINDINGS AND PRELIMINARY ANALYSIS

Supermarkets in these areas devoted considerable space to bottled water. Most stores had at least 127 units on their shelves.

No brand appeared dominant in the market. Sweet and Pure was in only five of the six stores, while H_2O Perfect was in only four. The bottled water market may be vulnerable to a new entry.

In the total store sample, Sweet and Pure and H_2O Perfect had almost even shares of facings;* however, Sweet and Pure sales were stronger in three stores and H_2O Perfect in two. Since we have excellent distribution contacts in four of the stores for our soft drink and these supermarket contacts also handle bottled water, we can expect some advantages in facings at four stores. The one-gallon container predominated, with a total facings share of 74.3 percent.

The most frequent price of the two major brands (Sweet and Pure and H_2O Perfect) for the one-gallon bottle was 73 cents. Sweet and Pure ranged from 68 to 75 cents per gallon, while H_2O Perfect ranged from 73 to 75 cents per gallon. Minor brands ranged from 47 to 65 cents per gallon, while vending machine water went for 35 cents per gallon. At 67 cents a gallon, our price is slightly higher than the minor brands and lower than the two national brands. We have name-brand recognition with those consumers as an excellent local soft drink and water manufacturer.

In five stores the bottled water section was next to the soft drink section. One store shelved bottled water above the frozen food section. Vending machines for purified water were found outside all six stores visited.

*Facings are the number of bottles that face the aisle. For instance, five facings means that five bottles are displayed (with a depth of several bottles behind). Manufacturers bargain for facings when selling to stores because the number of facings relates to how well the product sells.

THE BASICS OF REPORT WRITING

See *"Recommendations That Don't Follow from the Question the Reader Wants Answered,"* pp. 408–410, for Exercise 8.

8. Linda Barton, a real estate analyst and manager, asked you to review the first and last sections of a report she wants to submit to her employer, Northern Services, Inc. (NSI). NSI is a company with diverse holdings in the Northeast. These include undeveloped land, restaurants, and apartment buildings. The company has sent Linda to Ohio and Indiana to investigate how it should go about investing in real estate in these states. Here is the draft of the introductory section of the report she wants you to review:

DRAFT

The assignment you gave me had several parts:

- Locate the most attractive properties as determined by investment criteria
- Identify the best deals
- Recommend purchase of one or more properties
- Assist in negotiating and closing the deals

In the body of the report, Linda identified criteria that she thought the company should use in determining whether to buy a property. These included location, size, amount of down payment, and ratio of purchase price to gross revenues. She concluded the report in this way:

Here are my conclusions based on my assignment. Although some of the following deals don't meet our investment criteria, I include them as a sample of my work:

- Happy Hunting Lodge: Does not meet our investment criteria.
- Meadowland Motel: Meets investor criteria but difficult to negotiate.
- The Midwest's Best: Meets investor criteria and can be negotiated. It is our best possibility.

What advice would you give her to improve the opening and final sections of her report?

See *"Poorly Organized Data,"* pp. 410–412, and *"Irrelevant Data,"* pp. 412–413, for Exercise 9.

9. A group of four business majors found summer employment doing a study for Health and Education Cinematique (H&E), a small film production and distribution company that specializes in the sale and rental of health care films and children's educational films. H&E's primary customers are schools, universities, hospitals, and health care organizations.

Since H&E's primary customers—educational and health institutions—were decreasing their purchase and rental of the company's films, the company president, Frank Cordner, wanted to know whether the firm should expand into the home video market.

Here are two paragraphs from the students' final report to Frank. According to the students, this passage demonstrates that the data they collected and analyzed substantiate their recommendation that H&E should *not* enter the home video market.

> Our team first consulted industry publications and general business research sources to get an overview of the home video market for health and educational films. From these sources we learned about films currently sold in the home video market; producers and suppliers of films most like those sold by H&E; wholesale, retail, and rental prices; sales volume of films similar to those handled by H&E; and frequency and length of rentals of these films. We didn't draw any conclusions from these sources about whether H&E should enter the home video market until we did some research of our own.
>
> So we then did two limited surveys, one surveying your competitors, local area distributors of health and educational films, and the other surveying your current and potential customers. As you might guess, the first survey proved unsuccessful. Your competitors were by and large unwilling to respond to our questionnaire. However, results of the customer survey indicate that the market is limited for health and educational films among home video owners. Only 20 percent of the owners polled said they would rent such films, no more than 5 percent said they would purchase them. Therefore, we recommend that H&E should not enter the home video market.

Does this passage support the team's recommendation that H&E should not enter the home video market? What changes would you suggest to the team for improving these paragraphs?

See "Meeting and Trip Reports," pp. 413–420, for Exercise 10.

10. Comment on the report in Figure 9.16, written by a student intern to his instructor and classmates following his first day on the job. The report is supposed to summarize what he learned about the work he will be doing as an intern.

Figure 9.16

STUDENT INTERN'S REPORT

1

My internship is under the overall direction of Ms. Peggy Withers, director of human resources for Action Cable (AC). Ms. Withers reports to the director of personnel and is responsible for ongoing training and staff development. She has been with AC for less than two years. Formerly she was dean of students for student affairs at Mississippi State University. She was an undergraduate at Denison College in Ohio and has a graduate degree in counseling from the University of Michigan. She is exceptionally articulate, personable, and conscientious. I had the impression that her areas of responsibility were still in the process of being established with AC.

Ms. Withers has set up my internship in two parts, both of which will involve project development in specific areas. The first consists of my developing a questionnaire for a market survey to gather data on programs that people would like to see offered on cable TV. This project will be under the direction of Ms. Ruiz, whose undergraduate studies were at Princeton (Urban Studies, '85) and who now serves as director of corporate development for AC. She reports to Mr. Steven Cooperman, senior vice president. She came to AC two years ago after working in the mayor's office in Indianapolis, where she was part of the city's team of negotiators with the cable TV industry as it was being established and expanded in the city. Her primary area of concern at this time is with the establishment of communication between the corporate office in Indianapolis and the myriad small, recently acquired cable TV franchises across the country. But she is also involved in overseeing the expansion of market research. As part of her effort to enhance communication and establish standards, she has me working on the draft of a newsletter that will discuss current legislative issues facing the industry from the corporation's point of view.

The second part of my internship will be with the Marketing Department. I have not yet met the staff I will be working with, but I have been informed that Marketing wants me to do a comparative study of our program offerings over the past six months and those of our two major competitors. Marketing is very interested in learning which programs received the highest ratings within particular age brackets and geographical areas.

(continued)

(STUDENT INTERN'S REPORT continued)

> 2
>
> I went to lunch with Mr. Lloyd Dempsey, director of community relations for AC. About two years ago, he came to the corporation from the phone company where he had been a manager in the Accounting Department. He has an MBA from Harvard along with a Harvard BA in Government ('84). His responsibilities include extensive travel to represent AC in franchise negotiations with local municipal governments. He has a wealth of experience in actual field operations that others at corporate headquarters lack. His sophisticated knowledge of the cable TV industry as a whole reflects his educational background.
>
> My first impressions have been positive. The cable TV industry is growing, as is AC. The company's optimism and enthusiasm reflect its expansion.

See "Progress or Status Reports," pp. 421–424, for Exercise 11.

11. Figure 9.17 is a quarterly report written by the affirmative action director of the Personnel Department at a major corporation. The report concerns the company's compliance with the federal Equal Employment Office (EEO) and affirmative action regulations. The purpose of the report is to tell management how well the company is complying with the federal regulations, and to make recommendations for improving the company's affirmative action record.

The first section gives an overview of all employee groups that have been monitored for compliance with affirmative action. The second section shows the distribution of these groups according to job designations as defined by the EEO. In each of the next two sections, "Minorities" and "Women," these groups are considered by overall employment trends, employment according to EEO categories, goals that the company has achieved, and goals it must achieve in order to comply with federal regulations. The concluding section summarizes the major findings: the company had made "positive gains in employment of minorities" but is "falling behind in the employment of women," several of whom must be hired in categories designated by the EEO.

After reading the report, discuss how it could be improved.

Figure 9.17

A STATUS REPORT

EEO AND AFFIRMATIVE ACTION
STATUS REPORT
QUARTER ENDED SEPTEMBER 30, 199_

AFFIRMATIVE ACTION MONITORING

Employment Data

The group that was monitored includes employees in all corporate departments and all divisions, with the exception of non-L.A.-based diversified operations employees, non-L.A.-based employees, and the chemical companies. Employment decreased by 2.2% from April 1, 199_, compared to an increase of 2.9% during the same period last year. Only the technicians category showed an increase. The largest decreases were in the service workers (32.3%), laborers, (7.6%), and operatives (7.4%) categories.

Work Force Distribution

Professional and office and clerical employees are the largest groups in our work force. The following table shows the overall distribution of employees by EEO category:

EEO Category	Percentage
1 Officials & Managers	16.5
2 Professionals	21.6
3 Technicians	6.8
4 Sales Workers	.9
5 Office & Clerical	17.9
6 Craft Workers	17.3
7 Operatives	14.2
8 Laborers	4.6
9 Service Workers	.2

Minorities

Minority employment increased 2% between April 1, 199_ and September 30, 199_, despite the overall decrease in employment.

1

(continued)

A STATUS REPORT (continued)

2

Minority employment increased in all job categories except sales workers, operatives, craft workers and service workers.

Minority representation (i.e., the percentage of minorities in the work force) increased by 4.6% to 13.7%. Minorities represent 15.3% of all blue-collar employees (EEO Categories 6–9), 23.4% of all white-collar clerical employees (EEO Category 5), and 8.4% of all white-collar nonclerical employees (EEO Categories 1–4).

Midway through the AAP year, goals have been achieved for technicians, craft workers, operatives, and service workers. To meet projected goals for minorities in the remaining categories, the following additional employees should be hired or promoted: 2 officials and managers, 7 professionals, 3 office and clerical, and 7 laborers, a total of 19 minorities, a decrease of 6, or 24%, from the last quarter.

Women

Female employment increased .06% between April 1, 199_ and September 30, 199_, despite the overall decrease in employment. Female employment increased in all job categories except professionals, office and clerical, and laborers.

Female representation (i.e., the percentage of females in the work force) increased by 2.2% to 23.4%. Females represent 4.1% of all blue-collar employees (EEO Categories 6–9), 83.5% of all white-collar employees (EEO Categories 5), and 15.2% of all white-collar nonclerical employees (EEO Categories 1–4).

Midway through the AAP year, goals have been achieved for technicians, sales workers, office and clerical, laborers, and service workers. To meet projected goals for women in the remaining categories, the following additional employees should be hired or promoted: 4 officials and managers, 21 professionals, 11 craft workers, and 3 operatives, a total of 39 women, an increase of 2, or 5.4%, from the last quarter.

CONCLUSIONS

At the halfway point of the AAP year, we appear to be making positive gains in the employment of minorities. However, it does appear that we are falling behind in the employment of women. For the quarter ended June 30, 199_, we needed 17 female professionals and 11 female craft workers. We will monitor this during the next quarter.

See "Reports on Procedures," pp. 425–429, for Exercise 12.

12. Write a report on the procedures for handling one of the following situations:

- Registering for classes
- Applying for an interlibrary loan
- Using computer search services in the library
- Petitioning for taking more than the normal course load

See "Proposals," pp. 430–435, for Exercise 13.

13. Write a proposal to the appropriate decision-making group on your campus for changing one of the following:

- Recent increases in tuition
- One or more aspects of the admissions policy
- The allocation of funds for a student organization (choose one you belong to)

10 THE FORMAL REPORT: GOAL, READER, IDEAS, AND INFORMATION

PREVIEW

This chapter should help you to

1. Set the goal of a formal report
2. Assess the readers of the report
3. Make a schedule to complete the report
4. Gather information and generate ideas for the report by
   - Consulting library sources
   - Making observations
   - Conducting experiments
   - Conducting surveys
   - Designing and administering questionnaires
   - Conducting interviews

As Mark White, a senior majoring in business, read the syllabus for his course in organizational behavior, his eye immediately caught the one starred item, a ten- to twenty-page research report due on the last day of class and worth 50 percent of the grade. Instructions for the report indicated that he was free to choose any topic in organizational behavior, as long as it concerned something that would interest graduating students who plan to go into business. He also had to use research methods he would learn during the term. "This is going to be a tough assignment," he thought to himself. "I don't have any idea what I can write about."

Like Mark, you may be asked to write a formal research report for a class or on the job. In college, writing a formal report gives you the opportunity to pull together the major concepts taught in a course and to apply them to a specific topic you investigate. On the job, formal reports provide information and recommendations to managers and help them make decisions. Major studies in any area of business often appear as formal reports.

Some formal reports require work on the part of many researchers and writers and can result in massive documents running hundreds of pages. These reports are costly in time and staffing but can contribute significantly to a company's productivity.

Although most formal reports do not run hundreds of pages, they can involve extensive research and large time commitments by several people. Since you may be asked to write all or part of a formal report at some point in college or in your career, mastering the basics of the formal report is important.

As with other writing tasks, you can plan the formal report using the activities of the writing process you are already familiar with, from setting the goal to revising and editing. And since writing the formal report has much in common with writing the short report, you can apply what you learned in Chapter 9. Like the short report, the formal report must answer a key question your primary reader wants answered. The report must also include relevant supporting information organized so as to be understandable and convincing to the reader.

In addition to drawing on what you already know about writing, several other important writing activities are particularly relevant to the formal report: making a schedule to manage your time and carry out the subtasks necessary to complete the report, using a variety of research techniques, designing a format for the formal report, and writing in groups.

The formal report is discussed in two chapters. In this chapter, we consider the early stages of report writing:

- Setting the goal
- Assessing the reader
- Making a schedule
- Gathering information and generating ideas

In this chapter we also introduce time management and research techniques. In Chapter 11, we consider the later stages of the writing process:

THE FORMAL REPORT: GOAL, READER, IDEAS, AND INFORMATION

- Organizing ideas and information
- Writing a draft
- Revising

In Chapter 11, we also discuss the use of formats and group writing.

SETTING THE GOAL AND ASSESSING THE READER

In business, your superiors typically will ask for the report and will tell you its purposes. In college, your instructor may provide you with a list of topics or may allow you to choose your own topic.

Whether your report is for work or for school, you must define your subject according to your primary reader's needs. Once you have determined the question your primary reader wants answered, write a goal statement, a statement that clarifies what your report is to accomplish with this reader. By doing so, you can focus your research activities.

Before Mark could write his goal statement for the formal report required in his organizational behavior course, he needed to find a topic that would interest his classmates and would be narrow enough that he could do the research and write the report in a few months. Since he knew that doing research would take a long time, he decided to get an early start on the project by budgeting the first two weeks of the term for exploring possible topics.

Given the requirement that his report must interest graduating students planning to enter business, Mark found that his friends and roommates who intended to pursue careers in business provided him with his best leads. He learned that, like himself, most students were concerned about getting a good job after graduation, so any aspect of the job search interested them: writing resumes, choosing the best industries and organizations given students' career goals and abilities, making contacts with companies, interviewing. He chose to investigate interviewing. From a discussion with the head of career counseling at school, he found out that his subject was much too large. After further thought and some preliminary library research, he tentatively narrowed his topic to the on-campus recruitment interview. He was then ready to formulate his goal statement: "I want to tell students the important characteristics recruiters look for in job candidates."

Assessing readers was easy for Mark. His classmates would be looking for the kind of information he himself would find useful about recruiters' criteria for evaluating job candidates. His instructor, another primary reader, would also want to see whether Mark could apply in his study the research methods he had learned in class.

When you assess readers for a formal report, your task may be less easy than Mark's. For instance, you may have some difficulty assessing your readers' knowledge of your subject or their attitude toward your findings. But since the formal report resembles the short report in this respect, you can use the same set of questions about readers for both reports (see Checklist for Assessing Readers of Reports on p. 398).

MAKING A SCHEDULE

A schedule is useful for completing any writing assignment. But for the formal report a schedule is critical because you need to manage a variety of activities, some of which can take weeks or even months to complete. For this reason, we recommend that you make a schedule to complete your report.

If, as in Mark's case, you must first find a topic, set aside time for exploratory research. Since it can take several weeks or months to write a formal report, limit the time you spend on this stage. Mark set aside two weeks to do exploratory research. In this period, he discussed with senior business students topics of interest to them and interviewed the director of career counseling (one hour for preparation, one hour for interview, one hour for review of notes). During the same period, he did some preliminary library research (one week), such as reviewing handbooks that offered general information on campus interviewing.

Mark's exploratory research helped him find a subject and narrow his focus. Once he had determined the purpose of his report—"to tell students the important characteristics recruiters look for in job candidates"—he could put together the rest of his schedule. It consisted of tasks and subtasks needed to complete his report, their sequence, and the time each would take:

- Do further library research (one week)
- Design questionnaire on recruiters' and students' perceptions of the job interview (two weeks)
- Identify sample of business students and recruiters (two weeks)
- Test and revise questionnaire (1 week)
- Mail questionnaire to sample (two weeks turnaround time)
- Interview five students and five recruiters (five days)
- Analyze data (one week)
- Outline report and write a draft (two weeks)
- Revise (one week)
- Type, prepare preliminaries, and proofread (one week)

After putting together this schedule, Mark turned it into a **time line,** a visual aid to help him picture the various tasks as he moved through them. He taped the schedule shown in Figure 10.1 over his desk to serve as a reminder during the term.

Notice that Mark's schedule suggests several important time management principles involved in making a schedule:

1. *List all the tasks you need to do*. Although you may have to add to the list as a project develops, by listing at the beginning of your work all the activities needed to complete the report, at least you will know early in the project what you have to do.

2. *Break down complex tasks into smaller, manageable units*. After you have listed the tasks you need to do to complete the report, see which ones need to be broken

THE FORMAL REPORT: GOAL, READER, IDEAS, AND INFORMATION

Figure 10.1

TIME LINE OF MARK'S SCHEDULE

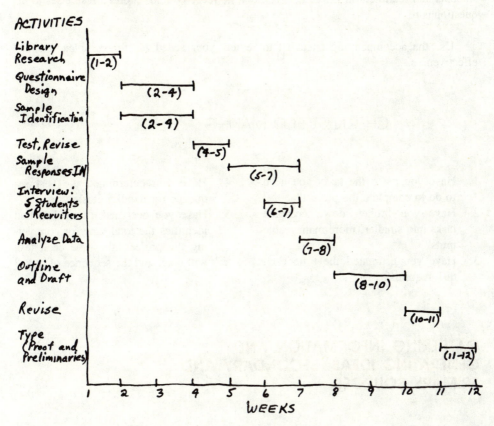

down. Mark broke down a complex task, his questionnaire, into several subtasks: designing, identifying a sample, testing and revising, and mailing.

3. *Assign an approximate time to each task.* List approximate times for completing each of your tasks, keeping in mind the extra time you may need for tasks that depend on the schedules of other people. Mark gave each task a time limit. Since several tasks—such as interviews and questionnaires—required coordination with other people, he budgeted time for contacting them and for awaiting their responses.

4. *Determine the best sequence for handling tasks.* Figure out the best order for completing your tasks. Remember that some tasks must be done before others. On the other hand, a number of tasks may be handled during the same time period.

Mark's time line shows the order in which he needed to complete tasks. The order was especially important because earlier activities could determine later ones. For instance, if, through library research, Mark had found a study done on his subject, he would not have had to design and administer a questionnaire.

Mark also scheduled some tasks during the same time period because the results of one set of activities did not depend on the results of others. For instance, he interviewed students and recruiters in the same week that he received and recorded responses to his questionnaire.

Use the accompanying checklist to review your schedules for completeness and effectiveness.

CHECKLIST FOR MAKING A SCHEDULE

1. Have you listed the tasks you need to do to complete the project?
2. Have you broken down complex tasks into smaller, more manageable units?
3. Have you estimated the time each task requires?
4. Have you determined the best sequence for handling tasks?
5. Have you designed a time line that identifies the total time for completing the project, the time each task will take, and the sequence of tasks?

GATHERING INFORMATION AND GENERATING IDEAS: SECONDARY AND PRIMARY SOURCES

Understanding your goal and your reader's needs should help you determine the scope of your report and allow you to get your research under way. Report writers have two sources of information available to them: secondary and primary sources. The term **secondary sources** refers to any information that has been gathered by another researcher. It includes books, articles, company reports, brochures, manuals, and dissertations. **Primary sources** refers to any information that you yourself gather firsthand. Such information includes what you learn from personal observation, experiments, questionnaires, and interviews.

The library is a good place to begin your research. Sometimes the problem you are trying to solve, or a similar one, has already been solved, and the solution is reported in a published study. A few hours spent doing library research, then, can save you weeks or even months in duplicating work that has already been done. At other times, you will find either that no one has studied the problem or that the previous work on the problem has been insufficient for your purposes, so you will want to conduct primary research.

THE FORMAL REPORT: GOAL, READER, IDEAS, AND INFORMATION

Ten Types of References to Consult

The library contains several kinds of secondary sources that you may wish to consult in gathering information for your report. Acquaint yourself with the ten types we identify here:

ENCYCLOPEDIAS

Since articles in encyclopedias give a quick overview of your subject and frequently include a short bibliography, they are sometimes a good place to begin your research.
Among the general encyclopedias that can can help you gather information are:

- *Encyclopedia Americana*
- *Encyclopaedia Britannica*

Among specialized encyclopedias are:

- *The Accountant's Encyclopedia*
- *The Encyclopedia of Banking and Finance*
- *The International Encyclopedia of the Social Sciences*

DICTIONARIES

Dictionaries that give definitions of specialized terms used in business disciplines include:

- *Concise Desk Book of Business Finance*
- *Dictionary for Accountants*
- *Dictionary of Data Processing*
- *Dictionary of Economics*
- *Thomson's Dictionary of Banking*

HANDBOOKS

Like encyclopedias, handbooks offer a quick overview of a subject and often include articles (with bibliographies) written by experts in the field. Business researchers may consult some of the following handbooks:

- *Accountants' Handbook*
- *Business Executive's Handbook*
- *Credit Management Handbook*

- *Financial Handbook*
- *Handbook of Auditing Methods*
- *Handbook of Business Administration*
- *Handbook of Industrial and Organizational Psychology*
- *Handbook of Insurance*
- *Handbook of International Organizations in the Americas*
- *Handbook of Modern Manufacturing Management*
- *Handbook of Modern Personnel Administration*
- *Handbook of Work and Industrial Psychology*
- *Industrial Accountant's Handbook*
- *Management Handbook*
- *Marketing Handbook*
- *Personnel Handbook*
- *Production Handbook*
- *Purchasing Handbook*
- *The Real Estate Handbook*

YEARBOOKS AND ALMANACS

Yearbooks and almanacs give a range of information on issues and events during a single year. For business purposes, they include:

- *Commodity Yearbook*
- *The Dow-Jones Mutual Fund Yearbook*
- *The Insurance Almanac*
- *The Stock Exchange Official Year-Book*
- *World Almanac and Book of Facts*
- *Yearbook of National Accounts Statistics*

BOOKS

Libraries use a traditional card catalog or, more recently, computer and microfiche catalogs. To locate a book in the library, check the card catalog for the stack number, then go to the stacks, or if your library's stacks are closed, write a call slip so that the librarian can retrieve the book for you. You will find books listed in your library's card catalogs in three ways: by author, by title, and by subject.

If you have picked up a reference from reading an encyclopedia, a magazine, or other source, you have the name of the author and the title of the work, so you can find the catalog card by either author or title.

For the author listing, look in the author section of the card catalog under the author's last name. On an **author card,** the author's name appears first followed by the title (see Figure 10.2). To find a title card, look in the title section of the card catalog under the first word of the title, omitting such words as "the," "a," and the like. The **title card** contains the same information as the author card, but with a few changes in

THE FORMAL REPORT: GOAL, READER, IDEAS, AND INFORMATION

References can be located by looking through a card catalog or, in some libraries, by checking a computer screen.

Figure 10.2

SAMPLE AUTHOR CARD

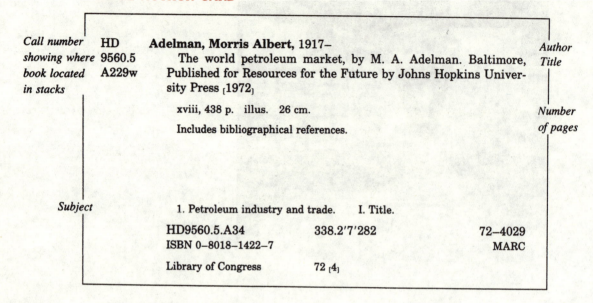

the order of presentation (see Figure 10.3). The title appears on the top line, with the author and the title below.

If you don't have the authors or titles of specific works, but you want to consult books in a general topic area, consult the library's subject catalog. Figure 10.4 shows the subject card for the same book as appeared in Figures 10.2 and 10.3. The **subject card** is filed alphabetically under the subject, in this case, "Petroleum industry and trade." A book can also appear under other subject headings. When it does, it is listed at the bottom of the card.

ARTICLES, ABSTRACTS, BOOK REVIEWS

Titles of business articles relevant to your research can be found in **indexes** for newspapers and periodicals. (Business periodicals are journals devoted to various business subjects.) Summaries of articles also appear in volumes called **abstracts**.

Indexes are usually published annually in bound volumes; softcover supplements may come out during the year. Abstracts give brief summaries of articles (and books as well), in addition to listing where the articles can be found. Common indexes and abstracts include:

THE FORMAL REPORT: GOAL, READER, IDEAS, AND INFORMATION

Figure 10.3

SAMPLE TITLE CARD

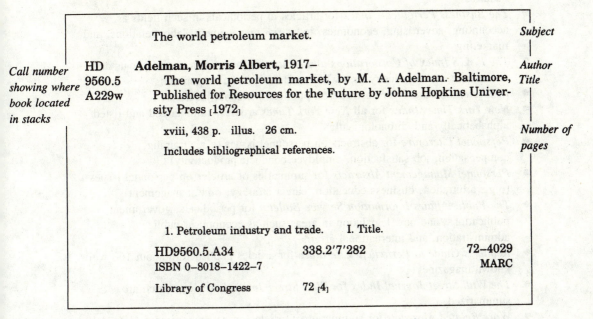

Figure 10.4

SAMPLE SUBJECT CARD

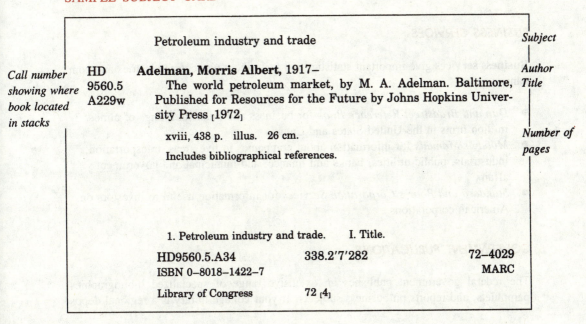

- *Accountants' Index* for articles, books, and pamphlets on accounting
- *Area Business Databank Abstracts* for summaries of articles on all aspects of business
- *The Business Periodicals Index* for articles in periodicals in such fields as accounting, advertising, economics, industrial management, labor relations, and marketing
- *The F & S Index of Corporations and Industries* for articles in periodicals and newspapers on an industry as a whole and on specific corporations
- *Insurance Literature* for abstracts on publications about insurance
- *New York Times Index* for all *New York Times* articles, summarized and listed alphabetically and chronologically
- *Personnel Literature* for abstracts on personnel issues (e.g., training, compensation, job satisfaction, employee conduct, productivity)
- *Personnel Management Abstracts* for summaries of articles on personnel issues (e.g., arbitration, business education, career strategy, time management)
- *The Public Affairs Information Service Bulletin* for periodicals, government publications, and new legislation in areas such as economics, public administration, and international affairs
- *Reader's Guide to Periodical Literature* for articles published in about 160 well-known magazines
- *The Wall Street Journal Index* for *Wall Street Journal* articles, which are summarized
- *Work Related Abstracts* for summaries of articles on personnel issues (e.g., labor-management relations, labor and industrial history, compensation and fringe benefits)

BUSINESS SERVICES

Business services give important statistics and facts about particular industries and companies:

- *Dun and Bradstreet Reference Book* for business and financial ratings of almost 3 million firms in the United States and Canada
- *Moody's Manuals* for information about companies in five areas: transportation, industrials, public utilities, banks and finance, and municipal and government affairs
- *Standard and Poor's Corporation Services* for information useful to investors on American corporations

GOVERNMENT PUBLICATIONS

The federal government publishes an extensive range of specialized bibliographies, pamphlets, and reports on business subjects. If your college library is a regional depos-

THE FORMAL REPORT: GOAL, READER, IDEAS, AND INFORMATION

itory, it may contain copies of government publications. If not, write to the particular government agency for a copy of the publication you need.

BUSINESS AND CORPORATE DIRECTORIES

Business directories are both national and local. They identify companies, their addresses, officers, and products. Corporate directories give information about companies' finances and personnel.

COMPANY DOCUMENTS

Company documents include newsletters, annual reports, and other company literature. Companies with above a certain value of assets and number of shareholders are required to file a 10-K form annually with the U.S. Securities and Exchange Commission. The 10-K form details company finances and related information.

The ten types of secondary sources just named are central to much of business research; however, the list is by no means exhaustive. We recommend that you review your company's or college's library and ask the reference librarian or your instructor to direct you to the major holdings for the business topics you are researching.

Suggestions for Using the Library

When doing library research, keep in mind the following suggestions.

1. *Begin your library research by reading pertinent sections of general reference books to get an overview of what has been published on your subject.* General reference books include encyclopedias, dictionaries, and handbooks. Some references may summarize key issues related to your subject and may provide extended bibliographies. By first consulting reference books and jotting notes on 3- by 5-inch index cards, you will have specific subjects, titles, and authors to use in a computer search, and you will be able to formulate specific questions to ask your research librarian.

In Mark's case, he first looked at two handbooks that he thought might contain relevant general information on campus interviewing: *Handbook of Work and Organizational Psychology* and *Handbook of Industrial and Organizational Psychology*. The first contained an essay called "Interview Skills Training." The title seemed promising, but it turned out that the article had nothing on recruitment interviews. An essay in the second handbook, called "Recruiting, Selection, Job Placement," discussed interviewing but, again, did not discuss his topic, what recruiters are looking for.

2. *Find out from your librarian or instructor if computer services are available to do some of your search automatically.* Computers can help you find information efficiently, since they store vast amounts of information on your library's and possibly

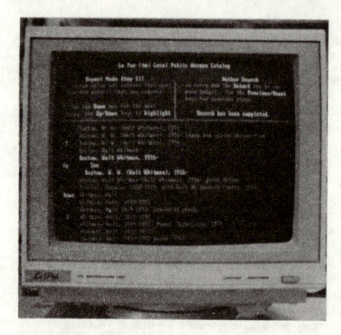

Computers offer a storehouse of information to researchers.

other libraries' holdings. But since a computer search can be costly, ask your librarian whether the service is free or is covered by student or academic fees.

If computer search capabilities had been available to Mark White through his library, he could have saved time by having the computer do much of the search he did on his own.

3. *Remember that you can consult the reference librarian for help in finding sources.* Reference librarians can help you locate sources that are difficult to find and can suggest relevant sources you may have overlooked. Don't hesitate to use their assistance.

4. *After you have reviewed general references, work with the library catalog or the computer services, for both locating references and discovering new ones.* When you use the library catalog or the computer services (or both if your library provides both), review the subject headings that your topic falls under, select bibliographical information that seems relevant, and note on 3- by 5-inch index cards the bibliographical information as well as the call number of the sources so that you can find them easily. Figure 10.5 shows a student's index card for the information shown on the subject card in Figure 10.4.

5. *Once you have done your initial search for titles, locate and skim the sources that seem particularly relevant to your subject.* Skimming a source usually means reading the introductory section, where the purpose of the book is summarized, and looking at the table of contents and the bibliography. As you skim a source, consider the following questions:

THE FORMAL REPORT: GOAL, READER, IDEAS, AND INFORMATION 465

Figure 10.5

STUDENT INDEX CARD

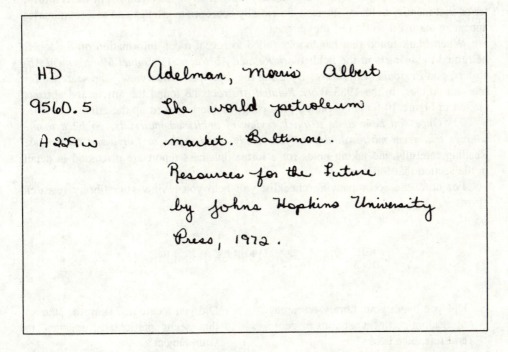

- Is the source frequently cited in other publications? If so, it may be an important publication on your topic.
- Is the work timely or out of date? Recent studies are generally better than older ones. The latest edition of a book is the one you should use.
- Is the author a well-respected authority in the field? You can check a biographical directory for information on the author. In addition, books and periodicals often give short biographical sketches of authors.
- In the case of a book, is the publishing company well respected in the field? In the case of an article, is the periodical a leading journal in the field? Usually your instructor or librarian can give you this information.
- Does the author document and support his or her views with references to major studies on the subject?

Be sure to jot down on 3- by 5-inch cards complete information on any source you plan to return to for a thorough reading. Your first set of notes on a source should indicate its possible relevance to your study, what it covers, and its likely strengths and weaknesses.

6. *Review indexes and abstracts.* Indexes provide you with titles of potentially relevant articles. Abstracts give you the names of books and articles and also summarize them. The opening pages of abstracts usually contain an alphabetical list of **descriptors,** terms that identify fields of interest. Potentially appropriate articles and their summaries appear in the main section of the abstract.

When Mark found that handbooks failed to reveal much information on his topic, he turned to abstracts in the field: *Work Related Abstracts, Personnel Management Abstracts,* and *Personnel Literature.* By using the descriptor "interview," he searched for relevant articles. In the 1983 *Work Related Abstracts* he found the article and abstract circled in Figure 10.6. This seemed promising, so Mark looked up the article.

7. *Once you have done a quick review of published materials, go back to the sources that seem most valuable to your study, read them carefully, and take notes.* Reading carefully and taking notes for a formal business report are discussed in detail in the section that follows.

For now, the accompanying checklist will help you review your library research efforts.

CHECKLIST FOR USING THE LIBRARY

1. Did you begin your library research by reading pertinent sections of general reference books?
2. Did you find out whether computer services are available to do some of your search automatically?
3. Did you consult the reference librarian for help in finding sources?
4. Did you work with the library's card catalogs or computer services?
5. Did you locate and skim the sources that seem particularly relevant to your subject?
6. Did you review indexes and abstracts?
7. Did you take notes on sources significant to your project?

USING SECONDARY SOURCES

As you read a relevant published source, you will want to review the source carefully and take good notes. You will also need to decide whether to quote, paraphrase, or summarize the source.

Taking Notes

Taking notes will help you retain what you have read and sharpen your understanding of the material. Your notes should consist of both the author's ideas and your reactions

THE FORMAL REPORT: GOAL, READER, IDEAS, AND INFORMATION

Figure 10.6

SAMPLE ABSTRACT

356 EVALUATING THE OLDER WORKER: USE OF EMPLOYER APPRAISAL SYSTEMS IN AGE DISCRIMINATION LITIGATION. M. H. Schuster and C. S. Miller. Aging & Work 4:229-43 n4 1981. Use of performance evaluations in age discrimination claims of older workers is analyzed. Three types of employment situations are examined; promotions, layoffs/retirement, and discharges. Authors question existing evaluation methods. Refs., tables.

357 RETIREMENT PLANNING PROGRAMS: ASSESSING THEIR ATTENDANCE AND EFFICACY. P. C. Morrow. Aging & Work 4:244-52 n4 1981. Findings indicate that those who complete program do not differ significantly from nonparticipants on most background factors, but have accomplished more general preparation activities and have more favorable attitudes toward retirement. Figure, table, refs.

358 ARCO CHIEF CITES LESSONS FOR BUSINESS IN NCOA SURVEY. W. F. Kieschnick. Aging & Work 4:226-7 n4 1981. President of Atlantic Richfield Co., which helped sponsor Natl. Council on the Aging survey conducted by Louis Harris and Associates, points to business' need for more information about elderly who will be increasingly important to business in 1980s and 1990s.

359 EEOC REPORTS INCREASE IN AGE DISCRIMINATION COMPLAINTS. Aging & Work 4:281-4 n4 1981. U.S. Equal Employment Opportunity Comm. has reported that in 1981 age discrimination complaints have "increased tremendously" since Jul 1, 1979 perhaps because of heightened public awareness of procedures.

360 ADEA AWARENESS VARIES AMONG RESPONDENTS. H. L. Sheppard. Aging & Work 4:224-5 n4 1981. National Council on the Aging finds that education is major factor in awareness of Age Discrimination in Employment Act of 1967, knowledge of its purpose, and evaluation of how 1978 changes will affect personal retirement plans.

361 TEN WAYS TO IMPROVE THE EFFECTIVENESS OF YOUR CAMPUS INTERVIEW. J. J. Phillips. SAM Adv Mgt J 47:56-62 n4 1982. Practical advice is given to graduating students on how to make favorable impression on company representatives during campus interview.

362 ADEA AND THE FUTURE OF RETIREMENT. M. H. Morrison. Aging & Work 4:253-7 n4 1981. Flexible coordinated employment and retirement policy is suggested. As result of enactment of Age Discrimination in Employment Act of 1967 (ADEA) and 1978 Amendments, recommendations include modifications in benefit structure of Social Security system, pension systems, personnel policies, and tax policies.

363 IN SICKNESS AND IN HEALTH, THE ABSENTEEISM DILEMMA. R. Dredge and P. Milton. Work & People 8:18-26 n1 1982. Two Australian case studies presented use regular collection of absence statistics, absence policy, communication of absence standards to employes, identification of absenteeism factors, involvement of supervisors, and monitoring of control attempts. Figures, refs., table.

364 HOW TO PREPARE FOR YOUR PERFORMANCE REVIEW. M. A. Bogerty. SAM Adv Mgt J 47:12-19 n4 1982. Analyzing role in company, conducting self-assessment, and preparing for interview are discussed. Two case studies of performance appraisals are given.

365 COMMUTING AND THE HOME LOCATION DECISION. M. R. Edwards and L. V. Hockley. SAM Adv Mgt J 47:23-5 n4 1982. Suggestions are provided for companies to help employes reduce commuting distance to work.

366 ECONOMICS IN PERSONNEL MANAGEMENT. J. Bridge. London, Inst. of Personnel Mgt., 1981. 264p. In attempting to integrate economics and personnel, author tries to give adequate coverage to such diverse topics as economics, optimization techniques, finance and planning. National economic policy in Britain is dealt with as well as work of Cyert and March (1963). Condensed from book review, Psl Psy 35:476-9 n2 1982.

367 WOMEN, WORK, AND WAGES: EQUAL PAY FOR JOBS OF EQUAL VALUE. D. J. Treiman and H. I. Hartman, eds. Washington, D.C., Natl. Academy Press, 1981. 136p. Committee on Occupational Classification and Analysis was established by Natl. Research Council to report to two government agencies on issues concerning job evaluation. Committee acknowledges that wage discrimination in employment may take many forms, but concentrates its attention on discrimination arising from sex composition. Final part offers two methods of implementing system of comparable worth compensation into organization's internal labor market. Condensed from book review, Psl Psy 35:458-61 n2 1982.

368 DESIGNING AND MANAGING HUMAN RESOURCE SYSTEMS. U. Pareek and T. V. Rao. New Delhi, India, Oxford & IBH Publishing, 1981. 347p. Central focus is on concept of human resource system designed to develop people and their competencies. Authors propose establishment of major department or management function to deal with four major human resources problem areas: planning and administration, jobs and salary, human resources development, and worker affairs. Elaborate model and its underlying philosophy are articulated by authors who are senior faculty members in premier management education institution in India. Condensed from book review, Psl Psy 35:446-50 n2 1982.

Section C, Abstracts 356-368
PERSONNEL MANAGEMENT   WRA, May 1983

to them. Note-taking is an opportunity to use writing as a way of thinking, to connect ideas on the page with your reactions to them in light of your subject. Handled in this way, your notes will give you a good start in identifying your major ideas and in organizing your report.

Reading a source carefully involves several activities:

1. *Think about how the source relates to the subject you are writing about.* To see the connections between your source and your topic, ask yourself questions about your topic and apply them to your reading. For Mark, this meant reading with questions in mind about the job qualifications recruiters expect in students: What job qualifications do recruiters say are most important? Do students view the same qualifications as important? If not, what are the differences in the views of each group?

2. *Read actively*. Imagine you are talking to the author. Question him or her about a conclusion, agree or disagree. Pay special attention to new information the author provides about your subject and whether this information changes or confirms what you have already learned.

3. *Weed out redundant material.* If after reviewing a source you find that it is not providing you with relevant information or that other sources have already given you the information, move on to the next source.

4. *Evaluate conflicting sources*. Should you come upon published materials that present conflicting viewpoints, identify the areas of disagreement and evaluate which sources are more valid.

We suggest that you take notes on 5- by 8-inch index cards, and bibliographical information on 3- by 5-inch index cards. The difference in the sizes of the cards will help you distinguish bibliographical information from notes on content when you begin organizing your report. Be sure to use some device (e.g., brackets, asterisks) to distinguish between your comments and the author's ideas. Put only one piece of information on a card, and label it with the name of the source and the subtopic. In this way, when you have finished your research, you will have a stack of cards you can group and order into an outline according to subtopics.

Quoting

Two situations call for a direct quotation: (1) when the author's opinions and recognized expertise in a field can support your own ideas, and (2) when the author's language expresses his or her ideas more powerfully than you could using your own words.

QUOTATIONS THAT SUPPORT YOUR IDEAS

Quoting an authority can lend support to your own ideas. After all, citing the opinions of experts who have investigated the problem you are studying gives credibility to your

THE FORMAL REPORT: GOAL, READER, IDEAS, AND INFORMATION

own inquiry. For this reason, Mark White quoted Barry Z. Posner's article "Comparing Recruiter, Student, and Faculty Perceptions of Important Applicant and Job Characteristics." Posner, a professor of management, had done primary research in Mark's subject, and his article explored his results. Because Posner is an authority, Mark decided to quote him directly; he took down the information verbatim on a note card (see Figure 10.7).

Notice that Mark uses quotation marks to indicate he is directly quoting Posner. He also labels the card with a subject heading so that he can readily identify the relevance of the quotation to his report topic when he begins to outline his report. In addition, he comments (in brackets) on the significance of the quotation; and he does this while it is fresh in his mind, rather than waiting until he outlines the report, at which point he may have forgotten why the quotation is important.

QUOTATIONS THAT EXPRESS IDEAS POWERFULLY

Quote a source if the author expresses ideas more vividly and memorably than you can by using your own words. Mark liked the persuasive appeal and forceful prose style of

Figure 10.7

SAMPLE NOTE CARD: A QUOTATION SUPPORTING A POINT

> Need for Research on My Topic   Posner
>
> p. 329 "While much has been written about how to recruit, sources of job applicants, interviewing techniques and the like (e.g. Glueck, 1978; Greco, 1975; Yoder & Heneman, 1974) very little is known about the factors, characteristics, and aptitudes which corporate recruiters consider in evaluating job applicants. Even less is known about the degree to which job applicants are aware of the factors considered important by recruiters. This may also be true for faculty members who offer advice and counsel to both students and recruiters."
>
> [Experts point out need to do study like the one I'm doing interviewing recruiters and students. Posner's a professor in management department at the University of Santa Clara.]

the quotation shown in Figure 10.8, taken from an article by Jack J. Phillips, who has directed recruiting programs for three companies at over twenty-five major universities.

Whether you are using a quotation to lend support to your ideas or for its memorable language, keep the quotation as short as possible and show its connections to the ideas you are developing in the report.

Paraphrasing

Except for the occasional instances when you need the exact wording of your secondary source, paraphrase passages. To **paraphrase** is to put the author's ideas in your own words, in order to condense ideas and to render an accurate substitute for the original. To remain faithful to the original, keep the same ideas and order of presentation as in the original, as Mark White does when paraphrasing from his sources (see Figure 10.9). When this information appears in his report, even though he does not quote directly, he identifies it by page number (see p. 518).

Figure 10.8

SAMPLE NOTE CARD: A QUOTATION
EXPRESSING AN IDEA FORCEFULLY

Importance of On-Campus Interview   Phillips

p. 56 "How you handle your campus interview may make a big difference in your career. The 30 minutes (to one hour) you spend with the recruiter not only may determine where you will first work but also may shape your entire future. The typical manufacturing corporation hires four graduates for every one hundred it interviews. Faced with these statistics, you can see the importance of conducting your interview effectively."

[strong, punchy statement]

THE FORMAL REPORT: GOAL, READER, IDEAS, AND INFORMATION

Figure 10.9

EXAMPLES OF PARAPHRASING

EXAMPLE 1

ORIGINAL

"The interview must elicit information that separates qualified candidates from unqualified ones, and it should determine whether the candidate will 'fit' the position."

PARAPHRASE

Interview as Selection Process — Ginsburg

p. 31 interview reveals: who's qualified
if there is a "fit" with company

(continued)

(EXAMPLES OF PARAPHRASING continued)

EXAMPLE 2

ORIGINAL

"What stands out most from the findings regarding important job applicant characteristics are not the differences, but rather the similarities between recruiters, students, and faculty. Communications ability and future potential are seen as the *most* important job applicant characteristics. Grades and work experience are somewhat in the middle in terms of importance, although these may be seen as predictors, or incorporated into the assessments, of 'future potential.' Extra-curricular activities and recommendations (personal as well as faculty/academic) were seen as the *least* important job applicant characteristics."

PARAPHRASE

> Future Potential & Communications Ability at Top of Recruiters', Students', and Faculty's List of Criteria   Posner
>
> pp 335-336 similarities in recruiters', students', and faculty's views
>
> — future potential & communications are top
> — grades & work experience
>   (though may be part of future potential)
> — extra-curricular activities & recommendations
>
> [compare his results to mine]

THE FORMAL REPORT: GOAL, READER, IDEAS, AND INFORMATION 473

As the examples in Figure 10.9 suggest, the paraphrase has several advantages over the quotation:

1. *The paraphrase can be more concise than the original.* Example 1 is two lines compared to three lines of the original. Example 2 is six lines compared to ten lines of the original.

2. *Paraphrasing can help you better understand the meaning of the original.* Since a careful reading of the original must precede a paraphrase of it, you can test your understanding of the idea as you grapple to put it in your own words.

3. *A paraphrase rather than a quotation is often easier for the reader to understand.* By putting the author's ideas in your own words, you retain your characteristic tone and style in the report, making it easier to read than a report in which the writer's voice is constantly interrupted by direct quotations from others. Save the quotations for when you need an authority's support or when you find that someone else's words express your ideas more powerfully than your own words can.

Summarizing

Rather than being a record of information at the paragraph and sentence level, as is a quotation or a paraphrase, a **summary** is a succinct restatement of the main ideas of a secondary source as it relates to the subject of your report. Unlike the paraphrase, the summary by necessity does not retain details and examples.

To summarize, review your source, noting its major divisions (chapters for a book, headings for an article). Then read the source carefully, underline the major ideas (if you are working from a photocopy), and make marginal comments (or comments on a separate page if you are not working from a photocopy)—such as how a major block of ideas in the source relates to your topic. Finally, go back over your comments and underlining to construct the summary. Notice how Mark used this technique to summarize a section of the article by Phillips, "Ten Ways to Improve the Effectiveness of Your Campus Interview" (Figure 10.10).

The accompanying checklist can help you review when to use quotations, paraphrases, and summaries.

CHECKLIST FOR QUOTING, PARAPHRASING, AND SUMMARIZING

1. Do you quote directly
   - When the author's opinions and recognized expertise in a field can support your own ideas?
   - When the author's language expresses his or her ideas more powerfully than you could using your own words?

2. Do you paraphrase in all instances except when the exact wording of your source is needed or when a summary is called for?

3. Do you summarize when you want a succinct restatement of the main ideas of a secondary source as it relates to the subject of your report?

Figure 10.10
AN EXAMPLE OF SUMMARIZING

> **ORIGINAL**
>
> I recently received a résumé with the following job objective: "A challenging and rewarding career in which I can utilize my experience and skills in personal contacts with professional and business people." What does that mean? If you try to include all your career objectives in one résumé, it leaves the impression that you really don't know what you want to do!
>
> ## Talk about your strengths and weaknesses
>
> Many recruiters will ask you about your strengths. The worst thing you can say is, "Well, I really don't know what my strong points are." That's not very impressive. Tally up your assets in different areas and talk about them. It may help you.
>   Be prepared also to discuss your weaknesses and how you might correct them. For example, suppose one of your weaknesses is report writing. A good response might be, "I'm not as good at report writing as I would like to be, but with some additional training I should be able to improve." Maybe your weakness is making presentations before groups. Stress that you're working on it, and with some additional practice, you should be able to master it. However, it's best to bring out weaknesses *only* if you are asked; but if you tell the recruiter that you don't have any weaknesses, he or she will question your honesty.
>
> ## The five-year plan
>
> Many recruiters and employment interviewers will ask, "What do you plan to be doing in five or ten years?" or "What are your long-range career goals?"
>   Let's look at some possible answers. If you say you're not sure, that leaves a bad impression. It will appear you're short on career planning or don't have enough career ambition to think that far ahead.
>   If you're totally honest and confess that you want to be in a job that's not related to one in the company, then you're out of the picture. For instance, suppose you're interviewing for an engineering job and your ultimate goal is to be a lawyer in ten years. No recruiter is going to hire you knowing that the company might soon lose you.
>   The best plan is to have an answer tailored to the job objective. If you are interviewing for a management-trainee position, a good five- or ten-year objective would be a department manager in the operations area of the company. Recruiters like to hear that. They like to think that you will come with them and stay forever.
>   I'm not suggesting you be dishonest. But it's true that many of us don't know exactly what we want to do in the future. Even if you want to be a lawyer ten years from now, by the time you get there you may change your mind. It's highly possible

[Margin note next to "Talk about your strengths and weaknesses":] Discuss them in order of importance to recruiters

[Margin note next to "The five-year plan":] Relate career goals to the job students are interviewing for

that the company employing you will provide the right challenges to keep you. Why place a shadow over your selection by giving information that may be irrelevant?

Don't criticize your former employer

Recently, we interviewed a candidate for a key first-line management job in the company. We had screened a number of résumés and found the one that seemed to have the best credentials for the job. He had the right education and experience and the initial telephone conversations were very favorable. However, during the interview, the candidate began to criticize his former employer's integrity, objective, and systems and procedures. For this reason, we turned him down.

> *"Those that make the best impression during the interview are likely to be invited for further interviews."*

Criticism of this type is received with mixed emotions. The candidate was a part of the system he criticized. He had helped to implement some of its programs; maybe that was an indication of his effectiveness! Or was he willing to sell his present employer short if it was to his advantage? In either case, we wanted no part of him. So regardless of what you think of your former employers, if any, and how you had been treated, don't be too critical. At the most, just indicate that you didn't agree with some of management's policies or actions or didn't see the opportunity for growth that you would like to have.

Future education plans

Most companies have tuition refund plans to assist employees in continuing their education. However, they're looking for someone to go to work and devote their attention to the job—at least for the first few years.

Unless you apply for a particular job where it's required that you get a master's degree or continue your education, don't bring up graduate school in your interview. If you do, a problem may surface. Your job usually requires your full attention, at least initially. For instance, suppose a recruiter is selecting someone for an opening in a plant in a small town in Arkansas. You say you want to begin an MBA immediately. Since there are no graduate business schools in that area of Arkansas, the recruiter knows you won't be satisfied. Or suppose the job involves some travel. You've indicated you want to settle down to work on a master's degree in engineering. Obviously, you'll be eliminated for that position.

(continued)

(AN EXAMPLE OF SUMMARIZING continued)

The best approach is to leave it out of the discussion and see what kind of opportunity becomes available. You may change your mind and not really want to pursue your MBA until you have had several years of experience. At that time, you could begin to fit your career plans in with the company.

Avoid discrimination issues

It's best to avoid the subject of discrimination during the interview, for a confrontation could label you as a troublemaker and block your further consideration. There are subtle ways to determine if a firm has had a past record of discrimination. Company brochures and literature usually address this issue. Look at the photographs to see if women and minorities are included.

Under no circumstances should you ask the recruiter if the company discriminates. It will get you nowhere. If you are concerned about it, ask to talk with other employees who have been recruited for this job or similar jobs. But don't ask the question on the basis of discrimination, say that you merely want to find out more about the company. Businesses are very touchy about this issue and most of them are trying to make progress.

Avoid the sensitive areas

It's best not to discuss salary in an initial interview unless you think the company won't offer a competitive one. If that's the case, you might ask a general question about the salary range for the job. Otherwise, stay away from it. When you have decided to give the company serious consideration, then you can negotiate salary.

Also, don't haggle over benefits beyond those that are normally offered. For instance, don't ask about moving expenses in an initial interview unless it's extremely important to you. Most companies provide moving expenses for their college graduates. It's best to get the job offer and then ask about moving expenses.

Other areas to avoid are religion and politics. It could offend the recruiter or show poor judgment on your part. Don't spend an excessive amount of time on your personal life unless questioned by the interviewer. These are common-sense items, but too many good applicants have been eliminated early because of the areas discussed during the interview.

THE FORMAL REPORT: GOAL, READER, IDEAS, AND INFORMATION 477

SUMMARY

Suggestions for Improving Interview Performance

Phillips advises students to discuss strengths but to avoid discussing weaknesses unless asked and, in that case, to show how to correct them. He also advises students to know how to talk about their career goals as they relate to the job they are interviewing for, to avoid criticizing former employers, to de-emphasize immediate educational plans, to avoid questions about discrimination, salary, and benefits.

[discuss assets in order of importance to recruiter]

Phillips, pp. 59-61

USING PRIMARY SOURCES

Much of the information for your report can be gathered from secondary sources. Sometimes, however, you will need to establish or supplement the main points of your report with primary sources—such as observations, experiments, and surveys conducted by questionnaire or interview.

Making Observations

Observation is useful for studying people's nonverbal behavior (e.g., gestures, tone, movement) and for learning firsthand about how people act, especially as compared to what they *say* about their actions in interviews and questionnaires. Since observation allows you to investigate behavior unavailable for study by other means, it supplements what you can discover through experiments or surveys.

Because achieving accuracy of observation is not simple, business people who make observations as part of their research are often specifically trained in the techniques of observation. We can, however, make some generalizations about how to conduct observations:

1. *Decide how observation will help you investigate the problem you are studying.* What is there about the problem that can be investigated by observation? Say you are trying to design a new ad campaign to increase local sales of a particular cereal in supermarkets. To determine whom to aim the ad at, it would be helpful as part of your market test in designated supermarkets to make observations of who purchases cereal and what kind. Or, say you are interested in studying how newly formed work groups in your company carry out tasks. It might be worthwhile as an observer to track the activities of sample groups.

2. *Identify the information you want to gather from your observations.* Since you cannot (and would not want to) focus on all aspects of the situation you are observing, decide beforehand which aspects are most relevant. Ask yourself what kinds of information you are looking for that observation can provide. Then focus your attention on only those elements of the situation. For instance, as a market researcher, you can jot down the number of shoppers buying cereals, which kinds they buy, and how long they deliberate.

3. *Take detailed notes on anything in the situation you are observing that pertains to information you need.* If your attention is focused on particular aspects of what you are observing, you can concentrate on recording the relevant details. For instance, if you are a market researcher studying purchases of cereal, then the age, sex, and apparent economic status of cereal buyers may be important.

4. *Beware of how your biases and preconceived ideas influence what you see and how you interpret it.* Expectations you may have of what you will observe can influence what you see. If you expect to observe poor relations between a manager and his subordinates, your bias may make you interpret neutral behavior as antagonistic.

5. *Be aware that your observing a situation may change it.* Once you enter a situation you are observing and identify yourself, your presence may change the situation. Thus even if you are not a participant in the activities, your presence may affect how people act. As a result, it can be difficult for you to get an accurate picture of the situation, and you may need to do other kinds of primary research.

To review your plans for observing a situation, use the accompanying checklist.

THE FORMAL REPORT: GOAL, READER, IDEAS, AND INFORMATION

CHECKLIST FOR MAKING OBSERVATIONS

1. Do you know how the observation may help your study?
2. Have you identified the kinds of information you want from your observation?
3. Are you planning to take detailed notes on anything in the situation you observe that pertains to information you need?
4. Are you aware of biases and preconceived ideas you may have that may interfere with your observations?
5. Are you aware that your presence may affect the situation you are observing?

Conducting Experiments

As an observer, you study an ongoing situation that may tell you something about the problem you are investigating, while trying your best not to change the situation. By contrast, as an experimenter, you deliberately change a situation to gather information and to test ideas about the situation. As with making observations, conducting experiments is a sophisticated procedure that requires special training.

In **experiments,** researchers attempt to control, or keep constant, all but one element in a situation. That element is called the **independent variable.** By manipulating the independent variable, researchers can measure its effects on another element in the situation, called the **dependent variable.** This second element is the one that researchers want to study. When conducting experiments, researchers work with the following assumption: If conditions can be controlled, change in the independent variable will cause changes in the dependent variable.

Suppose you were asked to report on whether or not setting up displays for disposable lighters will result in sufficient sales to justify the cost of the displays. By installing displays (the independent variable) in some selected retail outlets and not in others, you could determine if the display increases sales (the dependent variable) enough to justify its use in every store that sells the product.

Or suppose that your boss expects you to come up with a report recommending which direct-mail advertising the company should use. As part of your research, you divide a representative sample of customers into two groups. You advertise the same product to both groups, but you offer only one group a thirty-day trial period at no cost. If differences in sales occur between those who are offered the free trial period and those who are not, you would conclude that the free trial period was responsible for these differences.

Control of all elements other than the independent variable can be difficult to achieve. Unlike the scientist, the business researcher cannot duplicate in a business setting the controlled conditions of a lab.

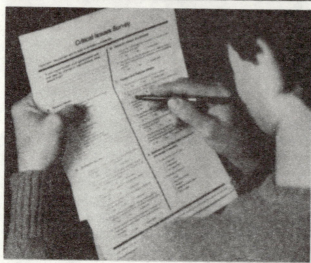

Data relevant to a business problem may be gathered through surveys, which can take place over the phone, face-to-face, or by a mailed questionnaire.

THE FORMAL REPORT: GOAL, READER, IDEAS, AND INFORMATION

Conducting Surveys

Surveys to collect information about a business problem may be conducted by mailed questionnaire, telephone interview, or face-to-face interview. Suppose you are a hospital administrator who needs to determine whether it makes sense for the hospital to expand the cafeteria and snack bar services it offers to employees. Surveying employees would help you see whether the current facilities are meeting their needs. Or suppose you are a wholesale distributor of children's toys and you want to increase business. You might survey present and potential customers to find out the criteria they use to choose a wholesaler.

Once you have determined that a survey can help you gather the information you want, decide on two things: (1) the population you want to survey and (2) the sample. The **population** consists of every person, organization, or object in the group you want to study (e.g., all hospital employees). Perhaps you can survey the entire population. If so, you do not need a sample. If, however, the group you wish to survey is so large that it would be impractical to reach everyone, survey a **sample**—that is, a subset of the population. The sample should contain characteristics identical to those of the population as a whole. On the basis of information you collect from the sample, you can draw conclusions about the population.

SAMPLING FOR SURVEYS

We cannot here deal fully with the issue of sampling, but we can provide a brief overview of three sampling techniques you may want to use.

Random Sampling. To set up a **random sampling,** first compile or obtain a list of every member of the group that you want to study. Then devise a system that guarantees every member the same chance to be selected for the sample. One way of producing a random sample is to put all the names of the members of a group being surveyed on slips of paper, toss the names into a hat, mix the contents, and pick a slip. Continue the process until you have enough names for your sample size.

As an example, let's consider Mark White's survey of students' and recruiters' perceptions of on-campus interviews. Mark chose a sample of sixty college seniors majoring in business, randomly selected from six Boston area schools and one New York school. He got the names from the campus directories of those schools. He also used random sampling in choosing thirty corporate recruiters; brochures from each college's job placement office listed recruiters who regularly interview business students.

Systematic Sampling. To do a **systematic sampling,** review a list of the population to be surveyed and select names at a set interval, such as every fifteenth customer or every twentieth student. As a hospital administrator doing a survey of employees' interest in expansion of food facilities, you could use the hospital's telephone directory of employees and select every twentieth name.

Stratified Sampling. To set up **stratified sampling,** first select mutually exclusive subgroups or "strata," from the population. Once you have done this, select from each subgroup a random sample. Its size should represent the subgroup's percentage of the population. If, for example, it is important to your survey of hospital employees that all income brackets be included according to the percentage each represents of the total population, you might work from the hospital's employee records to group the names of employees according to the salary bracket, and then give the percentage of employees that belong in each bracket.

Next you would choose employees randomly from each group, selecting the number of employees from each income bracket which represents that bracket's percentage of the total population—as shown in Table 10.1. Using stratified random sampling guarantees that all segments of the group being surveyed are represented in the proper proportion.

There are several other sampling techniques, but only a course in business statistics or marketing research can teach you those techniques thoroughly.

The accompanying checklist can help you put together a sample.

CHECKLIST FOR DEVELOPING A SAMPLE

1. If you are doing a random sampling, have you
   - Compiled or obtained a list of every member of the group?
   - Devised a system that guarantees every member the same chance to be selected?
2. If you are doing a systematic sampling, have you
   - Reviewed a list of the population to be surveyed?
   - Selected names at a set interval?
3. If you are doing a stratified sampling, have you
   - Selected mutually exclusive subgroups?
   - Selected from each subgroup a random sample in proportion to the total population?

Table 10.1

STRATIFIED RANDOM SAMPLE BASED ON INCOME

Salary Bracket	Number in Each Group	Percentage of Employees	Number in Each Sample
Less than $10,000	300	3	30
$10,000–$12,999	600	6	60
$13,000–$14,999	900	9	90
$15,000–$19,999	800	8	80
$20,000–$24,999	1,500	15	150
$25,000–$29,999	2,800	28	280
$30,000–$49,999	1,400	14	140
$50,000 or more	1,700	17	170

THE FORMAL REPORT: GOAL, READER, IDEAS, AND INFORMATION

Designing and Administering Questionnaires

To survey large numbers of people for information about a problem you want to solve, ask them to fill out a questionnaire. Since you can mail a questionnaire to all members of your sample (or to the full population if it is small enough), rather than having to conduct the survey in person, using a questionnaire can save time.

Mark White used a questionnaire to gather information for his study of how students and recruiters perceive the on-campus interview. The questionnaire was an efficient research tool for finding out from both groups what they thought recruiters looked for in job candidates.

If you have decided that using a questionnaire is the best way to elicit information from the population you want to study, design it carefully to ensure getting the results you want. When designing a questionnaire, keep in mind these suggestions:

1. *Decide precisely what information you can get from your respondent that will be useful.* Carefully formulate questions that will elicit the specific information you need. To design his questionnaire, Mark first identified the major questions he wanted answered:

- What criteria do recruiters use to judge job candidates at initial on-campus interviews?
- Are students aware of these criteria?

He then drew up a list of potential criteria that recruiters valued in job candidates and that students perceived to be valued by recruiters. To draw up his list, he looked at what other researchers had asked in similar surveys. Each criterion on his list became the topic of one question in his questionnaire. Among these were questions on grade-point average, personality, appearance, willingness to relocate, and college attended (see Chapter 11, pp. 533–536, for the full questionnaire). By pinpointing these criteria and asking about each of them individually, Mark hoped to learn from the sample of students and recruiters the relative importance to them of each criterion.

2. *Keep the questionnaire short.* Remember that your respondents are doing you a favor by taking the time to answer the questionnaire. For this reason, the shorter the questionnaire and the more concise each question, the more likely you will be to get a response. Avoid the temptation to ask questions that may be interesting but are extraneous to the purpose of your study. Weed out redundant questions, too, unless you think that by asking for the same information in two parts of the questionnaire, you will increase the validity of the responses.

3. *Decide whether closed or open questions are more appropriate.* **Closed questions** give the respondent a limited number of responses from which to choose. Use closed questions when you need specific information, when you are sure of the range of answers your respondents will give, and when you want to maintain strict control of topics.

Closed questions require the respondent to identify the appropriate, designated answer:

Would you recommend this travel agency to a friend or business associate?

Yes   No

Besides yes/no, closed questions can be multiple-choice:

In the past ten years, I have most frequently bought cars
   a. new from a dealer
   b. used from a dealer
   c. used from a friend or private party

Some multiple-choice questions allow for more than one answer:

How did you learn about the manufacturer from whom you bought your sewing machine? Check as many boxes as are appropriate.
- ☐ 1. Salesperson
- ☐ 2. Recommendation of another manufacturer
- ☐ 3. Advertisements in trade publications
- ☐ 4. Personally known manufacturer
- ☐ 5. Industry trade show/seminar
- ☐ 6. Advice from industry expert
- ☐ 7. Company brochure

Answers to closed questions can also appear as a scale to reflect the degree of the respondent's feelings about the topic. For instance, instead of simply asking respondents whether a criterion is important or unimportant, Mark White used a five-point scale to gauge people's reactions more accurately:

Directions: Answer these questions on the basis of how you feel the interviewer would be evaluating you. Rate each question below on a scale from 1 to 5 in degree of importance.

```
1————————5           circle one!
Most      Least
important important
```

1. How much importance do you place on grade-point average?   1 2 3 4 5
2. How important is the personality of the individual?   1 2 3 4 5
3. How much emphasis do you place on appearance?   1 2 3 4 5

Sometimes open-ended questions may be appropriate. **Open-ended questions** allow a respondent to answer in his or her own words and begin with such phrases as "What do you think about . . . . ?" or "How would you describe . . . . ?" Use open-ended questions when you cannot pinpoint the range of possible responses to a question. But keep in mind that answers are difficult to tabulate statistically.

You may decide that your questionnaire should combine both closed and open-ended questions. You might use the open-ended questions in the early sections of your questionnaire to explore the respondent's general attitudes about a specific subject, and the closed questions in the later sections.

4. *Word questions so that your respondents understand them easily.* As you would for any business communication, take into account your reader's knowledge and avoid *jargon* and *vagueness*.

JARGON

(questionnaire sent to consumer by market research firm)

Are you the appropriate target market for this product?

Not all consumers can be expected to know what "target market" means.

REVISION

Would you consider buying this product?

JARGON

(questionnaire sent to computer users who don't know the technology)

Do you want the architecture of the next processor you purchase to have memory mapped I-O?

This question should be omitted, since it is too technical to translate into terms that are understandable to nonspecialists.

Another pitfall to watch for is vagueness. Vaguely worded questions only confuse your respondents. What do you think the following question means?

VAGUE

What is your traveling behavior?

One respondent may think it asks how often he travels. Another may think it has to do with the way she acts when she travels.

REVISION

How often do you travel each year?
a. 5 times
b. 5–10 times
c. more than 10 times

A question may be vague because it tries to cover too much. Break down a general question into subquestions. For example, a computer manufacturer asking customers about the service the manufacturer of their current computer provides for its products might say:

VAGUE

Describe the extent of the support you received.

But customers may not know specifically what the manufacturer means by "support" or may not cover all areas thoroughly in their responses. So it would be better to write:

REVISION

Describe the extent of the support you received. More specifically, describe Telephone support: _____
_____

Technician's availability: _____
_____

Technician's expertise: _____
_____

5. *Ask only one question at a time so that each answer will correspond to one question.* Make sure that each answer can be attributed to one, and only one, question. Notice in the next example how the two-part question results in answers that cannot be clearly assigned to a specific question:

UNCLEAR

How important are food and accommodations in your choice of a hospital?
Not Important		Moderately		Very
1	2	3	4	5

REVISION

How important is food in your selection of a hospital?
Not Important		Moderately		Very
1	2	3	4	5

How important are accommodations?
Not Important		Moderately		Very
1	2	3	4	5

THE FORMAL REPORT: GOAL, READER, IDEAS, AND INFORMATION   487

6. *Avoid biased questions*. Sometimes the wording of a question can influence respondents to answer in a particular way. Notice how the following item appearing in a questionnaire will bias the respondent's answer:

BIASED

The U.S. trade deficit has increased so dramatically that many Americans have now begun buying more American products this year than last to help offset the imbalance of trade. Are you buying more goods produced in the United States this year than you did last year?

The introductory sentence suggests that Americans who are good citizens are buying more American products. To eliminate the bias, the researcher could omit that sentence and ask the question alone:

REVISION

Are you buying more goods produced in the United States this year than you did last year?

At other times, the values expressed in the question lead the respondent to answer in a particular way. For example, how do you think most people would answer the following question:

BIASED

Do you drink a moderate amount of alcohol?

People would tend to respond yes, since it is socially unacceptable to drink in excess (in addition to being bad for one's health). On the other hand, by giving people a choice, you are more likely to get an accurate response:

REVISION

Do you drink alcohol
1. Frequently? (5 or more times a week)
2. Sometimes? (1 or 2 times a week)
3. Seldom? (1 or 2 times a month)
4. Never?

7. *Avoid questions that may offend or embarrass the respondent*. You want to make your respondent feel comfortable and eager to answer your questionnaire, so avoid questions that build resistance or hostility.

OFFENSIVE

(to married female employees of a company)
Can you get your husband's permission to go on business trips?

Since no one asks a man if his wife will give him permission to go on business trips, this question is sexist and should be eliminated.

People generally resist answering questions that may put them in an unfavorable light, such as questions that concern their age, income, marital status, education, or employment. These questions may offend a respondent unless they are properly introduced.

OFFENSIVE

Do you plan to continue working at this company for the next
1. 1 year or less
2. 2 to 4 years
3. 5 years or more

For some respondents, their tenure at a company is a sensitive, personal issue. They may be unhappy at the firm, or they may not want to share their career plans with strangers. To make the question less threatening, assure people of the confidentiality of their responses, place the difficult question after several easy-to-answer ones, and let your respondents know the benefits that the questionnaire may eventually bring them. Notice how the writer of the previous question could improve his chances of getting a response by making such changes.

REVISION

(placed after several easy-to-answer questions)

Your answer to the following question will help us with our study to improve job satisfaction and to decrease employee turnover. All responses will be kept confidential.

Do you plan to continue working at this company for the next
1. 1 year or less?
2. 2 to 4 years?
3. 5 years or more?

8. *Order and group questions so that they are easy to read and motivate people to respond.* Order questions from least to most difficult, and group them in subsets. For good sequencing, begin with questions that are exploratory, easy to answer, and nonthreatening. Then move on to more focused questions that may raise sensitive issues. Once respondents have answered several questions, they are less likely to abandon the questionnaire than they would be if your beginning questions were difficult, potentially embarrassing, or threatening.

To make questions more easily understandable, group questions logically. For instance, questions about a product's performance should be in one section, those about the quality of the seller's service in another.

You may also find it useful to provide transitional statements between sections of a questionnaire, to show that you are moving from one group of issues to another:

THE FORMAL REPORT: GOAL, READER, IDEAS, AND INFORMATION

We have been discussing how you chose your current telephone service. Now we would like to discuss your evaluation of this service.

9. *Use a layout that is appealing to the eye and makes the questionnaire easy to respond to.* To increase the rate of response to the questionnaire, use generous white space and margins, and make the places for answering obvious to the reader. Good layout will also help you tabulate the responses. Notice how the layout of the questionnaire in Figure 10.11 encourages readers to respond and makes it easy for them to answer.

10. *Give the questionnaire a title that accurately summarizes the topic and appeals to the respondent.* Choose a title that tells the respondents what the questionnaire is about and that will motivate response. A title might stress reader benefits: "Analysis of Company Efforts to Improve Job Satisfaction." This title lets employees know the study concerns an issue of interest to them—their job satisfaction. A title can also emphasize the confidentiality of the study. "A Confidential Investigation of In-House Training Programs in Team Building."

11. *Use an introductory statement or cover letter to motivate people to respond to the questionnaire and to explain its purpose.* In addition to an appropriate title, a brief introductory statement attached to the questionnaire will encourage people to respond. For example:

Dear Patient:

We sincerely hope your recent stay at Harcourt Medical Center was as pleasant as possible. Because we continually strive to provide the best possible care and service, we ask you to fill out this short questonnaire. Your comments will guide us in improving the quality of service we can offer you and your family.

You can express your opinion on the other side of this questionnaire. Please return the completed questionnaire in the enclosed envelope by September 15 so that we can take into account your comments in improving our services.

But often the short courteous request is not enough to motivate people to respond. In these instances, use a cover letter to motivate them at the same time that you make your request. Mark White's cover letter for his questionnaire to students, shown in Figure 10.12, is an example of a well-written cover letter.

Figure 10.11

SAMPLE QUESTIONNAIRE

PLEASE CHECK ONE

	Excellent	Good	Average	Poor	COMMENTS
1. ACCOMMODATIONS					
a. Comfort	☐	☐	☐	☐	_____
b. Cleanliness	☐	☐	☐	☐	_____
c. Lighting	☐	☐	☐	☐	_____
d. Quietness	☐	☐	☐	☐	_____
2. FOOD					
a. Appearance	☐	☐	☐	☐	_____
b. Flavor (within diet limitations)	☐	☐	☐	☐	_____
c. Quantity	☐	☐	☐	☐	_____
d. Service	☐	☐	☐	☐	_____
e. Hot Food *Hot*	☐	☐	☐	☐	_____
f. Cold Food *Cold*	☐	☐	☐	☐	_____
3. NURSING STAFF					
a. Efficiency	☐	☐	☐	☐	_____
b. Promptness	☐	☐	☐	☐	_____
c. Courtesy	☐	☐	☐	☐	_____
d. Concern	☐	☐	☐	☐	_____
4. TREATMENT BY OTHER HOSPITAL PERSONNEL					
a. Interns and Residents	☐	☐	☐	☐	_____
b. Laboratory Technicians	☐	☐	☐	☐	_____
c. Inhalation Therapists	☐	☐	☐	☐	_____
d. X-ray Technicians	☐	☐	☐	☐	_____
e. Physical Therapists	☐	☐	☐	☐	_____
f. Explanation of Special Tests or Medical Procedures	☐	☐	☐	☐	_____
5. ADMITTING OFFICE					
a. Courtesy	☐	☐	☐	☐	_____
b. Promptness	☐	☐	☐	☐	_____
c. Explanation of Hospital Policies and Routines	☐	☐	☐	☐	_____
d. Explanation of Insurance and Financial Arrangements	☐	☐	☐	☐	_____
6. BUSINESS OFFICE					
a. Courtesy	☐	☐	☐	☐	_____
b. Helpful	☐	☐	☐	☐	_____
c. Consideration	☐	☐	☐	☐	_____
7. GENERAL IMPRESSIONS OF					
a. Hospital	☐	☐	☐	☐	_____
b. Volunteer Service	☐	☐	☐	☐	_____
c. Visiting Procedure	☐	☐	☐	☐	_____
d. Mail Service	☐	☐	☐	☐	_____
e. Television	☐	☐	☐	☐	_____
f. Telephone	☐	☐	☐	☐	_____

8. DID YOU WATCH PATIENT EDUCATION TV ON CHANNEL 6 ☐ Yes ☐ No

a. What films did you watch _____

b. Comments _____

c. What other patient education topics would you like to see _____

9. WOULD YOU RECOMMEND THIS HOSPITAL? ☐ Yes ☐ No

I would like to request that this information be kept confidential ☐

Room No. _____ Length of Stay _____ Was This Your First Stay With Us? _____

Name _____ Physician _____

THE FORMAL REPORT: GOAL, READER, IDEAS, AND INFORMATION

Figure 10.12

MARK'S COVER LETTER TO STUDENTS

Dear Graduating Senior,

If you're like me, you've spent years planning your future and many hours studying so you can qualify for the job of your choice. But you also know that your performance at a 30- to 45-minute job interview can determine whether you get the job you want.

Although you can read plenty of articles on how to prepare for a job interview, little is known about how recruiters actually evaluate job applicants. For this reason, I would like you to participate in a study I am conducting on the qualifications recruiters perceive as most important in job candidates. To participate, would you please fill out the enclosed questionnaire. All responses will be kept confidential.

Since you are one of a small representative group of students I am surveying, your responses will contribute significantly to my research. And I will be happy to share my findings with you so that you'll be able to focus your preparation for the job interview on the criteria that recruiters will use to judge you.

I have enclosed a stamped, addressed envelope for return of the completed questionnaire. Please put it in the mail by October 1 so that I can get my results to you by early December, when the heavy recruiting season begins.

Thank you for your cooperation. All of us will benefit from your efforts.

Sincerely yours,

Mark White

Mark White, Senior
Babson College

enc.

A review of Mark's letter strategy reveals techniques for writing a successful cover letter. They involve using the RTA formula for the special request.

Establish Rapport: Since asking people to respond to a questionnaire is a special request, build a bridge between your desire and their interest before making the request. Mark established rapport with the students by describing a common problem that greatly concerned them, getting a job of their choice:

> If you're like me, you've spent years planning your future and many hours studying so you can qualify for the job of your choice. But you also know that your performance at a 30- to 45-minute job interview can determine whether you get the job you want.

Influence Thinking: To influence your respondents' thinking and to motivate them further to respond, be specific about the purpose and scope of the questionnaire before making your request. Once Mark had established rapport with his potential respondents, he influenced their thinking by raising a specific issue that any job interviewee would like to know more about: the qualifications recruiters look for in job candidates. He also identified this issue as the focus of his questionnaire. He then explained the purpose of the study and stated his request, while assuring his respondents of the questionnaire's confidentiality:

> Although you can read plenty of articles on how to prepare for a job interview, little is known about how recruiters actually evaluate job applicants. For this reason, I would like you to participate in a study I am conducting on the qualifications recruiters perceive as most important in job candidates. To participate, would you please fill out the enclosed questionnaire. All responses will be kept confidential.

Encourage Action and Attitude: End your request by stating the importance of participation, showing how the study will benefit the respondent, and making it easy to comply with your request. It is usually a good idea to offer to share your findings with respondents to motivate them to answer the questionnaire. But sometimes the cost or confidential nature of the questionnaire won't allow you to do so.

Mark encouraged students to participate in his study by pointing out the importance of their contribution and by offering to share his findings with them:

> Since you are one of a small representative group of students I am surveying, your responses will contribute significantly to my research. And I will be happy to share my findings with you so that you'll be able to focus your preparation for the job interview on the criteria that recruiters will use to judge you.

After Mark urged his readers to answer the questionnaire and offered to share his findings, he made it easy for them to act and stipulated the deadline, thus ensuring promptness and a high rate of response to the questionnaire:

I have enclosed a stamped, addressed envelope for return of the completed questionnarie. Please put it in the mail by October 1 so that I can get my results to you by early December, when the heavy recruiting season begins.

Finally, he closed on a courteous note emphasizing reader benefits.

Thank you for your cooperation. All of us will benefit from your efforts.

Use the accompanying checklist to review your cover letter for completeness and effectiveness.

CHECKLIST FOR REVIEWING A COVER LETTER

1. Do you build a bridge between your request and your readers' interests?
2. Do you explain the purpose and scope of your questionnaire?
3. Do you state your request clearly?
4. Do you assure people that their responses will be kept confidential?
5. Do you emphasize the importance of the respondent's participation in the study?
6. Do you offer to share your findings if this is possible?
7. Do you specify a deadline for return of the questionnaire?
8. Are you enclosing a stamped, addressed envelope for easy response?
9. Have you closed on a courteous note?

12. *Pretest the questionnaire and cover letter, and revise before sending them to respondents.* Just as you would ask colleagues to review an important business communication, pretest your questionnaire with a small group. We recommend two rounds of pretesting, one in person and the other mailed. The first round should be with a small group similar to the people who will actually be answering the questionnaire. Work with this group in person, observing them as they fill out the questionnaire and noting the points at which they hesitate or seem to be confused. Later, ask them what they had difficulty with. When most of the problems arising with this first group have been ironed out, mail the questionnaire to a second test group and review their responses for problems. (If your first group has a lot of difficulty with the questionnaire it is advisable to repeat the first round of pretesting.)

In addition to pretesting the questionnaire and cover letter, review them yourself using the "Checklist for Reviewing a Cover Letter" above as well as the accompanying checklist on the next page.

CHECKLIST FOR REVIEWING A QUESTIONNAIRE

1. Do all the questions elicit specific information that you need?
2. Have you kept the questionnaire as short as possible?
   - Can any questions be eliminated?
   - Can any be made more concise?
3. Does your use of closed and open-ended questions allow for appropriate answers?
4. Is the wording of questions clear?
5. Are you asking only one question at a time?
6. Are any questions biased?
7. Will any questions offend or embarrass the respondent?
8. Are the questions in a logical sequence?
9. Is layout appealing to the eye?
10. Does the title explain the purpose of the questionnaire and motivate people to respond?

Conducting Interviews

WHAT INTERVIEWS CAN ACCOMPLISH

Interviews are an excellent way to accomplish any of the following objectives:

1. *To gather information about people's attitudes and feelings:* Interviews can help you get the kind of qualitative information that is difficult if not impossible to get through other research techniques. If you are an effective interviewer, a two-way, face-to-face session with a respondent tends to induce him or her to reveal attitudes and feelings to a greater extent than would, say, a mailed questionnaire. Among primary research tools, interviewing alone allows you to get immediate responses to your questions, to clarify confusing questions, and to ask respondents to explain and elaborate on their answers. Interviews also allow you to observe people's nonverbal behavior as they answer your questions, to see if it contradicts or complements their statements.

Among their many purposes, interviews are frequently used to do market research and to survey people's attitudes about conditions within their company. For instance, as a market researcher you might interview customers in the checkout line about what they like and don't like about the store. Or as an operations manager, you might conduct interviews to find out whether people prefer to work in groups that are heavily supervised or in relatively autonomous groups that determine their own schedules and tasks.

2. *To learn from experts in a field:* If published research on a topic is minimal or dated, you may want to go to experts to get the information you need. For example, to study corporate philanthropy, one researcher interviewed thirty individuals at major corporations who are at the forefront of this issue. The opinions of these individuals suggested future trends in corporate giving as well as the specific policies of their corporations.

3. *To learn from people with intimate knowledge of a problem or situation:* Interviewing may be useful when you are investigating a situation within a company or division. Then you will want to interview the people involved to learn about their attitudes and perspectives on the issue, since these people have intimate knowledge. For instance, if you are studying the effects of a new retirement policy, you may want to interview a representative sample of the company.

4. *To supplement information gathered from questionnaires, experiments, and observation.* Although more time-consuming than questionnaires, interviews can give you more personalized data, and the reactions of some respondents may open up new avenues of inquiry. For instance, one business person doing research on the marketing of a sports magazine gathered much of his data by sending out a questionnaire. But by interviewing a group of subscribers on their reasons for buying or not buying the magazine, he deepened his understanding of who buys the magazine, who does not, and why. Without the interviews, he would not have known that the personal stories of sports heroes was the magazine's strongest drawing card.

HOW TO CONDUCT AN INTERVIEW

If you have decided to conduct an interview for your report, keep in mind the following:

1. *Prepare a set of questions beforehand.* Use the principles outlined on pp. 483–490 to design your questions.

2. *Build and maintain good rapport with your respondents.* Help your respondents feel comfortable with you so they will be willing to answer your questions honestly and fully. You can establish good rapport with your interviewees in these ways.

First, *be cordial and relaxed.* Respondents may be busy or may feel ill at ease at the beginning of an interview. It can be a new experience for them, and they may feel inadequate for the task. Being friendly and relaxed yourself will put them at ease.

Second, *explain the reason for the interview and the selection process.* At the beginning of the interview, tell your respondent why you are conducting it and why he or she was selected. As in the cover letter for a questionnaire, if you can relate the purpose of the interview to the concerns of your respondents, you will encourage them to participate in the study. For instance, if the purpose of your interview is to recommend to top management changes in the reward system and salary structure, let the employees you are interviewing know that their opinions will influence management's decisions. If your interviewees' participation in a study will have a less direct impact on their home or work life, try to establish whatever connections may exist between the goals of your research and their interests.

Third, *listen attentively to the interviewees' responses, and don't judge them.* As an interviewer, your job is to gather information, not to influence opinions. Especially when your own opinions run counter to a respondent's, you may be inclined to argue with your respondent or to convey your dismay in subtle ways—for instance, by facial expression or body language. Arguments and criticism of a respondent's views have no place in an interview. To get people talking openly, show interest in what they are saying without adding your own comments or evaluating their opinions.

If the purpose of a survey is to determine attitudes and feelings, a face-to-face interview is preferable to an impersonal questionnaire.

Finally, *begin with questions people can answer easily and comfortably.* Using easy-to-answer questions at the beginning will put people at ease and make them less reluctant to give information of a personal nature later on in the interview. If you are including questions that may be embarrassing or threatening, be sure to introduce them with an explanation of their purpose, and assure people of the interview's confidentiality.

3. *Probe for clarification and elaboration of responses that warrant closer attention.* When conducting an interview, you have an opportunity to get a deeper understanding of important issues. Ask your interviewee to discuss further the responses that prove especially relevant to your research.

4. *Follow the same plan in conducting each interview.* To ensure the accuracy of your results, use a uniform approach in conducting each interview: Give the same introductory explanations and closing remarks. For an interview based on closed questions, ask the same questions in the same order.

THE FORMAL REPORT: GOAL, READER, IDEAS, AND INFORMATION

5. *Keep thorough records.* Since you want to get as much as you can from each interview, take detailed notes during the interview or, with the permission of the interviewee, record it. You may also want to jot down your impressions of each interview right after you have conducted it.

Interviewing requires more time and expense than does using a questionnaire and draws information from a more limited number of people. In addition, if you are not careful to keep your own judgments out of the process, you can bias people's responses. But handled carefully, interviews give you access to information that you cannot otherwise obtain.

When you are planning to conduct an interview, use the accompanying checklist to help you prepare.

CHECKLIST FOR PREPARING FOR AN INTERVIEW

1. Have you prepared a set of questions?
2. Are you prepared to build and maintain good rapport with your respondents by
   - Being cordial and relaxed?
   - Explaining the reason for the interview and the selection process?
   - Listening attentively to the interviewees' responses and not judging them?
   - Beginning with questions people can answer easily and comfortably?
3. Are you prepared to probe for clarification and elaboration of responses that warrant close attention?
4. Are you ready to follow the same plan in conducting each interview?
5. Are you prepared to keep thorough records?

SUMMARY

Writing a formal report is a matter of reapplying what you learned about writing the short report and mastering of several new activities. When you are involved in the early stages of formal report writing, these new activities include designing a schedule and learning to do secondary and primary research. The library is a good place to begin your secondary research. There you can consult a variety of references, some of which will provide relevant information on your topic. Taking good notes through the appropriate use of quotations, paraphrases, and summaries will give you a good start in identifying the major ideas of your report and in organizing it. To gather information for your report, you may also need to do primary research. This may consist of making observations, conducting surveys, designing and administering questionnaires, and conducting interviews.

EXERCISES

1. Suppose that you are a member of a faculty-student committee to improve college life. You have been assigned to investigate a specific problem that your college faces. From your knowledge of your own college's issues, define a problem that will require a formal report to be presented to the committee. Consider any of the following areas (or you may choose another topic):

- Admissions policy and procedures
- Alumni relations
- Computer facilities
- Counseling
- Cultural facilities and opportunities
- Curriculum development
- Faculty/student relations
- Outreach to the community
- Recreational facilities and opportunities
- Registration
- Student clubs

See "Suggestions for Using the Library," pp. 463–467, for Exercise 2.

2. Put together a preliminary bibliography for exploring the topic you selected in Exercise 1. Although you need not take detailed notes on your sources at this point, find out the names of publications available in your library on your topic. List ten possible sources on 3- by 5-inch index cards.

See "Setting the Goal and Assessing Your Reader," p. 453, for Exercise 3.

3. To help narrow your topic, interview several students, faculty members, or administrators on your proposed subject. Then write a goal statement for the report and assess your readers.

See "Making a Schedule," pp. 454–456, for Exercise 4.

4. Put together a schedule for completing your report. In designing the schedule, pay special attention to the time necessary to complete specific kinds of research for the report.

See "Taking Notes," pp. 466–468, for Exercise 5.

5. Summarize on 5- by 8-inch index cards an article that sheds light on the problem you must solve. Note precisely how the author's argument extends, describes, qualifies, or confirms what you already know and think about your subject.

THE FORMAL REPORT: GOAL, READER, IDEAS, AND INFORMATION

See "Quoting," pp. 468–470, for Exercise 6.

6. Choose passages to quote verbatim from one of your sources. Be ready to justify why you might want to use the author's words rather than your own in the report.

See "Paraphrasing," pp. 470–473, for Exercise 7.

7. Paraphrase a key section of a source pertaining to your topic, and indicate the relevance of the source.

See "Summarizing," pp. 473–477, for Exercises 8 and 9.

8. Test your understanding of an article by explaining to a classmate how it helps you develop the ideas in your report.
9. Assume that you are to write a formal report on the relative successes and failures of student entrepreneurs. Summarize the article in Figure 10.13 for your report.

See "Ten Types of References to Consult," pp. 457–463, for Exercise 10–12.

10. To familiarize yourself with sources available in the business section of your library, find the answers to the following questions:

- Who is the chief executive officer (CEO) of Arco?
- Where would you find studies on maternity leave? List three articles you find.
- What was the U.S. rate of unemployment for 1987?
- What kinds of financial institutions can give interest on checking accounts?
- Has U.S. paper production risen or fallen in the last twenty years?
- Name three companies that make compact disks.
- What is acid rain?
- What is the current status of acid rain legislation?
- What is a Eurodollar?
- What is the record of medical insurance claims filed against Aetna in the past five years?
- What is succession planning?
- Is the manufacturer of Adidas sneakers a subsidiary of another company?
- What is the financial rating of _____? (Choose a company you would like to work for.)
- Where can you find a record of children's shoe sales for the past ten years?
- How much industrialization is there in San Jose, California?
- How many people are employed by Kaiser Permanente?

11. Use the *Business Periodicals Index* to find three articles on one of the following topics:

- Corporate culture
- Entrepreneurship
- Executive search

- Mergers
- Telecommunications

12. Choose a business topic you might want to investigate. Then review *The Wall Street Journal Index* for three promising articles.

See "Making Observations," pp. 478–479, for Exercises 13 and 14.

13. Spend thirty minutes observing a group of students working on an assignment for class or a project for a club. Take notes on how well or poorly the group seems to achieve its goal.

14. Assemble a group of four students. One person should act as an observer who takes notes. Another should discuss a problem he or she is facing in doing research for a writing assignment. The other two should comment on and discuss this problem. As the observer, take down the key research problems identified by the researcher and discussed by the two students who comment. Note whether the two discussants help the researcher clarify and solve his or her problem and, if so, how. Then switch roles until everyone has had a chance to observe, present his or her problem, and comment. On the basis of your observations, prepare guidelines for solving research problems.

See "Conducting Experiments," pp. 479–481, for Exercise 15.

15. Design an experiment to test one of the following for a formal report you are writing:

- The speed with which students learn to use different word-processing packages (for a report on how computer technology affects the writing practices of students)
- The effects of videotaping on students' oral presentations (for a report on how students can improve their oral presentations)

See "Designing and Administering Questionnaires," pp. 483–495, for Exercises 16–21.

16. You have been asked by a local store selling sports cars, ice cream, spring break trips, camping equipment, or stereos (choose one) to survey members of your class to determine which kinds of products to keep in stock and which to drop or reduce. Put together the questionnaire for the survey.

17. Design a questionnaire to gather information on one of the following topics:

- The most popular major in your college or university (to assist a faculty committee in charge of courses)
- Why students chose to attend your college or university (to assist the director of admissions in recruiting students)
- Improvements that should be made in dormitory life (to help the director of student affairs decide on necessary changes in the dorm)
- Students' perceptions of campus social life (to help your student government select which activities to sponsor)
- Students' likely career or graduate school choices (to assist the director of placement to plan workshops and invite speakers and recruiters)

Figure 10.13

A *WALL STREET JOURNAL* ARTICLE FOR SUMMARIZING

On Campuses, Making Dean's List Comes Second to Making a Profit
by Karen Blumenthal

DALLAS—A Stephen F. Austin University student wants partners to drill oil wells. A Rutgers University student pushes a gift item for the authority-challenging collegian: a mounted screw and a blunt slogan. Other students talk of painting yachts, delivering birthday cakes or selling underwear emblazoned with school crests.

This is a convention of the Association of Collegiate Entrepreneurs, whose mushrooming membership reflects a growing reality: College students, once given to burning draft cards, are increasingly exchanging business cards. "It's become fashionable on campus to be 19 and say, 'I have my own company,'" says Verne Harnish, national director of the association.

Enterprising students have long been found on campuses, of course, particularly those working their way through school. But college professors and administrators say this generation shows more entrepreneurial fervor than they've ever seen.

Most charitably seen, it's an affirmation of belief in the nation as a land of opportunity. Most cynically, it's a reflection of a growing desire to get filthy rich young. It is, in any event, manifested by a change in campus heroes, from old Yippie outlaw Abbie Hoffman to young Apple Computer Chairman Steven Jobs.

The Association of Collegiate Entrepreneurs, a clearinghouse for entrepreneurial ideas, started with seven member colleges in 1983; it has more than 170 today. And student-run businesses are sprouting by the score. "I think they see this as an exercise that's going to prepare them for the big game," says Edward Birch, vice chancellor of the University of California-Santa Barbara.

Marketing to Students

Many collegiate entrepreneurs market to the customers whose needs they know best: their fellow students. At the University of Texas, for instance, men try to wow that special date by sending her flowers in advance. So junior Steve Schaffer decided to buy long-stem roses wholesale and deliver them.

In the best tradition of small businessmen, he undercuts the local flower shops with lower overhead. He advertises with cheap fliers and does most of the deliveries himself. Thus, he markets the posies for about one-third the price of the flower shops, sells about 25 dozen before each big dance and sees a nice profit.

At Texas A & M University, tradition holds that men give visiting mothers, sisters and girlfriends mums to wear at home football games. Student Mark Brown decided to provide an alternative, by selling East Texas roses at $3.50 a dozen (a dollar or two less than mums) and racking up big sales. In its first year of business, 1983, his Dixie Rose Co. sold more than 500-dozen roses on some football weekends.

(continued)

(A *WALL STREET JOURNAL* ARTICLE FOR SUMMARIZING continued)

But campus enterprises aren't immune to the reversals that the cold, cruel world can deal any business. Come 1984, the Aggie home games started being televised. Attendance dropped dramatically and so did Dixie Rose's sales, to about 150 dozen a football weekend. The venture still turned a profit, but on a much more modest scale.

Some businesses never make money. Last year, University of Arizona student A. David Zoller and a friend sunk $1,000 into an endeavor to sell personalized stationery. But they neglected to ask students—their target market—what products they actually wanted. They drew only 30 orders, prompting them to close up shop.

But there's a nice thing about campus entrepreneurship: The stakes aren't that big, the failures aren't that catastrophic and the students aren't generally afraid to try again. Mr. Zoller has just launched a new enterprise, selling electronic messageboards to local businesses.

Two freshmen at the University of California-Santa Barbara learned a business lesson last year, when they decided to put on dances for students too young for the local discos. They spent more than $1,000 up front, printing 5,000 invitations, renting a roller-skating rink and buying roses for the ladies. Only 350 students showed up. They were left with a loss and a lot of roses on their hands.

The students, David Glickman and Larry Vein, cut costs for the next dance by eliminating printed invitations and roses, and they raised revenues by selling advertisements on sheets distributed at the dances. By the third dance, with expenses pared to a few hundred dollars, they turned enough of a profit for the whole venture to break even. The partners have since turned to the more lucrative business of selling discount clothing on campus.

Some businesses that begin with only modest aspirations have become grand enterprises. Two-and-a-half years ago, another U.C.-Santa Barbara student, Dan Bienenfeld, borrowed $2,000 from his father to produce a calendar. It was to feature photos of some of the good-looking men about campus, an imitation of a popular calendar created by University of Southern California students. Though the photos were only black-and-white and though the distribution was limited to California, Mr. Bienenfeld grossed $10,000.

In early 1983 he aimed higher, taking on two partners and finding an investor to put up $80,000. They put out a glossy calendar called California Dreaming and enlisted professional salesmen to sell them nationwide. But theirs was just one of many products being pushed by the salesmen, and they garnered less than $20,000 of orders.

When you want things done right, the partners decided, sometimes you've got to do them yourself. Together with four employees, the three spent the summer doing their own selling: to card shops, beauty parlors, boutiques, book stores and more. And they did well for themselves, among other things getting the product placed in about 1,300 stores.

Calendar sales hit $200,000 in 1984, and this year College Look Inc., as it's now called, has added lines of posters, giftwrap, and a teddy-bear that sings "Love Me Tender" when hugged. Sales are expected to reach $3 million. "We've hit the home run," says 22-year-old Chip Conk, an original pinup boy and now one of the partners. "Now we just have to run the bases."

Rough Road

More typically, though, the young entrepreneurs find the road to riches neither

> short nor smooth. As a student at Babson College in Wellesley, Mass., Jed Roth ran a car-cleaning business on a shoestring and earned a modest $15,000 profit as a senior. But when he graduated and wanted to grow the business, he faced a stretch of frustration. Banks were loath to give him a loan, and costs like rent and insurance were daunting.
>
> Finally, Mr. Roth found an investor willing to stake him—a Porsche-driving customer—and with that boost the business has grown, to revenues of $100,000 last year. But he's working seven-day weeks, coping with constant pressures and finding the good life elusive.
>
> "I want my own Porsche, I really do," he says. "but I can get a van (equipped with a water tank and hoses) for the same price." Adds Mr. Roth wearily, "Sometimes I wonder what it would be like to be employed."

18. Locate, and if possible correct, errors in the following excerpt from a questionnaire sent by a retailer of computer packages. He wants to find out who his competitors are and what his customers find satisfactory and unsatisfactory about his product and service. The questionnaire is sent to customers who are first-time computer users.

- Are you generally satisfied with the package?
- Were vendor representatives available when needed during implementation?
- Did you evaluate other packages?
  If so, which ones? What did you find out?
- Was the package delivered on time?
- Why did you choose this package?
- How much downtime do you anticipate?
   a. 10 percent of operating time
   b. 25 percent
   c. 50 percent
   d. 75 percent
- Do you have trouble working with machines?

19. Here is a list of questions a personnel department wants to send to employees. The department needs to determine employees' job responsibilities (not just what the job description says) and their attitudes toward their responsibilities. Decide which questions to include, their sequence, wording, and layout:

- Tell us about your job.
- Do you have authority sufficient to carry out your job?
- How many people do you supervise?
- Do you have enough responsibility in your job? too much responsibility?
- Whom do you report to?
- What is your primary responsibility?
- How long have you been with this firm?
- How do you feel about your contributions to the company?
- What are your goals and objectives here?
- Do you feel you are making progress toward those goals?

- How do you see yourself as fitting into the organization?
- Are you doing any work that you think should logically be done by another person or department?
- Do you feel you have too much work to do?
- Do you feel you should carry additional responsibility?

20. What advice would you give a group of students working on a senior field experience who wrote the following cover letter for their questionnaire:

> Dear _____,
>
> As seniors in the management program at Michigan State, we would like your assistance in our study of your industry's present and future telecommunications requirements.
>
> We would appreciate your cooperation in completing the enclosed questionnaire. Because of your central position in the telecommunications industry of the Great Lakes Region, the information you provide will be especially valuable to us.
>
> We will be happy to share the summary information of our research with you. Confidentiality of individual responses will be strictly adhered to.
>
> Thank you for returning the completed questionnaire by April 15th.
>
> Sincerely,

21. As personnel director of Stanton Labs, Jeanne O'Grady is responsible for conducting the orientation program for new employees. The program tells them about the lab's entire operations and lets them know all about the company's benefit package. This year, however, Jeanne began noting that an increasing number of employees were calling her office to request repeats of information on benefits. Jeanne wondered if she could be doing a better job orienting new employees. To find out, she decided to survey the company's employees and personnel directors in companies similar to hers.

Jeanne designed a questionnaire that would elicit the information she needed. She now needs to write a cover letter that will be persuasive, but she is not sure how to go about it. Here is her first draft:

THE FORMAL REPORT: GOAL, READER, IDEAS, AND INFORMATION

Dear _____,

    As a fellow personnel director, I'm hoping you would be able to fill out the attached questionnaire regarding your orientation program. I would like to know how effective you are finding it.

    The information can help me design a more effective program that will enable employees at my company to understand our benefits package and to know where to look for further information when they need it.

    I can provide the results of my survey to you as soon as they are ready. Thank you very much for your cooperation.

Jeanne knew the letter asked precisely what she wanted, but she also knew it did not give other directors much of a reason to help her. Write a revised cover letter for her.

See "Conducting Interviews," pp. 495–498, for Exercises 22 and 23.

22. Interview a college librarian about the library's computer services or government publications. Your purpose is to include this information in a report to students on research assistance provided by the library.

23. Suppose you are doing a formal report addressed to your class and instructor on how to improve undergraduate business writing courses. Interview several classmates about what they want to learn from a business writing course and their attitudes toward the instructor's methods.

11
THE FORMAL REPORT: ORGANIZATION, DRAFT, FORMAT, REVISION, AND GROUP WRITING

PREVIEW

This chapter should help you to

1. Make an outline to organize your formal report
2. Write a draft
3. Put the report in a format that emphasizes its logical organization
4. Revise the report
5. Write a group report by
   - Coordinating your team's efforts
   - Working out when individuals and when the group as a whole should be involved in writing

In this chapter, you will see how to organize the formal report, write a draft, use report format, and revise. You will also learn about the special opportunities and challenges of writing reports in groups.

ORGANIZING

Organizing the formal report can be a big task because of the range and quantity of information and ideas you may have to work with. For this reason, we recommend that you make an informal outline or an analysis tree as early as possible. Your outline or analysis tree will give you the freedom to generate new ideas and new ways to order them while providing a structure for the report.

By the time you are ready to organize your report, you will most likely have amassed a stack of index cards. Mark had written over a hundred cards for his report. They represented:

- Authors' ideas (from secondary readings) and his reactions to them
- Results of his questionnaire and card-sort and his analysis of these results
- Results of his interviews with students and recruiters

By reviewing his research and analysis, Mark formulated several conclusions and recommendations about the qualifications students should demonstrate at on-campus interviews. He concluded that recruiters look for good communication skills and experience in group work and leadership. He also found that students recognize the importance recruiters place on communication skills but not on group work and leadership. Mark wanted to recommend several ways that students could improve their performance at on-campus interviews. With these conclusions and recommendations in mind, he had to organize his information to explain and support these conclusions and recommendations most effectively.

With the goal of his report in mind, he began an outline. To plan it, he carefully read and reread his note cards and grouped them, putting each in a stack according to

Hundreds of note cards may need to be organized for a report.

the subject it concerned. (As you may recall, he had labeled each card with a subject heading.) Each stack represented a potential major or minor idea in his outline.

As Mark reviewed his conclusions and recommendations, a pattern for organizing his report emerged: "I'll first show what recruiters look for, then what students think recruiters look for, and compare the two. In the last section, I'll describe what students can do to prepare for interviews."

If you recall Mark's method of data gathering (see Chapter 10, "The Formal Report: Goal, Reader, Ideas, and Information"), you will now understand how his method of research reduced his difficulty in outlining the report. While doing research, he collected information and recorded his ideas systematically. That is, he thought about how each piece of information related to others and to his subject. He also recorded these connections on his index cards as subject headings. The headings, then, suggested to him possible headings for the outline of his report. Here is the outline he came up with:

Do students know what qualifications they should demonstrate at on-campus interviews?
  I. What Recruiters Look For
      A. Communication Skills (see Posner and card-sort)
      B. Group Work and Leadership (see interviews)
  II. What Students Think Recruiters Look For
      A. Communication Skills (see Posner and Card-sort)
      B. Group Work and Leadership (further study needed)
  III. Comparison of What Recruiters and Students Think
  IV. How Students Can Prepare
      A. Long Range
          1. Communication Skills
          2. Group Work and Leadership
      B. Short Range
          1. Communication Skills
          2. Group Work and Leadership

This abbreviated outline represented the broad categories of his report, which he either filled in as he drafted the report or altered as new ideas emerged in writing the report. He used this informal outline to write a draft of his paper. Alternatively, he could have used an analysis tree, such as the one shown in Figure 11.1.

WRITING A DRAFT

Mark worked from his informal outline to write the body of his report. After several drafts he came up with the final version (Figure 11.3). As you read Mark's report, notice how he organized his ideas and information. Notice, too, the various parts of the report, which are discussed later in the chapter.

To accompany the report, Mark wrote a letter of transmittal (Figure 11.2).

Figure 11.1

MARK'S ANALYSIS TREE

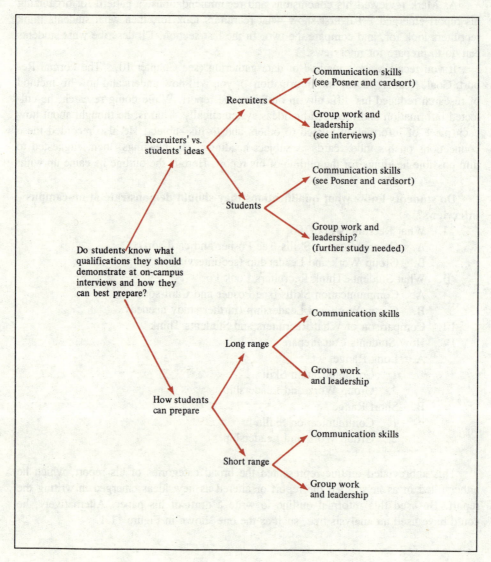

Figure 11.2

MARK'S LETTER OF TRANSMITTAL

Box 323
Babson College
January 11, 199_

Dear Professor Lancaster:

    To fulfill my research report assignment for Organizational Behavior 310 on a business problem relevant to college students, I have completed a report called "DO STUDENTS KNOW WHAT QUALIFICATIONS THEY SHOULD DEMONSTRATE AT ON-CAMPUS INTERVIEWS?" This report compares (1) the job qualifications recruiters look for in students and (2) the qualifications that students think recruiters look for. It also recommends how students can improve their performance at on-campus interviews.   *Reason for writing* / *Title* / *Goal*

    I was able to study several recruiters' criteria rather thoroughly. But due to time and budgetary constraints, I was unable to conduct research on all criteria recruiters find important.   *Scope and limits*

    You may find recommendations concerning curricular change to be of particular interest to you as you think about course content for communication courses and workshops.   *Special reader benefit*

    If you have any questions about the report, I would be happy to discuss them with you and am available at 6-9095.

Sincerely yours,

Mark White

Mark White

Figure 11.3

MARK'S REPORT—FINAL VERSION

DO STUDENTS KNOW WHAT QUALIFICATIONS THEY SHOULD
DEMONSTRATE AT ON-CAMPUS INTERVIEWS?

Prepared for
Professor Lancaster
Organizational Behavior 310

By
Mark White

January 11, 199_

OUTLINE

Do Students Know What Qualifications They Should Demonstrate at On-Campus Interviews?

I. Introduction: Why Study What Recruiters Look For in Job Candidates?

II. What Recruiters Look For
   A. Methodology
      1. Questionnaire and Card-Sort
         a. Selection of Subjects: Recruiters and Students
         b. Demographics
         c. Criteria Assessed
         d. Procedures
      2. Interviews
         a. Criteria Assessed
         b. Procedures
   B. Findings: Strong Communication Skills, Group Work, and Leadership
      1. Questionnaire and Card-Sort
      2. Interviews with Recruiters

III. What Students Think Recruiters Look For
   A. Methodology
   B. Findings: Strong Communication Skills
      1. Questionnaire and Card-Sort
      2. Interviews with Students

IV. Conclusions: Comparing What Recruiters and Students Think

V. Recommendations: How Students Can Prepare for On-Campus Interviews
   A. Long-Range Activities
   B. Short-Range Activities

i

(continued)

TABLE OF CONTENTS

Page

Executive Summary.. 1

Introduction: Why Study What Recruiters Look For in Job
  Candidates? 3

What Recruiters Look For 4
  Methodology 5
  Findings: Strong Communication Skills, Group Work, and
    Leadership 8

What Students Think Recruiters Look For 10
  Methodology 10
  Findings: Strong Communication Skills..................... 10

Conclusions: Comparing What Recruiters and Students Think.. 11

Recommendations: How Students Can Prepare for
  On-Campus Interviews.. 12
  Long-Range Activities.. 13
  Short-Range Activities 13

Notes.. 14

References 15

Additional Works Consulted.................................... 16

ii

Appendix I: 30 Recruiters from 23 Companies.................. 17

Appendix II: Recruiter's Questionnaire 18

Appendix III: Student's Questionnaire 20

Appendix IV: Distribution of Answers to Questionnaire 22

Appendix V: Recruiters' and Students' Responses
to Card-Sort.. 25

Table 1: Results of Recruiter Card-Sort: Personality and
Verbal Expression (Communication Ability) Ranked First
and Second by Recruiters 25

Table 2: Results of Student Card-Sort: Personality and Verbal
Expression (Communication Ability) Ranked First and Second by
Students 26

iii

(continued)

(MARK'S REPORT—FINAL VERSION continued)

EXECUTIVE SUMMARY

This report compares (1) the job qualifications recruiters look for in students and (2) the qualifications that students think recruiters look for. It then recommends how students can improve their performance at on-campus interviews.

Gives purpose and scope of report

The following research methods were used to study recruiters' expectations and students' knowledge of these expectations:

Identifies methodology

- Questionnaire and card-sort administered to recruiters and to seniors majoring in business at Babson and at comparable colleges
- Interviews with recruiters and students

Findings of the research show that recruiters look for strong communication skills, group work, and leadership in job candidates. Students are aware of one major criterion, communication skills, but may not be aware of the need for group work and leadership.

Summarizes findings

Students should become aware of all three major criteria recruiters value most in job candidates and should prepare for on-campus interviews in light of this knowledge. More research needs to be done to determine if, in fact, students are unaware of the importance of group work and leadership to recruiters.

Draws conclusions

Points out limitations

With knowledge of recruiters' expectations, students can participate in a program of long- and short-range activities to strengthen their communication ability and their group work and leadership experience:

Makes recommendations

1

1. <u>Long-range activities:</u> In their four years of college, students should take courses that teach them communication skills and should build their group and leadership activities.

2. <u>Short-range activities:</u> In the several weeks before the interview, students should practice their communication skills with the help of job placement and communication specialists.

(continued)

(MARK'S REPORT—FINAL VERSION continued)

INTRODUCTION: WHY STUDY WHAT RECRUITERS LOOK FOR IN JOB CANDIDATES?

Business students spend years planning their future and many hours studying so that they may qualify for jobs of their choice. Despite their preparation, however, they may not be hired for these jobs unless they know how company recruiters will evaluate them in a 30- to 45-minute interview, and unless they prepare for these interviews.

Shows importance of topic of report

Although research has been conducted on job interviewing, very little empirical work has been done on what recruiters actually look for in job candidates and what students think recruiters look for (Posner, 1981, p. 329). When research has been done, sample size has been very small. As Professor B. Z. Posner stated in the only major study on this subject,

Supports need for more research on topic

> Very little is known about the factors . . . which corporate recruiters consider in evaluating job applicants. Even less is known about the degree to which job applicants are aware of the factors considered important by recruiters (p. 329).

In his study, Posner investigated what those factors are and determined whether students recognized them.

When Posner compared students' and recruiters' perceptions of what recruiters look for in job candidates during interviews, he found that "What stands out most . . . are not the differences but rather the similarities [between perceptions of students and recruiters]" (p. 335). According to Posner, students <u>do</u> know the major criteria recruiters use to judge them. At the top of the list is <u>communication skills.</u>[1]

Summarizes results of the only study

Although Posner's study is thorough, it is dated (1981) and is not based on the Babson College student population.

Gives purpose of research

3

Therefore, to verify Posner's findings and to see whether they apply to Babson students, I conducted research on the criteria recruiters use to judge Babson students and similar populations during job interviews, and on whether students are aware of these criteria.

First, I questioned recruiters about what they look for in job candidates at on-campus interviews. To do this, I administered a questionnaire and card-sort to recruiters. During the same period, I investigated what students think recruiters look for in job candidates by administering the same questionnaire and card-sort. Then I interviewed five students and five recruiters on my topic. Finally, I did a preliminary review of pertinent secondary sources to find out how students might prepare for on-campus interviews.   *Gives preview of content of report*

The results of my research indicate that recruiters believe strong communication skills, group work, and leadership are most important. Babson College students are aware of the importance of communication skills to recruiters but may not be aware of the importance of group work and leadership experience. More research needs to be done to determine whether students recognize the importance of these two other qualifications. The need for such research emerged so late in the study that I was unable to carry it out.   *Gives conclusions of study*

WHAT RECRUITERS LOOK FOR

The results of my research confirm Posner's conclusion that communication skills are a major criterion recruiters use to evaluate students. My research also revealed the importance of group work and leadership experience.   *Summarizes results of research*

To determine the criteria recruiters value most, I used a questionnaire and card-sort as well as interviews with recruiters. A description of these research methods and the findings from the research follow.   *Previews sections that follow*

4

(continued)

(MARK'S REPORT—FINAL VERSION continued)

Methodology

Questionnaire and Card-Sort *Gives details of research design*

Selection of Subjects: Recruiters and Students

The study included two groups. The first group consisted of 30 recruiters who interview prospective employees in their common fields of business (e.g., an accountant interviews an accounting major). Recruiters were randomly selected; the only qualification was that they regularly interview business majors at Babson and at comparable colleges included in the study. The group included recruiters from the following well-known companies:

Prime Computers	Barry Wright
Zayre Corporation	R.C.A.
Arthur Andersen	First National Bank

In total, recruiters represented 23 companies. (See Appendix I for a complete listing of the breakdown by company.)

The second group consisted of 60 college seniors majoring in business, randomly selected from six Boston area schools and one New York school. The seven schools share comparable standing among the corporate employers used in the study, as determined by the percentage of students each company offers jobs to from each college. The Boston colleges (and the number of students per college) were:

Babson College (8)	Boston University (6)
Boston College (13)	Suffolk University (8)
Bentley College (13)	Northeastern University (6)

Adelphi University (6 students) was the New York school.

5

Demographics: Recruiters and Students

Recruiters ranged in age from 25 to 65. The mean age of participants was 50. Income brackets ranged from lower middle to upper class. The mean income was approximately $35,000 per year.

The student groups consisted of approximately 66 percent male and 34 percent female. The mean age of these college seniors was 21. They came from lower-, middle-, and upper-class income brackets, and various ethnic and racial backgrounds.

Criteria Assessed

To find out what criteria recruiters and students believe are important, I chose to assess those that previous researchers identified in studies of "criteria commonly used by recruiters when interviewing and hiring job candidates for entry-level positions (Anton and Russell, 1974; Hakel and Schuh, 1971; Kohn, 1975; Tschergi, 1973)" (cited in Posner, 1981, p. 332). I selected eleven criteria: grade-point average, personality, appearance, mobility, college attended, (verbal) expression, extracurricular activities, courses taken, content of the interview, goals, and part-time employment.

I used two questionnaires and eleven index cards. (See Appendixes II and III for copies of the questionnaires.)

The questionnaires were used to determine statistically whether a significant difference existed between what recruiters say they look for in job candidates and what students think recruiters look for. The average of each characteristic (questions 1–11) was taken and ranked in order of importance (most important to least). The means of recruiter and student were then compared to see if a significant difference existed.

(continued)

Recruiters and students received similar questionnaires. The only difference lay in the directions on how to answer the questionnaire. Whereas recruiters were asked to give their criteria for evaluating job candidates, students were asked to answer the questionnaire in the way they felt recruiters evaluate.

The card-sort required that each subject rank job criteria in order of importance. Eleven index cards, each containing one employment criterion (i.e., college attended, personality, etc.) were distributed with the questionnaire. After completing the questionnaire, the individual then arranged the eleven index cards in a sequence from most to least important. I recorded this ranking on the back of the participant's questionnaire. The data from these rankings were compared and averaged to derive a final mean and a final ranking.

Interviews

After the results of the questionnaire were determined, I conducted individual face-to-face interviews with five students and five recruiters who had participated in the questionnaire and card-sort, to see whether the findings of the questionnaire and card-sort would be verified and to find out new information.

<u>Criteria Assessed</u>

Criteria assessed consisted of (1) the eleven job qualifications identified in the questionnaire and the card-sort and (2) the qualifications students and recruiters deemed important that were not among the eleven.

<u>Procedures</u>

First, I asked each student and recruiter to rank-order the eleven criteria and to discuss their top choices. Then I asked the subject whether he or she could identify and discuss any other essential criteria not covered on the list.

Findings: Strong Communication Skills,
Group Work, and Leadership

Questionnaire and Card-Sort

The questionnaire yielded no significant results. (See Appendix IV for the distribution of answers to the questionnaire.) No significant difference between recruiters and students occurred in eight of the eleven items on a 95 percent confidence level when comparing the degree of importance each participant attached to each question. A significant difference did appear on three questions—#7 (extra-curricular activities), #8 (courses taken), and #9 (content)—but these criteria were in the mid-range in terms of importance to recruiters.

Gives results

The findings of the card-sort were significant. Whereas, when filling out the questionnaire, participants could place the same amount of importance on as many characteristics as they thought necessary, when doing the card-sort, they had to place the eleven characteristics in sequential order. (See Appendix V for distribution of responses on the card-sort.) The results of the card-sort indicate that recruiters rank personality and verbal expression—communication skills—as the top criteria. Table 1 shows recruiters' rankings of the eleven characteristics.

(continued)

(MARK'S REPORT—FINAL VERSION continued)

Table 1

Results of Recruiter Card-Sort: Personality and Verbal Expression (Communication Ability) Ranked First and Second by Recruiters

Card Name	Rank Assigned
Personality	1
(Verbal) Expression	2
Content of Interview	3
Appearance	4
Goals	5
Grade-Point Average	6
Courses Taken	7
Part-Time Employment	8
College Attended	9
Extracurricular Activities	10
Mobility	11

Interviews with Recruiters

Results of interviews with recruiters supported evidence gained from the card-sort: recruiters consider communication skills a major criterion in evaluating job candidates. Recruiters ranked personality and verbal expression first and second, respectively. When they described their choice, they said they were most concerned with gaining a general impression of the candidate's personality and getting the student to talk, before moving on to specific questions about his or her qualifications for a particular job. Recruiters revealed that most students who communicated poorly during the on-campus interview would not be offered jobs. The exceptions tended to be students with specialized technical expertise needed by the company. Recruiters also mentioned that their sense of the student's personality and ability to express ideas most influenced them in their decisions.

Interviews with recruiters also revealed two other major criteria of importance to recruiters, group work and leadership experience. In the questionnaire these factors may have been partially measured under CONTENT and EXTRA-CURRICULAR ACTIVITIES, but these categories are too broad to capture such information adequately. All five recruiters interviewed said that they asked students about their involvement in school and work groups and about offices and responsibilities they have held. As one recruiter summarized, "A derogatory statement [on the part of a student] about a work group shows not just lack of tact. It shows that the student is unable to work with others. Being a good team player is a must." All recruiters stressed the importance of students' group and leadership experiences.

WHAT STUDENTS THINK RECRUITERS LOOK FOR

Methodology

This has been fully described in the earlier methodology section (pp. 5–8). In brief, research methods used included (1) a questionnaire and card-sort and (2) interviews with students. Sixty college seniors majoring in business at seven schools responded to the same questionnaire and card-sort as did the recruiters. Five students were interviewed; they were asked the same set of questions as were the five recruiters.

Summarizes relevant part of methodology section

Findings: Strong Communication Skills

Gives findings

The results of my research show that students recognize communication skills as a major criterion but may or may not be aware of the importance of group work and leadership.

Questionnaire and Card-Sort

The results of the card-sort indicate that students recognize the importance to recruiters of communication skills: personality and verbal expression were ranked first and second by recruiters and students alike. Table 2 shows the students' rankings of each of the eleven criteria.

10

(continued)

(MARK'S REPORT—FINAL VERSION continued)

Table 2

Results of Student Card-Sort: Personality and Verbal Expression (Communication Ability) Ranked First and Second

Card Name	Rank Assigned
Personality	1
(Verbal) Expression	2
Appearance	3
College Attended	4
Content of Interview	5
Grade-Point Average	6
Goals	7
Courses Taken	8
Extracurricular Activities	9
Part-Time Employment	10
Mobility	11

Interviews with Students

Results of interviews with students supported evidence from the questionnaire and card-sort. At the interviews, students ranked communication skills first among the criteria recruiters judge important in job candidates. All five students reported that they felt recruiters gave serious attention to how well students express themselves. When asked about group work and leadership, students were divided in their opinions: two felt these criteria were important and three were unsure.

CONCLUSIONS: COMPARING WHAT RECRUITERS AND STUDENTS THINK

This study shows that Babson College business students recognize the importance recruiters place on communication skills but may or may not recognize the importance recruiters place on group work and leadership.

Summarizes findings

Further empirical research (e.g., questionnaires and a card-sort on job factors) should be used to determine whether students recognize the importance of group work and leadership to recruiters. Such research was not conducted for this study because the information emerged in interviews conducted after the questionnaire was distributed. It was then too late to include this information in the questionnaire or to administer another questionnaire that took into account group work and leadership.

Draws conclusions

My research also suggests that students may not do their best at the on-campus interview for two reasons:

1. They may not be aware of the importance of group work and leadership experience.
2. Even when they are aware of an important criterion (e.g., communication skills), they may not have adequately prepared themselves in the areas recruiters consider important.

Students should become aware of all the major criteria recruiters value most in job candidates and should prepare for on-campus interviews in light of their knowledge.

RECOMMENDATIONS: HOW STUDENTS CAN PREPARE FOR ON-CAMPUS INTERVIEWS

Students can prepare for on-campus interviews by building strengths in communication and in group work and leadership. On the basis of my preliminary library research on how students can prepare for on-campus interviews,[2] I recommend that students undertake several <u>long-range</u> and <u>short-range</u> activities.

12

(continued)

(MARK'S REPORT—FINAL VERSION continued)

Long-Range Activities

In their four years at college, students should

- Take courses or workshops that teach speaking, listening, and nonverbal skills (e.g., poise, posture, eye contact, gestures).
- Seek out opportunities to work in groups (e.g., clubs, part-time jobs, in-class teams).

Short-Range Activities

Several weeks before interviewing, students should practice their communication skills with the help of job placement and communication specialists. If help is not available on campus, there are consultants who do such work. All practice sessions should include the following five components:

- Discussions and demonstrations of good interviewing techniques
- Videotaping of individual students
- Role-playing and mock interviews
- Critiquing of students' verbal and nonverbal behavior
- Frequent practice of good interviewing techniques.

Further research is needed to determine better the scope and implementation of students' preparatory activities.

Gives specific recommendations

FOOTNOTES

1. Posner identified future potential as a top criterion as well, but I chose not to explore this factor in my research, since future potential is judged differently depending on a student's area of specialization (e.g., economics, accounting, finance).

2. My preliminary research yielded several articles that warrant further attention: Huegli and Tschirgi (1981) on "behavior modeling"—a technique involving identifying and practicing interviewing skills; Leach and Flaxman (1978) on the "self-rating sheet" for self, peer, and instructor evaluation of interviewing skills; and Phillips (1982) on effective responses to questions that interviewers frequently ask.

(continued)

REFERENCES

Huegli, Jon M., and Tschirgi, Harvey D. (1979). Preparing the student for the initial job interview: Skills and methods. ABCA Bulletin, 42 (4), 10–13.

Leach, James, and Flaxman, Nancy. (1978). Self-rating: An exercise for improving job interview skills. Balance Sheet, 59 (7), 303–305.

Phillips, J. J. (1982). Ten ways to improve the effectiveness of your campus interviews. SAM Advanced Management Journal, 47 (4), 56–62.

Posner, Barry Z. (1981). Comparing recruiter, student, and faculty perceptions of important applicant and job characteristics. Personnel Psychology, 34, 329–339.

ADDITIONAL WORKS CONSULTED

Forkner, Patricia A. (1981). The job hunt: Appropriate unit for basic business class. Business Educator, 35 (7), 11–12.

Taylor, Susan M., and Sniezak, Janet A. (1984). The college recruitment interview: Topical content and applicant reactions. Journal of Occupational Psychology, 157–168.

Tschirgi, Harvey. (1972–1973). What do recruiters really look for in candidates? Journal of College Placement, 75–79.

Vecchiotti, Dorothea I., and Korn, James H. (1981). Comparison of student and recruiter values. Journal of Vocational Behavior, 16, 43–50.

(continued)

(MARK'S REPORT—FINAL VERSION continued)

APPENDIX I

30 Recruiters From 23 Companies

Allison Corporation	North American Life Insurance
Arthur Andersen	
Avon	Prime Computer
Baker & Handler Insurance	RCA
Barry Wright Corporation	Ross Laboratories Inc.
Emerson West Company	South Shore National Bank
First National Bank of Boston	Suffolk Franklin Bank
Judge Electronics Service	Thorne Group
Littman & Futterman Accounting Firm	TJ Max
	World Wide Unlimited
Lot #1 of Boston	WROR
Million Dollar Corporation	Zayre Corporation
New England Telephone	

17

THE FORMAL REPORT: ORGANIZATION, DRAFT, FORMAT, REVISION, AND GROUP WRITING

APPENDIX II

Recruiter's Questionnaire

Directions: Answer these questions on the basis of how you would evaluate a student. Rate each question below on a scale from 1 to 5 in degree of importance.

<u>Circle one!</u>

```
        1                          5
      Most   _____     Least
    important                  important
```

1. How much importance do you place on grade-point average? 1 2 3 4 5
2. How important is the personality of the individual? 1 2 3 4 5
3. How much emphasis do you place on appearance? 1 2 3 4 5
4. How much importance do you put on the willingness of a person to relocate? 1 2 3 4 5
5. How much emphasis do you place on the college the individual attended? 1 2 3 4 5
6. How much emphasis do you place on the way the individual expresses himself or herself? 1 2 3 4 5
7. Do you insist on the individual having participated in extracurricular activities? 1 2 3 4 5
8. How much emphasis do you place on courses taken? 1 2 3 4 5
9. How much emphasis do you place on content in an interview? 1 2 3 4 5
10. How much significance do you place on the individual's future goals? 1 2 3 4 5

(continued)

(MARK'S REPORT—FINAL VERSION continued)

11. Is part-time employment during college important?   1 2 3 4 5

12. If there is any other important factor that you would include in an interview, what would it be?

13. What do you think is the most effective way of finding a job?

19

APPENDIX III

Student's Questionnaire

Directions: Answer these questions on the basis of how you feel the interviewer would be evaluating you. Rate each question below on a scale from 1 to 5 in degree of importance.

Circle one!

```
1 ──────────────── 5
Most              Least
important         important
```

1. How much importance do you place on grade-point average?   1 2 3 4 5
2. How important is the personality of the individual?   1 2 3 4 5
3. How much emphasis do you place on appearance?   1 2 3 4 5
4. How much importance do you put on the willingness of a person to relocate?   1 2 3 4 5
5. How much emphasis do you place on the college the individual attended?   1 2 3 4 5
6. How much emphasis do you place on the way the individual expresses himself or herself?   1 2 3 4 5
7. Do you insist on the individual having participated in extracurricular activities?   1 2 3 4 5
8. How much emphasis do you place on courses taken?   1 2 3 4 5
9. How much emphasis do you place on content in an interview?   1 2 3 4 5
10. How much significance do you place on the individual's future goals?   1 2 3 4 5

20

(continued)

(MARK'S REPORT—FINAL VERSION continued)

11. Is part-time employment during college important?   1 2 3 4 5

12. If there is any other important factor that you would include in an interview, what would it be?

13. What do you think is the most effective way of finding a job?

21

THE FORMAL REPORT: ORGANIZATION, DRAFT, FORMAT, REVISION, AND GROUP WRITING

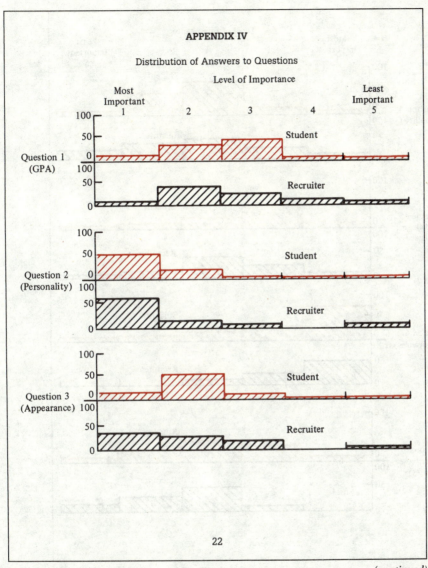

(continued)

(MARK'S REPORT—FINAL VERSION continued)

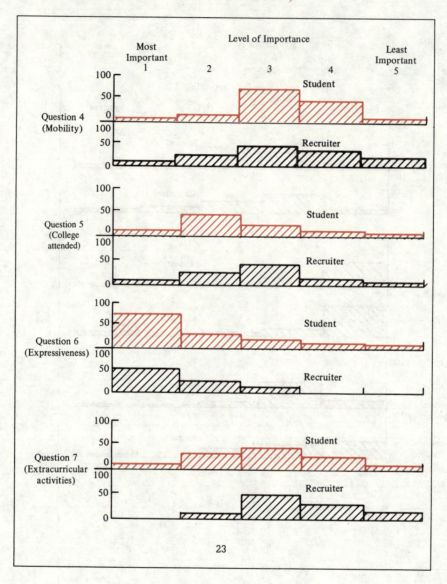

23

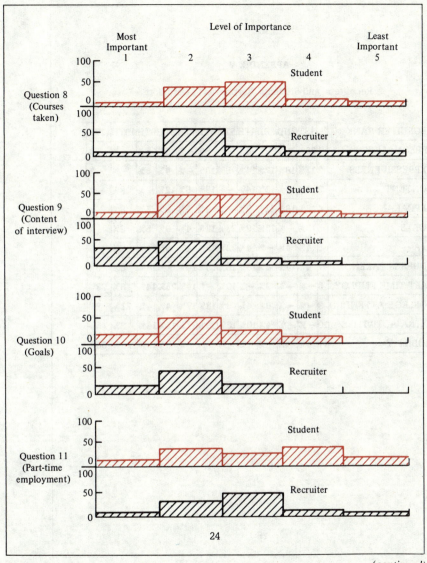

(continued)

(MARK'S REPORT—FINAL VERSION continued)

APPENDIX V

Recruiters' and Students' Responses to Card-Sort

RECRUITER RANK		1ST	2ND	3RD	4TH	5TH	6TH	7TH	8TH	9TH	10TH	11TH
PERSONALITY	1	36%	30%	9%	4%	–%	9%	–%	9%	5%	–%	–%
EXPRESSIVENESS	2	17%	18%	17%	14%	9%	13%	–%	4%	5%	–%	–%
CONTENT	3	9%	26%	13%	14%	–%	13%	5%	12%	–%	9%	–%
APPEARANCE	4	13%	18%	22%	9%	4%	4%	9%	9%	5%	8%	–%
GOALS	5	13%	–%	13%	13%	23%	13%	4%	9%	5%	8%	–%
GPA	6	4%	4%	–%	14%	22%	13%	14%	8%	14%	8%	–%
COURSES TAKEN	7	4%	4%	4%	18%	10%	13%	10%	–%	14%	8%	5%
PART-TIME EMPLOY.	8	–%	–%	9%	–%	10%	–%	14%	25%	14%	8%	23%
COLLEGE ATTENDED	9	–%	–%	9%	4%	9%	13%	17%	4%	14%	21%	9%
EXTRA ACTIVITIES	10	–%	–%	4%	10%	13%	9%	27%	12%	14%	8%	5%
MOBILITY	11	4%	–%	–%	–%	–%	–%	–%	8%	10%	22%	58%

25

STUDENT RANK		1ST	2ND	3RD	4TH	5TH	6TH	7TH	8TH	9TH	10TH	11TH
PERSONALITY	1	33%	40%	10%	10%	3%	–%	2%	2%	–%	–%	–%
EXPRESSIVENESS	2	26%	24%	15%	11%	5%	3%	2%	3%	–%	–%	–%
APPEARANCE	3	12%	7%	24%	16%	14%	3%	7%	7%	9%	–%	–%
COLLEGE ATTENDED	4	9%	5%	10%	10%	10%	12%	10%	16%	7%	2%	3%
CONTENT	5	–%	6%	15%	4%	19%	10%	14%	11%	10%	8%	3%
GPA	6	7%	7%	13%	10%	7%	10%	12%	9%	9%	8%	10%
GOALS	7	13%	3%	3%	7%	9%	9%	16%	12%	14%	5%	7%
COURSES TAKEN	8	–%	5%	7%	4%	17%	17%	7%	5%	19%	6%	9%
EXTRA ACTIVITIES	9	–%	–%	1%	13%	14%	12%	9%	13%	9%	17%	24%
PART-TIME EMPLOY.	10	–%	3%	2%	7%	2%	14%	10%	12%	14%	17%	17%
MOBILITY	11	–%	–%	–%	8%	–%	10%	11%	10%	9%	37%	27%

26

PARTS AND FORMAT OF FORMAL REPORTS

To be readable, a report needs to be subdivided into parts and to be well formated. Good formating emphasizes logical organization and allows readers to determine quickly which sections of the report are pertinent to their needs, which sections can be ignored, and which must be read in depth. Few readers will read everything. In general, managers read primarily for recommendations, and technical people read for methodology or for implementation of recommendations.

Include some or all of the following report segments in your report. The longer and more complex the report, the more of these report segments you will want to include.

INTRODUCTORY MATERIAL

    Letter of Transmittal
    Title Page
    Formal Outline
    Table of Contents
    List of Tables and Figures
    Executive Summary

BODY

    Introduction
    Discussion
    Findings
    Conclusions
    Recommendations

SUPPLEMENTARY MATERIAL

    Reference Citations in the Text
    Footnotes
    Bibliography
    Appendixes

Introductory Material

LETTER OF TRANSMITTAL

The **letter of transmittal** is a cover letter that introduces the report to readers. It can be less formal than the report—even conversational. Typically, it includes the following:

THE FORMAL REPORT: ORGANIZATION, DRAFT, FORMAT, REVISION, AND GROUP WRITING

- Reason for writing the report
- Authorization for the report
- Title of the report and its goal
- Acknowledgment of those who gave special help
- Scope and limits of the report
- Special reader benefits

Notice that Mark's letter (Figure 11.2 on p. 511) is written in a personal style and includes most of the above features.

TITLE PAGE

The **title page** should contain the title of the report, the name(s) and exact position or title of the writer(s), and reader(s), and the date. (See Figure 11.3, p. 512, for the title page of Mark's report.)

Effective titles clearly and concisely identify the focus of the report. Mark, for example, might have used a vague title such as "Important Criteria for Selecting New Employees," but the one he chose focuses the reader's attention on the exact topic: "Do Students Know What Qualifications They Should Demonstrate at On-Campus Interviews?"

FORMAL OUTLINE

A **formal outline** may be required in a college course but is usually *not* requested in business. Since Mark's instructor asked him to hand in a formal outline with his report, he followed the standard format you are probably familiar with (see p. 513):

Title of the Report

I. Major Point One
   A. Subpoint One Supporting Major Point One
      1. Support for Subpoint A
      2. Support for Subpoint A
II. Major Point Two
      etc.

If further subdivisions are required beyond the indented Arabic numerals, these successively smaller units should be indented from the previous level and appear as lower-case letters, then as numbers in parenthesis and then as lower-case letters in parenthesis.

The formal outline reveals the main points and supporting points as they are arranged in the report. Mark's outline (p. 513) helped him check the organization of his report and enabled his instructor to visualize its structure.

TABLE OF CONTENTS

The **table of contents** identifies for readers the major sections of the report in their order of appearance, followed by the supplementary material (e.g., footnotes, bibliography, appendixes). Page numbers are given for all sections.

Mark's table of contents is shown on pages 514–515. Note how the pages in his report are numbered:

- Lower-case Roman numerals (i, ii, iii, iv) to indicate the prefatory material
- Arabic numerals (1, 2, 3, 4) for the body of the report

Include the number of the first page of each section and subsection to the right of the name of that section or subsection. Use dots to separate the name from the page number.

If your report contains more than five or six graphic aids, you may want to include a separate **list of tables and figures.** (If you have less than five or six graphic aids, list them at the bottom of the table of contents.) The list of tables and figures should follow the table of contents on a separate page, as in Figure 11.4.

EXECUTIVE SUMMARY

The executive summary summarizes the report's essential information and allows readers to judge whether or not to read the entire document. The executive summary is often the only part of the report all readers will review.

Executive summaries should contain the following:

1. *Purpose and scope of your investigation:* The purpose refers to why the report has been written. The scope refers to what the report covers. This is how Mark began his executive summary:

> This report compares (1) the job qualifications recruiters look for in students and (2) the qualifications that students think recruiters look for. It then recommends how students can improve their performance at on-campus interviews.

2. *Methodology:* Methodology describes the research done to investigate the question you want to answer. Mark identified his research methods—questionnaires and interviews—in the second paragraph of his executive summary:

> The following research methods were used to study recruiters' expectations and students' knowledge of these expectations:
> - Questionnaire and card-sort administered to recruiters and to seniors majoring in business at Babson and at comparable colleges
> - Interviews with recruiters and students

Figure 11.4

SAMPLE LISTING OF GRAPHIC AIDS

LIST OF TABLES AND FIGURES

Figure 1: Scope of Services Offered by Urgent Care Centers ... 7
Figure 2: Space Allocations for Urgent Care Centers 9
Figure 3: Equipment Needed for Urgent Care Centers.......... 12
Figure 4: Staffing Needed for Urgent Care Centers 15
Figure 5: Estimated Demand for Physicians' Services in
           Orange County.. 23
Figure 6: Survery of Orange County Physicians................ 32
Figure 7: Largest Employees in Orange County................ 38
Figure 8: Perceived Deterrents to Health Care, Orange
           County 43
Figure 9: Estimated Market for an Orange County Urgent
           Care Center 46

10

3. *Findings:* Findings summarize what you have learned from your research. Mark included these right after he identified his methodology:

> Findings of the research show that recruiters look for strong communication skills, group work, and leadership in job candidates. Students are aware of one major criterion, communication skills, but may not be aware of the need for group work and leadership.

4. *Conclusions and recommendations:* Conclusions state what you have inferred from your findings. Recommendations state what you think the reader should do, on the basis of your findings and conclusions. Conclusions and recommendations make up a large part of the executive summary, as they did for Mark's:

> Students should become aware of all three major criteria recruiters value most in job candidates and should prepare for on-campus interviews in light of this knowledge. More research needs to be done to determine if, in fact, students are unaware of the importance of group work and leadership to recruiters.
>
> With knowledge of recruiters' expectations, students can participate in a program of long- and short-range activities to strengthen their communication ability and their group work and leadership experience:
>
> 1. <u>Long-range activities</u>: In their four years of college, students should take courses that teach them communication skills and should build their group and leadership activities.
> 2. <u>Short-range activities</u>: In the several weeks before the interview, students should practice their communication skills with the help of job placement and communication specialists.

In most cases, your reader is primarily interested in your conclusions and recommendations, so it is crucial to include them. But conclusions and recommendations should not be specified if you anticipate that your reader will reject or resist them. In those instances, you may want to state that conclusions and recommendations will be given in the report without identifying them in the summary.

5. *Implementation:* Many business reports demonstrate the feasibility of recommendations and outline the steps the organization must take to implement the recommendations.

Write your executive summary either before or after you write your report. If you write the summary *before* you write the report, you will be able to see if you have a sense of the whole report before writing it. If you write the summary *after* you write the report, first review your report carefully, paying special attention to headings and subheadings, since they should identify the key parts of the report, then write.

Try to keep your summary to one or at most two pages. Beyond that, it becomes too detailed and begins to read like the body of the report.

Use the accompanying checklist to review your executive summaries.

CHECKLIST FOR WRITING EXECUTIVE SUMMARIES

1. Have you stated the purpose and scope of your report?
2. Have you identified your research methods?
3. Have you identified your findings?
4. Have you specified your conclusions and recommendations?
5. Have you shown how your recommendations can be implemented?

The introductory material—the letter of transmittal, the title page, the table of contents, the list of tables, the formal outline, and the executive summary—introduces the report. Let's look now at the body of the report.

Body

INTRODUCTION

The opening section of the body contains the following items:

- Essential background information
- Definition of the problem
- Purpose of the report
- Scope and limitations of the investigation
- Description of the methodology
- Conclusions and recommendations
- Preview of the content and structure of the report

Mark's introduction can be found on pp. 518–519.

DISCUSSION

Usually the largest section of the report, the discussion should be organized to give logical support to your conclusions and recommendations. Your discussion section will provide such support if you have used an analysis tree or informal outline effectively. Mark's conclusions about students' preparation for on-campus interviews were based on what he covered in the discussion section, namely recruiters' expectations and students' knowledge of these expectations.

Previews and summaries can help your readers move efficiently through your discussion section. **Previews** inform readers of the major segment to follow and the ideas to be discussed. **Summaries** help readers recall the major points of earlier sections.

FINDINGS

The findings section identifies and sums up the results of your study. Mark presented his findings in two parts. He presented his findings about recruiters' expectations in the major section headed "What Recruiters Look For." He presented his findings about students' knowledge of these expectations in the major section headed "What Students Think Recruiters Look For."

CONCLUSIONS

The conclusion section draws inferences from your findings. These inferences should point to the recommendations. In the conclusion of his report, Mark compared his findings about recruiters and students, and suggested reasons why students may not do their best at on-campus interviews.

RECOMMENDATIONS

Recommendations, or what the reader should do about the problem you have investigated, should be based on your findings and conclusions. Mark's recommendations followed logically from his findings and recommendations. He found that recruiters looked for strong communication skills, group work, and leadership in job candidates. He also found that students were aware of one major criterion, communication skills, but might not be aware of the other two. He concluded that students need to become aware of all three criteria to succeed in on-campus interviews. He then gave specific recommendations based on these findings and conclusions. His recommendations concerned how students could prepare for the on-campus interview once they understood recruiters' criteria.

QUOTATIONS, PARAPHRASES, AND SUMMARIES IN THE BODY OF THE REPORT

Since formal reports often include references to outside sources, you will need to know how to present your sources in the body of the report.

Quotation. If a quotation is three lines or less, use quotation marks to signal its beginning and end, as Mark did in this instance:

> When Posner compared students' and recruiters' perceptions of what recruiters look for in job candidates during interviews, he found that

"What stands out most . . . are not the differences but rather the similarities [between perceptions of students and recruiters]" (p. 335).

Notice that the page number appears after the quotation. Notice, too, that the quotation fits smoothly into the sentence—in part because the author being quoted is introduced in the text, not in the reference citation.

If the quotation is more than three lines, indent it five spaces from the left margin and do *not* use quotation marks:

As Professor B. Z. Posner stated in the only major study on this subject,

> Very little is known about the factors . . . which corporate recruiters consider in evaluating job applicants. Even less is known about the degree to which job applicants are aware of the factors considered important by recruiters (p. 329).

Paraphrase and Summary. A paraphrase or a summary appears directly in the text. Place the page number of the source on which your paraphrase or summary is based right after the last word in your report containing the information you are summarizing or paraphrasing:

> Although research has been conducted on job interviewing, very little empirical work has been done on what recruiters actually look for in job candidates and what students think recruiters look for (Posner, 1981, p. 329).

Ellipses. An **ellipsis** consists of three spaced dots (. . .) It signals to readers that you have omitted some words from the quotation because they are not relevant to the point you are making:

> When Posner compared students' and recruiters' perceptions of what recruiters look for in job candidates during interviews, he found that "What stands out most . . . are not the differences but rather the similarities [between perceptions of students and recruiters]" (p. 335).

Use four dots if the omitted words include the end of one quoted sentence or the beginning of another, and be sure that what you have omitted does not result in a distortion of the writer's meaning.

Brackets. **Brackets** [   ] enclose words of your own that you have inserted in a quotation to clarify its meaning or to make the quotation fit the syntax of your sentence:

> "What stands out most . . . are not the differences but rather the similarities [between perceptions of students and recruiters]" (p. 335).

Supplementary Material

This includes reference citations in the text, footnotes, bibliography, and appendixes. The person who assigns the report to you may establish the requirements for the format and content of supplementary material. If not, we recommend using the guidelines provided by the American Psychological Association (APA).

REFERENCE CITATIONS IN THE TEXT

The patterns shown in Figure 11.5 are recommended in the APA guidelines. (For the full guidelines, see *Publication Manual of the American Psychological Association,* 3rd. ed.)

FOOTNOTES

Footnotes can be one of two types, depending on the function they serve:

1. *Copyright permission footnotes:* These document permission to quote copyrighted material, which, according to APA guidelines, is generally over 500 words.
2. *Content footnotes:* These provide comments that pertain to your ongoing discussion in the body of the text.

For copyright permission footnotes, you generally need written permission of the copyright owner, who is usually the author or publisher of the article. Try to secure permissions several weeks in advance of your deadline.

For content footnotes, you first need to decide whether the additional comments you want to make pertaining to your ongoing discussion should be placed in the body of the report or included as a footnote. If the comments would constitute a digression from your ongoing discussion, place them in a footnote. Such footnotes can give readers special technical information, indicate diverse points of view among experts in a field, or further discuss an article or idea related to a point you raise in the text.

Mark White used such footnotes in his report to give information on articles he thought the reader might want to refer to:

[2]My preliminary research yielded several articles that warrant further attention; Huegli and Tschirgi (1981) on "behavior modeling"—a technique involving identifying and practicing inerviewing skills; Leach and Flaxman (1978) on the "self-rating sheet" for self, peer, and instructor evaluation of interviewing skills; and Phillips (1982) on effective responses to questions that interviewers frequently ask.

Figure 11.5
STYLE OF REFERENCE CITATIONS

WORK BY A SINGLE AUTHOR

Place the author's name and the date of publication in parenthesis right after the section of the report referring to the publication:

Although research has been conducted on job interviewing, very little empirical work has been done on what recruiters actually look for in job candidates and what students think recruiters look for (Posner, 1981, p. 329).

If the author's name is included in your discussion, do not repeat it in the citation:

As Professor B. Z. Posner (1981) stated . . .

No parenthetical information is necessary if both the author and year appear in your report.

WORK BY MORE THAN ONE AUTHOR

If there are two authors, give both authors' names:

(Leach and Flaxman, 1978)

WORK BY UNKNOWN AUTHOR

If the author is unknown, cite the first few words of the title and the date of publication. If the source is an article, put the title in quotation marks. If a book, underline the title.

("Supermarkets and Scanners," 1979)

(The Modern Supermarket, 1985)

(continued)

(STYLE OF REFERENCE CITATIONS continued)

WORK BY AN ORGANIZATION

If you refer to a work by a government agency, a company, or a university, write out the full name in the first citation:

(City of Simi Valley, 1981)

If the organization is well known, put the abbreviation in brackets at the first citation; then use the abbreviation in subsequent references:

(Center for Disease Control [CDC], 1986)

(CDC, 1986)

REFERENCE TO SPECIFIC PART OF A SOURCE

If you are quoting or paraphrasing from your source, put the page number after the other information on the source:

(Posner, 1981, p. 329)

Note chapters in similar fashion:

(Hall, chap. 3)

Number footnotes consecutively in the report. Place the number to the right of and a half-line above the passage of the report the footnote refers to:

On the basis of my preliminary library research on how students can prepare for on-campus interviews,[2] I recommend . . .

(The footnote number *follows* all punctuation except the dash.) Put footnotes on a separate page directly after the recommendation section of your report. Call the page

"Footnotes." Indent the first line of each footnote five spaces, and be sure the number corresponds to the number in the report itself.

BIBLIOGRAPHY

A bibliography may include all the secondary sources you have cited in your report or may be more extensive, including works you have consulted but not used directly in the report. If you have kept accurate records of the sources you consulted as you did your research, your bibliography should be easy to compile.

The APA recommends that you include only the sources used for your research and writing, and that you call this list "References." Some instructors and managers expect you, in addition, to identify sources you have found pertinent to your study but have not used directly in the report, as well as sources for further reading. Mark's instructor wanted to see both the works Mark cited in his report and ones he had found useful but did not use directly. His instructor was interested in getting a sense of the scope of Mark's research as well as a list of sources to consult for further reading. To respond to his instructor's request, Mark submitted two bibliographies. The first contained references (secondary sources cited in his report). The second contained the sources he consulted but did not cite directly in the text. Check with your instructor or manager to find out what you should include in your bibliography.

Your bibliography should appear on a separate page following your footnotes. List entries alphabetically according to the last name of the author.

According to APA guidelines, the following information is listed for an article:

- Author's name listed alphabetically by last name
- Date of publication
- Title of article
- Name of journal, magazine, or newspaper
- Edition number for the journal
- Inclusive page numbers

A typical bibliographical entry for an article reads as follows:

Forkner, Patricia A. (1981). The job hunt: Appropriate unit for basic business class. Business Educator, 35 (7), 11–12.

Type the first line flush left and indent subsequent lines five spaces.

For references, the APA suggests the format shown in Figure 11.6.

Figure 11.6

REFERENCES IN APA STYLE

ARTICLE BY TWO OR MORE AUTHORS

Leach, James, and Flaxman, Nancy. (1978). Self-rating: An exercise for improving job interview skills. <u>Balance Sheet</u>, <u>59</u> (7), 303–305.

MAGAZINE ARTICLE

Yalamanchili, S., Malek, M., and Aggarwal, J. K. (1984, December). Workstations in a local area network environment. <u>Computer</u>, pp. 74–86.

NEWSPAPER ARTICLE

Blumenthal, K. (1985, April 4). Making dean's list comes second to making a profit. <u>Wall Street Journal</u>, Section 2, p. 1.

BOOK

Tubbs, Stewart L. (1978). <u>A systems approach to small group interaction</u>. Reading, MA: Addison-Wesley.

EDITED BOOK

Kolb, David A., Rubin, Irwin M. and McIntyre, James M. (Eds.). (1971). <u>Organizational psychology: Readings on human behavior in organizations</u>. Englewood Cliffs, NJ: Prentice-Hall.

Note that the editors' names appear in the author position.

ARTICLE IN A BOOK

Garfinkel, Harold. (1972). Remarks on ethnomethodology. In John J. Gumperz and Dell Hymes (Eds.), Directions in sociolinguistics: The ethnography of communication (pp. 301–324). New York: Holt, Rinehard, and Winston.

TECHNICAL OR RESEARCH REPORT

Flower, Linda, and Haynes, John R. (1984). Diagnosis in revision: The expert's option. Pittsburgh: Carnegie-Mellon University, Communications Design Center.

APPENDIXES

Appendixes contain supplementary material of various kinds, such as details of your research and technical or specialized information that is understandable or of interest to only a small number of readers. People should not have to read your appendixes to follow your line of thought in the body of the report.

Each appendix item should be referred to in the relevant section of the report so that readers will know how the material in the appendixes relates to the report proper. And each appendix item should be as carefully thought through and presented as is your main text. For instance, data presented need to be grouped logically and, when appropriate, interpreted.

Each item in the appendix exists as a separate unit and should be labeled "Appendix I", "Appendix II," and so on. The separate status of each appendix item is important because your readers may have reason to refer to a specific appendix on its own. Also, you may want to send out a particular appendix under separate cover.

Often you will be unable to decide what to put in the appendixes until you have outlined and drafted your report. The main ideas you want to convey should appear in the body of the report, along with supporting information, proofs, illustrations, and explanations. Anything supplementary goes in the appendixes.

Format

Headings and subheadings organize the report into manageable chunks for easy review, reading, and later reference. They also lay out the sequence of major ideas in your report. A reader should be able to grasp these ideas by reviewing your headings and subheadings. See, for example, Mark's headings and subheadings (p. 522).

The arrangement of headings and subheadings also shows the hierarchical organization of ideas in the report. Major ideas are the headings, supporting ones are the subheadings.

REVISING THE FORMAL REPORT

Several problems may arise in writing a formal report:

- Poorly developed conclusions and recommendations
- Excessive use of quotations, paraphrases, or summaries
- Lack of transitional paragraphs and sentences
- Secondary material put in the body of the report
- Organization according to sources or research design rather than by argument
- Irrelevant information
- Poor headings and subheadings
- Long executive summaries that rehash the whole report

In moving from the first to the final draft, Mark handled most of the problems mentioned above. Let's look at how he did this.

Poorly Developed Conclusions and Recommendations

The more extensive the research involved in doing a formal report, the more writers may forget that their *research is important only as it answers the reader's questions and supports recommendations the reader can act on*. Writers can get so immersed in data gathering that they give short shrift to the conclusions and recommendations that are the most important part of their research.

In an early draft of his report, Mark fully discussed his primary research: the questionnaires and cards he had sent to students and recruiters and his interviews with them. However, he spent little time on his conclusions and recommendations:

DRAFT

CONCLUSIONS

This study clearly shows that college business students are aware of one criterion recruiters use to judge them during on-campus interviews and may or may not be aware of two others. In that most important first interview, students can ruin their chances for a job by not emphasizing the correct characteristics. The individual may have the characteristics the company requires, but not let them be known due to ignorance of their importance.

RECOMMENDATIONS

I would like this report to be read by all those involved in the interviewing process, particularly in the business sector. I also think that this study will set a precedent for further research in the interviewing process for the employment of college graduates.

Although Mark drew an accurate generalization from his study (students are aware of one important criterion but may not be aware of others), his conclusions and recommendations are poorly developed. In his conclusion section, he did not mention the three criteria important to recruiters. In the recommendation section, he neglected to give specific recommendations based on his conclusions.

Before he came up with his final draft, Mark did some reading to find out how students can prepare for on-campus interviews. Note that in the conclusion and recommendation sections of the final draft (see pp. 526–528), Mark named the criteria important to recruiters and gave specific recommendations.

You can reduce your chances of making Mark's error if you keep your conclusions and recommendations in mind when you organize and write a draft. As you construct your outline (or analysis tree) and draft, think about how you want your readers to understand and accept your conclusions and recommendations. Do more research if significant gaps appear in these sections. Remember that decision makers are interested in actions they can take on the basis of your conclusions.

Excessive Use of Quotations, Paraphrases, or Summaries

Report writers sometimes fail to see beyond the information found in secondary sources to its implications for their analysis. In other words, they have not considered the relationship between what others have written and their own thinking about the topic. The reports of such writers give the impression that the writers are "hiding behind" secondary sources, using others' analyses in place of their own. These reports typically contain passages consisting of long quotations or a series of quotations, paraphrases, and summaries that are not integrated into the writer's arguments.

Even good writers may quote, paraphrase, or summarize excessively in early drafts. The overuse of sources indicates that these writers have not as yet mastered the material they have collected. Instead, they seem to use the ideas and words found in outside sources as a substitute for their own thinking about their subject. For the reader, the overuse of outside sources makes for difficult reading. In the following section from a draft of Mark's report, notice how the long quotations affect your ability to understand the point Mark is trying to make. In this section, he is trying to establish the need for a study of what recruiters look for in job candidates and what students think recruiters look for. How successsful is he?

DRAFT

At the end of one of his research studies on the interviewing process, Professor B. Z. Posner concluded:

> While much has been written about how to recruit, sources of job applicants, interviewing techniques, and the like (e.g., Gleuck, 1978; Greco, 1975; Yoder and Heneman, 1974) very little is known about the factors, characteristics, and aptitudes which corporate recruiters consider in evaluating job applicants. Even less is known about the degree to which job applicants are aware of the factors considered important by recruiters. This may also be true for faculty members who offer advice and counsel to both students and recruiters (p. 329).

Professor Harvey D. Tschirgi describes the problems a typical student confronts in approaching the initial interview with a company recruiter in the following way:

> Fred, master's-degree candidate in business at a large midwestern university, had just completed interviews with four manufacturing companies seeking candidates with graduate degrees for general management training programs. According to the candidate, each company's representative appeared interested in obtaining data from the other.
>
> "The first recruiter wanted my grades spelled out in detail; the second demanded to know what I did with my time outside classes; the third was more interested in how I'd thought out my future; the last recruiter simply asked whether I'd had any pertinent job experiences."

THE FORMAL REPORT: ORGANIZATION, DRAFT, FORMAT, REVISION, AND GROUP WRITING

As you read this passage, you probably found it extremely difficult to follow Mark's argument. The sheer volume of quoted material disrupts the flow of the report, forcing the reader to move abruptly from Mark's language and thought processes to those of the other writers. Notice how Mark controls his argument in his revision. He places a shortened version of the Posner quotation within the larger context of his argument, and he eliminates the second quotation entirely.

REVISION

Although research has been conducted on job interviewing, very little empirical work has been done on what recruiters actually look for in job candidates and what students think recruiters look for. (Posner, 1981). When research has been done, sample size has been very small. As Professor B. Z. Posner stated in the only major study on this subject,

> Very little is known about the factors . . . which corporate recruiters consider in evaluating job applicants. Even less is known about the degree to which job applicants are aware of the factors considered important by recruiters (p. 329).

In his study, Posner investigated what those factors are and determined whether students recognized them.

Secondary sources should support your argument, not be a substitute for it. If you think carefully about how ideas in your source relate to your own argument, you will avoid this problem.

Lack of Transitional Paragraphs and Sentences

Every business communication needs transitions. But they are especially important in a formal report because it requires readers to assimilate large amounts of material and to see connections between the parts of the report. Using previews and summaries can show readers the links between the sections of your report.

Writers frequently do not include enough transitions in their early drafts because at that stage they may not yet know what specific links to make between the parts of a report. But the absence of transitions from the final draft of a report will create gaps in the reader's understanding of the argument and will make it difficult for the reader to keep track of a report's major points. Check your drafts to be sure that whenever you move from one major section to the next, you show the reader the links between the sections.

Secondary Material Put in the Body of the Report

Sometimes writers put in the body of the report material that really belongs in appendixes. The material may be too technical or it may be unessential to the central argument. For instance, in an early draft of his report, Mark put his questionnaire in the body of the report. Later he saw that the questionnaire detracted from his main ideas, so he put it in an appendix, where it would be available to any reader with a special interest in it—for example, someone who might want to duplicate his study or check its accuracy.

Organization According to Sources or Research Design Rather Than by Argument

As writers collect data on each source they read and each research study they do, they may be tempted to organize the report chronologically, as though it were the story of their research efforts. This pattern of organization simplifies putting the report together but tends to obscure the main argument. Use data to support your argument. Refer to your analysis tree or outline to see where results can support your argument.

Irrelevant Information

Business people spend so much time and effort doing secondary research that some of them are tempted to include in the report everything they have reviewed. In an early draft of his report, Mark included an explanation of how he had decided on the eleven criteria he chose to study. He described at length his library research and his discussions with his instructor and the director of placement. In reviewing his report, he weeded out these nonessential details.

Poor Headings and Subheadings

Most business people know that a research report should be broken up with headings and subheadings, but sometimes their headings and subheadings are vague. If vaguely worded, a heading fails to specify for the reader the block of information it introduces. For instance, in an early draft of his report Mark labeled his first section "Introduction." Think how much more readers were told with his revised heading: "Introduction: Why Study What Recruiters Look For in Job Candidates?" The first title says little; the second identifies the subject and motivates the reader.

Long Executive Summaries That Rehash the Whole Report

Sometimes writers forget that an executive summary should distill essential information and present only the report's main argument. Instead, writers discuss the details of the report as well as the main points, repeating information that appears in the body of the report without condensing it. This problem arose in an early draft of the section of Mark's executive summary, where he discusses his research methods:

DRAFT

To verify Posner's findings and to see whether they applied to Babson students, I conducted research on the criteria recruiters use to judge Babson students (and similar populations) during job interviews and on whether students were aware of these criteria. The following research methods were used to study recruiters' expectations of students at job interviews and students' knowledge of these expectations:

- Questionnaire and card-sort administered to recruiters and to seniors majoring in business at Babson and at comparable colleges
- Interviews with recruiters and students

The study was conducted with two groups. The first group consisted of 60 college seniors majoring in business. These students were randomly selected from six Boston area schools and one New York school. The second group consisted of 30 recruiters who interview prospective employees in their common fields of business (e.g., an accountant interviews an accounting major).

In revising his executive summary, Mark retained only the second paragraph. He eliminated the details concerning Posner's study and his own sample.

Use the accompanying checklist to review your report for errors.

CHECKLIST FOR REVISING THE FORMAL REPORT

1. Are your conclusions and recommendations stated? Are they based on the research and analysis presented in the body of the report?
2. Do the secondary sources you cite support your argument? Should any be eliminated or shortened?
3. Do you use transitional paragraphs and sentences to show connections between the parts of the report?

4. Does any material currently in the body of the report belong in an appendix? Does anything in the appendixes belong in the body?
5. Is the report organized, as it should be, by argument and not by sources or research?
6. Can anything in the report be eliminated?
7. Do headings and subheadings specify the blocks of information in the report?
8. Is the executive summary succinct, and does it cover what it should?

GROUP WRITING

Mark's was an individual writing task, but sometimes you will work on group projects. In fact, a recent survey of 200 professionals revealed that 87 percent of the respondents write collaboratively.[1] Group work can have advantages over an individual effort, for group members bring varied expertise and points of view to identifying and solving a problem and to putting together a written response. For instance, one group member can be a good interviewer, another a computer buff, and a third may have a strong background in marketing research. As a result, a formal report written by this group can be better than one produced by a single member. In the words of one manager who frequently writes group reports, "They represent a higher order of thinking than can be achieved by individuals."

On the other hand, group writing presents special challenges in the coordination of group efforts and in the composing of the report.

Coordination of the Group's Efforts

Managing the writing of a formal report is especially difficult when the work of several people must be coordinated. When you are working in a group, be aware of the need to do the following:

1. *Discuss individual expectations*. Your group stands a good chance of working cooperatively on a writing task if team members share their individual goals and commitment to the task before the project gets under way. For some participants, the assignment may be a low priority; for others, an important project in their major area of work or study. Discussing individual goals and commitment increases mutual trust.

2. *Allocate tasks*. Your group should divide tasks equitably. This division of labor depends on the needs, interests, and commitment of group members and the individual expertise that members bring to the various tasks necessary for completing the report. Discuss these issues as they relate to each team member's responsibilities.

3. *Develop a schedule for completing all tasks*. Your group should first determine the components of the project and the time needed to complete the report. Then you should put together a schedule that lists

THE FORMAL REPORT: ORGANIZATION, DRAFT, FORMAT, REVISION, AND GROUP WRITING

Group writing requires regular meetings.

- The tasks and the amount of time each will take
- The individual team member responsible for each task
- The sequence of tasks

The schedule should look just like the one you would draw up for a report you write on your own, except that for the group report, each team member's activities should be identified.

4. *Decide in advance how you are going to handle recalcitrants*. Ideally, for a student group report the work is divided up equally and people share the same grade for the project. But sometimes, in college or on the job, people participate unevenly in the work. Then, if possible, they should be assigned credit according to the amount and quality of work they do. Your professor can suggest methods to ensure that credit for the project is assigned equitably. For instance, the professor may request each group member to evaluate both himself or herself and the others in the group in confidential notes submitted with the report.

5. *Determine procedures for making changes*. Since a project and an individual's involvement in it can change in midstream, set up a procedure for making changes that is acceptable to group members. Do this early in the project so the group is not stuck with working out a procedure at the same time that changes need to be made.

A group may decide that changes will be made democratically, with everyone having an equal vote in the proposed modifications and a 51 percent majority ruling. As an alternative, the group may appoint a leader who has the authority to renegotiate the workload.

6. *Meet regularly.* Given the length and complexity of a formal report, a group should meet regularly to keep track of new developments, to assess information that has been collected, and if necessary, to renegotiate the workload and redefine tasks.

We recommend that you begin discussing the above activities at your first group meeting. Groups that clarify the scope of the project, the tasks of individual group members, the credit each member will receive, and the procedures for making changes have a good chance of completing their work on time and to the mutual satisfaction of all.

Group Writing Within the Framework of the Writing Process

If we look at group writing within the framework of the writing process, we can identify those points in the process where it is preferable for the team to work together and those where individual writers should do the writing. Computer technology can assist teams at any stage of the writing process (see Chapter 15, "The Business Writer and the Computer").

SETTING THE GOAL AND ASSESSING THE READER

The group must begin by agreeing on the purpose of the report and the readers' requirements.

GATHERING INFORMATION AND GENERATING IDEAS

Research should be divided according to the expertise and interests of group members. When people do research in their areas of interest and expertise, the whole team benefits.

Although individual team members work on research tasks independently, the entire group should pool ideas and ongoing research so as to check for results, avoid unnecessary overlap in research and analysis, and move toward a consensus about conclusions and recommendations.

ORGANIZING

All team members should collaborate on an informal outline or analysis tree as soon as possible and on a *detailed* outline of the report once they have completed their research. The detailed outline should show the sequence of main and subordinate topics in the report. Individual team members should prepare notes on the detailed outline before the group meeting, especially on sections of the report they have researched.

THE FORMAL REPORT: ORGANIZATION, DRAFT, FORMAT, REVISION, AND GROUP WRITING

WRITING A DRAFT

Teams should appoint a coordinator and follow one of two methods to write a draft:

Method 1: Divide the writing task into several parts and have each team member write a section of the report.

Method 2: Appoint one person to write the entire draft.

REVISING

Regardless of the method used for writing a draft, a team should meet to review the draft for gaps and errors in content. One member of the group should be appointed editor to revise the whole for consistency in style and format.

If a group uses Method 1 to write a draft (several writers), revising can be easy if team members' writing styles are similar and if the group has successfully outlined connections between parts of the project. But Method 2 (one writer) is preferable if there are significant differences in the writing styles of group members.

Group writing of reports succeeds when a group plans its activities carefully, taking into account all phases of the writing process. Good planning helps the team avoid problems faced by teams that don't plan or plan poorly.

Pitfalls in Group Writing

1. *Poor project management:* The group may never finish the report, miss the deadline, or turn in a poor job if its plan is inadequate. Poor project management may mean that a group fails to divide the work fairly, neglects to design a schedule for completing the report, does not share findings regularly, or meets sporadically. To avoid these problems, plan thoroughly at the earliest opportunity, and discuss potential good and bad feelings you may have about working together as a group.

2. *Failure to agree about the goals and readers of the report:* No amount of research and analysis can compensate for failing to know how the report is going to help its readers and what their specific needs are. Groups make a big mistake when they launch into the research prematurely. One group we know wrote several drafts of a report and thought it was ready for final typing. Then a team member recognized that most of the information at the heart of the report was too technical for its intended reader. Knowing the goal and the reader is the only way to decide what kind of research is necessary and how to present it.

3. *Failure to achieve a single "voice" in the report:* Even if several people are involved in writing, reports need to sound as though they have been written by one person. When a report sounds as though it has been written by several writers, it is usually the product of a team that divided the writing of the report into several sections, had each member go his or her separate way to write a section, and failed to bring in a

single writer to review the final draft for consistency in content, style, and format. Regardless of how drafts are composed, one writer must be brought in to go over the entire report.

4. *Underestimating the writer's task:* Some groups that choose to have one person write the draft of the report think that all the writer needs to do is to take the results of the team's research and pour them into a prefabricated mold—a preexisting format and a ready-made style. Even the best writer working with a detailed outline needs the group to help with revising for organization, for conclusions, and for recommendations. Groups need to budget enough time for the writer to do a complete draft and to incorporate the changes that the group recommends.

5. *Isolation of the writer or writers from the research:* Even if one person is assigned the writing, he or she should be involved, if only as a listener, in the progress of the group's research and analysis. A writer brought in at the tail end of a project will have little sense of how to address the reader of the report, what to focus on in the writing, and how to flesh out even the most detailed of outlines so as to bring across the group's intended message.

By coordinating the group's efforts and organizing the writing of the report, you can avoid the problems faced by work groups that don't plan adequately.

Use the accompanying checklist to review your group writing efforts.

CHECKLIST FOR DOING GROUP WRITING

1. Have you coordinated your group's efforts by
   - Discussing individual expectations?
   - Allocating tasks?
   - Developing a schedule for completing tasks?
   - Deciding in advance how to handle recalcitrants?
   - Determining procedures for making changes?
   - Meeting regularly?
2. In writing the report, have you
   - Agreed on the purpose and the readers' requirements?
   - Divided research according to the expertise and interests of group members, and pooled research results?
   - Collaborated on an informal outline or analysis tree and later a detailed outline of the report?
   - Had each team member write a section of the report or had one person write the entire draft?
   - Reviewed the draft as a team for gaps and errors in content?
   - Had one person revise the report for consistency in style and format?

SUMMARY

Once you have gathered information and generated ideas for your report, you will be ready to organize it. Organization can be a big task because of the large amount of research you will have to integrate and present coherently and convincingly to your readers. An informal outline or analysis tree can help you organize your research and see the logical order of your report. An effective format will make this order clear to your readers. To design an effective format, you will need to become familiar with the various parts of the formal report and their uses. Group writing of formal reports involves special considerations: Take time to coordinate the group's efforts and to decide when it is preferable for the group to work together and when individuals should do the writing.

EXERCISES

1. As a member of a faculty-student committee to improve college life, you are investigating a problem your college faces. See Exercise 1 in Chapter 10 (p.498) for discussion of this assignment.

See "Organizing," pp. 508–510, for Exercise 2.

2. Write the outline for your report.

See "Writing a Draft," pp. 509–541, for Exercise 3.

3. Write a draft.

See "Parts and Format of Formal Reports," pp. 542–556, for Exercise 4.

4. Put together the final copy, including the letter of transmittal and supplementary material. (The report is to be submitted to the faculty-student committee, the group that can act on your recommendations.)

See "Executive Summary," pp. 544–547, for Exercises 5 and 6.

5. Read a classmate's formal report, then write an executive summary for it. Compare your summary to your classmate's. Discuss any discrepancies that appear between your summary and your classmate's.

6. Figure 11.7 is a draft of the executive summary to accompany a report on problems in a bank's management training program and on possible solutions to the problems. After reading the summary, revise it so that it conforms better to the aims of the study. Be sure to eliminate unnecessary information.

Figure 11.7

DRAFT OF AN EXECUTIVE SUMMARY

> This report examines the problem of unrealistically high expectations being created in management trainees at Fidelity Bank and suggests issues that should be addressed by policy makers so that recruiting efforts can be directed at filling personnel needs in the branch system. The opportunities for advancement expected by new management trainees do not correspond with the opportunities typically available to them. These unmet expectations were mentioned by personnel officers as a frequent cause of turnover.
>
> Factors contributing to these expectations prior to employment include a recruiting brochure that highlights head office positions and recruiters' enthusiasm about available career opportunities. Yet management trainees soon find themselves working in branch operations, and this work is demanding and inadequately rewarded. Interviews with operations supervisors who recently completed training indicated that few desire careers in the branch system and still fewer want to specialize in operations. This avoidance of operations is encouraged by the higher salaries and more rapid advancement opportunities perceived in credit positions. In addition, head office positions are preferred to branch positions by most management associates.
>
> Structural changes currently being implemented in the branch management hierarchy will increase the importance of developing operations skills in future managers. Hence the needs for branch management personnel will become even greater, while management trainees continue to prefer positions in the head office.
>
> Changing the expectations of potential trainees through the use of a recruiting brochure will not substantially improve the situation. It is more important at this point for policy makers in top management to work more closely with the personnel department to clarify the role of the Management Training Program in meeting changing needs for managerial talent. Currently, senior executives are concerned with the immediate need for operations skills, while the people being recruited have more long-term potential. If individuals with high potential are forced into undesirable positions because of short-term needs, then Fidelity Bank should be prepared to lose many good people.

> The following questions should be resolved to help establish the Management Training Program as a tool for meeting organizational goals: (1) What are the purposes of the Management Training Program? (2) How can Fidelity Bank identify and attract candidates for the program who will fit the existing organizational needs? (3) What can be done internally to motivate the best trainees to aspire to the needed positions? and (4) What can be done about present management trainees whose goals do not match organizational needs?
>
> The implications of these questions are discussed in the body of the report. Each is a complex issue deserving additional investigation. Accordingly, this report serves as a pilot study pointing to the needs for clarification and planning of the Management Training Program as it relates to overall organizational goals. If the role of the program is to fill needs in operations, then the jobs should be made more attractive to college graduates, or recruiting efforts should be restricted to people who will accept the lower status and recognition of operations.

See "Bibliography," pp. 553–555, for Exercise 7.

7. Put the following information in correct bibliographical form. In some cases, information is missing. Note those entries for which you need more information.

- Anne E. Fyfe Hospital Forum November/December 1981
- McCarthy, Joseph B. "Developing a Hospital Advertising Campaign"
- "Freestanding Clinics: Less Expensive, Less Crowded," Vol. 52 March 9 No. 10 March 9, 1981 J. C. Casey
- Deering's California Codes, Health and Safety Codes, San Francisco J. Deering ed. Bancroft-Whitney Co., 1975
- November 24, 1980 Medical Economics Vol. 57 J. Eisenberg No. 25 "Convenience Clinics: Your Newest Rival for Patients"
- Ambulatory Care Systems: Volume III Lexington Massachusetts R. J. Giglio Lexington Books 1977.
- Ohio State Medical Journal, Vol. 76, No. 10, October, 1980, "Urgency or Emergency."
- The National Ambulatory Medical Survey: 1977 Summary, United States, Vital and Health Statistics: Data from National Health Survey: Number 44, Series 13

See "Revising the Formal Report," pp. 556–562, for Exercises 8–10.

8. Roberta Johnson, a student in your business writing class, brought to class two paragraphs that she would like you to help her revise. Her subject is creative ways to finance summer vacations. What she has done is to write a one-sentence introduction to five paragraphs taken verbatim from the *New York Times* Real Estate Section.[2] First write a memo to her explaining why it would be preferable to present the information in the paragraphs without quoting all of them. Then revise the paragraphs for her. Here are the paragraphs:

House exchanges are one option for financing summer vacations. The <u>New York Times</u> had this to say on the subject:

Judy and Francis Furton, retired schoolteachers from Detroit who now live in Guadalajara, Mexico, are a couple with long experience in house swaps. They have been exchanging with homeowners in the United States and overseas for 20 years, they said by telephone from Guadalajara, and this year they plan to swap again.

They have been to Britain, Greece, Jamaica, Bermuda, Venezuela and Hawaii and more. Their one-story three-bedroom house in Guadalajara comes with maid and car—"Mexican charm with American comfort," as the Furtons put it in the home exchange directory.

"Your home is safer with people in it," says Mr. Furton, "and think of all the money you are saving."

The Furtons list their house in a catalogue prepared jointly by the Vacation Exchange Club, whose offices are at 350 Broadway in Manhattan; the Holiday Home Exchange of Milsons Point, Australia, and the Hawaii Home Interchange in Honolulu. These organizations in turn are affiliated with about 20 other exchange organizations in Europe, including Intervac International and The Directory Group. Over the years a number of similar organizations have been formed in this country and disbanded.

The Vacation Exchange Club, founded in 1960, charges an annual membership fee of $21. Members get catalogues in February and April listing the properties available for swaps. A member joining this month, for example, would get both catalogues, but his own home would be listed, assuming a listing were wanted, only in the April catalogue.[1]

9. Read a classmate's formal report. Then write a memo to your classmate explaining where and how the report can be improved. Refer to the checklist for revising the formal report (pp. 561–562) as you consider the strengths and weaknesses of the report.

10. Figure 11.8, pp. 572–584, is a formal report written by a group of students who acted as consultants to a summer camp program. The students' goal was to recommend ways that the camp could improve its competitive position. Among other things, the team suggested that the camp send a questionnaire to the parents of campers to determine how the parents choose a camp for their children. Read the report and consider any revisions that should be made to improve it. These may include adding, rewriting, eliminating, and reordering sections of the report. Consider, too, whether any of the

THE FORMAL REPORT: ORGANIZATION, DRAFT, FORMAT, REVISION, AND GROUP WRITING

appendixes should appear in the body of the report. The appendixes are not present, but their titles and the references to them in the body of the report should give you enough information to make this decision.

See "Group Writing," pp. 562–566, for Exercise 11.

11. Write a memo to your instructor analyzing the following features of a group writing project you are or have been involved in:

- The group's efforts to coordinate tasks such as sharing individual expectations, allocating tasks, developing a schedule for completing the project, handling recalcitrants, designing procedures for making changes, and conducting meetings
- The group's writing process, from setting the goal to revising and editing
- Any problems in group writing, such as poor project management, failure to agree on the goals and readers for the report, failure to achieve a single voice in the report, underestimation of the writer's task, isolation of the writer from the research

Figure 11.8

A SAMPLE REPORT

The Hancock Recreation Center
40 Central Avenue
Dover, MA 02030

<u>Attention</u>: Mr. Larry Reese, General Manager

The attached report of the summer camp program for the Hancock Recreation Center has been completed in accordance with the guidelines of the Hancock College Management Consulting Field Experience program. The camp industry data as well as the comparison with the competition are presented on pages 0 through 0. The full details of the pretest of the parent questionnaire and a methodology for implementing the full study are presented on pages 00 through 00. The need for further research is discussed on page 00.

We believe the material presented in the text presents the methodology to be followed when administering the parent questionnaire and gathering additional information on the competition. However, the study must be implemented in the fall of 198_ in order to take advantage of its full potential.

Further research is still needed in the area of competition. We recommend that further study be completed on the specialty camp industry. Also, a camper survey should be developed. Our recommendations for the implementation of the parent survey appear in detail, and we recommend focus groups merely as a precaution.

We hope the study will simplify your task of administering the parent questionnaire this fall. Because of the pretest results we are confident that the results of the questionnaire, coupled with the analysis of the competition, will have a positive impact on the summer camp program.

Sincerely,

Barbara Reilly   Tracy Roat

Kevin Soto   Brian Fullerton

MANAGEMENT CONSULTING FIELD EXPERIENCE:

THE HANCOCK RECREATION CENTER

SUMMER CAMP PROGRAMS

(continued)

(A SAMPLE REPORT continued)

TABLE OF CONTENTS

INTRODUCTION 1

INDUSTRY ANALYSIS 2
   History 2
   Competition 3
   Recommendations 4

PARENT QUESTIONNAIRE
   Pretest Design 7
   Methodology 7

FURTHER RESEARCH 10

APPENDIX A: BROCHURES OF COMPETITION 11

APPENDIX B: PROFILES OF COMPETITION 20

APPENDIX C: PARENT QUESTIONNAIRES 25

APPENDIX D: CODING FOR COMPUTER 27

APPENDIX E: COMPUTER ANALYSIS 32

APPENDIX F: PARENT PREFERENCES 36

i

INTRODUCTION

The summer camp program is a vital component of the Hancock Recreation Center organization. Therefore, it is essential that the camp meet the needs of the parents and camper as well as hold a competitive advantage over other camp programs. The purpose of this study is to present a methodology to investigate two aspects of the summer camp program: the competition and the decision-making process of the parents.

With respect to the competition, the coaches of each Hancock Recreation Center camp were contacted and a list of the competition requested. A profile was developed on each competitor, and a comparison was made with the corresponding Hancock Recreation Center camp. This comparison included such factors as the camp facilities, cost, meals, deposit due date, and giveaways.

As for meeting the needs of parents (and campers), a parent questionnaire has been designed. The survey attempts to answer three basic questions:

1. What is the decision-making process of parents in choosing a summer camp for their child?
2. Is the Hancock Recreation Center summer camp program meeting the needs of parents and camper?
3. What can the Hancock Recreation Center change or improve to make the summer camp program a more enjoyable experience for the camper and better meet the needs of parents?

It must be stated at this point and remembered throughout the reading of this report that its main purpose is to present a methodology to

(continued)

(A SAMPLE REPORT continued)

carry out a study. Any pretests or results that will be presented do not warrant definite conclusions because they are supported by the results of the large mailing scheduled for September of 199_. A survey has been designed and tested as well as the methodology for implementation in the fall. It is now up to the Hancock Recreation Center to proceed with the study.

This report will continue as follows. First, the camp industry will be analyzed, including a brief history, a comparison with the competition, and recommendations. Next, the pretest design of the parent questionnaire and its methodology will be explained. Finally, the need for further research will be discussed and the conclusion will be stated.

INDUSTRY ANALYSIS

History

Organized camping began in the late nineteenth century and has traditionally provided young people with activities designed to promote personal growth and development skills. Many types of camps exist, including day, overnight, privately owned, social agency, religiously affiliated, and specialty camps. Over 4 million young people participate in summer camps each year, and 4 million more young people and adults are involved in programs year-round.

The American Camping Association is a nationwide, nonprofit organization, committed to continuing values and benefits unique to the organized camp setting. Since 1910, the American Camping Association has developed and implemented its program of inspection and accreditation for general activity camps. To date, the association has accredited over 2,200 camps, consists of 5,000 members, and publishes a Parents' Guide to Accredited Camps. Unfortunately, the American Camping Association provides the only national program and does not offer accreditation to specialty camps, such as the Hancock Recreation

Center camps. No formal organization exists for specialty camps, making research more difficult.

Important differences exist between overnight, general activity camps (known as traditional camps) and day, specific-activity camps (known as specialty or clinic camps). While the number of children attending specialty camps is increasing, the traditional overnight camps still represent the majority of the country's 10,000 camps. Parents and their children have been attracted to traditional camps in the past by their emphasis on sportsmanship over performance and the extended length of the sessions, which allows the camper to develop friendships and skills. The average price, however, for a private traditional camp ranges from $1,800 to $3,000 for a seven- to eight-week session.

Recently, parents have been less inclined to send their children to the same traditional camp year after year. They have begun to realize the value of varied experiences, and they now alternate their child's summer activities between camp and family vacations. Also, as a result of the higher divorce rate, children often divide their summers between parents. Consequently, children may prefer to attend camps with shorter sessions, which then allow them to pursue other activities as well.

Competition

The coaches of each of the Hancock Recreation Center camps were contacted for a list of the competition. The following analysis concentrates on the lists provided by the coaches, but it is recommended that advertisements in local newspapers as well as the camps mentioned in the results of the large mailing of the parent questionnaire be included in the future.

The first step was to contact each camp and request information about this year's summer camp program. Some camps were eager to provide information and to field any questions. On the other hand, some camps were difficult or impossible to contact. The brochures which were

(continued)

(A SAMPLE REPORT continued)

received may be found in Appendix A. Because most camps are open only in the summer, they do not maintain an office staff year-round. In this respect, the Hancock Recreation Center enjoys a distinct advantage.

After accumulating the information on the competition, we developed a profile on each camp. This profile included the type of camp (day vs. overnight), the sex and age of the campers, the dates of their sessions, their facilities, the meals, the cost, the amount of any required deposit, the date that the full balance is due, and whether the camp gives away prizes, awards, certificates, etc. The profiles may be found in Appendix B. The camps within each sport category were compared to the corresponding Hancock Recreation Center camp.

Recommendations

Five recommendations can be made from the comparison of the Hancock Recreation Center camps with their competition. First, the pricing schedule should be reviewed. In general, the Hancock Recreation Center's prices are below their competitors. For instance, the price of Hancock Recreation Center soccer camp is 57 percent lower than the average price of its competition. The Hancock price for its basketball camp is 47 percent lower than its competition, and its tennis camp is 25 percent lower than the regular price and 52 percent lower than the member price. The Hancock price for its boys' hockey camp is 75 percent lower than its competition. Incidentally, the girls' hockey price at Hancock is the only camp priced higher than its competition. However, many factors must be considered when establishing a pricing strategy, so an immediate increase in prices at all Hancock Recreation Center camps may not be appropriate.

Second, a deadline for the full balance payment should be implemented. Most of the competition (except for soccer camps) require the entire payment by June 1 or July 1. While parents may prefer to pay later, establishing a due date will produce two positive results. First, the Hancock Recreation Center will have earlier use of the funds, and second, the center will be reinforcing the commitment made by parents for their

4

child to attend. The pretest questionnaire responses indicated that while most parents made their decision some time between January and June, the majority decided in March and April. As a result, asking parents to pay by June 1 will probably not affect their decision-making process.

Third, in comparison to the other camps, the Hancock Recreation Center camps did not provide as many giveaways or awards, especially for the soccer, basketball, and girls' hockey camps. For the soccer camp, Hancock provides a T-shirt, whereas the others give away a jersey, a ball, and an evaluation. For basketball, Hancock gives out trophies while the others give away T-shirts, evaluations, and awards. Whereas the competition gives jerseys to its girls' hockey camp participants, the Hancock Recreation Center camp gives nothing. The Hancock Recreation Center hockey camp for boys does give away jerseys. Of course, an increase in giveaways may affect the cost of the camp.

Fourth, parents complained, on the pretest questionnaire, that only soda was provided at lunch and that the refrigeration for the lunches was poor. They preferred that campers be able to choose juices or milk instead of soda. This suggestion does not apply to the tennis camp, as the Hancock Recreation Center provides the entire lunch.

Finally, the brochures should be revised. Some confusion arises over the titles on the front of the brochures for two reasons. First, while the basketball and soccer camps use one brochure entitled "boys and girls," the hockey camps are separated, with the girls' brochure entitled "women's ice hockey." Further, advertisements in local newspapers read, "girls' ice hockey." All brochures should be separated by sex and clearly designate either "boy" or "girl" in the title. Second, the brochures for hockey and soccer call their programs "schools," whereas the tennis and basketball programs are called "camps." Although it is not essential for all the brochures to be identical in appearance, a consistent format will eliminate confusion.

Although the brochures are an important information source, they are not the most important way for people to become interested in the

5

(continued)

(A SAMPLE REPORT continued)

Hancock Recreation Center camps. Most parents cited friends and neighbors first and advertising second. Because of this strong word-of-mouth advertising, promotion through youth programs in the area could provide effective results. It would also be advantageous to contact the recreation departments of the towns surrounding the Hancock Recreation Center for referrals. This strong word-of-mouth network emphasizes the importance of satisfying parents. By implementing research, such as this Management Consulting Field Experience project, the Hancock Recreation Center is showing parents that it does care about what they think. The Hancock Recreation Center probably stands alone in implementing a program to measure parent satisfaction.

A final comment on the competition brings up the question of why the Hancock Recreation Center allows a competitor, the Green Valley Hockey School, to use its facilities. While the prices for the Hancock and Green Valley boys' camps were comparable, the Hancock price for the girls' hockey camp was much higher than the Green Valley price.

In summary, the Hancock Recreation Center camps can improve their programs by considering five recommendations: checking prices, establishing a full balance due date, increasing giveaways, improving beverage selection, and revising brochures. Concern was mentioned over why the Hancock Recreation Center allows a competitor to use its facilities.

PARENT QUESTIONNAIRE

Pretest Design

A parent questionnaire (Appendix C) has been designed for two reasons. First, it will determine the decision-making process of parents in deciding which summer camp their child will attend. Second, the parent questionnaire will determine if the Hancock Recreation Center's summer camp program is meeting the needs of the parents. If it is not, it will be decided what should be changed or improved to meet the parents' needs more effectively. Copies of both the 199_ and 199_ questionnaires are also included in Appendix C.

At first glance, the questionnaire appears to be quite simple and straightforward. This was not always the case when it is realized that the final draft is the tenth draft of the questionnaire. Although many problems did exist in the original copy, it is believed that all the difficulties have been ironed out and the final draft is ready to be mailed to the parents of each camper of the 199_ season. The large mailing was not done at this time because timing is a critical factor in this case. It is important that the parents receive the questionnaire at the end of the camp season, when the strengths and weaknesses of the program are fresh in their minds. The best and most valid responses will be received at this time. Again, the task of this report is to outline the methodology for the large study. It is not to present survey results.

A large part of the efforts to ensure a simple and straightforward questionnaire was to pretest it. A random sample of 100 names was taken, using a table of random numbers, from a list of parents whose children attended camp during the 199_ season. The sample was stratified, so a proportionate number of names was taken from each specific camp depending on the percentage of the total who were enrolled in the camp. The questionnaire was mailed in March of this year. The response was quite surprising when compared with the industry average. Normally, a response rate of 15 percent is considered adequate. However, the summer

7

(continued)

camp survey achieved a response rate of 40 percent. These results can be attributed to the following three factors. First, parents in this area do show a great interest in the summer camp where their child is enrolled. By mailing out the questionnaire, the Hancock Recreation Center is reinforcing that they are doing all they can to provide the best camp possible. Second, four days after the questionnaire was mailed, members of the staff at the Hancock Recreation Center called those surveyed to stress the importance of the study and to remind them to return the survey. It was imperative to call recipients after the large mailing to ensure the high response rate. Also, a return stamp was metered on the envelope to facilitate the return procedure. The third factor that aided the high return was the questionnaire itself. As a result of the high number of drafts, the questionnaire was clear and concise. However, as expected, a few changes were incorporated due to the results of the pretest. The wording was changed on a question that proved confusing, and a question was eliminated that appeared redundant.

Methodology

The following section explains the methodology that was used in the pretest and that should be followed on the large mailing to analyze the data. The responses to the pretest questionnaire were coded and the data were entered into a VAX 1170 at Hancock's computer center. The statistical analysis was carried out using the software package "Minitab." The analysis that will be explained in detail was repeated for five sets of data. First, the entire data set—all the responses from every parent answering the questionnaire—was analyzed. Next, the responses from each camp were divided into separate data sets. These four separate sets of data, one for each specific camp, were analyzed using the same procedure as the analysis that was used on the large data file. In the pretest, the large data set had 40 respondents, but the individual data set responses ranged in size from 4 to 26. The pretest responses cannot serve as valid samples due to the small size, although in the large mailings, definite conclusions can be reached from the analysis.

Most of the questions have been set up to run simple histograms, or graphs showing the number of responses to each question. For many of the questions, the histogram will be all the information that will be needed to draw conclusions. For example, one question on the survey asks the parents to indicate which month they make the summer camp decision. Analysis of the histogram can reveal trends. This question can then be used to help the Recreation Center decide on an appropriate date on which deposits must be received to assure the camper a place in the camp.

Two questions within the survey (question 3 and question 9) have been designed for reasons of cross tabulation. One can see that the factors parents have to rank in question 3 directly correspond to statements parents must give an opinion on in question 9. Tables can then be printed that incorporate both questions. The analysis is presented in greater detail in Appendix E. Here we refer to the step-by-step process for implementing the survey:

STEP 1—Conduct focus group of five to seven.

- Allow parents to answer questionnaire without comment
- Open the discussion so members can discuss any problems they may have with respect to wording or content
- Incorporate any changes that result from the focus group into the questionnaire prior to mailing

STEP 2—Mail the questionnaire.

- Include a cover letter explaining the research. Emphasize the potential benefit their children will receive because of improvements that will be implemented as a result of the parents' answering the survey

9

(continued)

(A SAMPLE REPORT continued)

- Include a stamped, self-addressed envelope
- Mail the questionnaire at the beginning of September

STEP 3—Code the returned questionnaire, format the responses and enter the data into five data files. (See Appendix D.)

STEP 4—Complete computer analysis. (See Appendix E.)

STEP 5—Prepare a list of responses to the open-ended questions, by camp. A list of the responses from the pretest appears in Appendix F.

FURTHER RESEARCH

Further research should be completed in three areas. First, more information about the camp industry, particularly about specialty camps, should be gathered. Because no formal organization exists for specialty camps, contacts in the industry may be helpful. Second, focus groups should be held to ensure that no hidden problems exist in the parent questionnaire. A group of parents should be assembled to discuss the questionnaire and to eliminate the ambiguities. While the questionnaire is in its final form, a focus group is recommended as a double check before the large mailing begins. A second focus group to be held after the questionnaire has been administered is also recommended. Third, a camp survey should be developed. This questionnaire would be administered to each camper on the last day of camp. It should be carefully worded and presented so that every camper will be able to understand it and complete it properly.

12
SPEAKING

PREVIEW

This chapter should help you to

1. Understand the connections between writing and speaking, and decide when it is better to write and when it is better to speak in handling a communication task
2. Give oral presentations by moving through these activities:
   - Setting the goal of the presentation
   - Assessing your audience
   - Organizing the parts of your presentation
   - Rehearsing to revise and to polish your delivery
3. Conduct interviews
4. Hold meetings

Most of what you have learned so far in this book concerns writing. In this chapter, we turn to the speaking that business people do. Since the links between writing and speaking are strong, we look at several speaking activities as they relate to writing and to what you know about writing as a process.

In the business world, writing and speaking are closely linked. Whatever your purpose for communicating may be, you will often perform a *series of writing and speaking activities* in order to achieve your goal. In addition, you will judge the *relative merits of writing and speaking* in achieving your goal in a given situation, and then choose the action—speaking or writing—that allows you to communicate your ideas more effectively.

The first part of this chapter—the major part—deals with oral presentations. They closely resemble writing in the way you handle them, from the moment you decide to do a presentation to your delivery of the talk. The second part considers two other kinds of speaking activities, interviewing and conducting meetings.

LINKS BETWEEN WRITING AND SPEAKING

When we asked business people to discuss when they wrote and when they spoke, they seemed to agree that in the business world, writing and speaking cannot easily be separated.

"As a financial analyst, I give twenty to thirty talks a year to my corporate clients. These talks boil down the findings contained in my written reports. Generally a company gives me about thirty minutes to summarize my analysis and recommendations. Since I can't afford to skip a major point and I can't waste my clients' time, I always prepare my presentations carefully and give my clients an outline so they can follow along."

"I work in production. I'm big on quick meetings, phone calls, and face-to-face discussions to keep things rolling. If I waited to get people to respond to memos, we'd never be able to meet our deadlines. But I do use writing too. I've found that people need to have my instructions in writing. Writing things down helps people see whether they understand what they've heard.

"Occasionally I've got to work with someone who's not dedicated to the job. I try as many channels as I can to make the job objectives clear: I talk to the person and I write memos. If these efforts fail and I have to let the employee go, I keep my written records of the worker's performance to back up my decision."

"I chose to work in customer service because I love to talk. But I'm surprised by how much writing I have to do just to keep track of what I've said and what my customers have said. Since I spend most of my time on the road troubleshooting, I always keep a notebook handy to jot down customers' questions, complaints, and comments. In that way I don't forget important details. When it's time to do my report for the home office, my notes also keep me from wandering all over the place."

Financial analysts are often required to give oral presentations of their report findings.

SPEAKING

Managers of production must be proficient at issuing orders and motivating others to carry them out. Both speaking and writing are important.

Despite differences in the jobs of each of these business people, similar patterns emerge in the ways that writing and speaking help them do their work.

1. *Speaking and writing are mutually reinforcing and interdependent*. One common theme in these business people's comments is that talking leads to writing and writing leads to talking. Achieving your purpose—be it explaining a business's financial status, giving instructions, or solving a customer's problem—frequently requires a communication strategy that involves a mix of writing and speaking.

The financial analyst organizes a formal presentation based on his written report. He then gives his clients an outline of the talk to help them see the structure of his presentation as he delivers it.

The production manager gives orders orally to get his message across on time. He then reinforces his oral instructions with written ones that clarify the details and provide his workers with an easy reference. When he has to fire someone, he uses his memos as documented evidence of his attempts to do everything reasonable to retain the employee.

The service rep jots down notes to prepare for her interview with her company's clients and then takes notes during the interview. The key points she has taken down during the interview then become the basis for the trip report she turns in to her boss.

2. *As a means of communicating, speaking has relative advantages and disadvantages when compared to writing*. These business people's comments show that sometimes speaking is better than writing for achieving your purpose with an audience, and sometimes the reverse is true.

By speaking to clients, the financial analyst can synopsize information quickly, get an immediate response to his work, and communicate with his colleagues face-to-face. By speaking to workers, the production manager gets his message across immediately

Customer service representatives must speak well to gain the confidence of clients, but they must also write well to convey the substance of their customers' concerns to management.

and handles questions. He could never get his work done on time if he had to wait for people to respond to memos. By speaking to customers, the service rep can maintain and build business. Talking face-to-face with customers allows her to establish a personal rapport with them, which is so important to sales.

Choose to speak rather than write when you want to make use of the built-in advantages of speaking mentioned in Figure 12.1.

On the other hand, writing has exclusive advantages too. *Choose to write rather than speak* when you want to make use of the built-in advantages of writing mentioned in Figure 12.2.

Because good business communicators can distinguish between the uses and effects of speaking and writing, they can decide when it is better to talk, when it is better to write, and when it is better to do both. Knowing the comparative advantages and disadvantages of speaking and writing, and the ways they reinforce each other, can help you to make good choices.

ORAL PRESENTATIONS

An **oral presentation** is a relatively formal kind of talk requiring preparation and some amount of writing. Whether you are giving a formal presentation to a large audience or a short informal talk to a small group, you can build on your knowledge of writing as a process. Preparing oral presentations closely resembles the process of preparing written communications, as Figure 12.3 demonstrates.

Figure 12.1
ADVANTAGES OF SPEAKING

> Speaking allows you to:
>
> - Convey a brief message quickly
> - Learn immediately from the facial expressions and questions of your listeners whether your message is understood and well received
> - Adjust what you have planned to say in response to your audience's questions and nonverbal responses (e.g., facial expression, body language)
> - Establish a personal rapport with your listeners
> - Take advantage of the positive impression you can make on people by the way you look and speak
> - Clarify and reinforce written messages

Figure 12.2
ADVANTAGES OF WRITING

> Writing allows you to:
>
> - Think through problems and make decisions
> - Create a permanent record of your message
> - Be certain that the details of your message are communicated
> - Provide readers with a reference
> - Clarify and reinforce messages delivered orally

Throughout this chapter we point out what is special about speaking. Still, as the comparison shows, the similarities between writing and speaking are even more striking than their differences. Just as in writing, effective speaking requires that you have a clear sense of your purpose and your audience, and that you gather information, generate ideas, and organize your information and ideas. And just as you need to revise your writing, you will need to rehearse your presentation—to learn what to revise in your outline and to polish your delivery.

Figure 12.3

A COMPARISON OF WRITING AND ORAL PRESENTATIONS

Writing	Oral Presentations
Setting the goal	Setting the goal
Assessing the reader	Assessing the audience
Gathering information and generating ideas	Gathering information and generating ideas
Organizing	Organizing
Writing a draft	Writing the outline or the copy for the presentation and designing visuals
Revising	Rehearsing to revise outline and to polish the delivery

Setting the Goal

Business people usually give talks to inform, to persuade, or to entertain. Because informative and persuasive talks are more common to business, they are our focus.

Giving presentations may be part of your job. Speaking within your organization, your goal may be to *inform* subordinates of changes in procedures and policies or *explain* to associates a project's specifications and goals. You may also be asked to *recommend* to superiors a solution to a problem, or you may decide to take the initiative and *suggest* to your superiors a better way to perform a task or solve a problem.

Speaking outside your organization, your goal may be to *persuade* potential customers of your organization's proven track record or *defend* your company's policies against public attack. From time to time, you may be asked to *speak on a ceremonial occasion*—to encourage students to enter your profession, to welcome a new business to your community, to praise a colleague for her accomplishments, or to introduce a guest speaker at a banquet.

The person requesting you to speak will sometimes give you explicit instructions about who your audience is and what your talk is supposed to accomplish. If this occurs, listen carefully and then ask questions about anything that is unclear. If you are not given guidance, approach the person who has assigned the talk and ask for clarification.

Business people frequently are expected to give briefings to others in their organizations.

Managers, especially those higher up in an organization, must communicate with the public about their firm's policies.

In all instances, formulate a goal statement for yourself that answers the questions, What do I want my audience to think and how do I want my audience to act as a result of listening to my presentation? Such a goal statement helps you limit the ground you cover in your talk and thus prevents vague rambling. Throughout the speaking process, your goal statement should serve as the objective against which to judge what you plan to say and how you organize.

Assessing the Audience

As with the readers of your writing, knowing as much as you can about the audience for your presentations will enable you to give a talk that is both interesting and informative. In short, you need to assess your audience as you would for a writing assignment. Learn what you can about the following factors:

1. *Your audience's business relationship to you:* In speaking outside your organization, find out whether your audience has a business relationship with your company as, for instance, customers or potential job seekers. This information will help you determine what is relevant and interesting to your audience. In speaking within your company, think about your responsibilities and authority in relation to the people you are addressing. For instance, if you are making a recommendation to superiors, you will want to build solid support for it and prepare for their questions and comments. On the other hand, if you are explaining new procedures to subordinates, you will want to make sure your explanation is clear. You will not have to justify the change; but to induce your subordinates to cooperate, you will want to explain how the new procedures may benefit them.

2. *Your audience's knowledge of the subject:* How familiar is your audience with the subject of your talk and with specialized terms you may want to use? If your audience is familiar with your topic, don't repeat what people already know. If the material is new to them, take time to give people the necessary background to understand your findings and recommendations. If you are speaking as an expert to a lay audience, explain specialized terms.

3. *Your audience's expectations about how your talk should be presented:* What style of presentation does your audience expect? In general, the larger the audience and the more formal the occasion, the more formal the presentation should be. In fact, for some public speaking events, it is appropriate to write out your speech and read it to the audience. The smaller the group and the more informal the occasion, the more appropriate it is to talk **extemporaneously**—that is, from an outline. On some occasions, you will be called on to give an **impromptu** talk—one you are requested to do on the spur of the moment without prepared notes.

Your audience's expectations will also be influenced by the circumstances of your talk. For example, whether you are one of a number of speakers or the only speaker can affect your presentation. If you are one of a group of speakers, your position in the sequence of speakers and the topics others plan to cover will influence your talk. If you are the only speaker, there are no such constraints on your presentation.

In ordinary business contexts, the purpose of your talk will be to inform or persuade, and your topic will be well defined. But on ceremonial occasions, your audience may be less familiar and your topic wide open. For instance, you may be asked to speak at an awards luncheon honoring outstanding business majors, at a college graduation ceremony, or at the opening of your town's new chamber of commerce offices. If you are asked to do such a public presentation, the person or organization sponsoring your talk should be able to provide you with information about your general topic and audience.

4. *Your audience's attitude toward you and your message:* How does your audience feel about you, and how are they likely to feel about your message? If you anticipate a positive or neutral attitude on the part of your audience, use a direct approach in organizing your talk: present your recommendations first and then provide supporting evidence. If you anticipate a negative attitude, use an indirect approach: Build a case for your point of view first and then announce it.

The accompanying checklist can help you assess your audience.

CHECKLIST FOR ASSESSING THE AUDIENCE

1. What is your audience's business relationship to you?
2. How familiar is your audience with the subject of your talk and with specialized terms you may want to use?
3. What style of presentation does your audience expect?
4. What is your audience's attitude toward you and your message?

Gathering Information and Generating Ideas

You may need to gather information and generate ideas for your talk. If it is to be based on huge amounts of data, the biggest part of your preparation may be gathering information: reading books, periodicals, newspapers, company reports; talking to colleagues and interviewing experts; conducting surveys; or making observations. (See Chapter 10, "The Formal Report: The Goal, The Reader, The Ideas and Information," for a review of research techniques.)

To generate ideas for your talk, use the same techniques you use when you brainstorm to do a writing assignment: talk to an associate, use a tape recorder, write nonstop, or make lists.

Organizing

Once you have gathered information and generated ideas for your talk, you are ready to group and order your notes as you would for a written assignment. Let's look at how you might prepare the three sections that make up every talk: the introduction, the body, and the conclusion.

An introduction must gain interest, and preview the parts that follow.

THE INTRODUCTION: GAINING INTEREST

To gain your listeners' interest, consider using one or more of these attention-getting devices:

1. *Ask a question.* Asking a question prompts your listeners to think about an answer. As a result, they will become curious about how you will answer the question in the body of the presentation. Here is how Tom Peters, management consultant and coauthor of *In Search of Excellence,* began a speech at a UCLA awards dinner honoring him for his significant contributions to public understanding of business, financial, and economic issues:

> There is a hypothesis I want to throw out. Given the current economic environment, business news has become an enormous part of our daily lives. But why hasn't management news? What's the distinction between the two?

Another business person, Gloria Rodriguez, also opened her talk with a question. She used it to build her case for a liberalized immigration law:

> How many of you have parents or grandparents who were immigrants to the United States? [She waits to see how many people raised their hands.]
> That's what I thought. Many of the workers in the United States today are immigrants, whether documented or not. Incidentally, I prefer the term "undocumented immigrants" to aliens, which sounds as though they're from Mars or Jupiter.

And here is how a recent college alumnus launched his talk to a group of college students on how he began a successful chain of one-hour photo development stores:

> How do I make money in this business? That's a question all of us have to ask in thinking about starting a business.

2. *Use an unusual idea or comparison.* Presenting the ordinary in a new light through a novel idea or comparison can spark interest in a topic that might otherwise be greeted as the "same old subject."

See how John D. Lyon, executive vice president of an oil company, used a novel idea to encourage executives in his industry to think about an unpleasant topic, the gloomy state of the energy business. (We will be referring to this speech at several points in our discussion.)

> No government agency, as far I know, publishes an uncertainty index, but if there were such a thing as an uncertainty index and if it were used to measure the energy industry today, it would register off the top of the scale.

Similarly, a business analyst used a novel comparison to get his technical staff to begin thinking about a common problem they were having in explaining a new computer package to a group of nontechnical people:

> If you've ever been in a music group or watched one practice, you know that musicians "talk" a special language of their own. A guitarist who wants a different beat from a drummer taps it out on the music stand or hums it. A flutist will replay the melody if he thinks the clarinetist hasn't done it right. Like a music group, our staff communicates in a special language that only we understand. It's efficient for us, but it can sound as foreign as the talk of a music group to the people we're supposed to be assisting with new computer packages.

3. *Tell a story that reflects your listeners' needs and interests*. Almost everyone is receptive to a good story. Use a story that relates to your topic to gain your listeners' attention and to direct their attention to your major points. A spokesperson for a retired executives' group introduced her talk to a public meeting on senior citizens' rights with this story:

> Imagine yourself at 70. You've worked hard for years and may be thinking it's time to retire and get in some gardening, learn to play the piano, or enjoy your grandkids. Your company's ready for you to retire too. In fact, 70 is compulsory retirement age.
>
> But what if you don't like gardening, don't want to take up a musical instrument, or really don't want to spend time with your grandkids? What if your keenest pleasures come from work? Well, the law says you have no choice. You must retire.

4. *Identify how your subject directly affects your listeners in performing their jobs*. This device works especially well for introducing presentations within your organization. Your listeners have built-in motivation to listen to you, since the subject of your talk can directly affect how they perform their jobs. Launch your talk quickly by saying how your presentation meets your listeners' needs and goals. See, for example, how the top sales representative for Office of the Future, Inc., a company selling office automation equipment to small businesses, began his presentation to the marketing division of his company:

> I'm pleased to tell you the upshot of my meeting with our top customer, Bio Health Tech. They're very satisfied with their savings in labor and paperwork since they purchased our deluxe office automation package, and they're even more satisfied with the reliability and expertise of our support people.
>
> Six months after the installation of our system, Bio Health Tech reports a 20 percent increase in the productivity of their secretarial pool, a 15 percent reduction in the purchase of paper, and only one minor breakdown in equipment, which we repaired within twenty-four hours.

And here's how the head of an outside consulting firm began his talk to the top management of a museum on how the museum could improve its bookstore operations:

My task over the past few weeks has been to study the organizational structure of your bookstore. My recommendations, which I will present to you this afternoon, will help you implement an improved method of accountability, set better staffing and budgetary limits, and establish more efficient lines of authority.

5. *Refer to the occasion.* If you are giving a talk for a special occasion such as a graduation, an honorary dinner, or the opening of a new facility, the occasion may provide the attention-getting remark you need. By referring at the outset to the occasion, you can link your talk to its broader meanings. Notice how this technique operates in a ceremonial speech by the student president of the Babson College Chamber of Commerce at the annual ceremony honoring famous entrepreneurs:

We are here today to honor four very successful men. Each of them will have a different story to tell you, but the plot will be the same. They spotted a need and they capitalized on it. I'm sure that if you looked carefully at the personalities of these men, you'd find three qualities that each of them owes his success to. These qualities are uncommon courage, enormous self-confidence, and the desire to win. Some people would call it "the right stuff."

6. *Identify a problem.* If you open your talk by identifying a problem that is likely to concern your listeners, you will get them to think about the impact of the problem on them, its possible solutions, and the solution you are likely to present during the course of the speech.

This is how a head of Marketing opened her talk designed to motivate entry-level managers to attend a series of training sessions on how to give oral presentations:

What if you suddenly found yourself in Jack's position? Jack's boss has just told him, "Jack, we've got customers showing up any minute now. How about giving them a fifteen minute update on the improvements we've made in our product line?" As entry-level managers, you can usually feel confident that you *won't* be requested to speak off the cuff. But research as well as my own experience show that, as you move up the career ladder, your technical skills take a back seat. It's your communication skills that increasingly count.

A human resources manager, Beth Milwid, varied this technique for dramatic effect. She initially described an apparently problem-free situation and then identified a problem that existed beneath the calm surface:

The number of American women in professional jobs has skyrocketed during the past decade. As legal barriers to sex discrimination have been enacted, many women have gravitated toward previously all-male fields. The media document the achievements of "rising star" and "fast track" women who have advanced quickly, and with apparent ease. "Mary Cunningham" has become a household word. Today, everywhere we turn we see photographs of attractive female executives happily swinging their briefcases, competently chairing high-level meetings in corporate board rooms, or eagerly jumping out of their BMW's to catch last-minute flights. Such publicity would have us believe that for the majority of new professional women, opportunities abound and the path to success is now a blissful one.

Unfortunately this perspective overlooks the psychological realities of day-to-day work life. The truth is somewhat different. Often the beginning professional woman finds that she is the only female in her office. Suddenly she realizes that she has indeed entered a male work culture and must adapt to it somehow, or fail. Sometimes the woman enjoys great visibility and gratifying rewards. At other times she feels harried, discouraged, and decidedly out of place. The range of emotions that these women experience on the job is vast. The stresses on the individual can be intense.

THE INTRODUCTION: PREVIEWING THE MAIN POINTS

Following an attention-getting opening, it is important to set up your audience's expectations about the scope of your talk and the order in which you will discuss major points. This is the place to preview what you will cover in the talk, to prepare your listeners so they will have a framework in which to understand and remember your major points.

In energy executive John D. Lyon's talk on the oil crisis, this preview appeared right after his opening remarks on an "uncertainty index" for the energy industry:

> I want to talk on three subjects this afternoon: First, the scope and nature of the current confusion and uncertainty in the oil industry; second its causes; and finally, my own guesses about its duration and resolution.

Similarly, the head of Marketing previewed her talk right after identifying the problem managers will face in needing to give impromptu talks and formal presentations:

> Today I want to talk about the importance of presentation skills to your career advancement. First, I'd like to describe a a typical career path here at Lemco in terms of the increasing uses and expectations about your communication skills. Second, I want to discuss briefly two of the skills you'll need—giving formal presentations to large groups and giving impromptu talks like the one Jack's been asked to give. Third, I'm going to suggest the concrete steps you can take today to prepare for your advancement.

In the next example, an investment consultant previewed the services his company provides potential clients:

> You'll see how our investment counselors can help you (1) save on your taxes, (2) set up a low-risk, high-yield portfolio of investments, (3) plan for vacation and retirement, and (4) reduce the amount of personal time and effort you'd have to waste to manage your own investments.

Finally, notice how human resources consultant Beth Milwid highlighted the main points of her talk:

> I'll start by outlining briefly what the study involved. Next, I'll summarize the important findings of my investigation. For that portion of my talk I'll be using the subjects' own words as much as possible. My presentation will conclude with some very specific things that human resources managers can keep in mind when working with professional women.

THE BODY OF THE TALK

Getting your listeners' attention is a challenge. Holding their attention and at the same time influencing their thinking is even more difficult. There are several things you can do to ensure your success.

1. *Limit the main points you discuss.* Keep in mind that the listener's ability to assimiliate information is more restricted than the reader's ability to take in information. Readers can take in information at their own pace, backtrack to review difficult and important material, and rely on the document's headings and visual design to discover your central and supporting points. Listeners have none of these aids. For this reason, try to limit the body of your talk to two or three main points.

2. *Use transitional devices.* Because people are listening to rather than reading what you have to say, it is not enough to limit your talk to two or three main points. You also need to use transitional devices—transitional phrases, summaries, and previews—within the body of your talk to help your listeners grasp your main points. Notice the effective use of summary in John D. Lyon's speech on the energy business. The summary acts as a transition, reinforcing what listeners have just heard so that they can remember it before taking in another major point:

> I now turn to Tosco and to the Colony Shale Project, but before I do, I will summarize the three points I would like you to remember so far:
> One, oil is an ordinary kind of market commodity having no special mysteries.
> Two, the richest and largest shale oil deposits are those of the western U.S., especially northwestern Colorado.
> Three, technology of a dull and conventional character is available and proven for extracting shale oil, while at the same time there is limitless opportunity to tinker with approaches as exotic as you like.

A preview appeared a little later in the body of the talk. After analyzing his company's past strategies, Lyon turned to how the company's expectations about the energy business were or were not met:

> I will discuss with you some of the areas in which our expectations were, viewed as of today, too rosy, too gloomy, or just right.

Here, a human resources manager, talking to college students about the job satisfaction people seek, summarizes the main points of the body of his talk before moving on to his conclusions:

> What, then, are the needs of people on the job? First, they want to be appreciated for a job well done. Second, they need a sense of accomplishment within themselves. Third, they need a grievance process, a way to pour out the problems they face on the job. Fourth, they need to respect their boss's abilities and fairness.

3. *Use details to support your main points.* To develop the two or three key points in the body of your talk, you can use anecdotes, vivid illustrations, and, for persuasive talks, assertions to support your point of view. These details hold your audience's attention, enliven your talk, and, in the case of persuasive talks, build a convincing argument.

Lyon used a series of historical highlights to illustrate a key point about uncertainty in the energy business:

> Looking around the room, I don't see very many persons under the age of 10, so perhaps it's needless to review in any detail the astonishing recent history of oil. But so compelling is that history as a tale of uncertainty beyond all expectations, that a brief mention of key elements is in order.
>
> Four years ago, at this time of year, gas lines had become an accepted if unwelcome feature of life in California and a few other places but were still considered a great joke in Washington, D.C., which would not have its own gas lines until June.
>
> Three years ago, the world's largest corporation entered the synthetics industry with a rush of enthusiasm, publishing plans that called for production of 8 million barrels a day from oil shale in less than two decades. Gasoline prices had just cracked the dollar-a-gallon barrier.
>
> Two years ago, at the end of a decade of oil controls in the United States, alarmed critics predicted unconscionable increases in prices and renewed shortages, both of which would be sponsored by the wicked cartelists at home and abroad.
>
> Last spring, OPEC met repeatedly amid speculations that the market price would tumble to $20 when talks collapsed, never to recover in this century.

John Reilly, an insurance agent for a major airline, used vivid illustrations to explain a technical point about his work to a group of young airline personnel:

> Everyone is familiar with the role of the dice and the fact that there are probabilities associated with each possible outcome. But when outcomes are based on several intermediary events, figuring the outcomes becomes more complex. A common example of this complexity is the probability of success—or the probability you'll have fun on your next date. There are several probabilistic or uncertain events involved here: One, the chance he or she will accept the date. Two, the probability you'll have to talk with the parents. Three, the probability you'll be able to sneak a good-night kiss. There are techniques that help you model these events called Monte Carlo simulation.

I'll talk a little bit about Monte Carlo simulation by example. I was involved in a project in which we were trying to predict the number of crashes of our planes that would occur in 199_. The first thing we did was to identify the uncertain events that might occur in that year: First, the number of probable accidents based on our records for the last ten years. Then, given the number of accidents, we looked at the value of the aircraft, the possible extent of aircraft damage based on our aircraft histories, the likely number of people aboard, and the expense of the injuries per person. Once we had identified these events, we developed a computer program that modeled the following process:

First, the computer randomly selected a number of accidents. Let's say x was the number of accidents.

Second, for each of these accidents, the computer determined—again randomly—the value of the extent of damage to the aircraft, the number of people aboard, and the expense of the injuries per person. So, at the end of the process we had a dollar amount that was the estimate of insurable losses. We did this simulation fifteen hundred times and ended up with fifteen hundred individual estimates. We then combined these to form a sample probability distribution. And, as with any distribution, we calculated various statistics like the mean, the median, and the probability that the loss would be less than a certain amount.

Using this one approach, we can model uncertain events. So if anyone is having problems with a future date, I'll be happy to help.

Finally, let's look at the assertions a senior citizen activist built into his argument against mandatory retirement:

I say mandatory retirement is wrong. Individuals should have a choice. I have two reasons for advocating voluntary retirement. First, it's morally wrong to force people to retire. Our country was founded on the ideas of life, liberty, and the pursuit of happiness. To force people to retire is to deny them freedom of choice. Second, it can be economically costly to society and to the company to force some people to retire. Retired people are not productive, and they collect social security. As far as the company is concerned, their knowledge and expertise are lost to the company, which incurs significant costs in training replacements. In addition, companies sometimes have to resort to hiring their retired employees as consultants at a fee that is almost as high as their full-time salaries.

THE CONCLUSION

Too often a speaker trails off at the end of a talk because he or she doesn't realize the importance of a strong conclusion. Conclusions are crucial because people tend to remember best what they hear first and last. An effective conclusion can summarize and reinforce the main points that you want listeners to remember and can identify how you want your listeners to think and act.

You can use several devices to conclude your talk.

1. *Refer to the phrase, example, question, or story you used at the beginning of the talk.* A conclusion that echoes the opening and extends its meaning creates an effec-

tive closing for your talk. The following conclusion of a talk given by a spokesperson for Johnson & Johnson on the Tylenol poisonings both recalls the opening and moves listeners in a new but related direction:

INTRODUCTION

Leverage is a favorite "buzz word" for all of us in business. As a matter of fact, a lot of what we do in managing our businesses has to do with leverage—leveraging our assets—whether we are talking about the balance sheet, brand names, or the brain power of our people. I know of nowhere that leverage has been practiced with such extraordinary success as by the Ad Council. To take less than $2 million worth of advertising and to leverage it into more than $700 million worth of advertising—and all in the interest of the public—the idea itself is truly staggering.

CONCLUSION

I began my remarks talking about leverage and would like to end on the same thought.

I think the lesson in the TYLENOL experience, as well as the record of these 15 companies over the past 30 years, is the same, and that is that we as businessmen and women have extraordinary leverage on our most important asset—goodwill—the goodwill of the public. If we make sure our enterprises are managed in terms of their obligations to society, that is also the best way to defend this democratic capitalistic system that means so much to all of us.

2. *Restate the problem you introduced at the beginning of the talk and then provide a summary of solutions you have developed in the body of the talk.* A conclusion that restates the problem and then provides a summary of your solutions is especially effective for a problem-solution talk, since the conclusion emphasizes the link between your recommendations and the problem presented to listeners at the start. Observe how a consultant in public relations used this technique to conclude his talk to a group of company presidents:

What can you as chief executives do to make certain your company is creating a strong public image?

First, you can hire competent image builders—people who are experienced in public relations.

Second, give them clear-cut goals to reach, and while you're at it, make sure you make them part of the management team.

And finally, check your progress routinely to make certain you're on track.

3. *Use an apt quotation.* Quoting the words of an eloquent speaker, a famous person, or a well-known text can focus your listeners' attention on the key themes of your talk and close it with dramatic effect. This is how the student president of the Babson College Chamber of Commerce concluded his talk on the four business people Babson was honoring at its annual conference on entrepreneurship:

> As President of the Babson Student Chamber of Commerce, I encourage all students to get involved and start a business. What will it take? Some creativity, energy, commitment, a little bit of daring. Listen carefully today to what these four distinguished entrepreneurs have to say because they have done it. They have done it successfully. They have "the right stuff"—persistence in the face of uncertainty. As President Teddy Roosevelt once said, "Far better it is to dare mighty things, to win glorious triumphs, even though checkered with failure, than to take rank with those poor spirits who neither enjoy much nor suffer much, because they live in the gray twilight that knows not victory nor defeat."

And this is the way special guest speaker John Coleman used a passage from the Bible to sum up dramatically his talk to a group of college students, his theme being work, human dignity, and personal accomplishment:

> I know it's Wednesday rather than Sunday but I'm going to close with the Bible: the words of Ecclesiastes, "a time for this, a time for that" are terribly well known. If they're not well known to you, they should be. How many of you have read just a sentence or two beyond "a time for this, a time for that"? The next words are not typical of the writers of Ecclesiastes, who are by and large gloomy people. But the words that are important are these: "I know the only thing for man is to be happy and to lead the best life he can while he's alive." I like the words so much I'm going to say them all over again. "I know the only thing for woman is to be happy and to lead the best life she can while she is alive."

4. *Use humor*. If your subject and tone allow, you can end with a humorous remark that ties in with the main themes of your talk. Notice how John Hanson, founder of Hanson's Recreational Vehicles, played with the idea of "management by wandering around," MBWA, to conclude his talk to college students on the qualities that make for a successful entrepreneur:

> The theme of what I have to say today is, "Go out and do it." Find something that you're interested in.
> You hear about MBWA, management by wandering around. That sounds silly but it works out, and MBWA can be done in so many ways. In our case, we have sixty acres under one roof. You can do a lot of wandering around there. In fact, you can get lost. But, beyond that, you have to wander around America and the world to see what's going on. I realize that for a lot of you that's difficult, but for us who are in a business which is national and international, it's most important.

5. *Use an example*. A good example can provide the vivid detail that sums up the major point of your talk and gives your listeners a concrete illustration to remember. The example can be drawn from your personal experience, from business, or from the larger community. Heinz Nixdorf, owner of a major software company in Europe, drew on an example from business life in Germany to illustrate for his audience of U.S. college students business's responsibility for education:

> The more we invest in people, the more we do for our country. In my nation, Germany, ninety percent of all youngsters get qualified training. Twenty-five percent have a chance to go to the university and to become a manager. Nearly seventy percent have a

chance to be educated for three years as an apprentice at the expense of a company. We spend twenty thousand dollars per person over a three-year period, and in a plant of four thousand with twelve hundred apprentices, you can compute how much our investment is in the teaching of youngsters. The result at the end of three years is that they are skilled workers, able to make quality products. We get back our investment many times, not only in quality but also in the attitude of these workers. The seven hundred thousand apprentices we teach in three years time are free to leave the company that trained them after the three years. They can go to any company. On the one hand, you might say we get back nothing. On the other hand, there's no negative result! Every good company makes it because we can hire skilled workers developed in other companies too.

The accompanying checklist will help you review the organization of your talks.

CHECKLIST FOR ORGANIZING PRESENTATIONS

1. To gain your listeners' interest, have you done one of the following:
   - Asked a question?
   - Used an unusual idea or comparison?
   - Told a story that reflects your listeners' needs and interests?
   - Announced how your subject directly affects your listeners?
   - Referred to the occasion?
   - Identified a problem that is likely to concern your listeners?
2. Have you given your audience a preview of the scope and organization of your talk?
3. Have you limited the main points you discuss?
4. Have you used transitional devices within the body of the talk to help your listeners grasp your main points?
5. Have you used details to support your main points?
6. To conclude your talk, have you done one of the following:
   - Referred to the phrase, example, question, or story you used at the beginning of the talk?
   - Restated the problem you introduced at the beginning of the talk and then provided a summary of solutions you developed in the body of the talk?
   - Used an apt quotation?
   - Used humor?
   - Used an example?

Outlining or Writing Out the Copy for the Presentation

Speeches that are read word for word from a paper tend to be lifeless and stilted. That's why the most effective presentations are usually based on outlines.

PREPARING AN OUTLINE

Outlines give you the opportunity to speak conversationally and to fill in the main points and subpoints as you move through your presentation. Outlines also give you a structure to follow, making it easy to keep track of the main points you want to convey. The major divisions of the outline name the main points of your presentation.

In preparing an outline, use 4- by 6-inch index cards to record your main points and subpoints. Also, because beginnings, transitions, and endings are crucial and often hard to remember, write out in full the first sentence, the transitional sentences between and within sections of the talk, and the concluding sentence. Writing these complete sentences and having them before you is a good way to embed the sequence of your talk in your mind and will prevent you from forgetting your major ideas and the connections among them. Figure 12.4 illustrates how the outline of a talk can be structured.

Put no more than one or two main points (with their subpoints) on each index card so that you will be able to grasp quickly the structure of your talk as you give it. If cards are crowded with lots of details, it is easy to lose your place or to read the cards verbatim. Number the cards consecutively and label each card "INTRODUCTION," "BODY," or "CONCLUSION" in big, bold letters. Except for writing complete sentences for the opening, transitions, and the conclusion, use only key words to indicate main and subpoints. Key words will trigger in your memory the ideas you want to convey while helping you avoid the trap of reading verbatim from a text and failing to maintain eye contact with your audience. For each card, indent subpoints several spaces from the main point to show that the subpoints are subordinate to the main point. In this way you can quickly review the key points for a section of your talk and still concentrate on your audience.

Figure 12.5 shows the complete outline on index cards for John D. Lyon's twenty-minute talk, "The New World of Energy: Changes and Shakeouts," to a group of executives in the energy business. Notice how he:

- Distributes the speech over several cards, which are numbered
- Writes the labels of his cards in big, bold letters
- Uses complete sentences only for the opening, the transitions, and the conclusion
- Uses only key phrases for the main and subpoints

Outlining for "Impromptu" Talks. Most talks are prepared by making outlines. In fact, even when you are asked to give an impromptu talk—one you are requested to do on the spur of the moment—you can often have an outline ready if you anticipate the situations in which you may be called on to speak. One marketing rep explained to us that whenever important customers showed up or he landed in a branch office town, he would be asked to summarize the company's most recent marketing successes. As a result, he prepared a five-minute talk on note cards about the firm's top five marketing successes and updated his notes every month.

Figure 12.4
STRUCTURE OF AN OUTLINE FOR A TALK

1	INTRODUCTION

Opening Sentence (in full):

Anecdote:

Preview (in full):

2	BODY

Main Point 1:

    A. Supporting Point:

    B. Supporting Point:

Transitional sentence (in full):

(continued)

(STRUCTURE OF AN OUTLINE FOR A TALK continued)

```
3                          BODY


    Main Point 2:

        A. Supporting Point:

        B. Supporting Point:

    Review:
```

```
4                       CONCLUSION



    Summary:



    Concluding Sentence (in full):
```

SPEAKING

Figure 12.5
OUTLINE FOR JOHN D. LYON'S TALK

① INTRODUCTION:

"No government agency, as far as I know, publishes an uncertainty index, but if there were such a thing as an uncertainty index and if it were used to measure the energy industry today, it would register off the top of the scale."

② INTRODUCTION:

Brief description of uncertainty

(continued)

OUTLINE FOR JOHN D. LYON'S TALK (continued)

③ INTRODUCTION:

PREVIEW:

"I want to talk on three subjects this afternoon: First, the scope and nature of the current confusion and uncertainty in the oil industry; second, its causes; and finally, my own guesses about its duration and resolution."

④ BODY

MAIN POINT 1: SCOPE AND NATURE OF CONFUSION AND UNCERTAINTY

Review recent astonishing reversals in oil
- Four years ago, gas lines
- Three years ago, world's largest corporation enters synthetic industry
- Two years ago, predictions of increased prices and renewed shortages
- Last spring, OPEC talks collapse

⑤ BODY:
TRANSITION TO SECOND POINT:
"Which brings us to today, when many of us are not too proud to admit that our crystal ball acts like it's broken. Nevertheless, it is possible to review some of the current results of these reversals."

⑥ BODY:
MAIN POINT 2: CURRENT RESULTS OF REVERSALS AND CAUSES

Results
- Exploration activity reduced
- Gas wars returned

(continued)

(OUTLINE FOR JOHN D. LYON'S TALK continued)

⑦ BODY:
   MAIN POINT 2:
   Apparent Causes:
   — Falling demand
       caused by conservation
   — Conservation
       caused by rising costs

⑧ BODY:
   TRANSITION TO POINT 3:
   "That demand has fallen cannot be debated, but does that explain the turbulence and uncertainty in the oil industry? I think not."

⑨ BODY:
   MAIN POINT 2: REAL CAUSE IS INDUSTRY'S INABILITY TO MANAGE INVENTORIES AND RESPONSE TO MARKET.

   – Problem concealed by bureaucratic controls and steady demand increase
   – Previously, managing decisions made by integrated systems under central control of single corporations

⑩ BODY:
   MAIN POINT 2:

   – Now decisions made by people widely separated by place, interest, expectations
   – Now decisions have no organic connection to consumer market
   – Tosco's prediction that industry would stabilize wrong
   – Advocates of separation or disintegration of big oil wrong: won't stabilize industry

(continued)

① BODY:

SUMMARY OF MAIN POINT 2:

"This continuation of uncertainty disables planning and investment not only in the oil industry but also in autos, solar electricity, and nearly any other economic activity."

② BODY:

RECOMMEND:

Stability will help industry

⑬ BODY:
   TRANSITION TO MAIN POINT 3:

"I will now enter into the most dangerous part of our journey, passing from analysis to prediction."

⑭ BODY:
   MAIN POINT 3:

- Predict movement toward greater stability
- Movement clearly begun
- Construction of oil refineries
- Purchase of markets by crude oil exporters
- Purchase of crude gatherers by refiners
- Purchase of refining capacity by gas retailers

(continued)

(OUTLINE FOR JOHN D. LYON'S TALK continued)

⑮ CONCLUSION:

SUMMARY OF MAJOR POINTS:

Summarize results and their causes

⑯ CONCLUSION:

CONCLUDING SENTENCE:

"Many of these integrating moves will be novel. Many will be unrecognized, but taken all in all, they will serve to restore a measure of stability to oil, energy, and the economy."

You, too, may be called on to give an impromptu talk. For example, if you work on a group project, you may be called on to give an impromptu talk about your area of expertise. Or if you are the regular spokesperson for a group, you can assume you will have to speak to individuals and groups that work with your group. In such instances, preparing notes in anticipation of being asked to speak will give you confidence and improve the substance of your talk.

WRITING OUT A TALK

Occasionally you will be asked to give a talk that must be written out. Perhaps you are addressing a very large audience, or perhaps your argument is too complex or too important to risk error. Usually these talks are for a formal occasion—for instance, an annual company retreat or a celebration of a company anniversary—and may be printed in a company publication. In these instances, triple space the speech, leave generous margins, and number the pages. In addition, underline important words and phrases for emphasis, and "key" the speech with marks such as asterisks to indicate where to pause, slow down, speed up, and take a breath.

Rehearsing to Revise and to Polish Your Delivery

Once you have fully prepared the content and structure of your talk in an outline, you will be well on your way to giving a polished presentation. In fact, nothing can substitute for a carefully thought through outline. But as in turning out an effective piece of writing, giving an effective talk requires that you revise for content and structure. Rehearsing the talk can help you determine what needs to be revised. Rehearsing is also essential to developing a polished delivery.

Focus on different issues in your early and late rehearsals. In early rehearsals (the first and possibly the second), concentrate on revision. Mark your note cards where you feel you need to adjust your talk, and revise it before you practice again. In later rehearsals, focus on delivery.

QUALITIES OF A POLISHED DELIVERY

When either you or your associates are judging your rehearsal, you should have several questions to ask about your performance. How well do you do in:

- Projecting a relaxed, confident image
- Focusing attention on your listeners and not on your text or outline
- Adjusting the length and content of your talk to unforeseen circumstances
- Handling questions
- Using visual aids

Projecting a Relaxed, Confident Image. Since your physical presence and the quality of your speaking voice can be assets or liabilities when you speak to others, try to use appropriate dress, posture, gestures, facial expression, and voice.

1. *Dress:* Adjust your dress to suit the occasion and the dress code of your company or the group you are speaking to.

2. *Posture and gestures:* Stand straight, but not rigidly, to give a friendly, alert impression. Keep your feet several inches apart and your hands comfortably at your sides. If you are speaking from a lectern, don't clutch it. Stand behind it with your hands on top of it, behind it, or at your sides.

Use gestures that appropriately reinforce your ideas. For instance, when you are making a series of points, you can hold up one finger to make the first point, two for the second, three for the third, and so on.

Try to get rid of distracting and overblown gestures. If you tend to tap your pen on the desk or scratch your ear, don't. If you wave your arms too frequently, tone down this gesture. As a rule, work on making your gestures as natural as they are when you are speaking comfortably with others.

3. *Facial expression:* Remember that people can often read your emotions in your face. And if your emotions are at odds with the content of your talk, people will put more faith in what they see than in what you say. Therefore, try to appear relaxed, yet alert.

4. *Tone of voice, vocal stress, and inflection:* Develop a natural and friendly tone of voice to engage your listeners' interest. Try to speak with ease and enthusiasm. Your tone can encourage your audience to be enthusiastic too. Vary your tone, vocal stress, and inflection to avoid monotony and to stress points you consider important.

5. *Rate of speaking:* Use a conversational rate of speaking, and change it to avoid monotony and to emphasize important ideas. Pause before key words and transitional words (e.g., "therefore," "as a result"). Slow down as you shift your audience's attention to or away from your visuals. In general, speed up when giving information that is easy to understand, and slow down to convey information that is difficult to understand.

6. *Volume:* Maintain the necessary volume to allow your listeners to hear you without effort. If you speak too softly, they will soon stop making the effort to listen; if you are too loud, they will be annoyed. Varying your volume will help distinguish major points from minor ones and keep your listeners' attention.

7. *Word choice:* Avoid vocalized pauses (e.g., "er," "uh," "um," "you know"), since they can distract or annoy your audience.

Focusing Your Attention on Your Listeners. Good speakers spend a small percentage of their time looking at their notes and a large percentage observing how the audience is responding to what they are saying. To focus attention on your audience, establish and maintain good **eye contact.** Eye contact lets your listeners know that you are comfortable talking to them, have something important to tell them, and want to respond to their reactions. If you fail to use eye contact, you can seem evasive and uncomfortable, or not fully in control of your subject matter.

To establish eye contact, try, *before* you begin speaking, to spot people in different parts of the room who seem friendly, and look at each person briefly. To maintain eye contact, try to look for a few seconds at each person in the audience, but focus on those who seem most receptive, and move your gaze from one of these listeners to another while you are speaking.

Adjusting the Length and Content of Your Talk. To prepare for unexpected changes in schedule, see how you can lengthen or shorten your talk. You will need a shorter version of your talk if, for example, earlier speakers overrun their time, agenda items take more time than anticipated, or extra speakers or agenda items must be accommodated. The shorter version should retain your major ideas and leave out examples or other supporting points.

You may need a longer version of your talk if listeners ask for further explanation or illustration. But before you allow your talk to exceed the time limit, check with the group or with those in charge to see whether exceeding your time limit would be in order.

When you can extend your talk, use your listeners' questions and nonverbal reactions to guide you in adjusting its content and length. To judge their reactions, observe how your listeners are responding to what you are saying: Are they listening? Are there any glazed looks? Are they puzzled? If the audience seems confused, you may want to pause to illustrate or explain more fully what you mean.

Handling Questions. As you prepare your talk, it is a good idea to anticipate listeners' questions, to jot down possible questions, and to formulate your responses. When handling questions during your presentation, do the following:

- Consider people's nonverbal questions—such as confused or pleased looks—as well as their verbal questions.
- Be sure you understand your listeners' questions. If necessary, ask for clarification of a question you don't understand, or paraphrase it and ask the questioner to confirm whether your paraphrase is accurate.
- If some people in the audience cannot hear a question, repeat it before answering.
- If one person tries to monopolize the question-and-answer period by giving a little speech or asking a battery of questions, stop the speaker courteously and acknowledge someone else.

You may want to handle questions as they arise or at the end of your talk. There are advantages and disadvantages to each approach. If you allow listeners to interrupt you, you will be sure to hold their attention, since you are addressing their needs on the spot; however, such interruptions can cause you to lose your place, digress from the main point, consider issues out of sequence, or lose the attention of listeners who find the question uninteresting or irrelevant.

If you handle questions after the talk, you will have better command of the structure of your talk and the time schedule. If you choose this option, prepare to summarize.

your main points again *after the question period* so that your listeners will remember the main points of your talk rather than the questions others asked. At the beginning of your talk, let your audience know when you prefer to handle questions.

Using Visual Aids. Research shows that visual aids improve comprehension. They visually reinforce, illustrate, or explain the major points of your presentation. Since visual aids support your presentation, select and design them after you have completed your outline. (See Chapter 13, "Visual Aids," for a detailed discussion.) When reviewing the main points of your outline, you will be able to see where and how a visual aid could supplement your major points.

Since your audience has to read the visual aids while listening to your presentation, keep visuals simple to read and understand. In general, they should be less complex than the ones you would use in a report. Readers of reports have charts and graphs right in front of them and can review them at their own speed, but your listeners have only a limited time to review visual aids and may have to strain to see them.

Follow the same principles in choosing a graph, chart, or table for your talk as you would in choosing visuals for your written communications. The difference between visual aids for talks and for written communications is that those for talks should be simpler:

- No more than two columns for tables
- No more than three lines for graphs or charts
- No more than five lines of text

As with visuals for written communications, visual aids for talks should be clearly and accurately labeled, and they should be presented at the appropriate place.

When you practice using your visual aids, run through these questions:

- Is your equipment working properly, and do you have everything you need (e.g., chalk and eraser, screens, flipchart, extension cords, extra light bulbs for an overhead projector)?
- Are your visual aids easy to see from the back and sides of the room?
- Does the room have enough light?
- Is the speaker's area situated so that everyone can see you and your visuals?
- Are you speaking to the audience and not to the visual aid?

If colleagues are evaluating your speech, ask them to consider whether your visual aids suitably reinforce, illustrate, or explain your message, and whether they are properly sequenced and coordinated with your talk.

The accompanying checklist will help you see if your rehearsal is thorough.

CHECKLIST FOR REHEARSING PRESENTATIONS

1. Have you projected a relaxed, confident image?
2. Are all of the following appropriate and effective:
   - Dress?
   - Posture and gestures?
   - Facial expression?
   - Tone of voice, vocal stress, and inflection?
   - Rate of speaking?
   - Volume?
   - Word choice?
3. Have you focused your attention on your listeners and not on your outline?
4. Can you adjust the length and content of your talk as conditions change?
5. Are you prepared to handle questions?
6. Have you designed visual aids that enhance your talk, and do you know how to use them?

TECHNIQUES FOR REHEARSING

One or more of the following techniques can help you revise your talk and polish your delivery:

1. *Rehearse in front of a mirror.* If you are rehearsing alone, practice in front of a mirror to see whether your posture, facial expression, and gestures are appropriate. Also, practice using your visual aids (e.g., flipcharts, slides, overhead transparencies) to ensure your ability to integrate them effectively in your presentation.

Practicing a speech before a mirror can help you check the appropriateness of your body language to your message.

620 THE RANDOM HOUSE GUIDE TO BUSINESS WRITING

Practicing in the hall where you are scheduled to speak can help you get comfortable with the conditions.

2. *Rehearse in the room where the talk is to be given.* If you have access to the room where the presentation is to be given, or to a comparably sized room, practice there, imagining your audience in front of you. The more you can duplicate the conditions of your talk, the more you will be able to make adjustments to suit your purpose and audience.

3. *Tape or videotape your rehearsals.* When you rehearse, use a tape recorder, or better still, if your organization provides media services, a videotape recorder. If you can detach yourself sufficiently from your image on the screen and the sound of your voice, reviewing your taped delivery will let you hear and see yourself as your listeners will hear and see you. As you play back the tape, role-play your audience. Check to see whether you are speaking clearly and at an appropriate rate and volume. Listening to the tape will also allow you to detect a sing-song delivery, vocalized pauses (e.g., ''er'' or ''um'') or a monotonous tone, and to catch words you may have mispronounced. Mark your note cards where these errors occur, and practice correcting these errors in your talk before you rehearse the whole talk again. Keep taping your presentation until your delivery sounds as though you are talking naturally to your audience. If you use a videotape recorder, evaluate both your speaking and your body language.

4. *Have friends or associates review your presentation.* Ask your listeners to *evaluate structure and content first* and *then delivery.* Have them outline your talk as they

SPEAKING 621

By using videotape to rehearse, you can work to improve both your voice and your mannerisms.

listen to you. Then compare their outline of your main points and subpoints to your own outline, noting discrepancies. Question your listeners about differences between your outline and theirs, and adjust your outline and talk so that the main points you want to convey come through clearly in the structure of your talk. Ask your listeners to comment also on the effectiveness of your delivery.

OTHER COMMON SPEAKING TASKS

As a business person, you will be expected to handle speaking assignments other than presentations. The most common are interviews and meetings. The knowledge that you have gained about giving oral presentations will help you handle these other speaking tasks.

Conducting Interviews

An interview is a conversation that is set up to reach a specific goal. Common types of interviews include the **employment interview,** for selecting a job candidate; the **infor-**

mation-gathering interview, for gathering information or solving a problem; and the **appraisal interview,** for reviewing the job performance of a subordinate.

Interviewing resembles other communication tasks. It is a process that consists of setting your goal, analyzing the interviewee, gathering information and generating ideas, organizing, conducting the interview, and doing necessary follow-up.

SETTING THE GOAL

To figure out the information you need to bring to and obtain from an interview, determine beforehand exactly what you want the interview to accomplish. You may even want to write down your objective. For example:

EMPLOYMENT INTERVIEW

I want to decide whether this job candidate's performance at the interview warrants calling her back for a follow-up interview with my boss. More specifically, does the candidate meet three essential criteria: working knowledge of the area, good communication skills, eagerness to learn more and to work hard?

INFORMATION GATHERING INTERVIEW

I want to find out what kind of telephone answering service small companies need.

APPRAISAL INTERVIEW

I want Glenn to understand how well he handles the technical aspects of his job and how poorly he motivates his staff. I also want him to be receptive to my suggestions for improving his weakness.

ASSESSING THE INTERVIEWEE

Given the purpose of the interview, consider anything about the interviewee that may affect the success of the interview. Some or all of the following may apply:

1. *Business relationship:* What is the interviewee's business relationship to you? For an employment or information-gathering interview, your assumptions can set the tone of the interview. For instance, if you are interviewing a job candidate who has held middle-level management positions similar to yours, you can talk as to a peer. In an appraisal interview, you should keep in mind that you are the interviewee's superior. The interviewee will take what you have to say seriously because you can significantly influence his or her promotion, salary, and retention.

2. *Attitude:* How is the interviewee likely to feel about you as an interviewer? If you are interviewing job candidates, they may be apprehensive and feel anxious about how they will come across. At an appraisal interview employees may also feel anxious,

SPEAKING   623

At some time in your business career, you will either conduct an interview or be interviewed. You can become more effective in this situation by learning about the process of interviewing.

unless they know the appraisal will be extraordinarily positive. Since no one receives criticism comfortably, try to put job candidates and employees at ease. At an information-gathering interview, your respondents may be reluctant to spend the time on your questions because they perceive no obvious benefits in being interviewed. Therefore, you should indicate to interviewees the advantages of complying with your request.

3. *Knowledge:* How much information does the interviewee have about the purpose and scope of the interview? In an employment interview, interviewees may not know much about the job or the company beyond the job description and the information provided by company publications and company contacts. Interviewees will be eager to learn from you about details of the job—such as its responsibilities, benefits, challenges, and drawbacks. In an information-gathering interview, respondents should know something about the topics you will cover, but perhaps not at the depth you assume. Be prepared to explain your topic and the depth at which you plan to deal with it. In an appraisal interview, employees may know a little or a lot about your evaluation of their work, so be ready to shorten or to elaborate on your remarks.

4. *Expectations about the interview:* What are the interviewee's expectations about how the interview will be conducted? Interviewees expect an interview to be professional. In other words, they anticipate that the interviewer will be courteous and prepared, and that the interview will take place in a quiet, private setting. Ideally interviewees would like the interviewer to put them at ease, to listen carefully, to be understanding, to ask relevant questions, and to offer useful information.

GATHERING INFORMATION AND GENERATING IDEAS

The kind of interview you plan to conduct dictates the kinds of information and ideas you will need. For an employment interview, review the candidate's resume, the company's job description (e.g., qualifications needed for the job, job tasks, and responsibilities), and the job's "selling points." Also be prepared to discuss the details of the job. This may mean talking beforehand with the people the new employee will work with. For an information-gathering interview, do research to pinpoint the kinds of information you want to gain from your interviewee. (See Chapter 10, "The Formal Report: The Goal, the Reader, the Ideas and Information," on the information gathering interview.) For an appraisal interview, collect all pertinent information on the employee's performance, methods for improving it, and company policy on uses of the appraisal.

Types of Questions. As you gather data and think about the interview, you can begin devising questions to ask the interviewee. Questions may be closed, open-ended, or a combination of the two. **Closed questions** have a specific answer: yes or no, multiple-choice, or a single word or phrase. They are appropriate when you:

- Need specific information
- Are sure of the range of answers your respondent can give
- Want to maintain strict control of the topics discussed during the interview

Open-ended questions begin with such phrases as "How do you feel about . . . ?" "How would you describe . . . ?" or "What's your opinion of . . . ?" They have no preset answers. They are appropriate for exploratory research when your ideas are somewhat undefined and your knowledge of your respondent is limited.

Closed questions have several advantages over open-ended ones. Closed questions result in quantifiable data and can be replicated accurately; an interviewer asks exactly the same questions in exactly the same order to every interviewee. Closed questions are also easier for the interviewer to administer. The interviewer does not need special skill in asking probing questions, as does the interviewer administering open-ended questions.

Open-ended questions have advantages too. Since open-ended questions require more thought on the part of the interviewee, these questions can yield in-depth information. And if the response the interviewee gives seems particularly relevant, the interviewer can follow up with several more questions pertaining to the topic.

Whether you use closed or open-ended questions or a combination of the two, the phrasing of your questions deserves attention. Be sure that your wording is unambiguous and readily understandable to your respondent. If you must use specialized terms, define them. Check, too, that none of your questions will antagonize the interviewee.

After you have put together your own questions, draw up a list of questions that the interviewee is likely to ask and your answers. For an employment interview, such questions would relate to the nature of the job and the organization. For an information-gathering interview, the questions might relate to how the respondent's answers will be used, whether they are confidential, and when, if ever, the findings will be released. For an appraisal interview, the interviewee's questions would relate to the impact of the evaluation on retention, salary, and promotion.

ORGANIZING THE INTERVIEW

Once you have generated questions and topics you want to cover during the interview, group and order them in a sequence that is logical to interviewees and puts them at ease. For instance, in an employment interview, you can group questions according to such topics as education, work experience, and career goals. Sensitive questions can appear in the middle or at the end, to avoid making interviewees uncomfortable at the outset and resistant to answering.

CONDUCTING THE INTERVIEW

Regardless of the specific goals of an interview, one of your objectives is to establish a comfortable and productive session with your interviewee. Since an interview can be stressful, do what you can to reduce the interviewee's tension and to establish rapport. Choose a private, quiet, and comfortable place for the interview, and make sure that you will not be interrupted by others.

At the opening of the interview, introduce yourself to the interviewee (if you don't know each other) and smile. You may also want to make a few brief comments to put the interviewee at ease. Don't be afraid to speak of the weather, to show concern for the interviewee (Could she find the office easily?), and to tell the interviewee that you have been looking forward to your talk together.

Before you begin your questions, identify the purpose of the interview so that the interviewee knows what to expect. For example:

EMPLOYMENT INTERVIEW

Within the next hour I want to describe the position we've advertised. I also have several questions to ask you about your education, work experience, and career goals as they relate to the position that's open in our company. I would be happy to answer questions you may have about the position and about the company.

INFORMATION-GATHERING INTERVIEW

Good morning, Mr. Conklin. May I have a few minutes of your time to ask you some questions about the telephone answering services you require in your offices? I work for a not-for-profit organization, SAT Research, Inc., and we are doing a survey of owners of small companies like yours to find out your needs and to pass on this information to the telephone service companies in your area.

APPRAISAL INTERVIEW

Glenn, we'll spend the next hour discussing the results of your performance evaluation. We will look at your strengths and those areas in which you can improve. We will have time too to discuss anything on your mind about the evaluation.

Keep several essentials in mind as you conduct the interview:

- Use your questions to cover key issues.
- Take notes on the interviewee's responses and on your strongest impressions of the interviewee.
- Maintain eye contact with the interviewee as you would in ordinary conversation.
- Listen fully to the interviewee's responses before commenting or moving on to the next topic, and leave time for the interviewee to ask questions.
- Draw out the interviewee. Talk less than the interviewee does, and be tactful and sympathetic.
- Close the interview courteously. Thank the interviewee for coming, ask for further questions, and when appropriate, summarize the key points of the interview and mention specific follow-up.

FOLLOW-UP

After an interview, jot down notes summarizing your final impressions and evaluation of the interview. Note-taking will help you retain the main points of the interview, and will make it easy for you to summarize your thoughts for others who are interested in the outcome of the interview.

The accompanying checklist will help you evaluate your interviewing technique.

CHECKLIST FOR CONDUCTING INTERVIEWS

1. Do you determine exactly what you want the interview to accomplish?
2. Do you consider anything about the interviewee that may affect how you should conduct the interview?
3. Do you gather necessary information and devise questions to ask the interviewee that will enable you to find out what you want to know?
4. Do you group your questions in a sequence that will make sense to your interviewee and put him or her at ease?
5. Do you establish and maintain a comfortable, productive exchange with your interviewee?
6. Do you summarize your final impressions and evaluation of the interview?

Holding Meetings

To learn how to hold a meeting, you can draw on your knowledge of speaking as a process that begins with setting a goal and ends with a polished delivery.

SETTING THE GOAL

Every meeting should have specific and defined objectives. Since the expense of holding a meeting involves the dollar cost of the participants' salaries as well as the potential loss of goodwill if the meeting proves a waste of time, decide whether you really need a meeting before calling one.

If you call a meeting, keep its purpose clearly in mind as you plan it. Ask yourself what you want the meeting to accomplish and formulate a goal statement:

> We need to draw up a recruiting schedule and criteria for entry-level positions.
>
> Our goal is to clarify the staff's responsibilities during the boss's absence.
>
> We have to devise a better marketing strategy for our product line.

Use your goal statement to help you decide who and what to include in your meeting, what information to collect beforehand, and how to organize the meeting.

ASSESSING THE PARTICIPANTS

Invite to the meeting only those people who need to participate—for example, for the meeting on the recruiting schedule, invite the ones who should design the schedule and criteria for entry-level positions, clarify work responsibilities while the boss is away, or help design a marketing strategy. Once you have determined who should attend, consider:

- The business relationship of the participants to one another and to you
- Participants' knowledge of the topic and of you
- Participants' attitude toward the topic and toward you
- Participants' expectations about how the meeting should be conducted (e.g., Will there be formal rules and procedures? a formal agenda?)

GATHERING INFORMATION AND GENERATING IDEAS

All but very informal meetings should have an **agenda**—a list of things to be dealt with at the meeting. Do any research needed to put together the agenda. Your research may include talking to participants, reading reports, and interviewing experts.

ORGANIZING

The agenda should present in a logical order the items that should be covered at the meeting to allow you to achieve your goals.

To prepare participants for the meeting, send out a memo or letter announcing the agenda, giving information about scheduling—such as the day, time, participants, and

Figure 12.6

MEMO ANNOUNCING A MEETING

DATE: July 12, 199_
TO: Marketing Staff
FROM: Carol Okido, Senior Marketing Analyst *CO*
SUBJECT: Meeting to Design Marketing Strategy for New Christmas Line

There will be a meeting in the 3rd Floor Executive Lounge on Friday, June 9th, from <u>2 to 3:30 P.M.</u> to discuss the design of a marketing strategy for our new line of humorous Christmas cards. Here is the agenda for the meeting:

1. Review elements of our current marketing strategy. Marketing analyst Fred Martin to present findings of sample tests in two market segments, Southeast and Midwest.
(25 minutes)
2. Identify and consider alternate strategies
   - Catalogs vs. direct store sales
   - Establish lead vs. strong second
(25 minutes)
3. Allocate responsibilities for testing alternative strategies
(30 minutes)
4. Summarize decisions
(10 minutes)

meeting place. If you think it is possible and useful, include the time scheduled for each item on the agenda. Figure 12.6 on page 628 shows such a memo.

LEADING THE MEETING

Leading a meeting will bring into play your skills as a speaker and a listener. Figure 12.7 presents some tips for conducting meetings.

FOLLOW-UP

After the meeting, distribute to participants—and to anyone else who needs to know—a set of minutes or a summary of the outcome of the meeting. Be sure to put in writing points on which agreement was reached and the division of future tasks and responsibilities.

The checklist on page 630 will help you plan and lead meetings.

Figure 12.7
TIPS FOR CONDUCTING MEETINGS

1. *Keep to the agenda*. Begin and end on time, and plan the appropriate amount of time for each item on the agenda. But build some flexibility into your schedule too. Remember that some issues may demand more attention than you had predicted. Before the meeting, make a note for yourself of items you can drop, handle less fully, or postpone for another meeting.

2. *Establish a focused but participative forum for discussion*. Ideally, as the leader of the meeting, you should keep the discussion on target while ensuring that everyone gets a fair hearing and participates productively. This can mean keeping down an aggressive talker who wants to monopolize the meeting, or drawing out a timid participant who has much to offer.

3. *Summarize main points and key decisions*. If the meeting is long, summarize your progress between agenda items. In any case, before you adjourn, review the main conclusions, recommendations, and decisions.

CHECKLIST FOR HOLDING MEETINGS

1. Do you define what you hope to accomplish at the meeting?
2. Do you invite only those people who should attend the meeting?
3. Do you conduct the necessary research to create an agenda?
4. Do you draw up an agenda that names the topics that should be covered?
5. In conducting the meeting, do you keep to the agenda, establish a focused but participative forum for discussion, and summarize the main points and key decisions?
6. After the meeting, do you distribute a set of minutes or a summary of the outcome to the participants and to others who should be informed?

SUMMARY

As you face situations that require you to communicate with others, you will want to judge when it is preferable to write, when it is better to speak, and when a combination of speaking and writing will best serve your purposes. Your business career will present you with many occasions to give oral presentations. You will be able to apply what you have learned about writing as a process to handle your oral presentations effectively, but, in addition, you will need to become familiar with the special requirements for presentations. As a business person, you can also expect to conduct interviews and meetings. The knowledge you gain about giving oral presentations will help you handle these speaking tasks as will your understanding of their special requirements.

EXERCISES

See "Links Between Writing and Speaking," pp. 585–588, for Exercises 1 and 2.

1. You are working as a student intern for a co-op food store. The manager of the co-op, Lester Simmons, has asked you to do a marketing study. He wants to know who is shopping at the co-op and why. (Both member households and nonmembers may shop at the market.) Lester is also interested in the competitive position of the co-op in the neighborhood. The co-op's competition consists of outlets for two national supermarket chains within a five-block radius.

You have told Lester that interviewing customers would enable you to gather important information for the study. To conduct the interviews, Lester has agreed to allow you to train three of his store clerks as interviewers. (You would have liked to do all the interviewing yourself, but your time is limited.) None of the clerks has had experience as interviewers—or interviewees.

You are now planning to train the clerks. Would you give them instructions verbally, by memo, or by speaking and writing to them? Explain your answer.

2. You work for a local insurance company, General Insurance Agents, Inc. The company owns several investment properties in the community. You are training to be

an assistant manager for the small real estate division of the company that has recently been established to handle the management of these properties and others that the company plans to acquire.

Last week your boss, Judith DuBois, sent you to a series of town meetings on a community program for renovating the downtown area. Your company owns two office buildings and a block-long vacant lot there. At the meetings, you learned that the local government has designed and passed tax incentives and rezoned the area to encourage businesses to build downtown. The town would like to see a major business/industrial park there.

According to your assessment, the empty lot your company owns in the downtown area can now be sold at a 20 percent profit. If developed, the property might be worth even more. As for the two office buildings the company owns, which are now the only structures in good condition in the area, these could soon be surrounded by other large modern buildings. Both the vacant lot and the developed property have potential for even greater profits, but this can't be determined until renovation plans are under way and General Insurance Agents does a thorough assessment of the real estate value of its holdings.

You have been back in your office for two days now and have left two messages with your boss's secretary saying that you need to talk to your boss about the town meetings. Judith is either out of town or not answering calls. Her behavior is uncharacteristic; she usually responds quickly to your requests. What strategy do you use to get your message to her?

See "Setting the Goal," pp. 590–591, for Exercise 3.

3. You work for the insurance agency in Exercise 2. Your boss, Judith DuBois, is now able to see you for a quick (five-minute) discussion of your findings. Write the goal statement of the presentation you will give.

See "Oral Presentations," pp. 588–615, for Exercises 4–12.

4. Give an informal three-minute talk to your class describing a company you may be interested in working for. To prepare the talk, first analyze your audience's knowledge, attitudes, and expectations. Then review the company's annual report and recent articles published on it in several journals, magazines, and newspapers. Try to arrange an informational interview with someone at the company. Organize the presentation on note cards using the outline format described on pp. 604–615.

5. Choose an industry you would like to work in. Give an informal five-minute presentation informing your class about entry-level job prospects in the industry. Assume that your audience is also considering employment in this industry. If possible, to prepare for the talk, interview business people in the industry and do library research. Organize the talk in an outline, and hand in a copy of the outline to your instructor on the day of your talk.

6. Give a five-minute speech to your class explaining a piece of technical information or a specialized business term you have learned in another course.

7. Give a ten-minute presentation to your class in which you discuss an aspect of one of the following topics:

- Stock market investment for the 1990s
- Health care: industry or profession?
- "Office of the future"
- Competition with foreign countries for U.S. markets
- Best entry-level jobs in the 1990s
- Women in the work force
- Companies under public attack
- Entrepreneurship in the 1990s
- Value of the MBA degree
- Personal financial planning
- Hiring procedures for college graduates
- Truth in advertising
- The aging work force
- Career changes
- Real estate
- Robotics
- Personal computers
- Your choice

8. Identify a company or industry that is being investigated by the federal government or criticized by the public. Take the part of (a) the federal government, (b) the public, or (c) the company, and give a five-minute presentation to the class defending the position you have taken.

9. Prepare a five-minute presentation reporting on your progress in writing a research report assigned to you in this or another class. Your purpose is to encourage specific comments on your work-in-progress to help you write the report. Be sure to discuss problems and new issues that have arisen in the process of doing your research and writing.

10. Organize a three-minute speech introducing one of your favorite instructors to your class.

11. Prepare a four-minute after-dinner speech to be given to a group of bankers (for bankers you can substitute accountants, human resources managers, or your choice) who are interested in learning about college students' preparation for entering the business world.

12. Prepare a five-minute speech acknowledging the accomplishments of a friend, family member, instructor, or community leader.

See "Rehearsing To Revise and to Polish Your Delivery," pp. 615–621, for Exercises 13–16.

13. Rehearse one of your talks out loud in front of a mirror and check your gestures and posture.
14. Rehearse the same talk using a tape recorder or videotape and play back the tape

to check your tone of voice, vocal stress, inflection, rate of speech, and volume. Mark the places in your speech that need improvement, and go over them until you are satisfied with your performance. If you use a videotape, check for appropriate gestures, posture, and facial expression.

15. Attend a lecture and take notes on the speaker's ability to communicate his or her ideas to the audience. Using what you have learned about a good oral presentation, write a memo to your business writing instructor summarizing your evaluation of the lecture as an oral presentation. Don't assume that your instructor has attended the lecture or knows much about the speaker's subject. Be sure to evaluate the organization and delivery of the lecture.

16. Evaluate a classmate's rehearsals for one of the presentations in Exercises 4–12. As you listen to your classmate, keep in mind two principles:

- *Be an empathic listener as well as a critical listener*. Try to understand the speaker's point of view rather than being quick to argue with it. You will have time later to evaluate the speaker's presentation, and you will be more likely to give it an accurate evaluation if you are a receptive and thoughtful listener.
- *Focus your attention on the speaker*. Make an effort to focus exclusively on the speaker. Try not to be distracted, and resist the temptation to "tune out" mentally in order to prepare your own comments. To avoid breaking your concentration on the speaker, focus on retaining as much as you can of the central points, feelings, and opinions of the speaker.

Discuss the rehearsal with your classmate. Then write a memo to your classmate outlining the strengths and weaknesses of the delivery and giving specific recommendations to help him or her improve the presentation.

See "Conducting Interviews," pp. 621–626, for Exercise 17.

17. To help a classmate prepare for job interviews, conduct a mock interview. Interview your classmate for a hypothetical job in an organization or industry your classmate is interested in. To prepare for the interview, review your classmate's resume, do some research on the organization or industry, and put together a job description. Then design a series of questions to ask your classmate.

See "Holding Meetings," pp. 626–630, for Exercise 18.

18. Hold a meeting with three other students in your class. Have one person write an agenda for a thirty-minute meeting devoted to one of the following:

- Planning a spring-break vacation for you and several classmates
- Recommending criteria for selecting new students for your college or university
- Devising a procedure for registration at your college or university
- Your choice

A second person should chair the meeting. A third person should take the minutes. The fourth should write a memo summarizing the group's work.

13
VISUAL AIDS

PREVIEW

This chapter should help you to

1. Identify how visual aids can improve your written communications by showing you how to
   - Use tables to compare and contrast exact data
   - Use bar charts to compare precise data at precise time intervals
   - Use line graphs to demonstrate trends
   - Use pie charts to show the whole in relation to its parts according to percentages
   - Use organization charts to show the formal structure of a company
   - Use flow charts to display a process or procedure
   - Use maps to convey quantitative information about a geographical area
2. Identify how text visuals can help you convey key points in a talk
3. Recognize the benefits of computer graphics

Visual aids can help you get your ideas across more effectively. When coordinated with a text or presentation, visual aids can help to summarize, clarify, illustrate, reinforce, or explain information. Studies show that visual aids make data in written texts and oral presentations easier to understand and remember. And with the availability of graphics software for computers, you will increasingly be encouraged and expected to use visual aids to communicate your ideas.

This chapter focuses on the major types of visual aids and their functions. We show you how visual aids can help convey certain of your ideas better than would a written or oral communication alone. We also show you which kind of visual aid is best to use for a given purpose and how to create clear and accurate visual aids.

TABLES

Assistant finance analyst Charlie Langdon was puzzled about his boss's reaction to the statistics he had presented in his report. His boss, Nan Seward, had asked that he summarize the income generated by the banks that the company owned throughout Texas. Charlie prided himself on his mathematical ability, so he was surprised to see the comment Nan scrawled over the section of his report showing his figures: "I just can't make any sense out of these numbers. I thought you were going to help me compare the banks against each other."

635

Let's see how a table could help Charlie's boss compare their banks' financial situations. First, here is the section of the report showing the figures his boss couldn't make sense of:

If we consider the organizational contribution of the different banks in 199_, we come up with the following: In 199_, the income before securities transactions for Hamden Commerce Bank-Houston was $51.6 million, and the return on assets was 1 percent. For the 16 banks with assets over $100 million, the income before securities transactions was $47.4 million, and the return on assets was $1.5 million. For the 22 banks with assets under $100 million, the income before securities transactions was 11.7 percent, and the return on assets was 1.5 percent. For the parent and any other banks, the income before securities transactions was 7.7 percent. The total income before securities transactions in 199_ was $103 million, and the return on assets was 1.1 percent.

Presented in paragraph form, Charlie's quantitative information is all but impossible to understand. After reading the paragraph several times, we can see that he has classified the banks into several groups such as "16 banks with assets over $100 million" and "22 banks with assets under $100 million." For each group, he has considered two financial items: the income before securities transactions and the return on assets. He has also totaled these figures for all the banks.

Notice how much clearer the information becomes when presented in a table, Figure 13.1. First of all, the title identifies the main point: the income generated by the company's banks in 199_. Second, the rows and columns of the table effectively cluster and order the bank groups (rows) and the financial contribution of each bank group (columns). Third, the layout of the table lets Charlie's boss easily compare the financial situation of one bank group against another. And the number and percentages at the very bottom show the banks' totals, set apart from the subtotals by a double line.

Use a **table** if your purpose is to help readers compare and contrast precise data. As Figure 13.1 illustrates, a table presents information in rows and columns. They are the most effective way to help your readers interpret and remember exact quantitative information.

Design of Tables

Tables can be either formal or informal. Formal tables have titles and headings, are numbered with all other visual aids in the text, and are separated from the text by top and bottom rules. Figure 13.1 is a formal table.

Informal tables may have headings, but they have none of the other apparatus. They appear directly in the text, as shown in Figure 13.2.

VISUAL AIDS

Figure 13.1

A FORMAL TABLE

Table 1: Income Generated by the Company's Banks in 199__
(in millions of dollars)

	Income Before Securities Transactions	Return on Assets
Hamden Commerce Bank—Houston	$ 51.6	1.0%
16 banks with assets over $100 million	47.4	1.5
22 banks with assets under $100 million	11.7	1.5
Parent and other	7.7	—
Banks' Total	$103.0	1.1%

Figure 13.2

AN INFORMAL TABLE

Population

Population growth in Santa Monica since 1940 is illustrated in the following table:

Year	Population	% Change
1940	53,500	—
1950	71,595	+33.8
1960	83,249	+16.3
1970	88,289	+6.0
1980	88,314	—

Santa Monica experienced its largest growth between 1940 and 1950, when the population increased from 53,500 to 71,595, or by about 34 percent. From 1950 to 1970 the city continued to grow but at a much slower pace. Since 1970 there has been virtually no change in population base.

THE RANDOM HOUSE GUIDE TO BUSINESS WRITING

Here are several suggestions for designing accurate tables that make your point:

1. *Group information in the order in which you want readers to retain the information.* Figure out the order in which you would like readers to understand and remember the data, and then use this order in your table. Typically, tables show data either chronologically or in increasing or decreasing order of importance.

One common pitfall in arranging data is presenting them alphabetically (although alphabetical order is not always wrong). Business writers may develop this habit because they are accustomed to seeing many lists handled in this way. For example, marketing analyst Tom Sands, writing on trout production in several countries, listed the countries alphabetically in his first draft (Figure 13.3).

The **purpose** of the information should guide your choice of a sequence. Since Tom wanted to show the relative production of trout in these five countries, listing the countries by ascending or descending order of production was a better sequence, as shown in Figure 13.4.

2. *Be consistent in your use of categories and layout.* Since tables allow you to show precise quantities, be consistent in the scale you use. If, for instance, one country publishes production figures in metric tons and another in pounds, convert all the data to the same measure so that your numbers are consistent.

Keep the layout of your table consistent, too. Line up rows and columns. Align Arabic numbers on the right, and align decimal points directly under one another:

```
   567
    53
     4
    43
    45.7
 5,214.7
```

3. *Let your title identify your table accurately and succinctly.* The title of your table should clearly capture its main point so that readers can quickly grasp the table's meaning. Figure 13.5 was used in a report to top management by a research staffer in an oil import company. Notice how the title highlights for his superiors the main point of the table.

4. *Acknowledge the source.* If your table is taken from another source, indicate this by "Source:" followed by the name of the source. Figure 13.5 illustrates this point.

5. *Give totals and subtotals when they are useful information to the reader.* Totals and subtotals of your data usually appear to the right of rows and at the bottom of columns. A ruled single or double line separates totals from subtotals, as in Figure 13.1.

6. *Refer to the table and explain its purposes in your written text.* Mention the table right before it appears in the text. In addition, if you want to guide your reader's interpretation of the table or if you think the table needs further clarification, provide

VISUAL AIDS

Figure 13.3

FIRST DRAFT OF TOM'S TABLE

Table 1: Trout Production (199_)

Country	Metric Tons
Denmark	12,945
France	15,000
Italy	16,430
Japan	17,631
United States	12,000

Figure 13.4

TOM'S REVISED TABLE

Table 1: Trout Production (199_)

Country	Metric Tons
Japan	17,631
Italy	16,430
France	15,000
Denmark	12,945
United States	12,000

your comments after you present the table. Figure 13.6 shows how the researcher first explained the significance of the table in the body of his report and later revised the paragraph.

On rereading the report and thinking about his purpose and his readers, the researcher decided that he wanted to revise and add to the paragraph following the table, to emphasize to his superiors the need to consider importing residual fuel as well as crude oil. He knew that over the past ten years, the company had been ignoring the

Figure 13.5

TABLE WITH MAIN POINT HIGHLIGHTED
IN TITLE

Table 1:
DAILY AVERAGE IMPORTS OF CRUDE OIL AND
RESIDUAL FUEL OIL
(thousand barrels per day)

	Crude Oil	Residual Fuel Oil
1973	3,244	1,853
1974	3,477	1,587
1975	4,105	1,223
1976	5,287	1,413
1977	6,615	1,359
1978	6,356	1,355
1979	6,519	1,151
1980	5,263	939
1981	4,396	800
1982*	3,412	738

*First eight months.
Source: DOE Monthly Energy Review, October 1982.

country's demand for residual fuel oil and overestimating the demand for crude oil. That is why he used the table to show the imports of one against the other.

   7. *Don't crowd the table with excessive or unnecessary information.* Tables cluttered with too much information confuse readers. To solve this problem, get rid of unnecessary information and if necessary break up the tables into several tables. The table in Figure 13.7 is confusing because there is too much detail for the reader to assimilate. Since the writer wants to show the population in each of the urban agglomerations as well as to compare the total populations of the three, he should make three tables out of this one, each showing the data for one urban agglomeration and a fourth table that summarizes the totals from the other three. And he should leave out the information on the total population of Japan, since that information is unimportant to his boss. In addition, he might show the tables horizontally to make better use of the length of the page to spread out the data. Figure 13.8 shows what his revision might look like.

Figure 13.6

DRAFT AND REVISION FOLLOWING TABLE SHOWN IN FIGURE 13.5

DRAFT
Imports of residual fuel oil have been dropping steadily since 1973. If this winter is severe, the current low level of 738,000 barrels a day could foreshadow a shortage in the United States.

REVISION
Clearly the drop in residual fuel oil since 1973 and the possibility of a severe winter alert us to the possibility of a need for importing residual fuel oil on very short notice. If this winter is severe, the current low level of 738,000 barrels a day could foreshadow a shortage in the United States. In fact, it might be preferable to store larger inventories of residual fuel oil than we currently have instead of increasing our crude oil inventories, which are more than adequate for meeting our current and projected needs.

Figure 13.7
DRAFT: TABLE WITH TOO MUCH INFORMATION

Table 1:
The Three Largest Urban Agglomerations in Japan

Major Cities	Prefecture	Population	% of Population in Each Prefecture by Age Group						
			0-9	10-14	15-19	20-24	25-29	30-34	34+
Tokyo	Saitama	5,309,000	18.81	8.57	6.80	6.76	8.80	9.98	40.27
Yokohama	Chiba	4,617,000	18.04	8.01	6.84	6.78	8.69	9.75	41.91
Kawasaki	Tokyo	11,596,000	14.39	8.00	7.72	7.77	9.32	9.51	43.29
Kanagawa		6,809,000	17.18	8.37	7.06	6.89	8.94	9.77	41.78
	Total	28,331,000	16.48	8.20	7.25	7.21	9.03	9.70	42.14
	% of Total	24.40%							
Osaka	Kyoto	2,515,000	15.90	7.67	7.04	6.99	8.27	8.99	45.13
Kyoto	Osaka	8,487,000	16.96	8.46	7.29	6.74	8.41	9.65	42.49
Kobe	Hyogo	5,139,000	16.52	7.59	6.95	6.70	7.86	8.91	45.44
	Total	16,141,000	16.65	8.06	7.14	6.77	8.21	9.31	43.84
	% of Total	13.98%							
Nagoya	Gifu	1,945,000	16.35	7.76	7.40	6.48	7.45	8.28	46.27
	Shizuoka	3,420,000	16.73	7.34	6.81	6.70	8.01	8.74	45.61
	Aichi	6,176,000	17.55	8.48	7.29	7.06	8.32	9.46	41.82
	Mie	1,674,000	15.65	7.23	6.69	6.45	7.29	8.12	48.63
	Total	13,215,000	16.92	7.92	7.11	6.80	7.98	8.93	44.32
	% of Total	11.38%							
Total Population in the three largest urban agglomerations		57,687,000							
	% of Total	49.76%							
All of Japan		116,133,000	16.23	7.59	6.95	6.89	8.21	8.62	45.42

Figure 13.8

REVISION: ONE TABLE MADE INTO FOUR

Table 1:

Urban Agglomeration 1

Major Cities	Prefecture	Population	% of Population in Each Prefecture by Age Group						
			0-9	10-14	15-19	20-24	25-39	30-34	34+
Tokyo	Saitana	5,309,000	18.18	8.57	6.80	6.76	8.80	9.98	40.27
Yokohama	Chiba	4,617,000	18.04	8.01	6.84	6.78	8.69	9.75	41.91
Kawasaki	Tokyo	11,596,000	14.39	8.00	7.72	7.77	9.32	9.51	43.29
Kanagawa		6,809,000	17.18	8.37	7.06	6.89	8.94	9.77	41.78
	Total	28,331,000	16.48	8.20	7.25	7.21	9.03	9.70	42.14
	% of Total	24.40%							

Table 2

Urban Agglomeration 2

Major Cities	Prefecture	Population	% of Population in Each Prefecture by Age Group						
			0-9	10-14	15-19	20-24	25-29	30-34	34+
Osaka	Kyoto	2,515,000	15.90	7.67	7.04	6.99	8.27	8.99	45.13
Kyoto	Osaka	8,487,000	16.96	8.46	7.29	6.74	8.41	9.65	42.49
Kobe	Hyogo	5,139,000	16.52	7.59	6.95	6.70	7.86	8.91	45.44
	Total	16,141,000	16.65	8.06	7.14	6.77	8.21	9.31	43.84
	% of Total	13.98%							

(continued)

Table 3:

Urban Agglomeration 3

Major Cities	Prefecture	Population	% of Population in Each Prefecture by Age Group						
			0-9	10-14	15-19	20-24	25-29	30-34	34+
Nagoya	Gifu	1,945,000	16.35	7.76	7.40	6.48	7.45	8.28	46.27
	Shizuoka	3,420,000	16.73	7.34	6.81	6.70	8.01	8.74	45.61
	Aichi	6,176,000	17.55	8.48	7.29	7.06	8.32	9.46	41.82
	Mie	1,674,000	15.65	7.23	6.69	6.45	7.29	8.12	48.63
	Total	13,215,000	16.92	7.92	7.11	6.80	7.98	8.93	44.32
	% of Total	11.38%							

Table 4:

Comparison of the Three Urban Agglomerations

Urban Center	Population	% of Population in Each Prefecture by Age Group						
		0-9	10-14	15-19	20-24	25-29	30-34	34+
Urban Center 1 Total	28,331,000	16.48	8.20	7.25	7.21	9.03	9.70	42.14
% of Total	24.40%							
Urban Center 2 Total	16,141,000	16.65	8.06	7.14	6.77	8.21	9.31	43.84
% of Total	13.98%							
Urban Center 3 Total	13,215,000	16.92	7.92	7.11	6.80	7.98	8.93	44.32
% of Total	11.38%							
Total Population in the three largest urban centers	57,687,000							
% of Total	49.76%							

VISUAL AIDS 645

The accompanying checklist will help you review your use of tables.

CHECKLIST FOR USING TABLES

1. Have you chosen to use a table because you want to compare and contrast precise data?
2. Do you group information in the order in which you want readers to retain it?
3. Are your categories and layout consistent?
4. Do you identify the table accurately and succinctly?
5. If your table is taken from another source, do you indicate this?
6. Do you give totals and subtotals when they are useful information to the reader?
7. Do you refer to the table and explain its purposes in your written text?
8. Do you keep the table free from excessive or unnecessary information and divide a table into several tables if it is cluttered?

GRAPHIC AIDS: BAR CHARTS, LINE GRAPHS, AND PIE CHARTS

Each of the three common forms of graphic visual aids presented in this section has its particular strengths. Bar charts show comparisons of quantitative information in discrete time periods. Line graphs show trends. Pie charts show the whole in relation to its part.

Bar Charts

Susan Fowler, editorial trainee in publications for an aerospace company, was reviewing the report her division helped the Planning Department write for top management. As she read, she decided that some kind of visual aid could highlight the Planning Department's success. Turning to Bill Toulin, another editorial trainee, Susan remarked, "I want a way to play up our increase in revenues for each of the last five years. Our revenues have grown 91 percent since Planning implemented the strategic marketing concept five years ago. What kind of visual aid do you think would really bring this home?''

Susan wanted to find a visual aid to highlight the Planning Department's success. Bill knew a lot about visual aids, so he recommended a bar chart, because only a **bar chart** can show comparisons of quantitative information in several discrete time periods. Notice how the bar chart in Figure 13.9 helps Susan underscore both the dramatic increase in revenues year by year and the specific revenues for each of the five years.

Besides the simple bar chart Susan used for the Planning Department's report, there are several variations. Let's look at the specific functions that each can perform.

SIMPLE BAR CHART

A **simple bar chart** like Susan's helps you compare exact quantities. The length of each bar and the number at its top represent a quantity that can then be compared to other quantities, represented by the lengths of and numbers on the other bars.

GROUPED BAR CHART

To compare two or more variables, you can use a **grouped bar chart.** Suppose you wanted to compare percentage increases in sales of hamburgers by two large fast-food restaurants, McHenry's and The Ruling Burger, from June 1988 to January 1989. Using a colored bar for one franchise and a black bar for the other would yield a bar chart like the one in Figure 13.10.

SEGMENTED BAR CHART

Segmented bar charts allow you to display the portions of a *single* total quantity, represented by the whole bar, as you compare several total quantities, or bars. You can use shading to indicate the different portions of each bar. The segmented bar chart in Figure 13.11 shows world oil production for the period 1970–1982 according to the amounts produced by each of four groups.

BILATERAL BAR CHARTS

Bilateral bar charts allow you to show positive and negative values by using space below as well as above the zero line. Figure 13.12 illustrates how in the period 1982–1989 the earnings of a company soared and then turned into huge losses. Positive values, or earnings, appear above the zero line; negative figures, or losses, below it.

Line Graphs

Whereas tables show exact amounts of quantitative information, **line graphs** show trends or relationships between two or more sets of data. If your purpose is to illustrate, summarize, explain, or highlight one or more trends, you can use a line graph.

Figure 13.9

SUSAN'S BAR CHART

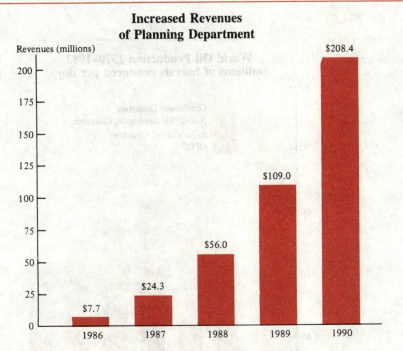

A simple bar chart compares quantitative information in several discrete time periods.

Figure 13.10

A GROUPED BAR CHART

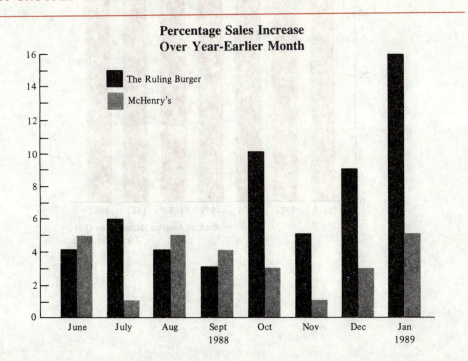

To compare two or more contrasting variables, you can use a grouped bar chart.

Figure 13.11

A SEGMENTED BAR CHART

A segmented bar chart allows you to display the portions of a single total quantity, represented by the whole bar, as you compare several total quantities, or bars.

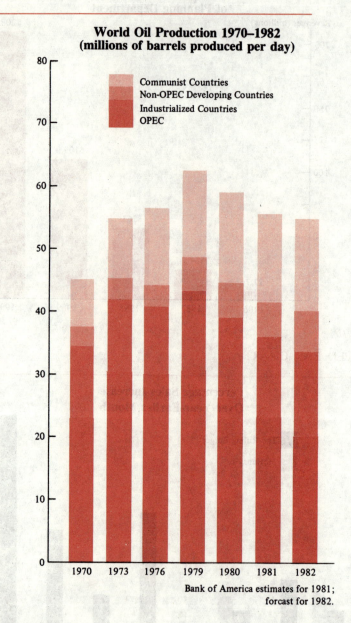

VISUAL AIDS **649**

Figure 13.12

A BILATERAL BAR CHART

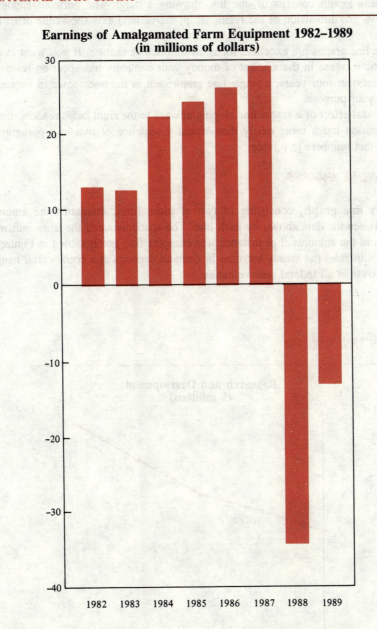

To show positive and negative values, you can use a bilateral bar chart.

SINGLE LINE GRAPHS

A **single line graph** consists of one line showing a trend. The horizontal axis of the graph shows one dimension of the relationship; the vertical axis shows the other dimension.

Single line graphs are excellent for showing rates of change. If you want to convey the dramatic increase in the amount of money your company has spent on research and development over four years, a single line graph such as the one shown in Figure 13.13 will serve your purpose.

The visual effect of a single line sloping upward to the right helps readers remember this information much more easily than would a sentence or two in a paragraph or a series of exact numbers in a table.

COMPLEX LINE GRAPHS

A **complex line graph,** consisting of two or more lines, compares the amounts of change between the data shown by each line. The space between the lines indicates the differences in the amounts. For instance, the complex line graph shown in Figure 13.14 succinctly illustrates the steady increase in demand deposits at a commercial bank relative to deposits at all federal reserve banks.

Figure 13.13

A SINGLE LINE GRAPH

A single line graph shows trends or relationships between two or more sets of data.

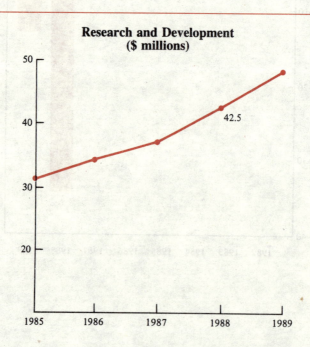

Figure 13.14

A COMPLEX LINE GRAPH

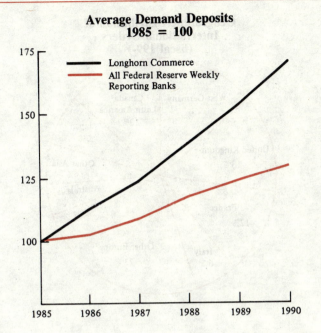

To compare the amounts of change between the data shown by each line, you can use a complex line graph.

Pie Charts

You can use a **pie chart** if your purpose is to illustrate a whole divided into its parts according to percentages. For example, the pie chart in Figure 13.15 illustrates the geographical distribution of international orders for a company's major product. Each slice of the pie represents a discrete geographical sales area.

When you construct a pie chart, label the percentage of the whole represented by each slice of the pie. In general, the most important position on the pie chart is right after 12 o'clock so put the information you want the reader to pay most attention to there. Also make sure that there is a match between the size of the slice and the percentage it represents—as is done in Figure 13.15.

Figure 13.15

A PIE CHART

A pie chart illustrates a whole divided into its parts according to percentages.

The accompanying checklist will help you review your use of bar charts, line graphs, and pie charts.

CHECKLIST FOR USING BAR CHARTS, LINE GRAPHS, AND PIE CHARTS

1. Have you chosen to use a simple bar chart to show comparisons of quantitative information in several discrete time periods?
2. Have you chosen to use a grouped bar chart to compare two or more variables?
3. Have you chosen to use a segmented bar chart to display the portions of a single total quantity as well as to compare several total quantities?
4. Have you chosen to use a bilateral bar chart to show positive and negative values?
5. Have you chosen to use a single line graph to illustrate one or more trends?
6. Have you chosen to use a complex line graph to compare the amounts of change between data?
7. Have you chosen to use a pie chart to show the whole in relation to its parts according to percentages?

GRAPHIC AIDS: ORGANIZATION CHARTS, FLOW CHARTS, AND MAPS

Besides tables, bar charts, pie charts, and line graphs, three other kinds of graphic visual aids are commonly used to help communicate ideas: the organization chart, which displays the formal structure of a company; the flow chart, which shows the stages of a process or procedure; and the map.

Organization Charts

When you are discussing the hierarchy within an organization, you can orient your readers by using an **organization chart** that pictures the formal structure of the organization. Organization charts can also be used to:

- Provide readers with a guide to a company's functional areas (e.g., accounting, marketing, finance) and the links between and within them
- Discuss relations of authority and responsibility among several members of an organization
- Explore a business problem that stems from the way a company is structured

Compare, for instance, the ease and ability with which you can understand the hierarchical structure of a division within the XYZ Company as presented in Figure 13.16 to the verbal explanation on page 654.

Figure 13.16

AN ORGANIZATION CHART

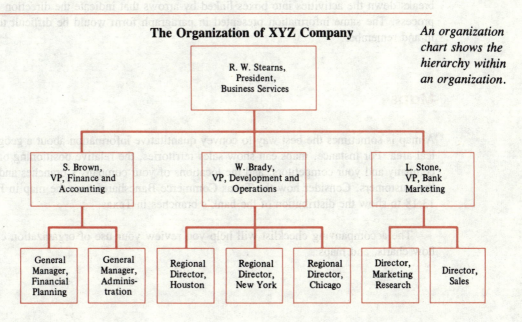

An organization chart shows the hierarchy within an organization.

The Business Services Division is headed by the president, R. W. Stearns. Directly below him are three vice presidents: S. Brown, vice president of Finance and Accounting; W. Brady, vice president of Development and Operations; and L. Stone, vice president of Bank Marketing. Each vice president has one or more operating divisions that report to him or her. Each division is headed by a general manager or director. The general manager of Financial Planning and the general manager of Administration report to the vice president of Finance and Accounting. The regional directors for the three branches (Houston, New York, and Chicago) report to the vice president of Development and Operations. The director of Marketing Research and the director of Sales report to the vice president of Bank Marketing.

The organization chart efficiently displays the functional areas and reporting relationships within the organization. Imagine how confused you would be if you had to rely on the verbal explanation alone.

Flow Charts

You can use a **flow chart** to represent a process or procedure. The flow chart in Figure 13.17 appeared in a report written by a film company's financial analyst. Top management asked him to explain the steps of the process that the Finance Department uses to develop a budget. With the flow chart to assist, readers can easily see all the activities in the budget process.

Especially when you want to coordinate the efforts of several people, a flow chart can show where their particular activities fit into the larger scheme. The flow chart breaks down the activities into boxes linked by arrows that indicate the direction of the process. The same information presented in paragraph form would be difficult to take in and remember.

Maps

A map is sometimes the best way to convey quantitative information about a geographical area. For instance, maps can show sales territories, the relative positioning of your company and your competitors, and the locations of your company's branches and your key customers. Consider how the Texas Commerce Bancshares uses the map in Figure 13.18 to show the distribution of the bank's branches in Texas.

The accompanying checklist will help you review your use of organization charts, flow charts, and maps.

VISUAL AIDS 655

Figure 13.17
A FLOW CHART

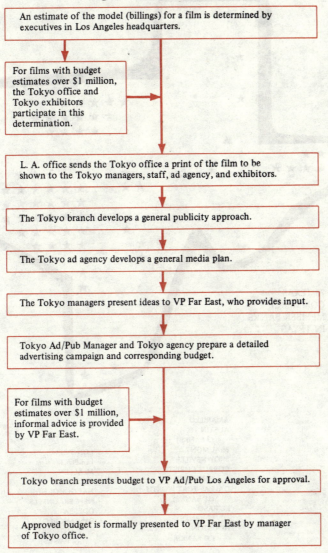

To represent a procedure or process, you can use a flow chart.

THE RANDOM HOUSE GUIDE TO BUSINESS WRITING

Figure 13.18
A MAP

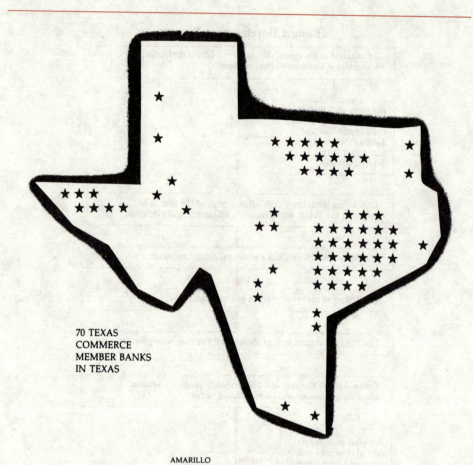

70 TEXAS
COMMERCE
MEMBER BANKS
IN TEXAS

AMARILLO
AUSTIN
   (3 BANKS)
BEAUMONT
BROWNSVILLE
CORPUS CHRISTI
   (2 BANKS)
DALLAS-FORT WORTH
   (15 BANKS)
EL PASO
   (7 BANKS)
HOUSTON
   (30 BANKS)

LONGVIEW
LUBBOCK
McALLEN
MIDLAND
NACOGDOCHES
NEW BRAUNFELS
ODESSA
SAN ANGELO
SAN ANTONIO
   (2 BANKS)

A map can convey quantitative information about a geographical area.

CHECKLIST FOR USING ORGANIZATION CHARTS, FLOW CHARTS, AND MAPS

1. Have you chosen to use an organization chart to do one or more of the following:
   - Show the formal structure of an organization?
   - Provide readers with a guide to a company's functional areas?
   - Discuss relations of authority and responsibility among several members of an organization?
   - Explore a business problem that stems from the way a company is structured?
2. Have you chosen to use a flow chart to represent a process or procedure?
3. Have you chosen to use a map to convey quantitative information about a geographical area?

VISUAL AIDS FOR ORAL PRESENTATIONS

Just as you would use visual aids to help convey key points in your writing, you can use these aids to enhance your oral presentations. A good visual aid will allow your audience to *see* your ideas while listening to you talk about them. Visual aids, then, reinforce visually what your listeners are hearing. As a result, your listeners will be more attentive and will better understand and remember your ideas.

In choosing visual aids for a presentation, follow the same principles as when choosing them for a written communication. But there is a difference. Compared to the visual aids you would use in your written communications, visual aids for your talks should be simpler. Readers can move at their own pace through a document and stop to study the details of a visual aid and its overall purpose in the communication. Listeners, on the other hand, must follow along at the pace you set for giving information, and they may be seated so far from a visual aid that it is hard for them to read it. Although you may be tempted to use a visual aid from your report on an overhead transparency, don't transfer the visual aid to your presentation without making adjustments for your audience.

Given the special needs of listeners for visual aids that are simple and clear, use:

- No more than two columns for tables
- No more than three lines for graphs or charts
- No more than five lines for a text visual

In addition, write in big, bold letters, and make sure that your visuals can be seen from all parts of the room.

Text Visuals

As Marjorie Brown, company chairperson for the United Way Campaign, prepared her in-house presentation, she wondered, "I've got forty-five pages of text in my report that I can't possibly pass out at the meeting. But I do want people to have some easy reference in front of them as I talk so they can follow along. What should I do?"

Marjorie wanted to figure out how to provide her listeners with a written guide for her talk. A text visual could solve her problem. A **text visual** consists of key phrases—on a handout, flip chart, or overhead transparency—that provide listeners with a preview of the presentation, show them the structure of the talk as they listen, and serve as a reminder of the key points. Marjorie might have used the text visual shown in Figure 13.19.

Instead of a single text visual, another possibility is to use a *sequence* of text visuals, as Roger Carson does for his thirty-minute talk. Roger is head of an internal consulting group, called Business Analysis, that provides technical services in data processing to all areas of a multinational corporation. But many employees don't know what the group does. Roger wants to explain the work of his group and, in particular, to outline the services his group can provide.

Early in his talk, Roger uses the text visual in Figure 13.20 to preview his main points. This visual gives Roger's listeners a framework for understanding the rest of his talk. To make it easy for his listeners to read the visual, he limits it to five lines. He also uses upper- and lower-case letters, rather than all capitals, because differences between the capitals and the small letters make it easier to read each word.

As Roger progresses in his talk, he uses additional text visuals to elaborate on each of the main points presented in his early visual. For each point, he first shows the early visual with the point he is about to address highlighted in boldface. This reminds people of how that point fits into the larger framework of the talk. So, for example, when he gets to his third main point, he displays the text visual shown in Figure 13.21, which is the early visual with the third point highlighted. The text visual that follows Figure 13.21 breaks down his third point into four key aspects, as shown in Figure 13.22.

In this thirty-minute presentation, Michael makes three major points. After his brief definition of the Business Analysis group as internal consultants (point 1), he discusses their training (point 2) and their service to other employees (point 3). Text visuals that remind his listeners of his main points, or that identify key details about each main point, help his listeners hold on to the structure of his talk as he introduces new material.

The checklist on page 663 will help you review your use of text visuals.

Figure 13.19
A TEXT VISUAL

REGIONAL VOLUNTEER RECRUITMENT PROCESS

- Big Successes in Regions I and III:
  10 Recruited in Each Region within Two Weeks

- In Some Regions Little or No Recruiting in One Month:
  Region II, No One Recruited
  Region IV, Only 6 Recruited

Figure 13.20
ROGER'S EARLY TEXT VISUAL

BUSINESS ANALYSIS DEPARTMENT

- Organized as an Internal Consulting Organization
- Trained in Development and Application of Computerized Tools and Techniques
- Assigned to Improve Clients' Productivity

VISUAL AIDS 661

Figure 13.21

EARLY TEXT VISUAL WITH POINT 3 HIGHLIGHTED

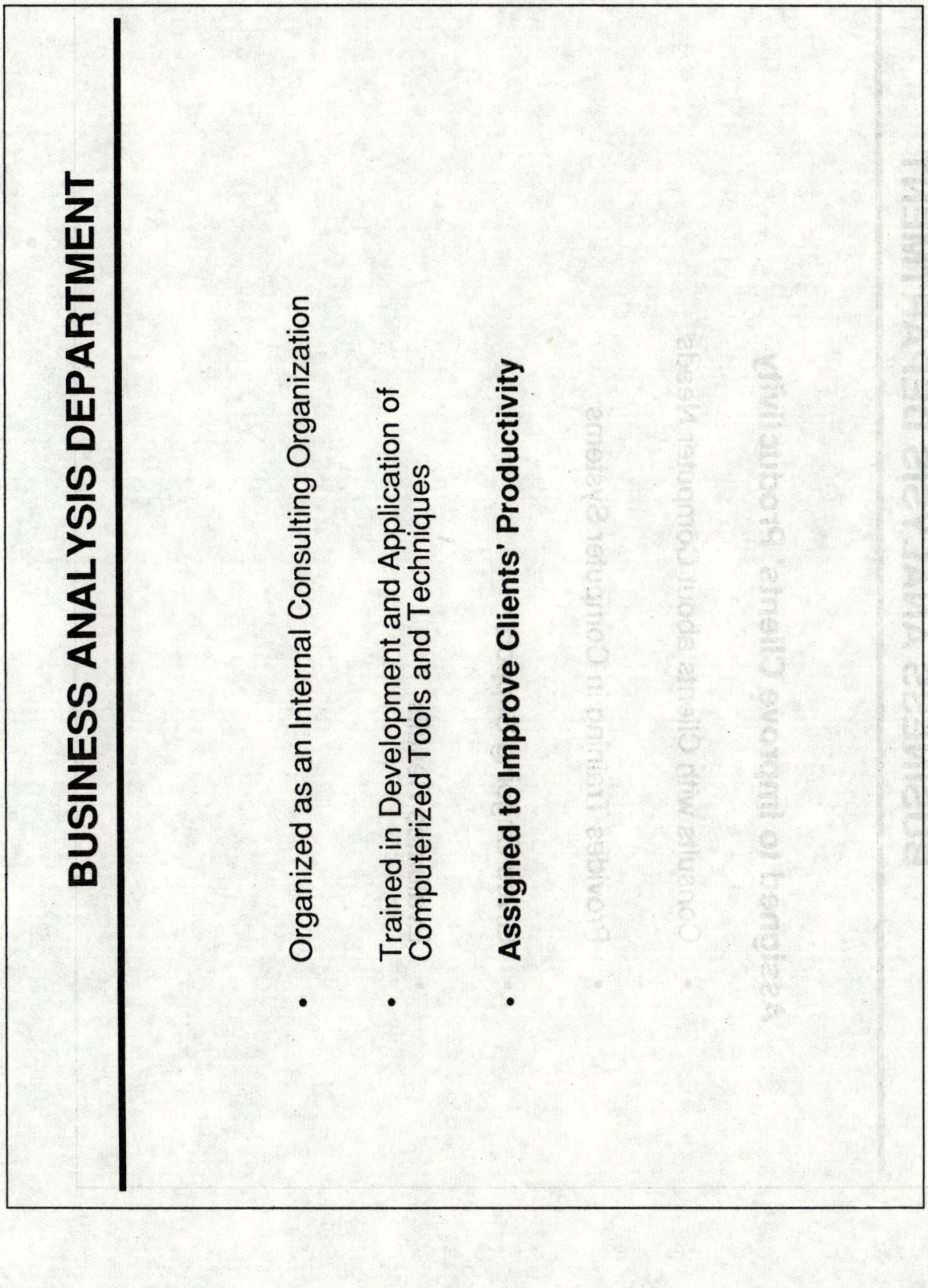

BUSINESS ANALYSIS DEPARTMENT

- Organized as an Internal Consulting Organization
- Trained in Development and Application of Computerized Tools and Techniques
- **Assigned to Improve Clients' Productivity**

Figure 13.22

ROGER'S TEXT VISUAL SHOWING SUBDIVISION OF POINT 3

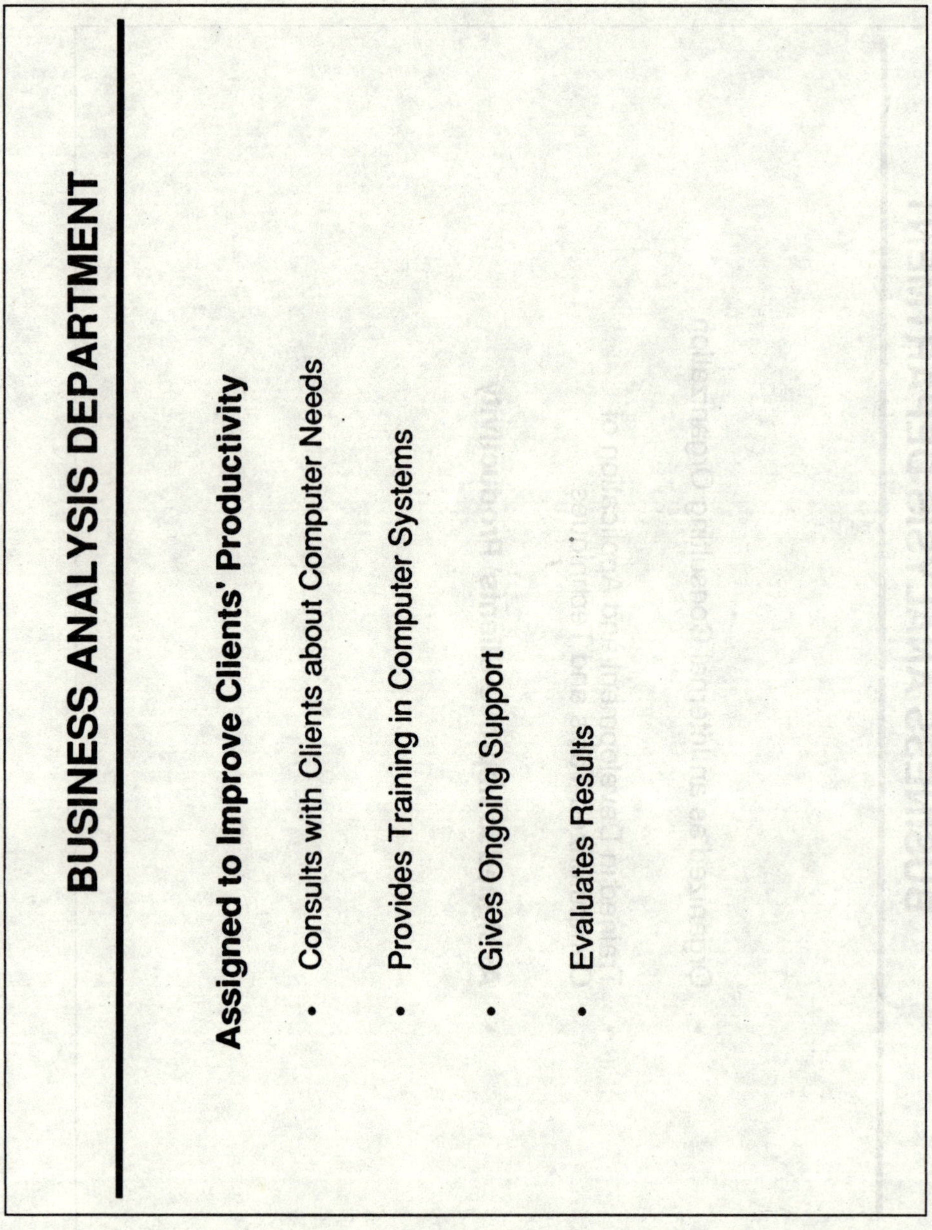

BUSINESS ANALYSIS DEPARTMENT

Assigned to Improve Clients' Productivity

- Consults with Clients about Computer Needs
- Provides Training in Computer Systems
- Gives Ongoing Support
- Evaluates Results

VISUAL AIDS   663

CHECKLIST FOR USING TEXT VISUALS

1. Is the visual no more than five lines?
2. Is it limited to key phrases?
3. Does it do one or more of the following things:

- Preview the presentation?
- Reveal the structure of the talk?
- Serve as a reminder of the key issues?

Displaying Visual Aids

How you present your visual aids usually depends on several things: the equipment at your disposal, your company's formal or informal policy concerning visual aids, the purpose of your presentation, and the size of your audience. You can display visuals in any of the following ways:

1. *Blackboard:* If you are brainstorming in a small, informal group, you may want to use a blackboard to jot down, rearrange, and record the group's ideas. The blackboard is easy to see, write on, and erase.

2. *Flip chart:* As with the blackboard, you can use a flip chart if you are working with a small, informal group. A flip chart can contain prepared visual aids as well as ones you create on the spot. Flip charts are also easy to carry and set up.

3. *Overhead transparencies:* You can use overhead transparencies when you want to show visual aids you have prepared beforehand as well as ones you compose as you talk to a group. Since your visual aids are enlarged by the projection, they can be more detailed than those you would present using a flip chart.

4. *Slide projection:* You can use slides for formal presentations. Slides that are professionally designed beforehand are likely to have a strong visual impact and can include elaborate photographs, organization charts, flow charts, and so on. But be aware that slides require a darkened room, so you will lose eye contact with your audience.

5. *Handouts:* You should use handouts when you want your listeners to have detailed information in front of them as they listen. Distribute a handout as you reach the topic it covers. The advantage of handouts is that listeners can write their notes under pertinent sections of the handout. Disadvantages are that rustling papers can be noisy and can turn the group's attention away from you or the screen.

COMPUTER GRAPHICS

Current computer technology can help you create professional-looking visual aids quickly and easily. Computer software allows you to create such visual aids by entering a series of commands into your computer.

Flip charts are effective for small, informal meetings.

FIGURE I:
A COMPUTER WITH VISUAL AID DISPLAYED

Using a computer allows you to create professional-looking graphics that can enhance your presentations and your letters, memos, and reports. Notice how the visual aid displayed on the screen uses colors and a three-dimensional layout to emphasize the extent of the smog problem and to pinpoint its locations. Color graphics packages will enable you to dramatize and highlight your message.
(Courtesy of Unisys)

FIGURE II:
A GRAPH USING SYMBOLS

Computer software graphics packages are available with a variety of preset symbols such as buildings, animals, people (men, women, or groups), borders, and signs. The graphic shown here is preprogrammed. However, this program also allows users to draw their own symbols freehand.
(Courtesy of Enertronics Research, Inc.)

FIGURE III: A GROUPED BAR CHART

This computer grapic uses colors and a three-dimensional layout to compare discount flights in the East, Central, and West United States regions. Compare the grouped bar chart here with the one in Figure 13.10 (p. 647), which was created without the computer. Are the colors necessary to convey the information? Are they helpful? Are three dimensions necessary or helpful?
(Courtesy of SPC Software Publishing Corp.)

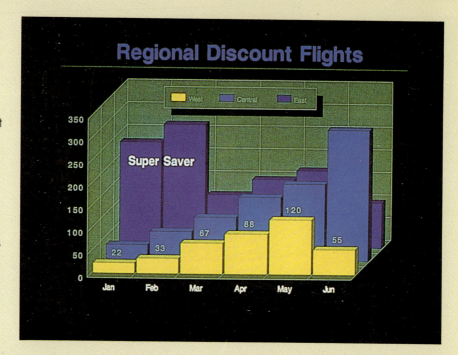

FIGURE IV: A SEGMENTED BAR CHART

Colors make the information in this segmented bar chart easy to grasp. By focusing on a color, the viewer can quickly compare the company's fixed costs, its variable costs, or its net profit in four regions. Notice how the more neutral background color (yellow) keeps the viewer's focus on the more colorful bars.
(Courtesy of Execucom)

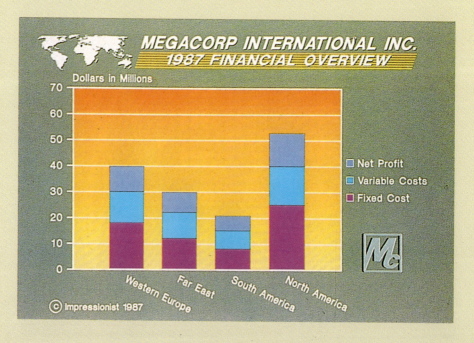

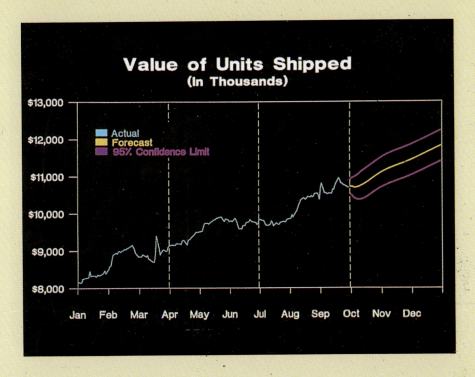

FIGURE V: A LINE GRAPH

In this line graph a past trend is distinguished from the future by the introduction of two new and contrasting colors, red and yellow.
(Courtesy of SAS Institute)

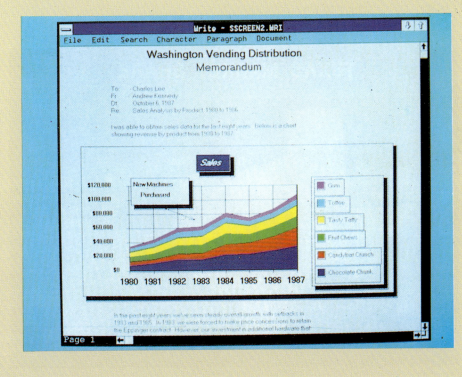

FIGURE VI: A LINE GRAPH EMBEDDED IN A MEMO

Thanks to integrated software packages that combine text and graphics, line graphs such as this one can be inserted into a memo immediately after the reference to it. Writers no longer have to create their graphics separately and insert them by hand.
(Courtesy of Microsoft Corp.)

**FIGURE VII:
PIE CHARTS**

The placement of these two pie charts next to each other helps to summarize succinctly an organization's entire financial situation. One computer graphic, the left-hand pie chart, distinguishes by color the sources of funds; the other, the right-hand pie chart, distinguishes by color the uses of funds. As long as pie charts are simple to read and compare, placing multiple charts together can be an efficient way to convey your message.
(Courtesy of Microsoft Corp.)

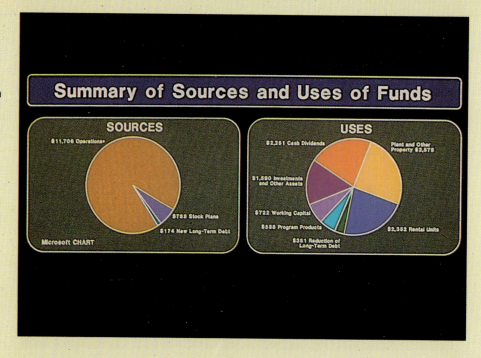

**FIGURE VIII:
A MAP**

The use of colors in this map of Texas quickly conveys precise information about American Business Systems' relative market share in specific counties of Texas.
(© 1985, 1986, 1987 by Ashton-Tate Corp. Portions © 1985 Mapmaker, Inc. All rights reserved. Reprinted by permission)

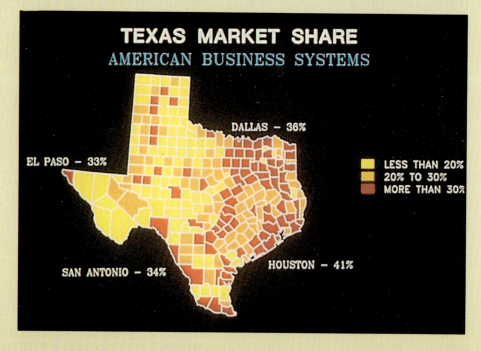

VISUAL AIDS 665

Business people making presentations can use a variety of visual aids to display information.

Because this software enables you to change the size, wording, type font, shading patterns, colors, and even the type of visual aid, the software will not only help you produce a high-quality visual aid, but it will also save you time by speeding up the revision and final production of your visual aids. For instance, if you discover that the data you have presented using a pie chart would be better presented by a bar chart, entering a new series of commands in the computer will turn the pie chart into a bar chart on the computer's screen. Once you are satisfied with your visual aid, a good computer printer can produce visual aids of a quality that was formerly possible only if done by your organization's graphics department or if you yourself had the necessary skills (see Figure 13.23). For some color examples, see the visual aids beginning opposite page 664. In addition, integrated computer packages can insert your visual aids into the ongoing text of your written documents.

Although the benefits of the technology far outweigh its costs, a few words of caution seem warranted. Creating charts and graphs is so simple using the computer that occasionally writers use visual aids when they are unnecessary. Some business people get so enamored of the technology that they develop overly elaborate visual aids—including rainbow-colored graphs, ornate type fonts, crosshatching on bar charts, and complicated borders (see Figure 13.24, for example). If you are tempted to overdo things, restrain yourself. Use your good judgment about what constitutes an *effective* visual aid to decide how yours should look (see Figure 13.25). Be aware, too, that some software packages don't allow you to develop adequate visual aids. For instance, you may not be able to include verbal information on a line graph, or above or next to a bar in a bar chart. To compensate for the inadequacy of these packages, experienced writers use the computer to print out the line graph or bar chart, and then neatly handwrite or type the additional information where it should be placed.

Computers can generate a wide assortment of visual aids quickly.

Figure 13.23
COMPUTER GRAPHICS

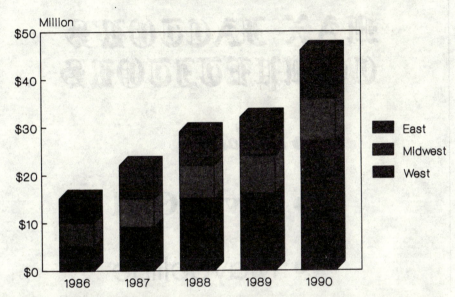

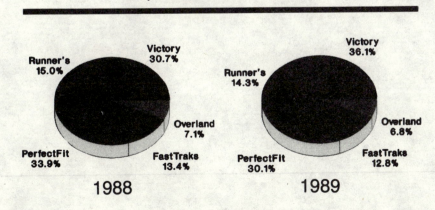

Figure 13.24

AN OVERLY ELABORATE GRAPHIC

𝕸𝖆𝖝 𝕱𝖆𝖈𝖙𝖔𝖗'𝖘 𝕮𝖔𝖒𝖕𝖊𝖙𝖎𝖙𝖔𝖗𝖘

- *Revlon*

- **Cover Girl**

- Maybelline

- L´Oreal

VISUAL AIDS

Figure 13.25
A COMPARISON OF TWO VISUAL AIDS

Which text visual is better, this one or the one on the next page?

Max Factor's Product Innovations

- Face Make-up

- Cover-ups

- Waterproof Cosmetics

THE RANDOM HOUSE GUIDE TO BUSINESS WRITING

(A COMPARISON OF TWO VISUAL AIDS
continued)

- FACE MAKE-UP

- COVER-UPS

- WATERPROOF COSMETICS

VISUAL AIDS

SUMMARY

When coordinated with your text or presentation, visual aids can help you present data and other information. Once you have decided that a visual aid will enhance your communication, choose carefully the one that best conveys your ideas and make sure that it is simple, accurate, and complete. Use tables to compare and contrast exact data, bar charts to compare precise data at precise time intervals, line graphs to demonstrate trends, pie charts to show the whole in relation to its parts according to percentages, organization charts to show the formal structure of a company, flow charts to display a process or procedure, and maps to convey quantitative information about a geographical area. Computer graphics can assist you in creating all of these visual aids.

EXERCISES

1. Review the visual aids in the *Wall Street Journal, Business Week,* or a good local newspaper. Decide whether they are effective, and explain why.
2. Review reports you have written for this or another class. Where could you have added a visual aid to communicate your ideas more effectively? What kind of visual aid would have helped?
3. Look at the visual aids in the annual report of a company, and decide whether they effectively communicate information to readers. Here are some questions to consider:

- Are the visual aids described accurately and sufficiently in the text and by labels in the aids themselves?
- Are they well placed?
- What makes the visual aids work? If they don't work, how could they be revised or what visual aids should replace them?
- Should any of the visual aids be eliminated?

4. Assistant human resources manager Brian Simpson has just collected data on the percentages of minorities who were hired by his company in 1986, 1987, 1988, and 1989. Brian's boss, Les Paulsen, has asked Brian to construct a visual aid for presenting this information in a status report advising Personnel about the company's hiring practices. (Les is the company's affirmative action officer.) Les is particularly interested in seeing the mix of jobs that minorities held, how this mix may have changed from year to year, and what percentage of the company's total work force is composed of minorities. Here are the notes on which Brian must base his visual aid:

> In 1989, minorities composed 18.2 percent of the work force. They were 18.4 percent in 1986, 17.8 percent in 1987, and 16.3 percent in 1988. Of the 18.2 percent minorities who composed the work force in 1989, 8.8 percent were officials and managers, 16 percent were professionals, 20.7 percent were technicians, 4.0 percent were sales workers, 22.9 percent were office and clerical workers, 16.1 percent were skilled craftspeople, 21.8 percent

were operatives (semiskilled workers), 19.8 percent were laborers (unskilled), and 30.6 percent were service workers. In 1988, 30.2 percent were service workers, 24.6 percent were laborers, 22.3 percent were operatives, 17.2 percent were craftspeople, 21.9 percent were office and clerical, 5.0 percent were sales workers, 19.4 percent were technicians, 15.1 percent were professionals, and 8.6 percent were officials and managers. Back in 1987, 8.0 percent were officials and managers, 14.0 percent were professionals, 18.4 percent were technicians, 5.2 percent were sales workers, 21.6 percent were office and clerical, 17.0 percent were skilled craftspeople, 21.0 percent were operatives, 26.4 percent were laborers, 29.0 percent were service workers. Finally, in the first year under consideration, 1986, 29.7 percent were service workers, 22.9 percent were laborers, 19.6 percent were operatives, 14.6 percent were craftspeople, 20.0 percent were office and clerical, 4.2 percent were sales workers, 18.0 percent were technicians, 12.6 percent were professionals, and 7.5 percent were officials and managers.

What kind of visual aid should Brian use to organize his data? Why would you recommend this kind of aid rather than another kind? Construct the visual aid for him.

5. Suppose you are a research assistant for Will Jeffrion, head of Overseas Marketing for an aerospace company. Will has just made a request: "Let me know how our international assets have changed country by country from 1988 to 1989. I need to add this information to my marketing plan for overseas operations." Through your research, you have turned up the following information:

Measured in millions of dollars, in 1989, assets were 5.6 for Argentina, 30.9 for Australia, 94.6 for Brazil, 85.7 for Canada, 50.1 for France, 303.3 for Germany, 13.4 for Italy, 70.6 for Japan, 20.5 for Spain, 23.2 for Switzerland, 148.5 for the United Kingdom, and 63.7 for all others. In 1988, they were 54.9 for all others, 177.5 for the United Kingdom, 28.2 for Switzerland, 27.5 for Spain, 67.8 for Japan, 17.8 for Italy, 18.4 for Holland, 332.2 for Germany, 57.6 for France, 77.3 for Canada, 105.0 for Brazil, 33.1 for Australia, and 12.8 for Argentina. Total assets for 1988 were 910.1, and they were 1,010.1 for 1989.

Design a visual aid that will help your boss convey all this information in his report to top management.

6. Each of the following examples includes (1) a description of the business situation and the purpose for which a visual aid is to be used, and (2) information presented in paragraph form that can be conveyed better in a visual aid. Read each example, construct the visual aid, and write the text that should accompany the aid for the written document or oral presentation in which the aid is to appear.

a. You are a management trainee in health care administration at a local nursing home. Since you are also a recent college graduate majoring in business, your college has asked you to give a talk to seniors on career opportunities in the health care professions. You want to use the following information in your talk:

In 1963, 1973, and 1977, information was gathered on the uses of nursing homes by the elderly, who were classified in three age groups: 65–74, 75–84, and 85 and over. Out of every 1,000 people in the United States between ages 65 and 74, 8 in 1963, 12 in 1973, and 15 in 1977 were in nursing homes. Of every 1,000 people between ages 75 and 84, 40 in 1963, 59 in 1973, and 68 in 1977 were in nursing homes. Of every 1,000 people 85 years and over, 148 in 1963, 254 in 1973, and 216 in 1977 were in nursing homes.

b. You are an assistant to the vice president of New Acquisitions at a company that produces cereals and breads. The company is considering the purchase of a grain supplier business to help stabilize its grain costs. Your boss wants to include the following information—on the monthly average cost of grain between 1987 and 1989—in a proposal to top executives persuading them to buy the grain supplier:

The cost went from about $2.45 per bushel up to $2.50 mid-year of 1987 and then down again to about $2.45 at the beginning of 1988. Although remaining stable through the early part of 1988, the price dipped to about $2.00 per bushel in mid-1988, and then rose sharply and steadily to about $3.00 by the beginning of 1989.

c. As an assistant market researcher, you have gathered the following data for your superior. She is writing a report to the vice president of Marketing, who must decide whether the company's advertising budget has been appropriately allocated. Here are the data:

Out of a total budget for selectively advertising four breakfast cereals, 1 percent is used in Houston, 2 percent in Dallas, 22 percent in Boston, and 75 percent in New York.

d. You are a junior member of a software company's task force. The task force was formed to try to get a number of venture capitalists to invest several million dollars in the company's expansion plans. The following information is to appear in a proposal to the venture capitalists:

Net earnings (in millions) rose gradually to about 25 million from the founding of the company in 1970 to 1980. From 1980 to 1990, net earnings in millions rose at a steady pace another 275 million.

e. A group of students doing an internship report on a pharmaceuticals company's sales of headache remedies in the Far East wants to include the following information in the appendix of their formal report:

We interviewed everyone in the international sales division. We began with the highest manager, Bill Soto, the executive vice president of International Sales. Then we talked to Kim Nakomoto, the vice president of

Far East Operations, and Shao Wu, the vice president of Advertising, Publicity, and Promotion. Both of them report to Sam Yamagato, the executive vice president of Sales. From our discussion with Kim Nakomoto, we decided to interview his immediate subordinate, Shunjiro Itagaki, the manager of the Tokyo office, and her subordinates, Yasuhiro Okubo, Naoyuki Karasawa, and Masahiro Haraoka.

f. You work as an assistant financial analyst for a medium-sized investment company. You have been asked to brief your boss, who is new to the company, on your company's sale of land and buildings over the last few years. The following information goes into your presentation:

Reviewing chronologically the company's land sales in 1989, we see that in February, a store at the northwest corner of Santa Monica Boulevard and Bundy consisting of 10,000 square feet was sold at $115.28 per square foot. Then, in March, we sold a factory on the Northwest corner of Wilshire Boulevard and San Vicente Boulevard consisting of 66,647 square feet for $205 per square foot. In June, an office building on the southwest corner of Wilshire Boulevard and Bundy consisting of 46,750 square feet went for $214 per square foot. In August, property at 1315 Wilshire Boulevard consisting of 5,000 square feet went for $90 per square foot.

g. You are a junior executive working on your company's annual report. The following information needs to be turned into a visual aid.

Here is a review of our operating revenues for our major divisions: publishing and related distribution, filmed entertainment, recorded music and music publications, and consumer electronics for 1984, 1986, and 1988.

In 1984, 5 percent of our total revenues of $22 million resulted from publishing and related distribution, 30 percent from filmed entertainment, 60 percent from recorded music and music publications, and 5 percent from consumer electronics.

In 1986, 5 percent of total revenues of $43 million resulted from publishing and related distribution, 40 percent from filmed entertainment, 45 percent from recorded music and music publications, and 10 percent from consumer electronics.

In 1988, 5 percent of total revenues of $90 million resulted from publishing and related distribution, 35 percent from filmed entertainment, 25 percent from recorded music and music publications, and 35 percent from consumer electronics.

h. As a junior member of the technical staff of a semiconductor manufacturer, you are including the following information in a report to new sales reps explaining the company's mix of products:

As you can see, semiconductor production equipment is needed for processing, testing, and assembling. Significantly, from 1984 to 1988, the steady rise of sales in assembling equipment from approximately $1 to $2 million has been paralleled by a steady rise of sales in testing equipment that is three times as large and in processing equipment that is four times as large.

7. Comment on the text visual (shown in Figure 13.26) that a product manager wants to use to present the steps in developing a new product. He is giving an introductory talk to a group of management trainees who want to learn about different aspects of the company before selecting the area in which they would like to be assigned. None of the trainees has worked in product development.

Figure 13.26
A TEXT VISUAL IN NEED OF REVISION

STEPS IN NEW PRODUCT DEVELOPMENT

IDEA GENERATION

EVALUATION

- FINANCIAL

- STRATEGY

PRODUCT DESIGN

- MARKET RESEARCH—BENEFITS SOUGHT

    PERCEPTIONS OF COMPETITIVE PRODUCTS

    UNSATISFIED NEEDS

- SELECTION OF A POSITION—CONCEPT

- TRANSLATION OF CONCEPT TO PHYSICAL PRODUCT

- MARKET RESEARCH—TEST IMPLEMENTATION

PRODUCT LAUNCH

14
THE JOB SEARCH

PREVIEW

This chapter should help you to

1. Prepare for your job search by showing you how to
   - Devise a schedule to prepare for and conduct your job search
   - Do a self-assessment and do research to explore career options
   - Write a resume
2. Conduct your job search by showing you how to
   - Read want ads
   - Do library research on specific companies and positions
   - Speak to business contacts about openings in their companies or other organizations
3. Complete your job search by showing you how to
   - Write letters of application
   - Interview
   - Write thank-you letters
   - Write a letter of acceptance
   - Write letters of refusal

Winter quarter had just begun, and Michael Eaton, a senior at UCLA, knew he had to begin his job search if he hoped to land a job by graduation. Michael had had a number of part-time and summer jobs since high school, but he had never done a job search for full-time employment. "Where do I begin?" he wondered. "And what do I have to do to get a good job?"

Like Michael, you may wonder, How do I carry out a job search? This chapter will show you the major elements of the job campaign. You will first see how to prepare for a job search by making a schedule of necessary activities, by exploring career options, and by writing your resume. You will then learn how to conduct the search itself. Finally, you will see how to interview and write the letters related to the job campaign.

MAKING A SCHEDULE

In planning your job search, begin by making a schedule of the various tasks necessary to your search. A schedule should take into account the deadline by which you want to complete your search, the tasks involved, and the time and sequence for these tasks.

Career counselors suggest beginning the job search as early as possible. According to one career counselor, once the initial preparation (self-assessment, research on career goals, and resume writing) is complete, it can take an average of two to six months to secure a position; but it may take more, depending on the job candidate's interests, preparation, and mobility, as well as market conditions.

Michael knew that he wanted to complete his job search by the end of June. He had six months and could devote approximately five to ten hours a week to it. With this deadline and time commitment in mind, Michael listed everything he had to do, the estimated time each activity would take, and the sequence of activities. (He learned about these activities, their sequence, and the approximate time each would take by talking to a counselor at his job placement center.) Michael's list is shown in Figure 14.1. After putting together the schedule, Michael designed a time line to help him visualize what he had to do and when (see Figure 14.2).

Notice that Michael's schedule suggests certain characteristics of the job search:

1. *It involves several overlapping activities*. To increase your efficiency, you can do several job search activities during the same time period—for example, conduct preliminary library research, check college placement services, and contact business people and professional associations. Later on, you can do research on specific companies during the same weeks that you check wants ads, write letters of application, interview, and write thank-you letters following your interviews.

2. *It requires flexibility*. A schedule for a job search must be flexible enough to accommodate unforeseen delays and your inability to control when offers will come in. Michael gave himself over four months to find a job once he completed his resume. He also established a contingency plan. If a full-time job did not materialize by the end of this period, he would seek temporary employment by the end of June to pay his bills until he received an offer. (The dotted lines on his schedule indicate that his job search may have to go beyond the six months.)

EXPLORING CAREER OPTIONS: SELF-ASSESSMENT AND RESEARCH

Exploring your career options requires you to set aside time for self-assessment and for research, using college placement services, libraries, business contacts, and professional associations.

Figure 14.1

MICHAEL'S LIST OF JOB SEARCH ACTIVITIES

First 1½ months for the following activities:
- Do self-assessment (1 week)
- Do research on career goals by using
    - College career counseling services or career assessment (3 weeks)
    - Library (3 weeks)
    - Business contacts (6 weeks)
    - Professional associations (6 weeks)
- Write resume, have it reviewed by college placement counselor and business contacts, and revise (3 weeks)

4½ months plus for the following activities:
- Read want ads
- Do library research on specific companies and positions
- Speak to business contacts
- Write letters of application
- Interview
- Write thank-you letters
- Write letters of acceptance and letters of refusal (final week)

Figure 14.2

MICHAEL'S TENTATIVE SCHEDULE

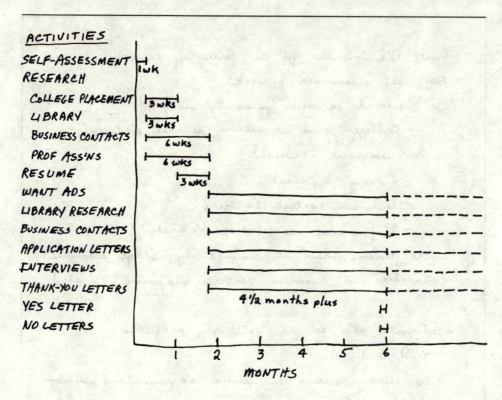

Self-Assessment

Before you look at job opportunities, you will benefit from considering what you do well, what you enjoy doing, and what skills and education you would like to use and develop on the job. Your self-assessment will help focus your job search and is useful not only for the initial job but also at various points in your career when you are thinking about changing your occupation.

To do a self-assessment, ask yourself some questions about those aspects of your life that pertain to your choice of work—such as your education, accomplishments, and skills—and then see whether any pattern of interests emerges from your responses. Let your questions first stimulate your thinking about broad issues of your background and personality—such as education, accomplishments, skills, qualities, and interests; then let the questions help you focus more narrowly on issues pertaining to job choice—such as work values, preferred geographic area, and preferred work environment. Use the questions in Figure 14.3 as a guide. To give you an idea of how one person used the questions, Michael's responses follow each question.

Figure 14.3

QUESTIONS FOR SELF-ASSESSMENT AND
MICHAEL'S ANSWERS

Education: *What was your major? your minor? Have you taken special courses or had special training? What were you most successful in, and what did you enjoy?*

Major—sociology. Minor—business. Liked English, marketing, social science, and communication studies; best grades in those subjects

Personal accomplishments: *Can you name seven to ten accomplishments you are most proud of? What did you do in each case? What gave you a sense of pride? Can you rank your accomplishments in order of importance?*

— Salesman for Casual Ware—ended up in top 10 percent of salespeople; good at multiple sales—a guy would ask for a sports coat and I would sell him the pants, shirt, cuff links, and tie, to go with it.
— State of California ocean lifeguard—tryout was tedious and competitive. 300 guys started out. We had to swim one mile in the ocean. It was February. The temperature was around 55 degrees, the surf about 8 feet, and the current at 2 to 3 knots. 150 eliminated in that first test. The ones remaining had to run, swim, and run. We ran 500 yards in deep sand, swam 500 yards around a buoy, and ran 500 yards again. The judges then interviewed the top 100 people. Asked me to respond to mock situations in the interview: "If a person with a dog came on the beach and the dog was not allowed, how would I handle it?" 60 guys remained after the interviews. We went through a week-long training program of 10 hours a day—competed every morning and spent 8 hours in class learning first aid, CPR, and procedures on the beach. The last day we were tested and they picked 24.
— Manager, UCLA basketball team—managed the team when we were on the road, controlled the budget and in charge of selecting and buying food for the pregame meal and postgame snacks.
— Got an A in speech—went from being afraid to talk in front of groups to being one of the best speakers in the class. Don't have to memorize speeches anymore. I just write down the important info on cards and go with it.
— Waiter at a prestigious hotel—worked one summer as a regular waiter for a major restaurant with an internationally known chef, helped organize dinner parties.
— Gourmet cook—taught myself how to cook starting with easy recipes. Now cook gourmet meals (even Mexican and Chinese) for my friends.

(continued)

(QUESTIONS FOR SELF-ASSESSMENT AND MICHAEL'S
ANSWERS continued)

— Improved my GPA with a tight schedule—brought my GPA up to 3.4 even though I was working part-time.
— Paid for half of my college education—had a variety of summer and part-time jobs (waiter, salesman, lifeguard).
— Ranking of Accomplishments
  1. State lifeguard
  2. Improving my GPA
  3. Manager, UCLA basketball
  4. Salesman
  5. Paid half college education
  6. Waiter
  7. Gourmet cook
  8. A in speech

Skills: *What skills did you use to achieve your accomplishments (e.g., computer, financial management, foreign language, initiative, leadership, negotiation, project management, research, training, sales, speaking, writing)?*

— Physical and psychological endurance and athletic ability for state lifeguard test.
— Teamwork in pulling up my grades (worked in study group).
— Communication skills for passing lifeguard exam, working as a salesman and a waiter, managing the team, and getting an A in speech.
— Analytical skills for improving my GPA.
— Organizational and financial management skills in managing the basketball team on the road and for paying half my college education.
— Negotiation and leadership skills in managing the basketball team.
— Sales skills for job at Casual Ware.

Personal qualities: *How would you describe your personality (e.g., competitive, creative, enthusiastic, good with people, interested in ideas, organized, practical, responsible, self-confident)? What are your most outstanding characteristics?*

— Ambition, dedication (even have the word "ambition" on a sign tacked over my bed); am an easygoing guy socially—I get along well with people and I like them.

Interests: *What hobbies and extracurricular activities do you pursue? What do you like best?*

— Water sports competition, gourmet cooking, and spending time with friends.

> **Work values:** *What is most important to you (e.g., status, job security, creativity, teamwork, money, structured routine, challenge)?*
>
> — I'm a team player (e.g., my study group at school—work with friends, give each other help); managing basketball team's trips.
> — Challenge—love to take on difficult tasks I enjoy and to succeed.
> — Persistence—I pick a goal and go for it.
>
> **Preferred geographic area:** *Do you prefer living in a city, the country, or the suburbs? Do you have a favorite place where you would like to work? Will family or other obligations require that you work in a specific location?*
>
> — Flexible—I'd like a job that gives me some training and experience and allows me to move up.
>
> **Preferred work environment:**
>
> a. *Do you see yourself happiest working for a large, medium, or small company?*
>
> — Large firm because of the training opportunities and potential for upward mobility.
>
> b. *Would you like to be your own boss or do you prefer working on a team?*
>
> — Work best on a team.
>
> c. *What kinds of problems would you like to solve?*
>
> — Marketing and people-oriented problems—I enjoy figuring out how potential customers make choices, what makes products sell, and how to increase sales; I like thinking about people issues and working with people.
>
> d. *Do you prefer taking directions from others or managing your own workload?*
>
> — For the next few years I want to work for some great managers so I can learn the ropes. Later on work for myself.

Answering questions such as the ones in Figure 14.3 will stimulate your thinking about the skills and experience you bring to the job market and the kinds of work you would like to do and are qualified for. After answering these questions, review your responses to see whether you can pinpoint what you like doing, what you do best, and what skills and experience you would like to use and develop at work.

Michael took several days to review his responses, looking to see if he could clarify for himself his career interests. Since he had typed his responses, he circled key points in each one to help himself think through the career areas that might interest him, and he paid special attention to the last few questions, which pertained specifically to work. Here are the responses he circled:

Education: sociology, business

Accomplishments: lifeguard, improving GPA, manager of basketball team, salesman, paid half college education, waiter, gourmet cook, A in speech

Skills: physical endurance, athletic ability, teamwork, communication skills, analytical skills, organizational and financial management, negotiation and leadership

Qualities: ambition, dedication

Interests: water sports, gourmet cooking, friends

Work values: team player—study group, persistence

Geographic location: flexible

Preferred work environment: large firm, team, marketing or sales, people problems, work under experienced manager

Michael thought about what he enjoyed most, what skills he would like to use, and what kind of work might give him the greatest satisfaction. By working through this self-evaluation, he could see that marketing might be an area that would interest him. He already had experience in sales and knew he liked solving marketing problems and working with people.

By reviewing his responses to the self-assessment questions, he could also see that he enjoyed teamwork and was successful at it. He noticed, too, that he got satisfaction from completing challenging tasks that required dedication and brought into play such business skills as analysis, communication, financial management, and sales. When he looked carefully again at the last several points that stressed work values—large firm, opportunity for learning, marketing—he realized that, for the first few years at least, a large, established firm might be the right environment for him.

As you work through a list of self-assessment questions, your career interests may surface as readily as Michael's did. If not, you may want to ask people who know you as a college student, a friend, or an employee to go over your assessment and to give you a second opinion. Especially if the people you choose are well acquainted with what you can do, your reviewers may be able to see patterns in your background that you have missed. But even if you don't come up with major career interests from your self-assessment, you can still learn a lot by looking for *common themes* among your interests, skills, and accomplishments. Knowing these themes will help you as you seek further assistance in defining your career interests and determining the fit between your interests and the needs of companies.

THE JOB SEARCH 685

As career counselors advise, don't skip this step of self-assessment. Too many students plunge prematurely into writing their resumes and sending out letters. These students are usually the ones who take any job that comes along and who return to their campus placement centers one to five years later discouraged by their unhappy work situations. On the other hand, with preparation, you will have a sense of direction in the job search and a sense of authority in job interviews.

Research

In addition to working on your own to discover the kinds of careers that may best suit you, several resources are available to help you find a match between your career goals and what the marketplace is looking for. These resources include college placement services, libraries, business contacts, and professional associations. As you use each of them, try to discover the possible fit between your career interests and the needs of specific industries and companies.

COLLEGE PLACEMENT SERVICES

Most college placement offices offer a variety of resources to job candidates:

- Career counseling
- Instruction in resume writing and interviewing
- Information about which industries and functional areas are hiring people with your background
- Listings of job offers and internships
- Videotapes done by company recruiters describing their companies and discussing career opportunities
- Computer programs that serve as career planning tools
- On-campus interviews with company recruiters
- Special programs for minorities

Before you begin your job search, find out what services your placement center provides.

If you seek the help of a counselor to think through your career interests, we recommend that you do some self-assessment on your own beforehand so that you will be able to ask questions relevant to your particular job search. For example, when Michael came to his appointment at the placement center, he already knew that he wanted to work in some area of marketing for a large, growing company. His counselor informed him that many large companies offer formal training programs for young college graduates that might appeal to him. The counselor also suggested that, on the basis of his interest in sports and good food, he might want to market products that he himself was experienced with and felt enthusiastic about.

LIBRARY SOURCES

Libraries often maintain a collection of books that are helpful for a job search. Portions of the books listed in Figure 14.4 are especially useful.

For articles on specific fields, consult the *Business Periodicals Index*, the *New York Times Index*, *Public Affairs Information Service*, the *Reader's Guide to Periodical Literature*, and the *Wall Street Journal Index*.

In addition, if you have not as yet begun reading major business publications such as *Business Week*, *Forbes*, and the *Wall Street Journal*, this is a good time to begin. Reading them will bring you up-to-date on the latest information about particular organizations and industries, and about political, economic, and social events and trends that affect business. For example, you may find out about mergers and acquisitions, new product lines, and new tax laws and government regulations that affect business. You will also assimilate the language and concepts that educated business people use, which will be useful to you in interviewing and in writing letters.

BUSINESS CONTACTS

To find out more, interview friends, acquaintances, professors, college alumni, on-campus speakers, and authorities in your fields of interest. In Michael's round of discussions with business contacts, he spoke to a friend of his parents who works as manager for a large food company in Los Angeles, and to several business people whom he heard speak at the undergraduate marketing club. Because Michael already knew something about the career area that interested him, he could ask his contacts specific questions about the training their companies provide and the typical career progression for young college graduates. These contacts, in turn, led him to others in marketing.

To get the most out of your interviews with business contacts, career experts Susan Bernard and Gretchen Thompson recommend that you come prepared with a list of specific questions. Figure 14.5 lists sample questions you may want to use to find out about an occupation, an industry, or a company. Using these questions, along with what you know about how to conduct an interview (see Chapter 10, pp. 494–497, and Chapter 12, pp. 621–626), should give you valuable inside information about occupations, industries, and companies that interest you. Such interviews may also lead you to re-evaluate your career interests if you find, for instance, that there is little demand for the occupation that appeals to you, or that an occupation, industry, or organization that seemed attractive to you does not, on closer examination, suit your needs. On the other hand, you may confirm your interest in a career choice or discover new areas of interest. Interviewing for information will also give you practice in employment interviewing, and it may result in job leads.

Figure 14.4

BOOKS EXPLORING CAREER CHOICES, EMPLOYMENT FIELDS, AND CAREER OPTIONS

Career Choices

Bernard, Susan, and Thompson, Gretchen. *Job Search Strategy for College Grads: The 10-Step Plan for Career Success.*

Bolles, Richard Nelson. *What Color Is Your Parachute?*

Djeddah, Eli. *Moving Up: How to Get High-Salaried Jobs.*

Flores-Esteves, Manuel. *Life After Shakespeare: Careers for Liberal Arts Majors.*

Good, G. Edward. *Does Your Resume Wear Blue Jeans? The Book on Resume Preparation.*

Gould, Christine A. *Consider Your Options: Business Opportunities for Liberal Arts Graduates.*

Holland, John. *Making Vocational Choices: A Theory of Careers.*

Irish, Richard K. *Go Hire Yourself an Employer.*

Jackson, Tom. *Guerrilla Tactics in the Job Market.*

Malnig, Lawrence, with Anita Malnig, *What Can I Do with a Major in . . .? How to Choose and Use Your College Major.*

Payne, Richard A. *Market Yourself for Success: How to Develop a Personal Marketing Plan to Be in the Right Place at the Right Time, Get the Job You Want, and Move Ahead in Your Career.*

Shingleton, John, and Bao, Robert, *College to Career: Finding Yourself in the Job Market.*

Employment Fields and Career Options

Occupational Outlook Handbook, U.S. Department of Labor. Covers 200 occupations and describes job responsibilities, educational preparation, opportunities for advancement, job outlook, and salaries.

Dictionary of Occupational Titles. U.S. Department of Labor. Gives definitions of almost 17,500 occupations.

Encyclopedia of Careers and Vocational Guidance, 2 vols. Gives information on how to evaluate career interests and identifies job opportunities in major industries.

Guide for Occupational Exploration. U.S. Department of Labor Employment and Training Administration. Provides information on skills, training, and aptitudes necessary for success at jobs in 12 interest areas and 66 work groups.

Figure 14.5

QUESTIONS TO ASK YOUR CONTACTS

FOR INFORMATION ABOUT AN OCCUPATION

1. How did you decide on the career you've chosen?
2. What do you do on a daily basis?
3. What percentage of your time is spent doing what?
4. What are the jobs you've had that led to this one?
5. What are the skills that are most important for a position in this field?
6. What are the entry-level jobs in your area?
7. What kind of people do you hire to fill these jobs?
8. What are the advancement opportunities?
9. What is the salary range?
10. What types of training do companies give to people entering this field?

FOR INFORMATION ABOUT AN INDUSTRY

1. What do you like about working in this industry?
2. What don't you like?
3. How is the economy affecting this industry?
4. What is the employment picture like in this industry?
5. Are there a lot of jobs in this industry?
6. What is the largest area for growth in the future?
7. What should a college graduate know about your industry before he [or she] applies for a job?
8. What are the professional associations your company belongs to?
9. Does your professional association sponsor any career day events?
10. What publications or periodicals should I be reading to acquaint myself with what is happening industry-wide?

FOR INFORMATION ABOUT THE COMPANY

1. Why did you decide to go to work for this company?
2. What do you like most about this company?
3. How does this company differ from its competitors?
4. What kinds of people work for your company? With what kinds of backgrounds?
5. What divisions do you have?
6. How many college graduates do you hire each year?
7. In which divisions are college graduates most likely to be hired?
8. What should college graduates know about your company before applying for a job?
9. Where can one get this information?
10. What advice would you give to someone who wants to break into your field?

Source: Susan Bernard and Gretchen Thompson, *Job Search Strategies for College Grads: The 10-Step Plan for Career Success* (Boston: Bob Adams, 1984), pp. 48–50.

PROFESSIONAL ASSOCIATIONS

Occupations and academic disciplines often have professional associations that may provide you with information about job openings and about trends in the profession. You may be allowed to join or to attend meetings where you can make business contacts. For listings of associations, check either the *Career Guide to Professional Associations: A Directory of Organizations by Occupational Field* or *National Trade and Professional Associations of the U.S. and Canada.*

In using the *Career Guide,* Michael found two promising listings, including addresses and phone numbers: the Food Industry Association Executives and the Sales and Marketing Executives International (See Figure 14.6). He wrote to these associations for information about opportunities for employment in the profession, and about meetings and special programs their local chapters might run.

The accompanying checklist will help you evaluate how well you have explored your career options.

CHECKLIST FOR EVALUATING CAREER EXPLORATION

1. Have you asked yourself questions about your
   - Education?
   - Personal accomplishments?
   - Skills?
   - Personal qualities?
   - Interests?
   - Work values?
   - Preferred geographical area?
   - Preferred work environment?
2. What career interests emerge from reviewing your responses?
3. Have you used the services of your career placement office?
4. Have you reviewed secondary sources that give advice about the job search?
5. Have you spoken to people who work in your fields of interest?
6. Have you written to relevant trade associations for information about employment opportunities, meetings, and programs?

WRITING YOUR RESUME

Once you have explored your career choices, you are ready to write your resume. Putting it together will help you further examine your career interests and the qualifications you bring to your future employment. As with other business communications, you can use the activities of the writing process to compose your resume.

Figure 14.6

CAREER GUIDE LISTINGS RELEVANT TO
MICHAEL'S JOB SEARCH

FOOD INDUSTRY ASSOCIATION EXECUTIVES
1701 LaSalle
Waco, TX 76706
Career Field: 189
Career Aid: Prof. (N)

SALES AND MARKETING EXECUTIVES INTERNATIONAL
380 Lexington Ave.
New York, NY 10017
Tel. 212-986-9300
Purpose: To promote free enterprise and further professionalism in sales and marketing. Founded 1939. 22,000 members; no student memberships. Publication: *Marketing Times* (bimonthly). Meets semiannually.
Career Fields: 164, 18, 19, 25, 26, 27, 29
Career Aids: Literature; Awards; Ed.; Ethics & Standards*

*KEY TO ABBREVIATIONS
  Aids—Provides career aids: (1) literature (books, pamphlets, etc.); (2) audio-visual materials; (3) speakers.
  Awards—Offers awards and prizes for excellence in the profession.
  Ed.—Educational assistance: (1) sponsors courses, seminars, workshops; (2) sponsors apprenticeship and on-the-job training; (3) offers scholarships and financial aids to students; (4) engaged in research activities.
  Ethics & Standards—Establishes ethics and standards for the profession.
  Prof.—Professional society: (I) international; (N) national; (R) regional.

Reprinted from *Career Guide to Professional Associations: A Directory of Organizations by Occupational Fields*, 2d ed., © Copyright 1980. Compiled and edited by the staff of The Carroll Press.

Setting the Goal

A resume is a persuasive document. You use it to get an interview with a prospective employer. This goal is, according to one career counselor, "a tall order for one or possibly two sheets of paper." For a resume to work as your "selling instrument," it has to highlight those skills and accomplishments that demonstrate to a recruiter your qualifications for the job you are seeking.

Assessing the Reader

The primary reader of your resume may be the person you will report to, a member of the personnel department, or a member of a hiring committee. In some companies, the first person to see your resume is a secretary or assistant assigned to weed out unqualified applicants to save time for the primary reader.

No matter who your reader is, he or she is a busy person. If you are applying for an entry-level position, your reader is probably faced with hundreds of resumes and has less than a minute to read your resume. Given this situation, your reader wants a resume that

- *Is easily readable:* Your reader should have no trouble identifying key elements in your resume.
- *Matches your education, accomplishments, and skills to the job requirements:* Your reader wants to see quickly how your background fits the job requirements. For this reason, if you are applying for different positions, your resume may need to be modified for each position.

Michael, for example, modified his general resume to highlight selective aspects of his background that best demonstrated his preparation for each of three different jobs: one in product management for General Mills, another as marketing representative for Adidas, and a third in marketing and promotions for Red Onion restaurants.

Since managers are often faced with hundreds of applications for a position, they are drawn to those applications that are easily readable and systematically match an applicant's background to job requirements.

Gathering Information and Generating Ideas

If you have carefully explored your career options, you will have much of the material for your resume: information about your education, accomplishments, and skills. In addition, as you consider the specific details for each category of your resume, new information will come to mind.

Organizing the Resume

You can organize your resume by putting the appropriate information under each of the categories mentioned in Figure 14.7. Some items are mandatory, such as the heading and education sections; others are optional. You also have some flexibility in the naming of sections and in the order in which you present information.

OPENING SECTION

Your opening section consists of a heading and, if you so choose, a job objective.

Heading. As long as you include your name, address(es), and phone number(s), you may choose among several effective headings for your resume. Here are two, one a simple listing of information, the other tailored specifically to a company and position.

>MICHAEL EATON
>17412 Margate Street
>Encino, California 91316
>(818) 555-3113

>KIMBERLY MANNING'S QUALIFICATIONS as
>MANAGEMENT TRAINEE FOR
>BOISE CASCADE
>219 4 Street, NE
>Washington, D.C. 20002
>202-555-7542 (o)
>202-555-2261 (h)

To make it easy for a potential employer to reach you, include a work number as well as a home number if possible. (If employers have difficulty reaching you, they are likely to move on to other applicants.) If you are seldom at home and don't have an answering machine, include a phone number for messages so that you won't miss a potential employer's call. The following heading includes a number for messages, a

Figure 14.7

SUGGESTED PARTS OF THE RESUME

> Opening Section
> > Heading
> > Job Objective
>
> Education
> Work Experience
> Skills and Accomplishments
> Activities, Interests, Awards (Optional)
> Personal Background (Optional)
> References (Optional)

home phone number, a present address, and a permanent address—since the job candidate is moving after graduation.

<u>Larry O'Neill</u>

Present Address	6170 Larchwood Ave. Philadelphia, PA 19143	Telephone: 215-555-1812 215-555-9001 (messages)
Permanent Address as of June 15	23 West 13th St., New York, N.Y. 10011	212-555-3786

Job Objective. The section "Job Objective" should focus on several things:

- The level of job responsibility you seek
- The kind of work you are looking for
- The industry you prefer

This section may also identify the skills you want to use, the company size you prefer, the responsibilities you seek, and even the name of the company where you would like employment and your long-range career goals. In one of Michael Eaton's resumes, the job objective read as follows:

JOB OBJECTIVE:
Entry-level position in product management at a large company specializing in sports equipment

Ultimate goal: Manage major product line

Here are several other examples:

> JOB OBJECTIVE: A challenging management-trainee job as data processing manager
>
> Long-range goal: Director of Data Processing division in medium-size company.
>
> CAREER GOAL: Assistant manager in hospital administration, with the eventual aim of top administration at large urban hospital.

Career Objective

Entry-level position in insurance at Allstate. Particularly interested in using quantitative and marketing skills. Eventual goal: director of division.

GOAL

Assistant Human Resources Manager which can expand to include:
—designing training packages
—implementing personnel policy
—organizing management development seminars

Career Goal

To enter arts organization as an assistant in the public relations division. Ultimate goal: manage not-for-profit arts organization in medium-size city.

There is some disagreement as to whether students need to identify a job objective. We recommend that you include a job objective for two reasons:

1. Constructing a job objective will help you select and organize information around a specific goal. The job objective then acts as the major theme under which you can include elements of your background that reinforce the theme.
2. Especially if your background is mixed—for example, if you have a little work experience in several fields—the job objective will make it easy for a potential employer to see how your background fits his or her needs.

In the following example, a student who had held a number of jobs and participated in several school projects found it helpful to write a job objective. By stating in the "Job Objectives" section that he was interested in management training and development, he was then able to group the experience that followed under a single category.

Job Objective

Entry-level position in human resources. Particularly interested in using communication and counselling skills in training and development.

EXPERIENCE IN TRAINING AND DEVELOPMENT

- Peer tutor in writing
- Counselor for student hotline
- Research assistant in social psychology
- Summer internship in personnel, Hughes Corporation
- Camp counselor

If the student had listed his experience without formulating a job objective, he would have given the potential employer little sense of his preparation for the job. Moreover, if he had put peer tutoring and counseling under "Work Experience" or "Activities," research under "Education", summer internship under "Work Experience" and "Education," and camp counselor under "Work Experience," he would not have revealed his preparation for work in human resources.

If you are applying for different jobs, put together a job objective for each opening. Notice in Figure 14.8 how Michael designed different job objectives to match the different positions he was applying for. In these job objectives, Michael incorporated the language used in the companies' descriptions of the positions. His attention to detail showed potential employers that he had prepared his application carefully and suggested how well suited he was for the particular position.

EDUCATION

If education is your key qualification for a job, place "Education" right after "Job Objective." In this way, the strongest support for your application appears right after your job objective.

This section names in reverse chronological order colleges from which you received degrees. You may include the names of other colleges you attended if this information strengthens your resume. Include the following information:

- Name of college(s) from which degree expected or received
- Degree, or degree expected, and date of graduation
- Area(s) of concentration
- Grade-point average (GPA) if a B or above
- Honors
- Relevant courses (optional)

Figure 14.8

MICHAEL'S DIFFERENT JOB OBJECTIVES

Notice how Michael's job objective echoes phrases from the Red Onion ad.

FIELD MARKETING POSITIONS
1. Red Onion Restaurants seek marketing professionals to work with management and corporate office on the development of local marketing plans with focus on local promotion planning in Palm Desert and other Red Onions. Successful candidates will have 1-2 years' marketing experience with agency or restaurant company, need energetic, self-motivated individuals. Excellent salary and benefits. Please send resumes to:

The Red Onion
Attn: Promotions Manager
1139 E. Dominguez St., Suite H
Carson, CA 90746
(No phone calls, please.)

1. Job Objective: Field marketing position at The Red Onion. Interested in developing local marketing plans.

Michael identifies a position in his job objective from the company's brochure on career opportunities.

2. As a member of a brand group, you'll run one of General Mills' key businesses. Right from the start, you're an essential part of the corporation's line management that has bottom-line responsibility. Marketing people are catalysts for change in the product lines, which means you move the brand forward. You'll tackle a variety of challenging assignments, from established products like Wheaties to a newer product like Fruit Corners Fruit Bars. All offer you ample opportunities for growth as a marketing professional.

As an entry level marketing assistant, you'll execute the brand's strategy while learning about the product, its markets and competition. The pace will be non-stop, as you develop sales merchandising materials, attend product development meetings and analyze promotion programs. You'll often lead a team of professionals—marketing researchers, scientists, engineers and ad agency people—in solving problems and capitalizing on opportunities.

2. Job Objective: Entry-level marketing assistant at General Mills. Ultimate goal: Product manager

> A promotion to assistant product manager means you'll still execute the brand's strategy, but you'll accomplish this by training and supervising marketing assistants. At the same time, you'll plot your brand's future strategy.
>
> Reaching the product manager level means you'll manage the bottom line of a dynamic consumer foods business. You'll concentrate on strategic planning while managing the brand's resources to achieve short-range objectives. For those who demonstrate exceptional qualifications, further opportunities exist at the marketing director and vice president, general manager levels.

In presenting his educational background, Michael chose to include his major and minor, his grade-point average, and relevant courses. Each of these details supported his application for a position in marketing.

EDUCATION: University of California, Los Angeles, 1989
B.A. Sociology with minor in Business
Grade-point average: 3.4

<u>Relevant Courses</u>

Speech	Accounting
Business Writing	Marketing
Small-Group Communication	Statistics

Overall, the section showed that he had strong verbal, interpersonal, and quantitative skills—all of which are needed in marketing.

Like Michael, you may want to name the specific courses you have taken if they demonstrate your expertise in the field of your potential employment. In the following example, the student is looking for a position in personnel. Notice how he highlights his academic preparation for such work:

EDUCATION

Georgetown University—B.S. Business Administration, 1988
Major: Human Resources (35 hours)

Special Courses

Human Resources
Small-Group Problem
  Solving
Human Resources
  Accounting
Human Resources
  Management
Organizational Psychology

Other Relevant Courses
Business Statistics
Decision making and
  Planning
Formal and Informal
  Organizations

Senior thesis on quality of work life

You may also want to list relevant internships, extension courses, and company-sponsored seminars. In the next example, the student is seeking work in economic forecasting at a major financial institution:

Education and Training

BA, Hofstra University, 1988
Major: Economics
3.6 GPA on a 4-point scale

Courses include microeconomic theory, econometrics, macroeconomics, elementary management statistics, and business communications

Internship at Citicorp on economic forecasting

If your grades in your major are high (B or above) but your overall average is low, you may include only your average in your major:

Education: University of Maryland
    B.S. Finance, 1988
    3.7 in major
    Bank of America Scholarship for Outstanding
    Business Student

Education

B.S.   University of Kentucky, B.S. Engineering, 1988
    Grade-point average in major: 3.4
    Ranked in top 2% of students enrolled in Management
    Science courses

WORK EXPERIENCE

The section "Work Experience" demonstrates to a potential employer how your past work experience qualifies you for the position you are seeking. Most recruiters expect to see the following information in reverse chronological order (but see pp. 706 and 708 for advice about using functional ordering):

- Name and location of company where you held a position
- Dates of your employment
- Your functional title
- Your responsibilities
- Your most important skills and accomplishments

If you have done volunteer work closely related to the work you are pursuing, you may want to include your volunteer work in this section as well. If this is the case, call the section "Experience" or "Related Experience" rather than "Work Experience."

The most challenging part of the work experience section is to describe your skills and accomplishments. It may include any of the following:

Computer: Did you program or use one or more computer languages?

Conflict management: Did you settle arguments? Were you successful in resolving conflicts between people of diverse backgrounds, values, or attitudes?

Financial management: Did you control a budget?

Foreign language: Did you use a foreign language on the job?

Initiative: Did you launch a project? Did you suggest an improved policy or procedure? Have you started a small business?

Leadership: Were you in charge of a staff or a project?

Negotiation: Did you represent a position or group of people successfully?

Project management: Did you successfully complete a project on schedule?

Research: Did you collect or analyze data?

Sales: Were you a salesperson?

Speaking: Did you give presentations or conduct meetings?

Training: Did you instruct others?

Writing: Did you write letters, memos, reports, or company publications?

To generate ideas for this section, list all the jobs you have held, and name as many as possible of the responsibilities, skills, and accomplishments related to each job. You can narrow the list later and selectively include items in different resumes. If you have spent time doing some self-evaluation, as Michael did, you will already have generated some of this information (see Figure 14.3 on pages 681–683).

When choosing items to include in the "Work Experience" section of your resume, be selective. Especially if you have held a number of jobs, describe only those that support the particular job application. For example, in applying for a position with Adidas, Michael did not discuss his work as a waiter. He did, however, describe it in his application for a position with The Red Onion and General Mills, because he felt that his knowledge of the restaurant and food industry, and his experience with the consumer, would support his application for work in the food industry. For these two positions, Michael showed his work experience in the following way:

WORK EXPERIENCE

Retail Salesperson and Assistant Manager   10/88-5/89
Casual Ware
Westwood, CA

Created multiple sales achieving 30% profit over last year. Managed staff of five sales assistants. Assisted in storewide promotions increasing sales 20% over previous five years. Co-authored marketing plan for store expansion.

Waiter   7/88-9/88
Le Chateau Hotel
Los Angeles, CA

Served at table restaurant with world-famous chief Pierre Girard. Planned seven dinner parties for 30 to 35 people at $50/person.

State of California Ocean Lifeguard   7/87-8/87
Huntington Beach, CA

Responsible for 500 swimmers. Enforced state safety laws.

Head Manager, Basketball Team (20 members)   9/85-6/87
University of California, Los Angeles

Coordinated over 400 meals with restaurant managers. Ordered and maintained athletic equipment. Managed $3,000 budget for on-the-road expenses. Developed leadership skills by supervising staff.

THE JOB SEARCH

Giving numbers to substantiate his accomplishments and using specific action verbs made Michael's presentation of his work experience effective. You can present your work experience effectively by doing the following:

1. *Give measurable results* by quantifying your accomplishments. For example:

—Increased Club membership by 20% in six months.

—Recruited, trained, and supervised staff of 75 for Girl Scouts.

—Improved operation of paper embossing machine that resulted in 8% reduction in operating expenses.

—Started painting business employing 25.

—Sold 30% more than . . . .

—Supervised 10-person research staff for biweekly newsletter.

—Wrote and edited 30 articles each month.

2. *Use specific action verbs:* Those shown in Figure 14.9 on page 702 may be helpful. In combination with numbers, action verbs indicate precisely what the job seeker has accomplished.

ACTIVITIES, INTERESTS, AWARDS (OPTIONAL)

Your extracurricular activities, interests, and awards can demonstrate to a potential employer the skills you bring to a job. If you have minimal work experience but your extracurricular activities are strong, use this section of your resume to bring out your preparation for a business position. Among your activities, interests, and awards, select those that show the skills needed in business. These activities may be similar to those you have done for paid work, but here they relate to volunteer and school activities. (See p. 699 for a list of these activities.)

The "Activities" section of Michael's resume was brief, since most of his pertinent experience was included under "Education" and "Work Experience."

ACTIVITIES

Sigma Chi Fraternity: Assistant Rush Chairman
Undergraduate Business Society

Figure 14.9

ACTION VERBS FOR USE IN RESUMES

accelerated	implemented	recommended
achieved	improved	reduced
administered	increased	reorganized
analyzed	influenced	ran
	initiated	
	installed	
completed	interviewed	scheduled
conducted	introduced	served
consulted	invented	set up
controlled		solved
coordinated		strengthened
correlated	launched	succeeded
created	led	supervised
conducted		sold
	managed	
delegated	maintained	trained
demonstrated	mastered	
designed	mediated	
developed	motivated	unified
directed		
	negotiated	won
earned		wrote
established		
evaluated	operated	
expanded	ordered	
	organized	
	overcame	
formed		
formulated		
founded	participated	
	performed	
	pinpointed	
generated	pioneered	
	proposed	
	provided	
headed	programmed	

Notice how the following entry demonstrates the job candidate's teamwork, sales, and counseling skills:

ACTIVITIES

—Cocaptain varsity swimming team.
—Rush chairman for college fraternity. Helped increase membership 30 percent.
—Freshman sponsor. Counseled 10 freshmen.

The next entry demonstrates the student's commitment and outstanding achievement in her field of interest, accounting. It also shows her good communication skills.

Activities and Awards

—Wrote 15 articles on local restaurants for college newspaper
—"Speech Fellow": Tutored 5 students/week in oral presentations
—Dean's List junior and senior years
—Beta Alpha Psi (accounting honorary society)
—Member, Accounting Club

In the above entry, the student explained an item her reader might not understand—that Beta Alpha Psi is the honorary society for accounting. Include explanations in your resume for unfamiliar items.

The next entry shows the job candidate's initiative, high achievement, and strong verbal and financial management skills, as well as his outstanding background in a foreign language.

Activities, Interests and Awards

—Honors Thesis in Economics
—Phi Beta Kappa
—Phi Beta Lambda (business honorary society)
—Drama Club
—Fluent in Spanish
—Started dog-walking service earning over $1,500 a year for student government

The next example stresses the job candidate's business skills, leadership and financial management, by using them as general categories.

ACTIVITIES

<u>LEADERSHIP</u>: Chairman, United Way Campaign
—Designed first all-campus campaign for student contributions
—Recruited and trained 25 student volunteers
—Raised $15,000

<u>FINANCIAL MANAGEMENT</u>: Dorm treasurer
—Managed $10,000 budget
—Developed new accounting procedures that reduced operations cost 10 percent.

PERSONAL BACKGROUND (OPTIONAL)

Personal background may include military service, age, marital status, weight, health, hobbies, special skills, personality traits, and other pertinent information you have not been able to list elsewhere. If you include military service, cite your date of enlistment, location(s) of service, highest rank achieved, achievements, and date of discharge.

About your personal background, we recommend that you give only information that demonstrates your qualifications for the work you seek. For example, Michael mentioned his hobby of preparing gourmet food in his application for work at Red Onion Restaurants and at General Mills; he felt that this hobby would suggest to the company his special knowledge of and interest in food products. But he did not mention this hobby in applications he sent to companies outside the food industry.

Notice how in each of the following entries the personal background of the job seeker enhances his or her chances of attracting a potential employer's interest. In the first example, the job candidate is seeking employment at a firm that does a lot of business in South America:

PERSONAL BACKGROUND

<u>Fluent in Spanish. Lived in Argentina and Peru for two years.</u>

In the second example, the student is applying for work at a company that uses sophisticated computer applications in financial analysis:

<u>Personal Data</u>: Computer buff. Have written programs for personal financial planning.

In the third example, the job candidate is applying for a sales position that involves a significant amount of travel:

PERSONAL BACKGROUND

AGE: 22
MARITAL STATUS: Single
Enjoy travel and eager to relocate in large Midwest city.

THE JOB SEARCH   705

The student's age suggests that he has the physical stamina to travel, and his marital status indicates that he is free of family commitments.

REFERENCES (OPTIONAL)

References are people who have taught or worked with you and can recommend you for the work you are seeking. They include business associates, faculty members, and employers. When putting together a list of references, include at least one employer if you can, because businesses like to know how you performed in a work situation.

Potential employers may call or write to your references to find out more about your background and preparation for the job you seek. Before giving a potential employer the names of your references, contact them by mail, by phone, or in person for their consent, discuss your job interests and opportunities with them, and show them your resume. By giving your references this background information, you will help them speak on your behalf or write letters of recommendation that best show how you are suited for the work you seek. (See Chapter 5, pp. 185–188, on requesting and writing letters of recommendation.) If you are graduating, before you leave campus be sure to get in touch with instructors who will serve as your references.

At the end of your resume, you may state that your references are available on request; and if you have letters of recommendation on file, include the address of your college placement office. Alternatively, you can include on your resume the names of your references and full information on how to contact them—the title, organization, business address, and phone number of each reference. We recommend that you choose the first option, mentioning the availability of references but without listing them. In this way, you save space on your resume.

The accompanying checklist will help you review your resume.

CHECKLIST FOR WRITING YOUR RESUME

1. *Opening:* Have you given your
   - Name?
   - Address?
   - Phone numbers?
   - Future address and phone number (if applicable)?
2. *Job Objective:* Have you focused on
   - The level of job responsibility you seek?
   - The kind of work?
   - The industry?
3. *Education:* Have you included
   - The name of the college(s) from which you expect or have received a degree?
   - The degree or degree expected and date of graduation?
   - Area(s) of concentration?
   - Grade-point average if B or above?
   - Honors?
   - Relevant courses?
4. *Work Experience:* Have you included
   - Name and location of company?
   - Dates of employment?
   - Functional title?
   - Responsibilities?
   - Most important skills and accomplishments?

5. *Activities, Interests, Awards* (Optional): Have you included those activities, interests, and awards that show your preparation for the job you seek?
6. *Personal Background* (Optional): Have you included those aspects of your personal background that show you are qualified for the job you seek?
7. *References* (Optional): Have you included the names of people who have taught or worked with you and can recommend you for the work you are seeking? Or have you indicated that references are available on request?

Writing the Draft

Once you have decided what to include in each section of your resume, consider the overall effect you want your resume to have on a prospective employer. Go back over the information you have listed and using your job objective as the central idea you want to communicate to your reader, see what information you can highlight, what you can delete, and how you can best order the sections of your resume to create the effect you want. Then write a draft of your resume on one or at most two 8½- by 11-inch pages. Figure 14.10 shows how Michael's resume for General Mills looked after several drafts:

A CHRONOLOGICAL VERSUS FUNCTIONAL ORDERING

Michael used reverse chronological order to show his work experience. But if you are several years out of college and have had a number of jobs in diverse organizations, you may want to use a functional rather than a chronological approach. A **functional resume** groups your experience by job categories. It therefore highlights the continuity in your work experience and plays down the diversity in the jobs you have held or types of companies you have worked for.

Stuart Remington, class of 1980, chose to organize his experience by function to highlight his preparation for a management position in computer operations and com-

Figure 14.10

MICHAEL'S RESUME FOR GENERAL MILLS

Michael Eaton
17412 Margate Street
Encino, California 91316
(818) 555-3113

OBJECTIVE Entry-level marketing assistant at General Mills.
Ultimate goal: Product management.

EDUCATION **University of California, Los Angeles**   1989
B.A. Sociology with minor in Business
Relevant Courses: Speech, Business Writing, Small-Group Communication, Accounting, Marketing and Statistics. GPA 3.4

WORK EXPERIENCE **Casual Ware**   10/88 - 5/88
Westwood, CA
Retail Salesperson and Assistant Manager
Created multiple sales achieving 30% profit over last year. Managed staff of 5 sales assistants. Assisted in storewide promotions increasing sales 20% over previous five years. Coauthored marketing plan for store expansion.

Le Chateau Hotel   7/88 - 9/88
Los Angeles, CA
Waiter
Served at table restaurant with world-famous chef Pierre Girard. Planned 7 dinner parties for 30 to 50 people at $50/person.

State of California, Huntington State Beach   7/87 - 8/87
Huntington, CA
Ocean Lifeguard
Responsible for 500 swimmers. Enforced state safety laws.

Basketball Team   9/85 - 6/87
University of California, Los Angeles
Head Manager
Coordinated over 400 meals with restaurant managers. Ordered and maintained athletic equipment. Managed $3,000 budget for on-the-road expenses. Developed leadership skills by supervising staff.

ACTIVITIES Sigma Chi Fraternity, Assistant Rush Chairman.
Undergraduate Business Society.

PERSONAL Self-taught gourmet cook. Paid for half of my college education.

REFERENCES Available on request.

puter planning. Compare his functional resume (Figure 14.11) to the chronological resume that he might have used (Figure 14.12)? Can you see why a functional approach is better in Stuart's case?

In Figure 14.11 Stuart consolidates the information he wants to convey to prospective employees by presenting his experience according to categories (computer operations, computer systems planning, personnel supervision) that transcend specific industries. He thus shows how his work experience prepares him for a position in computing, regardless of industry. (His education appears at the bottom of his resume because education is less relevant than experience to the positions he is applying for.) In Figure 14.12, the chronological resume that Stuart does not use obscures his technical preparation for work in computing because of the variety of companies, industries, and job titles. His experience in computing comes across as a hodge-podge of unrelated activities and these activities, not the range and consistency of his computing work, will be foremost in the minds of potential employers reviewing his resume.

Resumes are so important that students often ask instructors or experienced business people to review them.

Figure 14.11

STUART'S FUNCTIONAL RESUME

STUART REMINGTON
834 F St. Charles Ave. NE
Atlanta, Georgia 30306
(h) 404-555-5490
(w) 404-555-3227

OBJECTIVE: A management position in computer operations and computer systems planning.

EXPERIENCE:

Computer Operations
Scheduled jobs to be run. Responsible for computer maintenance. Coordinated with computer repair people, sales, and service organizations. Designed efficient means of scheduling batch processing, which reduced clerical personnel by 20%.

Computer Systems Planning
Determined requirements for new computer system. Supervised computer installation. Gathered product information from computer vendors. Recommended new systems to top management.

Personnel Supervision
Supervised computer staff of 20. Scheduled and conducted training seminars in computer operations: rated in top 5% of trainers.

EMPLOYERS:
New South Bank Atlanta, Georgia	1987 - present
Blue Cross Washington, D.C.	1985 - 1987
U.S. Navy Bureau of Personnel Washington, D.C.	1983 - 1985

EDUCATION: Georgia Technological Institute
B.S., Industrial Management.
June 1983.

ACTIVITIES: Coordinator, internship program for 10 college students, New South Bank. Adviser in data processing, local Chamber of Commerce.

REFERENCES: Furnished upon request.

Figure 14.12

STUART'S CHRONOLOGICAL RESUME

STUART REMINGTON
834 F St. Charles Ave. NE
Atlanta, Georgia 30306
(h) 404-555-5490
(w) 404-555-3227

CAREER OBJECTIVE A management position in computer operations and computer systems planning.

WORK EXPERIENCE

New South Bank   1987 - present
Atlanta, Georgia

Assistant Manager of Data Processing Operations. Determined requirements for new computer system for automated teller windows. Supervised computer staff of 20. Recommended new computer systems to top management for processing checks and maintaining other financial records. Scheduled and conducted training seminars in computer operations: rated in top 5% of trainers.

Blue Cross   1985 - 1987
Washington, D.C.

Computer Facilities Section Head. Scheduled computer jobs to be run. Designed efficient means of scheduling batch processing, which reduced clerical personnel by 20%. Recommended to top management new computer systems for storing health insurance records.

U.S. Navy Bureau of Personnel   1983 - 1985
Washington, D.C.

Lt (jg). Responsible for computer maintenance. Coordinated with computer repair people, sales, and service organizations. Supervised computer installation. Gathered product information from computer vendors.

EDUCATION Georgia Technological Institute   June 1983
B.S., Industrial Management

ACTIVITIES Coordinator, internship program for 10 college students, New South Bank. Adviser in data processing, local Chamber of Commerce.

REFERENCES Available upon request.

The Appearance and Format of Resumes

All resumes share a number of features:

1. They are typed or professionally printed on good-quality 8½- by 11-inch paper in a typeface that is easy to read.
2. They are preferably one page but no more than two pages.
3. They use white space, capitalization, indenting, underscoring (or italicizing and boldface, if available) to emphasize the key points.
4. They use short, concrete phrases and action verbs.

As long as you keep these principles in mind, you can use a variety of formats for your resumes. We recommend that you experiment with format until you find the one that best highlights your job preparation. Figures 14.13 and 14.14 illustrate different formats.

Revising

As with most business communications, the first draft of your resume will not be your final one. To review your resume, you can use the two techniques we recommend for revising any business communication:

1. *Have a friend, associate, or instructor read your draft.* Ask someone experienced in reading resumes to review a draft of yours. Give your reader relevant information about the work you are seeking (e.g., the ad, the section of a company brochure, notes you have taken from interviews with company contacts and from reviews of relevant literature).
2. *Role-play the reader of your resume.* Go over your resume, imagining that you are your potential employer, and ask yourself whether the reader will be interested enough to go further with your application. To review your resume, ask yourself the questions in Figure 14.15.

As you review your resume, try to avoid the following common errors:

1. *Including irrelevant information.* Some job candidates think their resumes should be as complete as an autobiography. It is as though they are telling the employer, "Here's everything I've done. You make something of it." This strategy does not work. A summer at camp or piano lessons may be personally important, but they generally have no place in a resume. Irrelevant information creates clutter, forcing your reader—if he or she still remains interested—to ferret out those elements of your background

Figure 14.13

SAMPLE RESUME 1

LISA G. HAMILTON 5869 Chariton Ave.
Los Angeles, California 90056
(213) 555-2633

OBJECTIVE: Entry-level management position in a progressive toy and hobby store with an opportunity to advance to upper management.

EDUCATION: University of California, Los Angeles
B.A. Economics, June 1990

Course work includes: Statistics, Accounting, Pascal Computer Language, Mathematics, Social Science, Business Writing.

EXPERIENCE: <u>Leadperson</u>   8/87 - present
Karl's Toys
Culver City, California

- Learned how to operate a retail store and the management techniques required to run the store in the absence of management.
- Mastered merchandising techniques, inventory control, and paperwork.
- Trained 10 college interns in customer relations.

<u>Cook</u>, <u>Cashier</u>, <u>Leadperson</u>   2/84 - 1/87
Round Table Pizza
Culver City, California

- Became familiar with operations of a fast-food restaurant.
- Learned financial responsibilities of restaurant management.

<u>Cashier</u>, <u>Salesperson</u>   8/82 - 2/84
Fabrics & Fashion
Inglewood, California

- Gained retail experience, including knowledge of fabric department, inventory control, and public relations.

SKILLS: Bookkeeping and word processing.

REFERENCES: Will be furnished on request.

Figure 14.14

SAMPLE RESUME 2

Diane Mullen
6637 Rhodes Avenue, #1
North Hollywood, CA 91606
(818) 555-9030

CAREER OBJECTIVE   A position in animation with special emphasis on program development and creative affairs.

EDUCATION   **University of Southern California**
B. A. History with minor in Business, June 1989

EMPLOYMENT   January 1989 – Present   **Marvel Productions**
Los Angeles, CA

Assisted in program development and creative affairs. Reviewed submissions, production videotapes, artwork. Assisted "voice-over" department with audition and recording sessions.

September 1988 – January 1989   **Marcucci Productions**
Los Angeles, CA

Responsible for collating and submitting daily actor job sheets. Reviewed literary materials, scripts, films and videotapes.

RELATED SKILLS   Knowledge of Pascal and Basic computer languages.

REFERENCES   Available on request

that qualify you for the job. Make your reader's work easy. Keep your resume short and targeted to a specific job by weeding out what is irrelevant and by focusing on skills and accomplishments that make you a desirable candidate.

2. *Giving vague descriptions of your job objective, work experience, or personal data*. Avoid vague descriptions—such as this one drawn from an early draft of one student's resume:

ORIGINAL:

    CAREER OBJECTIVE: To gain practical experience in various aspects of the banking industry

An employer would not know where to place this student. The "career objective" could pertain to almost any position with the bank. Notice how the revision specifies the student's interest:

REVISION:

    CAREER OBJECTIVE: A management trainee position in the marketing division of a bank

3. *Including information that eliminates you from consideration*. Do not include information that may eliminate you from consideration, such as specific salary requirements, desired geographic location, political party, or religious affiliation. You are better off not applying for a job that does not meet your minimal requirements. Once you decide to apply for a position, remove anything from your resume that will exclude you from consideration.

4. *Sloppy appearance*. A job applicant will not receive serious attention if his or her resume contains spelling and grammatical errors, is poorly reproduced, or is poorly designed (e.g., poor format, and lack of underlining, capitalization, or boldface to set off important information). Lack of attention to the appearance of a resume communicates to employers that a job applicant is careless with details, writes poorly, and does not take the job search seriously. Spend the time and money to ensure that your resume looks professional.

THE SEARCH

Once you have completed your self-assessment, initial research, and resume preparation, you will be ready to look for specific job positions. In the early weeks of February, one month after the winter quarter began and after he had determined his career objectives and drafted a resume, Michael launched his search by looking through want ads and researching companies.

Want Ads

Although many openings are not advertised, it pays to look at want ads in major newspapers and trade journals. Not only will you learn which companies and industries are seeking new employees, but you will also get a sense of the extent to which your skills are in demand. To find want ads, look at the classified and business sections of the Sunday edition of major newspapers, special weekly editions of newspapers that publish only during the week, and job listings of trade journals.

Since Michael was not restricting his job search geographically, he reviewed the following publications:

- Sunday sections of several major metropolitan newspapers (*Boston Globe, New York Times, Los Angeles Times, Chicago Tribune,* and *Washington Post*)
- The Tuesday Job Mart ads for all regional editions of the *Wall Street Journal*
- Advertisements in several marketing and advertising journals (*Ad Week* and *Ad Age*)

For each publication, he first skimmed the job classification section to see how jobs were listed. Then within the relevant sections, he reviewed each ad carefully to see whether his qualifications and interests matched the job description. Michael answered the Red Onion ad (see p. 696) because the position it described matched his skills, background, and interests.

Figure 14.15

QUESTIONS TO CONSIDER IN REVIEWING YOUR RESUME

- Is the job objective tailored to the position you are applying for?
- Does each section highlight your qualifications for the job?
- Is the resume succinct? Could anything be omitted?
- Should anything be added?
- Do entries use action verbs and give quantifiable results?
- Does the appearance (e.g., use of white space, boldface, italics, underlining, etc.) contribute to the overall effect?
- Has the resume been carefully proofread for correct grammar, spelling, punctuation, and usage?
- If you were the employer, would you interview the job candidate whose resume you are reading? Why? Why not?

In choosing ads to respond to, use the following criteria:

1. The ad should describe a specific job, including job responsibilities and the candidate's qualifications. The Red Onion ad specified that the company sought a person to fill a field marketing position and required the candidate to have one or two years of marketing experience with an agency or restaurant.
2. Your skills, background, and interests should match the job qualifications (but see the second item in Figure 14.16). For the most part Michael's did. (Although he did not have a full year's marketing experience, he had several summers' worth, as well as experience working in a restaurant.)
3. The ad should give the company's name and address or a box number. When companies use box numbers instead of giving their names, it is usually because they do not want to be bothered by follow-up phone calls from interested candidates. In most cases, these ads are legitimate.

The Employment Management Association, a nonprofit educational organization made up of personnel executives, offers some further suggestions for responding to want ads. They are shown in Figure 14.16.

Figure 14.16
SUGGESTIONS FOR RESPONDING TO WANT ADS

- Don't hesitate to answer ads placed by companies to which you might have responded earlier. Many firms do not have tracking systems, and those that do such filing are not infallible. A "No Interest" letter does not mean that you are rejected forever.
- Look for companies that are running large ads or doing considerable hiring. Even though your qualifications do not match those jobs being featured, there might be other positions available. Employers do not publicize all of their openings in one ad.
- Become aware of ads by firms which are expanding or moving into an area. There might be plans to hire someone with your background at a later date. These staffing plans might be advanced if the employer learns that such an individual is currently available.
- Watch for ads placed by companies that employ friends or acquaintances. A recommendation by an employee can help you greatly.

Source: Overlooking Help Wanted Ads Costly to Many Job Hunters,"
Employment Management Association (October 4, 1982): 2.

Research on Specific Companies

Earlier, in your exploratory research, you may have come upon companies and specific positions that interested you. Now is the time to focus your research on such companies and positions in order to determine which opportunities are most desirable.

To make an informed judgment about a company that interests you, gather information about the company's

- History
- Financial stability
- Growth possibilities
- Goals
- Geographic locations
- Size and position in the industry (or industries)
- Employment record (salaries, opportunities for promotion, benefits, training, etc.)
- Responses to social, economic, or political trends that may affect it

Knowing these characteristics, along with the criteria you consider important in assessing a prospective job, will help you sort out the companies that are most desirable to work for. For instance, if you are looking for a company that is expanding into the "high-tech" industry and you find that this is a primary goal of a firm you are researching, this firm may be particularly appealing to you. Or if a firm's location, size, and record of promotion from within are especially important to you, you can assess which among several firms are strongest in these categories. Such information will also help you to write your letters of application and to prepare for interviews, since companies are attracted to informed job candidates.

To gather information about specific companies, check the annual reports and career brochures at your career placement center, as well as publications and directories available at the library. Companies owned by shareholders usually produce annual reports, and if the companies recruit at school, they often provide the placement office with annual reports and other literature such as company newsletters. Other sources of information include the *Business Periodicals Index* and the *Wall Street Journal Index*. They list articles on recent company issues. Figure 14.17 lists publications that also provide information on specific companies.

Michael got a copy of General Mills's annual report. He also found several pieces in the *Wall Street Journal* and a *Business Week* article on General Mills that he felt might be relevant to his job campaign. For information on General Mills, Michael checked, among other publications, both the *Career Employment Opportunities Directory* and *The Almanac of American Employers* (see Figures 14.18 and 14.19).

Figure 14.17

PUBLICATIONS THAT PROVIDE INFORMATION
ON SPECIFIC COMPANIES

The Almanac of American Employers. Provides name of company, location, type of businesses, number of employees, sales and earnings, average monthly salaries, benefit plans. Gives information about financial stability and room for promotion.

Career Employment Opportunities Directory, 4 volumes. Vol. 1 for graduates in liberal arts and social sciences, vol. 2 for graduates in business administration, vol. 3 for graduates in engineering and computer sciences, vol. 4 for graduates in the sciences. Discusses career opportunities, special programs, and benefits at major companies; identifies people to contact.

College Placement Annual. Gives addresses and names people to contact at almost 2,000 organizations.

The College Placement Directory. Describes around 1,500 firms (including addresses) and kinds of employees they are looking for.

Million Dollar Directory, 4 volumes. Classifies alphabetically, geographically, and by industry 160,000 companies with a net worth of over $500,000. One volume, the "Top 50,000 Companies" looks at companies with a net worth exceeding $1,850,000.

Standard and Poor's Register of Corporations, Directories, and Executives. Gives for approximately 45,000 companies their addresses, phone numbers, names and titles of executives, division names and functions, descriptions of products and services, number of employees, and financial information. Gives names, affiliations, and titles of approximately 72,000 executives.

Thomas Register. 19 volumes. Lists names of companies, phone numbers, and addresses by products and services. Gives company profiles listed alphabetically by company and includes branch locations, assets ratings, company officials, and brand names.

Figure 14.18

SELECTION FROM *THE ALMANAC OF AMERICAN EMPLOYERS*

GENERAL MILLS INC

PO Box 1113, 9200 Wayzata Boulevard
Minneapolis, MN 55440 **TOTAL POINTS EARNED:** 834.70
(612) 540-2311 **OVERALL RANK:** 114

Locations:
  National: Nationwide
  International: Worldwide
Type of Business: Diversified manufacturer of grocery products, with additional operations in toys, restaurants, and fashion and specialty retailing. Selected brand names include Red Lobster, York Steak House, Parker Brothers, Betty Crocker, Gorton's, Izod, Ship 'n Shore, Monet, Eddie Bauer.

	Rank
Number of Employees: 81,186	44
Sales: $5,550.80 million	91
Earnings: $245.10 million	117

SALARIES/BENEFITS

	Points
Average monthly starting pay, college grads (est.):	
nontechnical: $1,798	89.91
technical: $2,302	115.08
Defined benefit pension?	50.00
Annual pension for a 35-year, $200,000 recent annual earnings employee: $100,000 (est.)	
Stock ownership plan?	50.00
Thrift plan?	0.00
The company's proxy statement refers to a "savings plan," but does not elaborate on it.	
Discount stock purchase plan?	0.00
Profit-sharing plan?	0.00
Salaries/Benefits Total:	**304.99**
Rank:	**296**

FINANCIAL STABILITY

	Points
Years profitable: 5	100.00
Earnings retained: 62.18%	31.09
Long-term debt: 37.80%	42.20
Average return on equity: 18.48%	184.78
Increase in sales: 48.22%	48.22
Increase in earnings: 66.73%	83.42
Comments: Financial data is for the years 1978–1982.	
Financial Stability Total:	**489.71**
Rank:	**130**

(continued)

(SELECTION FROM *THE ALMANAC OF AMERICAN EMPLOYERS* continued)

ROOM AT THE TOP	Points
Cash bonus plan for key execs?	10.00
Stock options or SARs?	10.00
Approximate common stock held by control family directors, officers, and others: 0%	20.00
Comments: Cash and equivalents paid to the two highest-paid execs:	
1. $834,270	
2. $591,427	
Total: $1,425,697	
Room at the Top Total:	**40.00**

OTHER CONSIDERATIONS

   A highly regarded company with a very good long-term record of profitable growth.

   General Mills donated $8.3 million to charitable causes in 1983.

   Ask for the company's brochure, "Change and Continuity: The General Mills Story."

   Employment increased by 10,000 from 1981 to 1983.

   16% of the work force are minorities. There is a black woman on the board of directors. 54% of the work force are women.

FOOD FOR THOUGHT

12 paid holidays • 10 days vacation after 1 year, 11 days after 2, 17 days after 5, 22 days after 14 • Insurance includes medical, disability, and dental • Free life insurance equals 100% of salary • Promote-from-within policy • Tuition reimbursement plan • Minneapolis headquarters employees enjoy an apple orchard, ponds, forests, an employee store, and an employee auto service center on the grounds

Reprinted from the Almanac of American Employers © 1985 by Jack W. Plunkett, with permission of Contemporary Books, Inc., Chicago.

Business Contacts

You may have talked to business contacts as part of your exploratory research. During the job search, you may want to go back to some of those you spoke to earlier and ask about openings in their company or in other organizations. At this point, you can be specific about the kind of work you are looking for.

Figure 14.19

SELECTION FROM *CAREER EMPLOYMENT OPPORTUNITIES DIRECTORY*

General Mills Restaurant Group

General Information:
The General Mills Restaurant Group is composed of diverse restaurant companies (Red Lobster Inns, York Steak House, Casa Gallardo, Darryl's, and The Good Earth) as well as two organizations that help support growth: a seafood procurement and distribution company as well as SigmaCon, a full-service construction company that designs, builds, and equips the restaurants. The Restaurant Group employs more than 38,000 people nationwide with more than 500 restaurants in operation coast to coast.

Career Opportunities:
The General Mills Restaurant Group offers career opportunities for qualified graduates in a variety of areas. The Restaurant Group maintains three major divisions to which graduates may become associated: Operations, Marketing, Finance and Control as well as career areas in Management Information Services, Menu Planning, Purchasing, and Quality Control.

Graduates on the operations team are the link between the final product and the guests. As management trainees, they receive a comprehensive training program with additional responsibilities available in management levels to general management positions with salary increases according to advancement. Advancement to general manager normally takes from one and a half to three years. Operations employees come from a broad variety of educational backgrounds but graduates in business administration, accounting, and related fields are especially desirable.

The Marketing team identifies the customer base, determines their needs and desires, interfaces with other departments to ensure total product satisfaction, and maintains and develops demand through increased customer awareness and understanding. A graduate degree in business administration combined with a thorough knowledge of business principles combined with effective communications and human relations skills is a requirement for the successful marketing manager. Individuals with a solid marketing background may become involved in such key areas as marketing research, marketing planning, regional marketing, and advertising.

The Finance & Control team focuses on a management philosophy that includes strict financial controls and strong financial planning to help assure continued growth and stability. Financial managers provide input regarding sales forecasts, pricing structures, accounting procedures, budget planning, and capitalization requirements. Major departmental areas include Corporate Planning, Investment Analysis, Operations, and Corporate Accounting, and Operations Analysis. Assignments may include such projects as exploring alternative restaurant expansion strategies, evaluating new restaurant site and construction proposals, measuring the financial impact of projected menu changes, or analyzing restaurant capacities from a financial viewpoint. A helpful background for a career in Finance & Control would be a degree in business administration with interests in accounting, marketing, and/or operations analysis.

Graduates may find employment in other career areas such as Menu Planning and Purchasing where graduates in hotel and restaurant administration or business administration as well as other related fields would be an asset.

Special Programs:
The General Mills Restaurant Group provides an educational gift matching program with reimbursed tuition and fees upon completion of coursework related to present or future job responsibility and a relocation reimbursement program.

Location of Employment:
The General Mills Restaurant Group has headquarters in Orlando, Florida, but there are headquarters and regional offices for the individual restaurants coast to coast.

Benefits:
The compensation package includes a comprehensive employee benefits program. The employee becomes eligible for most benefits on the first day of employment. The package covers: medical and dental insurance, long-term disability insurance, life insurance, accidental death and dismemberment insurance, survivor income benefits, profit sharing & savings plan, and a retirement plan providing a monthly retirement income in addition to Social Security.

For Further Information:
Contact the Director of Personnel at the appropriate company:
Red Lobster Inns of America
6770 Lake Ellenor Drive
Orlando, Florida 32809

York Steak House Systems, Inc.
2255 Kimberly Parkway East
Columbus, Ohio 43227

Casa Gallardo Restaurants
1009 Executive Parkway Drive
St. Louis, Missouri 63141

Darryl's Restaurants
2209 Century Drive, Suite 400
Raleigh, North Carolina 27612

General Mills Restaurant Group, Inc.
P.O. Box 1431
Orlando, Florida 32802

The Good Earth Restaurants
800 Trafalgar Court, Suite 380
Maitland, Florida 32751

SigmaCon
8100 Presidents Drive
Orlando, Florida 32809

The accompanying checklist will help you review your job search efforts.

CHECKLIST FOR REVIEWING JOB SEARCH EFFORTS

1. *Want Ads:*
   - Are you looking at want ads in major newspapers and trade journals?
   - Are you responding to ads that
     - Describe a specific job?
     - Describe a job for which your skills, background, and interests match the job's qualifications?
     - Give the company's name and address or a box number to reply to?
2. *Research on Specific Companies:* Have you gathered information about the company's
   - History?
   - Financial stability?
   - Growth possibilities?
   - Goals?
   - Geographic location?
   - Size and position in the industry?
   - Employment record?
   - Response to social, economic, or political trends affecting it?
3. *Business Contacts:* Have you contacted business people you know about openings in their companies or in other organizations?

LETTERS OF APPLICATION

Once you have decided that a company or a job might be for you, write the letter of application. There are two kinds of letters, solicited and unsolicited. A **solicited letter** is sent in response to a specific job opening. An **unsolicited letter** is sent to a company that interests you but has not advertised.

Whether solicited or unsolicited, all your letters of application should be sales letters. The "product" you are selling in this case is yourself—your skills and experience as they meet a company's needs.

The Solicited Letter

Consider these activities of the writing process as you put together a solicited letter.

SETTING THE GOAL AND ASSESSING THE READER

Since your goal is to gain an interview, appeal to the reader by first determining your potential employer's specific needs and then how you can fill them. If you are responding to an ad, a good way to determine the company's needs is to make a list of key words in the ad that either pinpoint these needs or identify the kinds of qualifications expected of the job candidate. Figure 14.20 shows how Michael used this approach to respond to The Red Onion ad he found in *Ad Week*. The ad specified these qualifications: someone to do local marketing plans and local promotion planning, with 1–2 years of marketing experience, with knowledge of the restaurant industry, and with energy and self-motivation.

Figure 14.20

MATCHING YOUR SKILLS WITH THE COMPANY'S NEEDS

Company Looking For	My Qualifications
— Local marketing plans	Helped plan store expansion
— Local promotion planning	Assisted in storewide promotions — profits up 20% Educational experience allowed me to write promotions and help in planning
— 1–2 year's marketing experience	At Casual Ware
— knowledge of restaurant industry	At Le Chateau and as manager of UCLA basketball
— Energy and self-motivation	Worked while attending college, maintained high average; lifeguard competition

GATHERING INFORMATION AND GENERATING IDEAS

To decide what to include as your central selling points, identify the key words in the ad that suggest the company's needs and the candidate's expected qualifications, and answer the following questions:

- What skills and experience is the company looking for?
- How can you fulfill their needs?

Michael reviewed his resume and notes from his self-assessment to determine his qualifications for the job. He placed these to the right of the list of qualifications the company was looking for (see Figure 14.20).

ORGANIZING

To organize your letter, pinpoint one or two selling points around which to build your appeal by reviewing the list of qualifications the company is looking for and your qualifications. Then use the RTA formula to organize your letter. In reviewing his list (Figure 14.20), Michael decided that his work and education qualified him for the job at The Red Onion. He then used the RTA formula to organize his letter.

Establish Rapport: To establish rapport,

- Identify the publication in which the ad appeared (if you are responding to an ad).
- Address the letter to a specific person. (If only the company's name is given in the ad, phone the company to see if you can get the name of the person or persons who had the ad listed.)
- Identify the position you are applying for.
- Mention your central selling points (i.e., qualifications for the job).

Michael began his letter to Red Onion in this way:

                                                    17412 Margate Street,
                                                    Encino, California 91316
                                                    March 6, 199_

Dear Mr. Fernandez:

    This morning's <u>Ad Week</u> carried your ad for "marketing professionals to work . . . on local marketing plans with focus on local promotions planning." Both my work experience and my educational background prepare me well for the position.

Notice that in his opening paragraph, Michael named the source in which the ad appeared, the position he was applying for, and his central selling point—that his work and education make him a desirable candidate.

Here are several other openings that identify the publication where the ad appeared, a specific addressee involved in the hiring process, the position the job candidate is applying for, and the applicant's central selling point:

Dear Mr. Lyons:

    Because of my work experience and coursework in economics, I can be the economic forecaster you advertised for in Sunday's <u>Baltimore Sun</u>.

Dear Ms. Booth:

    A degree in computer science and two years of work in a university computer center qualify me to become your data processing center's assistant manager, a position you advertised in June's <u>Office Management</u>.

Influence Thinking: To influence thinking, develop your central selling points by showing how they will enable you to benefit the company. Remember, too, that although you will be referring to the past (your previous accomplishments, experience, and education), your letter should be forward-looking to demonstrate how what you have done will serve the company in the future. Also if you are responding to an ad, make sure that you have addressed the key points in the ad.

In the body of his letter, Michael presented facts to show that his selling points—his work experience and educational background—would enable him to contribute to Red Onion's future efforts as advertised:

    In the past year as a salesperson and assistant manager at a retail clothing store, I assisted in storewide promotions that brought in a 20 percent profit over the previous five years. I also co-planned a successful store expansion that identified and capitalized on our increasing customer base. In addition, my coursework emphasizing research, writing, and speaking has prepared me for the analysis and communications work essential to all successful marketing efforts.
    I also have first-hand experience in the restaurant industry and have seen it from two perspectives. As a waiter at Le Chateau restaurant, I learned the essentials of customer service and of planning for large business amd social parties. Then as manager for UCLA's basketball team, I worked with the staff of over fifty restaurants nationwide, planning meals for our team on the road. This gave me valuable lessons in the competitive approaches restaurants can take in serving their customers.
    Besides the experience and education, I have the energy and self-

motivation to be your marketing professional. My successful competition as a swimmer for a lifeguard position, as well as my working part-time to pay half of my college education while maintaining a 3.4 grade point average, demonstrates that I thrive in challenging and competitive situations.

Notice in the next two examples how the job applicants develop their central selling points. In the first example, the applicant wants to show how his work experience and education prepare him for a position as an economic forecaster, a job requiring a strong applied research background and high grades.

> I have had considerable experience applying economic theory to practice during the past two summers. As a research assistant for the Rand Corporation, I worked on a study of employment trends in energy industries, using statistical packages to analyze data. I attended all project meetings, fully understood the rationales for all project decisions, and assisted the project manager in the production of the final report.
>
> Besides my work experience, I have completed a comprehensive program in macroeconomics with a GPA in my major of 3.4. I feel especially prepared and eager to contribute to your research on the environmental impact of diverse energy sources, since my senior thesis involved several research techniques that are useful to economic forecasting on energy issues.

In the next example, the job candidate demonstrates how his coursework and work experience prepare him to become an assistant manager for a data processing center.

> I have the technical knowledge and the ability to work with people essential to an assistant manager of data processing. As a computer science major at Michigan Technological University, I studied how to <u>manage</u> information systems, as well as the systems themselves. My senior thesis required me to demonstrate both capabilities. It involved developing a training manual and a workshop to teach undergraduate business majors how to use spreadsheet and database management packages.
>
> Working in the computer center at the university gave me experience in communicating technical information to people of varying abilities and needs. Because most of the students were interested in computer applications and not in the technology, I successfully devised ways to communicate how the various packages could assist them.

With my formal training and work experience, I am confident that I
can meet the technical and interpersonal demands of the position you
seek to fill.

Motivate Action and Attitude: To conclude your letter, ask for a specific action that will advance your application at the company. You may also want to reinforce your reader's positive attitude toward your application by emphasizing the benefits you bring to the company. Consider Michael's conclusion:

As my resume shows, I have been motivated and effective, both as an
employee and as a student. I would like to have the opportunity to apply
my abilities and experience to a full-time position with you. Will you
please call me to discuss the possibility of my working for you.

In the example that follows, the candidate decided to take the initiative by stating that he would call the company for an appointment:

The enclosed resume provides further information about my
background. I will call you on June 15 to see if a meeting can be arranged
to discuss the position you advertise.

In the next example, the job candidate decided to include his current and future phone numbers on the letter, so that the company representative would have no trouble reaching him when he moved:

Please let me know when we can discuss the opening in your finance
division. I can be reached before 5 P.M. any weekday at 205–555–5470 until
June 1, or after 6 P.M. and on weekends at 205–555–1442 after June 1.

The Unsolicited Letter

When you do research on specific companies, you may come across companies that interest you but that are not advertising openings at this time. You may then want to write an **unsolicited letter**—a letter requesting an interview from a company that has not advertised for job applicants.

Even if it has no openings, a company will routinely receive and even welcome unsolicited letters to save time and advertising costs and to build a pool of applicants to choose from when a position does become available. Or, a company may have an unadvertised opening, usually filled by the company's employees or through personal contacts. In this case a well-written unsolicited letter can bring a strong candidate's qualifications to the company's attention. And finally, although this is rare, companies have been known to create a job on the basis of a good letter and résumé.

Writing an unsolicited letter is very similar to writing a solicited letter except for the opening.

Establish Rapport: Since the potential employer has not actively sought letters of application, the opening of your letter must motivate him or her to read on. There are three ways to open an unsolicited letter:

1. *Refer to a pertinent publication.* Information about a company's current situation that you find in a magazine, newspaper, or company publication may provide you with a subject you can use to spur your reader's interest. In the opening of his letter to General Mills, Michael used an article about that company to get his reader interested in his application:

> According to a feature story in the December 23 issue of <u>Business Week</u>, General Mills is planning to reach a goal of 6 percent annual growth by promoting its packaged food and restaurant divisions. With my background and interests in both of these industries, I am prepared to help you reach these goals by serving as an entry-level marketing representative.

Michael presents himself as both knowledgeable about the company's situation and capable of contributing to its new goals. His research efforts and his ability to show the fit between the company's needs and his background would certainly encourage the reader to look closely at his application.

2. *Present those of your qualifications that would benefit the company most.* Stating immediately the abilities and background you can bring to meet a company's needs is likely to gain your reader's interest. For instance, Michael could have opened his letter to General Mills in this way:

> Are you looking for someone with experience in the food and restaurant industry who is interested in marketing your Big G cereals or Red Lobster Inn Restaurants? If so, you will find that I have the qualifications to meet your needs.

3. *Refer to a mutual business acquaintance.* Referring to a mutual business acquaintance can cause your reader to pay attention to your letter, if the business acquaintance is someone the reader has confidence in. Michael could have begun his letter to General Mills by mentioning the name of a General Mills representative who had spoken at a meeting of his business club.

Last month Dan McCally, one of your college representatives, spoke to the UCLA Marketing Club about career opportunities in marketing at General Mills. His discussion of General Mills' marketing emphasis leads me to think my skills and experience would enable me to contribute to your marketing division.

Influence Thinking: As in the solicited letter, present information to show that you can assist the company and to demonstrate your knowledge of what the company needs. However, since you are not responding to an advertised job description, first be explicit about the kind of position you seek. Michael organized the body of his letter to General Mills by first naming the kind of position he was interested in, then demonstrating how he was qualified for such a position.

My work experience and educational background demonstrate that I can be the energetic, consumer-oriented marketing professional General Mills has relied on for its success. As a salesperson and assistant manager for a retail clothing store, I sold the full product mix and assisted management in sales promotions and in expansion of the store. Our quarterly promotions resulted in a 20 percent increase in sales over the previous four years. As an assistant manager, I also trained a team of five sales assistants in customer service.

In working with restaurants, I also learned the value of high-quality food, good customer relations, and effective restaurant management—values that General Mills is known to represent. As a waiter for an exclusive restaurant, I saw how the high-quality food and good customer relations led directly to the growth of the business. As manager for the UCLA basketball team, I dealt with the management of over fifty restaurants in coordinating the team's meals and learned valuable lessons for managing in the competitive restaurant business.

Through coursework in business and in sociology, I have also acquired the research, organization, and communication skills necessary for contributing to your product management groups. Business courses provided me with conceptual tools for analyzing the kinds of business problems in sales and accounting that marketing managers often face. Also, as a sociology major, I learned how to analyze and organize data and to present information clearly and convincingly—skills I used in coauthoring a marketing plan for the retail store I worked for.

Motivate Action and Attitude: To ensure your reader's interest in your application and to motivate him or her to follow up, close on a courteous note, perhaps referring to an outstanding quality of the company, and request a specific action from the reader. In closing Michael complimented General Mills on its reputation and courteously requested a response:

> General Mills has an international reputation for high-quality consumer products. I would like to contribute my energy and skills to your winning team. Please consider me for an entry-level marketing position. Would you write to me at the address shown above to discuss how I might best assist you in your marketing efforts.

Revising Letters of Application

In revising your letters of application, watch out for several commonly made errors:

1. *Emphasizing your needs rather than the company's.* The letters of some job candidates are too self-centered. Such letters focus on how the job candidate hopes to benefit from the job, rather than on how his or her skills and experience can assist the company. Companies respond best to letters that show what the job candidate can do for the company rather than what the company can do for the candidate. Make sure that your letters are reader-oriented: Demonstrate how your background prepares you to benefit the company in the position you are applying for.

2. *Being vague.* Vague statements tell the reader practically nothing about the candidate. Avoid such statements as "I was an assistant at Crocker Bank," or "I worked as a manager at Lockheed." Instead, give specific information about your experience: "I was an assistant credit officer at Crocker Bank" or "I managed a small research and development proposal at Lockheed."

3. *Making unsupported statements.* Avoid making general statements about your experience without backing them up with evidence. For example:

ORIGINAL

> I feel I will make a successful junior tax accountant and am highly motivated to do this work.

Beyond the candidate's personal belief, what evidence is there that he or she will succeed? The letter needs information to back up the assertion:

REVISION

> Coursework in tax accounting and financial planning prepare me to be the junior tax accountant you are seeking.

4. *Retelling the resume.* Some application letters merely repeat the facts presented in the resume. Such letters overemphasize past performance and training. Instead, your letters should be future-oriented. They should show how your past experience prepares you for the job opening.

5. *Omitting important details.* Application letters need to include all relevant information. To ensure that your letters are complete, ask yourself the following questions:

- Have you addressed a specific person in the company?
- Have you included the name of the company, the position sought, and the date you are available?
- Have you discussed the key qualifications you offer the company?
- Have you included an easy way to get in touch with you?

6. *Using an inappropriate tone.* The tone of an application can undermine it. Some letters sound overly humble or apologetic, emphasizing the candidate's deficiencies:

> Although my senior thesis doesn't directly relate to economic forecasting, I feel that the thesis has at least some connection to the economics of health organizations.

> I have not taken formal courses in computing, but I think I have a good aptitude for programing.

Other letters err in the opposite direction by sounding arrogant or overblown:

> You made a mistake when you ignored my application the first time I applied.

> I have made financial planning the center of my life.

> There is an extraordinarily strong fit between my skills and the qualifications you seek.

In writing letters of application, try to establish a tone of confidence based on information that demonstrates your qualifications.

The accompanying checklist can help you review your letters of application.

CHECKLIST FOR WRITING LETTERS OF APPLICATION

1. For the solicited letter:
   - Have you appealed to the employer by first determining his or her specific needs and then by showing how you can fill them?
   - To decide what to include as your central selling points, have you identified key words in the ad that suggest the company's needs and the candidate's expected qualifications?
   - To organize, have you pinpointed one or two selling points around which to build your appeal, and used the RTA formula?
2. For the unsolicited letter of application:
   - Have you used one of the following openings:
     — Referring to a pertinent publication?
     — Presenting your strongest qualifications that would benefit the company?
     — Referring to a mutual business acquaintance?
   - Have you organized the rest of the unsolicited letter as you would a solicited letter?
3. In reviewing letters of application, have you:
   - Emphasized what you can do for the company rather than what the company can do for you?
   - Been specific in giving information about your experience?
   - Supported general statements about your experience with evidence?
   - Avoided retelling the resume by emphasizing how your past experience prepares you for the future?
   - Used a tone that is neither apologetic nor arrogant?

THE JOB INTERVIEW

The job interview is your chance to show a company why you are the best person for the job. At the same time, the interview gives you the opportunity to learn whether the job is right for you. As with all significant speaking activities, you will want to plan for the interview and to rehearse. Then you will know fairly well what to expect at the interview.

Planning for the Job Interview

All of the homework you have done thus far for your job search will serve you well as you prepare for job interviews. By doing a self-assessment and preparing resumes and letters of application, you know what you can offer a company. By doing research on specific companies, industries, and fields, you have some idea of the companies you would like to work for, and you can present yourself as an informed job candidate.

Your major task in planning for a *specific* interview, then, is to apply your research on yourself, the company, the industry, and the field to the interview situation so that you will be able to come across well and learn what you need to know about the job and the company. To plan, we recommend that you do the following:

1. *Consider how your skills, accomplishments, background, and career goals match the company's needs.* Now is the time to *narrow* your focus to the specific company about to interview you. To begin, review the company's job description (and any other statements about the job you are applying for), your letter of application, and your resume, and take notes that may help you at the interview.

To illustrate, let's consider what Michael did to prepare for his interview with Dress for Success, a nationwide men's and women's clothing company with thirty locations across the United States and annual sales of approximately $55 million.

Michael first reviewed the company's job description, which appeared on the bulletin board of his university's placement center (see Figure 14.21). He then noted that in his resume and his letter of application, he had stressed skills, accomplishments, and those aspects of his background that matched the company's needs. Specifically, he had mentioned:

- His sales experience at Casual Ware (where he had been in the top 10 percent of salespeople and had become accomplished at multiple sales)
- His interest in solving marketing problems and his experience in designing marketing plans
- His communication skills (the A he received in speech, his work as a waiter, and most important, his work in sales)
- His ambition and dedication
- His enjoyment of working with people

Figure 14.21

JOB DESCRIPTION

OUTSIDE SALES

Will call on business and professional people in their offices. Clientele-building business emphasizing service to client, clothing selection, and consulting.

Degree required, any major. Must have inside sales experience in clothing or outside sales experience.

Since he felt that these factors would make him a particularly desirable job candidate for Dress for Success, he noted them on a note card he would take with him to the interview. Bringing notes would help him remember to mention some or all of these things.

From reviewing his resume and letter of application, Michael also noticed how he was careful not to state things that might make him less desirable to the firm, such as his preference to work for a large company. (Dress for Success was a medium-sized firm.) He planned to exercise the same care at the interview. Like Michael, you will want to avoid volunteering information about yourself that would influence the interviewer negatively.

2. *Review literature and speak to contacts about the company, the industry, and the field*. Reading and talking to others will give you an informed perspective on the job and the company. Be sure you know these basics about the company:

- Its products and services
- Its size
- Changes in the industry to which it belongs
- Changes in the company itself
- Major company activities in the last year
- The location of headquarters and its main branches
- The chief officers (chairman, president, chief executive officer)
- Its financial performance

This information is readily available for large companies (see pp. 717–718). For smaller companies, you may have to write to their public relations departments for samples of company communications (e.g., newsletters, addresses of officers, media releases) and speak to business contacts acquainted with the firm.

From reviewing some of the internal communications of Dress for Success, Michael learned that the company was expanding in the Far West and putting out a new line of leisure apparel for business and professionals. From a recent article in the *Wall Street Journal*, he also learned that professional women spent a larger percentage of their discretionary income on clothing than did men. These facts (expansion in the Far West, new line of leisure clothes, spending habits of women professionals) might help him respond to questions and to formulate questions of his own.

3. *Prepare answers to potential questions*. An excellent way to prepare for the questions an interviewer is likely to ask is to prepare answers to some commonly asked questions (see Figure 14.22). Some of the questions may be more difficult to answer than others. General open-ended questions are perhaps most difficult because you are given no clue as to what the interviewer is looking for. For instance, how would you answer a question such as "Tell me something about yourself?" You can use your response to such a question as an opportunity to show why you are a strong candidate

Figure 14.22
COMMONLY ASKED INTERVIEW QUESTIONS

1. What are your major strengths and weaknesses?
2. What can you tell me about yourself?
3. How does your college career prepare you for your work life?
4. Why did you choose your major?
5. What courses did you enjoy most? Why?
6. What kind of extracurricular activities are you involved in? How does what you accomplished outside the classroom add to your education?
7. How do your skills relate to our needs?
8. What are your hobbies?
9. Have you had previous employment in this or a related field?
10. Why would you like to work for this company?
11. What interests you about the company's products or services?
12. What criteria do you use in choosing a job?
13. Why should we hire you?
14. Is there anything you would like to know about the company?
15. What kind of salary are you looking for?
16. Can you work under pressure?
17. What is your ideal job? Why?
18. What have you learned from previous jobs?
19. Do you prefer any particular geographic location?
20. Where do you see yourself in five years?
21. Do you have any questions?

for the job. For instance, you might bring up information about your achievements at work or at school that show your suitability for the position. In his interview with Dress for Success, Michael answered this question by discussing his interest in solving marketing problems and in working with people, two aspects of his background that he knew were important to a clientele-building business such as Dress for Success.

In addition to open-ended questions, questions about sensitive areas of your background may also be difficult to answer. When asked such a question, you can point out the positive things about what may appear to be a liability. For example, if you dropped out of school for a few years, can you discuss what you learned during that time through work or volunteer activities? If you changed jobs frequently, can you emphasize your desire to find permanent long-term employment now? If you lack direct experience in the job you are seeking, can you identify related experience you have had? In Michael's case, he was asked whether, because of his youth, he would be comfortable working with an older clientele. He responded by stressing his success in selling to such a group when he worked at Casual Ware.

4. *Prepare your own questions.* In addition to selling yourself to the company, you can use the interview to learn what you can about the job and the company. Remember that it is just as important for you to feel comfortable with the company as for the company to find you acceptable. John D. Erdlen, an expert in the job interview process, recommends that you ask the questions listed in Figure 14.23.

Figure 14.23

QUESTIONS FOR CANDIDATES TO ASK DURING AN INTERVIEW

> 1. Where is this organization going? What plans or projects are being developed to maintain or increase its market share?
> 2. Who are the people with whom I will be working? May I talk with some of them?
> 3. When and why do you have to fill this job? Where is the former incumbent?
> 4. Why are you not promoting internally? Do you have a job-posting system?
> 5. May I have a copy of the job description? What might be a typical first assignment?
> 6. Why do you think this job might be the right spot for me?
> 7. Do you have a performance appraisal system? How is it structured? How frequently will I be evaluated?
> 8. What is the potential for promotion in the organization?
> 9. What type of training will I receive? Will I be reimbursed for taking formal courses related to my job?
>
> Source: John D. Erdlen, *Career Opportunities News* (November, 1984): 2.

As you formulate your list of questions, be careful not to include questions you can find answers to by doing a little research on your own. *Do* formulate questions that show you have done research on the firm, and try to demonstrate through your questions that you may have special skills or other background that will be an asset to the company. For example, Michael asked, "Since, as I've read recently, you are expanding your sales efforts in the Far West, do you consider Los Angeles one of your growth areas?" This question showed he had done research on the company. It also allowed him to discuss his knowledge of Los Angeles as a sales territory and to find out whether he could begin work at Dress for Success in the geographical area familiar to him. Michael also formulated this question: "A recent article in the *Wall Street Journal* suggests that women professionals spend a greater percentage of their income on clothes than do men. What is the company doing to target the professional women's market?" Not only did this question show his knowledge of the industry and of marketing issues, but it also allowed him to probe the marketing sophistication of the company.

5. *Learn about the interview situation.* In general, companies conduct at least two interviews, one on campus and one at the company. Campus interviews tend to be short

(about thirty minutes) and are often conducted by members of Personnel or by a recruitment team whose job is to weed out unqualified candidates and to recommend strong ones for further interviews. At the company site, you may be interviewed by your potential boss and co-workers, either individually or in groups. If you interview at the company, you will be able to see how the organization conducts business.

Before going on an interview, try to find out the company's interview procedures. Ask the person who contacts you whether this is a preliminary interview, one in a series of interviews, or the final interview. Michael learned that his interview with Dress for Success would be a preliminary thirty-minute on-campus interview. If successful, he would be called for further interviews.

6. *Learn about the interviewer*. The more you know about the interviewer, the better you will perform. If your interviewer is a member of Personnel, he or she may know little about the specifics of the position but probably knows a great deal about company policy. If the interviewer is an expert in your field, you can expect to be questioned in detail about your preparation for work in the field. If the interviewer is your potential boss, he or she will be able to spell out your duties and will most likely ask how your skills and background prepare you for the job.

All interviewers are interested in learning how well you present yourself, how well you are likely to get along with others in the organization, and if you are a hard and responsible worker. For the interview with Dress for Success, Michael learned that he would be interviewed by a senior sales representative. He surmised that his interviewer would probably be eager to learn about his marketing experience and would understand the jargon of the field. He also felt that he could ask detailed questions about the company's sales operations.

Rehearsing

Rehearsing will help you build your confidence and improve your performance. To rehearse, role-play the interview session with an experienced friend or member of the placement office acting as the interviewer. Prepare your mock interviewer beforehand by providing him or her with a list of questions you are likely to be asked and with essential background information about the job, the company, and the interview situation. Have the interviewer critique both the content of your remarks and the quality of your questions. Also, ask him or her to comment on your eye contact, confidence, voice projection, and posture. To make the most of your practice session, videotape it and review the tape with your interviewer.

At the Interview

On the day of your interview, make sure you know the exact location of the interview and give yourself enough time to get there. Bring two copies of your resume, your notes, and a pen and pad.

DRESS

How you dress is the first impression you will make on the interviewer. Dress conservatively: a suit or conservative sports jacket and slacks for men; a suit, conservative dress, or skirt and blouse for women.

THE INTERVIEW SEQUENCE

Job interviews generally consist of three parts: introductory remarks, a question-and-answer exchange, and concluding remarks.

In the first few minutes of an interview, you can expect that the interviewer will introduce him or herself, shake hands, and in some instances, outline the purpose and scope of the interview. These first minutes are also your opportunity to make a good first impression by appearing relaxed and attentive.

The question-and-answer exchange is at the heart of the interview and will, in the case of a thirty-minute interview, usually last about twenty to twenty-five minutes. When you are asked questions, try to give a clear and concise answer, speak confidently and enthusiastically, and show by your body language (e.g., posture, gestures, and facial expressions) that you are responsive to the interviewer's concerns. If you don't understand a question, ask for clarification. If you feel that the interviewer has not understood your response, rephrase it. Remember that the interviewer will be judging *how* you listen and respond as well as what you say.

During the question-and-answer period, your interviewer may give you an opportunity to ask questions. (If not, ask for a few minutes at the end of the interview.) When asking questions, be sure to choose the ones that are most important to you since your time will be limited.

At the close of the interview, the interviewer may outline the next steps of the hiring process, such as the company's timetable for making a decision and the scheduling of further interviews. If this information is not forthcoming, ask for it and offer

Dress is crucial to a successful interview.

follow-up information on yourself such as the names, addresses, and phone numbers of your references.

During or after the interview, take notes on key points and on your interaction with the interviewer. (The main reason not to take notes during the interview is that you may focus more on note-taking than on making a good impression and learning what you can about the job and the company.) Good notes will help you remember important details. They are essential to your own decision making and to the effectiveness of your follow-up with the company.

The accompanying checklist can help you review your preparation for and performance at a job interview.

CHECKLIST FOR PREPARING FOR AND PERFORMING AT A JOB INTERVIEW

1. Have you prepared for the job interview by:
   - Considering how your skills, accomplishments, background, and career goals match the company's needs?
   - Reviewing literature and speaking to contacts about the company, the industry, and the field?
   - Preparing answers to potential questions?
   - Preparing your own questions?
   - Learning about the interview situation?
   - Learning about the interviewer?

2. Have you rehearsed for the interview by:
   - Role-playing the interview session?
   - Videotaping and reviewing the session?

3. At the interview, did you
   - Dress appropriately?
   - Appear relaxed and attentive?
   - Speak confidently and enthusiastically?
   - Give clear and concise answers?
   - Ask important questions?
   - Take notes on key points and on your interaction with the interviewer?

THANK-YOU LETTERS

Since not all applicants send letters of appreciation, just sending one right after each interview will increase your chances of obtaining a job offer. But an effective letter can accomplish much more than just saying thank you. Let's see how you can move through the activities of the writing process in composing the letter. As an example, we will analyze Michael's experience in writing to Dress for Success.

Setting the Goal and Assessing the Reader

Besides saying thank you, your letter's goal is to maintain a company's interest in your candidacy. Your letter must demonstrate professional courtesy and show that you are seriously interested in the position. Assessing your reader before you write is important since the letter also provides you with an opportunity to add information that might strengthen your candidacy. This information could counteract reservations the interviewer may have expressed about your qualifications and offer details supporting your application that you did not have time to bring up at the interview.

Michael's goal was to maintain the company's interest in his application. As for his reader, Michael knew the company's representative would be pleased to have the letter but had at least one reservation about his candidacy.

Gathering Information and Generating Ideas

Thank-you letters that lack concrete details seem formulaic or insincere and show that the writer has not put much thought into the interview or letter. We recommend that you write down your strongest impressions of the interview right after the session. By reviewing your interview notes, you may discover details to include in your letter that will demonstrate your sincere interest in the company. You may also want to do some nonstop writing or use a tape recorder to generate ideas.

Michael had taken notes on his interview with the company's representative, so he had a good idea of what she was looking for and what she saw as his assets and liabilities. He could rely on these notes to help him generate ideas for his letter. He went back over his notes putting a check mark next to anything he might want to include:

- Seems concerned that I may be too young to work with older clientele
- Likes my experience in marketing plans and promotions

Organizing

Once you have thought about your goal and your reader and have some ideas for expressing your appreciation, use the RTA formula to organize your letter and to come up with more ideas.

Establish Rapport: Establish rapport by thanking your reader immediately. It is also a good idea to include the title of the position and the name of the company in your opening statement.

> Thank you for talking to me about career opportunities as an outside sales representative at Dress for Success, Inc.

Influence Thinking: Demonstrate your interest in the company and your qualifications by mentioning significant information you learned from the interview. If you can, clear up any concerns the reader may have about your qualifications. Michael's interviewer wondered whether he could effectively sell to people in their forties and fifties.

> From what I learned from you about the Dress for Success focus on marketing high-quality men's and women's apparel, I would be proud to work as your outside sales repesentative. The challenge of selling to the mature-age market nationwide is particularly appealing to me, since I have had great success selling apparel to this age group in Los Angeles. I would like to transfer this ability to the larger market.

Motivate Action and Attitude: End your message by reinforcing your interest in the company and looking toward the future.

> Your comments on the retail clothing industry and the place of Dress for Success in the market made me realize how much I would enjoy working for you. Please consider me in your plans.

THE LETTER OF ACCEPTANCE

Once you have accepted a job offer, send the company a letter of acceptance. Begin by stating your pleasure in accepting the position, then follow up in the succeeding paragraph(s) with any details you may want to confirm, such as salary and the date you begin work. Close on a positive note by reaffirming your interest in joining the company. Michael's letter of acceptance to The Red Onion appears in Figure 14.24.

LETTERS OF REFUSAL

When you decide not to accept an offer, write a letter refusing the job, and if possible, let the reader tactfully know why you have declined. Letters of refusal follow the bad-news or indirect letter pattern. To buffer the bad news, begin by expressing appreciation for the job offer. Then in the next paragraph(s), explain your reasons for refusing and state your refusal. In the concluding paragraph, express your appreciation. As one example, see Figure 14.25, the letter of refusal Michael wrote to Dress for Success.

Figure 14.24

MICHAEL'S LETTER OF ACCEPTANCE

                                  17412 Margate Street
                                  Encino, CA 91316
                                  June 6, 199—

Mr. John Fernandez
The Red Onion
1139 East Dominguez Street, Suite H
Carson, CA 90746

Dear Mr. Fernandez:

    I am very pleased to accept a position as assistant marketing representative with Red Onion Restaurants.

    As we discussed, I will begin work at your Palm Desert location on June 15. I look forward to contributing to your efforts to expand the business into the local markets.

                                  Sincerely yours,

                                  Michael Eaton

                                  Michael Eaton

Figure 14.25

MICHAEL'S LETTER OF REFUSAL

>
> 17412 Margate Street
> Encino, CA 91316
> June 6, 199—
>
> Ms. Leslie Norton
> Dress for Success, Inc.
> 3440 Wilshire Boulevard
> Los Angeles, CA 90010
>
> Dear Leslie Norton:
>
>   Thank you very much for offering me a position as assistant marketing representative at Dress for Success.
>
>   The opportunity to join your sales force and work on a nationwide marketing campaign is very appealing to me. After considering your offer carefully, I have decided, however, to join the marketing staff of another company, The Red Onion Restaurants. My decision is based on my belief that my future lies in the restaurant industry rather than in retail clothing.
>
>   I appreciate the time you and your colleagues have taken to explain career opportunities at Dress for Success. You taught me a great deal about marketing as well as about retail clothing.
>
>   Best regards,
>
>   Michael Eaton

SUMMARY

Good planning and careful, persistent follow-through will help you conduct a successful job campaign. Begin by assessing your interests and qualifications and by doing research on your career goals. Then design your resume to emphasize those aspects of your background that demonstrate to employers your qualifications for the positions you are interested in.

Once you have done a self-assessment and research on your career goals and have prepared your resume, you can conduct your job search. The search will include reading want ads, doing library research on specific companies and positions, speaking to business contacts, writing letters of application, and interviewing. Following the search, you will need to write thank-you letters, an acceptance letter, and letters of refusal.

EXERCISES

See "Making a Schedule," pp. 678–680, for Exercise 1.

1. If you are beginning a job search, make a schedule that includes all the tasks you must complete successfully, the estimated time required for each task, the sequence of tasks, and the date by which you want to secure the job.

See "Self-Assessment," pp. 680–685, for Exercise 2.

2. Explore your career choices by answering questions about those aspects of your life that pertain to your potential choice of work. See Figure 14.3 for the list of questions.

After responding to these questions, review your answers to see if you can discover any patterns in your responses that suggest particular career interests. Have a friend or family member who knows you well review your responses and the career interests you are considering, and then discuss your self-assessment.

See "College Placement Services," pp. 685–686, for Exercise 3.

3. Visit your college placement center to find out what resources are available to students seeking summer, part-time, or full-time employment.

See "Library Sources," pp. 686–687, for Exercise 4.

4. Visit your college placement library or your general library to find out what publications are available on the job search. Note those that may be applicable to your needs.

See "Business Contacts," pp. 686–688, for Exercise 5.

5. If you have identified one or two of your career interests, interview a business contact (a friend, acquaintance, professor, or college alumnus) about the occupation, industry, or company that your business contact belongs to and that interests you.

If you want information about an occupation, industry, or company, consider asking those questions listed in Figure 14.5 that are relevant to your needs.

See "Professional Associations," pp. 689–690, for Exercise 6.

6. Check either the *Career Guide to Professional Associations: A Directory of Organizations by Occupational Field* or *National Trade and Professional Associations of the U.S. and Canada* for listings of associations in fields that you may be interested in entering on graduation. Then write a letter to one of the associations asking for information about local chapters, meetings, and possible participation by students.

See "Writing Your Resume," pp. 689–713, for Exercise 7.

7. Assume you are to apply for summer, part-time, or full-time employment. Write your resume for a job of your choice. Ask a classmate, a member of the career placement staff, or your instructor to review your resume.

See "Revising," pp. 711–714, for Exercises 8 and 9.

8. Exchange a draft of your resume with a classmate. Review your classmate's resume and write a memo to your classmate on how his or her resume could be improved.
9. A classmate of yours, Jamie Malone, is interested in applying for a management training position in international banking that would allow her to use her economics and computing background in her work. She has asked you to review her resume before she sends it out. After reviewing the resume (Figure 14.26), write a memo to Jamie recommending changes she should make.

See "Want Ads," pp. 715–716, for Exercise 10.

10. Over the next week or two, look through the want ads of two or three newspapers and trade journals. Locate five ads for positions you may be interested in applying for now or after graduation. Identify how your skills, background, and interests match the job's requirements.

See "Research on Specific Companies," pp. 717–721, for Exercise 11.

11. Identify a company you may be interested in working for on graduation. Review company publications, recent articles, and other relevant publications to find out important information about the company. See p. 717 for the kind of information you might seek.

Figure 14.26

JAMIE'S RESUME

```
              Jamie Malone
              4612 Larchwood Ave.
              (215) 555-1953

                 OBJECTIVE

A position in a financial institution that uses my economics and
computer skills.

                 EDUCATION
TEMPLE UNIVERSITY   Philadelphia, PA  May 1989
Bachelor of Arts in Economics and Spanish Literature
Courses:       International Economics, Intermediate Macroeconomics,
               Computer Science, and Statistics.
Activities:    International Association of Students in Economics and
               Business Management

UNIVERSIDAD DE SEVILLA, Seville, Spain.  January - June 1988.
Semester program with course work in Spanish literature.

                 RESEARCH
ADMINISTRATIVE ASSISTANT -- Dining Services,
Temple University, 1984 - 86
Process new meal contracts and solved student user problems.
Assisted with catering department in invoice preparation and executed
phone and mail- order payments.  Typed financial statements for
controller.

RESEARCH ASSISTANT -- Temple Econometrics Forecasting Associates,
Inc.
Philadelphia, PA  1988
Obtained data from original sources and compiled data bases of Latin
American countries.  Performed data analyses used for computer
econometric models designed to forecast Latin American countries.
Used Temple University software to generate graphics and tabular
outputs.  Worked under minimal supervision of economists.  Coauthored
Venezuelan report in semiannual, Latin American Outlook.  Collected
recent data via telephone from Latin American Central banks.  Fully
responsible for preparing Monthly Economic Indicators publications.
Set up Latin American Debt simulator model in personal computer.
Assisted clients with data information.

Computer Experience:  Knowledge of Temple Econometric Software
Systems (designed for time series data analysis), SPF on 3278
terminals, JCL, VisiCalc and 1-2-3 software.  Used IBM 370/168 and
3081 operating systems, IBM personal computer, VAX 780, and VAX 750
(in-house system).  Familiar with FORTRAN.

                 PERSONAL
Native of Houston, Texas.  Proficient in Spanish.  Travels include
Lisbon, Madrid, Paris, and Mexico City.  Enjoy photography, drama,
and dance.
```

See "The Solicited Letter," pp. 722–727, for Exercises 12 and 13.

12. Write a letter of application for a job of your choice advertised in a newspaper or trade publication, announced on the bulletin board of your career center, or made known to you by an acquaintance.

13. The admissions office at your college has put an ad in the campus newspaper for student assistants to lead discussion groups with high-school students who are considering applying to your college. Discussion groups will cover such topics as academic majors, core courses, campus clubs, part-time and summer employment, and ·social events sponsored by the college. Since you are interested in the position, write a letter of application to accompany your resume.

See "The Unsolicited Letter," pp. 727–730, for Exercise 14.

14. Write a letter of application for a job at a company that you would like to work for but that may not have a specific job opening.

See "Revising Letters of Application," pp. 730–732, for Exercises 15 and 16.

15. Suppose that you are Barbara Goldstone, a member of the committee for hiring the public relations manager at Southside Medical Center. You have just received several letters of application for a position you advertised two weeks ago in the *Orlando Sentinel* (see Figure 14.27). On the basis of the letters you received (shown in Figures 14.28 through 14.33), which of these applicants would you be interested in interviewing and why? What problems do you find in the letters?

16. Tom Landers, a classmate of yours, has drafted on his word processor an unsolicited letter to William Reynolds, the director of Marketing at Portland Stand. Tom had leafed through a brochure in the career placement office on career opportunities at Portland Stand, a forest product company headquartered in Portland. Tom decided that it might be the right company for him. The most pertinent part of the brochure concerns career opportunities in marketing and sales (see Figure 14.34). On the basis of Tom's resume (Figure 14.35) and letter (Figure 14.36), decide what kind of research he still needs to do to write an effective letter. Even with the limited information he has given you, consider what suggestions you would make to him for thinking through a revision of his resume and letter.

See "The Job Interview," pp. 732–739, for Exercise 17.

17. You and two of your classmates are going to prepare for your job interviews by staging a thirty-minute mock interview. One of you will be the job applicant. This person should prepare for the interview and should hand his or her resume and letter of application to the others. The second person will play the part of the interviewer. The third person will act as observer and will write down the strengths and weaknesses of the job candidate's performance. After conducting the interview, the observer should

review his or her comments with the other two. The interviewer and interviewee should also offer their assessment. Rotate the roles of interviewer, interviewee, and observer until everyone has played all parts.

See "Thank-You Letters," pp. 739–741, for Exercises 18 and 19.

18. Assume you have been interviewed by a company of your choice. Write a thank-you letter expressing your appreciation and giving additional information to support your application.

19. You have been interviewed on campus for a summer internship in marketing at a large bank. The recruiter for the bank has told you that, if chosen, you would be one of ten interns assigned to either an international or regional marketing group. During the course of the summer, you would work for a marketing analyst who would serve as your mentor, and you would be expected to complete a small marketing project (e.g., on customer satisfaction with a new automated teller service or on customer interest in having an assigned personal banker). You also learned that good performance during the summer internship often leads to a permanent position after graduation. Write a letter to the recruiter thanking him or her for the interview. Be sure to add information about your skills, experience, or background that might strengthen your chances for a job offer.

See "The Letter of Acceptance," pp. 741–742, for Exercises 20 and 21.

20. Assume that you have been offered a job that you would like to accept. Write a letter accepting the position.

21. Anthony Pollock, a recruiter for a pharmaceuticals company, received the letter of acceptance shown in Figure 14.37 from a job candidate. Suggest how it might be revised.

See "Letters of Refusal," pp. 741 and 743, for Exercises 22 and 23.

22. Assume that you have been offered a job that you do not want to accept. Write the letter telling your interviewer no but expressing your appreciation for the time he or she and the company took to meet with you.

23. A classmate of yours has just handed you a draft of the letter he wrote rejecting a job offer (see Figure 14.38). He would like you to review it before he sends it out. Read the letter and write your friend a memo explaining the changes you would suggest.

Figure 14.27

BARBARA GOLDSTONE'S WANT AD

PUBLIC RELATIONS MANAGER

PUBLIC RELATIONS MANAGER

Southside Regional Medical Center, in Ocala, Florida, is seeking an energetic and creative individual to coordinate all community related activities. Responsibilities for this position include development of public information programs, media releases, creation of brochures and displays and representing the medical center in various civic functions. A bachelor's degree in Communications, Journalism, or related field is required. Prefer 2-3 years experience. The position is compensated by an excellent salary and benefits package. For consideration please submit resume to:

SOUTHSIDE REGIONAL MEDICAL CENTER

Attn: Barbara Goldstone
P.O. Box 4000
Ocala, FL 32678

Equal Opportunity Employer

Figure 14.28

LETTER OF APPLICATION 1

34 Garden Avenue
Franklin Park, NJ 08823
September 20, 199_

Barbara Goldstone
Southside Regional Medical Center
P.O. Box 4000
Ocala, FL 32678

Dear Ms. Goldstone:

I hope you find the enclosed resume helpful in your search for a public relations manager. Judging from the qualifications mentioned in your advertisement in the <u>Orlando Sentinel</u>, I feel there is an excellent chance I am well suited for the position.

I am currently employed in a position that is totally unrelated to my job skills. It simply keeps the bills paid while I look for a position I can really become involved in and enjoy. I am free to leave at any time. I am available for an interview on Wednesdays, and would enjoy a chance to discuss this with you further. I can be reached at my home phone number any time on Wednesday, and before noon on Tuesday. Thank you very much for your time. I hope to hear from you soon.

Yours truly,

Bernadette Robinson

Bernadette Robinson

Figure 14.29
LETTER OF APPLICATION 2

                                      315 Mill Neck Road
                                      Williamsburg, VA 23185
                                      September 23, 199_

Barbara Goldstone
Southside Regional Medical Center
P.O. Box 4000
Ocala, FL 32678

Dear Ms. Goldstone:

    The enclosed resume emphasizes, unfortunately, extensive knowledge and experience in the tools-skills of public relations, marketing, and advertising—but does not say much (except by implication) of the capacity for long-range planning, conception, execution, *and* evaluation which molds those skills into working programs. A significant part of my master's work involved application of principles of problem solving with internal and external publics.

    The Governor's Award, by the way, was in the highly technical field of printing economies, but it involved perception of a need and creative adaptation of concepts to a specific approach. Nobody taught me how to do *that*; it's the kind of thing employers love to have on tap, and rarely get.

    By way of explanation: I've been involved for two years in an estate matter. It's been hugely time-consuming, expensive, and heartbreaking—all three. While so distant from what I had been doing, I resolved I no longer wanted to go on doing what had largely become design and illustration. I was using too few of the capacities of an analytical and creative mind. And so I have reentered the job market in search of greater challenge and greater satisfactions.

    I don't need to tell you Ocala is in one of Florida's most beautiful areas. I always welcome those rolling hills, just like those outside Williamsburg.

                                                      Sincerely yours,

                                                      Brian Nash

Figure 14.30

LETTER OF APPLICATION 3

150 New Mark Esplanade
Rockeville, MD 20850
September 22, 199_

Barbara Goldstone
Southside Regional Medical Center
P.O. Box 4000
Ocala, FL 32678

Dear Barbara Goldstone:

Communication is the most fascinating and important field in today's business world. I am proud to say that I have made communications my life. In my television work, I am deeply involved with promotional, commercial, and public service production. I also have dealings with commercial clients. I have enjoyed my work in television, but my future goals do not include the broadcasting industry.

I have been known as a people person, and nowhere is this characteristic more important than in public relations. Public relations has been a goal of mine for some time, especially in the medical field. I have a special tie to the medical field, being a kidney transplant recipient out of Shands Hospital in Gainesville. This is my opportunity to fulfill professional and personal goals. I have infinite knowledge and energy within me and no outlet to release them. Combine this with over 3½ years of communications experience, and I am your next public relations manager. I anxiously wait to hear from you. Thank you.

Sincerely,

Lee Harrison

Lee Harrison

Figure 14.31

LETTER OF APPLICATION 4

132 East Fulton St.
Long Beach, NY 11561
September 21, 199_

Barbara Goldstone
Southside Regional Medical Center
P.O. Box 4000
Ocala, FL 32678

Dear Barbara Goldstone:

Your Sunday's advertisement for a public relations manager sounds almost as if you were writing to me personally. There is a remarkable parallel between your requirements and my background. So despite the fact that I am currently vice president of administration at Golden Works Golf and Country Club, I feel almost obligated to respond to your notice.

I do have a degree in journalism from the University of Nebraska, and I certainly have more than your required minimum experience. I was Director of Communications for the PGA of America for nine years and have had extensive experience in advertising, marketing, and public relations in the Chicago area. I moved to Long Island to continue working with the PGA. Subsequently, as an independent contractor, I served Kemper Sports Management as its regional manager on Long Island. In that capacity, we made a presentation to Golden Works, and I was hired by that company as administrator to help move the development to completion.

At the advertising agency I was with before becoming involved in golf and with the PGA, I was creative director, public relations director, and subsequently vice president and account supervisor. I have written for the print media, and prepared speeches . . . and I like people.

I am married and our current permanent home is in Long Beach, New York, but my wife and I have fallen in love with Ocala. If you have not yet filled the position, perhaps we should discuss the possibility.

Yours truly,

Scott McKelvey
Scott McKelvey

Figure 14.32

LETTER OF APPLICATION 5

55 Spring Valley
Orlando, FL 32678
September 28, 199—

Barbara Goldstone
Southside Regional Medical Center
P.O. Box 4000
Ocala, FL 32678

Dear Ms. Goldstone:

This is in response to your recent advertisement in the <u>Orlando Sentinel</u> for a Public Relations Manager. I am seeking a challenging professional position in the north central Florida area and find my skills and interests well suited to your needs.

My professional experience in publications and public relations has included assisting the director of communications services for a national public relations trade association in an extensive audiovisual and print marketing program. Our marketing campaign resulted in a 20 percent increase in membership in comparison to the previous five years. I have also worked closely with the editor of an educational clearinghouse, where I am solely responsible for all phases of their newsletter. In my current work for a local consulting firm, I prepare presentations and marketing materials for their technical teams.

In addition, my education in the magazine curriculum of Florida College of Journalism and Communications provided an ideal combination of newswriting and public relations courses. Coursework provided experience in photography, publications development for a hospital corporation, and press releases.

As the wife of a professor of health and hospital administration and as a daughter and sister of three registered nurses, I believe I would bring to your organization a sensitivity and awareness of the increasingly important role of public relations and marketing in the health care industry. I would welcome the opportunity to work with Southside Regional Medical Center in developing an effective public relations program in the challenging environment that exists today.

I look forward to hearing from you and hope to discuss this further at a mutually convenient time. I can be reached at 555-2936 (home) or 555-3318 extension 308 (work).

Sincerely,

Ellen Greene

Ellen Greene

Figure 14.33

LETTER OF APPLICATION 6

>514 Hidden Valley Road
>Wilmington, NC 28406
>September 28, 199_

Barbara Goldstone
Southside Regional Medical Center
P.O. Box 4000
Ocala, FL 32678

Dear Ms. Goldstone:

My name may ring a bell, inasmuch as the job you are now advertising is not new to me. And, while your selection discrimination process bypassed me earlier this year when this job was previously available, I still believe I'm strongly qualified for the position and would again like to be considered for it.

To review, I have extensive public affairs and corporate public relations experience, much of which represents a level of "professional criticality" beyond that necessitated in a hospital environment. In other words, the bulk of my experience and expertise is generic in nature and is particularly compatible with your professional environment because of the similar technological representation needed within a "matrix sensitive" information management.

You didn't talk with me that last time we covered this ground, and I'm sure you made that decision based on your bias toward the medical community and against practitioners from other fields. There's only one way I can deal with that kind of discrimination and that's straight ahead with complete frankness. I was brought up in a medical family, and while a Flintwood public relations manager in Baltimore, I worked with PR officials in some of America's finest medical institutions. I **KNOW** I can do the job as well as anyone you consider, regardless of their background in the medical community.

(continued)

Figure 14.33

(LETTER OF APPLICATION 6 continued)

Barbara Goldstone
page 2
September 28, 199_

    If you still have my last letter on file, as you should, you have a pretty good description of how my work interacted strongly with the Baltimore medical community as a corporate gifts-and-grants administrator. Not only was there a great deal of that kind of work, but my professional relationship with those hospital PR directors led to some friendships that allowed me ample opportunity to explore and develop an understanding of what public relations work is like in the medical community. There is also a "personal" attitude that you should give some value to. I watched surgery as a child, and took many aptitude exams that indicated I should have gone into medicine. I therefore have an essential understanding of the administration requirements, the management and public sensitivities involved, and the technologies being applied within your community—and very probably to an extent of intensity many PR practitioners already established within the medical community don't have because they simply haven't been exposed to the number of such professional problems I've experienced.

                                       Sincerely yours,

                                       Lori Mathiesen

                                       Lori Mathiesen

Figure 14.34

A SECTION FROM THE PORTLAND STAND
RECRUITMENT BROCHURE

In most of our businesses, we're looking for people with sales, marketing, or other business-related degrees who are interested in marketing and sales as a career.

Excellent career opportunities exist for persons in all our product groups. We're interested in individuals who not only sell a product, but who can sell service and who put a premium on dependability and quality. Our salespeople must be people-oriented—they must be willing to establish long-term relationships with their customers and be able to work out creative ways to solve their customers' individual problems.

You could be hired by one of our packaging divisions to meet customer needs in an assigned area, which could be anywhere from coast to coast; or by our Business Marketing Division, which has one of the largest commercial sales forces in the corporation. Besides our numerous manufacturing facilities, we have sales and distribution facilities for most of our product groups in almost every major U.S. city at all points of the compass—from California to Florida, from Hawaii to Maine.

Your first job in sales at Portland Stand will usually be as a sales trainee. During your initial training period, you'll learn everything there is to know about the products you're going to sell; you'll learn the basic business procedures at your location; and you'll learn who your customers are. Training can be on the job, as well as in the classroom.

Depending on available opportunities and your performance, you'll move first to sales representative, responsible for a specific geographical territory or set of accounts. Then it's on to jobs in merchandising, advertising, marketing management and sales management. Sales management jobs include field sales manager and region sales manager. A career in marketing and sales can also ultimately lead to operations or general management positions.

Or you could be hired as a sales/management trainee by the Home Construction Division. This job could lead to an opportunity with management responsibility for one of the division's numerous retail or wholesale building materials facilities. You'll start out in a training program, which includes on-the-job training at a location and classroom-type instruction. Then you could move to jobs such as inside sales, product manager, outside sales and, ultimately, to location manager.

Figure 14.35

TOM'S RESUME

TOM LANDERS
4672 Sylmar Avenue
Sherman Oaks, California 91423
(818) 555-2339

CAREER OBJECTIVE	A position that will use my education and work experience as a basis for growth into management responsibilities.
EDUCATION	California State University, Northridge B. A. Psychology, June 1989
WORK EXPERIENCE 2/88 - present	Floor Manager, <u>Sign of the Cat Restaurant</u> Evening floor manager at an established English restaurant. Customer service responsibilities, including daily reservations and party planning; supervising dining room and bar personnel, including cash security.
4/87 - 2/88	Management Trainee, <u>Northridge Associated Students Concessions</u> Acting manager of the food concession operation at California State University, Northridge. Responsible for customer service; planning and scheduling events; food purchasing; hiring, firing, and training; annual budge forecasting; cost controls; monthly account reconciliation. Supervised a staff of 12 student supervisors and 200 employees. Developed annual sales budge of over $300,000. Developed new sales items and capital improvements and performed sales/ attendance analysis.
6/86 - 4/87	Senior Student Supervisor, <u>Northridge Coffeehouse</u> Assisted manager in planning of events, supervised events staff, maintained food quality and cash controls, coordinated efficient operations, and motivated student personnel.
	Transportation Assistant, <u>Treeland Nursery</u> Coordinated weekend deliveries to customers and retail outlets for major wholesale nursery. Yard foreman; organized orders; supervised 15 employees; participated in long-term planning and expansion; organized weed abatement program; assisted at a choose-and-cut Christmas tree location.
SCHOOL ACTIVITIES	Alumni Relations Committee Treasurer, Sigma Kappa Alpha
HONORS	Sign of the Cat Employee of the Year
REFERENCE	Furnished on request

Figure 14.36

DRAFT OF TOM'S UNSOLICITED LETTER OF APPLICATION

Dear Mr. Reynolds:

I will graduate in the spring of 1989 with a major in psychology and am looking for a position with a well-established company such as Portland Stand. I hope to apply my background in psychology to work in one of your product groups.

I have taken courses in the following areas that may be applicable to a job you have open or plan to create:

Industrial psychology   Business finance
Statistics   Business economics
Small-group problem solving

These courses can help prepare me for a position at your firm.

In addition to coursework, my education includes service on the alumni relations committee and treasurer of my college fraternity.

While in college, I held several jobs that may relate to the qualifications you want in your marketing and sales professionals:

Floor manager for Sign of the Cat Restaurant
Management trainee for the Northridge Associated Students Concessions
Senior student supervisor for the Northridge Coffeehouse
Transportation assistant for Treeland Nursery

Your company has an international reputaton for excellence. If you are looking for someone who is eager to do a good job for you in one of your product groups, I'm the person.

I look forward to meeting you at your convenience.

Figure 14.37

LETTER OF ACCEPTANCE

1310 Waverly Road
Rome, NY 13440
September 24, 199_

Anthony Pollock, Senior Accountant
Barton Pharmaceuticals
13 West 11th Street
New York, NY 10011

Dear Mr. Pollock:

I am pleased to accept your job offer. I've already begun shipping my things to New York and will be at work on the date and at the time you stipulated.

Sincerely,

Madeleine Forester

Madeleine Forester

THE JOB SEARCH

Figure 14.38

DRAFT LETTER OF REFUSAL

Dear _____,

I regret to inform you that I am unable to accept your job offer. As much as I enjoyed interviewing with you, I found another firm's offer more to my advantage.

Thanks once again.

23. A classmate of yours has just handed you a draft of the letter he wrote rejecting a job offer (see Figure 14.38). He would like you to review it before he sends it out. Read the letter and write your friend a memo explaining the changes you would suggest.

Figure 14.38

DRAFT LETTER OF REFUSAL

Dear _____,

I regret to inform you that I am unable to accept your job offer. As much as I enjoyed interviewing with you, I found another firm's offer more to my advantage.

Thanks once again.

15
THE BUSINESS WRITER AND THE COMPUTER

PREVIEW

This chapter should help you to

1. Understand the benefits that computer technology offers business writers for their individually written assignments
2. See how computer technology can assist you in your group writing tasks.

A survey on computer use estimates that in the 1990s there will be 15 million personal computers in business, 6.8 million in the home, and 2.5 million in schools.[1] People are increasingly realizing that, as computer prices continue to decline and computer capabilities continue to expand, the productivity of the new technology outweighs its expense. Even if you do not have a computer at home, at school, or at work, the technology will most likely be part of your future office environment.

Some of you have been using computers for your writing assignments and already know how it can save you time and help you improve your writing. By itself, the computer cannot make you a good writer, but using the computer can help you enhance your writing skills and make you more efficient. As sales representative Adrienne Bernstein of Hewlett-Packard told us, "Your average business person turns out copy four times faster using word processing rather than a typewriter." And if you include turnaround time for a secretary to type and retype drafts, the time saved is even greater.

If you have not used computers yet, you will need to be acquainted with several terms before reading further about how the computer can assist you in your business writing. Figure 15.1 presents a glossary of selective computer terms. If you have used computers, these terms should already be familiar to you.

Figure 15.1

GLOSSARY OF SELECTIVE COMPUTER TERMS
FOR BUSINESS WRITING

communications network: A system of computers that can communicate with one another through electronic links. If your *word processor* is connected to other computers, it is part of a communications network.

data base: A continuously updated *file* of information—often large—on a specified topic.

disk: A device for storing computer programs (instructions) and data. Information stored on a disk can be reviewed on the display monitor, can be processed (for example by a *word processor*), or can be printed.

electronic mail or **electronic messages:** Messages sent electronically that can include anything from a one-word message to a full-text document (see Figure 15.2). Messages can be sent from other *terminals,* such as in a library or other research facility belonging to the same *communications network*.

electronic mailbox: A storage area for receiving and holding electronic messages. *Electronic mail* can be stored in your general mailbox or sorted into special mailboxes according to topics of your choosing (see Figure 15.3). For instance, you might have a mailbox designated for all messages pertaining to a project you are working on and call the mailbox "PROJECT."

electronic messaging: The process of sending and receiving messages. If your *terminal* is connected to other units via a *communications network,* you can send messages by typing them into your terminal and then typing a command to send them over the network to another computer terminal in your communications network. Messages you receive may appear on your display monitor or in printed form.

file: A set of related information treated as a unit.

hardware: The physical computer equipment—such as the display monitor, the keyboard, and the printer.

modem: A device between your telephone and your computer that allows you to communicate via telephone with other computers.

software: The instructions to the computer that enable it to carry out specific operations. For example, word processing software provides instructions to the computer that enable it to insert, move, change, delete, or store words, sentences, paragraphs, and complete texts.

terminal: Usually a display monitor and keyboard. Terminals are used to enter and display data.

word processor: *Hardware* and *software* used to create, modify, store, and print documents. Documents may include text, numbers, and graphics. The word processor's *hardware* usually consists of a *terminal,* computer, and printer. The word processor may be linked to other word processors or computers by a *communications network*.

THE BUSINESS WRITER AND THE COMPUTER

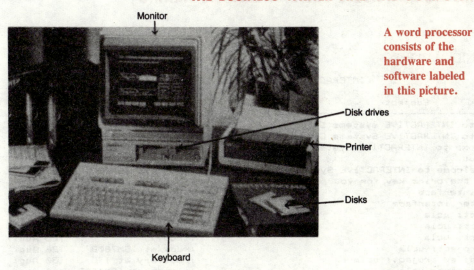

A word processor consists of the hardware and software labeled in this picture.

Figure 15.2

AN ELECTRONIC MESSAGE

```
             UCLA - GRADUATE SCHOOL OF MANAGEMENT
                      TEAMate Mail System


Message # : 357  Message prepared Nov  5 09:24:18 1986

Author : Admin
Subject : Uploading Weekly Logs
-----------------------------------------------------------------

Field Study Teams:


We have decided that sending your weekly communication logs to adminresearch
is too much of a hassle, not to mention that it has a bad history.

From now on, please upload your weekly communication log to your team's
sub-topic under the topic "Weekly Communication Logs."

This will allow all of you to create the log in Framework and simply upload
that document into the outline, thus avoiding Uniplex.

If you have any problems, please send me a message right away.

doug


-----------------------------------------------------------------
Read by : reese       : at Wed Nov  5 14:46:10 1986
          markus      : at Wed Nov  5 17:10:09 1986
          smb         : at Wed Nov  5 18:29:13 1986
          siegel      : at Wed Nov  5 19:56:39 1986
```

766 THE RANDOM HOUSE GUIDE TO BUSINESS WRITING

Figure 15.3

ELECTRONIC MAILBOX

```
                      INTERACTIVE Electronic Mail

         Subject                            From/{To}          Date
+------------------------------------------------------------------------+
|Welcome to INTERACTIVE systems D          |diane at ISM70    |13 Aug|
|Welcome to INTERACTIVE Systems Corporation|diane at ISM70    |13 Aug|
|Re: Welcome to INTERACTIVE Systems Corporation|{diane at ISM70}|13 Aug|
|thank you                                 |{diane}           |13 Aug|
|Re(2): Welcome to INTERACTIVE Systems Corporation|diane at ISM70|13 Aug|
|I set up the print key for you            |forman at ISM780B |13 Aug|
|printer interface                         |{Diane}           |14 Aug|
|Re: printer interface                     |diane at ISM70    |15 Aug|
|em project: ucla                          |{briane}          |25 Aug|
|em project: ucla                          |{claire}          |25 Aug|
|em project: ucla                          |{rudy}            |25 Aug|
|Re: em project: ucla                      |rudy at ISM780B   |26 Aug|
|Forwarded: em project: ucla               |rosemary at ITO   |30 Aug|
|Re: em project: ucla                      |claire at ISM780B | 8 Sep|
|writing projects                          |{claire}          |17 Sep|
|ad project                                |{claire}          |17 Sep|
|printing files at home                    |{Claire}          |23 Sep|
|Re: printing files at home                |diane at ISM780B  |24 Sep|
|Re: ad project                            |claire at ISM780B |24 Sep|
|Forwarded: printing files at home         |claire at ISM780B |24 Sep|
|Forwarded: printing files at home         |jafar at ISM780B  |24 Sep|
|New mailbox in your area                  |claire at ISM780B |29 Sep|
|Re: Forwarded: Forwarded: printing files at home|eric at ISM780B|30 Sep|
|UCLA research project                     |claire at ISM780B | 8 Oct|
|Forwarded: Re: UCLA research project      |claire at ISM780B | 9 Oct|
|Re: UCLA research project                 |rickc at ISM780B  |10 Oct|
|Forwarded: Re: Attention Baseball fans!   |claire at ISM780B |11 Oct|
|Attention Baseball fans!                  |joanne at ISM780B |11 Oct|
|Forwarded: Re(2): Attention Baseball fans!|claire at ISM780B |11 Oct|
|Forwarded: Re(3): Attention Baseball fans!|claire at ISM780B |11 Oct|
|Forwarded: Forwarded: Re(3): Attention Baseball fan|claire at ISM780B|11 Oct|
+------------------------------------------------------------------------+
```

THE BENEFITS OF COMPUTER TECHNOLOGY

To illustrate the benefits that computer technology offers business writers, let's look at the versions of a writing task without and with such technology.

WITHOUT COMPUTER TECHNOLOGY

As a member of the marketing staff for a fitness center headquartered in Miami, Beth Johnson is in charge of writing sales letters and ads to bring in new customers to fitness center locations across the nation. As she finished the draft of a new sales letter (about two pages long) that her boss wanted to send out as soon as possible, she called in her secretary, Mary, to type it. Mary had it ready within three hours (she was interrupted by phone calls and other typing). Beth then made several corrections in pen on the clean copy. Once her secretary had retyped the draft the following morning, Beth was able to send the sales letter and a cover letter (outlining the goals of the sales letter and several questions) to her counterparts in the cities where the fitness center has locations.

Two weeks later Beth received comments from three out of four reviewers. One wanted a catchier sales pitch: "There are a lot of fitness centers out there saying exactly the same thing. We need to get across that we have a unique set of fitness programs tailored to individual needs and designed under the guidance of experts in sports medicine." Another commented: "We need to focus on our unique training programs and downplay our equipment. All the competition has similar equipment, but no one has got as extensive a line of programs." A third noted, "You mention the saunas we've installed at all our locations, but the one here in Indianapolis is still under construction. If the builders get further behind the schedule, you'll have to hold off on that part of the sales pitch."

"All good advice," Beth thought as she reread these comments alongside the draft of her letter. An hour later she had a revised letter ready for typing once again by her secretary. When she received the clean copy from her secretary the following day, she made several sentence-level changes, had the letter retyped, and then sent off the revised letter to her boss. The whole process took about three weeks.

WITH COMPUTER TECHNOLOGY

Even though she is a slow typist (less than 40 words a minute using the hunt-and-peck method) and makes lots of errors, Beth composed a draft of a new sales letter on her computer. She then printed out the draft. Working with the printed copy, she revised the letter: she moved a paragraph, added an introduction resembling one that had worked in an earlier letter, and made several sentence-level changes. Beth then typed in her changes and corrected errors in spelling and grammar using two software packages designed for these purposes. Finally, with a few commands, she sent her revised copy over her modem to the computer terminals operated by her counterparts in Chicago, Indianapolis, New Orleans, and Birmingham. She asked them to review her text and return their comments as soon as possible.

The following day she checked her electronic mailbox to find that three of her reviewers had commented on her letter by typing in boldface capitals right under the section of the letter their comments concerned. When she did not receive her fourth reader's comments within three days of sending her first message, Beth sent a brief reminder note by electronic mail. The fourth reviewer's comments showed up that afternoon. Armed with the four sets of comments, Beth revised her letter. Again she wrote her revisions on a printed copy but entered the changes into the computer. Two drafts later she sent off her revised copy to her boss. The whole process took less than one week.

Several differences emerge when we compare Beth's writing process with and without the computer. Most obviously, composing on a computer that was part of a communications network *allowed her to get the job done sooner*. Even though Beth is not a fast typist, she composed the draft of her sales letter more quickly using word processing than by hand because she could by-pass her secretary and insert the changes herself on the draft already typed in the computer. To make these changes, she preferred working with a printed copy because the full text exceeded the length of the screen. She also had easy access to earlier effective sales letters she had written because she had stored them on disks and could retrieve them as she began composing the new letter. To hasten the review process, she sent the letter instantaneously by electronic mail to the marketing staff in other fitness centers, instead of mailing it. In turn, her reviewers inserted their comments directly onto the text and returned them over the modem.

In addition to increasing her efficiency, Beth's use of the computer most likely *improved the quality of her letter* for several reasons. First, she received all her reviewers' comments. (People in her company are less likely to avoid or misplace messages they receive by electronic mail than messages taken over the phone.) Second, she could revise her letter several times because of the ease with which she could insert changes. Finally, she could use software packages to help check her grammar, usage, spelling, and typographical errors.

Keep in mind Beth's use of the computer as we review how the computer can assist you through all the stages of the writing process.

THE COMPUTER AND THE WRITING PROCESS

Setting the Goal and Assessing the Reader

Software currently available can help you set the goal of your communication and assess your reader by asking questions relevant to specific business documents. These programs also ask you to put this information in a summary statement you can refer to as you write the communication.

Gathering Information and Generating Ideas

If your computer is linked to a communications network that includes various data bases, your terminal can help you do research. If company literature, business information sources, and internal communications are part of the data base, you will be able to review these materials on your display monitor. Some computer systems can store large bodies of reference data, such as encyclopedias, and include software that allows you to access the material randomly and associatively. As college libraries begin to store materials electronically, students with computer terminals will be able to "call up" research information on their display monitor rather than going to the library stacks to do their research.

Even without such a network, you, like Beth Johnson, will be able to "call up" on your screen previous communications you have written that are applicable to the one you are currently composing. Because your old communications are stored on disks rather than in files—or worse still, lost in a stack of papers—your efficiency in gathering this kind of information for your writing will increase.

Computers can also assist you if you are involved in conducting primary research. They can speed up your analysis of data and increase your accuracy. For example, if you are doing marketing analysis, the computer can tabulate the results of questionnaires in seconds, calculations that would take you hours to do without a computer. Computers can also do sales forecasts involving multiple products and multiple markets; without the computer you would have to limit the scope of your analysis to one product or one market segment at a time.

As you generate ideas, the computer can encourage you to write nonstop, since changes in the text are so easy to make with the computer. Several software packages also stimulate freewriting activities. One package actually times pauses in your writing and begins to insert X's if too long a time elapses between keystrokes. Other software helps you generate ideas by asking questions about your topic and readers, and providing you with a transcript of the questions and your answers.

Organizing

Because the computer allows you to rearrange, delete, and add items easily, you can quickly make adjustments in an outline or analysis tree as you consider how to group and order ideas. In addition, software is available that specifically helps writers build analysis trees or outlines. Often such capabilities are part of a word processing package.

Writing a Draft

For those business writers who have problems writing a draft because they believe that their first draft must be their final one, the computer takes the drudgery out of writing by removing the need to transcribe using pen and paper. Texts written on the computer can be changed easily.

The computer is also a flexible tool. It can be used during all of the writing process or during only part of it, so writers can retain their individual styles of composing and still use the computer. For instance, writers can compose first drafts on legal pads with felt pens and use the computer as they revise. Or they can do everything from their initial note-taking to final editing on the computer.

For some business positions, the computer's merging capabilities are an important asset. For example, most marketing representatives find themselves covering the same information in introductory letters, sales demonstrations, follow-up letters, and contract bids. The computer allows these business people to take sections from one text and use them for another. You will also be grateful for the availability of a computer if you write customized form letters. Final copy of these repetitive writing tasks becomes especially easy because you can write the form letter and make the few necessary changes in the basic text for different readers.

Revising

Since, when using the computer, your drafts no longer have to be recopied or retyped, revising should be more efficient. The computer can save you time whether your style is to write one draft, perfecting every paragraph before moving on to the next, or whether you write several whole drafts, revising large chunks before perfecting each small section. Revisions can be made on the original and on subsequent drafts by entering commands (e.g., "delete," "insert,") that make changes on the section of the text displayed on the video screen or on larger chunks of text you have blocked off. You can review each corrected draft—either as it appears on the screen or in a printed copy while saving the text in the computer.

In addition to increased efficiency, business writers report that the quality of their revising improves when they use the computer. Many writers would agree with what one writer has said: "I'm such a sloppy writer that after a point I can't see through my arrows, asterisks, and cross-outs. Before word processing, I lost track of my thoughts because of all the cutting and pasting I had to do." For the writer who does extensive revision, the computer's ability to supply fresh copy for each new draft is a great boon.

If you include asking associates to review your writing as part of your revising process, electronic mail enables you to solicit opinions about your draft simultaneously from multiple readers located at computers in the next office or around the world. Like Beth Johnson, you can use electronic mail to send full drafts of your writing to readers; they in turn can send you their comments, which can be displayed on your screen or printed. Depending on the software, reviewers may interpolate comments in that part of the text they are referring to or in "windows"—boxed off areas juxtaposed to your text. When using windows, reviewers can place their comments so that they appear next to but set off from the text.

Editing, Proofreading, and Formating

Once you are satisfied with the text as a whole, you will find several software packages useful for editing sentences and correcting spelling. Current software can help you identify problems in grammar (for example, subject-verb agreement, pronoun case, punctuation) and style (for example, word choice, use of the verb "to be," sexist language, clichés, wordiness), as well as spelling and typographical errors.

As part of your editing process, you may also want to use software packages that help you design the format of your communication. If you are writing a report, software is available to help in numbering pages and in formating the table of contents, tables of data, footnotes, bibliographies, appendixes, and headings and subheadings. For example, to compose a table of contents, the computer can scan the headings and major subheadings of the report, along with the page numbers on which they appear, and create the table of contents from this information. For shorter or simpler communications, the computer can help you with format (boldface, underlining, centering). If you are interested in testing the effectiveness of different formats, computers help here too. You can try out different formats by entering a few commands.

Since the mid-1980s "published" quality written communications have been possible through the use of Desktop publishing equipment (DTP). With DTP equipment, you can now produce copy that looks professionally typeset and printed.[2]

FIGURE 15.4
AN EXAMPLE OF DESKTOP PUBLISHING

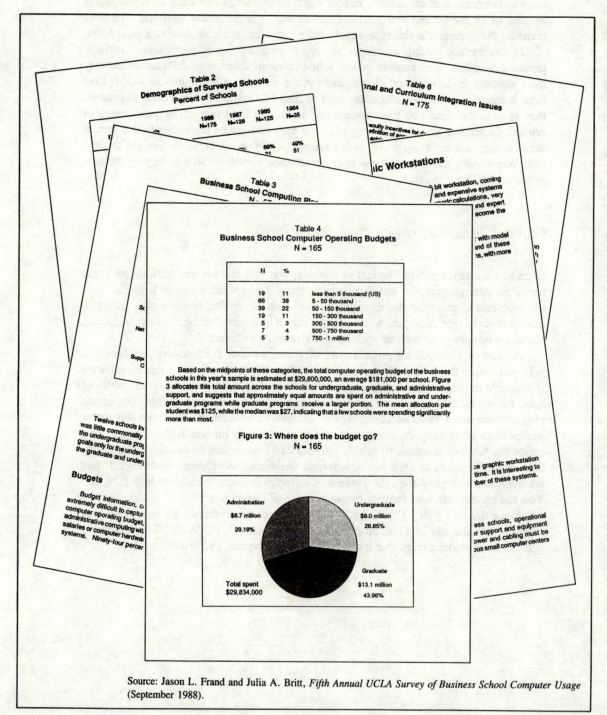

Source: Jason L. Frand and Julia A. Britt, *Fifth Annual UCLA Survey of Business School Computer Usage* (September 1988).

COMMON ERRORS IN USING THE COMPUTER FOR BUSINESS WRITING

Most students find learning to use the computer worth the effort. Both the quality of their writing and their efficiency improve. Despite these gains, some difficulties can arise either in learning to use the computer or as a result of using it incorrectly.

Focusing on the Mechanics Rather Than on Writing

As in acquiring any new skill, computer novices must be prepared to focus initially on how the equipment operates, rather than on how it can assist them in writing. Since the equipment and the manuals keep improving, however, it will take less and less time to learn to use the computer for writing purposes. Focusing on the mechanics of the computer rather than on writing is, then, usually a temporary problem associated with learning how to use the equipment.

Inappropriate Use of Electronic Mail

Sometimes writers try to solve disagreements using electronic mail as the medium of communication. Unfortunately, disagreements tend to escalate—or "flame," as those in the computer world call this phenomenon—when they are not handled face-to-face. When you want to settle an argument, try to meet with people; this is an occasion when your physical presence (your tone, gestures, appearance) can serve your purpose well. At such times, electronic mail is too impersonal.

Revising Only What Appears on the Display Monitor

Some writers revise only what appears before them on their display monitor. This technique is fine for short documents and for sentence and paragraph editing, but for texts that exceed the length of the screen (typically twenty-four lines, though sometimes sixty-six lines) the technique may be harmful. For long texts, whatever appears in front of you at any given moment is just an arbitrary chunk of the larger text. To do a holistic revision of such texts, consider printing the whole piece, making or outlining your changes on the hard copy, and then inserting the changes in the computer.

Computer-Generated Errors

Perhaps because the computer makes it so easy to add, delete, and shift words, sentences, and paragraphs, writers sometimes forget to erase a line or word they have changed, or they transfer only part of a section they want to move within a text. Most grammar and spelling software packages do not pick up these errors. Even though you may have made only a few changes since you last proofread the text, you will have to proofread your final copy.

THE COMPUTER AND GROUP WRITING

As well as personal productivity, computers can increase the productivity of groups. Computer systems are now available to help business people work on their group writing projects and allow teams to realize greater efficiency and flexibility throughout the writing process. A recent issue of *BYTE* magazine devotes a full section to "groupware"—software that helps groups carry out their work collaboratively.[3]

When the computer of each team member is linked to those of others in a communications network, members can efficiently exchange ideas, information, and text by sending electronic messages. For example, a writer can send a single message simultaneously to all group members, so that everyone is informed of the project's status, and all team members can keep this and other electronic messages as an ongoing record of changes. The ease with which people can exchange ideas and information can also cut down on meetings. As one manager told us, "By using electronic messaging you can dispose of scene setting, so a two-hour meeting becomes one hour. There's 'precommunication' about the subject, so people are better prepared to meet and discuss."

Besides increasing efficiency, electronic messaging can increase flexibility. For instance, two parties exchanging information do not have to be simultaneously available. You can be having lunch while your teammate is sending you a message. Without electronic messaging, team members are usually at the mercy of one another's schedules, and the discrepancy in schedules often leads to telephone tag.

In addition, working on the same communications network allows for geographical dispersion of team members. Since computers in the same network can be located at vast distances from one another, members of a team can work in different cities. You are able to work with people whose expertise and experience you value but whose participation on a project was previously very difficult, if not impossible, because of geographical distance. For example, in a marketing group at a high-tech firm, two of seven key members had their offices outside of Los Angeles headquarters: the manager in charge of graphics for brochures and ads was in Boulder, Colorado, and the head of international marketing was in Toronto. Despite the geographical distance, these two team members worked smoothly with the rest of the team and even felt a sense of team spirit because they could exchange informal as well as business messages. In the words of the head of International Marketing, "Being on the network counteracts the loss of camaraderie."

Computer systems can have a variety of uses throughout the group writing process. At any point in the process, groups can share ideas and information about the goal of the communication, its readers, its content, and its structure. Although groups may prefer to meet face-to-face in the initial stages of writing in order to clarify goals and readers and to work out schedules, groups that work together frequently on similar tasks are likely to use electronic mail to handle even these early writing activities. Software is now available to help groups coordinate schedules, track writing projects, and follow up on details.[4]

In the later stages, if the writing task is divided among several team members, they can use electronic messaging to exchange drafts for review and to merge a final document. And because everyone can share the same word-processing software, the one team member who is responsible for editing the document can merge and revise the work of the others.

Even as you read our suggestions for how the computer can assist you in writing your business communications, new advances that assist writers are being made in computer technology. These include software packages that allow writers to review files that consist of text graphics, *sound*, and *animation*; color screens that enhance graphics and formating; and new idea-generating and editing software packages. If you familiarize yourself with the stages of the writing process and learn the basics of word processing, we believe that you will be ready for the new technology.

SUMMARY

Once you have some familiarity with computer technology, you will find that it is a useful tool in handling individual and group writing assignments. Business people have been especially impressed by how the technology helps them in drafting and revising individually written documents and in exchanging ideas, information, and text in their group writing efforts.

EXERCISES

1. Visit your college's computer facilities and find out about the word processing and electronic mail capabilities available to students. Write a memo to the class summarizing what you have learned.
2. If you know how to use word processing, use it to write a business communication. Be prepared to discuss in class the ways in which the technology may have affected your writing of the communication (e.g., techniques you used, time required, quality of final product).

3. Interview a college administrator or a business person about his or her uses of the computer for handling writing tasks. Prepare for the interview by making a list of questions that cover the following issues:

- The kind(s) of writing the individual does using the computer
- Why he or she uses the computer
- The advantages and disadvantages of using the computer

Write a memo to your instructor describing that person's uses of the computer for writing.

4. Assume that your college is going to purchase personal computers for student use and that you are a student member on the Computer Purchasing Committee. At least fifty computers are needed, and the school can spend $100,000 ($2,000 per computer including hardware and software).

Interview five students who regularly use the computer for handling their writing assignments, and ask the students what they would advise the school to purchase, given its budget. Then consider what kind of technology you would want to use to handle your class assignments. After assessing the results of your interviews, check the equipment available in your price range at several local computer stores. Then write a short report to the committee recommending a personal computer for the college.

5. Interview a business person who uses electronic messaging. Request to see some samples, and ask the following questions:

- How long have you been using electronic messaging and how did you learn to use it?
- When and why do you use electronic messaging?
- With whom do you communicate using electronic messaging?
- Who in your organization uses electronic messaging to communicate with you? How frequently? For what purposes?
- Does company policy or informal agreement among employees exist on when and why to use electronic messaging?
- What advantages and disadvantages do you see in using electronic messaging?
- When do you prefer meeting face-to-face or using a telephone instead of electronic messaging, and why?

Prepare a ten-minute presentation discussing your findings.

Appendix A
WRITING RESPONSES TO CASES

PREVIEW

This appendix should help you to

1. Solve the business problem(s) presented in a case by
   - Determining the question the reader wants answered
   - Analyzing the problem
   - Establishing criteria for selecting the best alternative among the possible solutions and evaluating and choosing among alternative solutions
2. Write a response to a case by
   - Keeping your purpose and reader in mind
   - Gathering information and generating ideas that support your solution
   - Organizing your information and ideas
   - Avoiding common pitfalls in the write-up

Undergraduate Jill Kellerman has been assigned a case on "the boss who won't listen." Next week she has to turn in an analysis of the case. The case asks her to play the role of Susan Woodward's friend and, using business theory, to advise Susan about the kind of corrective measures she can take to get the boss's attention. As Jill reviewed her assignment, she wondered how she would find the right answer, relate the answer to theory she was studying in class, and determine how much role playing she needed to do.

Like Jill Kellerman, you may be asked to write about cases in business classes. A **case** is a story, complete with details of setting and characters, that is centered around a conflict in a business organization. Cases range in length and complexity from one-paragraph handouts to elaborate stories that include quantitative data and exhibits. Typically, case assignments require you to identify the problem, make recommendations for solving the problem, and support your recommendations with information from the case and sometimes from related assigned articles and lectures.

Since cases attempt to simulate the imperfect real-life conditions in which business decisions are made, some of the facts and points of view given in the case are incomplete, obscure, or irrelevant to solving the problem. Therefore, effective responses to a case begin with a careful reading of the case to determine what is important.

When you are assigned a case, read it through once to get an overview of the contents and a preliminary sense of the "big picture"—key potential problems, main characters, nature of the industry and organization, and important exhibits (e.g., financial statements, organization charts). Once you have made this broad sweep, go back over the case asking yourself which details seem to be important clues about the central problem you are asked to identify and solve.

The case assignment is an academic version of the problem-solving business report, but in addition to obvious similarities between the case write-up and the report, several features distinguish writing a response to a case from writing the problem-solving report. Figure A.1 shows these similarities and differences, grouped under considerations of purpose and audience.

PROBLEM SOLVING AND CASE ASSIGNMENTS

The process Jill Kellerman went through to write a case response for her general management course allows us to compare the problem-solving business report and the case analysis. Jill was given the case shown in Figure A.2. Her instructor handed her the following assignment in class:

> Assume you are Susan's friend and business associate. Susan has just called you to ask your advice about how to deal with her boss. Since you are leaving town in about three hours and you and Susan cannot schedule a meeting time on such short notice, you decide to write her a short report analyzing her problem and suggesting remedies. (You have also considered that, given the delicate nature of the matter, Susan might better receive your suggestions if you give them to her in writing before talking over the situation with her.) In writing your response, use what you learn from your course readings.

In a real classroom situation, part of your assignment can involve selecting relevant readings among those assigned in class. Jill found an article called "How to Manage Your Boss," by Allen R. Cohen, devoted to common problems that can arise between a subordinate and a superior, with suggested solutions. One section of the article, reproduced in Figure A.3, seemed particularly relevant to her case write-up.

Since the case assignment is an academic version of the problem-solving report, you can use the three-part problem solving approach described in Chapter 9 to help you find the best solution to the problem. Let's see how Jill used this approach to handle her assignment.

APPENDIX A WRITING RESPONSES TO CASES

Figure A.1

A COMPARISON: THE CASE WRITE-UP AND
THE PROBLEM-SOLVING REPORT

The Case Write-Up	The Problem-Solving Report
Purpose	
1. Solves the problem and recommends the best action to remedy the problem	1. Same
2. Gives convincing reasons that support your analysis, and displays your analytical abilities and your knowledge of the course's concepts, vocabulary, and readings as they apply to solving the problem	2. Gives convincing reasons that support your analysis
3. [Optional (depending on the instructor)]: Explores in detail alternative solutions to the problem and ways to implement recommendation(s)	3. Same (depending on manager you report to)
Audience	
Instructor as evaluator who is interested in whether you have (a) found and substantiated the best among possible solutions (although often there is no one "best" solution) and (b) understood the key concepts and readings in the course	Decision maker who is interested in getting the best solution to the problem

Determine the Question the Reader Wants Answered

Jill had two readers, the character Susan Woodward and Jill's instructor. They both had questions Jill needed to answer. First, Susan, Jill's associate, wanted to know, "How can I improve communication with my boss?" Second, Jill's instructor had questions: He wanted to see whether Jill could analyze Susan's problem and suggest remedies while role-playing Susan's friend and associate, and he wanted to see whether Jill could apply ideas drawn from Cohen's article to her write-up.

Figure A.2

THE CASE ASSIGNED TO JILL

After being on the road for nearly a month, Susan Woodward, a young assistant market researcher for a soft drink company, has been back at her Houston office only a week. On the road, she had been checking the discount supermarkets in several Midwest towns where her company was market testing a new line of diet soft drinks.

For the first time in her career, Susan had been involved in designing a market research questionnaire. (A manager from another part of the company had even praised her for her contribution.) In addition, she herself had interviewed customers at all six stores where the company was running the test and spent time talking with store employees. Susan had three ways to confirm that the soft drink was going over—her observations, the results of the questionnaire, and her discussions with stock clerks and store managers. She was so encouraged by customer responses to the new product that she couldn't wait to tell her boss about the product's success.

"I'd bet that Bart wouldn't have guessed I'd be so successful," Susan thought, "and there's little chance he knows what I found out about our competitors." Their competitors were planning to market test a nearly identical product in the coming weeks in that same Midwest area.

Sometimes Susan felt intimidated by Bart's experience as a market researcher. In his ten years at the company, he had managed the market testing for eight of their ten top soft drinks. Recently she had also been discouraged because she felt she had been overlooked for a promotion. The company had hired someone from the outside. Due to the success of her work in the Midwest, Susan for the first time felt she could speak up with confidence about what she had accomplished and could give Bart important news about their competitors. This was crucial information he surely hadn't gotten wind of but would need for his May status report.

For several mornings since her return, Susan has had little success in getting through to Bart. On the basis of past experience with him, Susan found this problem strange. As a rule, Susan and Bart met every Monday and Friday for about ten minutes to discuss new developments in marketing. And during lunch hours, Bart was always friendly; he liked to swap stories about their mutual interest—jogging.

Just this morning, a Monday, Susan was surprised when Bart interrupted her after the first five minutes of their normally scheduled ten-minute meeting. "Sorry, Susan, that's all the time I have. I've got this status report due on Thursday and a briefing to give on Friday." Susan, who had just begun telling him how exciting it had been to go back to her college town in Ohio—one of the places where the soft drinks were marketed—was dumbfounded. "Bart, you're going to be interested in what I found out in Ohio." "Great," Bart answered as he walked her to the door, "let's pick up on this next week."

Later that day Susan remembered how Bart had been fidgeting in his chair and looking at his watch a number of times from the moment she had walked in the door. His lack of interest seemed uncharacteristic of him, even though she felt that he never gave her quite the attention her work warranted, especially when she knew how attentive he could be when his own boss had something to say.

During the course of the day Susan called Bart's office several times in the hope that she could reschedule the meeting. "After all," she thought, "this is the first time I managed a market test and, between my observations and our analysis of the questionnaire, it's obvious that our soft drink's a winner. But if our competitors find out in advance, they could ruin our chances of capturing the market."

Bart's secretary apparently gave Susan's messages to Bart. Susan also sent him an electronic message, but he didn't get back to her. Susan's frustration increased as Tuesday passed with no return call. She felt especially anxious because this project represented six months of labor. If she couldn't persuade Bart of its significance, she felt she had little chance of a raise and promotion at her next performance review. What made Bart's silence even worse was that Susan's findings were important information to him. Her success in the Midwest and her news about their competitors would influence what he had to say in that status report to top management that he was so pressed to write.

Figure A.3

EXCERPT FROM "THE BOSS WHO WON'T
LISTEN" BY ALLEN R. COHEN

Though some people have "hearing" problems no matter what setting they are in, even managers who are by nature more sympathetic and receptive listen less and less when they are overwhelmed. Under pressure, it is easy for managers to begin to feel that every new contact, even with people who are bringing good news, is a nuisance because it prevents them from doing something else. Managers in that position often radiate impatience and avoid listening in order to reduce their own feeling of overload.

Some managers, as a screening method, deliberately make it hard for their staff to influence them, so only the important matters come to their attention. Unfortunately, this often leads the staff to accelerate the intensity of their requests in order to get past the boss's protective barrier, which in turn makes the boss feel even more overwhelmed and less willing to listen.

If your boss is overloaded, carefully consider what it is you want and need that cannot be supplied by anyone else.

Keep in mind that if the boss is suffering from overload, even sociable contact that under normal circumstances would be reassuring is a nuisance.

So think about other ways to communicate with your overloaded boss.

- Could you write a memo that summarizes important points and focuses on exactly what action steps are needed?
- Can you better plan meetings with your boss? Think through carefully what it is you want to say and exactly what you need. Then tell the boss exactly how much time you will require and for what.

A crisp statement—for instance, "I can give you the highlights on this problem in about three minutes, and I'll only need two pieces of information from you"—can be very freeing to the boss, since she or he may then anticipate the end of the contact and perhaps plunge into it more wholeheartedly if it promises to be short and to the point.

Find ways to decrease the distance between you and your boss.

Not all bosses who don't listen well are victims of overload. Particularly when there are great discrepancies in power between boss and staff, bosses have a tendency to discount the value of what a staff member has to say and, instead, to attribute all successes to their own cleverness. If this is the case, try to decrease the distance between you and the boss, not by pulling the boss down but by enhancing your personal capacity to get work done. You need to take greater initiative to increase your access to information and resources. Making contacts with people in other parts of the organization can lead to the acquisition of more information that allows you to be more effective in your job. Similarly, building relationships around the organization may give you more access to resources as you need them.

Be confident about what you have to say.
Sometimes people don't get heard because they act as if they're less powerful or knowledgeable than they actually are. For example, some women have conflicts about calling attention to themselves or are afraid to upset others. Assertiveness techniques won't necessarily help. It's more a matter of being convinced that what you have to say is indeed important and that the boss needs to hear it. Expressing yourself clearly usually follows from that. It is a rare boss who can resist listening to a staff member who says, "I've got something here that can help us meet our departmental goals."

If none of these strategies work, make an appointment to talk straightforwardly with your boss.
Schedule an hour, and say that you want to talk about how you can improve your effectiveness. Take care not to begin the conversation by putting your boss on the defensive. Instead, acknowledge the possibility that there could be something in your behavior that is blocking your communication. And rather than complaining in general about never being listened to, you should provide several specific examples so that the boss is clear on what you are talking about. Use the specifics to get to the more general point. You can say something like: "I'm concerned about my effectiveness because I have the impression that you aren't finding my comments valuable. Here are four instances when I had trouble getting your attention [then list a, b, c, d]. If there is something that I am doing wrong, I'd like to know about it so that I can find a better approach. . . ."

Again, it is hard for any boss to resist a staff member who wants to learn how to perform more effectively and who approaches difficulties looking at the possibility that she or he might be responsible for part of the problem. This implied openness to learning often reduces the boss's defensiveness and allows her or him to acknowledge her or his own part in the problem.

Sometimes the boss will genuinely not know what you are doing, either because you hide your light under a bushel or because she or he is too removed from your day-to-day activities to appreciate your work. But occasionally people find themselves working for a boss who maliciously tries to take all the credit for what goes on in her or his unit and deliberately underplays the contributions of staff members. In such a situation you may have to take deliberate steps to build alliances outside your area through service or company-wide committees or task forces, informal social contacts,

(continued)

THE BOSS WHO WON'T LISTEN continued

and job-related contact with peers, managers, or senior executives from other areas within the organization.

Plan a campaign to make yourself noticed.

If the problem with your boss is simply due to an innocent failure to see your contributions, you need to make yourself noticed. Coming to the boss for a quick response to something you have been working on is one perfectly legitimate way to initiate contact. Not only does it allow you to demonstrate what you know, but it is also possible that you will get helpful advice. If you are working on something with your co-workers, and there is a chance to present your findings to the boss or higher-ups, volunteer to make the presentation. As long as your peers don't see you as trying to look good at their expense, they are not likely to refuse your offer.

Volunteer to take on certain chores that your boss does not like to do or finds repetitive.

You can, after carefully assessing the strengths and weaknesses of your boss, try to find an area in which you have complementary skills. For example, a boss who hates to write might delegate first drafting to an assistant with writing skills, thereby getting rid of a burdensome task, and giving the assistant recognition—and useful access to advance information.

Analyze the Problem

To analyze the problem, Jill reviewed the details of the case, her own experience, and Cohen's article. They provided her with several ways to consider the poor communication between Susan and her boss. As a result, Jill created the analysis tree shown in Figure A.4 to visualize two possible sources for the problem.

To answer the first set of questions about the boss, Jill searched the case for clues. (A) Several details about Bart's behavior led her to infer that he must have been overloaded. Both his abrupt ending of the meeting with Susan and his failure to answer her calls seemed irregular. He also mentioned to Susan the impending deadline for the status report, which was most likely a requirement made by his superior. (B) The case contained conflicting information about whether Bart generally listened to Susan's advice. On the one hand, they had a brief meeting twice a week. With the exception of the week in question, the appointments seemed to be kept. On the other hand, Susan felt that Bart was capable of paying more attention to what she had to say than he did, since she observed him listening with much greater concentration to his boss.

As for the second set of questions, about Susan as the source of the problem, the case again provided information from which Jill could draw some conclusions. (C) First, Susan believed that her news about the company's product was vital to her boss. She was, in fact, eager to tell him of her accomplishments on the company's behalf. (D)

Figure A.4

JILL'S ANALYSIS TREE FOR SOLVING SUSAN'S
PROBLEM WITH THE BOSS

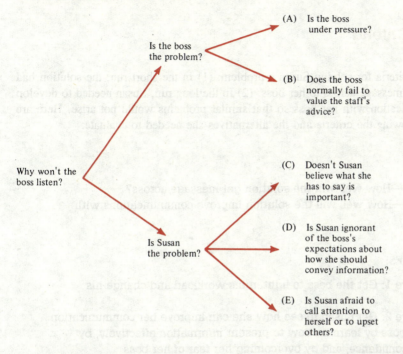

Susan was most likely unaware of her boss's expectations about how she should convey information, especially when he is under pressure. During their meeting, she failed to get immediately to the point that concerned him most, even though she observed his impatience and his sense of urgency. (E) She was intimidated by Bart's experience and felt slighted by the recent hiring of a person for a slot she hoped to fill. These feelings might have caused her to lack confidence in presenting her achievements and to fear angering Bart were she to insist that he listen to her even after he had closed the meeting.

Jill then summarized what the analysis tree revealed about the sources of the problem to see whether the summary suggested possible solutions. The boss *and* Susan seemed to contribute to the problem. The boss was under pressure but, even in the best of circumstances, might not take Susan's advice seriously. For her part, Susan believed in the importance of the information she wanted to convey to her boss, but she was most likely unaware of how best to convey it. She might also have lacked confidence in presenting her achievements and feared angering Bart by raising the issue of his abruptness during their meeting.

On the basis of her analysis, Jill concluded that the situation could be remedied by focusing on the boss, Susan, or the two of them as sources of the problem. For instance, the boss might be able to lighten his workload and begin to listen to Susan. Or, Susan could improve her communication with the boss in several ways. She could learn how to present information effectively to him, build confidence in what she had to say, and overcome her fear of Bart.

Establish Criteria

Jill saw two criteria for solving Susan's problem: (1) In the short run, the solution had to get Susan's message across to her boss. (2) In the long run, Susan needed to develop good communication with her boss so that similar problems would not arise. Here are Jill's notes showing the criteria and the alternatives she needed to evaluate:

CRITERIA:

    Short Run—How well will the solution get message across?
    Long Run—How well will the solution improve communications with boss?

ALTERNATIVES:

    Alternative 1: Get the boss to lighten his workload and change his attitude
    Alternative 2: Get Susan to see how she can improve her communication with her boss by learning how to present information effectively, by building confidence, and by overcoming her fear of her boss

Both alternatives could meet these two criteria, but only one could be implemented. Susan's solution had to depend on how easily and realistically she, as a subordinate, could change the situation.

The accompanying checklist will help you review your analysis of a business problem presented in a case.

CHECKLIST FOR SOLVING A BUSINESS PROBLEM PRESENTED IN A CASE

1. Have you determined the question the reader wants answered?
2. Have you analyzed the problem and done research to determine the sources of the problem and to uncover possible solutions?
3. Have you established criteria for selecting the best alternative among possible solutions and evaluated and chosen among alternative solutions?

THE PROCESS OF WRITING A RESPONSE TO A CASE

As with the problem-solving report, writing a response to a case requires that you have your goal and your reader clearly in mind. Then you need to gather support from the case and from related materials to back up your recommendation.

Setting the Goal

Jill had two purposes: to analyze Susan's problem and recommend to her practical ways to get the boss to listen, and to show her instructor that she could incorporate in her short report appropriate ideas from Cohen's article.

Assessing the Reader

Jill had two readers, Susan and the instructor. Jill had to role-play a friend and business associate of Susan's and write a short report advising Susan about what to do to get her boss to listen.

Jill also had to consider the instructor, who would be "reading over the shoulder" of Susan, so to speak. Like readers in the business world, instructors have certain expectations about what an answer should contain and how it should be organized. In all instances, instructors want the case write-up to be a persuasive document that identifies and analyzes the key underlying problem and makes recommendations, supported by evidence, for solving the problem. Beyond this expectation, instructors' requirements vary.

Some instructors, including Susan's, want a write-up that approximates a realistic business communication, that is, a problem-solving report that you would produce on the job. Among these instructors, some may give you leeway in choosing the format, the coverage, and the sequence of topics you address. In fact, to them, part of the exercise is to test your skills in determining the content and structure of your write-up. Other instructors stipulate a set way to do the case write-up: for instance, put recommendations up front, followed by supporting evidence, then give alternative solutions and their pros and cons; or, build a case for your point of view first and then conclude with your recommendations.

A significant number of instructors want something that more closely resembles an academic essay. These instructors expect you in your case write-up to name and discuss theoretical principles and examples drawn from lecture notes and outside readings.

Susan's instructor had identified what he was looking for in the way of a written response. Jill underlined the key points of the assignment to help her remember them: *"Assume you are Susan's friend and business associate. . . . Write her a short report*

Instructors have different expectations about what should be included in a case write-up.

analyzing her problem and suggesting remedies. . . . Use what you learn from your course readings.'' Jill's instructor wanted to see not only an effective written response to Susan, which should resemble a realistic problem-solving report, but also Jill's ability to apply assigned readings and principles learned in class to solving the problem presented in the case. Since Jill's response had to resemble an authentic business communication, she could *not* quote from the readings or lecture notes.

Gathering Information and Generating Ideas

Given the purpose and readers of her report and the work she had done to solve Susan's problem, Jill had gathered the material she needed to write her response. She knew to what extent the boss and Susan had contributed to the problem. She now had to decide how to organize her material.

Organizing

Jill constructed the analysis tree shown in Figure A.5 to help her group and order her ideas.

Figure A.5
JILL'S ANALYSIS TREE FOR HER MEMO TO SUSAN

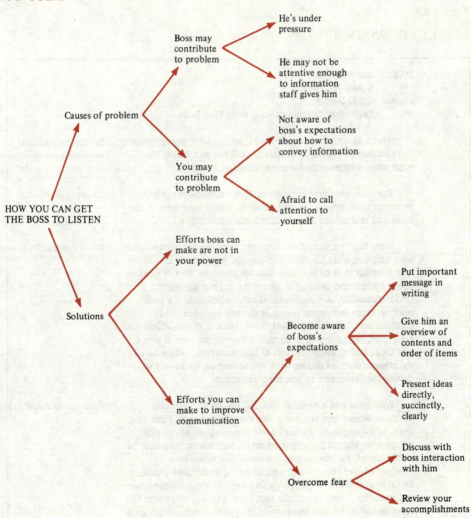

THE RANDOM HOUSE GUIDE TO BUSINESS WRITING

Writing a Draft

Jill used her analysis tree as a guide in putting together her write-up. Notice how she took up all the ideas shown in the analysis tree and appropriately emphasized the efforts Susan could make to improve communication with her boss. After two major drafts and some editing, Jill turned in the case write-up shown in Figure A.6.

Jill successfully completed all aspects of her assignment. First of all, she was convincing in her role as adviser to Susan Woodward. Jill analyzed Susan's problem and presented Susan with concrete solutions. Second, Jill presented herself to Susan as receptive and knowledgeable, and remained sensitive to Susan's ego, fears, and frustra-

Figure A.6

JILL'S CASE WRITE-UP

DATE: April 9, 199_ TO: Susan Woodward FROM: Jill Kellerman RE: Improving Communication with Your Boss	
Susan, in an effort to assist you, let me offer my analysis of the problem you have with your boss, Bart, and follow this with some suggestions for remedying the situation.	*Subject, purpose, and organization of the report*
The disappointing outcome of your encounters with your boss can have several causes, some of which your boss is the source of and others for which you are responsible.	*Causes of problem*
From Bart's unusual abruptness in ending his conversation with you and from his failure to answer your phone messages, it is possible that he is under intense pressure. Bart is anxious about completing the status report for top management. Understandably, this professional responsibility is his first priority, since his status report is directly relevant to his position with top management. As a result of the deadline for his report, he discourages contact between the two of you at this time. But in even the best of circumstances, when he has the time to discuss issues with you at leisure, he seems to devote less attention to you than you merit.	*Boss's contribution to problem*
Your boss has a hand in creating the communication problem, Susan, but you have also contributed to it. First, you seem to be unaware of your boss's expectations about how information should be conveyed when he's under pressure. In all likelihood, he has no time for small talk when he's overloaded, yet you opened your meeting with him by talking about how much you enjoyed going back to your college town of Columbus, Ohio, one of the test sites. Second, you seem to be intimidated by Bart because of his years of experience as a	*Susan's contribution to problem*

successful market researcher. As a result, you're perhaps not confident and straightforward in delivering your important news to him.

To alleviate your communication problems with Bart, I recommend that you follow a course of action that involves improving your end of the communication process, since these changes are under your control:

Recommendations for improving communication

1. Precede each meeting by sending a memo that summarizes your objectives, sets priorities, and outlines the amount of time needed to consider each one.

   Put important message in writing

2. At the beginning of a meeting, give him an overview of what you want to cover, the order in which you want to raise issues, and the time you'll need. He's more likely to listen if you grab him with the importance of your findings early on and limit the amount of time you take.

   Give him an overview

3. Capture Bart's attention by presenting your ideas directly, succinctly, and clearly. Remember that you now possess information that is critical to his immediate objectives. Get to it immediately and avoid wasting his time by talking about your personal experiences. Using such small talk to break the ice may be interpreted as a nuisance by your boss. What's personally important to you is not important to Bart, but the results of the market test and the news about the company's competition are important to him.

   Present ideas directly, succinctly, and clearly

4. If these first three suggestions fail, discuss with your boss the nature of your interaction with him. Schedule a meeting at a time convenient for your boss, and talk about the gaps in communication between the two of you. Airing the problem may reduce your fear of him and help build your confidence. But be careful not to put him on the defensive. Initiate conversation by explaining that you feel your meetings are not as effective as they could be. Ask for suggestions to help you improve your behavior. To illustrate the problem and substantiate your concern, use your last meeting as an example.

   Overcome fear and build confidence by discussing with boss interaction with him

5. Finally, review your accomplishments. Put aside a little time to go over in your mind what you've achieved in the last six months. You've helped design a great questionnaire, conducted interviews with a range of personnel, made careful observations, come up with positive results, and verified your findings. Try to keep these accomplishments in mind the next time you speak with Bart. You may not have his marketing experience, but there's no reason to fear him and every reason for you to feel confident about your ability and the results you've achieved.

   Overcome fear and build confidence by reviewing accomplishments

tions. Third, Jill used relevant ideas from Cohen's article without quoting it, since doing so would have been inappropriate for the realistic business communication she was assigned to write. Fourth, Jill's write-up was well organized and persuasive. She announced her purpose, discussed Susan's problem, and presented several recommendations that were logically developed from her analysis of the problem. Susan would have no trouble following Jill's logic.

The accompanying checklist will help you review your response to a case.

CHECKLIST FOR RESPONDING TO A CASE

1. Have your decided on the purpose of the write-up?
2. Have you determined who your reader is and assessed your reader's knowledge of the situation, attitudes toward you and your message, and expectations about how the write-up should be presented?
3. Do you have the appropriate information and ideas?
4. Have you determined the best way to group and order ideas and information so that they are accessible and convincing to the reader?

Revising a Case Write-Up

Since writing a response to a case may be a new kind of academic assignment to you, you may discover one or more of the following errors in your draft.

1. *Retelling the case*. No matter what the requirements of your assignment, your instructor is interested in a *cogently developed argument,* a document that defines the problem and persuasively supports your recommendations for solving it. Failing to build such an argument may be the result of a common misunderstanding—that you must retell the case.

Here's how one of Jill Kellerman's classmates began her write-up of the same case:

> During our recent conversation, you expressed your concern about the difficulty that you had experienced when you tried to inform your boss about the results of your market research. You stated that Bart had not been very attentive or responsive to what you were saying. You also mentioned that your boss had appeared somewhat preoccupied during your meeting.
>
> You had relevant information that could have helped Bart prepare his status report. Unfortunately, Bart did not listen attentively to what you

were trying to tell him. In fact, he did not even give you the opportunity to describe your test results and findings because he was worried about his other responsibilities, namely, his status report.

This summary of the case just fills up space in the write-up. Assume your reader knows the facts of the case, and begin immediately with your analysis.

2. *Inadequate role-playing*. Several of Jill's classmates had trouble role-playing Susan's friend and adviser. Here, for instance, is the opening of one student's report:

> It is imperative to your career that you brief your boss immediately on the information necessary to his report. Go directly to his office. Tell him you gathered some information on your trip that is vital to his report and that you can take only ten minutes to report this information to him. State the critical information in a brief, organized manner. At the end of the meeting, tell Bart you will give him a full report at your usual meeting time. Then leave promptly.

Regardless of how sound the advice may be, any reader would be offended by the authoritarian tone. The writer sounds more like a dictator giving orders than like an associate giving some friendly advice.

When assigned a case to respond to, you will often be asked to take on a role in the case and write from this point of view to another character in the case. If you are supposed to be a friend, be informal and show your sensitivity to the situation. On the other hand, should you be asked to role-play a consultant with particular expertise, demonstrate your knowledge and impartiality. Whatever role you play, keep your reader in mind so that you convey the appropriate tone and the right kind and amount of information to support your argument.

3. *Poorly organized data*. In the following paragraph by one of Jill's classmates, notice how you have to pick your way through the details to discover the writer's major point.

ORIGINAL

> At the beginning of your meetings with your boss, you should define a time span and your main points. If you do this consistently, he will expect clear, useful presentations from you and will increase his attention. Your confidence in the content of what you have to say will build. Eventually, a closer working relationship will develop. As an assistant to the market researcher, you have the responsibility to report information as quickly as possible.

Jill's classmate needs to decide on the main idea he wants to convey in the paragraph, state that idea first, and then develop it. The information in the case suggested that efficient reporting would improve Susan's communication with her boss. This should be the main point presented in the paragraph. Here is one possible revision:

REVISION

Quick reporting of important information to your boss should improve your communication with him, because he will appreciate your sensitivity to the limitations on his time and your ability to select and relay important information to him. At the beginning of your meetings with your boss, let him know the time you will need and the main points you want to discuss. If you do this consistently, he will expect clear, useful presentations from you and will increase his attention. Your confidence in the content of what you have to say will also build.

The main idea is the need for quick reporting of information. Positioned at the head of the paragraph, this main idea organizes the details that follow concerning *how* Susan can report information quickly.

Presenting lots of poorly organized details is perhaps instructors' most common complaint about students' case write-ups. Using an analysis tree will help you set up a hierarchical structure that frames the information you want to present and will help you to avoid slipping in irrelevant data, or new data under the wrong general heading. When you have doubts about the organization of your case write-up, try to write an analysis tree based on your write-up; then check to see if the tree shows a logical structure for your argument.

4. *Failure to answer the question fully.* One of Jill's classmates analyzed the problem but forgot to give recommendations. Another student did the reverse, presenting recommendations without setting them in the context of his analysis of the problem. Neither of them used Cohen's article.

Be sure to answer all parts of an assignment. If Jill's classmates had underlined the subparts of the question, they might have given a complete answer. We suggest that you read your assignment once through and then review it slowly, underlining key instructions (e.g., "identify," "analyze," "discuss," "give supporting evidence for," "make a recommendation"). Let's look at two other examples of case assignments and students' attempts to figure out their instructors' requirements:

EXAMPLE 1

(The case concerns a young, successful firm that sells personal computers and is preparing for a major expansion.)

Assignment

You're an <u>outside consultant</u> for this entrepreneurial firm. <u>Drawing on your understanding of the growth of the firm</u> over the past five years, <u>identify</u>

APPENDIX A WRITING RESPONSES TO CASES

for your client <u>potential hazards</u> in company morale and productivity that may arise as the company doubles its staff in the next six months. <u>Make recommendations</u> to help the company avoid potential problems. Suggest ways your client can <u>implement</u> your recommendations.

Student Response

The student approached this question by underlining key terms and thinking about the directions. Clearly he needed to

- Role-play a consultant
- Explain how growth of the firm would lead to potential problems
- Make recommendations, based on the analysis, to avoid the problems, and substantiate these recommendations
- Suggest ways to implement the recommendations

EXAMPLE 2

(The case concerns a U.S. bank that has international customers and several branches outside the United States.)

Assignment

You are <u>Roger Burns, assistant to the vice president of personnel and training</u> at the bank. Your boss wants to know <u>how to select and train bank personnel for overseas assignments</u> more effectively because the company is experiencing rapid turnover and low productivity abroad. <u>Use lectures and outside readings</u> to help you analyze the bank's problem. <u>Consider alternative ways</u> to select and train employees. <u>Decide on a course of action to recommend</u> to your boss.

Student Response

The student realized that she needed to

- Consider her business relationship to the vice president
- Solve the problem that is given in the case—the need to select and train employees for overseas assignments more effectively
- Determine the relevance of principles and examples from lectures and outside readings to analyze the problem
- Discuss the pros and cons of alternative solutions before making her recommendations
- Make recommendations

For most case write-ups, instructors want you to use the concepts presented in the course and to demonstrate the reasoning process you used to reach your conclusions and make your recommendations. When you are in doubt about the directions for an assignment, ask your instructor to clarify them. This is particularly important because there is no set format for a case write-up.

5. *Quoting outside readings excessively.* Another professor assigning the case "The Boss Who Won't Listen" did not want students to role-play. Instead, she asked students to address the write-up to the professor, and name and discuss outside readings and lecture notes. But one student relied too heavily on outside readings without showing their relevance to her argument. Here is one section of her write-up:

ORIGINAL

RECOMMENDATIONS

Bart's priority is to complete his status report. Since he doesn't have much time for Susan, she should find ways to limit her contact with him and at the same time to get her message across. According to Allan R. Cohen in "How to Manage Your Boss," Susan should think of other ways to communicate with [her] overloaded boss" (1981, p. 28). Here are some questions Professor Cohen asks his readers to consider that Susan should consider as well:

- Could you write a memo that summarizes important points and focuses on exactly what action steps are needed?
- Can you better plan meetings with your boss? Think through carefully what it is you want to say and exactly what you need. Then tell the boss exactly how much you will require and for what.

A crisp statement—for instance, "I can give you the highlights on this problem in about three minutes, and I'll only need two pieces of information from you"—can be very freeing to the boss, since she or he may then anticipate the end of the contact and perhaps plunge into it more wholeheartedly if it promises to be short and to the point (pp. 28–29).

In quoting the article so extensively, the writer weakens her analysis. Much, if not all, of the quoted passage could be summarized and included in the writer's ongoing analysis. Here is one possible revision:

REVISION

Bart's priority is to complete his status report. Since he doesn't have much time for Susan, she should find ways to limit her contact with him yet to get her message across. According to Allan R. Cohen in "How to Manage Your Boss," these include

- Writing him a memo that summarizes her findings and makes recommendations
- Planning an agenda for the meeting and sharing it with him
- Previewing for him at the beginning of the meeting the topics she wants to cover and her time requirements (198–, p.–).

When you use outside readings in your case write-ups, quote sparingly. Use direct quotations for two reasons: (1) when the actual words of the author convey the information better than you can by either paraphrasing or summarizing it; (2) when the author's recognized expertise in a field can support your own ideas especially well if you cite the expert *in his or her own words*.

The accompanying checklist will help you revise your case response.

CHECKLIST FOR REVISING A CASE RESPONSE

1. Have you avoided retelling the case and, instead, developed a cogent argument?
2. Have you taken the role assigned for you in the case and written from this point of view?
3. Have you organized data to support your recommendation(s)?
4. Have you answered the question fully?
5. Have you effectively integrated outside readings?

SUMMARY

Case assignments are often used in business courses to teach problem-solving skills and the application of business principles to practical situations. Like the problem-solving report, the case response first requires that you solve the business problem (or problems) presented in the case. Once you have determined the solution (or solutions) to the problem, you can write an effective case response by keeping your purpose and reader in mind, gathering and generating ideas that support your solution, organizing that information and those ideas, and being careful to avoid common errors in putting together a case response.

EXERCISES

See "Assessing the Reader," pp. 787–788, for Exercise 1.

1. As a student, you have probably figured out what your instructors want when they ask for a written response to a case. Consider a current assignment and think about what

your instructor expects in the way of your responses to a particular writing assignment. Discuss in class your understanding of your instructor's expectations.

See "Problem Solving and Case Assignments," pp. 778–786, and "The Process of Writing a Response to a Case," pp. 787–792, for Exercises 2 and 3.

2. You are a member of your company's Personnel Department. Your company is looking for a new director of Personnel, and you are on the search committee. Here is an ad the company recently ran in a local paper:

> The director will be responsible to the president of a software company (2,000 professionals, 500 support staff) for activities of the personnel office. Duties include staff recruitment, employee relations, fringe benefits, affirmative action, and training. B.A. required. Applicant must show administrative potential, be able to speak and write well, and enjoy a "high-tech" research environment.

The search committee received over two hundred applications. You have received data on the three top candidates. The data (shown in Figure A.7) include (1) the chief features of each candidate's resume and (2) the head of the hiring committee's notes from his review of the candidates' applications and from his preliminary interviews.

Figure A.7

DATA ON THE TOP THREE CANDIDATES

---

1. Steve Lancaster

Data from Résumé:

Age: 30

Education: Harvard Business School, MBA; Michigan State University, BS

Experience: 2 years, assistant to the VP, Harvard
1 year, assistant director of Personnel, small Boston-based computer firm

General: High achiever in college; excellent managerial potential

Points from Letters of Recommendation: Thrives in a professional environment of other highly talented people; takes the initiative—successfully designed and proposed to top management a computer-based collection of data on personnel

2. Janet Mizuo

Data from Résumé:

Age: 31

Education: University of Illinois, MS; University of Illinois, BS

> Experience: 3 years, employee relations director for Louisville, Kentucky, firm
>
> 4 years, social worker for Cleveland's inner-city area
>
> General: Extensive public speaking experience and training in team building; negotiates labor contracts; hard-working, precise, demanding
>
> <u>Points from Letters of Recommendation</u>: Unusually capable of handling white-collar/blue-collar tensions; adapts easily to new work environments
>
> 3. Donald Marshall
>
> <u>Data from Résumé</u>:
>
> Age: 34
>
> Education: New York University, BS
>
> Experience: 1 year, May Company
>
> 3 years, Legal Aid Society of Model Cities, Unit Affirmative Action
>
> 2 years, junior high school teacher
>
> General: Excellent listener and writer
>
> <u>Points from Letters of Recommendation</u>: Ambitious, hard-working, and eager to enter young thriving industry; willing to "do homework" in a new job; quiet

You were invited to interview all three candidates. Your notes summarizing your impressions of their performances at the interviews are shown in Figure A.8.

Figure A.8

YOUR NOTES ON THE CANDIDATES

> 1. Steve Lancaster
>   - Asked only a few questions about his job responsibilities
>   - Wanted to know about vacation, fringe benefits, and policy for promotion
>   - Came up with several excellent and original ideas

(continued)

YOUR NOTES ON THE CANDIDATES continued

>   for executive seminars in stress management, team building, and personnel assessment
>   - Seemed arrogant, quick to brag about his accomplishments
> 2. Janet Miguo
>   - Had read annual report
>   - Seemed knowledgeable about the job
>   - Knows very little about software
>   - Easy to talk to
>   - Eager to take on a new position
>   - Wanted to know what I saw as the strengths and weaknesses of the department she'd be working for
> 3. Donald Marshall
>   - Asked good questions about job responsibilities
>   - Hard to get him to talk about previous work experience as it relates to career change
>   - Little knowledge of job titles and typical personnel procedures
>   - Owns personal computer and is obviously an enthusiast
>   - Likes the location of the firm and the chance for a change of job

Whom would you recommend? Write a memo to the head of the hiring committee justifying your choice?

3. You are Patrick Jackson and have a B.S. in computer science. Your company is a consulting firm in tax and accounting. You are in your first job as an entry-level manager for the computer application division, a division of twenty young staffers whose job is to keep up with state-of-the-art software and hardware technology and its

application to business. Your department's functions include updating computer equipment and explaining its uses to the company's professionals, who are predominantly nontechnical people.

Lately you have seen that other staffers at your level were acting less friendly toward you. In your early days on the job, you had been a regular member of after-hours gatherings. At those times, there was plenty of complaining about the firm's accountants and tax attorneys. In the words of your friend Steve, "Those guys never appreciate how neat our new computers are—lots more memory, and they can number crunch faster than ever before." And another entry-level staffer, Bob Johnson—a self-proclaimed "computer nerd" who spent all his free time creating new software for his home computer—added, "These accountants and lawyers are back in the Dark Ages. I just can't believe this accountant I worked with yesterday. He wasn't interested in this new accounts payable and accounts receivable package that would make his job twice as easy." As your friends talked, you thought to yourself, "That's funny. I never have trouble with the accountants I'm assigned to." Lately, though you weren't sure of the reasons why, your buddies had begun to leave you out of Happy Hour at the local bar. Even Steve, your friend in the department, seemed close-mouthed. At the same time, you realized that the other staffers were reviewing software half the day while you were constantly on the phone talking to the nontechnical professionals.

Last week your boss, Frank Taylor, told you, "I don't know what you're doing right, but when any of the accountants want help in using new software, they're unhappy working with anyone but you. My boss, Jack Shrader, has been so impressed by your work that he's created a new position—an interface function between us techies and the accountants and tax people. You're being promoted. It's your job to show the staffers what you do."

"But I've never trained anyone to do anything."

"We know that. We don't expect you to be an expert in training, so we want you to work closely with Ned Hancock from Human Resources. And, Pat, maybe you'll have a better sense of the kinds of skills you do have—and that we definitely need to learn—after you've looked over this memo I was sent recently concerning your work. I don't want you to get a big ego, but this is just one of five memos I've received in the same vein."

The memo Frank showed to Pat appears in Figure A.9.

Figure A.9

MEMO TO FRANK CONCERNING PAT'S WORK

DATE: March 15, 199_
TO: Frank Taylor, Director of Computer Applications
FROM: Hal Summerhill, V.P. of Accounting
SUBJECT: Performance of Computer Group Assigned to My Department

As you know, four members of your staff—Nan Carpenter, Pat Jackson, Bob Johnson, and Hank Stoller—have been assigned to my accountants to help them learn the new software packages we've just purchased. I've observed your staffers at work since they began and must report to you that, with the exception of Pat Jackson, the group's performance has been unsatisfactory.

Nan, Bob, and Hank seem to know the software well but have tremendous problems explaining how it works. I attended training seminars given by each of them and know they failed with my accountants. All three of them had trouble communicating <u>how</u> the equipment works and what it could do for us. A few things stand out in my mind. Nan's visuals were unclear. Bob didn't seem interested in people's questions. Hank got sidetracked several times by the details of the software design and lost my staff, who just aren't interested or prepared to follow his explanations.

On the other hand, I am pleased to report to you that Pat Jackson's done a great job with my people. Most of them are middle-level managers in their mid-forties and didn't have an opportunity to work with computers during college. Several are computer phobic, and none of them relishes being trained by a staffer fifteen years their junior. But despite their initial lack of receptivity, Pat's won their respect.

From conversations with my staff and my own observations of Pat's work (I was a participant in two of his sessions), I would credit his success rate to several qualities:

- His willingness to listen and respond to our software needs and our problems using it. In his training sessions, Pat left ample time for our questions and was patient in explaining instructions that were unclear in the software manuals.

- His good judgment in avoiding digressions on the intricacies of the new equipment. Pat told us how the equipment can <u>help us</u>, not how its parts work. Most of us <u>don't care</u> how the equipment works. We just want it to help us do tax planning.

- His ability to communicate technical information in a way that was understandable to us. Too many of your staff speak "computerese" rather than English. We have no idea what they're saying about the equipment and find it impossible to follow their instructions.

- His awareness of our middle managers' resistance to typing. Our managers entered business when secretaries were the only ones who typed. As a result, my managers hated the "typing" necessary to use the computer. Pat made things easier for them by

APPENDIX A WRITING RESPONSES TO CASES 803

> showing how a minimum amount of data entry (he never called it typing) results in quick answers it used to take us a day to get by other means.
>
> I am impressed by the maturity and communication skills of Pat Jackson, and I'm disappointed with the performance of the other three staffers. I suggest that perhaps you can find a way to help Nan, Bob, and Hank learn from Pat's success with us.
>
> HS/cg

As Pat Jackson, you are now ready to announce the first of several training sessions to the entry-level staffers. Your fear is that some of them may be so resentful of your rapid promotion that they will sabotage your efforts to train them.

Write a memo to the entry-level staffers explaining the design and purpose of the training sessions and the topics to be covered. You will be working with Human Resources Manager Ned Hancock, who will help the staffers develop their interpersonal skills through role-playing. The two of you will be sharing the burden. Ned will look carefully at the staffers' ability to communicate. You will be looking for how they handle the technical explanations.

As you plan your message, remember the motto of the computer applications division, made up over a few beers one Happy Hour: "Number Crunchers are Number 1. We're proud to be Computer Nerds." In addition, take into account the broad outline of topics for the training sessions that you worked out with Ned, shown in Figure A.10.

Figure A.10

NED AND PAT'S OUTLINE OF TOPICS
FOR THE SESSIONS

RELATING TO YOUR CLIENTS

- Assessing their background, needs, and attitudes
- Establishing goals and timetables for reaching them
- Building client confidence:
  - Handling computer phobia
  - Making computer terminology understandable
  - Building client motivation
- Conducting applications sessions at one-month intervals to review people's skills and to see how successful the training has been

---

See "Revising a Case Write-Up," pp. 792–797, for Exercises 4 and 5.

4. A classmate of yours has responded to the case presented in Exercise 2. He has asked you to review his write-up. Write a memo to your classmate suggesting how he might improve his response, which follows:

> Steve Lancaster is an extraordinarily bright man. Although he can come across as a bit arrogant, his quick intelligence would win over our professionals. At the interview, he came up with several ways to handle problems with stress and with team building that we've been having with our computer scientists. His kind of creativeness and initiative may be exactly what we need to develop the professional talent in our organization.
>
> From my interview with Janet Mizuo, I thought she had done her homework thoroughly. She had read the annual report and asked specific questions about the structure of our organization and about Personnel's place within it. Judging from the interview, I think she would have an effective style for entering our organization; she observes and asks questions before making a big move. Although she knows very little about software, she is so eager to take on the position that she will probably spend time learning about our products.
>
> Don Marshall was a bit hard to talk to about his previous work experience, but he may have just been nervous about interviewing for this job. Although his work experience has been in the public sector, he knows a lot about personal computers. I can imagine he'd have an easy time dealing with all the other computer buffs in the firm—about 95 percent of us. He struck me as ambitious, hardworking, and willing to spend a lot of time and effort to learn about our industry.
>
> Each of the candidates has significant strengths, but Steve Lancaster is my first choice because he is the candidate most likely to gain the respect and cooperation of our professional staff. His intelligence and innovative ideas will stimulate the professional staff to attend training sessions, which they so badly need, and will create goodwill between the personnel department and the technical areas where Steve's kind of analytical intelligence will be valued.

5. One student's response to the case presented in question 3 is shown in Figure A.11. After reading the response, write a memo to the student indicating how the response could be improved.

Figure A.11

ONE STUDENT'S RESPONSE TO THE CASE
OF PAT JACKSON

DATE: April 5, 199_
FROM: Pat Jackson, Manager of Computer Applications Training
TO: Computer Applications Staff
SUBJECT: Training Sessions on Client Relations

Since complaints have reached our department about the general performance of most of the staff in their client relationships, top management has created a new position, Manager of Computer Applications Training, and has asked me to take on this job.

The seminars I am to direct are to help eliminate some of your major failings identified by our accountants and attorneys. After all, they are our clients. You must learn how to listen and respond to their software needs and refrain from talking about the sophisticated design and capacity of the software. You've got to learn how to speak our clients' language rather than "going on in computerese." I am hoping that the seminars will teach you to improve.

Here is an outline of the sessions I worked out with Ned Hancock of Human Resources. I think the outline will give you an idea of the topics we'll cover.

RELATING TO YOUR CLIENTS

- Assessing their background, needs, and attitudes
- Establishing goals and timetables for reaching them
- Building client confidence:
    - —Handling computer phobia
    - —Making computer terminology understandable
    - —Building client motivation
- Conducting applications sessions at one-month intervals to review people's skills and to see how successful the training has been

I look forward to working with you.

Appendix B
A Brief Guide to Grammar and Punctuation

ABBREVIATIONS

Use abbreviations sparingly, but the following abbreviations are appropriate.

1. With names, abbreviate *Mr., Mrs., Ms.* (not strictly an abbreviation but used in the same way Mr. and Mrs. are used), *Dr., Rev., Jr.,* and *Sr.,* but spell out titles of governmental and military leaders. Abbreviate degrees such as M.D., Ph.D., C.P.A., but avoid duplicating information.

Dr. Barbara Campbell
Barbara Campbell, M.D.
Susan Meyers, Ph.D.
Henry Johnson, C.P.A.
Captain William Shultz
Senator Richard Shelby

2. Abbreviate names of agencies, groups, people, places or objects commonly referred to by capitalized initials.

U.S. Senate
Washington, D.C.
NFL
TV
IBM

3. For less common names of agencies or groups or for technical terms that are going to be used repeatedly in a letter or report, spell out the name in full for the first use and introduce the abbreviation parenthetically immediately after. Then use the abbreviation throughout the document.

The National Fire Protection Association (NFPA) has recently announced the appointment of Corpus Christi Fire Chief Ken Lavey as a principal member of the NFPA Technical Committee on public fire service operation.

APOSTROPHE

1. Use an apostrophe to mark the omission of letters in a contraction.

it is	it's
should not	shouldn't
she will	she'll
do not	don't

2. Use an apostrophe to form the possessive case of most nouns and indefinite pronouns.

If a noun (singular or plural) does not end in *s,* add an apostrophe and *s.*

corporation's profits
fabric's construction
Israel's future
everybody's business
women's achievements

If a name or a singular noun ends in *s,* add an apostrophe and *s* only if the second *s* does not make pronunciation difficult; otherwise, add only an apostrophe.

success's trappings	Jess's memo
class's schedule	boss's desk
headquarters' personnel	business ethics' dilemmas
Archimedes' theorem	*Times'* publisher

If a plural noun ends in *s,* add only an apostrophe.

Salomon Brothers' employees
dancers' movements

To indicate joint possession, make only the last noun possessive.

Karen Warner and Paula Winthrop's new company

If a noun is compound, make only the last word possessive.

chairman of the board's responsibility
somebody else's situation
department head's discretion

CAPITALIZATION

1. Capitalize the first word of a sentence and the first word of a sentence in a direct quotation.

Long ago it was said, "Bed is a bundle of paradoxes: we go to it with reluctance, yet we quit it with regret."

2. Capitalize proper nouns and their abbreviations. Proper nouns are the names of specific people, places, or things that set them off from the species (e.g., *Clara Owens,* instead of the common noun *person; Hyatt Regency,* instead of *hotel*). Consider the following categories of proper nouns.

PEOPLE

Katherine Graham
Lee Iacocca
Ayn Rand

ETHNIC GROUPS, NATIONALITIES, LANGUAGES, RELIGIOUS BODIES, AND SACRED BOOKS

Afro-Americans
Chinese
Arabic
Vatican Council
Talmud
Koran

PLACES

    West Germany
    Wall Street
    Harvard Square
    Ozarks
    Garden of Eden

Although directional terms (north, south, east, west) are not capitalized, when such terms are used to designate specific geographical areas or have reference to such areas, they are capitalized.

    Northeast
    Midwesterner
    Deep South

ORGANIZATIONS

    Union of Concerned Scientists
    National Organization for Women
    Securities and Exchange Commission
    American Automobile Association

HOLIDAYS, DAYS OF THE WEEK, HOLY DAYS, AND MONTHS OF THE YEAR

    Veterans Day
    Halloween
    Wednesday
    Yom Kippur
    February

NOUNS THAT REPLACE A PROPER NAME

Even though Father promised to accompany me, the captain said no.

3. For titles of pieces of writing and works of art or architecture, capitalize the first and last words, the first word that follows a colon or semicolon, and all other words except articles, conjunctions, and prepositions of fewer than five letters.

    Richard Cantillon: Entrepreneur and Economist   the Pietà
    Two Years Before the Mast   the Parthenon
    Of Mice and Men

COLON

1. Use a colon to indicate that what follows will illustrate, explain, or clarify. What follows may be a list, a series, a quotation, a clause, or a word.

The confusion was massive: trucks, cars, bicycles, and pedestrians moved indiscriminately about the square.

The message from the EPA was clear: the corporation would be fined heavily unless it cleaned up the toxic wastes from its dump site.

There's only one word to describe his proposal: brilliant.

Make certain that a complete sentence precedes the colon. (But in introducing lists, the use of a phrase preceding the colon is becoming more acceptable.)

Faulty: We had everything: desks, chairs, lamps, computers, telephones, that we needed to start processing orders.

Correct: We had everything we needed to start processing orders: desks, chairs, lamps, computers, telephones.

Faulty: Features of the compiler include: optimal code, complete libraries, and built-in functions.

Correct: Features of the compiler include optimal code, complete libraries, and built-in functions.

Acceptable: Features of the compiler include:
    optimal code,
    complete libraries, and
    built-in functions.

2. Use a colon to follow the salutation in a business letter.

Dear Ms. Scott:

3. Use a colon to separate titles from subtitles.

Stemming the Tide: Arms Control in the Johnson Years

COMMA

1. Use a comma to separate independent clauses joined by a coordinating conjunction (*and*, *but*, *or*, *for*, *nor*, and sometimes *so* and *yet*).

Upon arrival, they were less educated than the native population, *yet* their children are better educated than those of the native-born.

2. Use a comma to set off most introductory phrases and clauses.

As to the prospects for reform, no one can be sure.

But short introductory phrases may not require a comma.

Within a month at least four division heads had left the firm.

3. Use a comma to set off nonessential (nonrestrictive) phrases or clauses, appositives, and phrases expressing contrast.

Margaret Thatcher, who recently won reelection, will increase her number of foreign trips next year.

His computer, an IBM-PC, can run the packages we need.

My blue shirt, not my gray one, needs pressing.

4. Use a comma to set off participial modifiers at the end of a sentence.

Carol spent the week on the financial statement, adding columns, checking figures, and formating the spreadsheet.

5. Use commas to set off *yes, no,* tag questions, words of direct address, and mild interjections.

Yes, I'm ready to make the presentation to the stockholders.

I think we should reconsider our offer, don't you?

Mr. Rodriguez, how are you voting on this proposal?

Really, did your boss say that?

6. Use a comma between items in a series.

A fight is not, as some writers claim, an erotic ballet, a primitive ritual, or a chess match.

He will reduce bureaucratic power by giving each division the right to determine what they will produce, how much they will produce, and how they will use the resulting profits.

7. Use a comma to separate a series of adjectives when they modify the same noun.

His was an overbearing, oppressive, and power-hungry personality.

The tall, new, glass office building overshadowed the historic church.

8. Use a comma to set off a direct quotation from the clause that names the source of the quotation.

"The Soviet bureaucratic problem," according to Galbraith, "is our own writ large."

9. Use commas to separate items in an address, a place name, or a date when the month, day, and year are included.

For further information, write to 624 Brattle Street, Cambridge, Massachussetts 02138.

Akron, Ohio, is the home of the Soap Box Derby.

We took these photographs on December 18, 1987, just before we began renovations. [But no comma is required when using only the month and the year: We began renovations in January 1988.]

10. Use a comma to prevent misreading, even when no standard punctuation rule applies.

Spectators experienced in driving fast cars, carefully selected their seats for the Indy 500. [The comma is necessary to avoid creating the impression that spectators drove fast cars carefully.]

Long before, Mike had visited the Grand Canyon. [The comma prevents the reader from thinking the sentence will describe something that happened long before Mike's visit.]

COMMA SPLICE

A comma splice is the error of joining two independent clauses with nothing but a comma.

They graduated from business school, all they could think of was a long vacation.

Readers expect the same sentence to continue after the comma, but here they find themselves reading a second sentence before they know the first one is finished. In other words, two sentences have been spliced together with a comma. To correct a comma splice, do one of four things:

1. Put a conjunction after the comma.

They graduated from business school, and all they could think of was a long vacation.

2. Replace the comma with a semicolon.

They graduated from business school; all they could think of was a long vacation.

3. Replace the comma with a period, making two separate sentences.

They graduated from business school. All they could think of was a long vacation.

4. Subordinate one clause to the other, using a subordinating conjunction.

When they graduated from business school, all they could think of was a long vacation.

Often comma splices are caused when the writer uses a conjunctive adverb to join two independent clauses. To join two independent clauses with a conjunctive adverb, you must use a semicolon. Otherwise use a period to make two separate sentences. Common conjunctive adverbs include:

accordingly	instead
also	likewise
anyway	meanwhile
besides	moreover
by this means	namely
certainly	nevertheless
conversely	next
consequently	nonetheless
finally	now
for example	on the other hand
further	otherwise
furthermore	similarly
hence	still
however	then
in addition	thereafter
in fact	therefore
incidentally	thus
indeed	undoubtedly

APPENDIX B A BRIEF GUIDE TO GRAMMAR AND PUNCTUATION

Faulty: The phenomenon is difficult to explain, *nevertheless*, most market analysts agree on its importance.

Correct: The phenomenon is difficult to explain; *nevertheless*, most market analysts agree on its importance.

Correct: The phenomenon is difficult to explain. *Nevertheless*, most market analysts agree on its importance.

It may be difficult to know whether you have a conjunctive adverb, which does require a semicolon, rather than a subordinating conjunction, which requires only a comma. **To test,** see if you can move the conjunction to a location within the clause that it introduces. If so, you have a conjunctive adverb.

Correct: The phenomenon is difficult to explain; most market analysts, *nevertheless*, agree on its importance. [Because *nevertheless* can be relocated within the clause it modifies, it is a conjunctive adverb and the sentence requires a semicolon.]

Correct: The phenomenon is difficult to explain, *although* most market analysts agree on its importance. [*Although* is not a conjunctive adverb since it would not make sense to say "market analysts *although* agree on its importance." The sentence requires only a comma.]

DANGLING AND MISPLACED MODIFIERS

In general, modifiers should appear as close as possible to the part of the sentence they are modifying. Modifiers are *dangling* if what they should logically modify does not appear in the sentence. Modifiers are *misplaced* if they appear to modify the wrong part of the sentence, or if one cannot be certain what part of the sentence they modify.

DANGLING MODIFIERS

While walking around the store, the laser printer caught my eye. [The laser printer was not walking around the store. The introductory phrase modifies *I*, which does not appear in the sentence.]

After buying a computer, his typewriter seemed unnecessary. [His typewriter did not buy the computer.]

Being a good driver, her car didn't slide off the icy road. [Her car is not the good driver.]

My suitcase was stolen before leaving on vacation. [The suitcase did not leave on vacation.]

MISPLACED MODIFIERS

He cooked steaks for the picnickers on the grill.
[*On the grill* appears to modify the picnickers rather than the steaks.]

Many students are passed by professors who don't turn in their homework.
[*Who don't turn in their homework* appears to modify professors, rather than students.]

At department meetings, the manager only looked at Bruce. [This sentence appears to mean that the manager only *looked at* Bruce, as opposed to, say, speaking to him; but did the writer intend that the manager *looked only at Bruce* and did not look at anyone else?]

Consumers who sued corporations frequently received large settlements. [Does this mean *consumers who sued frequently,* or *consumers frequently received?*]

In general, don't let modifiers separate a verb phrase or split an infinitive.

Faulty: The copywriters *had,* by working all day on the brochure, *finished* it on time.

Correct: The copywriters, by working all day on the brochure, *had finished* it on time.

Faulty: The sales personnel had expected prices *to not increase.*

Correct: The sales personnel had not expected prices *to increase.*

DASH

1. Use a pair of dashes to give special emphasis to parenthetical remarks.

This tick variety proved extremely difficult to spot—especially in its earliest stage—because it is far smaller than the familiar dog ticks.

2. Use the dash or a pair of dashes to indicate an abrupt shift in sentence structure or thought.

Should the workers try again to settle grievances—after all, management walked out of the first meeting—or just go on strike?

3. Use a dash to set off introductory lists or summary statements.

Slide projector, screen, slides, script—had she remembered everything for the trade show?

APPENDIX B A BRIEF GUIDE TO GRAMMAR AND PUNCTUATION

FRAGMENTS

A sentence fragment is a group of words that looks like a sentence—it begins with a capital letter and ends with a period—but isn't. It lacks either a subject or a verb, or it is a dependent clause attached to no main clause. Most fragments are caused by the writer improperly punctuating parts of the sentence preceding or following them.

Faulty: I can imagine expedient ways of reducing the feline population. Although perhaps not without harm to my relations with the neighbors.

Correct: I can imagine expedient ways of reducing the feline population, although perhaps not without harm to my relations with the neighbors.

Faulty: There is bound to be friction with the United States. Regardless of which party rules South Korea in the future.

Correct: There is bound to be friction with the United States, regardless of which party rules South Korea in the future.

Faulty: Our car offers all these features as standard equipment. Resulting in an automobile that responds quickly and efficiently.

Correct: Our car offers all these features as standard equipment, resulting in an automobile that responds quickly and efficiently.

Faulty: The design reflects the work of fifty years. Basic engineering and safety research.

Correct: The design reflects the work of fifty years of basic engineering and safety research.

HYPHEN

1. Use a hyphen to spell some compound nouns (e.g., *print-out, slip-up*), adjectives (e.g., *water-repellent, high-test*), and verbs (e.g, *ice-skate, weather-strip*). The conventions governing the spelling of compound words can vary considerably. For example, compound words may be written as two words, like the noun *time deposit,* as one word, like the noun *timecard,* or as a hyphenated word, like the noun *time-out.* To be sure of the spelling, consult your dictionary. The following rules, however, are reliable for forming compound adjectives.

A hyphen can form a compound adjective when two or more words serve together as a single modifier before a noun.

>   little-known opera
>   Chinese-speaking faculty
>   out-of-print directory

Note that the hyphens are unnecessary when the adjectives are used after the noun.

>   The directory is out of print.

Hyphens can form an adjective that is coined for a single use.

>   Her boss gave her a don't-interrupt-this-meeting-or-you're-out look.

2. Use a hyphen to attach prefixes and suffixes when a prefix is combined with a capital letter or to prevent misreading or confusion.

>   pre-Raphaelite
>   co-worker
>   re-refrigerated
>   anti-inflammatory

3. Use a hyphen to divide a word at the end of a line only when absolutely necessary.

- Divide words only at the end of a syllable. (Consult a dictionary for syllabification.)
- Do not divide a word so that a single letter stands at the end of one line or one or two letters at the beginning of the next line (e.g., a-cre, phobi-a).
- Divide compound words into the words that make them up, or at the hyphen. (e.g., guide-books, long-range, post-modernist).

ITALICS (OR UNDERLINING FOR ITALICS)

In printing, type that slants to the right is known as *italic type*. To indicate italic type in handwritten or typed materials, use underlining.

1. Italicize titles of books, magazines and journals, newspapers, plays, films, works of art, long poems, pamphlets, musical works, movies, television and radio programs, and record albums.

The Queen's Prize: The Story of the National Rifle Association
the *New Republic*
the *Wall Street Journal*
A Chorus Line
Gone with the Wind
the *McNeil/Lehrer Newshour*
Sgt. Pepper's Lonely Hearts Club Band

Note that except in book titles, the article (the) is not included in the title.

2. Italicize ships, aircraft, and spacecraft.

the *Titanic*
the *Spirit of St. Louis*
Apollo IX

3. Italicize foreign words and phrases that have yet to be accepted into the English language.

deus ex machina
affaire de coeur

4. Italicize letters, words, and numbers used as words.

Phantom begins with a *p*, not an *f*.

The word *home* means different things to different people.

Don't confuse a *three* with an *eight*.

5. Use italics for emphasis; but use sparingly, since too much emphasis is no emphasis at all.

NUMBERS

1. In general, use words instead of numerals for numbers under 100. But spell out large round numbers.

three years' experience   a faculty of 326
twenty-four acres   ten thousand soldiers

2. If some numbers in a paragraph (or section) are over 100, use numerals for all.

The school had 198 Asian students—122 from Japan, 60 from India, 12 from Taiwan, and 4 from South Korea.

3. Use numerals with *million* and *billion,* for money amounts, for ages, and for percentages.

5 million people
a 20-cent increase
a 50-year-old president
a 10 percent profit

4. If a sentence begins with a number, spell out the number. But if this is awkward, rewrite the sentence to avoid beginning with a number.

Awkward: Two hundred and twenty thousand square feet should be ample office space.

Better: Office space of *220,000* square feet should be ample.

5. In addresses, use numerals for street numbers, except *one,* which should be spelled out.

One East Tremont
57 South Main Street

When the street name is a number, use words for streets from one to ten, use numerals for streets from eleven up.

155 East Tenth Avenue
4288 North Fourth Street
230 West 57th Avenue
22 South 122nd Street

When no direction separates the number from the street, use a dash.

348—52nd Street
1708—53rd Avenue

APPENDIX B A BRIEF GUIDE TO GRAMMAR AND PUNCTUATION

PARALLELISM

Similar or coordinate elements in a sentence should be similar or parallel in form. Parallelism reinforces the equal importance of coordinate parts in a sentence.

In the days when oil was | accessible, plentiful, and cheap, | our business boomed.

In a single year | the Filipinos threw out Ferdinand Marcos, the people of Hong Kong pressed the British government for direct elections, and South Koreans forced democracy on their rulers.

For | pulling tiny bones from fish, turning bacon or fillets in the skillet, or getting the last olive out of a narrow jar, | these tweezers are great.

1. Use parallelism when elements are linked by coordinating conjunctions.

Faulty: The manager advocated the development of a corporate strategy, writing a resource allocation plan, and to evaluate investments.

Revised: The manager advocated developing a corporate strategy, writing a resource allocation plan and evaluating investments.

To test for correct parallelism, make sure that each parallel phrase that follows the introductory word would read smoothly if it stood without parallel elements.

Faulty: The scholar described his love and dedication to the study of Impressionist art.

If we try to read each parallel element alone, the first does not read smoothly.

The scholar described his ⟨love / dedication⟩ to the study

[It does not make sense to say *his love to the study,* so the parallelism must be corrected.]

Correct: The scholar described his *love for* and *dedication to* the study of Impressionist art.

Sometimes, to avoid confusion, the introductory word(s) must be repeated.

Confusing: The judge showed leniency by not imprisoning the officials and fining the company. [Did the judge show leniency by only fining the company or by not fining the company at all?]

Revised: The judge showed leniency by not imprisoning the officials and by not fining the company.

2. Use parallelism when elements are linked by correlative conjunctions such as *both . . . and, not only . . . but also,* or *either . . . or.*

Faulty: He told her that he would *both* give her a raise *and* would let her hire an assistant.

Revised: He told her that he would *both* give her a raise *and* let her hire an assistant.

Faulty: Either the markets would have to coordinate their margins and clearing systems *or* live with inefficiency.

Revised: Either the markets would have to coordinate their margins and clearing systems *or* they would have to live with inefficiency.

3. Use parallelism when elements are being compared or contrasted.

Weak: Sam was satisfied with a C in accounting rather than study for an A.

Revised: Sam was satisfied to receive a C in accounting rather than to study for an A.

4. Use parallelism when items are listed or outlined.

Weak: Deregulation of the airline industry was marked by:
1. A decrease in some air fares.
2. The number of carriers increased.
3. Greater number of near misses in the sky.

Revised: Deregulation of the airline industry was marked by:
1. A decrease in some air fares.
2. An increase in the number of carriers.
3. An increase in the number of near misses in the sky.

POSSESSIVE PRONOUNS

The following are possessive pronouns. They indicate possession and do not require an apostrophe.

>   my, mine
>   your, yours
>   his, her, hers, its
>   our, ours
>   their, theirs

Because *its* and *it's (it is)* are similar in form, they may cause confusion. **To test** whether you have the correct form, substitute *his* for *its* and *he's* for *it's*. If the sentence sounds grammatically correct, you have the correct form.

>   Architectural style has turned its back on modernism. [Turned *his* back is grammatically correct, so *its* is the correct word.]

>   It's reduced to a manageable problem. [*He is* reduced is grammatically correct, so *it's* is the correct word.]

PRONOUNS

Pronouns take the place of nouns or of noun phrases that have already been used.

>   Harriet thought that she would be offered the job.

>   The colonel embodied a world in which nothing had changed since the glorious victory at Iwo Jima.

1. Be sure that pronouns refer clearly to their antecedents.

Faulty: The personnel in Public Relations included the statistic in the annual report. They later took *it* to the stockholders' meeting. [Does *it* refer to the statistic or the report?]

Revised: The personnel in Public Relations included the statistic in the annual report that they later took to the stockholders' meeting.

2. The pronouns *this, that, they, it, which,* and the like can occasionally be used to refer not to a specific word or phrase but to a whole idea expressed in a preceding clause or sentence.

>   Helen was not intimidated by the outbursts from some of her colleagues or by the

apathy of others. She had too much experience, education, and confidence for *that*. [*That* refers to the whole idea expressed in the preceding sentence.]

But using pronouns for such broad references is often misleading and should be avoided.

Misleading: Dr. Roberts explained that Americans took the Constitution for granted as the logical outcome of the Revolution, *which* was not true. [Was it Dr. Roberts's explanation of Americans' opinion that was not true, or the idea that the Constitution was granted as the logical outcome of the Revolution?]

Revised: Dr. Roberts explained that Americans took the Constitution for granted as the logical outcome of the Revolution, but his view was faulty.

Revised: Dr. Roberts explained that Americans took the Constitution for granted as the logical outcome of the Revolution, but they were wrong.

Faulty: Genetic research can result in tremenduous profits but is expensive and could take years to show a return on investment. Above all, it frightens the public. *This* will keep most firms out of it. [Does *this* refer only to the fact that it frightens the public?]

Revised: Genetic research is expensive and could take years to show a return on investment. Above all, it frightens the public. These factors will keep most firms out of it.

PRONOUN AGREEMENT IN NUMBER

Pronouns must agree in number with their antecedents.

1. Use a plural pronoun when two or more antecedents are joined by *and*.

Sarah *and* Jim have studied for *their* exam.

2. Use a singular pronoun when two or more antecedents are joined by *or* or *nor*.

Either David *or* Bruce will bring *his* calculator.

3. When one of two antecedents joined by *or* or *nor* is singular and the other is plural, make the pronoun agree with the nearer.

Neither my roommate nor my classmates *have* planned for spring vacation.

Neither the children nor my father brought *his* own car.

APPENDIX B A BRIEF GUIDE TO GRAMMAR AND PUNCTUATION

    4.   When a collective noun, such as *group, faculty, team, family, audience,* or *committee,* is referred to, make the pronoun singular if the group as a whole is being referred to.

    The appraisal committee finished *its* evaluation. [The committee *as a whole* finished the evaluation.]

    Make the pronoun plural if members of the group are being considered individually.

    The division broke up when it became clear *they* could not divide their responsibilities amicably.
    [*Individual members* of the division could not divide their responsibilities.]

PRONOUN CASE

Some personal pronouns, as well as relative pronouns, have separate forms, depending on whether they are used in the subjective or objective case.

	Singular	Plural	Relative
Subjective:	I, you, he, she, it	we, you, they	who
Objective:	me, you, him, her, it	us, you, them	whom

    1.   Use the subjective form when a pronoun is the subject of a sentence or a clause.

    After *I* phoned Tony, *I* called the theater.

    2.   If you have trouble determining whether the pronoun in a compound construction is subjective or objective, **test** each pronoun singly.

    After *she and I* phoned Tony and Steve, we left to meet them at the theater. [**Test:** Should you say, "After *her and me* phoned Tony and Steve"? No, because you would never say, "After *her* phoned" or "After *me* phoned."]

    3.   Use the subjective form when the pronoun is a subjective complement following a form of the verb *to be (am, is, are, was, were, been.)*

    The ones who organized the trip were Gary and *I.*

    It was *she* whom the faculty tenured last fall.

4. Use the objective form when the pronoun is a direct object, an indirect object, or an object of a preposition.

They encouraged the vice president to hire *him*.

5. Compound objects often cause writers problems. To determine the correct form, **test** each pronoun singly to see if you would use that form by itself.

They encouraged the vice president to hire him and me. [**Test:** Should you say, "They encouraged the vice president to hire *he and I*"? No, because you would never say, "They encouraged the vice president to hire *he*" or "They encouraged the vice president to hire *I*."]

6. Use the appropriate case of the pronoun after *than* or *as* in a comparison, depending on the implied clause.

We remembered that she was taller *than* he. [The implied clause at the end of the sentence is *than he was tall* and takes a pronoun in the subjective case.]

In the following sentence, the appropriate case is essential for clarity because two different clauses are implied, depending on the case of the pronoun.

Monica believed Lynn as much as *him*. [Implied clause: as much as *she believed him*]

Monica believed Lynn as much as *he*. [Implied clause: as much as *he* believed Lynn]

7. Make the case of the pronoun in appositive constructions agree with the case of the noun that follows.

He bequeathed the stock to *us* heirs.

Heirs is in the objective case (as an object of a preposition) and requires the objective form of the pronoun. **To test** whether *us* is appropriate, drop the noun that the pronoun identifies. If the sentence reads correctly, the pronoun form is correct.

He bequeathed the stock to *us*.

8. In using *who, whoever, whom,* or *whomever,* determine the appropriate case of the pronoun by determining its function in the clause in which it appears.

People who read detective novels would probably enjoy this one. [The clause is *who read detective novels*. *Who* is the subject of the clause and so takes the subjective form.]

The dealers whom people know to be honest get the most repeat business. [The clause is *whom people know to be honest*. *Whom* is the direct object of the clause and so takes the objective form.]

To test whether you have the correct form, turn the clause into a question, then answer the question with the words *he* or *him*. If the answer is *he*, the clause takes the *who* form; if the answer is *him*, the clause takes the *whom* form.

She chose a lawyer who she knew had experience. [Who did she know had experience? *He* had experience. Therefore the correct form is *who*.]

Mr. Peterson, whom Sharon recommended for the job, is the best qualified. [Whom did Sharon recommend? Sharon recommended *him*. Therefore the correct form is *whom*.]

Whom do you wish to see at the meeting? [You wish to see *him*. Therefore the correct form is *whom*.]

QUOTATION MARKS

1. Use quotation marks to enclose direct quotations from speech or writing.

"You can't ask too many questions," she advised.

It was the hiring manager who said, "You mean no one has checked his references!"

2. Use single quotation marks to enclose a quotation within a quotation.

Berman explained his terminology: "I use 'communist' loosely to denote leftists who regard dictatorship as a suitable expression of socialist ideals."

3. Use quotation marks around titles of articles, essays, chapters in books, short stories, short poems, and songs.

"The Piper at the Gates of Dawn" (Chapter 7 of *The Wind in the Willows*)

"Blood Lust in Academia" (article in the *New Republic*)

4. Use quotation marks to indicate that a word or phrase is being used in a special way.

Considering shareholders' sentiments, was the stock split really such an "opportunity"?

"Liberation," in this case, had little to do with increased wages.

5. Avoid using quotation marks to apologize for trite expressions or slang. If the word is appropriate, use it without quotations. If it is inappropriate, replace it.

Faulty: We recommend going into production "full steam."

Faulty: The new project would be "a piece of cake."

6. To punctuate quotations:

- Place commas and periods inside quotation marks.
- Place colons and semicolons *outside* quotation marks.
- Place dashes, question marks, or exclamation points inside when they apply to the quotation, and outside when they apply to the whole statement.

I asked, "When should I do it?"

Did you say, "Do it now"?

RUN-ON SENTENCES

A run-on sentence runs together two main clauses without using any punctuation. Correct run-ons in the same way as comma splices: provide a coordinating conjunction, use a semicolon, make each clause a separate sentence, or change one of the main clauses to a subordinate clause.

Faulty: I wore a conservative suit I wanted to blend in with the bankers.

Revised:
1. I wanted to blend in with the bankers, so I wore a conservative suit.
2. I wore a conservative suit; I wanted to blend in with the bankers.
3. I wore a conservative suit. I wanted to blend in with the bankers.
4. In order to blend in with the bankers, I wore a conservative suit.

SEMICOLON

1. Use a semicolon to join independent clauses that are closely related.

The court ruled in his favor; he had nothing more to worry about.

The agreed tax-reform package will give the temporary boost needed; it will cut taxes and ensure higher demand.

APPENDIX B A BRIEF GUIDE TO GRAMMAR AND PUNCTUATION

2. Use a semicolon to separate main clauses joined by a conjunctive adverb such as *however, nevertheless,* and *therefore* (see a more complete list of conjunctive adverbs on p. 814).

Edward delivered the marketing plan; however, he didn't stay to discuss it.

You can distinguish conjunctive adverbs from other connectors by realizing that they can be moved to other positions in the clause without affecting the clause's meaning.

Edward delivered the marketing plan; he didn't stay to discuss it, however.

3. Use a semicolon to separate elements in a series if some of the elements themselves contain commas.

The product line included plastic ketchup bottles, which the company was advertising heavily; toothpaste tubes; cans without lead seams; and jars.

SUBJECT-VERB AGREEMENT

Subjects should agree in number with their verbs. Some grammatical patterns require careful attention if you are to avoid agreement errors.

1. When words or phrases come between the subject and verb, make sure the verb agrees with the real subject.

Hours of study *were required* to pass the CPA exam. [The verb must agree with the subject, *hours,* not the nearer word, *study.*]

The shelf full of files, ledgers, and boxes *was sagging* to the floor. [The verb must agree with the subject, *shelf,* not the nearer word, *boxes.*]

2. When singular subjects are joined by *or* or *nor,* use a singular verb. If the subjects differ in number, make the verb agree with the subject nearer to it.

Either the controller or the lawyer *was* to submit the report.

Neither the president nor the vice presidents *were* aware that it hadn't been submitted.

3. Singular indefinite pronouns—such as *another, anybody, anyone, anything, each, either, everybody, everyone, neither, nobody, none, no one,* and *one*—take singular verbs.

Everyone is at lunch.

Neither is likely to give in.

Everybody wants to take a break.

4. The indefinite pronouns *all, any, most, more, none,* and *some* take either a singular or a plural verb, depending on their meaning in the sentence.

Some of the program code is faulty. [*Some* refers to the singular noun *code*.]

All of the diskettes are ruined. [*All* refers to the plural *diskettes*.]

None of it is well documented. [*None* refers to the singular pronoun *it*.]

None of the programs are well documented. [*None* refers to the plural noun *programs*. But note that for strict grammarians, *none* always means *no one* and therefore should always be considered singular.]

5. When the subject is a collective noun, use a singular verb when referring to the group as a single unit, and a plural verb when referring to the individual members of the group.

The staff *responds* to the general manager. [The staff acts together as a single unit.]

The staff *leave* work at different times. [Members of the staff act independently.]

The board of directors *has read* the annual report. [The board has acted together.]

The board of directors *like* different parts of it. [Members of the board think independently.]

6. When using linking verbs, be sure the verb agrees with its subject, not with a complement.

The most popular part of the annual report *is* the photographs. [The subject is the singular noun *part*.]

Variable rate mortgages are now a bargain. [The subject is the plural noun *mortgages*.]

APPENDIX B A BRIEF GUIDE TO GRAMMAR AND PUNCTUATION

7. When *here* or *there* delays the subject until after the verb, make sure the verb agrees with the subject.

Here *rests* the source of so many of our troubles. [The subject is the singular noun *source*.]

There *are* more profits to be made [The subject is the plural noun *profits*.]

8. When using the relative pronouns *who, which,* and *that* as subjects, make the verb agree with the antecedent.

They are the night workers who *get* so much done. [*Who* refers to the plural noun *workers*.]

Be especially careful when using the phrases *one of* and *only one of*.

Afghanistan is one of the countries that *are* affected by Islamic fundamentalism. [That refers to *countries*, of which Afghanistan is one.]

Afghanistan is the only one of the countries that *is* affected by Islamic fundamentalism. [That refers to *the only one,* that is Afghanistan.]

9. With subjects that are plural in form but singular in meaning, use a singular verb.

The *corps* is ready to attack.

Politics requires idealism and pragmatism.

Liberal arts is a popular major.

Sons and Lovers was made into a movie.

10. Subjects indicating quantities—such as sums of money, measurements, or distance—usually take singular verbs.

Three quarters of the boxcar *was* full of sawdust.

Forty yards of reinforced nylon *is* ready for stitching.

Twelve inches *is* not much of a clearance.

But when the items in a quantity are thought of as separate units, they usually require a plural verb.

Half of my stocks *have* done very well this year. [The stocks did well separately.]

One-third of the households *use* liquid soap. [Households use soap individually.]

NOTES

CHAPTER 1

1. Martha H. Rader and Alan P. Wunsch, "A Survey of Communication Practices of Business Graduates by Job Category and Undergraduate Major," *Journal of Business Communication 17* (Summer 1980): 40; and Marie E. Flatley, "A Comparative Analysis of the Written Communication of Managers at Various Organizational Levels in the Private Business Sector," *Journal of Business Communication 19* (Summer 1982): 48.

2. R. L. Jenkins, R. L. Reizenstein, and F. S. Rodgers, "Report Cards on the MBA," *Harvard Business Review 5* (September–October 1984): 28.

3. Ross M. Stolzenberg, John Abowd, and Roseann Giarrusso, "The Myth of the Modern MBA Student," *Selections,* Autumn 1986, 9–21. Graph from preliminary draft of article.

4. Lester Faigley and Thomas P. Miller, "What We Learn from Writing on the Job," *College English 44* (October 1982): 559–560.

5. Lisa S. Ede and Andrea Lunsford, "Collaborative Learning: Lessons from the World of Work," *Writing Program Administrators 9* (Spring 1986): 21.

6. James Paradis, David Dobrin, and Richard Miller, "Writing at Exxon ITD: Notes on the Writing Environment of an R&D Organization," in *Writing in Nonacademic Settings,* ed. Lee Odell and Dixie Goswami (New York: Guilford Press, 1985), 281–307.

7. Robert B. Mitchell, Marian C. Crawford, and R. Burt Madden, "An Investigation of the Impact of Electronic Communication Systems and Organizational Communication Patterns," *Journal of Business Communication, 22* (Fall 1985): 9.

8. Flatley, "A Comparative Analysis," 39.

CHAPTER 3

1. Thomas L. Kent, "Paragraph Production and the Given-New Contract," *Journal of Business Communication 21* (Fall 1984): 45–66.

2. Thomas J. Peters and Robert H. Waterman, Jr, *In Search of Excellence: Lessons from America's Best-Run Companies* (New York: Harper & Row, 1985).

3. See Joseph M. Williams, *Style: Ten Lessons in Clarity and Grace*, 3rd ed. (Glenview, Ill.: Scott, Foresman, 1989), 26–27. Williams is professor of linguistics at the University of Chicago.

4. For the information in this section, we are indebted to Francine Frank and Frank Anschen, *Language and the Sexes* (Albany: State University of New York at Albany, 1983), and especially to Casey Miller and Kate Swift, *The Handbook of Nonsexist Writing: For Writers, Editors and Speakers* (New York: Barnes and Noble, 1980).

5. Joseph Schneider and Sally L. Hacker, "Sex Role Imagery and Use of the Generic 'Man' in Introductory Texts: A Case in the Sociology of Sociology," *The American Sociologist 8* (1973): 12–18, as reviewed in William R. Todd-Mancillas, "Man-Linked Words and Masculine Pronouns: A Review of Literature and Implications for Speech and Communication Teachers and Researchers," ERIC Publication #ED 186955, April 1980, 4.

CHAPTER 4

1. Jeanne Halpern and Sarah Liggett, *Computers and Composing: How the New Technologies Are Changing Writing* (Carbondale: Southern Illinois University Press, 1984), 9.

2. John D. Gould, "Experiments on Composing Letters: Some Facts, Some Myths, and Some Observations," in *Cognitive Processes in Writing,* ed. Lee W. Gregg and Erwin R. Steinberg (Hillsdale, N.J.: Erlbaum, 1980), 102.

CHAPTER 6

1. "Statistical Abstracts of the United States," *United States Department of Commerce: Bureau of the Census Statistics for 1986, 1988.*

2. C. Gilbert Storms, "What Business School Graduates Say About the Writing They Do at Work: Implications for the Business Communications Course," *ABCA Bulletin,* December 1983, 13–18.

3. Quoted in Geoffrey Bailey, "Direct Hit," *Canadian Business,* February 1984, 76.

4. Quoted in Bailey, "Direct Hit," 76.

5. Readers may notice that what we are calling psychological appeals, logical appeals, and appeals based on authority correspond to Aristotle's categories of appeals based on pathos, logos, and ethos. Although we have put testimonials in a separate category for pedagogical reasons, strictly speaking testimonials are a kind of ethical appeal.

6. Jim Powell, "The Lucrative Trade of Crafting Junk Mail," *New York Times,* June 20, 1982, section F, 7.

7. Study cited in Stephen Fox, *The Mirror Makers: A History of American Advertising and Its Creators* (New York: Morrow, 1984), p. 328. Fox's source for the study is the American Association of Advertising Agencies (AAAA) study of 1,600 ads in *Commercial Connection,* ed. Wright, 53.

8. Quoted in Powell, "Lucrative Trade," 7.

9. ATRON, "A Bugbuster Story" advertisement in *Technical Journal,* (December 1985) (slightly modified).

10. Quoted in Powell, "Lucrative Trade," 7.

11. Quoted in Powell, "Lucrative Trade," 7.

12. Quoted in Bailey, "Direct Hit," 75.

13. This case is based on the situation confronted by Dow Chemical Canada, Inc., in 1980, as recounted in D. R. Stephenson's articles, "How to Turn Pitfalls into Opportunities in Crisis Situations," *Public Relations Quarterly,* Fall 1982, 11–15; and "Internal PR Efforts Further Corporate Responsibility: A Report from Dow Canada," *Public Relations Quarterly,* Spring 1983, 7–10. A few details have been changed or added to the case so as to feature the writing problems that Dow's situation presented.

14. For a fuller description of where public relations experts stand on the necessity for honesty in public relations, see the Public Relations Society of America's "Code of Professional Standards for the Practice of Public Relations with Interpretation," reprinted in Doug Newsom and Alan Scott, *This Is PR: The Realities of Public Relations* (Belmont, Calif.: Wadsworth, 1976), 265–268. For a quick introduction to the complexity of the issue of honesty in public relations and for further references, see Hugh M. Culbertson, "How Public Relations Textbooks Handle Honesty and Lying," *Public Relations Review 9* (Summer 1983): 65–73.

15. Harold L. Johnson reviews current thought on business's social responsibility in "Ethics and the Executive," *Business Horizons 24* (May–June 1981): 53–59, relying especially on John Simon, Charles W. Powers, and Jon P. Gunneman, *The Ethical Investor: Universities and Corporate Responsibility* (New Haven: Yale University Press, 1972). See also Joseph Nolan, "Protect Your Public Image with Performance," *Harvard Business Review 53* (March–April 1975): 135–142, which confirms Johnson's views. Our entire discussion of business ethics relies heavily on Johnson.

16. Johnson, pp. 56–57, cites several studies: Frederick D. Sturdivant and James L. Ginter, "Corporate Social Responsiveness: Management Attitudes and Economic Performance," *California Management Review,* Spring 1977, 30–39; Milton Moskowitz, "Social Responsibility Portfolio 1973," *Business and Society,* January 1974, 1; Moskowitz, "Profiles in Corporate Responsibility," *Business and Society Review,* Spring 1975, 28–42; Moskowitz, "46 Socially Responsible Corporations," *Business and Society,* July 1974, 8. We would also add Moskowitz, "The Corporate Responsibility Champs . . . and Chumps," *Business and Society Review,* Winter 1985, 4–10.

17. Erika Wilson, "Social Responsibility of Business: What Are the Small Business Perspectives?" *Journal of Small Business Management 18* (July 1980): 17–24.

18. Wilson, "Social Responsibility," 24.

19. Wilson, "Social Responsibility," 24.

20. Johnson's article demonstrates this.

21. Carl Gerstacker, chairman of Dow Chemical, as quoted in Stephenson, "Internal PR Efforts," 7–8.

22. This case is based on the situation confronted by Revlon, Inc., in 1980, as revealed in the following articles: "Use of Rabbits in Testing Cosmetics Draws Protest," *New York Times,* May 14, 1980, section B, 2; "Cosmetics Firms Feel Heat over the Draize Test," *Chemical Week 127* (September 10, 1980): 18–19; "Revlon Grant Seeks Humane Testing," *New York Times,* December 24, 1980, section B, 3; "Revlon Concedes to Critics, Funds Search for New Eye Test," *Drug and Cosmetic Industry,* February 1981, 52; "Johns Hopkins Is Selected as Site for Center for Animal Test Alternatives." *Drug and Cosmetic Industry,* November 1981, 42, 109. A few details have been changed or added to the case so as to feature the writing problems that Revlon's situation presented.

CHAPTER 7

1. Thomas J. Peters and Robert H. Waterman, Jr., *In Search of Excellence: Lessons from America's Best-Run Companies* (New York: Harper & Row, 1985), 239.

CHAPTER 9

1. Flatley, "A Comparative Analysis," 35–49.

CHAPTER 11

1. Lisa Ede and Andrea Lunsford. "Collaborative Learning: Lessons from the World of Work," *Writing Program Administrators 9* (Spring 1986): 17–26.

2. *New York Times,* February 7, 1982, Real Estate Section, 1.

CHAPTER 15

1. Greggory S. Blundell, "Personal Computers in the Eighties," *BYTE*, January 1983, pp. 170–172.

2. Joel P. Bowman and Debbie A Renshaw, "Desktop Publishing: Things Gutenberg Never Taught You," *Journal of Business Communication* 26 (Winter 1989): 57–77.

3. In *BYTE* 13 (December 1988), see Douglas Engelbart and Harvey Lehtman, "Working Together," 245–252; Terry Winograd, "Where the Action Is," 256A–258; Jonathan Grudin, "Perils and Pitfalls," 261–264; and Susanna Opper, "A Groupware Toolbox," 275–282.

4. Opper, "A Groupware Toolbox," 275.

INDEX

abbreviations, 807–8
ABCA Bulletin, 834n
Abowd, John, 833n
abstracts, 460–62, 466, 467
Accountant's Index, 462
action verbs, 701, 702
active voice, 69–70, 72–75
Ad Age, 715
address formats, 146–49
adjustments:
 requesting, 191–92
 see also claims
adverbs, conjunctive, 814–15
advertising:
 extent of, 234
 see also direct mail
Ad Week, 715
affirmative duty of businesses, definition of, 282
agenda:
 definition of, 627
 for meetings, 627
 for revision, 56
The Almanac of American Employers, 717, 718, 719–20
almanacs, 458
American Association of Advertising Agencies (AAAA), 835n
American English, 82
American Express, 201
American Psychological Association (APA), publication guidelines of, 550, 551–52, 553
American Society for Personnel Administration, 124
The American Sociologist, 834n
AMS simplified format, 140–41
analysis, case writing and, 784–85
analysis trees:
 case write-ups and, 784–85, 789, 790
 computers and, 770
 formal reports and, 508, 510
 letters and, 114–115
 memos and, 352, 353
 organization trees and, 35n
 paragraphs and, 59–63

problem-solving reports and, 393–95, 399–400, 408
 structure of, 35–39
 see also organization trees
anecdotes:
 requesting favors and, 252
 in sales letter, 235
 in speaking, 595, 599, 600
animation, computers with, 774
announcement memos, 371, 372
Anschen, Frank, 834n
apostrophe, 808–9
appeal, collection series, 266, 269, 274–75
appeal, urgent, collection series, 266, 276, 277
appeal, sales letters, 229–33
 authority or trustworthiness, 229–31, 232–33
 logical, 232–33
 psychological, 229–31, 233, 234
 testimonial, 233, 235
appendixes, of formal reports, 555
application letters, 722–32, 750–56
 assessing readers of, 722–23
 central selling points of, 724, 725–26
 checklist for writing of, 732
 conclusion of, 727, 729–30
 establishing rapport in, 724–25, 728
 organization of, 724–27
 presenting information in, 729
 revision of, 730–31
 RTA formula and, 724–27, 728–30
 solicited, 722–727
 unsolicited, 722, 727–30
 want ads and, 722–23
Area Business Databank Abstracts, 462
Aristotle, 834n
articles, magazine, 460–62
assessing the reader:
 of application letters, 722–23
 of business letters, 108
 of case write-ups, 779, 787–88
 checklists for, 23, 398
 of collection series, 265–66
 with computers, 769
 in controversy, 282–84

839

INDEX

assessing the reader, (*continued*)
  of direct-mail advertisements, 228–29
  of formal reports, 453
  of goodwill letters, 309
  of memos, 348, 350–51
  of problem-solving reports, 397–98
  in requesting favors, 251
  of resumes, 691
  of sales letters, 228–29
  technique of, 21–23
  of thank-you letters, 740
Association for Business Communication, 2, 225
associations, professional, 689
ATRON, "A Bugbuster Story," 835*n*
audience:
  assessment of, 592–93
  attitude of, 593
  expectations of, 592
  questions of, 617–18
  speaker relationship to, 592
  see also readers
author card, 458, 460

Babson College, 596
bad news:
  direct letter pattern and, 172–73
  letters of, 167–73
  memos of, 359–63
Bailey, Geoffrey, 834*n*, 835*n*
bar charts:
  bilateral, 646, 649
  definitions of, 645–46
  examples of, 647–49
  grouped, 646, 647
  segmented, 646, 648
  simple, 646, 647
Bernard, Susan, 686, 688
Better Business Association, 266
bibliography:
  of formal reports, 553–55
  style of, 553–55
bilateral bar charts, 646, 649
blackboards, 663
block paragraphs, 370
Blumenthal, Karen, 501
Blundell, Greggory S., 837*n*
body:
  of formal reports, 518–28, 547–49, 560
  of letters, 109–10, 113–18, 145

  of oral presentations, 598–600
book reviews, 460–62
Bowman, Joel P., 837*n*
brackets, use of, 549
brainstorming, 25–27, 769
bullets:
  definition of, 369
  in memos, 370
Business and Society, 835*n*
Business and Society Review, 835*n*
business directories, 463
business ethics, 282–84, 287
Business Horizons, 835*n*
Business Periodicals Index, 462, 686, 717
business services, 462
Business Week, 43, 671, 686
business writing, *see* writing, business
BYTE, 774, 837*n*

California Management Review, 835*n*
Canadian Business, 834*n*
capitalization, 809–10
  in memos, 370
carbon copy notation, 146
career choices, books on, 687
Career Employment Opportunities Directory, 717, 718, 720
career exploration, *see* job search
Career Guide to Professional Associations, 689
Career Opportunities News
case write-ups, 777–805
  analysis and, 784–85
  analysis trees and, 784–85, 789, 790
  argument of, 792–93
  assessing readers of, 787–88
  checklists for, 786, 792, 797
  choosing data for, 787–88
  completeness of, 794–96
  definition of, 777–78, 787
  drafting of, 790, 792
  establishing criteria for, 786
  goals of, 787
  information gathering for, 788
  organization of, 789, 793–94
  problem solving in, 778–79
  vs. problem-solving reports, 778, 779
  quotations in, 796–97
  reader expectation and, 779
  revision of, 792–97

INDEX

role-playing in, 793
summary in, 785, 792–93
types of, 787–88
catalogs, library, 458, 460, 464
central selling point:
  application letters and, 724, 725–26
  determining, for sales letters, 230–31
charity requests, 206, 255–56, 257, 260–62
charts, 651–55
  bar, *see* bar charts
  flip, 663
  flow, 654, 655
  organization, 653–54
  pie, 651–52
checklists:
  for assessing audience, 593
  for assessing memo completeness, 356
  for assessing reader, 23
  for assessing readers of reports, 398
  for communicating in controversy, 292–93
  for conducting interviews, 626
  for developing sample, 482
  for doing group writing, 566
  for editing sentences, 86
  for evaluating career exploration, 689
  for formulating goal statement, 21
  for gathering information and generating ideas, 27
  for holding meetings, 630
  for making observations, 479
  for making schedule, 456
  for organizing business communications, 39
  for organizing presentations, 603
  for preparing for and performing at job interview, 739
  for preparing for interview, 497
  for quoting, paraphrasing, and summarizing, 473
  for rehearsing presentations, 619
  for requesting favors, 257
  for responding to case, 792
  for reviewing cover letter, 493
  for reviewing job search efforts, 722
  for reviewing memo format, 371
  for reviewing questionnaire, 494
  for reviewing report format, 406–7
  for revising case response, 797
  for revising formal report, 561
  for revising holistically, 58
  for revising memos for tone, 366
  for revising problem-solving report, 412
  for solving business problem, 397
  for solving business problem presented in case, 786
  for using bar charts, line graphs, and pie charts, 652
  for using library, 466
  for using organization charts, flow charts, and maps, 657
  for using tables, 645
  for using text visuals, 663
  for writing collection letter, 276
  for writing executive summaries, 547
  for writing good-news letter, 167
  for writing goodwill letter, 312
  for writing indirect bad-news letter, 171
  for writing letters of application, 732
  for writing memos that give bad news or persuade, 363
  for writing memos that give or request information, 355
  for writing problem-solving report, 405
  for writing resume, 705
  for writing sales letter, 247
Chemical Week, 836n
chronological order:
  of reports, 410–11, 414
  in resumes, 710
citations, style of, 457–58, 460–63
claims, 191–200
  direct letter pattern and, 192, 193
  indirect letter pattern and, 192, 194–200
  making, 191–94, 195–96
  responding to, 194, 196–200
clarification, memos of, 379, 380
clichés, 85–86
closed questions, 483–84, 624
Cognitive Processes in Writing (Gregg and Steinberg, eds.), 834n
collaborative writing, *see* group writing
collection series, 263–80
  appeal of, 266, 269, 274–75
  assessing readers of, 265–66
  debtor classification and, 266
  definition of, 263
  establishing rapport in, 267
  generating ideas for, 267–68
  goals of, 263–64
  indirect letter pattern and, 267–68

INDEX

collection series (*continued*)
  inquiry, 266, 269, 271–73
  motivating action in, 267–68
  organization of, 267–68
  reminder in, 266, 268–69, 270
  RTA formula and, 267–68
  stages of, 265–66, 268–76
  ultimatum in, 266, 276, 278, 279
  urgent appeal in, 266, 276, 277
College English, 833n
College Placement Annual, 718
College Placement Directory, 718
college placement services, 685–86
colon, 811
comma, 812–13
commands, in sales letters, 236
comma splice, 813–15
Commercial Connection, 835n
communicating in controversy, 280–92
communications network, 764
company documents, 463
company logo, 368, 369
comparison, of products or services, 232
complex line graphs, 650, 651
complimentary close, 145
computers, 763–76
  analysis trees and, 770
  animation with, 775
  assessing readers with, 769
  benefits of, 767–68
  drafting with, 770
  editing with, 771
  errors made with, 774
  formats and, 771
  generating ideas with, 769
  glossary of terms for, 764
  graphics of, 12, 665–66, 667–70, 775
  group writing with, 774–75
  information gathering with, 769
  libraries and, 463–64
  nonstop writing and, 769
  organizing with, 770
  outlines and, 770
  proofreading with, 771, 774
  research and, 769
  revising with, 770–71, 773
  setting writing goals with, 769
  sound with, 775
  technology of, 12–13, 775

Computers and Composing: How the New Technologies Are Changing Writing (Halpern and Liggett), 834n
conclusions:
  of application letters, 727, 729–30
  of formal reports, 526–27, 546, 548, 556–57
  of oral presentations, 600–603
condolence, letters of, 328, 329–31
confirmation, memos of, 377–79
congratulations:
  occasions of, 312–13
  writing letters of, 313–18
conjunctive adverbs, 814–15
contacts, job search and, 686, 688
contributions, letters requesting, 255–56, 260–62
controversy, causes of:
  changing social values, 287–91
  public misperception, 281–86
controversy, letters in response to, 280–92
  assessing readers for, 282–84
  crisis do's and don't's in, 293
  establishing rapport in, 285
  goals in, 281–82
  indirect letter pattern in, 285
  information gathering and, 284
  organization of, 284–85
  RTA formula and, 284–85
  truth in, 281
copyright permission, footnotes for, 550
corporate directories, 463
courtesy: *see* tone
cover letters:
  checklist for review of, 493
  examples of, 431–32, 491
  proposals and, 430, 431–35
  questionnaires and, 489, 491–93
  RTA formula and, 492–93
Crawford, Marian C., 833n
credit, 201–5
  approving, 201, 203
  references, 201, 202
  refusing, 203–5
  replying to checks of, 201
credit cards, 201
credit rating services, 201
credit references, definition of, 201
Crisis do's and don't's, 293

INDEX 843

see also controversy, letters in response to
criteria:
    case write-ups and, 786
    definition of, 395
    for questionnaires, 483
    problem solving reports and, 395–96
Culbertson, Hugh M., 835*n*

dangling modifiers, 815
dash, 816–17
data:
    in case write-ups, 793–94
    irrelevant, 412
    organization of, 410–12
data base, 764
Davis, Anita, 120, 134
debtor classification, collection series and, 266
delinquent accounts, definition of, 263
dependent variable, definition of, 479
Desktop publishing (DTP), 771–72
descriptors, 466
dictation, 121–25
    equipment for, 121
    myths and facts about, 123–24
    technique of, 121–22
dictionaries, 457
direct letter pattern:
    approving credit with, 201, 203
    bad news and, 172–73
    claims and, 192, 193
    good news and, 160–67
    ordering products and, 173, 175
    ordering services and, 173–75
    requesting information and, 173, 176–77
    requesting recommendations and, 185–88
    technique of, 160–67, 172–73
direct mail, 224–25, 228, 239
discussion section, of formal report, 547–48
disks, computer, 764
Dobrin, David, 7, 833*n*
Dow Chemical, 836*n*
Dow Chemical Canada, Inc., 835*n*
drafts:
    computers and, 770
    function of, 39–40
    of business letters, 120
    of memos, 363–66
    of problem-solving reports, 400

    of resumes, 706–8
    of tables, 636–41
Drug and Cosmetic Industry, 836*n*
Dun and Bradstreet Reference Book, 462

Ede, Lisa S., 7, 833*n*, 836*n*
editing, 49–103
    with computers, 771
    postponement of, 41–42
    see also revision
education, resumes and, 695, 697–98
electronic mail, 12, 771, 773
electronic mailboxes, 764, 766
electronic messages, 764, 765
ellipsis, definition of, 549
Ellison Machinery Company, 4
emotional appeal, in sales letter, 234
employment fields, books on, 687
Employment Management Association, 716
enclosure notation, 146
encyclopedias, 457, 458
endorsements, 233, 313
Engelbart, Douglas, 837*n*
envelopes:
    address formats of, 146–49
    for automatic processing, 147–49
    for sales letters, 243–46
Erdlen, John D., 736
essays, business writing compared with, 15–16
The Ethical Investor: Universities and Corporate Responsibility (Simon, et al.), 835*n*
ethics, business, 282–84, 287
exams, business writing compared with, 15–16
executive summary, 516–17, 544, 546–47, 561
experiments, 479
explanatory memos, 371, 374, 375
expressions:
    padded, 78
    pretentious, 78, 79
    redundant, 78, 80
Exxon Corporation, 7
eye contact, 616

The F & S Index of Corporations and Industries, 462

INDEX

Faigley, Lester, 833*n*
favors, requesting of, *see* requesting favors
files, computer, 764
findings, of formal reports, 523–24, 525–26, 546, 548
Flatley, Marie E., 833*n*, 836*n*
flip charts, 663
flow charts, 654, 655
footnotes:
    for copyright permission, 550
    in formal reports, 550, 552–53
Forbes, 43, 686
formal outline, 513, 543
formal reports, 451–584
    analysis trees and, 508, 510
    appendixes of, 555
    assessing reader of, 453
    bibliography of, 553–55
    body of, 518–28, 547–49, 560
    checklist for revision of, 561–62
    conclusions of, 526–27, 546, 548, 556–57
    conducting experiments for, 479
    conducting interviews for, 494–97
    conducting surveys for, 481
    discussion section of, 547–48
    drafting of, 509
    examples of, 512–41, 572–84
    executive summary of, 516–17, 544, 546–47, 561
    findings of, 523–24, 525–26, 546, 548
    footnotes in, 550, 552–53
    format of, 542, 556
    goals of, 453
    group writing and, 562–66
    headings in, 560
    inclusiveness of, 560
    index cards and, 508–9
    information gathering for, 456–58, 460–63
    introductions of, 518–19, 547
    introductory material of, 511–17, 542–47
    letter of transmittal and, 511, 542–43
    libraries and, 463–66
    list of tables and figures of, 544, 545
    making observations for, 478–79
    methodology and, 520–22, 525, 544, 548
    organization of, 508–9, 560
    outlines of, 508–9, 513, 543
    overview of, 452
    paraphrases in, 470–73, 549
    parts of, 542–55
    primary sources for, 477–97
    questionnaires for, 483–94
    quotations in, 468–70, 548–49
    recommendations of, 527–28, 544, 548, 556–57
    revision of, 556–61
    schedule of, 454–56
    secondary sources for, 559
    summary in, 473, 474–77, 548, 549, 557–59; *see also* executive summary
    supplementary material of, 529–41, 550–55, 560
    table of contents of, 514–15, 544
    table of tables of, 544, 545
    title page of, 512, 543
    topic of, 453
    transitions in, 559
    see also oral presentations; problem-solving reports
formats:
    AMS simplified, 140–41
    computers and, 771
    envelopes, 146–49
    of formal report, 542, 556
    full block, 134–35
    of letters, 134–41
    of memos, 366–71
    modified block, 136, 137–38
    for problem-solving reports, 405–7
    of resumes, 711
    semiblock, 136, 139
Foster, Bob, 4
Fox, Stephen, 835*n*
fragments, 817
Frank, Francine, 834*n*
frankness, requesting favors and, 254
full block format, 134–35

gender, terms of, 82–85
generating ideas:
    for business writing, 25–27
    for case write-ups, 788
    for collections series, 267–68
    for communicating in controversy, 284
    with computers, 769
    for formal reports, 456–94
    for goodwill letters, 309–310
    for interviews, 623–24

for the job search, 724
for letters, 108–9
with lists, 27
for letters requesting favors, 251–52
for meetings, 627
for memos, 351
for oral presentations, 593
for problem-solving reports, 399
for resumes, 692
for sales letters, 229–33
techniques of, 25–27
for thank-you letters for interviews, 740
generic terms, 82–85
Gerstacker, Carl, 836n
Giarrusso, Roseann, 833n
Ginter, James L., 835n
goals:
   of business letters, 107
   of case write-ups, 787
   of collection series, 263–64
   computers and, 769
   in controversy, 281–82
   of formal reports, 453
   of goodwill letters, 308–9
   of interviews, 622
   of letters, 107
   of meetings, 627
   of memos, 348
   of oral presentations, 590–91
   of problem-solving reports, 397
   requesting favors and, 251
   of resumes, 690
   of sales letters, 228
   shared, 253, 361
   statements of, 19–21, 453
   of thank-you letters for job interviews, 740
good news:
   direct letter pattern and, 160–67
   letters of, 160–67
goodwill letters, 307–46
   of appreciation, 319, 320–27
   assessing readers in, 309
   of congratulations, 312–13, 314–18
   generating ideas for, 309–10
   goals of, 308–9
   organization of, 310–11
   RTA formula and, 310–11
   of season's greetings, 328, 332–33
   stationery and, 311

   of sympathy, 328, 329–31
   of thanks, 319, 320–27
   of welcome, 334, 335–39
goodwill memos, 382–84
Goswami, Dixie, 833n
Gould, John D., 834n
government publications, 462–63
Graduate Management Admissions Council, 2
grammar, 807–31
   see also specific topics
graphics:
   computer, 12, 665–66, 667–70, 775
   sales letters and, 243–46
graphs, line, 646, 650–51
Gregg, Lee W., 834n
grouped bar charts, 646, 647
groupware, 774
group writing, 564–66
   checklist for, 566
   with computers, 774–75
   coordination of, 562–64
   of formal reports, 562–66
   problems of, 565–66
   process of, 564–65
Grudin, Jonathan, 837n
guarantees, 232
Gunneman, Jon P., 835n

Hacker, Sally L., 834n
Halpern, Jeanne, 834n
The Handbook of Non-Sexist Writing: For
      Writers, Editors, and Speakers (Miller
      and Swift), 834n
handbooks, 457–58
handouts, 665
hardware, 764
Harvard Business Review, 2, 833n, 835n
headings:
   in formal reports, 560
   of letters, 143
   of memos, 366–68
   problem-solving reports and, 405–6
   of resumes, 692–93
holistic revision:
   computers and, 773
   letters and, 124–25
   RTA formula and, 124–25
   technique of, 50–59
"hook," in sales letter, 234

human relations, business and, 308
hyphen, 817–18

ideas:
  generating, *see* generating ideas
  grouping and ordering of, 29–33, 38
  organization of, 29–38, 63; *see also* organization
  transitions and, 63
impersonal agents, 75
implementation, of report recommendations, 546–47
Inc., 245
independent variable, definition of, 479
index cards, 468
  formal report and, 508–9
indexes, 460–62, 466
indirect letter pattern:
  bad news and, 167–71
  claims and, 192, 194–200
  collection series and, 267–68
  controversy and, 285
  refusing credit and, 203–5
  refusing requests from charities and, 206–7
  replying to orders and, 176, 178–84
  technique of, 167–71
information:
  in application letters, 729
  gathering, *see* information gathering
  given vs. new, 65–67
  logical order of, 114–15, 410–12
  organization of, 27–39; *see also* organization
  psychological order of, 117–18
  sources of, *see* primary sources; secondary sources; sources
information gathering
  for business writing, 23–25
  for case write-ups, 788
  for communicating in controversy, 284
  with computers, 769
  for formal reports, 456–58, 460–63
  for interviews, 623–24
  job search and, 724
  for letters, 108–9
  for letters requesting favors, 251–52
  for meetings, 627
  for memos, 351
  for oral presentations, 593

  for problem-solving reports, 399
  for resumes, 692
  for sales letters, 229–33
  techniques of, 23–25
  for thank-you letters for interviews, 740
inquiry, in collection series, 266, 269, 271–73
In Search of Excellence: Lessons from America's Best-Run Companies (Peters and Waterman), 66–68, 308, 594, 833*n*, 836*n*
instructional memos, 371, 373–74
Insurance Literature, 462
interviewee, assessment of, 622–23
interviews, 621–26
  accuracy of, 496
  advantages of, 494–95
  appraisal, 621, 625
  assessment of interviewee and, 622–23
  checklist for conducting of, 626
  checklist for preparation of, 497
  conducting of, 495–97, 625–26
  establishing rapport in, 494–96, 625
  following up on, 626
  goals of, 622
  information gathering for, 621–22, 623–24, 625
  job, *see* job interviews
  organization of, 625
  records of, 497
  types of questions in, 624
  uses of, 494–95
italics, 818–19

jargon, 81–82
Jarvis, Jean, 9, 10
Jayme, William, 243–45
Jenkins, R. L., 833*n*
job interviews, 732–39
  assessing interviewer and, 737
  checklist for, 739
  companies and, 733–34
  conducting of, 625
  dress for, 738
  goals of, 621, 622
  planning for, 732–37
  procedures and, 736–37
  questions and, 734–36
  rehearsing for, 737

sequence of, 738–39
job search, 677–762
  books on, 687
  business contacts and, 686, 688, 720
  characteristics of, 678
  checklists for, 689, 722
  choosing a company and, 717
  college placement services for, 685–86
  information gathering and, 688
  interviews and, *see* job interviews
  letters of acceptance and, 741, 742, 781
  letters of application and, 722–32, 750–56
  letters of refusal and, 741, 743, 762
  library sources for, 686, 687
  professional associations and, 689
  questions for, 688
  research for, 678, 685–89
  schedule for, 678, 679, 680
  self-assessment and, 680–85
  thank-you letters and, 739–41
  want ads and, 715–16, 749
  see also resumes
Job Search Strategies for College Grads: The 10-Step Plan for Career Success (Bernard and Thompson), 688
Johnson, Harold L., 283, 835n, 836n
Journal of Business Communication, 2, 833n, 837n
Journal of Small Business Management, 283, 836n
"junk mail," 225

Kaufman-Broad, 9, 10
Kent, Thomas L., 833n

language:
  appropriateness of, 80–86
  conversational, 133
  in letters, 133
  sexist, 82–85
  specialized, 81
Language and the Sexes (Frank and Anschen), 834n
layout:
  memos and, 369–70
  of questionnaires, 489
  of tables, 638
Lehtman, Harvey, 837n
length:

  of memos, 369
  of oral presentations, 617
  of paragraphs, 131
  of questionnaires, 483
  of sales letters, 238
  of sentences, 131–33
letters, 105–346
  of acceptance, 741, 742, 761
  analysis trees and, 114–15
  application, 722–32, 750–56
  assessing readers of, 108, 228–29, 309, 722–23, 740
  bad-news, 167–73
  body of, 109–10, 113–18, 145
  business, RTA formula and, 108–20, 124–25
  carbon copy notation of, 146
  for claims, *see* claims
  closing of, 118–20
  collection, *see* collection series
  complimentary close of, 145
  of congratulations, *see* congratulations
  cover, *see* cover letters
  on credit, 201–5
  direct pattern of, *see* direct letter pattern
  drafting, 120
  enclosure notation of, 146
  envelopes and, 146–48
  establishing rapport in, 109, 110–13
  formats of, 134–41
  functions of, 106
  goals of, 107
  good-news, 160–67
  goodwill, *see* goodwill letters
  heading of, 143
  holistic revision of, 124–25
  indirect pattern of, *see* indirect letter pattern
  influencing readers of, 113–18
  information in, 107, 113–18, 160, 162
  of inquiry, 176, 177
  inside address of, 143–44
  local revision of, 125–34
  mixed messages in, 166
  openings of, 111
  for ordering products, 173, 175
  for ordering services, 173–75
  paragraph length in, 131
  parts of, 141–46

INDEX

letters (*continued*)
   of persuasion, 223–305
   positive attitude in, 107, 118–19, 129–30
   on products and services, 173–84
   protest, 287–91
   recommendation, 185–91
   of refusal, 206–7, 741, 743, 762
   replying to orders, 176–84
   for requesting favors, *see* requesting favors
   requesting information, 173, 175–77
   resale in, 180
   revision of, 124–34
   sales, *see* sales letters
   salutation of, 144
   of season's greetings, 328, 332–33
   selling substitute products, 180, 183–84
   sentence length in, 131–33
   signature of, 145–46
   solicited, 722–27
   structure of, 109–10
   style of, 125, 131–34
   subject line of, 144
   of sympathy, 328, 329–31
   of thanks, *see* thank-you letters
   tone of, 125–31
   of transmittal, 511, 542–43
   typist's reference section of, 146
   unsolicited, 722, 727–30
   of welcome, 334, 335–39
libraries:
   checklist for use of, 466
   computers and, 463–64
   formal reports and, 463–66
   reference sources in, 456–58, 460–63
   sources for job search in, 686, 687
   use of, 43, 229, 458, 460, 463–66
library catalogs, 458, 460, 464
Liggett, Sarah, 834*n*
line graphs, 646, 650–51
Lipton, Rick, 5–6
lists, of tables and figures:
   for formal reports, 544, 545
   for generating ideas, 27
local revision:
   letters and, 125–34
   technique of, 59–86
logical appeal, 232–33
logical order, of report, 410–12
logo, company, 368, 369

Lunsford, Andrea, 7, 833*n*, 836*n*
Lyon, John D., 20, 594, 597, 598, 599

Madden, R. Burt, 833*n*
magazine articles, 460–62
mail:
   direct, 224–25, 228, 239
   electronic, 12, 771, 773
   guidelines for automatic processing of, 147–48
   "junk," 225
mailboxes, electronic, 764, 766
mailing lists, 228–29
maps, 654, 656
MasterCard, 201
meetings, 626–29
   agendas for, 627
   assessing participants of, 627
   checklist for holding of, 630
   conducting of, 629
   following up, 629
   goals of, 627
   memos for, 627, 628, 629
   organization of, 627, 629
   reports of, 413
memos, 347–90
   analysis trees and, 352, 353
   announcement, 371, 372
   assessing readers of, 348, 350–51
   of bad news, 359–63
   bullets in, 370
   capitalization in, 370
   of clarification, 379, 380
   completeness of, 356
   of confirmation, 377–79
   content of, 350
   definition of, 1, 347
   direct vs. indirect approach, 356, 359
   drafts of, 363
   explanatory, 371, 374, 375
   formats of, 366–71
   functions of, 371–84
   for giving or requesting information, 351–55
   goals of, 348
   goodwill, 382–84
   heading of, 366–68
   importance of, 347–48
   information gathering for, 351

instructional, 371, 373–74
layout of, 369–70
length of, 369
for meetings, 627, 628, 629
organization of, 351–55, 359
to peers, 361
persuasive, 359–63
of reminder, 379, 381
revision of, 363–66
for routine requests, 374, 376–77
stationery and, 368, 369
structure of, 350
style of, 350, 370–71
to subordinates, 359, 360
to superiors, 361, 362
tone of, 363–66, 370–71
underlining in, 370
messages, electronic, 764, 765
methodology, formal reports and, 520–22, 525, 544, 548
Miller, Casey, 834n
Miller, Richard, 7, 833
Miller, Thomas P., 833n
Million Dollar Directory, 718
Milwid, Beth, 596, 598
The Mirror Makers: A History of American Advertising and Its Creators (Fox), 835n
Mitchell, Robert B., 833n
misplaced modifiers, 815, 816
mixed message, in letters, 166
modem, 764
modified block format, 136, 137–38
modifiers:
  dangling, 815
  misplaced, 815, 816
Moody's Manuals, 462
Moskowitz, Milton, 835n
moral minimum, definition of, 282
multiple-choice questions, 484

National Trade and Professional Associations, 689
New York Times, 715, 834n, 836n
New York Times Index, 462, 686
Newsom, Doug, 835n
Nolau, Joseph, 835n
nonstop writing:
  computers and, 769

technique of, 26–27
note-taking, 24–25, 466, 468
nouns:
  all-purpose, 77–78
  clusters, 76–77
  verbs and, 71
numbering, in memos, 370
numbers, use of, 819–20

observations, technique for making, 478–79
Odell, Lee, 833n
Office of the Future, Inc., 595
Old English, 82
open-ended questions, 484–85, 624
Opper, Susanna, 837n
optical character reader (OCR), 148
"oral cultures," 7
oral presentations, 585–621
  assessing audience of, 592–93
  audience's questions on, 617–18
  body of, 598–600
  checklist for organizing, 603
  conclusions of, 600–603, 604
  connecting introduction and conclusion of, 600–601
  definition of, 588
  delivery of, 615–18
  evaluation of, 620–21
  eye contact and, 616–17
  generating ideas for, 593
  goals of, 590–91
  humor in, 602
  impromptu, 604
  information gathering for, 593
  introductions of, 594–98
  keying of, 615
  length of, 617
  limits of, 598
  openings for, 594–97
  organization of, 593–603
  outlining, 604, 615
  preview of, 597–98
  quotations in, 601–2
  rehearsal of, 6, 15, 619–21
  revision of, 615
  speaker image and, 616
  summary in, 601
  transitions in, 598–99, 604
  use of details in, 599–600

oral presentations (*continued*)
   using examples in, 602–3
   visual aids and, 618, 657–65
   writing compared to, 590
   writing out, 615
orders:
   for products and services, 173–76
   replying to, 176, 180–84
organization:
   of application letters, 724–27
   of case write-ups, 789, 793–94
   of collection series, 267–68
   computers and, 770
   in controversy, 284–85
   of data, 410–12
   of formal reports, 508–9, 560
   of goodwill letters, 310–11
   of ideas, 29–38, 63
   of information, 27–39
   of interviews, 625
   of meetings, 627, 629
   of memos, 351–55, 359
   of oral presentations, 593–603
   of problem-solving reports, 399–400, 410–12
   of questionnaires, 488–89
   requesting favors and, 252–57
   of resumes, 692–706
   of sales letters, 233–39
   of thank-you letters, 740–41
organization charts, 653–54
organizations:
   expectations of, 7–10
   reputations of, 232, 253
   writing and, 7–13
organization trees, 35*n*
   see also analysis trees
outlines:
   computers and, 770
   of formal reports, 508–9, 513, 543
   of oral presentations, 604, 615
   paragraphs and, 62
   structure of, 38
overhead transparencies, 663
"Overlooking Help Wanted Ads Costly to Many Job Hunters," 716

padded expressions, 78
page layout, memos and, 369–70
Paradis, James, 7, 833

paragraphs:
   analysis trees and, 59–63
   block format of, 370
   coherence of, 62–68
   completeness of, 59–62
   focus of, 67–68
   given vs. new information in, 65–67
   indentation of, 370
   length of, in letters, 131
   organization of, 59–62
   outlines and, 62
   style of, 370
   transitional, 559
parallelism, 821–22
paraphrasing:
   definition of, 470
   examples of, 471, 472
   excessive use of, 557–59
   in formal reports, 470–73, 549
   quotation vs., 473, 548–49
passive voice, 72–75
periodicals, 460–62
permissions, copyright, footnotes for, 550
Personnel Administrator, 123–24
Personnel Literature, 462
Personnel Management Abstracts, 462
persuasion, definition of, 223–24
Peters, Thomas J., 66–68, 308, 594, 833*n*, 836*n*
Phillips, Jack J., 470
phrases, conversational, 133
pie charts, 651–52
placement services, college, 685–86
Posner, Barry Z., 469
possessive pronouns, 823
Postal Service, U.S., guidelines for automatic processing of mail, 147–48
Powell, Jim, 834, 835*n*
Powers, Charles W., 835*n*
presentations, oral, *see* oral presentations
previews, 548
primary readers, 21
primary sources:
   definition of, 24, 456
   experiments, 479
   of formal reports, 477–97
   interviews, 494–97
   observation, 478–79
   questionnaires, 483–94
   surveys, 481–82

INDEX

problem-solving reports, 392–413
  analysis trees and, 393–95, 399–400, 408
  analyzing the problem and, 393–95
  assessing reader of, 397–98
  case write-ups vs., 778, 779
  checklist for revision of, 412–13
  checklist for writing, 397, 405
  defining the problem, 392–93, 407–8
  definition of, 392
  drafting of, 400
  establishing criteria for, 395–96
  formats for, 405–7
  formulating subquestions for, 393–95
  goal of, 397
  headings and, 405–6
  information gathering for, 399
  irrelevant data in, 412
  organization of, 399–400, 410–12
  recommendations of, 408–10
  revision of, 407–12
  systematic approach to, 392–97
  title of, 405
procedure reports:
  writing, 425–26
process, writing, 7–47, 49–103
products and services:
  analyzing features of, for sales letters, 230–31
  comparison of, for sales letters, 232
  description of, for sales letters, 232
  guarantees of, for sales letters, 232
  offering samples of, 232
  orders for, 173–84
  trial periods and, for sales letters, 232, 239
professional associations, 689
progress reports:
  writing of, 421, 423
pronouns, 823–27
  agreement in number of, 824–25
  cases of, 825–27
  gender and, 85
  possessive, 823
  reference of, 823–24
proofreading:
  with computers, 771, 774
  postponement of, 41–42
  technique of, 86
proposals:
  cover letters and, 430, 431–35
  definition of, 430
  marketing, 49
  writing, 430
protest letters, responding to, 287–91
psychological appeal, 229–31, 233, 234
public:
  attitude toward business, 282
  misperception of companies, 280, 281–86
The Public Affairs Information Service Bulletin, 462, 686
Publication Manual of the American Psychological Association, 550
Public Relations Society of America, 835n
Public Relations Quarterly, 835n
Public Relations Review, 835n
punctuation:
  "open," 134
  see also specific punctuation marks

questionnaires, 483–94
  checklist for review of, 494
  cover letters and, 489, 491–93
  criteria for, 483
  designing, 483–94
  example of, 490
  introductory statements and, 489
  layout of, 489
  length of, 483
  offensive questions and, 487–88
  organization of, 488–89
  pretesting of, 493
  question types for, 483–85
  question wording and, 485–87
  RTA formula and, 492–93
  title of, 489
questions:
  biased, 487
  closed, 483–84, 624
  interviews and, 624
  job interviews and, 734–36
  job search and, 688
  multiple-choice, 484
  offensive, 487–88
  open-ended, 484–85, 624
  requesting favors and, 254
  rhetorical, 112–13
  in sales letter, 236
  types of, for questionnaires, 483–85
  wording of, 485–87
quotation marks, 827–28

quotations:
   in case write-ups, 796–97
   excessive use of, 557–59
   that express ideas, 469–70
   in formal reports, 468–70, 548–49
   paraphrasing vs., 473, 548–49
   that support ideas, 468–69

Rader, Martha H., 833n
random sampling, 481
rapport, establishment of, 109, 110–13, 267, 285, 495–96, 724–25, 728
   see also RTA formula
readers:
   assessment of, see assessing the reader
   attitudes and emotions of, 117–18, 159
   expectations of, 779
   influencing of, 113–18
   primary, 21
   secondary, 21
Reader's Guide to Periodical Literature, 462, 686
reader-writer relationship, in letters, 119
recommendation letters:
   requesting, 185–88
   writing, 188–91
recommendations, of formal reports, 527–28, 544, 548, 556–57
recruitment brochure, 757
redundancy, 78, 80
reference books, general, 463
reference citations, style of, 550, 551–52
reference librarian, 464, 465
references, research, types of, 457–58, 460–63
references, resumes and, 705
rehearsing:
   for job interviews, 737
   of oral presentations, 6, 15, 619–21
   technique of, 619–21
   videotapes and, 620
Reilly, John, 599–600
Reizenstein, R. L., 833n
reminder, collection series, 266, 268–69, 270
reminder memos, 379, 381
Renshaw, Debbie A., 837n
reports, 391–584
   basics of, 391–449
   chronological order in, 410–11, 414

   definition of, 1
   formal, see formal reports
   meeting, 413
   problem-solving, see problem-solving reports
   procedure, 425–29
   progress, 421–24
   proposal, 430–35
   research, 23, 24, 43
   short, 413
   status, 421–24
   trip, 413–20
   see also oral presentations
requesting favors, 247–62
   anecdotes and, 252
   appealing to reader and, 250, 251, 252, 254–55, 257
   assessing readers and, 251
   attitude and, 256–57
   contributions and, 255–56, 260–62
   establishing rapport and, 252–54
   frankness and, 254
   generating ideas and, 251–52
   importance of, 247–48
   motivating action and, 256–57
   objections to, 255–56
   organization and, 252–57
   questions and, 254
   refusal of, 206–7
   RTA formula and, 252–57
   setting goals and, 251
   speakers and, 255, 258–59
   testimonals and, 253–54
   timing for, 255
resale message, 180, 269
research, 23–24, 43
   computers and, 769
   for formal reports, 477–97, 559
resumes, 689–714
   appearance of, 711, 714
   assessing reader of, 691
   awards and, 702, 703–4
   checklist for writing of, 705–6
   descriptions in, 714
   draft of, 706–8
   education section of, 695, 697–98
   extracurricular activities in, 701, 703–4
   format of, 711
   functional, 706–708

INDEX 853

goal of, 690
heading of, 692–93
inclusiveness of, 700, 714
information for, 692
irrelevant information in, 711–14
job objective statement of, 693–95, 696–97
list of parts of, 693
military service and, 704
opening section of, 692–95
organization of, 690–706, 692–706
personal background and, 704–5
personal interests and, 701, 703–4
quantifying accomplishments in, 701
readability of, 691
references and, 705
review questions for, 715
revision of, 711–14
as "selling instrument," 690
skills and, 699
suitability to job requirements of, 691
verbs in, 701, 702
work experience and, 698–701
reviews, book, 460–62
revision, 49–103
agendas for, 56
of application letters, 730–31
of case write-ups, 792–97
with computers, 770–71, 773
of formal reports, 556–61
holistic, *see* holistic revision
of letters, 124–34
local, *see* local revision
of memos, 363–66
of oral presentations, 615
paragraph, 59–69
of problem-solving reports, 407–12
receiving others' opinions for, 41
of resumes, 711–14
sentence, 69–86
of tables, 641
techniques of, 40–41
Revlon cosmetics, 229, 836*n*
Revson, Charles, 229
rhetorical questions, 112–13
Rodgers, F. S., 833*n*
routine request memos, 374, 376–77
RTA formula:
application letters and, 724–27, 728–30
bad-news letters and, 169–71

business letters and, 108–20, 124–25
claim letters and, 192, 194, 196–99
collection series and, 267–68
controversy, letters in response to and, 284–85
cover letters and, 492–93
definition of, 35
good-news letters and, 162–67
goodwill letters and, 310–11
holistic revision and, 124–25
letters of recommendation and, 185–86, 188–89
letters about credit and, 203–4
letters replying to orders and, 176, 180, 183
letters requesting information and, 173, 175–77
letters selling substitute products and, 183
questionnaires and, 492–93
requesting favors and, 252–57
sales letters and, 233–39
technique of, 109–20
thank-you letters and, 740–41
run-on sentences, 828

sales letters, 224–47
anecdotes in, 235
appeals based on authority and trustworthiness in, 229–31, 232–33
assessing reader of, 228–29
central selling point of, 230–31
closing, 239
commands in, 236
emotional appeal in, 234
envelopes for, 243–46
establishing rapport in, 234–37
examples of, 240–45
gathering information for, 229–33
generating ideas for, 229–33
goal of, 228
graphics and, 243–46
guarantee and, 232
"hook" of, 234
length of, 238
logical appeals of, 232–33
mailing lists of, 228–29
motivating action with, 238–39
organization of, 233–39
presenting costs in, 237–38
proposition of, 228

INDEX

sales letters (*continued*)
  psychological appeals of, 229–31, 233, 234
  "pulling power" of, 241
  questions in, 236
  RTA formula and, 233–39
  scenarios in, 234
  technique of writing, 224–39
  testimonials and, 233, 235
  testing, 241–43
salutation, 144
samples, developing, for surveys, 481–82
scenarios, in sales letter, 234
schedules:
  checklist for making of, 456
  for formal reports, 454–56
  for job search, 678, 679, 680
Schneider, Joseph, 834*n*
Scott, Alan, 835*n*
season's greetings, 328, 332–33
secondary readers, 21
secondary sources:
  definition of, 24, 456
  of formal reports, 559
  summarizing of, 473–77
  types of, 457–58, 460–63
  using, 466, 468
Securities and Exchange Commission, U.S., 463
segmented bar charts, 646, 648
Selections, 833*n*
self-assessment, for the job search, 681–84
  education and, 681
  importance of, 685
  interests and, 682
  personal accomplishments and, 681–82
  personal qualities and, 682
  preferred geographical area and, 683
  questions for, 681–84
  skills and, 682
  work environment and, 683
  work values and, 683
selling point, central, *see* central selling point
semiblock format, 136, 139
semicolon, 828–29
sentences:
  comma splice and, 813–15
  confusion in, 73
  fragments and, 817
  impersonal agents in, 75
  length of, 131–33
  in letters, 131–33
  parallel, 821–22
  run-on, 828
  subject of, 70, 72, 75
  transitional, 559
  word order in, 76
  wordy, 73, 76–80
sexist language, 82–85
short reports, definition of, 413
signature, 145–46
Simon, John, 835*n*
simple bar charts, 646, 647
single line graphs, 650
slide projection, 663, 665
social values, companies and, 280, 287–91
software, 764, 774–75
solicited letters, 722–27
sound, computers with, 775
sources:
  library, for job search, 686, 687
  researching, 464–65, 466, 468; *see also* primary sources; secondary sources
speakers, requesting, 255, 258–59
speaking, 585–633
  advantages of, 589
  extemporaneous, 592
  image and, 616
  impromptu, 592, 604
  writing vs., 7, 10, 15, 25–26, 585–88, 589
  see also audience; interviews; meetings; oral presentations
Standard and Poor's Corporation Services, 462
Standard and Poor's Register of Corporations, Directories, and Executives, 718
stationery:
  goodwill letters and, 311
  memos and, 368, 369
statistics, for persuasion, 253–54
status reports, 421–24
Steinberg, Erwin R., 834*n*
Stephenson, D. R., 835*n*, 836*n*
stereotyping:
  in language, 82–84
  in usage, 82–84
Stolzenberg, Ross M., 833*n*
Storms, C. Gilbert, 834*n*
stratified sampling, 482

Sturdivant, Frederick D., 835*n*
style:
   appropriateness of, 80–86
   of bibliography, 553–55
   definition of, 125
   "gobbledygook" and, 69–70
   of letters, 125, 131–34
   of memos, 350, 370–71
   of paragraphs, 370
   of reference citations, 550, 551–52
   see also formats
Style: Ten Lessons in Clarity and Grace (Williams), 833*n*
subject card, 460
subject line, 144
subjects:
   of sentences, 70, 72, 75
   verb agreement with, 829–31
summaries:
   in case write-ups, 785, 792–93
   definition of, 473, 548, 549
   excessive use of, 557–59
   executive, 516–17, 544, 546–47, 561
   in formal reports, 473, 474–77, 548, 549, 557–59
   in oral presentations, 601
   of secondary sources, 473–77
supplementary material:
   of formal reports, 456–97, 529–41, 550–55, 560
   see also appendixes
surveys:
   conducting, 481
   sampling for, 481–82
Sutton, Nat, 6
Swift, Kate, 834*n*
sympathy, letters of, 328, 329–31
systematic sampling, 481

table of contents, of formal reports, 514–15, 544
tables, 635–45
   checklist for use of, 645
   design of, 636–40
   examples of, 638–44
   information in, 638
   layout of, 638
   lists of, 544, 545
   revision of, 640, 641

   source of, 638
   text and, 638, 639–40
   title of, 638
   totals in, 638
   use of, 636
tape recorders, 25–26, 27, 46
Technical Journal, 835*n*
terminal, computer, 764
terms:
   for computing, 764, 834*n*
   of gender, 82–85
   generic, 82–85
testimonials:
   definition of, 229
   requesting favors with, 253–54
   sales letters and, 233, 235
text visuals, 658, 663, 775
thank-you letters:
   goodwill and, 319–327
   job search and, 739–41
This Is PR: The Realities of Public Relations (Newsom and Scott), 835*n*
Thomas Register, 718
Thompson, Gretchen, 686, 688
time lines, 454, 455
time management, principles of, 454–55
title card, 458–60, 461
title page, of formal report, 512, 543
Todd-Mancillas, William R., 834*n*
tone:
   definition of, 125
   of letters, 125–31
   of memos, 363–66, 370–71
transitions:
   in formal reports, 559
   ideas and, 63
   in oral presentations, 598–99, 604
   in paragraphs, 63–64, 559
   sentences as, 559
transmittal letter, 511, 542–43
transparencies, overhead, 663
trip reports, 413–420
truth, in controversy, 281

ultimatum, of collection series, 266, 276, 278, 279
underlining:
   for italics, 818–19
   in memos, 370

United States Department of Commerce: Bureau of the Census Statistics for 1986, 1988, 834*n*
unsolicited letters, 722, 727–30
urgent appeal, collection series, 266, 276, 277
usage, stereotyping, 82–84

variables:
   dependent, 479
   independent, 479
verbs:
   action, 701, 702
   nouns and, 71
   in resumes, 701, 702
   strong, 69–72, 701, 702
   subject agreement with, 829–31
   weak, 72
videotapes, for rehearsals, 620
Visa, 201
visual aids, 635–77
   bar charts, 645–46, 647–49
   blackboards, 663
   computer graphics, 665–66
   displaying of, 663, 665
   flip charts, 663
   flow charts, 654, 655
   handouts, 665
   line graphs, 646, 650–51
   maps, 654, 656
   in oral presentations, 618, 657–65
   organization charts, 653–54
   overhead transparencies, 663
   pie charts, 651–52
   slide projection, 663, 665
   tables, 544, 545, 635–45
   text visuals, 658, 663
vocabulary:
   stereotyping, 82–84
   technical, 81
voice:
   active, 69–70, 72–75
   passive, 72–75

Wall Street Journal, 43, 501–3, 671, 686, 715
Wall Street Journal Index, 462, 686, 717
want ads:
   application letters and, 722–23

   finding, 715
   responding to, 716
Waterman, Robert H., Jr., 66–68, 308, 833*n*, 836*n*
welcome, letters of, 334, 335–39
Williams, Joseph M., 833*n*
Wilson, Erika, 836*n*
Winograd, Terry, 837*n*
word processing, 12, 764, 770
   dictation and, 121
   see also computers
words:
   conversational, 133
   emphatic order of, in sentences, 76
   needless, 77–80
   repetition of, 68
Work Related Abstracts, 462
writer's block, 25, 39–40
writing, business:
   advantages of, 589
   career and, 3–6, 7–13
   with computers, 12–13; *see also* computers
   definition of, 1
   experience and, 14–16
   group projects of, 14–15, 562–66; *see also* group writing
   importance of, 2–7
   introduction to, 1–16
   managing workload of, 10–12
   nonstop, *see* nonstop writing
   office environment and, 10–13
   oral presentations compared to, 590
   as process, 17–47
   speaking vs., 7, 10, 15, 25–26, 585–88, 589
   style, *see* style
   as way of thinking, 3, 6–7
"writing cultures," 7
Writing in Nonacademic Settings (Odell and Goswami, eds.), 833*n*
Writing Program Administrators, 833*n*, 836*n*
Wunsch, Alan P., 833*n*

Xerox, 4, 234

yearbooks, 458

ZIP + 4 code, 147–48